ANTHROPOLOGY
AN INTRODUCTION · FOURTH EDITION

ANTHROPOLOGY
AN INTRODUCTION · FOURTH EDITION
LOWELL D. HOLMES   KIM SCHNEIDER

WAVELAND
PRESS, INC.

Prospect Heights, Illinois

For information about this book, write or call:

Waveland Press, Inc.
P.O. Box 400
Prospect Heights, Illinois 60070
(312) 634-0081

Contents

Preface

This textbook is designed for use in the general, or basic course in anthropology. It presents facts, concepts, and examples drawn from the full range of anthropological literature to provide college students with an introduction to the nature and scope of anthropology, and to acquaint them with the biological, social, and cultural nature of the objects of its inquiry—human beings. The purpose of this volume is to lay a cross-cultural and historical foundation for understanding world and national issues and for coming to rational decisions concerning individual, social, and cultural alternatives for action.

This book, initially published in 1965, was one of the first to include a comprehensive chapter on the American cultural configuration. We believe that this chapter has even more importance today than in the past because of the increasing tendency for American anthropologists to study industrial societies, particularly their own. One of the great benefits of studying other cultures is that we come to understand our own better. We have also related anthropological concepts to American culture throughout the book to make its reading a more relevant learning experience. We are interested in describing the behavioral characteristics of *people,* not just those few that seem exotic and live in far-off lands. That was what anthropology used to deal with when it was described as the study of "primitive man."

Chapter 2 presents the student with a history of anthropology. This chapter is placed at the beginning because we believe it can provide a basis for understanding why anthropologists think the way they do and what they are trying to achieve. Many of the ideas discussed in this chapter were advanced many years ago and have never been improved on. Some people have questioned why such a detailed chapter is even included in a text like this. There is an increasing number of young anthropologists today who are operating under the impression that very little of theoretical importance was discovered prior to the end of World War II. Some would even claim that the important breakthroughs began with the advent of "the new archeology" or "the new ethnology" in the mid-1960s. For these reasons it is important that students of anthropology be aware of the cumulative heritage of their science, which goes back as far as the ancient Greeks. If we may be forgiven for taking great liberties with a famous quote by Santayana, we would like to suggest that those who do not know the history of anthropology are destined to re-invent it.

We find ourselves very much in the debt of many friends and colleagues who have assisted us in the production of this book. For the basic theoretical perspectives on which this volume and its earlier editions were built, we are indebted to our mentors at Northwestern University and Ohio State University.

Thanks are also due to our students who assisted in this revision by challenging our ideas and making us clarify issues. Our debt of gratitude also extends to colleagues Don Blakeslee, who suggested ways we might update the sections on prehistory, to Loy Neff, who did the line drawings for Chapter 3, and to Ellen Holmes, who assisted in editing the manuscript. We are particularly indebted to Dr. Wayne Parris, Professor Emeritus, who was co-author of the Third Edition of this text. We extend our thanks for his contributions and we wish him a long, happy and productive retirement.

Lowell D. Holmes
Kim Schneider
Wichita State University
Wichita, Kansas

Anthropology and Its Perspective 1

Human geography
History
Psychology

Anthropology is the study of the physical and cultural development of the human species from prehistoric through modern times.[1] Historical in perspective, anthropology also seeks answers to scientific questions about the nature of people in Western, Eastern, and developing societies. Anthropology traditionally is described as a broad and general discipline; its many specialized aspects display the characteristics of a biological, a social, and a physical science. It can even be considered a humanistic discipline, in its interest in art, literature, music and dance, value orientations, and philosophical systems.

Anthropological Specializations

Anthropologists come in many varieties. Linguists study the forms of human speech and their symbolic meanings. They believe that the extraordinary capacity to use language symbols sets the human animal apart from all other animals in the quality of its communication.

Archeologists, thought by some laymen to be the only "real" anthropologists, spend long hours digging up the bones and old stones of prehistoric cultures and past civilizations and even longer hours in their laboratories analyzing and classifying their excavated evidence in an attempt to determine how and when the people of these societies lived and died.

The physical (biological) anthropologist's interests center on all aspects of human biology through time and space. Traditional areas of research have included paleoanthropology (the study of human and nonhuman primate fossils), human variation and population biology, and skeletal biology. However, today the fields of inquiry in physical anthropology have grown to include interests such as genetics, growth and development, demography, nutrition, medicine, and nonhuman primate behavior.

By far the largest number of anthropologists today perform under the banner of "social" or "cultural" anthropology. While they always remain on speaking terms with the physical anthropologists, the linguists, and the archeologists, the social and cultural anthropologists view the societies of the contemporary world as case studies which can illuminate the nature of human behavior and suggest ways in which many of the world's problems can be solved. That is, they look upon societies all over the world as "mirrors for man" (Kluckhohn 1949) wherein they may view the human animal in its infinite va-

---

[1] The word *anthropology* derives from the Greek *anthropos* meaning "Man" and *logia* meaning "systematic study" or "science."

riety and ponder both its wisdom and its folly. Most social and cultural anthropologists have a particular geographical interest, for example, in the peoples of Polynesia, or the American Indians, or city dwellers of North America, or the peoples of West Africa, etc., and they have probably lived among and studied one or more of these types of societies sometime during their professional careers.

Social and cultural anthropologists have become so diversified in their interests that the scope of anthropology is commonly described as "what anthropologists do." They may identify themselves as specialists in "cognitive anthropology," in "the anthropology of aging (gerontology)," in "cultural ecology," or in a number of hyphenated interest areas such as ethno-botany, ethno-musicology, ethnohistory, ethno-science, or socio-linguistics. Many of these socioculturally oriented scholars also make practical applications of their science; as "applied" or "action" anthropologists they take the findings of anthropology and apply that knowledge to the solution of social, economic, political, and medical problems.

The Task of Anthropology

For a hundred years at least, the natural habitat of the anthropologist has been the museum or the college classroom, but today you can find anthropologists almost anywhere—at the public health department, on a mental health diagnostic or therapy team, on the city manager's staff, or on the family guidance council. They are still found in colleges and universities, and in greater numbers than ever before, but even in their classrooms, today's anthropologists are making their discipline more relevant, more oriented to our society in all of its modern, urban, industrial complexity.

Anthropology and "Primitives"

Anthropology—at least the variety that deals with contemporary human behavior—was once known as the "science of primitive man," but the science is changing. No longer is it the discipline which studies mostly remote and little-known societies which practice exotic and colorful customs. The forces of modernization and industrialization are making such societies difficult, if not impossible, to find. The term *primitive* is quite out of fashion these days in developing nations, and many such countries are not very cordial to anthropologists,

People like this Indonesian tribe-man were once the major focus of anthropology. Although still cross-cultural, anthropologists often study industrialized societies today (Courtesy Willis Tilton.)

since they have the reputation of studying "primitive" peoples. Some anthropologists (mostly European) have even insisted on using the word *savages* or at best *natives*, and progressive citizens of African and Asian independent nations are more than insulted by these references. While most anthropologists have at one time used the word *primitives*, it was used merely to designate non-Western peoples, living in small traditional and conservative societies with no system of writing of their own development and therefore having only orally transmitted tradition. Nonanthropologists, unfortunately, often assume that the term means what most dictionaries record as the definition—"crude," "simple," "childish," "backward," or even "stupid."

"Primitives" are a vanishing breed, but anthropology was never dependent on their existence anyway. Anthropological methodology and theory can easily be adapted to studying Samoan Islanders living in San Francisco, tribal East Africans living in copper mine settlements, Nova Scotian fishermen, bums on skid row, Wall Street stockbrokers, or elderly people living in a retirement community in southern California. The one thing that remains unchanged about anthropology in the modern world is that its practitioners still believe that no generalization about human behavior can be made on the basis of observations of a single society; only through cross-cultural comparisons can the true nature of the human animal be discovered.

The Anthropological Perspective

College courses in anthropology have been described as the epitome of liberal arts education. Anthropology is generally not preprofessional education, and its main purpose is to give students a new and broader perspective of the cultural world of *Homo sapiens* with all its variety. One might say that anthropology is a discipline trying to broaden horizons and reduce myth-based prejudices. Moreover, anthropology has a perspective which is unique among all social science and humanistic disciplines. This is because it is (1) cross-cultural, or comparative, (2) holistic, (3) concerned with both subjective (emic) and objective (etic) perspectives and, (4) case study oriented (Hunter and Whitten 1979:1).

CROSS-CULTURAL COMPARISON

Why anthropology is committed to cross-cultural, comparative analysis might best be explained by considering an episode from Andre Gide's classic work, *The Counterfeiters*. In this novel the author presents a conversation between two university students of science concerning a particular kind of fish that, due to its unique biological composition, is destined to live out its entire life at a certain depth of water. It lacks the ability to rise to the surface and experience contact with air and it can't descend to experience contact with mud and sand at the bottom of the ocean. While the characters in the novel do not comment on the fact, a perceptive student might quickly realize that the fish in question would have no insight into its environment. Many people in this and other societies suffer the same predicament as that fish. They lack insight into their own way of life because they have never been exposed to any other way of life. Anthropology helps this kind of person to break through the shell of cultural isolation and thus see his or her own behavior and that of others more clearly.

CROSS-
CULTURAL
PRECEDENTS

The precedent for anthropology's comparative approach goes back to the work of people who were not even recognized as anthropologists. A scholar like Ibn Khaldun, the Islamic economist and historian of the fourteenth century, studied a score of Middle Eastern and African societies and searched for predictable laws of social behavior which might be common to all human beings. "These laws," he maintained, "can be discovered only by the gathering of many facts from past history and contemporary situations in many societies." According to Ibn Khaldun, differences in human behavior between Arabs and Jews should not be attributed to racial differences but to differences in their past history and traditional life styles (culture). Not only was Ibn Khaldun comparative in his cross-cultural study of contemporary societies (often referred to as a *synchronic* approach) but he was also interested in looking at a given culture at many time periods (a *diachronic* approach).

An American lawyer and amateur anthropologist, Lewis Henry Morgan, built an entire school of theoretical thought on the comparative method. While representing the Iroquois Indians in a land claims case, he was compelled to do a thorough study of the kinship system to better understand Iroquois patterns of inheritance of property. The more he investigated the system the more he was struck by similarities between Iroquois kinship and that of the Greeks and Romans. Intrigued and puzzled that people so separated in time and space could have such similar patterns of social organization, Morgan began to collect more and more information about the nature of kinship systems the world over. He sent letters of inquiry to missionaries, government officials, and traders around the world requesting information about family and genealogical systems of local aborigines. He ultimately used knowledge gained from these responses, from several field trips to the western plains states, and from long hours in the library to produce the cross-cultural, comparative classic volume known as *Systems of Consanguinity and Affinity of the Human Family* (1870). After making further comparisons of other aspects of behavior of peoples at various levels of cultural development, Morgan set forth a theory of worldwide cultural evolution. While a substantial percentage of modern anthropologists would not agree that Morgan's evolutionary theory was sound, all agree that the comparative method he utilized so extensively *is* sound and that a science of human behavior based on observations of but a single culture would be worthless.

Comparative analysis is often used in anthropology to determine whether a given behavioral phenomenon is cultural (learned) or inherited through the genes. This procedure is best illustrated by the Samoan study of Margaret Mead. In the introduction to *Coming of Age in Samoa* (1928) Mead states the nature of her approach in testing the G. Stanley Hall contention that adolescent personality problems have a physiological basis (resulting from chemical changes in the body associated with puberty). Believing that adolescent temperament difficulties have a cultural base, Margaret Mead chose

> to go to a different civilization and make a study of human beings under different cultural conditions in some other part of the world. For such studies the anthropologist chooses quite simple peoples, whose society has never attained the complexity of our own. In this choice of primitive people . . . the anthropologist is guided by the knowledge that the analysis of a simpler civilization is more possible of attainment. (1928:7—8)

From such societies, different from one's own in historical development, language, and religious ideas "it is possible to learn many things about the effect of a civilization upon the individuals within it" (Mead 1928:8).

THE HOLISTIC APPROACH

Probably no other discipline studying peoples examines them so thoroughly, from so many angles, as anthropology. Anthropology simultaneously scrutinizes the human animal socially, culturally, biologically, ecologically, psychologically, spiritually, and historically. To ignore any of these dimensions is believed to distort the picture. Anthropologists think that the quality of any particular trait, complex, or cultural institution cannot be evaluated apart from the total cultural configuration in which it is found. The nature of a human family, for example, is influenced by methods of subsistence, by moral and religious ideals, by demographics (the balance of males and females), and by concepts of authority and of status and role. Anthropology's configurational or *gestalt* approach often loses sight of a few trees (details) but has the advantage that the forest (pattern) becomes more discernible. As Alfred L. Kroeber, the dean of American anthropology, once put it:

> We anthropologists will never know China as intensively as a Sinologist does, or prices, credit and banking as well as an economist, or heredity with the fullness of the genetic biologist. But we face what these more intensive scholars only glance at intermittently or tangentially, if at all: to try to understand in some measure how Chinese civilization *and* economics *and* human heredity, *and* some dozens of other highly developed special bodies of knowledge do indeed interrelate in being all parts of "man"—flowing out of man, centered in him, products of him. (1953:xiv)

An analytical net that is not cast wide enough runs the risk of producing explanations for phenomena which are distorted or inadequate. Deterministic thinking, for example, is reductionist and simplistic analysis that does not consider the full range of variables. Comparative and holistic studies, on the other hand, have proved to be an effective weapon against this kind of faulty reasoning. An analysis of the history of social and cultural thought reveals that all too frequently scholars without an acquaintance with all the facts (or perhaps without a desire to take all the facts into consideration) have arrived at inadequate premises. Classic examples are the racial determinism of Arthur Jensen and William Shockley who maintain that race determines IQ and intellectual achievement, the biological determinism of Desmond Morris, Robert Ardrey, and Konrad Lorenz who believe aggression and even warfare are innate human characteristics, and the geographical determinism of Montesquieu and Huntington who explained cultural levels of development and even particular cultural institutions in climatic terms.

EMIC AND ETIC ANALYSIS

Anthropology has never been guilty of using a lot of special jargon but the terms *emic* and *etic* have, during the past decade, become well established as useful ways of describing the manner in which anthropologists relate to the cultural systems they are investigating. Credit is usually given to the linguist Kenneth Pike for shortening the linguistic terms *phonemic* to *emic* and *phonetic* to *etic* and applying these special terms to investigative approaches of social and cultural anthropologists.

To the linguist, the word *phonetics* has always meant the study of the way language sounds are produced. It involves such considerations as whether a sound is voiced or unvoiced, whether it is labial or dental, or whether it is nasal or non-nasal. The study of phonetics reveals, for example, that human speech may include "clicks" like the clucking sounds Kalahari Bushmen make, glottal stops like Polynesians and New Yorkers produce, or rolled r's like the ones that come off the tongues of West Africans or Italian opera singers.

Phonemics, on the other hand, is the study of the significant sounds that make up a particular language, or as linguists put it, the study of sounds that are characteristic of a particular "speech community." While the human body is capable of making hundreds of sounds which could be used in speech, the average language consists of from 15 to 75 sound symbols, and no two languages have exactly the same number and combination. Thus *phonetic* refers to speech sounds *in general* and *phonemic* refers to a particular set of sounds that relate to each other in a given language system.

Translated into anthropological nomenclature for describing investigative procedures, *etic* refers to the objective or scientific perspective of a people's behavior which the anthropologist enjoys as a result of his knowledge (often from library research) of the cultural systems of a large number of human societies. The *emic* perspective, on the other hand, is the insider's or people's perception and appreciation of the culture. Here the cultural definitions and ways of categorizing experience are those of the participants, not the scientific classifier. Anthropologists attempt to obtain a special view of culture through prolonged residence with, and participation in the lifeways of the people they study.

The two concepts have been useful in emphasizing the need to view a cultural system as a unique creation of a given people with special meaning and value to them, on the one hand, and the need to view that same culture from the perspective of the scientist whose knowledge of many societies and their lifeways permits him to put it in its proper place in the overall scheme of things.

THE CASE STUDY APPROACH

Anthropology's reliance on the case study approach may be compared to the same approach, used effectively, in the field of social work, another social science. Just as social workers discover first hand the life styles of the families making up their case loads so anthropologists personally observe and experience the circumstances of the peoples and cultures they wish to study. Frequently they are not entirely sure of what they will find, what aspects of the culture they will study, or precisely what methodological approaches they will be able to use. But they know that there will be difficulties in establishing rapport, in understanding the value system of their subjects, and in comprehending the complexities and subtleties of communication. So they settle in for an extended period of what is called *participant observation*. By involving themselves as much as possible in their subjects' lives, keeping their eyes open, and constantly seeking explanations for perplexing behavior anthropologists achieve a depth of understanding of the culture rarely possible in other social science disciplines.

Just as social workers write thorough and penetrating case study reports on each of the families which make up their case loads and seek answers to the families' social and personal problems, anthropologists also seek explanations of human behavior in holistic and exhaustive analyses of social process.

As Hunter and Whitten put it,

> Though of course anthropologists appreciate the power of statistical analysis as much as other social scientists, their orientation, to a large degree, is to look for the rich description of setting, and behavior which are to be found in case studies. (1977:6)

Although anthropologists tend toward particularism—explaining each item of human behavior as understandable only in terms of its unique cultural configuration—deep involvement in a people's lifestyle ensures a humanistic concern and may help solve troublesome social and international issues. Most anthropologists speak of the

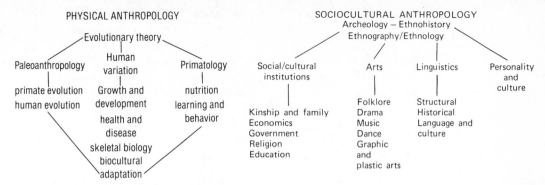

Figure 1-1 The panorama of anthropology.

people with whom they have lived and worked as "my people," and the case study (ethnography) that they produce as the result of this association helps them understand and predict developing patterns of behavior. It differs little from the case study procedures of good social workers who also study, learn to feel and therefore anticipate the social problems of "their families." Often the solutions lie in the wealth of data which comprises the case history.

The Divisions of Anthropology

As this chapter pointed out earlier, the scope of anthropological interests is enormous; therefore anthropologists must specialize. Anthropology has two major divisions: physical and sociocultural. (See Fig. 1-1.) Physical anthropology developed out of the study of human anatomy and race classification and became a recognized scientific discipline early in the nineteenth century. Sociocultural anthropology, on the other hand, developed out of social philosophy and did not become an established academic discipline until almost the turn of the present century. Although sociocultural anthropology has had a shorter history of growth and development, it is now more widely taught in American universities and colleges, and sociocultural anthropologists outnumber physical anthropologists by about ten to one.

PHYSICAL ANTHROPOLOGY

While new specialties continually develop within the major branches of anthropology, the following subdivisions or subject matter areas are usually regarded as traditional in physical anthropology.

Paleoanthropology. The appearance approximately 65 million years ago of primates gives the paleoanthropologist an important time perspective on the sequence of events which led to the emergence of modern humans *(Homo sapiens sapiens)*. By studying fossil remains and evaluating them with the cooperation of other specialists (for example, geochemists for soil analysis and palynologists for plant and pollen analysis), paleoanthropologists give us glimpses of our collective primate past in order that we may better understand our present. The paleoanthropologist is not only interested in the morphology (form) and age of fossil primates, but is also interested in the evolutionary mechanisms which have produced the diversity observed.

Primatology. The recognition of our place within the order Primates should lead to an obvious conclusion — the study of other members of the order is a likely place to begin if we are interested in understanding human biology and behavior. Evidence of our close genetic relationships with living apes (chimpanzee, gorilla, and orangutan) further underlines the importance of comparing and contrasting humans with other primates.

Human Growth and Development. This subfield of physical anthropology has a long history, and its goal is "to learn in what ways human groups differ (Tanner, 1951), why they do so, and how size and form are attained and modified (Garn, 1957, Tanner, 1966)" (Beall, 1982:447). Since the ways in which we grow and develop is affected by genetics, nutrition, climate and exercise, physical anthropologists involved with this research often are trained in a variety of biomedical disciplines. This type of training is not pursued because the physical anthropologist is a frustrated physician or biochemist. Rather, the anthropologist is interested (as always) in a holistic approach to the specific issues of human growth and development, and desires to include a wide variety of data bases, techniques, and specialities to understand these phenomena.

Human Variation. Recognizing that humans come in many different shapes, sizes and colors, physical anthropologists historically have been interested in understanding how we have come to be as we are today. Human variation studies have included studies of populations which live in particularly stressful environments, and which appear to have specific physical and physiological characteristics which allow them to survive. Human variation allows us to evaluate biological responses to temperature, altitude, diet, and even overcrowding and noise. Another important focus of this subfield is understanding why certain human populations have different risks to diseases such as cancer, mental illness and cardiovascular disease.

Physical anthropologists are involved with many other areas of research. As a matter of fact, just about any topic which is related to human biology is of interest. For example, studies of health and disease among prehistoric peoples (paleopathology), dental morphology and dental diseases (dental anthropology) and the application of anthropological methods to mass disasters and homicide investigations, specifically in identifying victims from skeletal and dental remains, (forensic anthropology) are each specialities which have developed in physical anthropology. The recent explosion of new methods and equipment capable of detecting variability among populations and the application of some of these techniques even to fossils has given rise to another new area of specialization, molecular anthropology.

Some view these specialized areas as increasingly narrowing the subdiscipline of physical anthropology. They argue that physical anthropology is becoming too specialized, and that it no longer can "relate" to the rest of the discipline. On the contrary, data generated from these areas of research furthers our understanding of human biology and are critical within the discipline. If anthropology is truly holistic, then each new avenue of investigation improves our understanding of ourselves.

SOCIOCULTURAL ANTHROPOLOGY

Anthropologists who concern themselves with human behavior rather than human biological characteristics are called *cultural* or *social* anthropologists. Occasionally they even hyphenate their identification to read "socio-cultural." The differences in perspective and method between social and cultural anthropologists are minor and seem to relate to the theoretical emphasis of the university in which they were trained. Social anthropologists lean more toward the functional traditions of the British while cultural anthropologists are more historical in orientation and are inclined more toward the theoretical position of Americans such as Lowie, Kroeber, and Franz Boas, who, in spite of the fact that he was German-born, is commonly referred to as the "Father of American Anthropology."

To add to this confusion, the position of archeology in relation to social or cultural anthropology is unclear. The layman often thinks that every anthropologist is an archeologist, but some archeologists tend to think of archeology as a separate and distinct discipline apart from social and cultural anthropology. Some universities have even established separate departments of archeology.

ARCHEOLOGY

Archeology is definitely a branch or subdivision of sociocultural anthropology because it studies the cultural behavior of past populations. It attempts to reconstruct the history and life styles of nonliterate peoples (who therefore left no written records) by digging up the material products (artifacts) of their culture, for example, their tools, house remains, and art works. Archeology is the area of anthropology that seems to have the greatest public appeal. In fact, one writer has referred to archeologists as "the glamour boys" of the an-

Excavating the squares of a grid. (Courtesy Wichita State University.)

thropological world. Anthropological archeology is primarily prehistoric archeology because it tends to investigate ancient peoples who never developed a written history of their own. Therefore, anthropologists dig up American Indian villages or South Sea island ceremonial centers but leave Greek and Roman ruins to *classical* archeologists (from history or classical language departments). In recent years anthropologists have occasionally excavated *historical* sites which date to American colonial, frontier, or Civil War periods.

The archeologist is hardly a treasure hunter. As a trained scientist, he/she knows that in order to understand why people have different economies, hold different religious views, and perceive the world in different ways, we must learn something of their cultural histories. He/she therefore carefully excavates and records the material effects of past populations as to location and level. Copious notes are a vital part of any archeological project, and after a location (called a *site*) has been dug it should actually be possible with these notes to put everything back just where it was found. Such attention to detail is necessary because the various levels of cultural material often represent various eras of cultural development.

ETHNOGRAPHY/
ETHNOLOGY

While archeology explores people's prehistoric past, ethnography and ethnology are concerned with the details of the cultural configurations of contemporary societies. Ethnography and ethnology describe the activities and interests of social and cultural anthropologists. The term *ethnography* refers to the empirical, fact-finding activities—observation and interview—carried out by anthropologists in the field. Derived from the words *ethnos* ("cultural group") and *graphy* ("description," or "picture of"), ethnography refers to the process of collecting facts about particular cultures in far-off lands or in subcultures within our own society, for example, blacks in urban ghettos, Appalachian migrants in Detroit, Amish in Iowa, old people in nursing homes, or even top executives ("gamesmen") in American industry.

In the word *ethnology* we find *ology* ("pertaining to science") replacing *graphy*. Thus we find that ethnology is the science of culture or cultural group behavior, and this activity involves comparing cultural descriptions (ethnographies) from a number of societies for the purpose of making generalizations and testing hypotheses about the nature of the human species.

Ethnohistory. Ethnohistory fills the gap between the knowledge that is normally supplied by archeologists and that supplied by social and cultural anthropologists studying their contemporaries. Ethnohistory tends to be a library-centered discipline rather than a field-centered one. It attempts to document the lifeways of preliterate people of the historical past by consulting missionary accounts, military journals, ships' logs, explorers' reports, etc., to piece together information concerning the fortunes and cultural adjustments made by indigenous peoples after the coming of the white man (or some other literate population). Details of the operation of the Iroquois Confederation, or the economic impact of the fur trade in North America, or London Missionary Society successes and its impact on island culture in Polynesia would be typical interests of ethnohistorians.

Ethnography, ethnology, and ethnohistory (and archeology) are all basically concerned with documenting how societies and cultures structure (or structured) their institutions—family, education, religion, government, economics; how they communicate through language and gesture; how they relate to the world of form and beauty through their arts; and generally how they conceptualize the nature of the world around them.

Sociocultural Institutions. It has been traditional in social science to categorize the roles, values, and patterns of human behavior into what are called *institutions* (or aspects) of culture. It is equally traditional to break up the totality of cultural behavior into the following categories: "family and kinship," "government," "religion," "education," and "economics." Of course this practice can distort somewhat our understanding of how life is actually lived. Who is to say, for example, whether going to work every day is "family" behavior or "economic" behavior? While Americans tend to be religious mainly between 11:00 A.M. and noon on Sunday morning (or on Friday evening, if Jewish) religion among most nonWestern people is more apt to be part and parcel of most everyday actions. In categorizing human behavior as we do we can handle data more easily and we have a convenient system for titling chapters in anthropology textbooks but we run the risk of presenting a spurious picture of human life.

Of all the institutional categories, family and kinship has been the one anthropologists have favored. This is because when anthropology began as a science it was primarily concerned with the study of "primitive" or nonliterate peoples, and in studying such societies an understanding of kinship was often the key to understanding the structure and operation of the society, particularly with respect to the assignment of roles and status.

The Arts. While anthropologists consider themselves to be scientists, they give considerable attention to areas that are normally thought to be the proper preserve of humanists associated with the fine arts. But since folklore (oral literature), drama, dance, music, and the graphic and plastic arts are cultural products of human beings, anthropologists, in their holistic approach to the whole individual, are vitally interested in these products—particularly in regard to the manner in which they relate to other aspects of life such as religion, social organization, or education. Rarely do anthropologists return from fieldwork in some non-Western society without a collection of carvings, pottery, or woven objects; and few would feel that the research experience was complete without collecting a volume of myths, legends, and folktales or substantial film footage of indigenous dances or the drama of ritual.

Linguistics. The human species' capacity for language more than any other ability sets it apart from all other animals and makes possible the existence of culture. Cultural anthropologists explore the varieties of communication utilized by human beings around the world. Although scientists have studied the phenomenon of language for many years through the disciplines of philology (literary history) and etymology (word origins), anthropological linguistics is unique because it concentrates on the more exotic languages of the world such as African Swahili and Bantu, American Indian Algonkian and Athapascan, and South Sea island Malayo-Polynesian, to mention but a few. Most of the languages anthropologists study are not written,

The study of music and the dance is an integral part of cultural anthropology.

and therefore, special methods are used for recording and analyzing them. A study of hundreds of individual languages around the world shows that no two languages have been put together in exactly the same way. Each is a selection of different sets of sounds (phonemes) and combinations of sounds (morphemes), and each has its unique grammatical structure (syntax).

One of the more outstanding contributions of anthropological linguistics has been the new understanding of the relationship of language and culture. We know, for example, that language greatly influences our philosophy of life, our values, and even our perception of reality. It has also been established that there is no relationship between levels of cultural development and linguistic complexity or efficiency. No language is superior to any other. Each provides reasonably adequate communication channels for its speakers.

Some linguists have concentrated on the historical development of languages, and although historical linguists can only speculate on how, when, or where language began, they have provided valuable insights into historical contacts of various societies by analyzing similarities and differences in their languages and the nature of linguistic change and diffusion.

Personality and Culture.   This interest area developed from a wedding of cultural anthropology and psychoanalytic theory in the late 1920s. While it has enlisted fewer researchers than other areas of anthropological concern, it has greatly enhanced our understanding of how personality development is influenced by cultural environment. The perspective differs somewhat from that of psychology in that there is less concentration on individual personality than on the extent to which personality types are shared within given societies or nations. Starting with such pioneer studies as Margaret Mead's investigation of adolescent personality development in Samoa and America (as described in *Coming of Age in Samoa* (1928) and Ruth Benedict's application of psychological theme labels to select American Indian and Pacific Island societies in her book *Patterns of Culture* (1934), workers in this area have increasingly contributed to the understanding of the nature and causes of mental illness, the influence of childhood experiences on adult behavior, and the extent to which common cultural and ideological forces influence the production of similar personality types among the citizens of industrial nations.

APPLIED ANTHROPOLOGY

Applied anthropology (sometimes called "action" anthropology) involves the practical application of the findings, concepts, methods, and theories of sociocultural and physical anthropologists to social, political, economic, educational, and medical problems in this and other cultures. Just as medicine has its Dr. Salks (doing laboratory research) and its general practitioners (treating patients), anthropology has both theoretical and practical proponents. A perusal of *Human Organization*, the official journal of the Society for Applied Anthropology, will acquaint the newcomer to anthropology with the many types of work being carried on by applied anthropologists.

Some of the earliest applied efforts were carried out in Africa where anthropologists were commonly used by Great Britain's Colonial Office as advisors on government policy for native populations. The establishment of "indirect rule," whereby Britain ruled through local hereditary leaders (who became paid government officials), is

Figure 1-2 The difference between applied and theoretical anthropology. (© 1960 United Feature Syndicate, Inc. — used with permission.)

the kind of contribution these "human engineers" made. They also worked directly with the people as liaisons between the indigenous population and the colonial administrators. Applied anthropologists also have been utilized by the American government in its dealings with Micronesian Trust Territory populations and with Native Americans through the Bureau of Indian Affairs.

In recent years applied practitioners of anthropology have contributed greatly in the medical and public health field (emphasizing cultural factors in illness and treatment), in the area of public housing and manpower training, and in understanding drug abuse and rehabilitation. In nearly all cases anthropologists tend to emphasize the importance of cultural traditions on a people's behavior and why it is important to know and work within the cultural system in seeking solutions to the problems of ethnic Americans or of peoples in other cultures.

Physical anthropologists also have their areas of applied contributions. They may engage in forensic medical investigations, in anthropometric research to provide clothing manufacturers with more realistic size categories, or in studies of American posture and posteriors so that better seat designs might be achieved for buses, trains, and planes. They have also been known to study the effects of space travel on the human organism. Just as the engineer who designs the space vehicle must know the strengths and weaknesses of construction materials so the applied anthropologist must be able to predict the qualities of the astronauts (or future commercial passengers) who may someday ride these machines into the far reaches of the universe.

Anthropology Among the Social Sciences

Having explored the scope and flavor of anthropology as a discipline let us now look at what kind of scholarly company it keeps. Anthropology is usually classified as a social science although earlier scholars in this field thought of it as natural history. As a social science anthropology shares its interest in the human animal and its lifeways with sociology, political science, economics, human geography, history, and psychology.

ANTHROPOLOGY AND SOCIOLOGY

Anthropology and sociology have long been considered sister sciences, and a number of universities and colleges in the United States have combined departments. John Bennett and Kurt Wolff once observed that the two disciplines tended to behave much like political parties, having separate professionalized bodies and ideologies. We might also add that like political parties they both have people's interests at heart but have somewhat different ideas about how to serve them best.

The beginning student often has difficulty understanding how the two disciplines differ, because anthropologists and sociologists often confuse the issue themselves by invading one another's territory. (See Fig. 1–4.) Indeed, sociology has even been referred to as "the anthropology of civilized society." Although sociology is becoming more international in its interests, traditionally it has been mostly concerned with Western European civilization, particularly the variety associated with the United States. Until recently, few sociologists engaged in worldwide comparative research although their borrowing of an anthropological fact has not been unusual now and then to document some theoretical principle. Sociologists today pay a great deal of attention to ethnic enclaves within our own society, and they have learned to work with value orientations very different from those of mainstream America. But generally they have been accustomed to working within a society they understand because they grow up operating within its traditions and unique ways of comprehending the world. While this familiarity is, on the one hand, an asset, because they can anticipate behavioral responses, it is also a handicap because

	American Sociological Association	**American Anthropological Association**
Special Interests	Criminology Uses of the Computer Socialization Social Stratification Marital Separation and Divorce Problems of the Working Class Social Mobility Social Movements and Collective Movements White Collar Workers Racism in American Society Statistical Models and Methods Housing	

American Sociological Association	**American Anthropological Association**
Aging and Retirement	Anthropology of Aging
Status of Women	Female Status: A Multidimensional Space
Sociology of Sport	Aspects of Sports in American Culture
Political Sociology	Political Anthropology
American Indians	American Indians: Indian-White Relations
War and International Conflict	Views on Aggression and Conflict in Man
Urban and Rural Migration	Migration and Social Change
Sociology of Law	Anthropology and American Legal Process
Health Care: Policy and Delivery	Health Care and Social Stress
Medical Sociology	Topics in Medical Anthropology
Social Psychology	Psychological Anthropology
Ecology and the Social Uses of Space	Living Space and Perception Management
Symbolic Interaction	Symbolic Analysis
Kinship and Society	Kin, Class and Social Structure
Cultural Symbols and Belief Systems	Religion in Social and Political Organization
Social Demography	Population Anthropology
Sociology of the American Labor Market	Industrial Ethnography in the U.S.
Mass Communication and Propaganda Analysis	Ethnography of Communication
Fertility Behavior	Factors Affecting Fertility and Population

The second portion of this listing is labeled **Shared Interests**.

American Sociological Association	American Anthropological Association
Historical Demography	Demographic Variable in Cultural Evolution
Arts in Modern Society	The Structural Study of Art
Sociology of Development: Africa	Africa: Method and Social Change
Sociology of Education	Anthropology of Education

Special Interests

- Primate Behavior and Communication
- Archeology of North America
- Recent Developments in Old World Prehistory
- Anthropological Sexology
- Studies in Biogenetic Structuralism
- Empirical Perspectives on Evolutionary Theory
- Ethnohistory—The Fur Trade and Native Americans
- Museum Collections as a Research Resource
- Subsistence Economies of Oceania
- Birth and Interaction
- Biosocial Anthropology

Figure 1-3 Titles of papers read at recent professional meetings.

their growing up within the system makes it more difficult for them to maintain objectivity. As a consequence sociology has developed a more quantitative and impersonal approach and has sometimes been called the "science of probabilities." Anthropology, with its origin in the study of primitive or tribal societies, initially developed a methodology well suited to the study of these simpler and more isolated societies. While anthropology concentrated on holistic studies of whole cultures, sociology was compelled to concentrate on aspects of the complicated civilization it had chosen to study. Any description which could document all aspects of Western civilization and how each was interrelated would be a monumental task. One scholar, Max Lerner, attempted such a project but complained in the forword of his *America as a Civilization* (1957) that

> whenever I have tried to chip off a fragment—on American government, on liberalism, on foreign policy, on morals—I found that it lost some of its

meaning when torn from the rest. Yet to attempt the subject as a whole seemed a formidable, even arrogant task. In 1945 I finally overrode my hesitation and started the book on its present scale. It has been more than a decade in the writing. (1957:xi)

Lerner also cites another major problem associated with his study—the one that has resulted in sociology's more quantitative and "scientific" methodology. He writes, "No American can achieve detachment in studying America. . . . The best you can do to achieve perspective is to keep a certain emotional distance from your subject" (1957:xii).

Matters of time perspective also set the two disciplines apart. Modern sociology deals primarily with events that have occurred within the last few hundred years, whereas anthropology attempts to reconstruct history and analyze its effect on human cultural development back to the very dawn of time. Because of this emphasis, anthropologists frequently have been labeled antiquarians, and it is interesting to note that while there are numerous anthropological museums there are few sociological ones.

POLITICAL SCIENCE

American political scientists, like sociologists, are primarily concerned with understanding and documenting Western political behavior, particularly that of citizens of the United States. Although political science departments have long offered courses called "comparative government" not until recently did such courses do more than compare constitutional systems in North America and Europe. Now such courses have moved more to analyses of a greater range of political behavior (with examples from developing countries) emphasizing decision-making processes and analyses of how and by whom rules of government are formulated. While political scientists occasionally utilize anthropological materials for the purpose of making comparisons between tribal and national political systems they have done very little in the way of fieldwork in nonWestern societies. American political scientists see their job as developing and dispersing a body of knowledge useful in understanding our own political problems and our own voting behavior. They do not pretend to be a political science for the entire human species.

ECONOMICS

Although anthropology frequently draws upon economic theories, most anthropologists have found difficulty in incorporating the major share of economic theory into a cross-cultural science of people. Because economics is probably among the most culture-bound of the social sciences, all of the models and instruments of analysis (such as the price system or market phenomenon) have been developed in terms of a European set of values. Economics is very much a matter of values and rational choices, and Western Europeans tend to make different kinds of choices than do people who were raised in other traditions. Therefore much of the theory and methodology economists use in predicting economic behavior and its consequences would not apply well to a South Sea island people or a West African group.

Still another very fundamental difference separates economics and anthropology. Economics focuses on a single aspect of modern European culture and, while this specialization has its advantages, it also has its disadvantages. The discipline, in its efficiency of specialization, often loses sight of the greater picture, for example, the way economic life relates to other facets of life such as art, religion, and sex and family behavior. However, anthropologists, with their more holistic approach (which reveals form and interrelation of institutions), are often pathetically inept at describing and analyzing purely economic phenomena. Both disciplines could profit from more excursions into one another's territory.

HUMAN GEOGRAPHY

While the older variety of geography—physical geography—was basically concerned with climatic zones, varieties of soil, topographic features such as mountains, steppes, plateaus, and the relationship of land masses to bodies of water, human geography is interested in many of the same things that concern cultural anthropologists. The primary interest of human geography is the study of how human populations adjust to the variety of environmental problems found on our planet. Human geographers share an interest in the concept of culture with anthropologists, and their studies are often cross-cultural. It is no coincidence that in some circles human geography is referred to as *anthropogeography*. Geographers have both drawn upon and contributed to the knowledge that anthropology has developed concerning the ways human beings relate to the land.

HISTORY

Although history has often been characterized more as a humanity than a social science, it maintains a close alliance with anthropology. Indeed, the scholar F. W. Maitland (1911) once stated that anthropology had the choice of being history or nothing. By this he meant that anthropology should be a particularizing rather than a generalizing discipline, since laws of human behavior would probably never be discovered. It should be pointed out also that anthropologists often feel much more at home with historians than they do with sociologists. To begin with, Herodotus has been referred to as the "father" of both history and anthropology, and the first formidable theoretical school of anthropological thought in America (established by

Franz Boas) was known as the American Historical School. Even today a large number of American anthropologists identify themselves as ethnohistorians.

PSYCHOLOGY

Psychology is sometimes referred to as a social science but is more commonly known as a behavioral science. It is the study of the individual and his unique pattern of responses to stimuli of many kinds, including cultural and social, and focuses on sensory, motor, and cognitive behavioral characteristics of human beings.

Social psychology, an outgrowth of sociology and psychology, tends to place more emphasis on the influence of the social environment (family, crowd, or community) on individual behavior and personality development than on cultural factors. Neither psychologists nor social psychologists have been as prone to deal cross-culturally with people as have culture and personality specialists whose research into human psychological makeup has been carried on as a part of sociocultural anthropology.

Summary

Anthropology is the scientific study of the physical and cultural development of human beings from early prehistoric to modern times. It is a broad and complex discipline that studies people in all their biological, social, and cultural dimensions. Anthropology's interests and procedures reveal that it is simultaneously a natural science, a social science, a historical science, the science of culture, and a humanistic discipline with interests in the arts, in value orientations, and in philosophical systems. Anthropology is a generalizing science of broad scope but its practitioners have numerous specializations. Basically, anthropology is divided into two major subareas or divisions: physical anthropology, & sociocultural anthropology.

Anthropology's perspective is unique among the social sciences in that it is cross-cultural, or comparative, holistic, concerned with both subjective (emic) and objective (etic) analyses of cultural phenomena, and committed to a case study approach in the gathering of data. Although once thought of as the science of exotic and primitive peoples anthropology today refuses to restrict itself to any particular kind of people or to particular levels of cultural development or complexity.

Perhaps the most important of anthropology's contributions to the study of human beings has been its role in integrating a variety of disciplines. It has drawn together data from the humanities and the natural and behavioral sciences, to analyze them in relation to the human animal. With the concept of culture at the heart of their varied research activities, anthropologists have tended to concentrate on overall problems, feeling that studying people in terms of special aspects of behavior impedes the following of problems wherever they might lead.

The History of Anthropological Thought 2

Functionalism

    Structural anthropology

    Malinowski's functionalism

    Configurationalism

Neo-evolutionists

    Multilinear evolution

    General or universal evolution

    Cultural ecology

    Evaluation of evolution today

Neo-diffusionists

    Evaluation of diffusionism today

Current anthropology

Anthropology is a very young science, at least when compared with astronomy, chemistry, biology, or social philosophy—disciplines which came into being in Classical times or at least during the Middle Ages or the Renaissance. Scholars have only been identifying themselves as professional anthropologists for a little over one hundred years, and most anthropology departments are products of the twentieth century. The subject matter of anthropology—customs, social and political organization, human physical variation and race, ritual, human value systems—however, has interested the learned since before the time of Christ. Although a mere youngster among the sciences, anthropology has been around long enough to have experienced a period of growth in which a variety of theoretical perspectives or "schools" of thought have influenced the direction and scope of the discipline. There is still some "school" thinking around today, but generally anthropology has discarded much of the early foolishness and retained much of the wisdom in formulating a remarkably eclectic science of human beings and their works. To better understand the perspective of modern anthropology let us review the ideas and activities of the hundreds of men and women who have contributed to the discipline as it is practiced today.

Ancient Writings

Long before anyone conceived of a field of study called "anthropology," ancient scholars were turning out detailed descriptions of the peoples and cultures that occupied the then-known world—mostly the lands that bordered the Mediterranean. In the fifth century B.C. the Greek historian Herodotus qualified as the "father of anthropology" by documenting Egyptian patterns of dress, division of labor, religious ceremonies, racial type, and language. This material, which appears in *Euterpré,* is but part of his total writings which include ethnographic descriptions of Babylonians, Scythians, and other Middle Eastern peoples.

About this same time Xenophanes was making cross-cultural studies of religion and Thucydides was doing historical research, delineating cultural survivals of barbarian days which he claimed had preceded Greek civilization. The concept of survivals would, many years later, become an important aspect of both cultural evolutionary and functionalist theory. Xenophanes, on the other hand, was clearly conceptualizing a position of cultural relativism. About 520 B.C. he wrote,

> Yes, and if oxen and horses or lions had hands, and could paint with their hands, and produce works of art as men do, horses would paint the

forms of the gods like horses, and oxen like oxen, and make their bodies the image of their several kinds. . . . . The Ethiopians make their gods black and snub-nosed; the Thracians say theirs have blue eyes and red hair.

Somewhat later in time (63 B.C. to A.D. 21) the Greek scholar Strabo spent considerable time traveling through Asia Minor making systematic comparisons of temperaments, clothing styles, dwellings, and life styles of a variety of societies, paying particular attention to the relationship between culture and geography. His books *Historical Memoirs* and *Geography,* written about 7 B.C., might be considered the first works on cultural ecology or anthropogeography.

The Roman philosopher Lucretius (98–55 B.C.) equally qualified as an anthropologist when he speculated on such theoretical questions as the origin of speech, religion, and the arts. Concerning the development of the arts, he wrote:

> A garment tied on the body was in use before a dress of woven stuff. Woven stuff comes after iron, because iron is needed for weaving a web; and in no other way can such finely polished things be made, as heddles and spindles, shuttles and ringing yarnbeams. And nature impelled men to work up the wool before womankind; for the male sex in general far excels the other in skill and is much more ingenious; until the rugged countrymen so upbraided them with it, that they were glad to give it over into the hands of the women and take their share in supporting hard toil. (1873)

Lucretius's speculations concerning the sequence of metal and weaving, the origin of a division of labor, and the natural aptitudes of the sexes, while grossly in error, represent an intriguing chapter in the development of scholarly interest in the nature of Man and culture.

Less speculative and more description in nature was the work of the Roman historian Tacitus, who in A.D. 98 wrote a splendid ethnographic account of the German people. While this account deals with nearly all aspects of indigenous German culture, a single example of his work—that dealing with family life—will reveal an approach very much like that found in modern anthropological monographs.

> Their marriage code . . . is strict, and indeed no part of their manners is more praiseworthy. Almost alone among barbarians they are content with one wife, except a very few among them, and these not from sensuality, but because their noble birth procures for them many offers of alliance. The wife does not bring a dower to the husband but the husband to the wife. . . . The young men marry late, and their vigour is thus unimpaired. . . .
> . . . Nor are the maidens hurried into marriage. . . . Sister's sons are held in as much esteem by their uncles as by their fathers . . . but every man's own children are his heirs and successors, and there are no wills.

. . . The more relatives he has, the more numerous his connections, the
more honoured is his old age. (1942:717−19)

The Middle Ages

Considering the flourishing state of "anthropological" thought during
the Greek and Roman antiquity, the period from the third to the fifteenth centuries can only be described as dismal. The Western world
was fettered by the orthodoxy of the Christian church, which saw no
need to search beyond biblical interpretations to understand people's
physical and cultural development. While there were contacts between Europeans and other cultures during the crusades and through
exploration and trade (e.g., Marco Polo), missionary activity, and warfare, very little of this experience found its way into scholarly works
or theoretical formulations. There was, however, a florescence of
Arab scholarship during this period. Especially noteworthy was the
work of Ibn Khaldun (discussed in the previous chapter) and Ibn Ba-
tuta (1304–1378) who both traveled to Europe, the Far East, Africa, and
Indonesia and studied variations in governmental systems and religious practices.

The Renaissance

Intellects and intellectual inquiry began to revive during the Renaissance (fourteenth and fifteenth centuries) when European scholars
(mostly Italian) began to acquire a more secular perspective. New interests in classical antiquity developed, and numerous artists and language and literary scholars began making comparisons between the
contemporary cultures of Europe and those of ancient Greece and
Rome. Some even engaged in archeological research in their search
for historical evidence. The result was a clearer perspective of the nature of culture and cultural differences and of the dynamics of cultural change. But Renaissance scholarship, centered on a limited
number of societies, was narrow in its scope, albeit the research had
the advantage of being diachronic.

The Age of Exploration

The Age of Exploration which followed close on the heels of the
Renaissance changed what had previously been the provincial nature
of the inquiry into cultures and their works. And during this period

the vast boundaries of the discipline which would become anthropology were established. Moreover it was a time when data about the diverse lifeways of the world's peoples began to be accumulated. The Renaissance had established a valuable frame of reference for the gathering of scientific data about people, and the Renaissance studies of classical languages and cultures became models for collecting similar types of information all over the world. Comparisons with the past had established a methodology which could now be used cross-culturally.

Beginning to be gathered during the explorations of the African coast promoted by Henry the Navigator of Portugal between 1441 and 1456, and continuing to be gathered on the voyages of Vasco de Gama, Christopher Columbus, Magellan, and dozens of others up through the Captain James Cook expeditions (1768–1779), a great volume of ethnographic data was amassed and made available to governments, scholars, and the general reading public. While most maritime explorers were more at home with their compasses and swords than they were with their pens, some produced excellent accounts of the exotic folk they encountered along the way. Many early voyagers included natural scientists in their expeditions. Men such as Joseph Banks and John and George Forster, who traveled with Captain Cook, kept excellent journals describing not only flora and fauna but also aborigines. They recorded many accounts of indigenous peoples, including not only descriptions of culture—strange customs and manners—but also the physical types of the people they met. It was believed that through an analysis and comparison of racial characteristics they could solve the mysteries of geographic origins and migratory histories. They foreshadowed the development of a science of anthropology with its interests in both cultural and biological phenomena.

Missionary Ethnographers

Colonization often quickly followed the discovery of new territories, and with the colonists went Christian missionaries—Spanish Catholics to North and South America and British and American Protestants to the islands of the Pacific. Worthy of special note are two monks, Fray Bernardino de Sahagún (a Franciscan friar) and José de Acosta (a Jesuit).

In 1529 Fray Bernardino de Sahagún arrived in Mexico. The Aztec nation had recently been conquered by the Spanish, and Sahagún had been sent to participate in the conversion of the Indians. He immediately became intrigued with the customs and history of these

Mexican people and made it his first priority to learn their language, Nahuatl. Rationalizing that evangelizing the Indians would be more successful if the native culture were known, he set about recording data in the aboriginal tongue, consulting old pictorial records (codices), training Aztec assistants to collect information, and chronicling the Spanish conquest from the Indian point of view. His *General History of the Things of New Spain* (in preparation from 1547 to 1577) has been pronounced one of the most comprehensive cultural descriptions of a non-European population at that time in history.

While Sahagún was primarily an ethnographer, content to investigate and record the facts of Aztec history and culture, Acosta was, in addition to being a collector of cultural data, also something of a theorist. Acosta postulated an evolutionary sequence in human history and delineated three major stages of development. His scheme placed "real savages" who were without complex government or writing in the bottom category of human beings. This category was divided into "higher savages" and "lower savages" depending on whether they were peaceful or warlike. Above them on the developmental scale were peoples like the Mexicans and Peruvians, who lived in stable settlements with complex governments but lacked the knowledge of writing. The Chinese and Japanese, with literacy and "civilization," came next but they were seen as being somewhat less genuinely the real creatures of "civilization" when compared with the Europeans. Acosta's formulations were ethnocentric, with value judgements favoring his own society, but he was probably the first scholar ever to combine actual field observation (ethnography) with cross-cultural comparison and theoretical conceptualization (ethnology). His *Natural and Moral History of the Indies*, written in 1590, uses the term *moral history* to describe systematic description and comparison of *mores,* or customs.

In North America the most outstanding early missionary-ethnographer was undoubtedly Joseph-Francois Lafitau (1681–1746). This French Jesuit worked among the Canadian Iroquois, and in 1724 published *Customs of American Savages Compared with Those of Earliest Times*. This volume is so detailed, and of such high quality, that it is a prime source for ethnohistorians today. In addition to providing a record of Iroquois culture Lafitau advanced the theory that the American Indians had their origin in the Old World, and that cultural differences between American Indian cultures and Old World cultures were due primarily to changes in environment, isolation, and the tendency for customs to fall into disuse and be forgotten over an extended period of time. Lafitau was a true ethnologist in that he devoted much of his life to comparing customs of Indians with those practiced in the Old World as described in the classical literature.

Much of what Lafitau wrote about the indigenous peoples of

North America found its way into a rather remarkable archive series, called *Jesuit Relations*. This series of publications ran to seventy-three volumes and covered a period of missionary observation and study of Indians from 1610 to 1791.

Another outstanding contributor to *Jesuit Relations* was Fr. Paul Le Jeune, who studied the tribes in the area of Quebec not as "savages" or even under the general category "Indians," but rather in terms of accurate tribal identifications—Montagnais, Huron, and Iroquois—making a special point to stress their cultural uniqueness. Fr. Jacques Marquette was the first to describe the beautiful calumet (peacepipe) ceremony among the Indians of the southern plains, and Fr. Maturin Le Petite produced a remarkably systematic description of the religion, political organization, and social structure of the Natchez of Louisiana.

Just as capable, although somewhat later in time, were the Protestant missionary scholars in the Pacific such as George Brown, who worked for forty-eight years among the Samoans and several Melanesian island groups, and William Ellis, whose *Polynesian Researches* (1831) recorded every phase of Pacific island life in the Society Islands, Hawaii, and New Zealand. Unlike most missionaries of his time, Ellis seemed disinclined to compare Polynesian cultural traits with European forms for purposes of stressing their inferiority. Ellis approached Pacific cultures with respect and admiration, and this resulted in the kind of rapport which permits quality data collection.

Scientific Societies

Exploratory voyages such as those of Captain Cook, Bougainville, La Perouse, Kotzebue, and others were creating a good deal of interest in the non-Western world during the late eighteenth and early nineteenth centuries. The accounts of maritime explorers and missionaries were best sellers in European book stores and scholars in Europe and America, interested in scientific inquiry, were founding special societies in which they could exchange information and ideas about remarkable new discoveries of exotic societies and peoples.

The first of these was the American Philosophical Society, founded by Benjamin Franklin in 1743. The purpose of the society was the promotion of research with special attention to be given to the Indians of the United States. Thomas Jefferson, president of the society from 1797 to 1815, formed a committee of members to send letters to persons associated with American Indians, requesting information concerning "the Customs, Manners, Languages and Character of the Indian Nations, ancient and modern, and their migrations."

The Society of Observers of Man was established in Paris in 1800. This was followed by the American Ethnological Society (in Philadelphia) in 1842, the Ethnological Society of London in 1843, and the Smithsonian Institution in 1846. These societies established a tradition of anthropological study when there still was no anthropological profession per se. Typical of the activities of these groups was the production of *Notes and Queries on Anthropology* by The Royal Anthropological Institute of Great Britain and Ireland. This book contains questions on all aspects of culture which colonial administrators, explorers, missionaries, or traders could use to produce a comprehensive ethnographic account of local indigenous populations. Another society, the Hakluyt, was founded in 1846 to promote the publication of explorers' journals.

The Amateur Anthropologists of the Enlightenment

The eighteenth and nineteenth centuries were without doubt times when there was growing interest in the nature of nonliterate societies. Concerning this development Clyde Kluckhohn writes:

> The first systematic anthropologists were gifted amateurs—physicians, natural historians, lawyers, businessmen—to whom anthropology was a hobby. They applied common sense, the habits they had learned in their professions, and the fashionable scientific doctrines of their day to the growing knowledge about "primitive" peoples. (1949:3)

Thomas Jefferson is a good example of these pioneers in the science of anthropology. Jefferson had grown up among Indians and had developed a deep interest in their history, physical type, language, culture, and welfare. His greatest interest was the comparative study of languages, and he personally collected vocabularies of over fifty Indian tribes. Jefferson's interest in Indian prehistory had also prompted him to engage in considerable archeological research, and he is believed to have been the first to employ the concept of *stratigraphy*, a major concern in nearly all modern scientific excavation. A fascinating but little known fact is that the ethnographic data collected by the Lewis and Clark expedition might not have been obtained without President Jefferson. In a section of Meriwether Lewis's orders marked "Ethnographic Information Desired," Jefferson stipulated the kinds of information he wanted the party to gather, and he gave full directions, including specific questions to ask, for recording the details of American Indian cultures.

Contrary to the attitudes of many of his contemporaries who considered the Indians to be literally savages and mentally incapable of acquiring the blessings of civilization, Jefferson held views which today would amount to *cultural relativism*. He maintained that differences in the level of development between Indians and whites could be accounted for by the circumstances which surrounded their lives. He wrote:

> Men living in different countries, under different circumstances and regimens may have different utilities; the same act therefore, may be useful, and consequently virtuous in one country which is injurious and vicious in another differently circumstanced. (Letter to Thomas Law, 1814)

Perhaps most unusual at this time in intellectual history was Jefferson's conceptualization of an evolutionary scheme for explaining various stages of human cultural development. In 1824 he wrote the following to William Ludlow:

> Let a philosophic observer commence a journey from the savages of the Rocky Mountains eastwardly towards our seacoast. These savages he would observe in the earliest stage of association living under no law but that of nature, subsisting and covering themselves with the flesh and skins of wild beasts. He would next find those on our frontier in the pastoral state, raising domestic animals to supply the defects of hunting. Then succeed our own semi-barbarous citizens, the pioneers of the advance of civilization and so in his progress he would meet the gradual shades of improving man until he would reach his, as yet most improved state in our seaport towns. This . . . is equivalent to a survey . . . of the progress of man from the infancy of creation to the present day.

Where, one might ask, could Thomas Jefferson ever have come up with a concept like this thirty-five years before the publication of Darwin's writings on biological evolution and thirty-eight years before those of Herbert Spencer on social evolution? Although we have noted that a concept of three stages of human development was held as early as 1590 by the missionary Acosta, the idea might have come from a group of Scottish philosophers.

The Scottish "Science of Man" Philosophers

During the mid-to-late 1700s there was a group of university professors, their star students, and friends, who met frequently in a tavern in Edinburgh to discuss such topics as human nature, progress, marriage and family relationships, religion, primitive customs, and the history of institutions. All of these issues were considered the subject matter of "moral philosophy" and were discussed utilizing cross-cultural data, which at this time was in fair supply thanks to the journals and reports of explorers, missionaries, and traders.

Comprising this group were David Hume (its intellectual leader),

William Robertson, Adam Ferguson, Dugal Stewart, Adam Smith, Lord Monboddo, and their patron, critic, and jester, Lord Kames. While all these scholars were cross-culturally oriented, Kames, Monboddo, and Robertson seem most interested in nonliterate people per se. Although each of the scholars had specific interests, the group's theoretical position might be generally described as follows: They believed that the main purpose of any Science of Man should be to understand "human nature," which they believed had ordered ways of behaving in accordance with the laws of nature. They posited a basic human nature, common to all human beings, and maintained that patterns of behavior resulted from this human nature and could be predicted. All institutions were judged to be products of natural laws and to operate to the glory of God, the satisfaction of the individual, and the welfare of the society. Basically evolutionary in their theoretical orientation, they believed that "progress" was natural to the human animal. Like any other animal, Man had the capacity for growth, but Man's growth was seen in his cultural achievements as well as in his physical maturation. Adam Ferguson maintained that progress was God's gift to all his intelligent creatures, and that it was within the competence of even the "lowest of human races."

Lord Kames's book *Sketches of the History of Man* (1813) used ethnographic data from such societies as the Caribbean Indians, Philippine Islanders, Tartars, Chinese, as well as from ancient Rome and Greece and from northern Europe. And from his analysis of this cross-cultural data he concluded that "just as there is with respect to individuals, there is a progress from infancy to maturity, so there is a similar progress in every nation, from its savage state to its maturity in arts and sciences."

William Robertson wrote a cultural history of the American Indians based on questionnaire responses from America as well as missionary and explorers' journals. He used an evolutionary frame of reference with specific categories of "savagery," "barbarism," and "civilization" to discuss various levels of development in social organization, language symbolism, and political organization.

Museums

Because anthropology began in part as the study of curiosities—exotic socities and strange races—museums logically play a large part in the formulation and encouragement of the discipline. People have always enjoyed viewing the artifacts of foreign people. Museums existed in Babylonia, Alexandria, and Rome in ancient times, and many of these contained not only material objects like tools and weapons but people as well—brought by their conquerors to amuse and pique the interest of spectators. In the mid-1800s it was demonstrated that the products of non-Western peoples could lend themselves to scientific treatment. In 1850, the Museum of Ethnology in Hamburg, Germany, was established, and in 1866 the Peabody Museum of Archeology and Ethnology came into being at Harvard University for the purpose of collecting and analyzing cultural materials. Although the National Museum of Natural History (the Smithsonian) was established in 1846 from a legacy of an English chemist, and although the museum's first secretary was a physicist, this government institution did much to sponsor ethnographic research on the American Indian.

In 1851, A. H. Pitt-Rivers, working at the University Museum of Oxford, arranged the tools and weapons of contemporary peoples according to quality of workmanship and complexity, in an attempt to illustrate how people had evolved or progressed in their technical abilities. About this same time, Christian Thomsen, a Danish scholar confronted with the problem of how to display a museum collection meaningfully, originated a scheme of classifying artifacts according to three ages—stone, bronze, and iron. Thus, the mere problem of how to exhibit non-Western artifacts forced museum people to develop theoretical frames of reference. Whereas early European museums often chose to display materials according to a developmental or evolutionary sequence, American museums (like those employing Franz Boas, A. L. Kroeber, or Clark Wissler) in the early part of the present century classified materials according to geographical regions—a procedure that ultimately led to the concept of culture areas (regions of common culture). Museums the world over have also been major subsidizers of anthropological research.

Social, Cultural, and Biological Evolution

No discussion about the growth of the science of anthropology is complete without dealing at some length with the nineteenth century philosophical and scientific concept—evolution. Seeds of evolutionary thought may be identified as early as the sixteenth century, but between 1840 and 1860 evolutionary ideas were popping up everywhere. In 1858 Charles Darwin learned that Alfred Russel Wallace, a botanist working in Indonesia, had independently developed a theory of biological evolution much like his own. As early as 1855 the sociologist Herbert Spencer maintained that societies are like organisms and they progress from simple to complex forms according to "invariable laws." During this same period a third scholar in the

United States, Lewis Henry Morgan, developed his own scheme of cultural evolution well before anything on biological evolution appeared in print by Charles Darwin.

With the development of this evolutionary frame of reference and a fund of data about primitive peoples available in museums and in travel accounts, all of the ingredients were now available for the emergence of a scientific study of the human animal. *On the Origin of Species* (Darwin 1859) had established humans as members of the animal kingdom subject to the same drives and needs that motivate other social animals, and Spencer had defined the task of the social scientist as that of tracing the development of human society from its most savage to its most civilized state. The force of evolutionary thought was not to be denied, and the result was the first theoretical formulation of cultural anthropology, the "school" of cultural evolution.

TYLOR AND MORGAN

Although many scholars were instrumental in formulating and advancing the evolutionary school of thought, Edward B. Tylor and Lewis Henry Morgan stand out above all others. Edward B. Tylor, an Englishman, was learning his father's brass foundry business when, as a result of a four month trip to Mexico, he became interested in the history and contemporary cultural behavior of non-Western societies. Upon his return to England he aligned himself with the Ethnological Society of London and spent the rest of his life researching anthropological questions.

On the other side of the Atlantic, a young lawyer in upstate New York, Lewis Henry Morgan, organized a social and literary society called the Grand Order of the Iroquois, and for some twenty-five years this group dedicated itself to the study of the life and history of the Indian peoples who occupied their region. Morgan made many visits to the reservations of the Iroquois (particularly the Seneca), observing games and ceremonies, studying their political organization and their kinship system, and recording their myths and legends. He also collected artifacts for the state museum at Albany.

When an unscrupulous group of businessmen, the Ogden Land Company, tried to swindle (with government help) the Senecas out of their lands, Morgan (as legal counsel) and the Grand Order of the Iroquois came to the aid of the Indians. This deep involvement in Iroquois affairs undoubtedly contributed to Morgan's knowledge of the society, and in 1851, he published *The League of the Ho-de-no-sau-nee,* or *Iroquois,* a monograph which was described by the head of the Bureau of American Ethnology, John Wesley Powell, as "the first scientific account of an Indian tribe ever given to the world."

In 1850 Morgan traveled to upper Michigan on personal business, but while there he spent considerable time investigating the Ojibwa Indian kinship system. Later fact-finding field trips to Kansas and Nebraska in 1859 and 1860 and trips to Winnipeg and the upper Missouri River territory in 1861 and 1862 allowed him to gather great amounts of data in his major interest of Indian kinship systems and other areas. Morgan proposed that comparison of kinship systems would be an excellent way of solving some of the anthropological mysteries of his day: Where did the American Indians come from? Were they created in the New World, or were they really remnants of Lost Tribes of Israel?

In 1871 Morgan published a monumental comparative work on kinship titled *Systems of Consanguinity and Affinity of the Human Family.* Beginning with data he personally collected, and adding what he could glean from classical literature and travel accounts describing societies in Europe, Asia, Oceania, and Africa, Morgan produced the book regarded to be that which created the science of kinship and established the nomenclature for all analysis of social organization. The book also represented the first evolutionary history of the human family, from promiscuous horde to monogamous domestic unit. His later book, *Ancient Society,* (1877) carefully spells out his theory of human cultural evolution on a worldwide scale. Actually it was primarily an amplification of the theoretical position set forth in his kinship book.

Edward Tylor's book, *Primitive Culture,* appeared in 1871, and although there seems to have been only minimal contact between the two men, their positions are remarkably similar. In the schemes of these early theorists and several of their colleagues, contemporary nonliterate peoples were considered representatives of the various stages of evolution of human culture. In *Primitive Culture* Tylor describes his method:

> By simply placing [European] nations at one end of the social series and savage tribes at the other, [and] arranging the rest of mankind between these limits . . . ethnographers are able to set up at least a rough scale of civilization . . . [representative of] a transition from the savage state to our own. (1871:26—27)

Culture, the evolutionists maintained, had evolved in successive stages, from a condition of savagery to one of civilization, and this succession of stages was essentially the same in all parts of the world. There had been, so to speak, a *unilinear* development of culture. This development was quite natural, since progress from simple to complex was the natural destiny of human beings. Not only was progress inevitable, but so was the order of stages of development, because of a *psychic continuity* among all human beings. That is to say, all peoples are not equal in their mental capacities (Tylor and Morgan thought some races were inferior) but that at the same stage of cultural development all human minds tend to think in similar ways and possess similar capacities. Tylor and Morgan never postulated any egalitarian "psychic unity" principle (this was Adolf Bastian's idea) although many anthropologists believe this was included in their theoretical position. Instead, Tylor and Morgan saw "savage" and "civilized" intellect as vastly unequal, and they maintained that primitive or savage man was to civilized man what a child is to an adult. They believed essentially that mankind had gone through what might be considered a childhood (savagery), a period of youth (barbarism), and a manhood (civilization).

In their discussions of the development of culture the evolutionists pointed to hunters and gatherers such as the Australian aborigines and Athapascan Indian tribes as being living examples of peoples at the savage stage of Man's development, while peoples like Eastern Woodlands Indians (with the art of pottery making) and Southwest Pueblo Indians (with permanent villages and plant and animal domestication) represented degrees of barbarism. The civilized stage (characterized by the use of a phonetical alphabet and the production of literary records) was divided into ancient and modern, the latter, of course, being represented by Western Europeans and the former, by the Romans and Greeks at a particular point in their development.

A characteristic activity of cultural evolutionists was speculation on the origins and development of such institutions as the family, law, private property, and religion. Morgan, for example, distinguishes five different and successive forms of family developing out of a stage of group promiscuity. He contended that matrilineal (mother's line) descent had preceded patrilineal (father's line), and that plural marriage had come before monogamy.

An important feature of the evolutionary method was the search for survivals, for example, elements in contemporary cultures that represent holdovers from former stages of culture. "Old folklore themes" and "superstitions" were construed as evidence of earlier lifestyles. Evolutionists believed that survivals revealed the history of mankind's cultural growth just as biologists used to believe that the growing foetus revealed the prehuman stages in the biological evolution of Man.

Although the reconstruction of human history according to the evolutionary principles of Tylor and Morgan has been rejected by the majority of modern scholars, this school of thought made a number of valuable contributions to the discipline of anthropology. These are the *comparative method* (cross-cultural analysis), the concept of *culture* (elaborated by Tylor), the framework for analysis of social organization (Morgan's concepts of *affinity* and *consanguinity*), and the establishment of a method of systematic classification and analysis of religious belief (by Tylor) which set a high standard of scholarship for others like Sir James Frazer (author of *The Golden Bough*) to follow.

Although Franz Boas (in America) and the German diffusionists accused the evolutionists of neglecting evidence of borrowing, in actuality Tylor was particularly interested in diffusion and did a detailed study of the similarity between the Aztec game *patolli* and the Indian game *pachisi* (our Parcheesi), concluding that Mexican civilization was "in large measure" the result of Asian influence (1878:128). In *Ancient Society* Morgan commented that in the course of human societal development "all of the tribes must have shared in each other's progress" (1877:39) and that evidence of diffusion in no way invalidated his evolutionary hypothesis. Tylor, in a similar vein, held that, "civilization is a plant much more often propagated than developed" (1958:I:53).

In addition to making the contributions cited above, Tylor, although not a university-trained scholar himself, was selected to occupy the first chair in anthropology at Oxford University, and anthropology in those days was often referred to as "Mr. Tylor's science."

In the Soviet Union Morgan is heralded as the greatest of all anthropological scholars because his book *Ancient Society* greatly influenced the thinking of Karl Marx and Friedrich Engels. Specifically Marx was impressed by Morgan's descriptions of the social structure of preclass society, his uncompromising evolutionism, and his characterization of primitive society as communistic (communal). Today Morgan's statue stands in Red Square, an ironic achievement for a more than financially comfortable capitalistic lawyer from upstate New York.

The Diffusionists

Convinced that history never repeats itself, and believing that the enthnographic facts failed to support the grandiose, nomothetic schemes of the nineteenth-century evolutionists, diffusion oriented scholars in Great Britain and Germany, and historically oriented scholars like Franz Boas in the United States were, during the latter part of the last century, vehemently opposing cultural evolution.

In Great Britain, people like W. H. R. Rivers, G. Elliot Smith, and W. J. Perry were not willing to admit that men were capable of independently inventing anything more complex than what would be invented at a hunting and gathering stage, and they maintained that most of the elements more complex than the simplest of survival skills had diffused from a single course. Smith and Perry, in particular, postulated that a number of cultural ideas such as kingship, irrigation, cremation, navigation, etc., derived from Egypt, their worldwide diffusion taking place when voyagers from this land circled the globe in search of precious gems.

G. Elliot Smith (1871–1937) had made an outstanding name for himself as an anatomist and physical anthropologist, but he made the mistake of going to Egypt to make a study of the brains of mummies. While in that country he became so impressed with the accomplishments of the ancient Egyptians that he credited nearly all of the cultural accomplishments in the world to them. These ideas were developed into a body of theory referred to as the Manchester or Heliocentric (sun-centered school of thought). Robert Lowie has summarized this diffusionist position as follows:

1. Man is uninventive; hence culture arises only in exceptionally favorable circumstances, practically never twice independently.
2. Such circumstances existed only in ancient Egypt; hence elsewhere culture, except some of the simplest elements, must have spread from Egypt with the rise of navigation.
3. Civilization is naturally diluted as it spreads to outposts; hence decadence has played a tremendous role in human history (1937: 161).

Smith and Perry maintained that nearly every important cultural trait known to man came from the ancient Egyptians but, as Lowie (1937:167) points out, they never quite explained how the Egyptians acquired the knowledge necessary to teach Eskimos how to build igloos or Siberians how to ski. While Smith and Perry had their day in England and even, surprisingly, attracted some good anthropologists to their theory, their school soon collapsed for want of supporting scientific data. In Germany, however, a much more convincing school of diffusionist thought was developing.

THE GERMAN DIFFUSIONISTS

The German diffusionist school commonly known as the *Kulturkreis* school ("cultural historical") gained recognition about 1925 through the writings of Robert F. Graebner and Father Wilhelm Schmidt. In comparison with the position of the cultural evolutionists and the British diffusionists the *Kulturkreis* school was scientific and scholarly. This school maintained that the cultures of the world had been built up by the spread of several core cultures (groups or clusters of traits) that diffused out of the Old World at various periods. For example, in the South Seas one complex of traits consisted of conical roofed huts, dugouts, spears, spearthrowers, and totemism, while a later unit was composed of yam cultivation, planked boars, gabled huts, heavy clubs, and the worship of the dead. The study of the cultural history of any particular group therefore necessitated making an analysis of its inventory of cultural traits. While modern day anthropologists credit this school with developing effective methods for assessing culture contacts, they deplore its disregard for geographical and psychological factors in the transmission of culture traits, its insistence on migration as the sole agent of diffusion, and its general tendency to utilize data supporting its theories while ignoring counterevidence. Although the culture-historical school scholars at one time exerted great influence on the work of German, Austrian, and Scandinavian anthropologists, their views are generally felt to be inadequate today.

AMERICA'S HISTORICAL DIFFUSIONISTS

In America Franz Boas and his students had rejected the cultural evolution school and were establishing a body of anthropological theory themselves. Boas, his students, and colleagues, while different in their points of view and in their anthropological activities, have frequently been described as representing a school of thought that has been called either the American diffusionist or the American historical school. Some of these pioneers in American cultural anthropology were museum people while others were professors of anthropology at various universities, but they all had one important thing in common: They were not armchair theorists. All believed in comprehensive field observation. Boas, for example, made prolonged field trips to the Eskimos of Baffin Island and worked with Northwest Coast Indians almost every summer for about thirty years. He constantly impressed upon his students at Columbia University that every aspect of culture, no matter how insignificant, should be recorded. He knew that he had left many gaps in his study of the Eskimos and was determined that his students should profit from his mistakes. American ethnographers felt that mastery of the native language was essential and that not only should the anthropologist speak like the people but ideally he or she should learn to think like the people so that culture could be studied from the people's point of view.

Anthropologists working in the early part of the twentieth century were especially concerned that American Indian groups, and indeed, "primitives" all over the world, were losing their cultural identity through contact with the West. Thus, there was a feeling of urgency, a desire to get out and record what still remained of the "old" cultures. Because many of the aboriginal customs had already been lost, there was an attempt to reconstruct the precontact culture by working with old people who remembered how things had been done in the more traditional past. These interviews were supplemented by archeological data, by analysis of folklore, and by delving into historical documents written by traders, missionaries, "squaw men," and explorers.

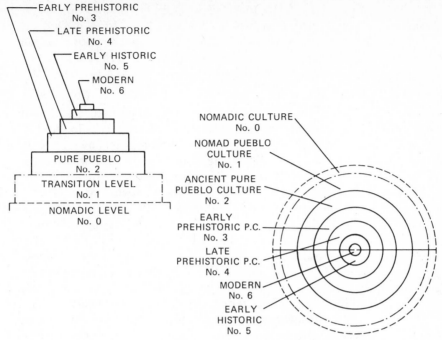

Figure 2-1 Principle of age-area illustrated by concentric distribution of pottery types in the Southwest, according to Wissler (1923:60, after Nelson).

AGE-AREA
CONCEPT

Where these methods were not considered adequate, some American scholars developed hypothetical schemes such as the "age-area" concept for the reconstruction of cultural histories. The "age-area" method involved the study of trait diffusion, and American scholars got their "diffusionist" label partly from this method. It assumed that cultural traits diffuse out from their point of origin in concentric circle patterns. By determining the areas of distribution of given traits, it was believed that their source and comparative age could be established. It was also believed that if the history of a number of traits could be determined they would add up to the history of a particular culture. (See Fig. 2-1.)

BOAS'S
HISTORICAL
APPROACH

Although the diffusionist label has been given to the work and theory of Boas and other pioneers in American cultural anthropology, their preoccupation with the diffusion of particular cultural traits was merely part of a historical approach to culture. Actually, the discovery of evidence of cultural borrowing from one tribe to another was but the first step in the development of a cultural history of a given tribe. Boas maintained that culture must primarily be understood in a historical context. In Boas's view, Hopi Indians do not live in permanent villages and farm the land because they have moved up the evolutionary ladder to that point but rather because of a unique set of historical circumstances—opportunities and limitations—coming from inside and from outside the culture which has shaped their lives.

BOAS'S GOAL FOR ANTHROPOLOGY

The American historical school has, of course, greatly influenced the growth and development of American anthropology. This is only natural since many American anthropologists have been greatly influenced by the work and teachings of Boas who made a number of major contributions to the growing discipline of anthropology. To begin with, Boas's insistence on exhaustive studies of cultures has provided modern anthropologists with valuable field data with which to test and document modern theoretical formulations concerning the nature of culture. He and his colleagues are largely responsible for the establishment of a systematic and orderly approach to the study of culture. Such concepts as culture traits, complexes, patterns, and areas have proved to be valuable research tools. While the American historical school tended to study separately the multiplicity of elements that make up a culture, these scholars always stressed a holistic study of culture and warned against thinking of culture as anything but a configuration of interrelated traits and complexes.

Although Boas and others were scientific in their methods and approach (Boas often used statistical analyses of data), they were not scientific in the sense that they were trying to discover "laws" of human behavior. Boas was often criticized for his failure to generalize on his findings. To such critics Boas replied that the ultimate goal of anthropology was the formulation of general laws of human behavior and cultural growth, but that more detailed studies of tribal cultures and histories were needed. Without all of these facts no valid generalizations could be ventured. As early as 1896 Boas's theoretical point of view had crystallized. He knew where he was going and how to get there. In a speech in that year he stated:

> It will be well to restate at this place one of the principal aims of anthropological research. We agreed that certain laws exist which govern the growth of human culture, and it is our endeavor to discover these laws. The object of our investigation is to find the processes by which certain stages of culture have developed. The customs and beliefs themselves are not the ultimate objects of research. We desire to learn the reasons why such customs and beliefs exist. (1948:276)

Boas was always concerned with why certain traits found their way into a culture and others did not. He also wanted to know how traits were incorporated into a new cultural context. In every case he thought that the reasons were historical, growing out of the unique cultural development of the group.

Functionalism

Any discussion of modern anthropological perspective must of necessity note the contribution of two European schools of theory which, in spite of their theoretical differences, have both been labeled *functionalism*. The earlier of these was the French sociological school of functionalism, which originated just prior to World War I with the work of the British anthropologist A. R. Radcliffe-Brown. Radcliffe Brown had been an admirer of the French sociologist Emile Durkheim, and the anthropological theory that he developed was strongly influenced by Durkheim's analysis of Australian aboriginal society. The functionalism of Radcliffe-Brown stressed the importance of group or societal behavior and all but dropped the concept of culture. In fact, the best statement of this theoretical position, Radcliffe-Brown's *The Andaman Islanders*, does not even list the word "culture" in its index. Tribal custom was interpreted in terms of social cohesion and integration, and the individual was virtually ignored in an attempt to discover laws of group interaction. The function or purpose of such customs as funerals, puberty ceremonies, and feasts was to contribute to group solidarity and survival. All systems existed primarily to maintain the social structure and enhance social integration. A good example of A. R. Radcliffe-Brown's position may be seen in his interpretation of mourning in the Andaman Island study:

> For the society a death is the loss of one of its members, one of its constituent parts. A person occupies a definite position in society, has a certain share in social life, is one of the supports of the network of social relations. His death constitutes a partial destruction of the social cohesion. The normal social life is disorganized, the social equilibrium is disturbed. (1948:285)

Thus, Radcliffe-Brown takes the position that death is less of a personal tragedy than a group tragedy. The response, therefore, is institutionalized mourning. This and many other human cultural habits were seen to grow out of the nature of group life. The group was stressed in his theories often at the expense of the individual. Functionalist theory looked upon society as something not unlike a biological organism and often drew analogies from biological terminology. For example the form or structure of society was often referred to as its "social morphology," whereas the nature of its activities or operations was referred to as its "social physiology."

The modern discipline of social anthropology, with its emphasis on social organization and social function, developed primarily from this school of functionalism. Anthropologists today are indebted to this school of thought for its theoretical and methodological contributions in the realm of family, kinship, and political organization analysis.

STRUCTURAL ANTHROPOLOGY

One of the most important developments in anthropological theory in recent years has been the work of the French anthropologist Claude Levi-Strauss, who has done much to integrate social and cultural anthropology under the title of "structural anthropology." Although influenced by the French sociological tradition of Emile Durkheim and Marcel Mauss, Levi-Strauss has developed highly original and productive methods for analyzing kinship structures, political systems, primitive classification systems, and mythology. In such works as *The Elementary Structures of Kinship* and *The Savage Mind* he expounds his thesis that culture is structured—just as language is structured—and that it is possible to isolate certain regularities analogous to the rules of syntax in a language. Through this logical cultural system members of the society come to recognize the world of nature and the human world as ordered, predictable, and comprehensible. The phenomenon of reciprocity is an example of the kind of general principle which Levi-Strauss maintains is observable in many aspects of culture in societies the world over. Principles such as this, Levi-Strauss believes, can serve as a basis for cross-cultural comparison of human behavior.

MALINOWSKI'S FUNCTIONALISM

Although the theory of the British anthropologist Bronislaw Malinowski has also been labeled *functionalism*, his point of view was quite different from that of A. R. Radcliffe-Brown. The most basic difference was that Malinowski was concerned with cultural traditions whereas Radcliffe-Brown was primarily interested in society and the interaction of its members. Malinowski maintained that individual cultures have a unity or equilibrium wherein every cultural trait is dependent upon, and interrelated to, every other, allowing society to function like a machine with every gear and cog in the proper place.

In one study of the Trobriand Islanders, *Argonauts of the Western Pacific*, he shows how economic activities relate to other facets of life such as folklore, religion, social organization, etc. This study was but one of his many exhaustive treatments of the Trobriand Island people, a group with which he spent a number of years doing firsthand research. Like Franz Boas, Malinowski stressed field investigation, seeing the culture from the native's point of view or, in Malinowski's own words, the anthropologist must "get inside the native's skin."

Malinowski not only emphasized the interrelated quality of the items in culture but maintained that the main function of each and every custom and institution was the satisfaction of biological, psychological, and social and cultural needs. Even though Malinowski's functionalism was psychological in approach, taking into consideration the factors molding individual personality and considering the conflict points in family and social life, he is often accused of being antihistorical. Malinowski is known to have emphasized the value of scientifically derived history in training his students; but he repeatedly went on record as opposing the kind of conjectural history that was utilized by the diffusionists and cultural evolutionists.

Not only did Malinowski refrain from engaging in historical reconstruction, but he almost totally ignored evidence of diffusion. His interest was the here and now, not the processes of cultural growth that produced the culture. Kardiner sums up Malinowski's position:

> The history of an institution, its form and distribution, its evolution and diffusion—all these problems are of secondary importance. The important questions are, How does an institution function now: How does it satisfy individual and cultural needs in a given society, and How is it related to other institutions? (1961:174)

Without doubt, the work of Malinowski added materially to the growing young discipline of anthropology in the late 1920s and the 1930s. He was, to begin with, the layman's anthropologist. He lectured widely and his books, always carrying catchy titles, were widely read. To professionals he had shown the value of a fieldworker totally submerging himself in the culture. Malinowski's own field methods—his use of interview, observation, and careful analysis of the native language—set a pattern for future research. By spotlighting the unity of culture, Malinowski did much to correct the misimpression of many, that culture is a fabric made up of "shreds and patches," that is, traits massed haphazardly as the result of diffusion.

CONFIGURATION-ALISM

Some anthropologists would claim that there was still a third functional school, that of the poet-anthropologist Ruth Benedict. While her approach has been termed *configurationalism*, it had many things in common with that of Bronislaw Malinowski. She approached culture in terms of its holistic and integrated quality, but unlike Malinowski she concentrated on whole cultures and not on their component institutions. The book *Patterns of Culture* illustrates her approach clearly. In this study she attempted to show how four cultures, Kwakiutl, Dobu, Zuni, and Plains, had a particular "pattern" or "theme" (terms borrowed from her background in esthetics) that ran through all institutions and customs and tended to mold the personalities of the society members to a particular, homogeneous form. Benedict maintained that just as the many cells of the body contain identical sets of chromosomes and genes, the many traits that make up a culture reflect the characteristics of the whole. All the traits work together to produce a certain type of culture and at the same time a common personality type. Culture, to her, had a master plan.

Benedict's writing not only emphasized the organic unity of culture but added still another dimension to the study of culture—the psychological aspect. With the use of such labels as *Dionysian, Apollonian, paranoid,* and *megalomanian,* Benedict attempted to characterize the "ethos" or psychological/emotional set of a culture.

Neo-Evolutionists

By 1945, many anthropologists were of the opinion that in rejecting unilinear evolution Boas and others had "thrown out the baby with the bath." Reevaluations of the concept of cultural evolution were being made by Julian Steward, Leslie White, Robert Redfield, and the British archeologist V. Gordon Childe. Most of the new theories that developed did not hold that all cultures in their processes of growth had gone through a series of identical stages. The new theories maintained that as peoples of various cultures developed their technology, broad trends, or similarities, in cultural development could be noted.

MULTILINEAR EVOLUTION

Julian Steward held, for example, that similar (but not identical) stages of development can be recognized in the cultural growth of such civilizations as the Inca, the Maya, the Mesopotamians, the Egyptians, and the Chinese. Steward's position, sometimes referred to as "multilinear evolution," stressed the fact that similar structures with similar core institutions may develop independently under analogous conditions and with analogous sequences of events.

GENERAL OR UNIVERSAL EVOLUTION

Leslie White, in contrast to Julian Steward, was primarily interested in the worldwide development of culture rather than individual cultures and even replaced the word *anthropology* with the word *culturology.* White ignored geographical and psychobiological facts and stressed the cumulative, collective force of culture. He explicitly identified the mechanism by which evolutionary change occurs, maintaining that culture advances as the amount of energy harnessed per capita per years increases, or as the efficiency of energy utilization increases.

V. Gordon Childe used archeological data to demonstrate that certain outstanding technological developments—plant and animal domestication, the invention of metallurgy, irrigation—produced revolutionary changes in every aspect of a society's life-style. More interested in the individual development of specific cultures than Leslie White, Childe tended to see an overall pattern of changes in the culture of mankind that was "progressive" in nature.

CULTURAL
ECOLOGY

Closely tied to modern evolutionary thought, particularly that of Julian Steward, is the theoretical approach known as *cultural ecology*, which is the study of the interaction of cultural processes with the biological and physical environment. Cultural ecologists maintain that different environments present different challenges and that these are met with different cultural responses of a technological, economic, social, and religious nature. They further believe that these responses will tend to represent the most efficient utilization of the natural resources, and, therefore, some responses are more likely to occur than others in certain kinds of environments. This is a holistic approach which considers the environment as an active, integral part of the cultural system rather than a passive, extracultural factor.

EVALUATION OF
EVOLUTION
TODAY

Present-day cultural anthropologists are far from agreeing on the usefulness of the concept of "evolution" as a frame of reference. The more traditional American anthropologists prefer to speak of "cultural change" and not "cultural evolution," believing the latter smacks too much of Tylor and Morgan and is all too often associated with biological evolution or with ideas involving value judgments such as "progress." One thing is certain—cultural evolution is once again on the anthropological horizon and will not easily be put down.

Neo-Diffusionists

Along with the increased interest in the work of Lewis Henry Morgan and in the concept of evolution in general has been the development of neo-diffusionism. While some of this has been promoted by people of German and Scandinavian backgrounds (where diffusionism has always been strong), some Americans have also become involved. Among the latter, for example, are Betty J. Meggers and Clifford Evans, who believe that the development of New World civilizations might very well have been affected by trans-Pacific contacts from Japan. Citing "striking parallels" between New World and Asian architecture, religious practices, and art styles, these two archeologists maintain that the explanation may lie in the diffusion of such ideas from Japan by fishermen who somehow arrived on the shores of Ecuador about 3000 B.C.

Pottery discovered by an amateur archeologist, Emilio Estrada, has been found to be remarkably akin to that from the Jomon Period from Kyushu, Japan. Similarities include comparable rim treatment (using castellations or peaks), general vessel shape, and decorative techniques. Both cultures decorated with incised parallel lines, zig-zags and "dog bone" impressions. This ceramic evidence plus the assumption that a typhoon blew a Jomon fishing party far enough out to sea that the prevailing winds and currents would carry them east and south has led Meggers and Evans to conclude that such an event did indeed occur and that Japanese contact "resulted in the introduction of different technologies, art styles, and patterns of behavior" and have "significantly modified the direction of indigenous cultural development in the New World" (Meggers and Evans 1966:35).

In addition to Thor Heyerdahl who has crossed two oceans—the Pacific on the raft *Kon Tiki* and the Atlantic on the reed vessel *Ra* —to establish the possibility of diffusion of culture by transoceanic migrations or expeditions, there is a more recent entry into the diffusionist arena by Robert Langdon, who has been described as having a "Sherlock Holmesian flair for noticing barely perceptible clues, and inexhaustible patience in seeking out facts." Moreover, he is described by his publisher as "someone unawed by experts and prepared to tackle such diverse subjects as astronomy, archaeology, anthropology, Basquology, botany, genetics, navigation, ship-building, linguistics, dog breeding and sixteenth-century Christian theology."

What this jack-of-all-trades proposes is that in 1526 four Spanish ships bound for the East Indies were separated by a storm just after passing through the Strait of Magellan. One vessel, the *San Lesmes*, was never heard of again. Langdon maintains that this vessel was wrecked on an atoll to the east of Tahiti. The surviving crew members allegedly married the local Polynesian women and over the following 250 years they and their descendants found their way to a great number of Pacific islands. Langdon claims that they established Hispanic-Polynesian dynasties, fused Spanish and Polynesian culture, and generally produced all of the cultural achievements for which Polynesians were heretofore credited. The Spanish sailors, for example, influenced canoe building and navigational techniques, brought writing to Easter Island, incorporated Biblical materials into Polynesian chants, and discovered New Zealand. The fleet of canoes which anthropologists have long believed carried Maoris from eastern Polynesia to New Zealand, was, according to Langston, really an expedition of sixteenth-century Spaniards trying to sail home via the Cape of Good Hope.

Perhaps the most startling of the ideas of latter day diffusionists are those of Erich von Daniken who claims that the origin of all things civilized is outer space. Although von Daniken is not a trained anthropologist, he deals almost exclusively with anthropological subject matter and his many books have sold into the millions. They have been accepted as legitimate anthropology by a large segment of the reading public of the Western World. He has been serialized in the *National Enquirer* and his ideas have been the subject matter of a television special and a movie. He accepts the idea of primate evolution but maintains that "all knowledge" came from outer space. Using a few hard facts and a great deal of liberal interpretation of myths, legends, and passages from holy books, von Daniken attempts to explain archeological "mysteries" of Easter Island, Mexico, Central America, Peru, and ancient China as being due to visitations from interplanetary beings. Von Daniken sees "integrated circuits" in the designs on ancient Chinese bronze discs, maintains that Sahara desert cave drawings depict creatures attired in spacesuits and helmets, and sees ray guns in the hands of stone figures at Tula, Mexico (although most anthropologists recognize them to be spear throwers). He interprets a petroglyph on Easter Island as a picture of a ramjet engine, and the Upper Paleolithic cave painting of a shaman wearing an animal head with antlers is, in von Daniken's interpretation, an extraterrestrial visitor in an antennaed space helmet. Most anthropologists who have analyzed his claims feel that every time he sees something he doesn't understand, he attributes it to extraterrestrial intelligence, and since he has read very little about prehistory, he sees evidence of this influence all over the planet.

EVALUATION OF DIFFUSIONISM TODAY

While many professional anthropologists take a dim view of most of these incredible schemes, they are usually hesitant to become embroiled in these kinds of controversies, since they are often accused of not being open to new ideas because of vested professional interests. Perhaps the best advice to the new student of anthropology in ascertaining the validity of what some have labeled "Sunday supplement" anthropology is to suggest the use of a do-it-yourself checklist such as that proposed by Professor James S. Trefil. It reads,

1. Are the facts really what the author says they are? (What do other authorities say?)
2. Is the author trying to overload your circuits?
3. Given the author's facts, is there a simpler explanation of them?
4. Does the whole thing boil down to being unable to prove a negative? (e.g. It is impossible to prove there are no unicorns.)
5. Are established scientists putting time in on the phenomenon?
6. Can you test the theory yourself? (Look at books on Peru and Polynesia and see if you see the same thing Heyerdahl does in regard to pyramid construction and stone carving.) (1978:20–21)

On the other hand, if you want to get into the act, and try your hand at breaking von Daniken's record for selling paperbacks, you may want to follow the advice of Professor John G. Douglas. It is:

1. Invent a conspiracy and expose it, thereby discrediting the authorities in the field.
2. Propose a Bold New Theory, which accounts for anything.
3. Collect some isolated oddities and pronounce them unexplained.
4. Give the appearance of documenting your statements.
5. Use inflated superlatives every chance you get.
6. Ask rhetorical questions at least once every three paragraphs.
7. Set yourself up as a persecuted intellectual martyr. (Graybill 1974:47)

Current Anthropology

Although the discussion thus far has stressed "schools" of theory developed by individuals or groups of anthropologists, there is little evidence that "school" thinking is present to any great extent in modern American anthropology. Social anthropology, which has found its greatest following in England, has been greatly influenced by the work of Durkheim, Malinowski, Levi-Strauss, and Radcliffe-Brown, but cultural anthropology seems to have selected the best contributions from the various "schools" of anthropological thought and combined them in a rounded, comprehensive study of humanity and its works. At its best, modern anthropology is functional, historical, diffusionist, psychological, and comparative; in other words, it has developed into an eclectic discipline.

Whether it is labeled "cultural evolution" or "cultural change," the study of the dynamics of culture has, without doubt, become the most important consideration in present-day anthropology. With the ever-increasing modification of primitive culture by Western contact the task of anthropology is felt to be the analysis of the processes and effects of cultural borrowing and assimilation. Because of this modification some anthropologists have even questioned the value of continuing to regard anthropology as the study of "primitives." There has been a developing emphasis on the cross-cultural aspect of the discipline and a decreasing insistence that anthropology should be concerned only with one kind of people. Today anthropologists commonly study peasant, folk, and even complex Western societies.

While the older approaches to the study of human populations and their cultures asked such questions as "What did they do?" and "When did they do it?" the modern approach is deeper and more searching. Now the question most frequently asked about the behavior of human groups is "Why do they do it?" Thus the areas of values, symbols, beliefs, and motivations have become prime subjects for anthropological research. Along with this trend there has been an increasing cooperation between anthropology and psychology, sociology, and social psychology in order to improve the quality of investigation of such topics as human interaction, personality formation, social structure, communication, cognition, and value orientation.

The trend toward working more closely with other disciplines may also be seen in the recent emphasis on the relationship between human biology and culture. This research has, of course, been directed toward explaining the existence of cultural universals (cultural items found in all societies) in terms of the biological nature of human beings. The titles of many new areas of anthropological specialization—ethno-musicology, ethnohistory, ethnobotany, chemical anthropology, ethnolinguistics—indicate the degree to which modern anthropology has joined forces with still other scientific and humanistic disciplines in order to explore ever deeper the biological, psychological, and sociological dimensions of the human animal.

Summary

Anthropology as a discipline is relatively new, but interest in the subject matter of anthropology goes back to ancient times when such scholars as Herodotus, Strabo, Lucretius, and Tacitus were writing about their contacts with foreign peoples and exotic lifestyles. During the first few centuries of the Christian era inquiry into human culture tended to be inhibited by the Church, but the Renaissance (fourteenth century) with its more secular trends of thought brought a renewed interest in human societies and cultures. This was followed in the sixteenth to eighteenth centuries with an Age of Exploration, during which scores of European voyages of discovery encountered and recorded the characteristics of numerous foreign cultural systems. This not only brought about speculation concerning human biological and cultural differences but provided a fund of ethnographic information which could be used to formulate and test theories concerning human nature and the growth of human civilization.

Beginning with the writings of the Scottish "science of man" philosophers in the eighteenth century and extending into the nineteenth with the work of Lewis Henry Morgan and Edward Tylor, the first formidable theoretical school, known as "cultural evolution," came to dominate the anthropological horizon. Only vaguely related to the biological theories of Charles Darwin, cultural evolution maintained that all contemporary nonliterate peoples around the world were representatives of various stages of evolution of human culture. Culture, they maintained, evolved through successive stages—savagery, barbarism, civilization—Western Europe, of course, representing the apex of human cultural development. Tylor is often credited with being the "father of anthropological science," and he occupied the first university chair of anthropology (at Oxford) from 1896 to 1909.

Believing that history never repeats itself and that the human animal is extremely uninventive, scholars in Germany, England, and the United States rejected evolutionary theory and were explaining the forms and growth of human culture in terms of diffusion of knowledge from one society to another. The German diffusionists thought in terms of the spread of bundles of traits, called *Kulturkreis*, whereas Britains Perry and Smith postulated worldwide contact by Egyptians, and Americans (mostly students of Franz Boas) attempted to understand the cultural history of American Indians by doing distribution studies (of diffused traits) and creating hypothetical formulations (like age-area) for reconstructing lost history.

During the early years of the twentieth century when American anthropologists were feverishly attempting to document the nature of dead and dying American Indian cultures, the British still enjoyed the luxury of observing functioning societies (in the colonies of the vast British Empire). One scholar, A. R. Radcliffe-Brown, had been strongly influenced by the sociological theories of Emile Durkheim and developed a position called *functionalism* which stressed group solidarity and social structure. A second school of functionalism also developed under the leadership of Bronislaw Malinowski, but he maintained that the primary function of every item in a cultural system is the satisfaction of biological, psychological, and social needs.

The end of World War II was marked by the rise of several new scientific theories. There was, for example, "neo-evolutionism," based to a large extent on the earlier ideas of Morgan and Tylor. Among this group were the multilineal evolutionist Julian Steward, the general or universal evolutionist Leslie White (who replaced the term *anthropology* with *culturology*), Robert Redfield, and V. Gordon Childe.

More recently there has also been a revival of neo-diffusionist theory with principal exponents being people like Meggers and Evans (stressing trans-Pacific contacts), Thor Heyerdahl (who sails rafts and reed boats across oceans to test migration feasibilities), and Erich von Daniken (who postulates diffusion from outer space).

Although the history of anthropology may be characterized as one of "school" thinking, modern anthropology tends to be highly eclectic, utilizing the best features of many theoretical positions. The modern discipline has shown increasing interest in value orientations, symbolism and cognition. There has been constant emphasis on understanding the culture from the people's point of view as well as an ongoing interest in removing ethnocentric bias and developing more objective methodology. Ecological and sociobiological interests have gained in popularity and there has been a greater emphasis on cross-disciplinary cooperation as evidenced by the titles of a host of sub-fields which have emerged, for example, ethno-musicology, ethno-history, ethnolinguistics, ethnobotany, etc. There has also been a movement toward greater specialization but this has not altered the basic perspective of anthropology which remains comparative and holistic.

The Human Animal Emerges 3

The Evolutionary framework

> Lamarck
>
> Darwin
>
> Mendel
>
> The modern synthesis

Human variation

> Polymorphism and "race"
>
> Adaptations to environmental stress
>
> Disease and natural selection

Primate evolution

> What is a primate?
>
> Early primates
>
> The appearance of hominoids
>
> Hominid characteristics
>
> The appearance of the genus *Homo*

Before Darwin

The development of biological evolutionary theory was essential to the growth of physical anthropology. Although we tend to associate the name Charles Darwin with evolution, many before Darwin tried to explain and understand biological diversity.

Evolutionary theory demands a particular view of nature, a point of view not often taken by early philosophers or naturalists. Prior to Darwin, virtually all who wrote about nature viewed each life form (species) as having its own essence, it's own fixity which could not change over time. This idea is central to many pre-Darwinian theories and is called *essentialism*. Proponents of essentialism (and these included people such as Aristotle, Descartes and Linnaeus) viewed the world in very static terms, and they did not believe that change of any kind could occur naturally. Another result of essentialistic thinking was the idea that there exists a great chain of being (the result of perfect creation) which logically progresses from "low" (simple) forms to "high" (complex) forms. Of course, humans were placed at the "high" end of the scale. Clearly, essentialism is incompatible with a concept of change, and the development of evolutionary theory had to await the erosion of this prevailing world view (Mayr 1982:310).

Not until the seventeenth and eighteenth centuries did the accumulation of biological and geological data truly propel naturalists into rejecting essentialism in favor of evolutionism. These data included an ever increasing list of fossils, increasing evidence of extinction of many forms, and a broader acknowledgement of the variability of flora and fauna. Each caused a growing discomfort with the long held notions of species fixity, perfect creation, the young age of the earth, and even the use of the Bible as a source of scientific explanation.

LAMARCK

Jean Baptiste Pierre Antoine de Monet, Chevalier de Lamarck (1744-1829) was a French biologist interested in plants. Early in his career, Lamarck believed in the fixity of species and was a traditional essentialist, but an academic appointment to study invertebrates (specifically worms) began to shape his ideas concerning diversity and change (Burkhardt 1977).

Lamarck was fascinated by the growing evidence of the extinction of many different forms of life. While extinct species were known to earlier naturalists, Lamarck found the prevalent explanations for extinction to be inadequate. Three explanations for extinction dominated natural science: 1) extinct animals were killed in Noah's flood, 2) extinctions were the result of human intervention (i.e., hunting), and 3) extinction was not really a fact because many of these forms were probably still living in unexplored areas of the world. The riddle-solving clue which led Lamarck to formulate a theory of evolution appears to have been his recognition of fossil species which closely resemble living species. Lamarck wrote "may it not be possible… that the fossils in question belonged to species still existing, but which have changed since that time…?" (1809:45).

One of the most important features of Lamarck's theory of evolution is that he recognized the importance of the environment as a factor affecting the biology of all organisms. Lamarck was struck by the balance and harmony each species has with its particular environment. Since he recognized that the environment constantly changes, he reasoned so too must species constantly change to maintain a perfect balance. This deduction most certainly led Lamarck to reject the essentialist's view of a static world.

By including time as a factor responsible for evolutionary change, Lamarck interpreted species diversity as a result of a long process of branching, with each change (branch) leading to a more perfectly adapted species. A central theme of Lamarck's theory is that as the environment changes, organisms must respond by acquiring new adaptations, appropriate for their new environments. This is called the *theory of acquired characteristics* or transformationism, and it is probably the most misunderstood aspect of Lamarck's theory. As a matter of fact, when discussing this topic, most textbooks erroneously attribute two ideas to Lamarck which have continued to belittle him as an evolutionist. The first is the commonly held belief that Lamarck accepted the idea that an organism can *will* a change to occur. Lamarck was not so naive as to believe that wishful thinking or an internal conscious "desire" could produce an adaptational response or a new anatomical structure. His complicated analysis argues simply that the organism *needs* (not *wants*) to become modified as the environment changes.

The second idea erroneously ascribed to Lamarck is that the environment can directly cause changes in an organism. Lamarck rejected this, and instead argued that "the environment affects the shape and organization of animals… in the course of time…(but the environment) does not work any direct modification whatever in the shape and organization of animals" (1809:107).

Why, then, do we not associate Lamarck's name with the theory of evolution? The most likely reason is that at the foundation of Lamarck's theory was an elaborate physiological model. It was his belief that subtle fluids are produced to satisfy biological needs that, although widely accepted at the time, is now known to be far from true. Other ideas held by Lamarck included: 1) a belief in *soft inheritance* (inheritance of features based on their use or disuse by the organism), 2) innate perfectibility, and 3) spontaneous generation. Without ignoring these obvious flaws, it may nonetheless be stated that Lamarck was an important forerunner of Darwin. He accepted evolution as a fact, he recognized the roles of time and the environment on biological change, and he provided a theory (although rejected today) to explain how evolution takes place.

DARWIN

Charles Darwin (1809-1882) was fascinated by nature and wanted desperately to spend his life as a natural historian. Born to a wealthy middle class English family, expectations were that he become a physician, not a naturalist. Darwin was, therefore, sent to the University of Edinburgh to study medicine. He quickly became bored with his lessons, and an alternate career in theology was selected. Darwin then entered Cambridge University in 1828 where he studied classics, theology, and mathematics, subjects which hardly lend themselves to improving skills in natural history. Darwin nonetheless completed his degree, all the while maintaining his avid interests in collecting beetles, keeping nature journals, and reading works on nature.

In 1831, after returning home from a geological mapping field trip, Darwin found what was to become the most important invitation of his life. Over the objections of his father, Darwin joined the voyage of the H.M.S. Beagle as the naturalist-on-board. Finally, he could devote all of his time to his favorite occupation, and he could do so with the added bonus of traveling around the world!

Darwin's observations aboard the Beagle as well as those he had accumulated during his life to that point, contributed to the development of his theory of evolution. He saw a variety of fossils while in Argentina, was awed by the spectacular Andes Mountains, and was fascinated by the species diversity of Galapagos finches. It was particularly this last point, species diversity, which became a central conceptual struggle for Darwin — How do species originate and why?

Borrowing from a paper by Thomas Malthus titled *Essay on Population* (1798), Darwin forwarded testable propositions and from these, then made two deductions: 1) if all things vary (as a quick glimpse around you will document) and 2) if populations have reproductive potential to increase dramatically, then what force keeps all of the variation which exists stable? The central core of Darwin's theory of evolution rests on his answer to this problem. Darwin deduced that there must be a constant struggle for existence. Individuals who survive the struggle are successful in an environment because of the particular characteristics they possess. In other words, they are naturally selected because their particular suite of features allow them to compete, survive, find a mate, and reproduce. This process, called *natural selection*, would gradually change populations through constant differential success at competing in the struggle.

Natural selection can also explain the origin of species. If a portion of a population were to enter a new environment or if individuals became geographically isolated from the original population, what would happen? Darwin argued that natural selection would work to produce future generations which would become modified (adapted) over time. If they could not survive, extinction would occur. Rather than proposing a goal-directed process leading to increasing perfection, Darwin simply argued that selection only operates to produce a "best fit" between individuals and their environments each generation.

While this basic thesis appears simple, it was revolutionary when published as a book titled *On the Origin of Species by Means of Natural Selection or the Preservation of Favoured Races in the Struggle for Life* in 1859. Before writing the book, Darwin learned that another naturalist, Alfred Russel Wallace had developed virtually an identical theory of evolution. Wallace also had read the Malthus essay and used its basic principles to develop the concept of natural selection. The coincidence of these two independent developments is surprising, but the result was that Darwin hurried to finish his draft before Wallace had an opportunity to beat him to publication. The race to publish was won by Darwin.

DARWIN'S DILEMMA

Darwin's theory of evolution challenged many long held beliefs about nature. Evolutionism created a great challenge to essentialists, as Darwin was able to demonstrate a logical alternative to species fixity, extinction and perfect creation. The obvious extension of natural selection to all living things, including humans, required a re-evaluation of our collective place in the natural order of things. For the traditionally educated 19th century student, placing humans at a level comparable to any other animal was at best distasteful and at worst, blasphemous. Nevertheless, as soon as essentialism was questioned, many ideas concerning nature had to be reviewed.

The most troublesome problem for Darwin was that he did not understand how nature produces the variation among individuals upon which natural selection must work. Why do all things vary? he asked himself. Even though offspring resemble their parents, they still look different. Where do these differences come from? These were questions without answers for Darwin. Darwin did not know how characteristics were inherited and therefore could never address these problems. A truly complete theory of evolution had to await the discovery of genetic principles.

MENDEL

Gregor Johann Mendel (1822-1884) was, in a number of ways, much like Charles Darwin. Mendel was intrigued by nature, and like Darwin, he believed that diversity was not chaotic and random but rather was ordered and even predictable. Searching for a profession which would secure a means of livelihood, Mendel entered an Augustinian monastery in 1843. It was then that Mendel had enough free time to devote himself to plant breeding, and eventually, to establishing the foundations of heredity.

Mendel's training and background provided an important key to his success. His father had taught him much about plants (he raised fruit trees) and his early schooling at the University of Vienna gave him a strong foundation in natural sciences. As is true of many great scientists, Mendel anticipated many possible problems before he began to experiment. For example, Mendel knew that he would have to choose an organism in which characteristics remained constant, that is, they had to be discrete. He wanted clear results, so the characteristics chosen would have to be equally straightforward. He also knew that he had to choose an organism which was easy to manipulate so that he could control mating. Obviously, if one is trying to understand patterns of inheritance, one must know both parents and their offspring, otherwise the pattern would be indiscernable. After some initial tests, Mendel chose the common pea plant for his experiments.

The first step of his experiments was to select the characteristics of the common pea which he would examine. Mendel focused his attention on seven characteristics, each of which had two, and only two expressions (Figure 3-1). He began his experiments by self-fertilizing plants to produce pure (true breeding) parents for each of the two expressions for the seven characteristics. For example, he bred a pure wrinkled plant and a pure smooth plant while ignoring all of the other of the pea's characteristics (height, seed coat color etc.).

Mendel proceeded by carefully fertilizing the two pure parents for the texture characteristic. The result of this cross (called a monohybrid cross) was that *all* of the offspring produced were smooth textured! What had happened to the wrinkled expression? Mendel had a pretty good idea of what had happened, but to support his theory, he executed the next step of his experimental design.

Mendel planted the offspring from the pure parental cross the next spring. He allowed them to fertilize themselves in the normal way, and when he harvested their pods, he found that they had produced both smooth and wrinkled peas. The wrinkled expression reappeared in the second generation! Mendel harvested these peas and counted them, again a step required in this well-designed experiment. He found 5,474 smooth peas and 1,850 wrinkled peas, a ratio of 74.7% to 25.3%, or 3:1 (Figure 3-2).

When he repeated steps one and two of his experiment using the other discrete characteristics of the pea, he discovered the following consistencies.

1. Each of the first generation offspring resulting from pure parental crosses possessed only one of the alternative expressions of the characteristic. Mendel termed the expression which appeared in these monohybrid offspring as the *dominant* expression.
2. The expression which was "lost" in the first generation offspring always reappeared in the second generation at approximately a 25%

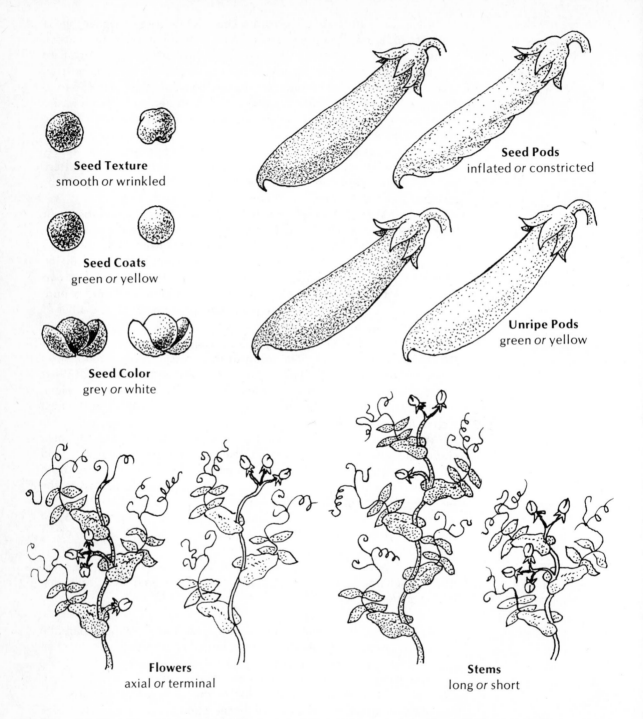

Figure 3-1 The seven characteristics of the pea plant chosen for analysis by Mendel (After Campbell).

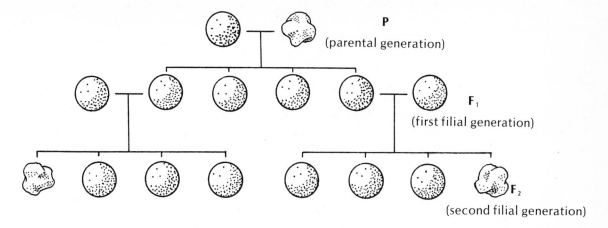

Figure 3-2 Results of the monohybrid cross using pea seed texture (smooth and wrinkled).

frequency. Mendel termed this expression of the characteristic the *recessive* expression.

3. Mendel found these consistencies in each of the tests of the seven characteristics, regardless of the sexes of the pure parents. For example, the results were the same if the pure smooth parent was either a male or a female.

What Mendel had demonstrated up to this point in his experiments was that the inheritance of traits follows distinct, understandable patterns. Being a smooth or wrinkled pea depends upon the contribution of factors from each parent. Characteristics are not a matter of blending fluids (a common idea prior to Mendel) or of chance. The inheritance of features follow straightforward, predictable patterns. Although Mendel could not actually see the units of inheritance which control the traits he observed, he reasoned that these units (he called them factors) must be particulate; that is, they behave as indivisible units, each with it's own integrity. He formulated his first law, the *Law of Segregation*, from these observations. The law states that the units (factors) controlling the alternate expressions of the characteristics separate or segregate independently from one another.

Mendel followed these experiments with another set of crosses. This time he examined two characteristics at a time. He followed the same procedure of first breeding pure parents for two of the characteristics at a time. He chose the characteristic of pea texture *and* pea coat color. He produced a pure smooth *and* yellow parent, and a pure wrinkled *and* green parent. Mendel proceeded once again to produce a first generation from the cross between these two parents. These crosses are called dihybrid crosses because two traits are being examined simultaneously.

The result of this cross yielded a 100% smooth and yellow first generation. All of these offspring resembled only one of their two parents. Mendel did not stop there, but rather proceeded to allow these first generation offspring to produce a second generation. The results of these plants (Figure 3-3) once again demonstrate that the recessive expression for both characteristics reappears just as wrinkly and just as green as in their grandparents. Furthermore, the texture trait does not alter the inheritance pattern of the color trait. This led Mendel to formulate his second law, the *Law of Independent Assortment.* Simply stated, no characteristic alters the inheritance of any other characteristic. In this example, color is inherited independently of texture.

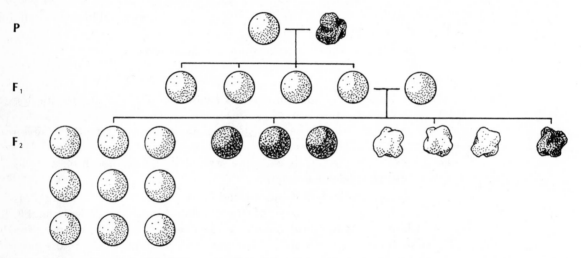

Figure 3-3 Results of the dihybrid cross using pea seed texture (smooth and wrinkled) *and* pea seed color (yellow and green).

Mendel presented the results of his plant hybridization experiments to the Brunn Society for the Study of Natural Science in 1865 and published them the following year, but they had no impact. The most likely reason for this is that Mendel had used a mathematical approach. Apparently, the logic of his discoveries escaped those who heard or read his publication. Furthermore, to understand Mendel's work demonstrating for the first time how traits are transmitted from parents to offspring, one had to believe that there exist particulate factors (too small to be seen) which direct the production and expression of characteristics. Mendel's ideas were just too hard to believe, and his work went unrecognized. Published at a time when Darwin could have found the missing principles to complete his theory of evolution, Mendel's work waited almost thirty years before being rediscovered.

GENETICS AFTER MENDEL

In March, April and June of 1900, three researchers independently rediscovered the work of Gregor Mendel. A Dutch botanist, Hugo DeVries, a German, Karl Korrens and an Austrian, Erich von Tschermak reintroduced Mendelian principles by presenting their results on plant hybridization to the German Botanical Society. Only DeVries knew from the beginning that a little-known monk originally had discovered the principles of heredity.

DeVries noticed that occasionally, the evening primrose plant would produce an entirely new variant. Although still obviously an evening primrose, he discovered a small cluster of plants in a field which had small oval leaves compared to the typical heart-shaped leaves he was familiar with. He called these new expressions *mutations*. DeVries argued that such novel characteristics help diversify populations, and they must play a vital role in evolution. Only when variation is present in a population can the more slow-acting, gradual process of natural selection act. Although Darwin rested his theory of evolution primarily on the force of natural selection, DeVries' evidence of the power of mutation was soon considered another equally important force of evolution.

THE MODERN SYNTHESIS

It was not until the 1950s that a holistic theory of evolution finally was developed. Why did it take so long and what factors were yet missing?

In 1902 Sutton and Boveri recognized that the dark staining bodies called *chromosomes* they observed in dividing cells were the probable units containing Mendelian factors. By 1953, F.H.C. Crick and J.D. Watson finally unraveled the mystery of chromosome structure. Chromosomes are long coils of deoxyribonucleic acid (DNA) containing the biochemical codes for each characteristic of an organism. The genetic makeup or *genotype* of an individual contains a specific code which directs the production of the specific protein producing each trait. This specific code is called a *gene*. The alternate expressions of a characteristic are caused by a variation in the code, and these are called *alleles*. Mendel could only record the expression of each of the seven characteristics in the pea plant by what he could see. This actual expression of the genotype is called the *phenotype*. But what Mendel knew existed, particulate factors turned out to be what we now recognize as genes.

DeVries was also right in arguing that mutation is an important force of biological change. Alleles are the result of changes which occur to the actual biochemical structure of DNA. Ultimately, all new genetic material is produced by mutation. Because natural selection must work on variability among individuals, mutation(s) may cause phenotypic differences which provide the diversity upon which natural selection acts.

Two other forces which can propel populations into biological change also were established. First, simple *migration* can produce biological change. Individuals possessing their own unique genotypes can alter the population's genetic diversity by introducing different alleles. Increasing the diversity of the entire population's set of alleles (called the gene pool) provides new possibilities of phenotypic variation.

The second force which can cause evolution is called *genetic drift*. If a small population becomes isolated from its parental population, alleles may be fixed at a particular frequency due to chance. Only some of the total allelic variation will likely be present among the individuals of this small population. Therefore, the new population's gene pool will be composed of a different selection of possible variants, causing potentially different consequences of natural selection.

THE PLACE OF EVOLUTIONARY THEORY IN PHYSICAL ANTHROPOLOGY

The development of evolutionary theory has been critical to the growth of all areas of physical anthropology. It provides the backbone to studies of human variation, of the primate fossil record, and of primate behavior. If we understand how biological change occurs, we can begin to explain rather than simply document and describe evolution.

Charles Darwin attempted to apply his theory of evolution by means of natural selection to humans in 1871, but at that time, principles of genetics were unknown. Even after Mendelian genetics was rediscovered, only a few researchers explored questions concerning human variation. The modern synthesis of evolutionary processes and population genetics occurred in 1937 when T. Dobzhansky united the facts of chromosome and gene action with observations on variation in natural populations (Dobzhansky et al. 1977:17). At last, many issues relevant to physical anthropologists could be addressed.

Human Variation

A major concern of the early founders of physical anthropology was to document and describe human diversity. From 1900 to 1930 the major focus of physical anthropologists was on describing the phenotypes of isolated peoples who were quickly being assimilated by Western colonization (Haas 1982:436). These data were used often to support or refute existing theories of racial variation. The entire concept of race grew not out of a tradition of evolutionary theory, but rather as an attempt to categorize variation. Differences among people's phenotypes were used to construct racial groups, each with their own recognizable "type." By assigning humans to these groups, similarities were of less interest than differences. Hair color and texture, skin color, and body shape (morphology) were primary features used in racial assignments (Figure 3-4).

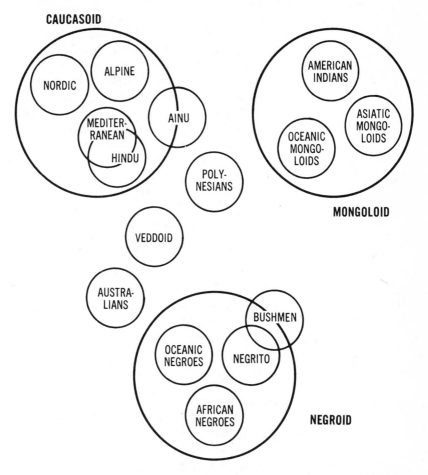

Figure 3-4 A.L. Kroeber's (1948) scheme for dealing with human "racial" variation. (From *Anthropology* by A.L. Kroeber. Copyright 1923, 1948, by Harcourt Brace Jovanovich and reproduced with their permission.)

This approach to diversity mirrors the efforts of early naturalists to establish and support species fixity. Remember that early naturalists viewed species as static, unchanging groups. Racial typologists were forced into drawing distinct boundaries among human groups, and in a similar manner, they made the diversity observed conform to strict, unchanging categories.

The establishment of the ABO blood group system in 1900 by Karl Landsteiner allowed researchers to study population differences for a genetically controlled characteristic. The ABO system easily is detected phenotypically by a simple test. Four different phenotypes can be recognized — types A, B, AB, and O. The trait is controlled by only three alleles, and these allele frequencies can be calculated from the populations phenotypes. A characteristic such as the ABO blood group system now allowed researchers to quantify racial differences and they hoped, support their designations of major racial groups throughout the world.

Genetic characteristics which vary in expression are called *polymorphisms*. During the 1940s and 1950s, many of these characters were examined (Crawford 1973). However, as new alleles were discovered and a growing number of genes were examined, it became evident that no consistent racial pattern existed. What had become apparent was that there is very little biological support for the existence of true racial groups. The distribution of human polymorphisms do not follow racially defined boundaries. A much more reasonable approach to the study of human variation is to consider in what way(s) genetic variants confer a selective advantage to the individual — in other words, how has natural selection produced the diversity we see?

ADAPTATIONS TO ENVIRONMENTAL STRESS

Humans live in diverse environments. Some areas are extremely cold for most of the year, while others are hot, humid, dry or temperate. Can any of the characteristics we observe be argued to have arisen through natural selection in these environments? Stressful environments appear to, in some degree, explain some features of population variation.

ECOGEOGRAPHIC RULES

Some fundamental principles which have been established can help us understand human adaptation to environmental stress. These principles hold true empirically for most mammals, humans included.

Bergmann's Rule is based on the observation that animals which live in cold environments have relatively larger body sizes than those which live in warm environments. For warm-blooded animals like humans, heat conservation is critical in a cold environment. Since body volume increases as a cubed dimension and surface area increases as a squared dimension, a larger body size will have a relatively smaller surface area. Because body volume produces heat and surface area is where heat is lost, higher volume to surface area ratio means efficient heat conservation.

Allen's Rule states that the relative size of appendages should decrease as a mean temperature of the environment decreases. Once again, body heat is lost from the surface areas of the body. In a cold environment, minimizing heat loss and conserving heat are at a premium. Individuals with relatively large trunks and short appendages would have a selective advantage over those of a different body type.

Gloger's Rule concerns pigmentation and the environment. Populations living close to the equator will have evenly distributed melanin and be phenotypically dark-skinned. As we move away from the equator, a more spotty distribution of melanin occurs, and individuals appear light-skinned. Melanin is a protective pigment produced in the basal layer of skin. The presence of this pigment protects the individual from harmful ultraviolent radiation. As this natural radiation can produce skin cancer, the protection gained from having an even screen of pigment is obvious.

HEAT AND COLD STRESS

Do humans follow the patterns expected by Bergmann, Allen and Gloger's rules? If we examine two extremes of human morphology, for example Eskimos and east African Nilotics (Figure 3-5), each prediction

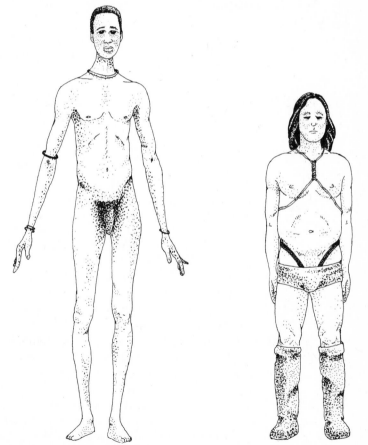

Figure 3-5 The Nilotic on the left and Eskimo on the right represent examples of Bergmann's and Allen's Rule. (Drawn to scale).

from the rules holds true. Eskimos tend to have stout, square-shaped trunks with relatively short appendages. These features are certainly adaptive in a cold environment. Nilotics tend to be extremely linear, with long trunks and long appendages. This morphology maximizes heat loss by increasing the surface of the body. The greater the surface area, the more efficiently sweating can occur to cool the body. Nilotics are also dark-skinned phenotypically, which protects them from the ill effects of ultraviolent radiation.

Although these two populations conform to our expectations, it is very important to recognize that such differences do not isolate these populations. An Eskimo and a Nilotic could have offspring, and their children would be able to survive and reproduce too. What we are stressing is that these differences are adaptations to environmental stress. They are not signs of speciation among human populations. Furthermore, variation between and among human groups is continuous. We have just compared two "ends" of the spectrum. Traits such as stature, skin and hair color vary among all human populations. As a matter of fact, there appears to be as much or more diversity within populations as there is between populations (Lewontin 1972; Latter 1980).

DISEASE STRESS

The presence of natural diseases has probably affected human populations for a very long time. No introduction to the field of physical anthropology would be complete without a discussion of human adaptations to an extremely well studied disease, malaria.

Malaria is caused by an infection of the malarial parasite, *Plasmodium*. The parasite lives in a mosquito host and enters the human bloodstream when the mosquito bites someone. Once inside, the parasite penetrates red blood cells (erythrocytes) and reproduces. It completes its life cycle in about four months. Because erythrocytes contain hemoglobin which plays an important role in transporting oxygen, the death of the red blood cell eventually causes the death of the infected victim.

In 1954 it was suggested that there may be some relationship between the geographic distribution of malaria and that of a genetic disease called sickle cell. Sickle cell is the result of a simple genetic mutation which alters the structure of the hemoglobin protein. Individuals with sickle cell genotypes appeared to be resistant to malaria as compared to individuals without these genotypes. It was soon established that individuals who possess one allele for sickle cell and one allele for normal hemoglobin (heterozygotes) were at a distinct advantage in a malarial environment. A portion of these individuals' red blood cells burst before the parasite can complete its life cycle. Even though the individual still is infected with malaria, the resistance provided by their sickle shaped red blood cells is sufficient to allow them to survive the disease (Figure 3-6).

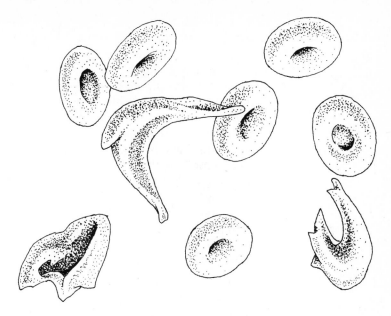

Figure 3-6 Sickled and normal hemoglobin.

Sickle cell is the classic example of human adaptation. A single mutation causing a variation of hemoglobin structure has the effect of improving the individual's chances of survival. Natural selection always acts to select those variants which improve the individual's chances of surviving and reproducing. Even though sickle cell has some negative effects on an individual's health by causing anemia, the advantages outweigh the disadvantages. Being anemic is certainly more adaptive than dying from malaria!

Human Variation in Evolutionary Perspective

Biological diversity which exists among human populations is best understood in light of evolution. What may appear to be unstructured or even harmful variations may, upon closer examination, reveal important adaptations. For example, particular genetic diseases have long been known to affect only certain human groups — cystic fibrosis among Europeans, sickle cell among some Africans, and Tay Sachs disease among Ashkenazim (eastern European Jews). Why do these diseases occur so frequently among these people? We know that these diseases are maintained at relatively high frequency because of mating patterns.

Why these diseases exist in the first place is another more difficult question. Evolutionary theory would predict that the presence of these genes confer some selective advantage. This should be measurable by examining if individuals with these genotypes produce more offspring than individuals without the genetic disorder. Practically, however, it is extremely difficult to demonstrate such selective advantage. Some reasons include the small family size of humans, and their particularly long lifespan. It is important to recognize, even with these limitations, that placing human variation in evolutionary perspective allows us to "make sense" of the diversity we see. Our understanding of genetic diseases can be applied in biomedical programs such as genetic counseling. Understanding growth and development patterns can be useful in recognizing growth disturbances or even in figuring out whether a youngster will be tall enough to compete in professional basketball or small enough to be a jockey. Each improvement in documenting and understanding human variation helps us view ourselves in biological perspective.

WHAT IS A PRIMATE?

Now that we have looked at modern human variation we need to ask how it is that humans have evolved. How have we come to be as we are today?

The first thing to recognize is that humans are just one member of a larger biological group. Humans are primates, and taxonomically we are classified along with other animals which share many characteristics in common. This grouping was established by Carolus Linnaeus (1707-1778) who spent his life developing a classificatory hierarchy. This classification system is still used today, but with some modifications. From broadest to most narrow, the levels of classification include kingdom, phylum, class, order, family, genus (plural genera), and species. Humans and all other primates are classified together at the order level (Table 3-1). As the levels become more and more restrictive, modern humans finally find a place of their own at the genus level.

Table 3-1. The Classification of Modern Humans.

Linnean System	Classification of Modern Humans
Kingdom	Animalia
Phylum	Chordata
Class	Mammalia
Order	Primates
Family	Hominidae
Genus	*Homo*
Species	*sapiens*

The naming of a species is called *binominal nomenclature* because two words (generally Latin) are given to each species. Sometimes a third name is given if the subspecies level is needed. Each group *(taxon)* has only one valid name, and for modern humans, our name is *Homo sapiens sapiens.*

What characteristics are shared among all primates? If we establish what these common characteristics are, we can begin to evaluate the fossil record of primate and eventually, human evolution.

1. Primates are extremely reliant on vision. Their senses of hearing and smell are much less efficient that their eye sight.
2. Primates have five fingers and five toes on each hand and foot. These mobile, grasping digits have nails instead of claws on one side and friction pads on the other. Gently rub your fingertips together to feel these friction pads (fingerprints) work!
3. Primate limbs are very mobile. Arms and legs can rotate and move in many directions.
4. Primates have unique dental characteristics. The number of teeth ranges in most groups from 32-36 teeth and they have distinct cusp patterns.
5. Primates tend to have a long period of infant dependency. Most primate parents must expend a lot of effort during their infants' early months or years.
6. Primates do not have large litters of offspring. Instead, primates have a low reproductive rate, permitting them to spend more time with each offspring.
7. Primates have relatively large and complex brains for their body size. Portions of the brain involved with muscle coordination, memory, learning and vision are more complex than in most other mammals.

THE EARLIEST PRIMATES

Around 65 million years ago during the geological period called the late Cretaceous, many life forms became extinct. Dinosaurs and many marsupials died, leaving open vast portions of the environment. One significant open arena was the arboreal environment, and some of the surviving mammal-like forms moved into these areas. They began to exploit portions of the arboreal environment, and they were successful.

The earliest primates were members of this invasion. They were small, insect eaters who used the terminal ends of tree branches to prey on flying insects. Using this portion of the arboreal environment (niche) certainly had some important consequences. Natural selection favored those forms who could maximize their reproductive success while still being able to compete with all of the other animals using the trees. The diet of these first primates would require agility, a high level of manipulative ability, a grasping hand to capture prey, and a refined sense of vision. Particularly stereoscopic vision, which allows an animal to perceive depth and distance, would be an adaptation to this lifestyle.

By the Eocene (53-37 million years ago), a widespread adaptive radiation of primate forms was underway. Diverse forms of primates were widely distributed throughout North America, Europe and Asia. Towards the end of the Eocene, however, competition in the arboreal environment increased. Rodents were beginning to become more prevalent, and these forms may have been in direct competition with primates. In addition, continents were drifting away from one another and the climate was becoming cooler. This would have the effect of altering many previously lush, tropical areas and would certainly have had an affect on the animals living in them.

The next epoch, the Oligocene (37-25 million years ago) was a period of dramatic speciation for primates. All of the fossil primate material comes from one locale, the Fayum. Located southwest of Cairo, Egypt, the Fayum remained a tropical rainforest, perfectly suited to primates (and to fossil preservation). Although much of the Fayum material is fragmentary, paleoanthropologists have argued that these fossils represent the separating evolutionary pathways of Old World monkeys (such as the baboon) and forms which would give rise to apes and humans.

THE EMERGENCE OF APE AND HUMAN ANCESTORS

During the Miocene (25-5 million years ago) primates who are probably ancestral to fossil and living apes and humans evolved. These forms, called *hominoids*, are found in Europe, China, and Africa.

One of the most discussed fossil hominoids is *Proconsul*. This fossil genus is best known from both cranial and skeletal remains. *Proconsul* (Figure 3-7) occupied a variety of niches in many areas, so it is fair to say that this genus was probably quite successful. Reconstruction of probable locomotion and diet suggest that *Proconsul* was quadrupedal (four-limbed locomotion) and a fruit eater (Morbeck 1975; Pilbeam 1979).

Historically, some paleoanthropologists have argued that *Proconsul* is ancestral to modern apes (chimpanzees, gorillas, orangutans, gibbons, and siamangs), while others have argued that it may be more closely related to humans. Because of the diversity of *Proconsul* fossils and these competing hypotheses, the taxonomic designation for *Proconsul* has been revised many times. The important issue to recognize is that agile, arboreal primates during the Oligocene were able to successfully survive and compete in the arboreal niche.

Another group of Miocene fossils has received a lot of attention. This group of hominoids is called *ramapithecines*, and it includes up to six different genera. These primates are found in Africa, Pakistan, China and even Greece and Hungary (Morbeck 1983). The majority of fossil evidence is limited to fragments of jaws and teeth, but these remains have generated much controversy. Much of the debate has centered on

Figure 3-7 *Proconsul africanus* (After Pilbeam).

whether these primates are the likely ancestors of our taxonomic family, Hominidae. Such forms are properly called *hominids*, designating their closer relationship to humans than to apes. As Milford Wolpoff states "ramapithecines are at the right place and in the right time span to be hominid ancestors" (1980:123). However, assigning them to the hominid status requires some concensus regarding exactly what an early hominid is, and many different opinions exist.

HOMINID FEATURES

In addition to the common features shared by all primates, hominids share a set of distinctive adaptations.

The lower trunk of hominids is unique. Pelvic, back, leg, and foot bones allow humans and their ancestors to do something very special — they stand erect. Bipedalism, a form of locomotion using only the legs, is a hallmark feature of all hominids. This adaptation had truly profound effects, as it allows the hands to be free for other activities, such as toolmaking. As we will see, hominids stood upright and moved bipedally approximately 1.5 million years before they began to depend on tools. Bipedalism, then, is the best marker in identifying a hominid because it appears to be the most important "first step" adaptation signaling the success of humans and their ancestors.

A second unique feature of our taxonomic family is intelligence. The evolution of intelligence generally is measured in terms of increasing cranial size and by increasing brain complexity. Sometimes a cast of the inside of a skull (an endocast) can be made from a fossil, and the imprints left on the surface by the brain itself can be seen. These endocasts can add information regarding intelligence because some of their features can be related to behavioral capabilities of the brain (Wolpoff 1980).

The third characteristic marking the emergence of hominids is a set of changes which have occurred to the face and teeth. Hominid teeth have unique morphologies. Compared to apes, hominids have relatively small canine teeth and shallow or flat faces. Their jaws can sustain greater chewing forces allowing them to efficiently grind and crush different types of food.

Finally, human behavior is unique. Culture has been defined in many different ways, but we can at least say that it represents a special kind of social organization, quite unlike that expressed in any other social organism. Acceptable standards of behavior, material goods such as tools, and a complex communication system (language) are some of the features we recognize as integral parts of culture. But how do we establish these features? Reconstructing behavior from fossil remains requires using comparative methods, analyzing aspects of material culture when items are found, and evaluating the environment in which early hominids lived. The early members of our lineage should not be expected to have looked or acted like contemporary humans. We simply must try our best to assess who they were and what they did from the evidence that they have left behind. There are no direct, simple answers to our questions about early hominid behavior or culture. Competitive hypotheses are generated constantly, and we should remember that, even when we learn about living cultures, we sometimes don't completely understand what we study!

AUSTRALO— PITHECINES

The first group of fossil primates which are considered hominids are called australopithecines. Their genus name is *Australopithecus* which means "southern ape," and this name reflects the early conservatism in recognizing these forms as human ancestors. Four species of *Australopithecus* are recognized. The earliest member of the genus is *A. afarensis*. Fossils of these species have been found in Ethiopia and Tanzania. The Ethiopian fossils, found at the Hadar site by D.C. Johanson and M. Taieb have been dated from 3.2 and 2.9 million years ago. The

Tanzanian material comes from a site called Laetolil and is composed mostly of teeth and jaws dated from about 3.7 million years ago. Unlike many other fossil collections, large amounts of bones and teeth have been found at both sites. The Hadar material includes a skeleton nicknamed "Lucy" (Figure 3-8). Lucy is the most complete fossil hominid yet found, and approximately 40% of her bones were preserved.

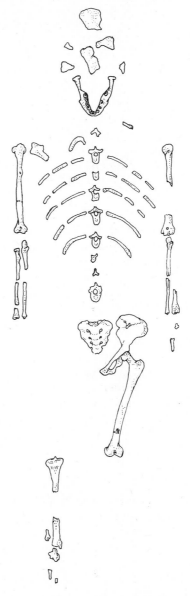

Figure 3-8 *Australopithecus afarensis, "Lucy".*

It is clear that these early hominids were bipedal. Lucy's pelvis, legs and feet indicate that she was an habitual bipedal primate (Johanson and Edey 1981). At Laetolil, Mary Leakey in 1977 and in 1978, found several sets of footprints preserved in the sand next to what had been a water hole. Volcanic ash had covered these imprints and preserved them. The footprints were made by a small, striding form, establishing that by 3.7 million years ago, a group of primates were depending on a uniquely hominid form of locomotion, bipedalism (Day and Wickens 1980).

By approximately 2 million years ago, australopithecines are represented by a diverse set of fossils found in eastern and southern Africa. Three species, *A. africanus, A. robustus, and A. boisei* represent what might grossly be stated as "variations on a theme." They are all small bodied, small brained (480-550 cc. cranial capacity), bipedal forms, some of which used stone tools (see Chapter 4). They were probably eating a primarily fruit-based diet, rather like that of a modern chimpanzee (Lewin 1984:45). Their diversity and widespread geographic locations can be interpreted as the result of favorable selection and their successful exploitation of the environment.

HOMO

At just about the same time, hominids at Koobi Fora in Kenya and Olduvai Gorge in Tanzania have been found. These fossils have cranial capacities of 650-800 cc., and are considered to represent the first members of our genus, *Homo*. Their taxonomic name is *Homo habilis*. From a distance, one would be hard-pressed to recognize *H. habilis* from some of the australopithecine fossils. However, upon closer examination we can see that *H. habilis* displays some important dental and facial characteristics, a larger brain, and that the concurrent discovery of many stone tools argues for the placement of these fossils in the genus *Homo*.

Chronologically, the next member of the genus *Homo* recognized is *Homo erectus*. These fossils appear in the record about 1.6 million years ago, and they have been discovered in Africa, Asia and Europe. Such a widespread geographic distribution of this form indicates that the specific features it had as a result of natural selection allowed its successful exploitation of a wide variety of environments.

Homo erectus has a cranial capacity which ranges between 800-1000 cc. The anterior teeth as compared to *H. habilis* are more modern-like, and its heavy build and robust bone structure argue that *H. erectus* was living constantly on the ground.

Probably the most important sets of characteristics discovered with H. *erectus* are changes in culture. Tear-drop shaped hand axes from sites in France and Kenya suggest local tool traditions were emerging. Sites in China, France and Hungary document the systematic use of fire from hearths which have been found. In Kenya, a camp site with fractured animal bones documents yet another aspect of *H. erectus* behavior. *H.*

erectus was hunting and eating animals, as evidenced by the large collection of baboon bones, together with large numbers of hand axes at the Olorgesailie site. Bones have cut marks on them, a clear sign that *H. erectus* was butchering animals and shifting to a meat-eating diet.

The evidence left by *H. erectus* leads us to a number of speculations concerning the emergence of culture. Some of these hypotheses include the presence of group dependence, food sharing, a more structured social unit, and possibly a division of labor. Many have argued that these activities and this lifestyle could not have been maintained without language. We will probably never know if *H. erectus* communicated with a spoken language, but we may suggest that the activities of *H. erectus* are more modern than any primate before them. The success of *H. erectus*, at the very least, attests to the selective advantage of our basic hominid characteristics.

The emergence of fossils belonging to our species occurred about 1.5 years ago, but the best known group of human ancestors belong to a different subspecies, *Homo sapiens neanderthalensis*. Depending on the locality, these fossils are dated from about 125,000-35,000 years ago. They are characterized by their strikingly modern anatomy, robust features, and large brains. Their brains, in fact, are larger on average than modern humans! Geographically, Neanderthals are found in Europe, Africa and Asia. Each of these areas underwent radically different environmental changes due to periods of relative cooling and warming caused by glaciation events. Such changes must have affected the survival of many of these groups, and predictably, not all of them survived.

Neanderthals left behind many clues to their lifestyle. A wide variety of tools, living structures, and other indicators of a complex culture exist (see Chapter 4). We know too, that some Neanderthals buried their dead and that they cared for aged and handicapped individuals in their social group. For example, an adult male fossil Neanderthal from the French site, La Chapelle-aux-Saints had severe arthritis and could not possibly have been able to help gather or hunt for food. He had lost all but two teeth and must have had difficulty eating, too. Yet he lived with these disabilities, and it is likely that other members of his group provided for him.

The transitions from Neanderthals to modern *Homo sapiens sapiens* are unclear. Modern humans belonging to the subspecies *sapiens* appear approximately 40,000 years ago. First found in 1868 in a rock shelter in France, these fossils were buried with flint tools and perforated shells and animal teeth, probably used as ornaments. The site is called Cro Magnon (named after a hermit called Magnon who had lived there), and it is located, as are many such sites, in an area rich in natural resources. The anatomy of these *H. sapiens sapiens* is indistinguishable from living humans, with a high vaulted skull and a cranial capacity comparable to

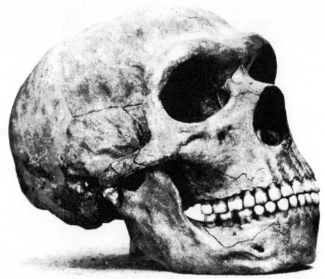

Skull of a classic Neanderthal. (Courtesy Field Museum of Natural History.)

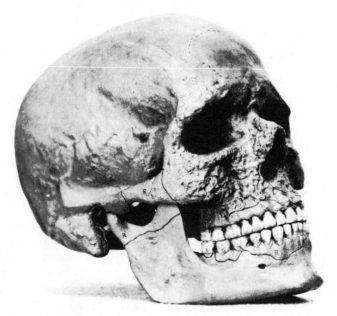

Skull of Cro Magnon Man, *Homo sapiens sapiens*. (Courtesy Field Museum of Natural History.)

that of modern humans. Culturally, mastery of making fire, dwellings, tools and clothing as well as evidence of painting, cave art, and a belief in magic all point to the fact that these early *H. sapiens sapiens* were hominids dependent on culture.

THE FOSSIL RECORD IN EVOLUTIONARY PERSPECTIVE

This summary of primate evolution is very abbreviated. Many diverse fossils have been omitted, as have many of these interesting issues and controversies which surround them. What should be apparent from this brief discussion is that primates have been evolving for only 65 million years, a mere "drop in the bucket" of time when put in perspective and compared to many other forms of life. Natural selection has worked to favor those primates throughout our short history who have been able to invade particular environments (first the trees, then the open terrestrial niche) and survive. Modern humans are not the result of a goal-oriented, directed pathway, but rather are the beneficiaries of many adaptive changes which have taken place in our taxonomic order. Natural selection always promotes those individuals and populations which simply function "best" due to their suite of characteristics, both biological and behavioral. In the case of primates, our ancestors' grasping hands, good vision, and complex brains comprised a "package" of characteristics which proved highly successful. Changes in locomotion, diet and social organization added new features which propelled populations down yet other evolutionary pathways. Some of the hominid "models" worked, and with variations through time, produced the only surviving hominid, ourselves.

Non Human Primates

Up to this point we have restricted our discussion primarily to humans and their probable ancestors. Humans are, however, just one taxon in the order primates. More than one hundred and fifty living species of primates inhabit Central and South America, Africa, and Asia including many islands such as Madagascar, Japan, and Java. When we include human primates, primate distributions range worldwide, and they testify to our order's great success.

Why should anthropologists study nonhuman primates? Normally, we tend to associate the disciplines of zoology, psychology or fields of medical research with interests in animal behavior and anatomy. Why have anthropologists who study nonhuman primates (called primatologists), claimed this endeavor as their own? The reasons should be obvious, but listing some of them may be helpful.

1. Anthropologists strive to see connections. Their holistic approach is

one which is used in all of the subdisciplines, not only in cultural anthropology. If we are interested in understanding human diversity, biologically and behaviorally, our closest relatives are likely to provide some insights.

2. The biological characteristics which have promoted human evolution are shared with other primates, particularly the great apes (chimpanzees, gorillas and orangutans). They provide important models for understanding the relationships between biology and behavior.

3. The most unique feature of humans is culture. Although it generally is agreed that other primates do not have culture, it is also recognized that they have extremely complex behaviors and social structures. Their behavior may help us to understand aspects of human behavior.

4. Nonhuman primates live in a wide variety of habitats. Examining their ecology and adaptations to their environments provides another dimension in understanding human adaptations.

Primatologists recognize the similarities between humans and nonhuman primates, but they also help identify characteristics which are unique to each. The uniqueness of humans has been a central issue historically in the discipline of anthropology. In our search to retain our separateness from other animals, humans have been identified as the only primate to make and use tools, hunt and even commit murder. Primatologists have shaken these claims by demonstrating through naturalistic field study that such features are not unique to humans. Other primates have been observed doing these very same things, and each time we have been forced to re-evaluate what the criteria should be for distinguishing humans from other animals.

PRIMATE SOCIAL GROUPS

Nonhuman primates live in a variety of social groups. Although some are solitary, most nonhuman primates live in social units of some type. The smallest social unit observed among nonhuman primates is the monogamous pair or family group. This social unit is composed of the adult female and male and their offspring. Another social organization is the uni-male group or "harem" structured to include only one adult male and multiple adult females and their offspring. Finally, multimale troops are social groups composed of several adult males and generally twice as many adult females. This is the type of social organization we generally associate with most nonhuman primates, and it is the most common type observed throughout the order.

In each of these social groups it is important to recognize that members stay together throughout the year and learn to know each other. They respond to each other, to predators, and to outsiders in specific ways which keep the group together and have the effect of improving survival. Although other animals are social (for example dogs, lions and even ants), primate social groups encourage interpersonal bonding, dependence and learning in unique ways.

SOCIAL BEHAVIORS

Even though the following characteristics are common features of primate social behavior, there are exceptions. These features are chosen because for many primates, they are key social adaptations. They are, as you will see, social solutions characteristic of human groups too.

Primate displays communicate many different messages. Happiness and anger require very different facial expressions, and many displays are expressed identically by humans, and in this case, a chimpanzee.

Almost all primates groom one another, but the role of grooming is more than simple hygiene. Grooming has been called the "social cement" of primates as it maintains close and friendly ties between individuals. Mothers groom infants constantly from birth, but as the infant grows it may exchange grooming behaviors with other individuals. In primates which maintain a social hierarchy such as baboons, grooming may reduce social tensions and maintain group cohesiveness.

As we have stressed, the significance of vision has been critical to the evolution of all primates. We all use visual cues and respond to them in different ways. Likewise, we make our emotions and responses clear by the use of what are called displays. Displays may communicate fear, aggression, danger, greeting, courtship and many other messages (Jolly 1972).

The most important social pair among primates is the female and her infant. Female primates particularly, invest a lot of time, energy, and effort into caring for their infants. In all primate groups, infants are very special, and the interactions they have with their mothers provides them with the foundation for their social learning (Poirier 1972). Infants are so important that in many groups, females who are not the mother may care for the infant. This behavior is called *allomaternal care* or aunting behavior. It may range from what may be considered short-term babysitting to adoption.

Social role separation between females and males and between adults and young is also common among primates. Social roles are learned as the infant grows up, and just as among humans, infant behavior is modified by the responses given by adults. For example, an infant squirrel monkey can cry vocally for its mother or aunt and one of them will retrieve it, but as the infant is weaned and joins its play group as a juvenile, these cries will be ignored.

PRIMATE TAXONOMY

The order primates is broken down into increasingly narrow groups (taxa) based on similarities and differences. Two suborders are recognized, Strepsirhini and Haplorhini (Table 3-2). Representative genera for each family in the order are included, but the complete list obviously is much longer. The suborder to which humans belong, Haplorhini, will be the focus of the following section. These genera are chosen because they are more closely related to humans both biologically and behaviorally. Representative examples are chosen to highlight these similarities and differences.

NEW WORLD MONKEYS

The forests of Central and South America are ideal environments for primates. Rich in natural resources, these areas are the home for a wide variety of arboreal monkeys.

Nonhuman primates of the Americas are called New World Monkeys, and they include representatives of three primate families; the Callimiconidae, Callitrichidae, and Cebidae. They are all arboreal and range in adult weight from a little over one half pound to about 13 pounds (Richard 1985). New World primate social groups include almost the entire spectrum, from parental family to multimale troop.

Table 3-2. Primate Taxonomy. *(Adapted from Richard 1985.)*

Order	Suborder	Family	Genus	Common name
		Cheirogaleidae	*Microcebus*	mouse lemur
		Daubentoniidae	*Daubentonia*	aye aye
	Strepsirhini	Indriidae	*Propithecus*	sifaka
		Lemuridae	*Lemur*	lemur
		Lepilemuridae	*Lepilemur*	sportive lemur
		Lorisidae	*Galago*	Bush baby
			Perodicticus	potto
Primates		Tarsiidae	*Tarsius*	tarsier
		Callimiconidae	*Callimico*	Goeldi's marmoset
		Callitrichidae	*Saguinus*	tamarin
		Cebidae	*Alouatta*	Howler monkey
	Haplorhini		*Saimiri*	squirrel monkey
		Cercopithecidae	*Papio*	baboon
			Macaca	macaque
		Hominidae	*Gorilla*	gorilla
			Pan	chimp
			Homo	human
		Hylobatidae	*Hylobates*	gibbon
		Pongidae	*Pongo*	orangutan

The Callitrichidae is unique because adult females and males usually are monogamous, bonding with each other and staying together to raise their offspring (Kleiman 1977). Unlike most other primates, marmosets and tamarins have twins regularly, and they sometimes have births twice a year because of a short sexual cycle. Another unique feature of callitrichid behavior is the social role of the adult male. Most primate fathers cannot possibly "know" their own offspring from any other in the troop because the female may mate with more than one male during her sexual cycle. Marmoset and tamarin fathers, however, do participate in raising their young, and they provide a lot of parental care when the infants are small. Their behavior is regulated strongly by hormone levels

(Dixson and George 1982) as are many behaviors directed towards infants.

OLD WORLD MONKEYS

Old World Monkeys, the Cercopithecidae, are the largest taxonomic family of primates. Members live in widely separate geographic areas (from Africa to Japan) and in very diverse environments (from dry, open grasslands to dense forests). One of the most widely studied taxa of nonhuman primates are members of the genus *Papio*, the baboon.

The savanna baboon lives in a multimale troop which can be between 10 to 200 individuals, but is usually composed of about 40 individuals. Stuart and Jeanne Altmann studying troops at the Amboseli Game Reserve in Kenya (1970) observed that the troop forages during the day, covering about 3.5 miles of their habitat. At night they return to the trees for protection from predators. The baboon troop is organized around a male and female dominance hierarchy. Males may change rank throughout their lives, moving up or down in social status. High-ranking males receive more grooming and are harassed less often than lower ranking males. Dominant males were thought to have the benefit of more frequent breeding with females. Recent data suggest that this benefit may not be associated with rank (Fedigan 1983). Female baboon hierarchies are a function of birth, as high-ranking females have daughters who assume high rank as adults (Altmann 1981). The most frequent grooming occurs between females, but the behavior is performed by all members of the troop. Generally, the higher one's rank, the more grooming received. The behavior is highly structured as are many other aspects of baboon social life, and appear to be important keys to the baboon's successful adaptation to an open, grasslands environment.

APES

The taxonomy presented in Table 3-2 reflects some important, recent evaluations of the respective places of humans and apes in the order primates. Traditionally the family Pongidae has included orangutans, gorillas, and chimpanzees, leaving humans as the sole representatives of the Hominidae. With the accumulation of biochemical data in recent years, new taxonomic designations have been suggested. Table 3-2 represents a classification based on recent molecular evidence. Although not listed, the family Hominidae is recognized by two subfamily designations, the Gorillinae consisting of the gorilla and the chimpanzee, and the Homininae consisting only of humans (Richard 1985). It should be stressed that this classification is far from unanimously accepted, as a quick survey of other introductory texts will show.

The recent molecular data are based on comparisons of proteins. Similarities between proteins of two species indicates similarities between their respective DNA. Differences between proteins and between actual DNA document that there are few differences between humans and apes, particularly between humans and chimpanzees. This evidence has given support to the evolutionary divergence of humans and apes in the fairly recent past (2.5-3 million years ago) (Stanyon and Chiarelli 1982; Sarich 1971).

Whether chimpanzees are placed in the same taxonomic family as humans or not, it is apparent that we share more in common with chimpanzees than previously thought. Chimps, which are found naturally throughout central Africa forests, were first systematically studied beginning in 1960 by Jane Goodall. As a consequence, chimpanzee behavior is now better documented than almost any other animal species.

Chimps live in fluid social groups composed of adults of both sexes and their offspring. A dominance hierarchy exists among males, although it is much less rigid than that of baboons. The most stable social unit is that of the mother and her offspring. Mothers and infants interact constantly, and for the first four years of life, infants are almost completely dependent on their mothers. Daughters remain dependent until about age seven and sons until about age ten, when they finally adopt adult behaviors and begin to mate. As is true for other primates, allomaternal behavior is expressed, and even adult and adolescent males occasionally take care of infants (Nishida 1983).

Chimpanzees have been observed on more than one occasion murdering infants and cannibalizing them (Goodall 1979). Although primarily herbivores, chimps also have been seen hunting, killing and sharing small mammals (Teleki 1973). Such behaviors have long been thought to be uniquely human, but intensive field study has demonstrated that these are not fortuitous or abberant behaviors among chimps.

Another human behavior once considered unique is that of toolmaking. Chimpanzees manufacture or alter stems of plants and they insert these probes into termite mounds. The termites bite at the foreign object, so that when the chimp carefully removes the probe, termites can be eaten in the same way we might eat corn on the cob! Chimpanzees also use leaves as bandages to dab scratches or wounds and as sponges to get drinks of water from tree hollows where water has accumulated.

A biological feature which makes tool use and toolmaking a possibility for chimps is their hand (Figure 3-9). The opposable thumb and dexterous fingers allow chimps to manipulate many objects. They have often been seen dragging or rolling branches, stones, and even camp equipment while displaying. Benjamin Beck (1980) reports that chimps will throw overhand, sidearm and underhand, and while not always very accurate, they can hit objects or other animals. The author has even seen captive chimps roll food or feces into small balls and shoot them at passers-by like shooting marbles!

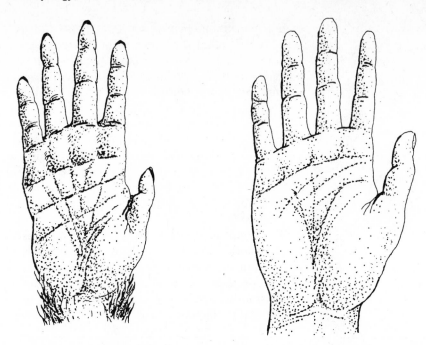

Figure 3-9 Hand on the left, chimpanzee and right, human.

Can chimpanzee behaviors be called culture? We think not, for a number of reasons. Culture is social and not primarily biological heredity. While chimps and other primates are capable of flexible learning, it would be difficult to argue that the behaviors discussed here are critical to their survival. Humans transmit their culture symbolically, through tradition and learning. Chimps must learn from seeing and doing through direct observation, whereas humans are not so restricted. Through language, we can just hear or read about something and we can try it ourselves. For example, consider the following. Humans are the only primates that can touch every finger to every other finger of one hand without using the other hand for help. You have just read this statement, and now you can try it yourself, without any model to copy. (By the way, don't worry if you cannot touch your index finger to your fifth (pinky) finger — lots of people can't)!

The Evolutionary Perspective

Physical anthropology is committed to studying primates through time and space. Primate evolution, modern human variation and primatology are just three of the eclectic areas of research pursued by physical anthropologists. Each dimension of the subdiscipline is linked together in a network by a reliance on fundamental evolutionary principles. When we understand the process of natural selection, the biological phenomena we observe make sense. Natural selection favors biological and behavioral features which work in particular environments. The naturally selected features which distinguish our taxonomic order have allowed for a relatively rapid evolutionary explosion over the past 65 million years. Evolution continues to be a process affecting all populations of primates, and humans are no exception. By understanding what has made us special, physical anthropologists can provide new insights into how we may deal with our ever-changing global environment.

Physical anthropology is important to the other subdisciplines of anthropology. For example, archeologists and physical anthropologists often work together. Human remains from prehistoric sites are analyzed by physical anthropologists. Evidence of disease, trauma, mortality, warfare and dietary stress can often be observed from the particular lesions which form on bones and teeth. This interest of physical anthropology includes specialties such as paleopathology and paleodemography, and results are useful to interpretations of the extinct cultures archeologists make.

Physical anthropologists and cultural anthropologists also have areas of common interest. For example, the study of ethnomedicine, the study of health practices and beliefs, is part of the cultural behavior studied traditionally by cultural anthropologists. While anthropologists have always included accounts of medical practices and beliefs about disease in their studies, physical anthropologists too have become interested in this area. Herbal medicines, drug-induced trance, and folk illnesses (called ethnic psychoses) have biologically relevant features which interest some physical anthropologists. Health is a measure of environmental adaptation (McElroy and Townsend 1985) and as such is a perfect area for coordination between cultural and physical anthropology.

Summary

Evolutionary theory provides physical anthropology with an important framework. Using the concepts of natural selection, migration, mutation and genetic drift, physical anthropologists can attempt to explain the biological diversity present in the primate order. Understanding these mechanisms of biological change allows physical anthropologists to evaluate genetic similarities and differences among human populations, and to explain various aspects of human biological adaptation. Rather than simply document differences of hair color, body shape, and skin color, today evolutionary principles help us explain this diversity as a result of adaptation to the environment.

The primate order, which includes prosimians, monkeys, apes and humans, emerged about 65 million years ago. Utilizing the arboreal environment, the earliest members of our order were able to compete and survive because of a group of unique features they possessed. Visual acuity, grasping hands and feet, and a relatively large brain are features firmly rooted in our primate past, and they represent a group of adaptations which allowed for and promoted the evolution of all primates, including humans.

The first hominids, australopithecines, evolved as early as 3.7 million years ago. These forms walked bipedally and began to move into new environments. By approximately 2 million years ago, hominids were altering their environments by using tools, exploiting animal rather than plant resources, and spreading geographically throughout Africa and Asia. *Homo habilis* and later *Homo erectus* came to depend more and more on cooperation between individuals, tools, and fire. Their success may have been more the result of these cultural adaptations rather than of biological adaptations. *Homo sapiens neanderthalensis*, a member of our species, emerged approximately 125,000 years ago. Neanderthals were culturally-dependent humans who manufactured high quality tools, hunted large animals, and buried their dead. The success of the Neanderthals documents the unique way in which culture has allowed humans to adapt in many diverse environments. Changes in locomotion, diet and social organization allowed hominids a means of competing and surviving what Darwin called the struggle for existence.

Nonhuman primates share many features in common with humans. Their dependence on social, group living and their close biological relationship to humans are two primary reasons anthropologists study nonhuman primates. By virtue of our common evolutionary history, nonhuman primates allow physical anthropologists to develop models of fossil hominid behavior. The apes, which include gorillas, chimpanzees and orangutans, are of particular interest because of our close genetic relationship with them, and field studies have documented that many behavioral similarities exist as well.

Physical anthropology adds an important dimension to the discipline of anthropology. Our holistic perspective required us to try to evaluate all possible variables which affect human culture and biology. Studies in physical anthropology certainly enhance and compliment our collective goal to improve our understanding of ourselves.

Archeology and Prehistory 4

Nearly 2 million years ago a beetle-browed fellow in Africa picked up a rock in each hand, banged them together until he chipped a sharp cutting edge on one, and then proceeded to use the tool to butcher a newly killed animal. While this action is not remarkable in terms of present-day technology, it represented the first step on the long road to civilization. Anthropology is very much interested in this long road and how it was negotiated. The journey tells us a great deal about ourselves. It tells how humans utilized their mental and physical capabilities in different times and in different places to create a more secure and comfortable existence for themselves and a more promising future for their progeny.

While all anthropologists are interested in the details of the human journey along the road to civilization it is the archeologist who has taken on the task of discovering, interpreting, and revealing the details of the trials and tribulations, the successes and failures, experienced by prehistoric individuals and societies.

There is no phase of anthropology that interests students and the general public more than the activities of the archeologist. The fact that this scientist is on a treasure hunt for valuable knowledge of the past makes him or her a romantic figure indeed. People are both impressed and mystified by archeological activities and their results. The mystifying aspect is reflected in the questions the archeologist is asked again and again—questions such as "How do you know where to dig?" "How can you tell so much about a people from a few stones, old bones, and pieces of broken pottery?" or "How do you decide how long ago these people lived?"

The answers to these and many other questions are being sought, not only in the digging of sites for specific evidence of people and their culture, but in attempting to reconstruct the environment in which they lived. We want to know how they responded to that environment in their search for food, shelter, clothing and other essentials for living; we want to understand the nature of their social organization, and why cities and civilizations came into being.

A wide range of investigative techniques have been borrowed from a number of disciplines outside of anthropology, including geology, meteorology, chemistry, physics, botany, zoology, and many more. Relating archeological evidence to life situations is the purpose of ethno-archeology, a subject in which the culture of contemporary traditional societies is compared in situations as closely related to the archeological setting as possible. In experimental archeology, on the other hand, there is an actual attempt to duplicate the artifacts of ancient societies. Famous archeologists, like Francois Bourdes, Don Crabtree, and others, have developed skills in the manufacture of stone tools and weapons. While it would be impossible in a chapter like this to discuss in detail the many methods that have been used by archeologists, we shall at least try to answer some of these questions and give the newcomer to archeology some insight into the science that snatches history from the dirt.

Archeological Methods

TYPES OF SITES*   The kinds of sites that archeologists investigate are extremely varied and may include simple campsites of nomadic hunting populations or extensive permanent villages of settled agricultural peoples. They might even rescue an ancient lost city from the jungle vegetation or from the alluvial mud of a flood plain. A cave or a rock shelter was often used as a temporary home by a roving band of hunters, and in many cases excavation of such sites reveals numerous layers of refuse which tell of the nature of the way of life of the caves' visitors over extended periods of time. Considerable knowledge about the tools and weapons of such people has also been acquired through research efforts at the spots where they quarried their flint, chert, or obsidian and at the "workshop" sites where they sat down to manufacture their lithic points, scrapers, or hand axes. Equally valuable are the "kill" sites and butchering areas where hunting populations dispatched and processed game. Such locations are usually littered with bones, broken points, and cutting blades and reveal facts about stone technology as well as about the sources of a people's food.

Interest in how people made their living and provided themselves with shelter is surpassed only by interest in how they worshiped, and few archeologists would pass up an opportunity to excavate a ceremonial center. They are often the products of remarkable engineering feats and are rich in evidence of art traditions and religious ideology. Indications of supernatural beliefs are also acquired through excavations of cemeteries, burial mounds, or tombs in pyramids. In many cases weapons or valuable ornaments were placed with the bodies, and the implication is that there was a belief that "you *can* take it with you" to your life after death. It is also assumed that the way a person was treated after death is a reflection of the status he or she held during life.

A paper read at a recent anthropology conference carried the unique title "Garbage, the Archeologist's Bread and Butter." While the title undoubtedly was conceived to evoke interest and a smile, it is true that garbage, or at least refuse, has been the most valuable source of information concerning early humans. Middens are the places where villagers deposited their broken pots, dinner bones, and worn-out sandals and thus left a record of their tastes and technology for today's archeologists to read.

*Site — any spot that contains evidence of past human activities.

WHERE TO DIG   In searching for the locations of the above types of sites the archeologists are guided in their knowledge of the general patterns of living of people who have faced similar subsistence problems in similar kinds of environments. For example, if they know that the prehistoric inhabitants of the area were a hunting population they would direct their attention to caves where they may have sought shelter or to the banks of streams or lakes where they may have set up temporary campsites out in the open. Streams and lakes provided hunters with drinking and cooking water, served as avenues of transportation, and were places where fish could be caught or animals killed when they came to drink. Other needs also influenced the locations of campsites. Hunters often located in places where they could obtain fuel for their fires and be protected from the elements or from human enemies. Camps were set up in the lee of hills which provided shelter from cold, cutting winds. Sometimes they were located on high ground, affording a view of the countryside, so that hunters could watch the movements of herds of game or have early warning of the approach of warlike neighbors.

Even though the archeologists may know approximately where to look for likely sites they still need a little luck and the cooperation of many citizens of the area if they are to be successful in locating actual sites. Unusual patterns in the vegetation may be discovered when viewing aerial photographs, and these may indicate the spots where early peoples built their houses or their village fortifications or where they cut into the earth to construct an irrigation system. The archeologist may choose to search the banks of streams looking for stone implements or bits of pottery that have become exposed through stream erosion. Many of the more important sites in both the Old World and the New have been discovered by farmers or construction workers who have uncovered ancient artifacts with a plow or a bulldozer and have been sufficiently aware of their importance to call an archeologist at a local university, museum, or historical society. Archeology owes a great deal to these concerned citizens.

DIGGING A SITE   Once a potential site has been located, the first step is usually to make a careful survey of the surface. Close examination may reveal numerous artifacts which have become exposed as a result of wind or water erosion or as a result of the land being disturbed by a plow. These surface finds as well as other clues such as variations in vegetation or unusual earth contours will help the archeologist decide just where the spadework should begin.

In the actual digging of a site there is no single right way to proceed, but there are many wrong ones. An amateur who digs without knowledge of proper methods is usually guilty of destroying valuable evidence forever. It is as though he had thrown away a rare historical document which can never be replaced.

Generally the procedure followed in preparing a site for excavation is to locate it geographically by taking bearings on surrounding buildings or natural features with surveying instruments. A map is then prepared showing how the site looked before excavation. It is on this map or one with larger scale that the various pits, trenches, or squares to be excavated will be plotted. (See Fig. 4-1.)

In most cases archeologists will construct a grid over the site at regular intervals, two or three meters or so on a side, along north–south and east–west base lines. Cords are stretched across the site in each direction forming squares four or nine square meters each (the size is not critical as long as consistency is maintained). The third dimension of depth is also maintained by digging to depths of ⅓ meter or so at each level. Depth is carefully recorded, but occupational or geological strata are noted as well. By maintaining this three-dimensional grid, the archeologist can record the exact location of every feature found in the site. Since excavation destroys the site, the importance of maintaining accurate records cannot be overstated. Since a site may have been occupied by several kinds of people (hunters, agriculturalists, and European settlers) over a long period of time the archeologist must be careful to record the exact level at which particular artifacts appear. He or she must also be careful to note characteristics of the natural stratigraphy (soil layers) in the site. This kind of analysis yields knowledge of the climatic conditions encountered by different peoples at different times.

When actual digging begins the soil is stripped off carefully with shovels or mattocks until man-made objects begin to appear. At this point the heavier tools will be forsaken for trowels (a pointed six-inch Marshalltown), grapefruit knives, ice picks, whisk brooms, or even half-inch paint brushes so that the artifacts may be uncovered without damaging them or removing them from their resting places. Samples of the soil itself are also saved for analysis, and some of the soil will be placed in a tank of water so that charred seeds and other tiny objects will float to the surface and be saved for examination. Once an artifact is uncovered its position within the grid and within the square being excavated will be carefully recorded on a map or a sheet of graph paper. Measurements are usually taken with steel tapes with metric markings. The archeologist may also want to photograph the artifact before it is removed. The find will then be numbered and placed in an appropriately marked sack.

Thus the excavation proceeds. The earth may be peeled away in measured layers, or excavation levels may be determined by the natural stratigraphy. The important thing to remember is that records must be painstakingly kept so that deeper excavation can take place with no loss

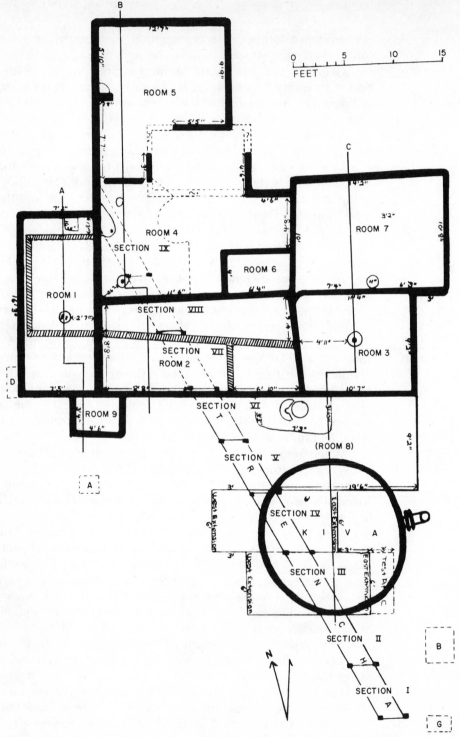

Figure 4-1 Site plan (*left*) of TA-26, a small pueblo site near Taos, New Mexico, excavated by Lucretia Vickery Ottaway.

of valuable data. It should also be noted that it is the relationships between the objects in the ground as much as the nature of the objects themselves, which may provide critical information.

When the archeologist reaches sterile earth, that is, where artifacts are no longer found, the task in the field is complete, except for tidying up. The site must be returned to the condition in which it was found. Farmers take a dim view of archeologists who leave gaping holes for cattle to step in and break a leg.

LABORATORY WORK

When the dig is over, the evidence in the form of artifacts and carefully kept notes is taken back to the archeologist's laboratory where it is studied, classified, and tabulated in preparation for the writing of a site report. Analysis and classification of data is oriented about considerations of (1) material used in the manufacture of artifacts, (2) techniques of manufacture, (3) form of the objects, (4) decorative characteristics, (5) the function of the artifacts, and (6) the state of preservation.

Let us say, for example, that the archeologist is studying a collection of materials recovered from an ancient Pueblo settlement in the Southwest. Projectile points would be analyzed in terms of kinds of stone used, how they were chipped or flaked, and what their general shape and size might have been. Decisions must be made as to whether they were spear points or arrowheads and how they were attached to shafts. The researcher would also calculate the percentage of these kinds of implements and compare it to the percentage of grinding stones and other tools normally associated with agriculture to make a somewhat educated guess as to the relative importance of the two kinds of economic activities.

Pottery would be analyzed in terms of kinds of clay and temper used, methods of firing employed, types of surface decoration if any, and the characteristic sizes and shapes. The archeologist will further try to determine whether the pottery was used only for everyday cooking and storage or whether it was also made for ceremonial or trading purposes.

After a complete investigation of the material has been made the archeologist will be prepared to describe the patterns of daily living of the people, the nature of cultural changes over an extended period of time, and the relationship of the people to other prehistoric cultures in the area.

DATING THE PAST

Whenever possible, the archeologist attempts to assign dates to his discoveries, and a number of techniques of relative and absolute dating have been developed. One of the more interesting methods of

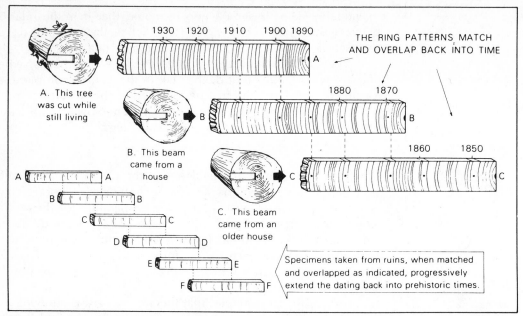

A. This tree was cut while still living

B. This beam came from a house

C. This beam came from an older house

1930 1920 1910 1900 1890   A

THE RING PATTERNS MATCH AND OVERLAP BACK INTO TIME

1880 1870   B

1860 1850   C

A   A
B   B
C   C
D   D
E   E
F   F

Specimens taken from ruins, when matched and overlapped as indicated, progressively extend the dating back into prehistoric times.

Figure 4-2 Deriving dates by means of tree-rings. (Courtesy Laboratory of Tree Ring Research. After Stallings, 1949.)

dating ancient settlements and habitations is *dendrochronology*—tree-ring dating. (See Fig. 4-2.) This technique, developed by A. E. Douglass, an astronomer, attempting to correlate sunspots with weather patterns, involves comparison of patterns of annual rings of growth in living and dead trees with those of timbers found in ancient dwellings. Since a tree grows wider rings in wet years than in dry it is possible to match up the patterns of wide and narrow rings and determine the exact year that a tree was cut. It was through dendrochronology that the period of occupation of Mesa Verde sites in Colorado was dated at A.D. 450 to 1300. Originally this method was used primarily in the American Southwest, but it subsequently has been applied in Europe and in the Arctic.

Another very satisfactory method of obtaining absolute dates for certain kinds of archeological specimens is *carbon 14* analysis. In the late 1940s Willard Libby discovered that radioactive carbon isotopes are present in our atmosphere (having been liberated through interaction of cosmic rays and nitrogen) and are present in the cells of all living organisms. During the organism's lifetime the process of oxygen exchange with the atmosphere results in an equilibrium of carbon 14 content, but at death the organism ceases to ingest the carbon 14, and the amount remaining in the material decays at a fixed rate. It has been established that in 5730 ± 30 years one half of the atoms will have disintegrated. Half of the remainder will decay in approximately the next 5730 years. Since the original content and the rate of disintegration are known, the task is to discover how long this disintegration has been going on by measuring the amount of carbon 14 present in a given sample. This is done by reducing the sample (charcoal, wood, bone, peat, or other vegetable or animal substance) to a gas or liquid and measuring its radioactivity in a special device that contains a circle of highly sensitive Geiger counters.

A contribution to archeology from the field of paleobotany is the technique of dating site strata through *pollen analysis* called *palynology*. Pollen from flowering plants and trees becomes deposited in lake sediments and in soils, and the nature of this pollen can reflect climatic changes which have occurred in a region over an extended period of time. Different kinds of flora grow during glacial advances than during interglacial periods, and as geologists become more knowledgeable concerning the dates of climatic fluctuations the archeologist also profits by receiving more accurate dates for artifacts found in association with specific varieties of pollen.

A dating technique that does not result in a completely reliable absolute date but which must be resorted to occasionally is *cross-dating*. Where undatable artifacts from one area are found to be similar in form to those found at other sites where dates have been established on the basis of carbon 14 or other methods, the archeologist has some basis for assuming his undated artifacts are of approximately the same antiquity.

Numerous other methods of achieving temporal ordering of archeological data have been developed through the help of scientists of other disciplines. Spectrography, analysis of chemical content of bone (fluorine and nitrogen), amino acid racemization (change in optical properties of molecules), obsidian hydration, potassium-argon radioactivity measurement of volcanic ash, and association of artifacts with various geological phenomena are but a few of the advances made possible through this interdisciplinary cooperation.

A now popular method attempts to identify the usage made of certain objects by comparing similar tools, techniques, skills, etc. found in contemporary societies living in similar conditions to those found in an archeological context. Modern craftspeople duplicate the tools of the past, and from them comes information as to prehistoric usage. The inferences drawn from these techniques are a valuable addition to those techniques already a part of archeology and its interpretation.

With this brief summary of archeological procedures in mind let us move now to the product of these efforts—the story of the human animal's cultural growth and development from Stone Age hunter to agriculturalist and finally to urbanite.

A. Old World Prehistory

The Lower Pleistocene

The story of the development of human culture must begin on the continent of Africa approximately 2 million years ago and must, for want of other evidence, begin with an analysis of early man's tools and toolmaking techniques. While apes and other primates have proven themselves capable of altering natural objects to suit their needs and thus qualify as "toolmakers" of sorts, only humans seem capable of developing a consistent pattern of toolmaking, or a toolmaking tradition. Although nothing would please the prehistorian more than to discuss the beginnings of family, religion, language, and political organization among the human animals of the Lower Pleistocene, these aspects of culture are nonmaterial and thus cannot be dug up by archeologists.

OLDUVAI GORGE—A CRADLE OF HUMANITY

The earliest datable evidence of human culture thus far discovered comes from the Lower Pleistocene deposits of Olduvai Gorge in Tanzania, Africa. It was here that the late Dr. L. S. B. and his wife, Mary Leakey, climaxed a lifetime of research in East Africa with the discovery of the remains of *Homo habilis* in 1960.

Typical tools were those made by striking a few flakes from one face (and occasionally two faces) of a cobblestone core, thus forming a jagged edge for use in cutting or scraping operations. While this pebble chopping tool is most typical of the Oldowan tradition, various sites have produced other forms such as flake scrapers. The Olduvai hominids carefully selected the raw materials for their tools, for the large pebbles were apparently transported to the place where they were worked and are foreign to the natural deposits lying about at these locations.

At Olduvai and at other early sites in the Rift Valley the remains of the australopithecines are found commingled with pebble tools, flakes and bones of a wide variety of animals. Recently, close study of the animal remains has indicated that most of the meat eaten by the australopithecines came from scavenging rather than hunting. Cut marks on animal bones from stone tools are sometimes found on top of the tooth marks of large predators. Apparently, our ancestors competed with hyenas and vultures for the scraps left by lions and other predators. Australopithecines probably also killed smaller game, such as the fawns of antelope that they found in the grasses of the savanna.

Two kinds of early sites suggest the practice of food sharing, a typically human form of behavior. In one kind of site most of the bones of a single large animal are found with a few stone tools. These appear to

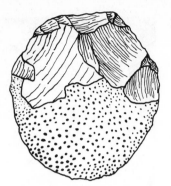

Oldowan pebble tool.

be butchering sites where meat from a predator's kill was scavenged. The other kind of site contains bones from many different animals, but often only one or two bones from a given animal. They also yield large numbers of stone tools and occasionally the remains of an australopithecine. These are thought to be base camps to which the foragers returned to share their finds of meat with others in their group. If we can extrapolate from later human cultures, the males may have searched for the meat while females gathered vegetable foods, with the latter providing the bulk of the diet.

Since the discovery of the Oldowan Pebble Culture in Tanzania, Lower Pleistocene tools of a similar type have been uncovered near Lake Chad, on the Vaal River in South Africa, near Casablanca in Morocco, at Ain Anech in Algeria, at Omo in Ethiopia, and even in western Hungary. We do not know as yet whether or not Olduvai was the original source of all these early cultural traditions or if there was a general pattern of independent development of simple pebble tools over an extensive area. At present the evidence indicates that the continent of Africa is the geographical locale where one branch of hominids first emerged as humans.

The Middle Pleistocene

The cultural remains of the Middle Pleistocene are those of *Homo erectus*. As discussed in Chapter 3, *Homo erectus* was invading new environments. They altered these habitats by exploiting animal resources for food. Using fire, natural swamps and cliffs, *H. erectus* killed large game including giant baboons and elephants, and they butchered them for their meat. At the sites of Olorgesailie and Torralba, large numbers of animal bones have been studied. Many animals, such as hyenas and leopards, leave distinct gnaw marks on bones, but the bones from these

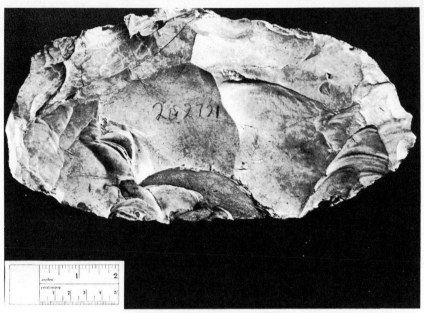

Acheulian handaxe. (Courtesy Field Museum of Natural History.)

sites have an unusual type of breakage. Recent studies of both animal bones and the associated stone artifacts indicate that *H. erectus* had developed a technology and the skill to exploit animal resources quite effectively.

HAND AX INDUSTRIES OF EUROPE AND AFRICA

The tool traditions of the *Homo erectus* of Africa and Europe have been labeled the Hand Ax, or Coup de Poing Industry. Within this general category are found the Abbevillian and the Acheulian traditions. The Abbevillian hand ax was a bifaced core tool produced by beating the core against a stone anvil. These tools show deep chip scars and are rather thick and bulky. In spite of this, they were a decided improvement over the Oldowan artifacts.

The Acheulian hand ax, named for the French site of St. Acheul, is a finely wrought flat pear-shaped implement with a cutting edge extending around the entire tool. An efficient cutting edge was achieved by removing small chips with a wooden or bone baton. In all cave deposits or open sites where Abbevillian or Acheulian bifaced core tools have been found there have also been great amounts of flake tools (see Fig. 4-3.) The flakes have keen cutting edges and must have fulfilled the function of knives or scrapers. Two distinct varieties of such tools existed during the Middle Pleistocene and have been given the names Tayacian and Clactonian.

It is likely that the Oldowan chopping-tool industry was ancestral

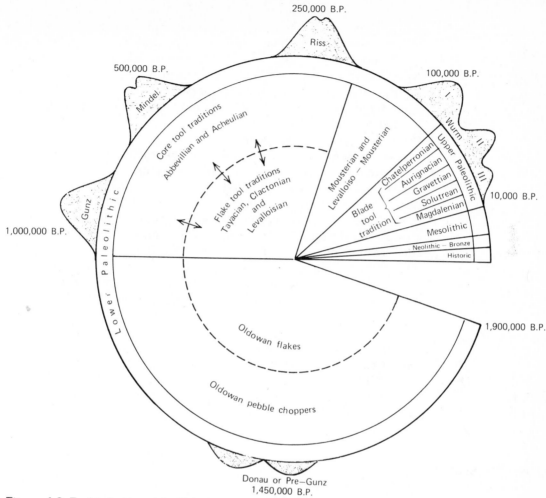

Figure 4-3 Tool industries of the Paleolithic.

to the hand ax industries which appeared during the Middle Pleistocene. The French prehistorian Bordes believes this development from pebble tools to hand axes took place very early in Africa (at Olduvai Gorge) and also in Casablanca and was accomplished by merely "extending the chipped-face first of all to the greater part of the pebble, then to its complete circumference" (1968:134).

THE CHOPPER-CHOPPING TOOL TRADITION OF ASIA

An early Pleistocene strata from a site on the Perak River in northern Malaysia has produced tools of the Oldowan pebble type, and these may have given rise to the Choukoutien and Soan chopping-tool industries of the Asiatic varieties of *Homo erectus*.

Chopper-chopping tools have come from India (Soan), Java (Patjitanian), Burma (Anyathian), and China (Choukoutien). They may be described as being heavy, broad scrapers or cleavers with an adze-type cutting edge. They were made from quartz, sandstone, and a poor grade of flint. While the choppers are most representative of the Asian traditions of toolmaking, it should be noted that most sites have yielded a selection of flake tools as well, in the form of scrapers, "chisels," "gravers," and "points."

Like their African and European counterparts, these *Homo erectus* were larger, stronger, and probably more intelligent than the australopithecines who preceded them. They were hunters who slew deer, rhinoceros, wild boars, and even elephants in some areas. It is reasonable to expect that they operated in small mobile hunting groups of a dozen families or so, making camp on the banks of lakes and streams and sometimes in caves. Since it appears that they knew the use of fire, they were more in control of their environment and further down the road to self-domestication through culture than any of the early humans who had lived up to that time. With this greater capacity for culture came a few bad habits — such as the unsavory tendency to utilize others of the species for nourishment (as evidenced by the presence of skulls bashed in at the base and split long-bones, which have been found scattered about the floor of caves).

Whether or not *Homo erectus* had any form of religion is unknown, but particles of red ocher found at several sites point to the practice of body painting.

Upper Pleistocene

MOUSTERIAN

During the third (Riss-Wurm) interglacial period we see in Europe, Asia, and possibly Africa, a new variety of human emerging — Neanderthals — and with them, new methods of tool manufacture. Mousterian traditions came upon the scene during the Upper Pleistocene, some 150,000 years ago.

The tools of this tradition show numerous advances over the simpler Acheulian artifacts. This is most easily seen in the Levallois technique typical of some Mousterian sites.

The Levallois manufacture method involved first the preparation of a turtle-shaped core. Then a large flake was struck having a convex side and a flat side (where it separated from the core). These flakes were used for scrapers or as points after they had undergone additional flaking. Mousterian tools included side-scraper flakes, triangular points, and small hand axes all struck from specially prepared cores.

Mousterian culture had a wide geographical distribution. While the traditions appeared to have been centered in France, similar tools have been identified in sites in Spain, Russia, central, south and east Africa, and in Asia.

Neanderthals were intelligent human beings (*Homo sapiens*). Their tools were efficient and made with obvious skill. They used fire to warm their caves or their campsites and they possibly used it as an aid to hunting. Their flake tools were probably used in the preparation of hides for clothing. Neanderthal was a courageous and skillful hunter, judging from the fact that a favorite game animal was the cave bear (eight feet tall). Mammoths, horses, deer, reindeer, and ibex fell before the fire-hardened or stone-tipped spears of groups of Neanderthal hunters. They were not only skilled but sensitive, and even religious. Those of their number who failed to survive the dangers of the hunt or the rigors of their harsh environment (peak glacial period) were carefully laid to rest, often with grave goods to aid them in some future life. Pollen found in the graves of Neanderthals at Shanidar Cave indicates that wildflowers were interred with the corpses. Decorative amulets discovered at a Mousterian site in Tata, Hungary, suggest the existence of religious concepts as does the stone chest filled with cave-bear skulls found in the Drachenloch cave in Switzerland. It is tempting to interpret this as evidence of totemism or even a formal cave-bear cult among these people. At Monte Circeo, a cave site in Italy, a Neanderthal skull was found inside a circle of stones. Since it was upturned and the base of the skull broken in order to remove the brain, some prehistorians have suggested the possibility of ritual cannibalism.

Homo sapiens sapiens, the direct descendant of Neanderthal, is the ancestor of all modern humans, regardless of race. This type is distinguishable from earlier relatives by a more prominent nose and chin, a globular skull, and by the absence of heavy brow ridges. The jaw is smaller and so are the teeth. Although our discussion will deal mainly with the cultures of Upper Paleolithic *Homo sapiens sapiens* in Europe and the Middle East, the reader should note that remains of these early forms of modern humans have been discovered in Africa (Florisbad), China (Peking Upper Cave), and the East Indies.

Upper Paleolithic

CHATELPERRON-IAN OR LOWER PERIGORDIAN (32,000–28,500 B.C.)

The first Upper Paleolithic culture in Europe is actually the Chatelperronian. The Upper Paleolithic has frequently been referred to as the period of the *blade* and *burin*, and it is therefore not surprising that the first tool industry which can be called Upper Paleolithic is one named after a particular type of knife blade discovered among other stone artifacts in the Perigord region of south-central France. Although long blades of flint struck from a prepared core with studied skill were its most characteristic and noteworthy tools, this culture also utilized a variety of flake scrapers, Levallois turtlebacks, Mousterian points, and rather primitive burins (engraving tools).

The Chatelperronians lived in open-air settlements and in caves throughout most of western Europe. Their economy centered about the hunting of wild horses and cattle (aurochs). Although they were not cave artists, they were artistic. They engraved pebbles with pictures of animals, produced pendants of carved bone, and very likely painted their bodies with red ocher for cosmetic, ceremonial, or burial purposes.

AURIGNACIAN (28,000–22,000 B.C.)

Following on the heels of the Chatelperronian culture (at least in France) is the culture known as the *Aurignacian.* This is the first tradition that is unmistakably that of *Homo sapiens sapiens* populations. It is predominantly associated with western Europe, but it has also been identified at eastern European and Middle Eastern sites.

The tool kit of the Aurignacians consisted of well-made blades, burins, triangular spearpoints, and a variety of bone and antler implements. Chatelperronian and Aurignacian cultures coexisted for some

Aurignacian artist at work in his Upper Paleolithic cave gallery. Diorama by Frederick Blaschke. (Copyright Field Museum of Natural History.)

time in different parts of Europe and had much in common. The distinguishing difference is that Aurignacians did not use the curved-back Chatelperronian blade but rather seemed to favor a variety of bone tools and flint burins. It is also believed that Aurignacians lived in larger settlements. They made pendants and beads out of shells, pebbles, and animal teeth and engraved large limestone blocks with line drawings of animals and with symbols which have been interpreted as being sexual in nature by some authorities. They also produced silhouette drawings of animals on cave walls. There is a possibility that during the later phases of this culture some female figurines (Venuses) were produced, but this is considered questionable. Although we know more about the archeology of Europe than other regions, it is worth noting that cave art also appears in South Africa at about this time.

GRAVETTIAN OR UPPER PERIGORDIAN (22,000–18,000 B.C.)

The *Gravettians* were a people who appear culturally related to both the Chatelperronians and the Aurignacians. Their tools were of the blade type—long, narrow flint points with a shoulder for hafting (lashing to spears), backed blades that could be used like a pen knife, and a variety of burins (often with several working edges). Art seemed to take a great stride forward during this period. Whether it was a magical exercise connecting art with success in hunting or whether it was merely an esthetic desire to reproduce the things most important in their lives, the hunters of this period painted animal silhouettes in excellent perspective on cave walls, modeled small animals out of clay, and carved human female figurines out of ivory and bone.

SOLUTREAN (18,000–15,000 B.C.)

This culture, which derives its name from the village of Solutré in France, developed at the height of the second Würm glacial fluctuation when the climate of Europe might be described as semi-arctic. Great herds of wild horses flourished in the open country, and herds of reindeer could be found on the fringes of the glacial ice. The Solutrean people responded to the rigorous climate with a culture very much distinct from any other Upper Paleolithic way of life we have described thus far. Flint tools were still of the blade variety, but the Solutreans developed the technique of pressure flaking (extracting small chips from the edge of a blade by applying pressure with a bone tool) and thus were able to produce long, narrow, and very thin spear and javelin points shaped like laurel and willow leaves.

Solutrean hunters were also artists and specialized in bas-relief sculpture in stone. At Le Roc de Sers, in southern France, these artists produced a frieze containing figures of horses, ibex, bison, and two humans. Solutrean culture was not widespread. Although it did extend beyond the borders of France into Spain, it never reached eastern Europe.

MAGDALENIAN (15,000–8000 B.C.)

Solutrean culture did not exert great influence on the course of European prehistory in spite of its revolutionary methods of fashioning flint into long, beautifully symmetrical blade forms. Rather, the Aurignacian culture, which had continued to function in many parts of Europe during the French Solutrean period, ultimately took over and gave rise to a new cultural tradition, the Magdalenian.

This culture, deriving its name from the La Madeleine cave site in southern France, came into fluorescence during the last of the Würmian (IV) glacial fluctuations. The culture appears to have originated in France, but in time it spread to Spain and to eastern Europe. Much of northern Europe was tundra at this time and Magdalenians apparently adapted to their environment by developing a way of life tied to reindeer hunting. The blade tools of Solutrean times, with their pressure flaked edges, were abandoned for bone tools. Harpoons with barbed points and the spear thrower (atlatl) were the weapons used in the hunt. Discovery of bone and antler awls and needles at Magdalenian sites allow us to assume that these people wore fitted clothing, perhaps like modern Eskimos.

Some artifacts from this period leave us completely puzzled, however. What, for example, was the function of *baguettes* (bone wands)? Were they used to remove snow and ice from clothing or were they symbols of authority, like a swagger stick? Perhaps they were religious objects. The *batons de commandment* of this period present us with still another mystery. These sections of antler with a large hole bored in one end could have served as a thong-stropper, a spear-shaft straightener, or as a ceremonial wand. Stone tools were also a part of the Magdalenian complex. Flint blades, burins, and scrapers were fashioned *a la* Aurignacian methods rather than along the line of Solutrean pressure flaking.

A number of open campsites have been discovered in Europe but Magdalenians were also cave dwellers, and cave art reaches a zenith during this period. In the deep recesses of caves artists toiled long and hard by lamplight reproducing the finest art of the Upper Paleolithic. Their reproductions of mammoth, reindeer, horses, bison, and occasionally people are masterpieces of line, perspective, and color. Many of the paintings occur in the same caves which had earlier been decorated by Aurignacian artists, and often the artists painted right over the earlier creations. Much of this art has been interpreted as being related to Magdalenian hunting goals, that is, by painting a wounded or dead bison they hoped for a magical transfer of what their painting depicted to a real-life accomplishment.

The Mesolithic

As the Würm glaciation drew to a close, large areas of Europe which had previously been tundra became covered with deciduous forest. As the flora changed so did the fauna. Animals of the open landscape—reindeer, bison, and wild horses—were replaced by red deer, elk, and wild boar—animals of the forest. People gradually adapted their hunting methods to the new conditions by making greater use of the bow and arrow, a weapon developed late in the Upper Paleolithic. Mesolithic societies also domesticated the dog for use in tracking and flushing animals. Stone tools were still in use, but many of them were drastically different from any we have encountered in the Upper Paleolithic tool traditions. This was the era of the *microlith* and heavy woodcutting tools. Microliths were tiny blades of flint struck from prepared cores and shaped like triangles, trapezoids, or half-moons. Often these blades were used by themselves in cutting operations, but more frequently several of them were inserted in slotted shafts of wood or bone to form a harpoon or a "sickle" for cutting wild grain. In some places heavy woodworking tools such as the tranchet (ax) or stone wedges were used in cutting and splitting timbers to be used in the construction of lean-tos or huts.

Throughout Europe, Asia, and Africa a variety of Mesolithic cultures developed, each exhibiting a slightly different manner of adjustment to the environment. We shall summarize four of these local cultural traditions, the Azilian, the Tardenoisian, the Maglemosian, and the Natufian.

AZILIAN

This was the earliest of the European Mesolithic cultures (10,000 B.C.). It extended over much of southern and central Europe and is named for a cave site, Mas d'Azil, in southern France. The culture is best known for its use of microliths of various geometric shapes. These tiny pieces of flint were set in the sides of wooden shafts to produce multiple or tandem barbed harpoons. Sometimes they were set in the end of a shaft to serve as a penetrating point. One of the unsolved mysteries of this period is what happened to art. The great Upper Paleolithic tradition of cave painting and sculpture seems to have been completely lost, for the artistic creations of the Azilians involved only the painting of simple geometric designs on river pebbles.

TARDENOISIAN

Tardenoisian culture was located to the north of the Azilian in the Feren-Tardenois region of northern France. Tools were of the microlith variety but it appears that these people did not utilize the small flakes in making barbed harpoon points. Nor did they decorate river pebbles. Their open campsites featuring pit houses roofed over with poles and skins were located along river terraces.

MAGLEMOSIAN

This culture, which has been identified at sites in Germany, Denmark, and other areas of Scandinavia, came into existence about 6000 B.C. Since Maglemosian settlements were located near lakes and streams or in swampy areas, this Mesolithic tradition is often referred to as the *big bog* culture. Equally responsible for the label is the fact that large numbers of their artifacts—canoes, rafts, and sledges (for use in winter)—have been recovered from peat bogs. Maglemosians were both hunters and fishermen. Hooks, barbed harpoons, and fish spears with microlith insets, were fashioned from antler and bone. To aid them in the hunt they had domesticated dogs similar to the Norwegian wolfhound.

An inventory of their heavy woodworking tools includes picks and axes made from red stag antler and a flint cutting ax known as a tranchet. It was with these that they constructed their log huts and lean-tos.

NATUFIAN

A Middle Eastern manifestation of the Mesolithic, known as Natufian culture, began about 8500 B.C. in the area around the present-day cities of Jerusalem and Jaffa. It is found on the eastern coast of the Mediterranean from Turkey to Egypt.

The Natufians were hunters, fishers and gatherers of wild grain. Using weapons of bone and antler with microlith insets they hunted gazelle, deer, bear, hyena, wild boar, and even leopard. Although 80 percent of the Mount Carmel artifacts consists of flint microliths, these people also produced larger flint tools such as burins, scrapers, and sickle blades. It is believed that the latter were used to reap grain, and this is based on the fact that these blades carry a kind of sheen which results only when a blade is used to cut grass or grain. Another variety of sickle was produced by mounting microliths in a curved rib bone. Further support for the theory that these people collected wild grain comes from the presence of mortars and pestles at Natufian sites. At a site in Israel called 'Ain Mallaha', they built permanent circular houses with stone walls. It would appear that Natufian culture was a truly transitional one, for it represents a bridge between the hunting ways of the Old Stone Age and the peasant ways of the New Stone Age. Even though there is no evidence for domesticated plants, the development of a sedentary way of life and the intensive harvesting of wild plants set the stage for that development.

The Neolithic

There is disagreement among prehistorians as to why humans began to experiment with the new techniques of food production. Life during the Paleolithic was not particularly difficult, and some major changes in the environment must have taken place to motivate people to experiment with new methods of securing food. Were there climatic changes? Did populations increase in number? Cause and effect are not always discernible from each other, but for whatever reason or combination of reasons, humans embarked slowly at first, but irrevocably upon a new way of life.

The Neolithic has often been described as a "revolutionary" era. It was a period of prehistory when humans developed new economic skills, new settlement patterns, and new material culture. The Neolithic is marked by the inception of deliberate planting and harvesting, of animal husbandry and herding, of pottery making and weaving, and of fabrication of new forms of stone tools by new methods such as pecking, grinding, and polishing. Human settlements became more permanent, life became more economically secure, and population expanded.

The word "revolution" when applied to the Neolithic is a good one, in that it implies great change, but a bad one in that it also tends to imply rapid change. Once experimentation with new subsistence methods began several thousand years passed before the new economy was completely established. Cultures experiencing the "revolution" still clung to many traditional methods. Men continued to hunt for wild game even though strides were being made to develop herds of domesticated animals. Women undoubtedly continued to collect wild roots, berries, and grains while they experimented with the cultivation of a limited number of crops. Stone tools continued to be chipped and pressure flaked even after new grinding, pecking, and polishing techniques were discovered. Although the shift to a new economic orientation came about slowly during the Neolithic, the period as a whole may be characterized as one of whirlwind change when it is viewed in the perspective of man's 2 million year history of hunting and gathering. Often people whose basic culture has changed because of culture contact will retain remnants of the old ways in ritual celebration. Some of the Pueblo peoples of the American Southwest who are and have been farmers for centuries hold summer dances and rituals for agriculture, but also have animal dances in the winter, commemorating a hunting way of life long abandoned.

The Middle East

Experimentation in plant and animal domestication was undoubtedly being carried out at a number of places in the Middle East between 10,000 and 6000 B.C. — at Jericho by the descendants of the Natufians, in the Zagros Mountains of Iran, in northern Iraq, and in the Taurus Mountains of Turkey. (See Fig. 4-4). The strata of an ancient settlement at Zawi Chemi Shanidar in northern Iraq reveals that its inhabitants had a goat- and gazelle-hunting culture with microlith points in 10,000 B.C., but by 9000 B.C. they were using mortars and reaping knives with microlith insets and had domesticated sheep and goats (suggested by the higher percentage of female animals). Flint sickles and chipped celts which might have been used as hoes have been found at other sites in this area, and while these artifacts hint at an agricultural economy, there is no definite proof. Emmer wheat has been found at Ali Kosh (a site in Iran) in strata that are from before 7000 B.C., and barley domestication has been positively identified at the Hacilar site in Turkey as beginning about 7000 B.C.

JARMO

One of the earliest permanent Neolithic village sites thus far discovered is Jarmo in the hills of Iraqi Kurdistan. It was first established

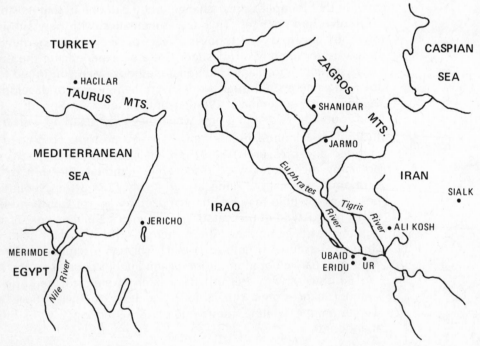

Figure 4-4 The Middle East.

about 6750 B.C. The village covered about four acres and was located on a bluff overlooking a small stream. Its houses, approximately 20 in number, were rectangular in shape with pressed mud walls. Some contained several rooms, but all the houses were relatively small in size. It is estimated that the inhabitants of Jarmo numbered somewhere between 150 and 200 people.

The Jarmo people cultivated barley and two kinds of wheat. They used flint sickles to harvest their grain, mortars to pound it, ovens to parch it, and stone bowls from which to eat it (probably in the form of gruel or porridge). They kept flocks of sheep and goats, and dogs may have aided them in their herding activities. Whether or not they also kept horses and cattle is still being debated.

While pottery vessels do not appear at the Jarmo site until relatively late in time, clay figurines in the form of animals and humans were being modeled from the very beginning. A favored type of figure seemed to be that of a pregnant woman somewhat reminiscent of Upper Paleolithic "Venuses." These figurines have been given the name *Mother Goddess* and have been interpreted as being cult objects or fertility symbols.

Neolithic Villages in Europe

The new economic revolution marked by plant and animal domestication promised a more secure and settled life, and it is not surprising to find Neolithic ideas diffusing out of the Middle East to peoples in Africa and Europe. There were agriculturalists and herders living in permanent villages in Anatolia (Turkey), Cyprus, and Greece as early as 5500 B.C. By 4500 B.C. the Neolithic had reached Egypt and North Africa. Five hundred years later agricultural villages could be found in central Europe, and by 2500 B.C. the New Stone Age had spread to England and Scandinavia.

DANUBIANS

In approximately 5000 B.C. agriculturalists from the Mediterranean area began moving into central Europe along the Danube and Rhine rivers. These people, who ultimately reached the Netherlands and southern Germany about 4200 B.C., are known to prehistorians as *Danubian I* people. The several hundred year period of their migration was one of great adjustment, for they were neither accustomed to the cold winter climate of central Europe nor to the heavy rainfall that occurred during the summer. Originally they had lived in a dry climate, and their houses, grains, and animals were adapted to the grasslands of eastern Europe. In central Europe they had to develop new forms of dwellings — rectangular longhouses made of sturdy timbers with walls of wood or mud and with roofs of thatch. These dwellings often measured over 100 feet in length and sheltered as many as 20 people. Some of the larger villages contained 20 or 30 of these structures. The 400 or so people thus accommodated were probably kinsmen. A village was very likely composed of a single lineage or clan, with groups of closely related families sharing a single longhouse.

These people were "slash and burn" agriculturalists, that is, they cut down the trees, burned over the wood and brush, and then made their plantings between the stumps. They used digging sticks and hoes with ground stone heads to turn the soil. Since Danubians used no fertilizer, and since the grains and vegetables they planted quickly depleted the loess soils along the Danube, these people were forced from time to time to move on to new areas with virgin soil. Their most important domesticated animals were pigs and cattle as these could prosper in a forested environment. Nothing in the way of spindle whorls or loom weights have been found at any of the Danubian sites so we must assume that they did not weave, although they did grow flax (probably for food). Danubians were, however, excellent potters, and they produced bowls and flasks decorated with incised parallel lines formed into spirals or meanders.

SWISS LAKE DWELLERS

Around 3000 B.C. a Neolithic population known as Swiss Lake Dwellers occupied settlements in the Alpine region of Europe. While much of our knowledge of these people has been derived from archeological excavations on the shores of Swiss lakes, the culture also extended into northern Italy and eastern France. Until recently it was believed that Swiss Lake Dwellers constructed their houses on pilings out in lakes, but more current opinions are that the villages were located along the lake shores or on dried-up lake bottoms. The manner of Swiss Lake construction would certainly lead one to believe the earlier theory, for long pilings were used in the construction of houses, and the house platforms were made of logs and extended out from the walls, thus forming a kind of deck on all sides. Furthermore, wooden walkways connected the house platforms, and these could easily be interpreted as being causeways or bridges. It would appear, however, that the long pilings driven deep into the ground and the heavy log platforms were necessary because the ground was often marshy and left much to be desired as a good firm foundation for building. The heavy log platforms seemed to have served as insulation from the dampness of the ground, and in many cases other forms of insulation were also employed, such as layers of bark laid down prior to the construction of the platform.

Why these people lived so close to the water is not entirely understood, but fishing was an important subsistence activity, and they manufactured such articles as wooden canoes, fishhooks of bone and

Swiss Lake Dwellers built their communities on lake shores and fished the waters with nets of flax twine. Diorama by Frederick Blaschke. (Courtesy Field Museum of Natural History.)

antler, and fishnets of flax twine for this enterprise.

Swiss Lake villages varied in size from 25 to 75 houses and therefore must have housed somewhere between 100 to 300 people. The inhabitants of these relatively stable hamlets were apparently quite secure economically. In addition to their fishing activities they hunted deer, bears, wild pigs, and cattle with bows and arrows, and they gathered nuts and acorns. Their agricultural activities included the growing of wheat (three varieties), barley, flax, and such fruits and vegetables as pears, apples, grapes, peas, beans, and lentils. Sheep, goats, and pigs were raised for food, but the most important domesticated animals were their cattle.

These lake dwellers were not only advanced agriculturalists but skilled craftsmen as well. They produced stone cultivating and hunting tools, ceramic vessels and figurines, and linen textiles, some of which they even embroidered. This was the Neolithic in full flower—a peasant way of life offering security through economic abundance and the promise of a long and fruitful future for European civilization.

B. New World Prehistory

Paleo-Indian Cultures

The story of human migration into North and South America is a matter of relatively recent prehistory. No human forms other than *Homo sapiens sapiens* have been discovered in the Western Hemisphere to date. Due to the time period of the initial migration, however, and on purely logical grounds, the possibility that East Asian Neanderthals were the first humans to enter the New World cannot be excluded. Whoever the first migrant hunters were, they utilized the same means of entering as did the mammoth and bison they hunted. They came to the New World by way of a land bridge across what is now known as the Bering Strait. We know that a drop in sea level of only 150 feet would have created a land bridge approximately 1000 miles wide, and such a phenomenon occurred during the Würm-Wisconsin glaciation which began about 70,000 years ago.

This "land bridge" (called Beringia) was no mere isthmus, but was of the proportions of a continental land mass, and in the several thousand years of its existence it was covered with grass and tundra and would have been indistinguishable from either continental Asia or North America. The migrations, probably as random as the movements of the animals the hunters were following, led over a long period of time into what is now North America. The entry was complicated by the fact that the land bridge was widest when the glacial ice was thickest and most widespread. Obviously when the entire northern part of the continent was covered, no access to the southern part was available. It is now known, however, that at least twice during the Wisconsin glaciation, there was an ice-free corridor along the eastern edge of the Rocky Mountains. The combination of land bridge and access routes occurred 36,000–33,000 years ago and 28,000–25,000 years ago, and these periods are quite likely to have been times of maximum migration, with the latter being the more probable. A scraper made from a caribou shinbone found in the Canadian Yukon has a carbon 14 date of 27,000 years ago and would seem to confirm this hypothesis, but there is some controversy about this site and all of the others that date before 12,000 years ago. Perhaps no aspect of archeology is more controversial than the dating of these early sites. Only those containing fluted points are accepted without dispute and these are dated at 11,000-12,000 years before present. Sites believed by some to date back to the time of the land bridge are much less agreed upon.

Undoubtedly these early hunters wandered into North America by accident, and at first they must have been few in number. There is considerable evidence, derived from sites in Alaska, that some of the earliest hunters were related to Siberian hunting peoples and were equipped with microlithic stone tools.

It would appear that once across the Bering Strait land bridge the movements of these Paleo-Indian hunters were largely determined by the areal distribution of the glacial ice sheet. The arctic coast of

Alaska was free of glacial ice and at times there was an unglaciated corridor leading south through the MacKenzie River Valley area. Once south of the Canadian ice shield of the Würm-Wisconsin glaciation, the early big-game hunters spread west and east from the Great Plains, and some groups continued south into Mexico and beyond. The earliest cultural remains of these Paleo-Indian hunters are barely visible, and evidence of their way of life will always be hard to come by since the numbers of these people were so small.

PLAINS CULTURE   The Paleo-Indian inhabitants of the Plains were big-game hunters who subsisted on the mammoth, the giant bison, the camel, and a small variety of horse. These people were nomadic, and the principal sites which reveal their way of life are mostly campsites or "kill" and butchering sites rather than permanent settlements. The cultures of the Plains during the period of 10,000 B.C. to 5500 B.C. are identified by forms of the various projectile points they used.

One of these Paleo-Indian projectile points is the *Clovis* point, a remarkable artifact identified at sites all over the unglaciated parts of North America. The Clovis point is the most characteristic tool of the Llano culture. They are long (often five inches) with concave bases and longitudinal fluting; that is, a channel that extends from the base halfway up the blade. This feature, which resembles that found in hollow-ground swords, perhaps facilitated hafting. Whatever the reason, the feature was perpetuated in a subsequent tool tradition known as *Folsom*. Folsom points are generally shorter, but the flute, or channel, extends nearly to the tip of the point. These lance or spear points were mainly used in the hunting of bison in New Mexico, Colorado, and Texas around 8500 B.C.

SANDIA POINT   CLOVIS FLUTED POINT   FOLSOM POINT
Early Paleo-Indian points.

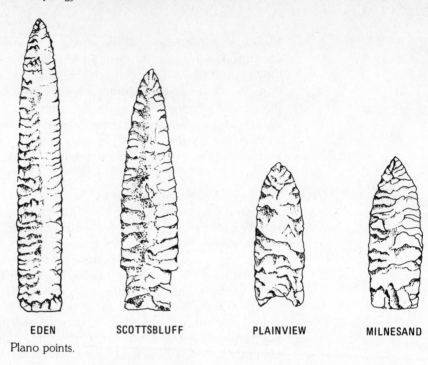

EDEN   SCOTTSBLUFF   PLAINVIEW   MILNESAND

Plano points.

The later Paleo-Indian Plains cultures have been labeled the Plano tradition. Plano people also made fine pressure-flaked tools, but they were not fluted. Their points were often as long as five inches and had nearly parallel sides. In the Plano tradition, a series of distinctive point-styles are found, and these are a good guide to the ages of the sites in which they appear. All are variations on a common theme, and all are dated as being in use between 8000 and 5500 B.C. Basically the Plano tradition is marked by the development of a variety of techniques for communal bison hunting — methods for killing whole herds at a time through the coordinated efforts of large groups of people.

Archaic

About 10,000 years ago the climate of North America began to change. As the great masses of glacial ice continued to melt in the north, temperatures rose. Much of the West and Southwest became arid or even desert-like. Concomitant with these environmental changes was a drastic reduction in the big-game population. During a period of 2000 years the woolly mammoth, the big-horned bison, the camel, the horse, and the giant sloth disappeared from the land. Just why this occurred is not clearly understood, but Paul Martin (1967) suggests that the demise of these animals was not due to climate alone. He feels that hunting techniques of Paleo-Indians, such as stampeding great herds of animals over cliffs, could quickly upset the ecological balance among animals already disadvantaged by the climate. Add to this the skill and technical proficiency of Paleo-Indian hunters and possibly the prestige factor (i.e. the acclaim and pride gained by a hunter for having killed a giant mammoth) and you have in the presence of early man in America what amounts to a super-predator with whom no dwindling species of big-game animal could cope.

Whatever the reason for their disappearance, the giant animals were not around by about 6000 b.c. Although Plano culture continued to exist for some time, archeological evidence indicates that a new way of life began to emerge throughout much of North America. This new cultural horizon has been given the label *Archaic.*

The new cultural horizon in the eastern part of the United States has been described as one of "primary forest efficiency" (Caldwell 1958), and, as it existed in the West it has been described as being "fully efficient up to the carrying capacity of the land" (Jennings 1974:130). What this means basically is that everywhere people slowly achieved great proficiency in exploiting their environment. They had developed a complex and versatile technology and were utilizing every resource known to them. Heavy woodworking tools allowed them to live in the forested areas of the East, and although societies in the New World did not have agriculture at this time, a combination of skillful hunting techniques and the careful harvesting of wild species of fruits, nuts, and vegetables made possible the existence of relatively permanent settlements. Nuts and seeds were ground into meal and made into cakes and mushes. Fish were taken in nets and on hooks, and a whole variety of traps and snares yielded quantities of rodents and fowl.

In the western part of the United States climatic changes had produced desert-like conditions much like those which prevail in the Southwest today. In spite of the hardships created by the environment, the people were no less proficient than in the East. At such sites as Danger Cave in Utah and at Gypsum Cave and Humboldt Cave in Nevada we see evidence of the adaptive nature of this desert Archaic. Here the people developed a way of life based on hunting small game and intensive gathering of vegetable foods. They wove baskets to collect and store seeds and nuts, and with the aid of manos and metates they ground them into meal. At Etna Cave, near Las Vegas, we find a curious phenomenon which reminds us of Old World religious practices associated with hunting. Excavations at this site have produced stick figurines of animals impaled on spear or lance points.

The Western, or Desert, Archaic extended over a vast area of America from Colorado to the California coast, and from Montana to the central plateau of Mexico. One region where this culture existed will be of particular interest to us later in our considerations of New World prehistory. That is the region of southeast Arizona and southwest New Mexico where the Archaic tradition has been labeled the Cochise culture. It was this Cochise culture that was destined to give rise to the great agricultural tradition of the Southwest. There is a growing belief, however, that one of these cultures, the Hohokam, may have been the result of a migration or of migrations from the Valley of Mexico, and ongoing contact with Mexico is suspected on the basis of numerous cultural traits shared by the two areas. These include ball courts, cast bells, stepped pyramids, and certain types of figurines.

New World Neolithic

The shift to agriculture in the New World was, as in the case of the Old World, a slow process. The archeological record reveals two relatively independent centers of incipient agriculture in the northern hemisphere: (1) Middle America and Mexico, and (2) the Woodlands area in the eastern part of the United States.

Middle America and Mexico

In the hill country of Mexico near Tamaulipas, preserved remains of what are believed to have been domesticated squash, peppers, and beans have been discovered in dry caves and dated as being somewhere between 9000 and 7000 years old. The first evidence for cultivation of maize (Indian corn), on the other hand, appears to have taken place first in southern Mexico (in the Valley of Tehuacan) about 5000 B.C. Within another 3000 years the practice had diffused to New Mexico. Although many early Indian populations in Mexico knew about agriculture, not until 1500 B.C. did they draw major support from farming.

The making of coiled baskets was an old and well established craft in North America, but pottery did not appear in America until agriculture developed. There seem to be two independent sources of New World pottery. An indigenous form of pottery is believed to have originated in South or Central America between 2500 and 2100 B.C., and then a second form, supposedly of Asiatic origin, appeared along the eastern coast of the United States about 2000 to 1500 B.C. As we have noted earlier, pottery tends to be associated with an agricultural economy, and this in turn tends to result in a sedentary way of life for those who practice it. Agricultural people develop stable communities, tend to collect things (like pottery and ceremonial objects), and seem prone to evolve formidable political institutions.

Woodlands of Eastern United States

In the eastern part of the United States the transition from an Archaic tradition to a *Formative* one (settled villages with agriculture) began about 5000 to 3500 years ago. In time other innovations appeared — special cemeteries and burial mounds, tobacco, and the tubular pipe. Although some Woodland peoples persisted up until historic times in what was essentially an Archaic tradition, there were two regions— the Ohio and Mississippi River valleys—where Indian peoples developed rich agricultural societies with sedentary villages

ADENA

The earliest of these Formative cultures was the *Adena*, with its heart in the central Ohio Valley. Originating about 700 B.C., this tradition is recognized for its elaborate burial practices and the construction of vast earthworks which normally consisted of high narrow ridges of earth fencing in large fields. In spite of the fact that Adena populations must have been fairly sizable to accomplish their earth moving projects, these people were only mildly agricultural. They did not cultivate corn, although their fields were planted with squash, pumpkins, gourds, sunflowers, and goosefoot. Corn was not grown in large quantities until perhaps A.D. 500. Additional food sources included deer, elk, bear, small game, fowl, fish and shellfish, and various nuts. Houses were round and measured from 20 to 80 feet in diameter. Their walls were constructed by weaving cane or brush around a circle of outer houseposts; a conical-shaped roof was thatched or covered with matting. Household furnishings included a cord-marked variety of pottery known as "Woodland."

The most notable feature of Adena culture was its burial mound complex. One such mound in West Virginia is over 65 feet high. In some cases the bodies interred in these mounds were placed in log tombs. The corpses were often coated with red ocher, but generally there was little in the way of grave goods placed with the body. A few ornaments have been recovered from these tombs, the most interesting of which have been small (3" x 4" x ½") stone tablets engraved with stylized bird motifs.

HOPEWELL

Adena and Hopewell cultures were contemporary from about 50 B.C. until A.D. 300. They were similar in many of their traits, but Hopewell

Hopewell soapstone effigy pipe, typical of mortuary goods recovered from burial mounds. (Courtesy Field Museum of Natural History.)

represented a more elaborate manifestation of the mound-building tradition. In addition to being a richer culture Hopewell was also more wide-spread geographically. Hopewell influence extended from its core areas in southern Ohio and Illinois to as far west as Kansas, as far south as the Gulf of Mexico, and as far north as the shores of Lake Superior. While sites over this broad area have been labeled Hopewellian, the reader should note that there was great variation in culture, and that this label actually refers to the presence of a common set of ideas having to do with death and the preparation of burial mounds and with the maintenance of a widespread trade system. It is therefore, difficult to describe "average" Hopewell tradition.

An analysis of a number of classic Hopewell sites in Ohio and Illinois, however, reveals data of a most extraordinary tradition which required not only a class of skilled craftpeople and artists but probably a priesthood or a body of priest-rulers as well. The surprising thing about these people is that they still relied in great part on hunting and gathering. It is suspected that Hopewell people did some farming, but there is little archeological evidence for intensive maize culture. Villages were made up of houses which were sometimes rectangular, sometimes oval, with domed roofs and mat- or bark-covered walls.

Though housing tended to be of simple construction, that of the resting places for the dead was not. Burial mounds were built in two stages—a low platform which contained a log tomb was topped with a conical hillock sometimes measuring 100 feet in diameter and 40 feet in height. Graves contained elaborate mortuary goods consisting of copper, mica, and shell ornaments, soapstone pipes carved in the image of birds and animals, and even quantities of freshwater pearls.

Hopewell pottery featured crosshatched rims and raptorial bird figure motifs. (Courtesy Field Museum of Natural History.)

Everyday pottery was a good quality Woodland ware embellished only with cord markings, but mortuary pottery was highly decorated with cross-hatched rims and raptorial bird and duck designs on the body of the pot.

Beautifully fashioned human figurines have been uncovered, and from these very realistic ceramic pieces we have learned much about Hopewell clothing styles, personal ornamentation, and even such details of motor behavior as sitting and standing postures. Like the Adena people Hopewellians constructed impressive earthworks, but they did so on a much larger scale. One type of earthwork consisted of long ridges of earth (often as much as 16 feet high) laid out to form circles, rectangles, octagons, or combinations of these. At intervals they were broken by openings or "gateways." Burial mounds are often found within the enclosures, and we may assume that the whole complex constituted some sort of ceremonial center.

MISSISSIPPIAN

The close of the Adena-Hopewell era marks the beginning of another mound-building tradition—temple mounds this time—in an area extending from Ohio south to Louisiana and from Tennessee to Arkansas along the Mississippi, Tennessee, Ohio, Missouri, and other major river courses. This culture, known as "Mississippian" emerged about A.D. 900 and proved to be the most colorful and elaborate that ever existed north of Mexico. In earthwork construction and general technological skill it was unsurpassed.

Sites such as Cahokia (southern Illinois), Spiro (Oklahoma), Angel (Indiana), Kincaid (southern Illinois), and Natchez (Mississippi) were centers which obviously were supported by large populations. Cahokia, which covered about six square miles, approached urban proportions. Typical temple mound sites of the Mississippi people consist of clusters of truncated pyramidal mounds grouped about a plaza. The mounds were built larger and larger over a period of time. In shape and function they were similar to the truncated pyramids of Mexico. On the flat tops of the mounds temples were built of wood, thatch, and mud. Monk's Mound at Cahokia is the largest of the temple mounds. It measures 1080 by 710 feet at the base and rises in several terraces to a height of 100 feet. It is calculated to contain nearly 22,000,000 cubic feet of earth—every ounce carried to the site by the builders.

There is some indication that Cahokia may have served as a solar observatory. Archeologist Warren Wittry has discovered a series of rather large and deep post holes arranged in large circles. Bearings taken along combinations of these post holes indicate that the posts once planted in them might have been used as vanes to sight the sun in determining summer and winter solstices and equinoxes.

The people who were responsible for all this were obviously engaged in intensive agricultural activities. Temple mound sites are nearly always found in fertile bottom lands, and archeology has revealed that corn, squash, and beans were the major foodstuffs grown. Preparation of the soil was accomplished through the use of large flint hoes. Baskets, skin utensils, and unpainted red, brown, and gray pottery were used in the collection, storage, or preparation of foods. Deer was the major source of meat, and fish and shellfish added variety to the diet.

Mississippians housed themselves in dwellings solidly built of wood with vertical wattled walls and gabled roofs covered with thatch. Floor plans were square, rectangular with rounded corners, oval, or round.

Mississippian burials have substantial amounts of associated grave goods. There are effigy jars and bottles, elaborately decorated pots, ornaments of copper, pearl beads (two gallons of them at Spiro Mound), and stone pipes — some with sculptured representations of the ruling class. One mound at Cahokia contains clear evidence of human sacrifice; wives, concubines, retainers and slaves all accompanied the chief in death. Although Mississippi temple mound culture suffered a decline about A.D. 1500 it is believed that this culture was carried on in modified form into historical times in the ways of life of such sophisticated societies as the Choctaw, the Chickasaw, the Natchez, and the Creek.

Formative Cultures of the Southwest

MOGOLLON

About 300 B.C. a hunting-gathering-farming culture known as *Mogollon* evolved out of an Archaic base in southeastern Arizona, southwestern New Mexico, and northern Mexico. The Mogollon were truly a Neo-lithic-type population, for they wove baskets, made pottery (brown undecorated ware), and lived in semisubterranean pit houses constructed of timbers covered with mats and surfaced with mud. Their economy was based on the hunting of deer and other small game, the gathering of sunflower seeds, acorns, walnuts, and yucca, and most important of all, the cultivation of squash, beans, and corn (of Mexican origin). Around the year A.D. 900 significant changes occurred in this culture as a result of the diffusion of ideas from a neighboring culture to the north—the Anasazi. From these people the Mogollon borrowed a new style of pottery—black on white ware—and the concept of stone masonry. It was this latter idea that brought about a shift to compact villages composed of adobe houses. Many of these structures had several rooms, and some even housed ceremonial chambers known as *kivas*. By the year A.D. 1350 Mogollon culture had become so mixed with traits of other Pueblo people that it lost its identity as a separate and distinct cultural tradition. It is generally agreed that the Zuni people are among the heirs of the Mogollon cultural tradition.

HOHOKAM

A second Southwestern tradition was the *Hohokam*. The people of this tradition, who may have been migrants from Mexico, established their villages along the Gila and Salt rivers of southern Arizona approximately 100 B.C. They lived in large rectangular houses with four supporting timbers and adobe-on-brush walls. The presence of milling stones at Hohokam sites implies an agricultural economy as do their extensive systems of canals.

At Snaketown (near Chandler, Arizona), one of the more important Hohokam sites, a massive irrigation feature has been discovered. A canal 35 feet wide and 10 miles long brought water from the Gila River. The undertaking of such a gigantic project suggests the availability of a great deal of manpower, a complex social and political structure, and a firm agricultural base for the economy. Excavations at Snaketown also uncovered a ball court measuring 100 by 35 feet and a rubber ball (undoubtedly of Mesoamerican origin). This court, of course, suggests Mexican influence as do numerous other artifacts such as ceramic figurines with "coffee bean" eyes, pyrite mirrors, acid-etched shell pendants, copper bells, and stone bowls carved in the shape of animals. A number of Hohokam sites contained small platform mounds which had been constructed in several stages until the final product measured 70 by 90 feet with a height of 10 feet. The sloping sides of the mounds had been plastered with adobe mud, and, where a building or "temple" had stood, there appeared to be a raised clay altar. Pottery over the 1500 years of Hohokam existence consisted of varieties of red-on-buff ware, often highly decorated with scroll, key, or stylized human and animal motifs.

The Hohokam people abandoned their villages on the Gila and Salt rivers about A.D. 1400 and their way of life faded and finally ceased to exist as a separate, distinct tradition. It is believed that the Pima and Papago people of today are the heirs of the cultural traits of Hohokam.

ANASAZI

To the northeast of the Hohokam there existed a cultural tradition known to us by the term *Anasazi*. The villages inhabited by these people were located in the "four corners" area where Arizona, New Mexico, Utah, and Colorado meet. Their tradition, which lasted some 1800 years, has been divided into two basic periods—Basket Maker and Pueblo. Although each of these has been subdivided (accurate dating being made possible by dendrochronology), there were generally two cultural manifestations.

Basket Maker (100 B.C.–A.D. 700). As the name implies, basket making was an important industry. Baskets were used for carrying water (when lined with pitch), carrying and storing agricultural products (yellow flint corn, squash, and sunflowers), and even in burials, when they were placed over the heads of the dead. In the earliest stages of Basket Maker culture there was no pottery.

In addition to agricultural activities and the gathering of wild seeds and nuts, the Basket Makers hunted small game. They used only spear throwers (atlatl) and light spears rather than the more efficient bow and arrow. Villages were not large, and it is believed that Basket Makers were seminomadic. Their houses were domed structures with walls constructed of horizontal logs laid in mud mortar. Pottery making was added to their fund of technical skills about A.D. 400, when they learned to produce a brown ware from the Mogollon people. Later they developed their own distinctive pottery tradition.

Pueblo (A.D. 700–1700) Drastic changes took place in Basket Maker culture in A.D. 700 — perhaps as a result of an influx of new people with new ideas. Whatever the reason, the next 200 years constituted a period of cultural revision. The atlatl and spear were replaced by the bow and arrow. Coiled pottery (decorated black-on-white) became widespread, and the first masonry structures appeared. Villages contained underground ceremonial chambers (kivas), often of great size.

Mesa Verde cliff house. (Courtesy of Wichita State University.)

Between A.D. 1100 and 1300 there were large pueblos at Chaco Canyon and along the Upper Rio Grande River in New Mexico, at Mesa Verde (Colorado), and in the Hopi and Zuni areas of northern Arizona. Pueblo Bonito at Chaco Canyon was a semicircular apartment building containing 800 rooms and rising 5 stories. It contained numerous courts, 2 major plazas, and 38 large kivas. Pottery making reached a high level of perfection in all Pueblo areas as did the weaving of cotton materials.

The year A.D. 1300 marks the beginning of the end for Pueblo prehistoric culture. At this time these people undoubtedly had the most advanced way of life in the Southwest, but a great drought resulted in the abandonment of many pueblos and a drastic constriction of Pueblo territory. By 1500 there were Pueblo settlements only along the Upper Rio Grande and in Acoma, Zuni, and Hopi areas. Shinkage of Pueblo territory and population was further accelerated by the invasion of Apache and Navaho people around 1500 and by the coming of the Spaniards in the 1600s. Although little definite, empirical evidence can tie contemporary Pueblo societies to the prehistoric cultures of the area, a large body of mythology plus material culture similarities between prehistoric and post-Spanish periods argues for a continuity with the past.

Summary

Archeology is the branch of anthropology that attempts to reconstruct cultures of societies of the past. In addition to excavation, careful analysis of recorded materials must take place and it must always be within a context of the times in which the people lived. Precise and detailed records must be kept since excavation destroys the original site. Attention must be paid to stratigraphic levels and the location of artifacts within the grid. Assessments of antiquity are made by comparing excavated material with similar material having known dates, by measuring carbon 14 residues in organic materials, or by using dating techniques such as dendrochronology, palynology, etc.

The oldest known cultural materials come from Old World sites in East Africa. In the Olduvai Gorge of Tanzania the earliest human-made tool industry has been discovered by the Leakey family and labeled "Oldowan Pebble" tools. These early artifacts are associated with australopithcines and are dated nearly 2 million years old. During the Middle Pleistocene hominids evolved a hand ax (core-biface) tool tradition in Africa, Europe, and western Asia and a chopper-chopping tool tradition in eastern Asia. The Upper Pleistocene finds Neanderthals utilizing core-biface and flake tools, called Mousterian, mostly in Europe whereas Cro-Magnon and other forms of modern *Homo sapiens* evolved a variety of blade traditions in a cultural period known as the Upper Paleolithic. A transitional period, the Mesolithic, bridged the hunting and gathering emphasis of the Paleolithic with the domestication of plants and animals in the New Stone Age, or Neolithic. The Neolithic Revolution as this new form of life is sometimes called brought increases and shifts in location of human populations. Over a period of several thousands of years village agriculture became the established way of life in the Near East and in Europe.

Human populations of hunters began to traverse a land bridge between Siberia and Alaska by the end of the Pleistocene and once in the New World they migrated to all parts of North and South America. The earliest peoples were known as Paleo-Indians, and their habitation sites have been found from Alaska to Cape Horn. Beginning as early as 7000 B.C. in Mexico and diffusing to much of Meso-America and even to Peru, agriculture based on corn, beans, and squash, established a basis for settled village life and ultimately for civilization.

In many parts of North America groups continued to hunt and gather well into historic times but in some areas—the Eastern Woodlands, the Southeast, and the Southwest agriculture (often combined with some hunting) made settled village life possible beginning about 1500 B.C. In some areas intensive agriculture was responsible for the growth of extremely advanced cultures with highly developed technical skills and elaborate ceremonial life. Such societies were the Missippian, the Mogollon, the Hohokam, and the Anasazi.

The Rise of Civilization: 5
The Urban Revolution

Civilization is a hard word to define. Some would define it in terms of humaneness, while others like V. Gordon Childe think of it mostly in terms of technological proficiency, complexity of political structure, urbanization, and more effective communication (e.g., the presence of writing). Paul Harvey maintains that the difference between "primitive" and "civilized" society is that in the former you can't drink the water and in the latter you can't breath the air. Some writers such as Alexander Goldenweiser escaped the problem completely by making "civilization" synonymous with "culture."

For our purposes let us follow the lead of Robert Braidwood and think in terms of a combination of criteria — technological, moral, and intellectual. Braidwood writes:

> To me civilization means urbanization; the fact that there are cities. It means a formal political setup—that there are kings or governing bodies that the people have set up. It means formal laws—rules of conduct— which the government (if not the people) believes are necessary. It probably means that after things get well established there are formalized projects—roads, harbors, irrigation canals, and the like—and also some sort of army or police force to protect them. It also means there is writing. . . . Finally . . . civilization seems to bring with it the dawn of a new kind of moral order. (1975: 143–150)

Stressing the intellectual aspect, sociologist Robert Bierstedt equates civilization with sophistication in the sense of a capacity for self-reflection, self-criticism, and other-awareness. In his thinking, primitive society has art but not esthetics, religion but no theology, techniques but no science, legends but no literature, language but no alphabet or ideograms; it has customs but no laws, knowledge but no epistemology; and it has a world view but no philosophy. Civilized humans, in Bierstedt's terms, reflect with a measure of objectivity on the meaning, nature, and dynamics of their thought systems, institutions, and lifeways, and this transcends the provincialisms of time, place, and circumstance (Bierstedt 1966).

In an attempt to learn something of how civilization developed in various parts of the world and what it meant to the people who lived under its influence we shall analyze five areas of incipient civilization—Mesopotamia, Egypt, the Indus Valley, Mesoamerica, and Peru.

A. Old World Civilizations

Mesopotamia

We have noted that the agricultural revolution came first to the highland areas of Turkey, Iraq, and Iran, and one might therefore expect that the highland people would be the ones to initiate the next step, the urban revolution and the development of civilization. This, however, was not the case, for civilization in the Middle East developed first in the semi-arid lowlands of the alluvial valleys of the Tigris and Euphrates rivers. While lack of rainfall was a problem in this area, the soil was remarkably fertile. When water was added either by way of irrigation or flooding it could produce high yields of agricultural products—particularly wheat and barley. The major problem was, however, that the Tigris and Euphrates rivers were very unpredictable water courses, and their silt laden waters could flow gently over their banks, thus providing farmers with valuable topsoil and moisture, or they could roar down the valleys destroying crops, villages, and anything in their path.

UBAID PERIOD
(4500-3500 B.C.)

In documenting Mesopotamia's rise to civilization we must first turn our attention to a period of prehistory (before writing) called the *Ubaid* Period. During this era Neolithic farming communities along the Tigris and Euphrates rivers grew into towns. At the center of these towns elaborate series of mounds were constructed and crowned with temples. These sacred structures ranged from very small sanctuaries only about 10 feet square in area to more impressive 60-foot-long structures with columns and altars. Often the temples were rebuilt or enlarged many times over the years. These edifices and the mounds on which they rested were known as *ziggurats*, and they apparently were the focal point of every town. Towns at this time probably served as ceremonial centers for a whole network of surrounding villages. They were also centers for trade and the residences of specialized craftsmen such as bakers, brewers, potters, boat builders, and heavy-construction workers. These towns also served as places of residence for numerous temple officials who had great influence in the political and economic life as well as in the religious life of the people.

PROTOLITERATE PERIOD
(3500-3000 B.C.)

As the name implies, this was the period when the first forms of writing appeared in Mesopotamia, but this innovation was only part of a steady and direct course toward urbanization and civilization. Another significant step along this course was the expansion of the temple mound complexes, and during this period we find such accomplishments as the construction of the White Temple of Uruk, which measured 58 by 83 feet. The edifice with its whitewashed mud-brick walls rested on a mound 40 feet high. It was truly a worthy monument to the sky god Anu. Another temple in the same town had an exterior decorated with ceramic cones colored red, black, and white. The ceramic cones appear to have marked administrative centers.

Temple building required large numbers of construction workers, highly skilled craftsmen, and substantial agricultural surpluses to pay the bills. In the countryside greater yields were being realized through the use of draft animals and the development of irrigation canals. In the towns, trade and craft specialization brought new wealth and the beginnings of class differentiation. Towns grew into cities, and political and economic life became more complex. The priests and other members of the divine households became more and more powerful as needs for planning and leadership became more important.

As the concept of church and private property became more significant there arose a need to document ownership and to keep track of economic transactions. This necessity resulted in the development of a system of numeration and pictographic writing on clay tablets and in the use of seals. The first forms of Mesopotamian writing were rather simple. A representative image of an ox head or an easily recognizable outline of a fish or a spike of grain was scratched into a slab of damp clay. Numerals were produced by pressing a hollow reed into the clay ($c = 1$, $o = 10$, $C = 60$). Seals, which were used to supply registration or identification of church or private property and to produce miniature works of art, were engraved stone cylinders that were rolled across wet clay.

During the Protoliterate Period metal made its appearance. Mesopotamian craftsmen began making tools and art objects of copper thus ushering in a period of human history known as the Chalcolithic, or Copper Age.

EARLY DYNASTIC PERIOD
(3000-2350 B.C.)

The Early Dynastic Period witnessed the rise of city-states—Ur, Uruk, Lagash, Erech, Eridu, and others—under the domination of kings or governors who, because they were the representatives of tutelary gods, also served as chief priests. These men did not entirely disrupt the influence of the "divine households," but they eventually became the principal purchasers of metal and luxury goods, the owners of large amounts of surplus land, and the controllers of military power. Since the agricultural lands surrounding the cities were considered the property of the city's principal god, the agricultural population was expected to return a portion of the surplus crop to the priestly households. This was undoubtedly shared with the rulers who protected the priests' interests and maintained order.

The cities at this time were walled communities with narrow, unpaved streets. Aside from the fact that the temples, palaces, and large homes of the wealthy classes were near the center of the city there was no recognizable plan. There was merely a jumble of large and small houses with a shop here and there. Most of the buildings were

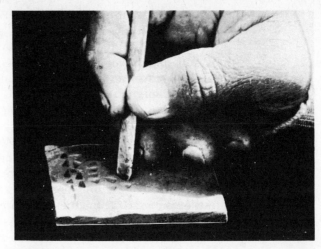

Cuneiform writing was produced by pressing a wedge-shaped stylus into soft clay. (Courtesy Field Museum of Natural History.)

of mud-brick construction. The larger houses were built around courtyards and some had two stories. There was so much litter and garbage in the streets that the level of the doorways had to be raised from time to time. Public buildings were also made of brick, but much skill and effort went into their construction. The temple at Erech, for example, rested on a platform 40 feet in height with an area of nearly a half a million square feet. Skilled craftsmen, either in the service of the temple officials or the ruling classes, produced luxury items in metal or semiprecious stone (lapis lazuli) to adorn the temples or be placed in the royal tombs. Some were engaged in production for export. Carpenters built boats, chariots, and furniture; brick makers produced the materials for the construction of public and private buildings; and potters produced ceramic goblets to decorate them. Craftsmen were not oppressed, but they were under the direct control of the civil and religious authorities.

As all this commerce and industry expanded there was greater and greater need for accurate record keeping, and scores of scribes labored at these clerical tasks. A new form of writing, called *cuneiform*, evolved. Instead of drawing pictures (pictographs) on tablets of soft clay, scribes now used a wedge-shaped stylus which they forced into the clay to produce a whole range of symbols, some conveying ideas very abstract in nature (e.g., "truth," "justice," "freedom," "prosperity").

Formal education produced an educated elite that developed a standardized system of weights and measures, a lunar calendar, a monetary system, and a highly evolved science of mathematics. Toward the end of the Early Dynastic Period metallurgists discovered that by combining copper and tin a much more durable metal, bronze, could be created. This resulted in the manufacture of better tools and better weapons. Commercial rivalries between city-states toward the close of this era resulted in armed conflict and the loss of political independence by some. This chaotic situation existed until about 2400 B.C., when a lasting unification was achieved under the Semitic ruler Sargon. After the reign of Sargon rival factions continued to compete for control of Mesopotamia until the area was again stabilized and unified under the rule of Hammurabi, who established the First Dynasty of Babylon in 1800 B.C.

Hammurabi has long been considered to have established the oldest legal code. "The code of Hammurabi," a detailed listing of offenses and punishments was based essentially on the *lex talionis*. This was a system of retaliatory procedures more or less equating punishment with offense, "an eye for an eye," "a tooth for a tooth," etc. Physicians were held responsible for the life of their patients, a requirement that must have discouraged many from the profession. An even earlier code of laws, dated about 2100 B.C. was that associated with the Sumerian King of Ur, Ur-Vammu. This legal code established honest weights and measures and tried to protect the poor from exploitation by the wealthy. Instead of resorting to the "law of the talon," it established money fines as payment for assaults (Kramer 1957). Both of these codes antedate the Ten Commandments by many centuries and most certainly were influential in the shaping of this famous Hebrew code of behavior.

Egypt

During the Pleistocene, the glacial advances captured so much of the water of the oceans that the eustatic sea level was lowered perhaps as much as 400 feet or more. This greatly affected the Mediterranean Sea basin. Because of the lowered sea level the flow of the Nile River was greatly accelerated and gorges were carved by the surging waters. When the sea level rose, the river greatly slowed resulting in the deposition of a broad delta of fertile silt. During the severe drought that followed the glacial retreat humans and animals moved into the area newly covered with wild grasses which ultimately would be domesticated as wheat and barley, making the delta one of the major Neolithic core areas of the Old World.

The civilization that developed in Egypt has sometimes been referred to as the "Gift of the Nile." This is a rather poetic way of emphasizing the fact that along the Nile there was an annual rebirth of the soil when the river overflowed its banks. But the Nile was both benefactor and thief, for a matter of a few inches in the level of the flood waters spelled the difference between ideal conditions of moisture and silt deposit and a raging torrent which could wipe out everything. The Nile was more predictable than the Tigris or Euphrates rivers, but still there were risks. Therefore, the great challenge to the Egyptian pharaohs and peasants alike was the control of the waters through irrigation and systems of drainage. The Egyptian and his river were inseparably joined. The Nile made a stable economy possible, and it provided a thoroughfare for trade thus expanding commercial and intellectual horizons. It challenged the Egyptian to develop a calendar to predict periods of high water and take protective steps.

VILLAGE-FARMING PERIOD (5200-3100 B.C.)

Much of the Neolithic history of Egypt is buried under many feet of silt deposits, but we do have some knowledge of the course toward civilization from the Merimde site on the Lower Nile which, remarkably enough, was not inundated by mud. The settlement at Merimde ("Place of the Ashes") dates from about 5000 B.C., and from the very beginning these people were farmers who cultivated wheat and barley and raised cattle, sheep, and goats. They lived in oval huts of wickerwork construction and kept their grain in large woven rush silos beside their homes. Their skills included the making of pottery—both undecorated "kitchen" ware and a finer polished variety decorated in red and black. Villages like Merimde were scattered all along the Nile from the delta to the Sudan. Each was economically self-sufficient and politically independent. These villages were organized in terms of clan affiliation, and they worshiped totemic deities.

Between the years 3600 and 3200 B.C. (an era known as the Gerzean Period) there was a unification of the many villages in both the Lower and Upper Nile regions. Each area, called a *nome*, had its own ruler and political administration. By the end of the period, the *nomes* had been united by a series of conquests into two kingdoms called Upper (southern) and Lower (northern) Egypt.

THE OLD KINGDOM (3100-2686 B.C.)

In the year 3200 B.C. the kingdom of Upper Egypt prevailed over that of Lower Egypt, and the entire country was united under Menes, who established the First Dynasty. By this time Egypt was well on its way to becoming a civilization. Contact with Mesopotamia and black Africa had triggered an expansion in technological knowledge and in the arts. A concept of pictographic writing was elaborated upon with the result that a hieroglyphic system emerged which incorporated the concept of phonemics. That is to say, the symbols designating sounds or words were often put together, thus creating more complex or abstract words. Just as in our language a picture of a bee and a leaf could be combined to make the word *belief*, the Egyptians could com-

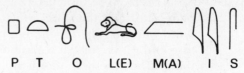

P   T   O   L(E)   M(A)   I   S

Figure 5-1 The name "Ptolemy" in hieroglyphics.

bine several sound symbols to produce words such as *Ptolemy*
(pharaoh of the third century B.C.) (Fig. 5-1). Writing of this sort was
done with reed pens and ink on papyrus, a paper made from rushes.

Egypt shared the concept of a divine king with their negroid
neighbors to the south. The king, or pharaoh, not only represented
the gods but was a god himself. He was believed to be the son of Re,
the sun god, but he was also associated with Horus, the hawk or fal-
con god, and with two goddesses of Upper and Lower Egypt. Theoretically the pharaoh worshiped the gods on behalf of the nation, but actually he appointed priests to carry out his sacred duties. There were
scores of local village temples throughout the country wherein
priesthoods worshiped not only the pharaoh and the national gods
but the local totemic ones as well.

The pharaoh was supreme ruler and overseer of all the land. He
and the members of his family supervised a civil service bureaucracy
which undertook great irrigation projects, mining operations, and the
construction of temples, pyramids, and public monuments. The top
official in this structure was the vizier who issued the royal decrees
for his pharaoh and served as chief justice of the courts. Below him
were the major officials, or ministers. There was the exchequer who
collected taxes and kept royal accounts, the royal sealbearer who
regulated Nile River traffic, the minister of agriculture, the royal con-
structor and architect and, of course, the chief priest.

The land was divided into provinces and each had its pharaoh-
appointed governor. Below the governors were the mayors of the individual towns and villages. Taxes to support this vast bureaucracy
were collected from agricultural surpluses, and there were levies on
the use of canals, wells, and on market transactions. Another form of
tax was the *corvee*. This was a system of forced labor where every
village had to provide a given number of men annually to assist in
canal building, pyramid construction, or labor in the mines.

One of the unique features about Egyptian civilization was that
there were no permanent cities until almost the beginning of the
Christian Era. There was the concept of the royal city—the capital of
the pharaoh—but after the death of a given pharaoh his successor
might choose to establish his headquarters elsewhere. The old capital
and its royal tombs would then be abandoned and a new one constructed to house a vast army of bureaucrats, priests, noblemen, pal-

Tomb inscriptions from Sakkara.

ace retinue, soldiers, craftsmen, and scribes who made the kingdom function. While these capital cities were densely populated with people of specialized skills and while they were places where ideas and goods were exchanged and where new knowledge was created, these urban centers were different from those of Mesopotamia or Indus Valley in that they did not have a long history of growth and development. They also had the potential of becoming ghost towns almost overnight.

When the pharaoh died it was believed that he returned to the host of deities from which he had come, and his immortality and divinity was symbolized by the grandeur and permanence of his tomb—the pyramid. The Old Kingdom period was the major era of pyramid construction, and the greatest pyramid of all was that built to house the remains of Cheops of the Fourth Dynasty, his retinue, and his objects of material wealth. It is estimated that this Great Pyramid took 100,000 men twenty years to build. If these men had averaged

Egyptian fresco depicting preparation of a mummy for interment in a royal sepulcher. (Drawing courtesy Field Museum of Natural History.)

$10.00 per hour as modern construction men do, the pyramid would have been worth roughly 40 billion dollars. While the pharaoh's labor undoubtedly came much cheaper than that, the expenditure of labor in these proportions for nothing more valuable than a monument does represent a great drain on the economy that cannot easily be accommodated by even a very great economic surplus.

It was perhaps because of such extravagance that the Old Kingdom crumbled at the end of the Sixth Dynasty in 2686 B.C. At this time priests and governors withdrew their support of the pharaoh as a divine and absolute ruler and established their own local dynasties. While unification was achieved at various periods, never again did a pharaoh exert complete political control or religious eminence over the land.

The Old Kingdom period had indeed been a glorious age. Civilization had come of age and had established a legacy for future generations. A highly efficient form of government with a code of laws had been evolved, a solar calendar with 365 days had been developed, a science of naval architecture had produced some of the first seagoing ships, the art of glassmaking had been discovered, and a tradition of classic architecture had been established which produced the column and the colonnade.

The Indus Valley

About the time of the fall of the Old Kingdom in Egypt, another great civilization, that of the Indus Valley, was coming into its own in West Pakistan and northwest India. The year 2500 B.C. marks the beginning of this tradition, which is known to us primarily from excavations at two large population centers—Harappa and Mohenjo-Daro. These two remarkable cities were laid out in careful grid patterns with straight parallel thoroughfares and intersecting avenues to form regular city blocks. Houses were two-story affairs either totally constructed of brick or with brick foundations. Most seem to have featured a central patio or courtyard. Houses had "plumbing" or at least a drainage system which led into large sewers under the main streets. While the cities were not walled or fortified in any way they did contain a single citadel which appeared to have served more as a ceremonial center than as a defense installation. Within the walls of the citadel was the Great Bath—a pool measuring 39 by 23 feet and with a depth of 8 feet—which may have been used for ritual bathing. On the other hand, this may have been the site of the world's first men's athletic club.

Indus Valley civilization was built on a grain economy (wheat and barley), for the cities contained numerous large granaries where commodities were stored for local use or for shipment. These early Indian peoples also raised a variety of domesticated animals including cattle, buffalos, sheep, goats, pigs, and horses. It is believed that the major cities were commercial centers with trade relations extending over thousands of square miles. Flat stone seals bearing the carved images of bulls and ox-like animals with a single horn are thought to be indicators of private property. Some of these seals are inscribed with pictographic symbols. Some 396 such symbols have been observed, but their meaning is still partly a mystery.

Indus Valley people appear to have been much too concerned with practical considerations to develop a very elaborate art tradition. There was nothing in the way of monumental sculpture or esthetic public works, and only a modest number of figurines (mostly mother-goddesses or bulls) or other objects of art have been recovered. We know very little about Indus Valley religion, but one seal has been found on which appears the image of a three-faced male god with horns and this has been interpreted as a prototype of Shiva, one of the more important gods in present-day Hinduism.

This civilization collapsed about 1800 B.C. Some scholars claim that population outdistanced the food production capabilities while others postulate desertification of a fragile environment.

B. New World Civilizations

Mesoamerica

The earliest experimentation with plant domestication in the New World is believed to have taken place in Mesoamerica. Pumpkins were being raised for food as early as 7000 B.C. at Tamaulipas (on the northern Gulf coast of Mexico), and maize was domesticated in the

Figure 5-2 Mesoamerica.

region around Puebla about 5000 B.C. Although squash, beans, and peppers also figured significantly in the diet of Middle American peoples, it was maize that was responsible for the growth of Mesoamerican populations and the development of civilization in various parts of Mexico, Guatemala, and British Honduras (now called Belize).

Maize was a most remarkable grain. It could be grown in mountainous terrain, in rainforest lowlands, or on arid plains. Its cultivation did not require large-scale irrigation projects, draft animals, or even the use of metal tools. It was possible to produce more than one crop of maize a year, and energy yields were greater than for any of the grains upon which Old World civilizations were built.

Between the years 5000 B.C. and 1500 B.C. the Mesoamerican people developed a full-blown Neolithic type of culture. By 2500 B.C. the Tehuacan people were producing pottery, and by 1800 B.C. they were living in permanent villages, producing baskets, and weaving textiles. The years 1500 to 100 B.C., known as the Formative Period, saw the establishment of agricultural settlements in all parts of Middle America—in the Southeastern Highlands at Chiapa de Carzo, in the Southern Highlands at Monte Alban, in the Yucatan Lowlands at Uaxactun, and in the Valley of Mexico at Tlatilco.

OLMEC

In the rainforest belt along the coast of the Gulf of Mexico people known as the Olmecs were simple farmers in 1300 B.C., but within 300 years they had developed what may be considered the first civilization in Mesoamerica. At La Venta they built a ceremonial complex featuring a pyramid 110 feet high, two paved courts, a series of mounds and platforms, and a tomb with stone columns. Four huge human heads with snubbed-nosed, infantile faces also are associated with this site. Each of these stone carvings weighs in the neighborhood of 50 tons and was probably transported some 80 miles from its point of quarry. The construction and maintenance of this ceremonial center was an extraordinary feat for a people who practiced only slash-and-burn agriculture. It is estimated that it must have taken a minimum of 18,000 people to support such a center. From a second Olmec site, Tres Zapotes, has come evidence of the New World's oldest calendrical system, and what is perhaps the oldest script form of writing comes from the Olmec phase at Monte Alban.

Certainly none of these achievements would have been possible had the Olmecs not had a high level of political, religious, and economic organization. Their art styles and religious ideas spread to much of Mesoamerica, influencing the futures of the people who inhabited the Valley of Mexico and the Maya located to the south and east.

The Classic Age of Civilization (100 B.C.–A.D. 900)

THE MAYA

Classic Maya sites have long been considered not to be true cities in that they did not have sizable resident populations. Thompson, in his book *The Rise and Fall of the Maya Civilization*, writes that after a big religious celebration there would be "a general exodus from temple and palace back to everyday-life. The city would lie deserted except for those who swept the courts and buildings or stored the masks and vestments, and for the priests on tour of duty. Then at the next market day the city would come alive again. (1954:60)

In recent years a number of anthropologists have come to oppose the view that Maya centers were not true cities. They argue that most archeologists have been so overwhelmed with the task of uncovering the spectacular ceremonial buildings that they have had little time for or interest in looking for evidence of the existence of the humble dwellings of the people whose agricultural and craft skills made the city operate. They further contend that the administration of a great city like Tikal or Palenque would require large numbers of government officials and priests, and, since these people were undoubtedly full-time specialists, they would require a great network of supporting people such as servants, artisans, merchants, and agriculturalists to satisfy their daily personal needs and to assist them in maintaining the city. While there may have been a great influx of rural people on ceremonial occasions or when the market functioned, it is only reasonable that such occasions could not have taken place without a great deal of preparation from people who lived and worked within the city.

The pattern of Classic Maya cities may have been something like that of Chichén Itzá, which the Spanish bishop Diego de Landa described in the sixteenth century. He spoke of the city having temples and "palaces" at the heart, sections of homes of ruling elite adjacent, then the homes of the wealthy merchants and artisans, and on the outer periphery of the city, the mud and thatch huts of the poorer classes.

Future excavations at the major Mayan sites such as Tikal, Copan, Palenque, Uxmal, and Uaxactun will undoubtedly shed more light on this topic of controversy. Until this information is available let us concentrate on the data at hand concerning the pattern of civilized life at these Mayan centers.

G. H. S. Bushnell describes the major ceremonial complex as follows:

> The centres were all composed of elements of the same kind—platforms and pyramids arranged round courts, ball courts, causeways and so on—but they differed greatly in execution. The towering steep pyramids of Tikal give a very different impression from the much lower ones of Palenque, and the flat tombstone-like stelae (stone column monuments) of Tikal are far from the rounded, sculptural forms of Copan. Palenque excels in low-relief carving and stucco modeling and Uxmal is famous for its long, low facades loaded with decoration in stone mosaic.
>
> Maya architecture as a whole is concerned with the grouping of great masses about open spaces, and little interest was taken in interiors. The temples which crowned the great pyramids were small and dark inside, roofed with wooden beams, or corbelled vaults in which each successive course of stone oversails that below it, until finally the remaining gap can be bridged by a single stone. A roof of either kind was generally crowned with a towering mass of masonry with a carved roof-comb at the top, designed purely for external effect. (1968:54–55)

Maya achievements in the areas of mathematics, astronomy, hieroglyphic writing, and calendrical calculation were closely linked to the ceremonial aspects of this civilization. Since their religion taught that the cycles of days and years could greatly influence the lives of men, great emphasis was placed on observations of solar eclipses and

Mayan Temple of the Sun at Palenque. Note the carved stone roof comb. (Courtesy Darrell Casteel.)

relative positions of other celestial bodies to establish astrological forecasts. The Maya used two separate calendars. One was the Sacred Calendar called *Tzolkin*, consisting of 13 "months" of 20 days (each with separate names) totalling 260 days. The other was the *Haab*, a solar calendar containing 360 days (eighteen 20-day "months") to which a five day period was added each year. The two calendars ran simultaneously and repeated themselves every 52 years (18,980 days). At the end of each 52-year cycle there were important religious activities to appease the gods and thereby insure that another such period would take place. Advanced systems of mathematics were devised to assist them in their complicated calculations. Their method featured place numeration based on 20 and the use of the cipher (nought) which for them stood for completion rather than zero. Mayan hieroglyphics were also developed for religious purposes. Many of the symbols stood for particular months in their calendar or for particular deities in their pantheon. Signs often were associated with sounds, as in the case of the symbol for "water" and for "to count." Since the sounds of the former noun and the latter verb were much alike, one symbol was felt to be sufficient.

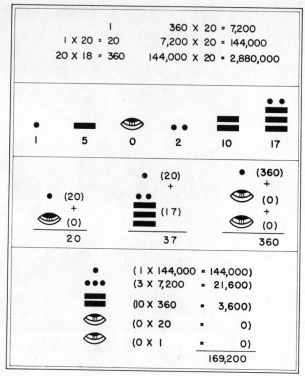

Mayan arithmetic vigesimal system, and numerals. (Chart courtesy Field Museum of Natural History.)

The religion which served to motivate the Maya scholars and architects was primarily centered about the worship of nature deities. Since the entire civilization was dependent upon success in the growing of maize, and since the production of this commodity entailed a constant struggle with the environment, their worship involved appeals to the gods of rain, wind, fire, and maize for good harvests. Particular days and months had patron deities associated with them, and the calendrical system they developed helped them keep the worship schedule straight. Offerings to the gods often included human blood drawn from the tongue, ears, or fingers, but human sacrifice was not practiced by the Classic Maya.

Every ceremonial center included a ball court, and it is known that the games played there had a sacred function associated with concepts of death and rebirth. Contestants could hit the ball with the hips, thighs, or elbows but not with the feet. How goals were made is not known but some of the later courts had stone rings set in the vertical walls.

THE VALLEY OF
MEXICO

While the Maya were developing their ceremonial centers in the low-lands of Guatemala and on the Yucatan Peninsula, another civilization, the Teotihuacán, was being established in the Valley of Mexico. Here without question we find true cities—ceremonial centers with resident populations. While the people of this region were dependent on maize like the Maya, this was open country rather than jungle, and with sufficient rainfall or irrigation large yields could be realized. Another factor that helps to explain the existence of a dense population at Valley of Mexico sites was the use of *chinampas* (sometimes called "floating gardens") which they maintained in five shallow lakes in the area. These gardens were actually platforms built up with layers of mud and aquatic plants and were kept productive by renewing the soil periodically with dredged-up mud.

The great city of Teotihuacán covered an area of over seven square miles. It was a planned city with broad avenues, spacious plazas, and soaring pyramids. Fronting on "main street" (the Avenue of the Dead) were the homes of the wealthy classes, the 210-foot high Pyramid of the Sun, the 136-foot Pyramid of the Moon, a 30-acre market place, an administrative center, and the Temple of Quetzalcoatl (the plumed serpent). Large groups of buildings near the ceremonial center housed multitudes of worshipers during the rituals. Worship was directed to natural phenomena. There was a fire god, a rain god,

Feathered Serpent carvings on the Temple of Quetzalcoatl, Teotihuacán.

"Los Danzantes" (The Dancers) figure from Monte Alban. They are interpreted by some to be protraits of ball court athletes. (Courtesy Darrell Casteel.)

a goddess of water, and gods of fertility and earth renewal; all of these were represented in stone sculpture about the plazas.

In addition to being a religious center, Teotihuacán was a governmental and trade capital dominating the Valley of Mexico for a hundred miles or more in every direction.

MONTE ALBAN

Still another Mesoamerican civilization of the Classic Age warrants our attention. This was the Zapotec civilization in the Central Highlands of Mexico. Here overlooking the Valley of Oaxaca, these people established the civic and religious center, Monte Alban. Monte Alban had a spacious plaza (940 feet by 630 feet) surrounded on four sides by pyramids, temples, platforms with tombs, and a ball court. The tombs, an important feature of this complex, contained ceramic urns with images of gods modeled on their sides, and rich grave goods. Interior walls of these burial chambers were finished with frescoes of deities and priests in ritual garb. The gods of Monte Alban were akin to those worshiped at Teotihuacán—a rain god, a maize god, and a feathered serpent. While Monte Alban was not a city in the sense that it had a large resident population, it was well on its way to becoming one judging from the hundreds of small house foundations that cover the slopes leading to the ceremonial center.

DECLINE OF THE
CLASSIC
CIVILIZATIONS

Between the years A.D. 800 and 900, the Classic Period came to an abrupt end. The Lowland ceremonial centers of the Maya were neglected and finally abandoned. Monte Alban was vacated by A.D. 900. During the seventh century the culture of Teotihuacán was destroyed by foreign invaders. The reasons for the fall of the Maya are not known. One theory blames their demise on epidemic diseases, while another postulates that the tropical soils were unable to support the dense population that had developed. Monte Alban's decline is also believed to have resulted from the inability of the Valley of Oaxaca to sustain an expanding population. Another theory holds that volcanic activity and earthquakes, interpreted as the anger of the gods, brought about the decline of Classic ceremonial centers. Most likely a combination of factors was responsible. Whatever the causes, the effect was a decline in population in the Lowland centers and a growth in population in the Yucatan Peninsula.

The Warrior Civilizations (A.D. 900–1521)

THE TOLTECS

During the tenth century a warlike people known as the Toltecs moved into the Valley of Mexico and established a capital city, Tula, north of the site of Teotihuacan. Although new to civilization, they managed to develop a ceremonial center with a plaza flanked by pyramids, temples, and a ball court. Carvings on the buildings and on numerous monuments seem to emphasize the themes of warfare, death, and reverence for the feathered serpent Quetzalcoatl.

After some 300 years of domination of the Valley of Mexico the Toltecs fell to a combination of troubles involving drought, rebellion and invasion by northerners called Chichimecs, in about A.D. 1200. From this time until the establishment of the Aztec state, the history of the Valley of Mexico is one of chaos.

During their period of domination, the Toltecs had managed to influence the cultures of people over a wide area. Their influence was felt as far away as the Yucatan Peninsula. The Maya city of Chichén Itzá was invaded by Toltecs in the tenth century, and they refurbished the site more to their own tastes with feathered serpent columns and relief carvings of warriors and jaguars.

AZTECS

After a long period of warfare between numerous factions in the Valley of Mexico, one Chichimec group, the Aztecs, gained control of the region and established their capital, Tenochtitlán, on the present-day location of Mexico City in about A.D. 1325. Within a period of about one hundred years their society evolved from one made up of 20 separate clans, each ruled by its own war chief, to one

Toltec warrior column at Tula.

with a centralized government, an absolute monarch, and a class of nobles. In time the nobility came to dominate policies of land tenure, agricultural activities, and trade.

The Aztec state has been described as a military theocracy. The major deities of the Aztec pantheon were rain and agricultural gods, the sun god, the war god, and an earth goddess. The sun god, Huitzilopochtli, was believed to be involved in a continual struggle with many other star deities. If he were not strong enough to repulse these forces, the world would be destroyed. Strength came from a constant supply of sacrificed human blood, and therefore, the Aztecs considered it their special duty to obtain prisoners in warfare and offer the blood and hearts of these captives to their paramount deity. These sacrificial ceremonies were performed with great fanfare on altars located on the tops of stepped pyramids while throngs of citizens watched from the plaza below.

Like the Maya, the Aztecs possessed both a system of writing and a calendar. They recorded their history in books, called codicies, with

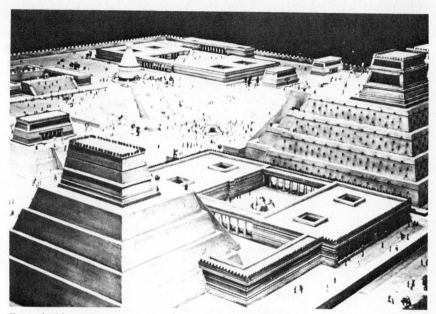

Tenochitlán, the Aztec capital city. (Drawing courtesy Field Museum of Natural History.)

pages made from inner bark fibers. The Aztecs maintained special schools for the training and education of craftsmen, priests, and scientists, and, although they achieved much in the areas of arts, letters, and sciences, their true interest was war. The army was a high calling and an excellent vehicle for moving up in the social and political structure. Valiant warriors wore elegant uniforms with elaborate headdresses and received great acclaim for their campaigns. For better than 200 years the Aztecs waged war and extracted tribute from their neighbors. They were indeed out for blood. It is quite understandable therefore that when Cortez arrived with his small army of 508 soldiers the enemies of the Aztecs rushed to join him in an effort to overthrow this "cruel and fanatic people." When Tenochtitlan fell in 1521 Mesoamerica had seen the last of its great indigenous civilizations. tions.

Cortez also was aided by a remarkable coincidence in the form of an ancient legend which predicted the return of the god Quetzalcoatl at almost the precise time that Cortez was landing at Vera Cruz. He was for a time believed to be that god.

Peru

There are few geographical regions in the world less likely to spawn civilization than the highland and coastal sections of Peru and yet this is precisely what they did. The coastal areas are arid desert and the highlands are extremely rugged with peaks rising to 20,000 feet. But much of the soil is rich and can be worked with digging sticks and hoes. Getting a living from the soil is far from easy, however, and it requires irrigation on the coast and terracing in the mountains and foothills.

KOTOSH

The move toward civilization in the New World seems to have taken place at Kotosh (about 200 miles northeast of Lima) in the year 2000 B.C. Here an ancient people built a 25-foot high platform and crowned it with a most remarkable temple. This edifice, which has been named the Temple of the Crossed Hands (because of a modeled pair on the interior of one wall), was rectangular in form, constructed of undressed stones laid in mud mortar. Its walls and floor were plastered over, and there was a sunken rectangular area in the center of the floor. Worshipers may have sat with their feet in this depression during ceremonies. Niches can be found at various places in the walls, and llama bones have been discovered in one of these. While we thus have evidence of domesticated animals at this early period, a search for clues of agriculture here has been scantily rewarded. We may assume, however, that a society capable of constructing and supporting a ceremonial feature such as the Temple of the Crossed Hands must have been agricultural. The earliest date for which we have indications of agriculture in Peru is 7500 B.C., but this comes from the highlands, not the coast.

Pottery in the form of gray bowls and jars was in use in Kotosh society after 1800 B.C. Some of the pieces were painted with red, yellow, or white pigments, and some were incised with geometrical designs. Kotosh is located part way up the eastern slope of the Andes, and its early inhabitants may have been a coastal people who migrated to higher ground where, because there was more moisture, they could establish a settled community based on herding and the cultivation of squash, peppers, beans, and potatoes, as well as the all-important maize and some domestication of fowl and animals.

CHAVIN

The next important cultural horizon on the Peruvian road to civilization is Chavin culture, which came into being about 1000 B.C. To study this culture we must turn our attention far to the north of Kotosh—to the northern Highlands—and to the principal site of Chavin de Huantar. This site is notable for its impressive stone architecture, best exemplified by the Castillo, a three-story building which forms part of a ceremonial plaza complex. The structure contains numerous rooms, galleries, and stairways and has a stone facade decorated with the carved heads of humans and jaguars. The jaguar motif was an important one in Chavin culture, and this feature serves to identify the spread of the tradition throughout Peru. Representations of the jaguar god were woven in textiles, painted on pottery vessels, and modeled in clay. The art style and presumably a set of religious ideas associated with it were adopted by many peoples in the northern Highlands and by peoples along a long stretch of the Peruvian coast. The Chavin tradition of art and craftsmanship was built on a sound economic base. These people grew a wide variety of foods including maize, and they herded llamas. The coastal Chavin also developed a pattern of efficient exploitation of the products of the sea.

It is assumed that Chavin villages were governed by priesthoods who directed the people's religious and artistic activities but probably did not have strong political power. The Chavin tradition survived in many areas of Peru until the beginning of the Christian Era and in some cases supplied a base out of which Classic Peruvian cultures evolved.

THE CLASSIC PERIOD OF MOCHICA, NAZCA, AND TIAHUANACO

The Classic Period in Peruvian prehistory began about the year A.D. 1 and continued for nearly 800 years. It was a period marked by the rise of Mochica, Nazca, and Tiahuanaco traditions. In many ways it represents an era much like the Classic Period of the Maya. It was a time of population increase and a time of florescence of arts and architecture. Religion was an important facet of life, and in numerous ceremonial centers priesthoods propagated the faith—a faith centering around the worship of a feline god. As trade and labor specialization increased so did wealth, and all Classic societies had their elite classes. Political power moved out of the hands of the religious leaders and into those of war leaders, and this power was utilized in organizing wars of conquest. Men were mobilized not only for war but for carrying out public works projects. It was during this period that a 75-mile irrigation canal and a huge aqueduct were built by the Mochica. At Tiahuanaco, in the southern Highlands near Lake Titicaca, a ceremonial center was built with a 50-foot pyramid faced with stone, a court which featured pillar-like statues, a carved stone gateway, and a large reservoir.

Unlike the Maya of the Classic Period, the Peruvians did not have a system of hieroglyphic writing. But their genius in the working of metals (gold, silver, copper, and their alloys), in the weaving of fine tapestries, and in the modeling and painting of portrait vases and stirrup jugs must command our respect.

The period from A.D. 800 to 1400 is one of unrest and warfare for many Peruvian cultures, for it was a time when new states were forming and competing for power. One such state, the Chimu, built a

Inca stonework serves as foundation for buildings in present-day Cuzco. (Courtesy Eugene Savaiano.)

great city, Chan Chan, on the north coast. This great urban center covered 11 square miles and had streets laid out in a grid pattern. It contained 10 walled compounds each with its own pyramid, palace, reservoir, and residential section.

THE INCA

The central Highland area around the city of Cuzco was the setting in which the next dramatic cultural development took place. This event was the rise of the Inca Empire, with its highly evolved political organization (see chap. 14) and its proficient military machine. The word *Inca* is the name given the ruling tribe of Quechua people who, through their genius and their ability to build upon the cultural traditions of the past, came to dominate a vast territory of coastal and highland Peru between the years A.D. 1438 and 1532.

The Inca were accomplished engineers, and they built roads

Machu Picchu, the ancient fortress of the Incas perched high in the Andes above Cuzco. (Courtesy Kim Schneider.)

(with suspension bridges) connecting all parts of the Empire to facilitate caravan travel and to expedite the movements of armies. And nearly all roads led to Cuzco, the magnificent capital of the Inca Empire. The city's palaces, temples, and fortifications were constructed of perfectly dressed but irregularly shaped stones fitted together (without mortar) so expertly that even today the blade of a knife cannot be slipped between them. Some of these individual construction blocks were over 20 feet in height, and how they were moved into place with nothing more than human muscle is still not understood, though most impressive by any standards.

High in the Andes the city of Machu Picchu was built on a ridge connecting two soaring peaks. The city had several levels, and every structure—houses, temples, public buildings—seems to have been carefully located according to some well-conceived plan. The precipitous sides of the mountains were terraced to permit their cultivation, and an elaborate system of conduits supplied both the city and the fields with water.

In spite of the evident ability of Inca artisans to plan and execute almost impossible feats of construction there is no evidence that any system of notation or writing was available to aid them. The only thing that approaches a recording system involves the use of the *quipu.* This is a horizontal string from which vertical strings were hung. By tying knots at various points on the vertical strings it is believed that Incas could record numbers up to 10,000. The *quipu* might also have been used as a memory aid for men of government, science, or perhaps the arts. There are traditions which refer to the existence of series of pictures painted on wooden slabs and kept in a special library in the emperor's palace but these have never been found. If such things ever existed they may have represented something akin to the codex records of Mesoamerican peoples.

Although the Inca civilization appears too well organized and too far advanced technologically to have ignored the advantages of notation and writing systems, they might have placed their efforts entirely on developing their formal educational system wherein those who would serve the emperor as historians, craftsmen, artists, priests, and priestesses learned the specialized knowledge they were required to know through rote memorization. There was a school known as the Yachayhuasi for nobles, and other schools, known as Yanacuna and Allacuna, for commoners who would enter imperial service.

The complete totalitarian nature of the Inca Empire was apparently the cause of its undoing, for after its leader, Atahualpa, and many of his nobles were captured and murdered by Pizarro and his conquistadors, the people were helpless to act. Having been taught that the emperor would direct their every move in peace or war Inca citizens lacked the initiative or ability to function without his leadership. The Empire fell in 1532, but the Inca walls still stand at Cuzco, and the Inca roads still carry human and llama traffic. They are silent testimony that here there once existed a remarkable breed of men and women.

Summary

Civilization, equated with urbanization and a high level of technological proficiency, began along the Tigris and Euphrates rivers in Mesopotamia as early as 4500 B.C. and was soon followed by other similar manifestations along the Nile in Egypt, along the Indus River between India and Pakistan, and on the Huang Ho (Yellow) River in China. Although fertile river valleys appear to be places conducive to the growth of civilization they were by no means an absolute prerequisite, for great civilizations emerged in the central highlands of Mesoamerica and in the high Andes mountains of Peru.

In the Old World, civilization was based on cereal (wheat and barley) cultivation, and urban centers were focal points of trade and commerce. Occupational specialists included priests who maintained shrines and often played important political roles, craftsmen (organized in guilds) who created practical and luxury commodities for local consumption and export, political officials who governed in centralized systems and levied taxes, and military personnel who did the bidding of the politicians in maintaining or extending national boundaries.

In the New World, civilization was based on cereal agriculture but here the important grain was corn rather than wheat and barley. Urban centers equaled those of the Old World in size and grandeur. Priest-kings controlled the peasants by accurate predictions of the seasons, and eclipses and other astronomical phenomena. Cities were dominated by temples and plazas, ball courts, and astronomical observatories. Communities were often laid out according to well thought-out plans with broad thoroughfares lined with palaces, dwellings for priests, and service facilities for worshippers at the frequent ritual celebrations.

Beginning with the Olmec civilization in Mesoamerica and the Kotosh in South America, civilization grew and flourished among such peoples as the Aztec, the Toltec, the Maya, and the Inca for centuries until it was destroyed quickly and brutally by the Spanish in the early part of the sixteenth century.

The Concept of Culture

6

Culture has traditionally been defined in anthropology as the learned, shared behavior that people acquire as members of a society. In recent years, however, students of culture have shifted toward a more cognitive definition which presents culture as a set of rules, skills, and attitudes which people use to generate and interpret social interaction and to thereby function as effective members of the group with which they identify. Although culture is a key concept in many of the social sciences, it has been anthropology, more than any other discipline, that has led the way in defining and studying this abstract determinant of people's behavior and personality. As the above definitions imply, one can't study culture without also studying the nature of society. Thus we can see the importance of maintaining a close relationship between anthropology and sociology; the former focuses its attention on culture, the latter emphasizes the study of society.

In order to fully understand the concept of culture and, indeed, society, we shall break down our definitions of culture and analyze the component parts. First of all, culture is learned behavior; it is not biologically inherited. Nearly everything that people do is learned from others. As the infant grows into the child and then into the adult, he or she will begin to think and act like influential associates—family members, neighborhood playmates, school chums, and community members. If the people with whom the child interacts eat with knives and forks, worship in the Christian tradition, and speak English he or she will do the same. When the child has fully learned its culture it will behave very much like its contemporaries and not very differently from its ancestors.

Not too many years ago psychologists attributed a number of instincts to humans—mother love, pugnacity, gregariousness. But one by one, these have been stripped away and today it is known that individuals come into the world with very little that will predetermine their behavior and allow them to operate independently of other human beings. Within minutes, a newly hatched chick can get onto its feet and go looking for food, but a human child must learn to get food and even to walk from its parents or other members of its group. The importance of learning for human animals is dramatically stated by A. L. Kroeber:

> Take a couple of ant eggs of the right sex—unhatched eggs, freshly laid. Blot out every individual and every other egg of the species. Give the pair a little attention as regards warmth, moisture, protection, and food. The whole of ant "society," every one of the abilities, powers, accomplishments, and activities of the species . . . will be reproduced, and reproduced without diminution, in one generation. But place on a desert island or in a circumvallation two or three hundred human infants of the best stock from the highest class of the most civilized nation; furnish them the

necessary incubation and nourishment; leave them in total isolation from their kind; and what shall we have? . . . only a pair or a troop of mutes, without arts, knowledge, fire, without order or religion. Civilization would be blotted out within these confines—not disintegrated, not cut to the quick, but obliterated in one sweep. (1917:177–78)

Our definition of culture also states that culture is shared. Let us imagine that we are all anthropologists newly arrived in a West African village. Our purpose in being there is to describe the culture, or traditional customs, of the people. The people we encounter will probably be inhabiting a common territory (in this case, the village), they will be interacting with one another (rubbing shoulders, so to speak) in order to achieve a common set of goals. If these conditions are present, we can say that the people we see form a society. What about their culture? At first we see the people of this West African community engaged in a variety of daily activities. In one part of the village a man is busy thatching his roof; in another, a woman is disciplining a child. Outside the village a man is hoeing his garden. After we have lived in the village for some time, we begin to see that there is a tendency for all men to use much the same methods in roof-thatching; the majority of women seem to discipline their children in much the same way and for the same reasons; and all farmers seem to use the same tools, the same motor behavior, and the same methods in hoeing their fields. These uniformities or consensuses of behavior are what the anthropologist is referring to when speaking of the culture of a people.

Culture is an abstraction just as a map is an abstraction. A map depicts only the most important characteristics of a geographical region, and culture refers only to the most significant aspects of a people's behavior. All anthropologists are, of course, interested in more than just the main characteristics of culture. They know that there are always deviants who do not completely follow the traditional customs, but the idiosyncratic behavior of deviants, while it is also learned, is not shared by the members of the society, and therefore cannot be classed as cultural behavior. In describing a culture the anthropologist is interested in characterizing the true nature of a particular way of life and not in showing the exceptions to the rule. The purpose of a map is to guide and direct people, to increase a person's knowledge of an area. To do this the map must be accurately and scientifically constructed. Similarly, an accurate analysis of a culture makes it possible to find one's way around in a society, to anticipate what the people will do in a given situation and to understand the significance of what might at first appear to be curious ceremonies and customs.

In defining cultural behavior as shared behavior, one caution must be observed. There are some types of behavior that are shared by everyone but are not learned and therefore cannot be labeled cultural behavior. For example, if a flash gun went off in the faces of a number of people there would be a common response. The pupils of all of their eyes would grow smaller. If the light flash were accompanied by a loud report, the people would jump or show some sort of startle response. If a number of individuals are tapped with a mallet at a certain spot on the knee, we can expect their legs to jerk. These reactions are reflex responses and are due to the structure of the human organism. They are shared but not learned, and therefore they do not fit into our definition of cultural behavior.

The final part of our definition of culture maintains that one acquires culture as a member of society. Without society it is impossible to have culture, and without culture it is impossible for any human group to survive, because culture provides established, traditional means for solving certain basic human problems such as securing food, keeping warm, and producing and raising young. Although it is possible to study culture without direct reference to people (archeologists sometimes do so in their analysis of the material effects of past civilizations), it must be remembered that without people carrying a set of ideas in their heads, without people violating cultural norms, or without people being incensed by such infractions, culture could not exist.

Subcultures

In urban areas or in literate societies in general, large groups of culturally different people often live in close proximity. Where such a situation prevails we say that we have a *plural* or *multi-cultural* society. In any mass society it is possible to point to a dominant culture to which the majority responds, and to culturally divergent groups which can be identified as *subcultures* or *ethnic groups*. Cultural differences are not always apparent between the groups and there will be unity with the dominant culture at some level—often the economic. Some of these groups may be bilingual and some may not, but there will be differences from one to another in values and world views. To emphasize the variety of cultural experiences and knowledge found within each of these subcultures one anthropologist, James Spradley, uses the term *cultural scenes:*

> There are cultural scenes known to some people but not others. Our everyday lives are lived in different social situations, dealing with different problems, doing different things. The thousands of career specializations represent different cultural scenes. So do hobbies, clubs, service organizations and even different neighborhoods. Any single individual will have

knowledge of many cultural scenes and could serve as an informant for them. (1979:21)

What Spradley is describing is actually akin to the concepts of *status* and *role*, developed by Ralph Linton many years ago. While Spradley talks about participating in many cultural scenes Linton maintains that it is

> "quite correct to speak of each individual as having many statuses, since each individual participates in the expression of a number of patterns. . . . *The status* of any individual means the sum total of all the statuses which he occupies. It represents his position with relation to the total society. Thus the status of Mr. Jones as a member of his community derives from a combination of all the statuses which he holds as a citizen, as an attorney, as a Mason, as a Methodist, as Mrs. Jones's husband, and so on." (1936:113)

The behavior associated with each of these statuses is referred to as the *role*.

In attempting to understand the cultural complexity of a modern plural society the use of the concepts of cultural scenes or status and role may be a way to sort out the meaningful cultural contexts within which the many members of subcultures participate. This, of course, would call for an *emic* (insider's) approach, and from this perspective we might define culture as a code of learned and shared symbols and meanings which members of a society utilize to understand their own and others' behavior. A motorcycle group like the Hell's Angels will operate under a vastly different set of understandings and under a very different charter of behavior than will a college fraternity or a monastic order. Each of these groups would share certain features with the dominant culture, like admiration of technology, importance of social skills, or religious piety.

Culture and Communication (Linguistics)

Most social scientists would agree that culture is unique to humans. Although there is evidence that animals learn certain types of behavior through imitation,[1] most animal behavior is pretty much determined by

---

[1] The Kyoto Research Institute in Japan has been observing the behavior of 28,130 wild *Macaca fuscata* monkeys for 20 years. Several years ago these monkeys discovered that if they scrupulously washed the sand and dirt from their sweet potatoes they were more palatable. This habit was imitated by subsequent generations and today 90 percent of the animals carry on this ritual prior to eating. Until 1959 no monkey at Kyoto had ever attempted to swim in the waters surrounding the island where the research institute is located, but in that year several bold monkeys managed to paddle out and retrieve some peanuts. Today all the monkeys are capable of a modified form of Australian crawl and young monkeys are veritable water-babies (Lucas 1968).

the nature of the organism. While animals have given us a great deal of evidence that they are intelligent and in some respects more capable than humans, they fall down in one area. This is the area of abstract symbolic communication.

Language is essential to the development and transmission of human culture. It is well-known that animals are capable of a level of communication, but they do not have language. Stephanie Morgan (1968:38) reports that dolphins make specific sounds which appear to be expressions of emotions or reactions to particular immediate situations, but she does not believe that their communications approach the symbolic quality of human speech. Various primates can convey feelings of anger, fear, sexual desire, or their recognition of dangerous situations by emitting various types of cries or hoots, but again, this communication represents only a signal system and the utterances are only reactions to here-and-now events or feelings. Observations of communication systems of apes and monkeys in the wild led anthropologists to believe that although a primate could produce a mating call, he certainly did not have the language capacity to make a date for next Saturday night. Nor could apes warn their young about things that might happen in the future. Only human parents, it was assumed, could instruct their children about what to do if the house should ever be set on fire or warn them about the danger of playing with matches. And it was believed that only human beings were capable of storing up knowledge, speculating on future events, and then communicating that information to others through a series of abstract symbols representing ideas of things seen, unseen, and unseeable and thereby creating a special world known only to themselves, the world of culture.

WASHOE AND KOKO

In 1966 Allen and Beatrice Gardner at the University of Oklahoma acquired a chimpanzee named Washoe and began an experiment which explored the possibility of an ape acquiring human language skills. Since they knew that all earlier attempts to teach chimpanzees to talk had failed they decided to teach Washoe American Sign Language, the communication system used by some 200,000 deaf Americans. Within four years the ape had acquired a knowledge of 132 signs and used them in much the same way as a young child learning to use language. Yerkes Primate Research Center in Atlanta also had a communicating chimp named Lana who had learned to type out phrases on a specially coded keyboard.

In 1972 a Stanford University graduate student, Francine Patterson, tried her hand at teaching language to an ape but acquired a three-month-old gorilla, named Koko, instead of the usual chimpanzee. Six years later Koko, also using American Sign Language, had managed to learn 375 signs which she could use to make requests for food and objects, to refer to past and future events, to express feelings of happiness and sadness, and even to lie.

Now to what extent can we say that these apes were really using language the way human beings do? Let us evaluate their performances in light of Charles Hockett's characterization of human language ability. According to Hockett true language has

1. Productivity—ability to communicate an unlimited number of messages.
2. Duality of patterning—capability of combining meaningless sounds into meaningful words and messages.
3. Displacement—capacity to refer to other times and to other places.
4. Arbitrariness—where sounds of words bear no relationship to their meaning.
5. Transmission by tradition—capacity to be acquired by others through learning and not genetic inheritance. (1962)

In regard to *productivity*, Washoe understood and produced original messages. She once combined the signs for water and for bird to identify a duck, and Koko came up with the same combination for a swan. But since the signs Washoe and Koko learned did not involve sounds there is no way of knowing whether or not they might have been capable of *duality of patterning*. Washoe was apparently not capable of *displacement*, although the gorilla, Koko, managed the abstraction of time when she signaled "First pour that (milk). Later Koko drink." Because no sounds were used *arbitrariness* could not be tested. In regard to *transmission by tradition* Washoe did not try to converse with other apes in her colony using signs although all had been trained in their use. It was reported however that Washoe had been successful in teaching her adopted 17-month-old son Loulis 10 signs having to do with food and drink and that these basic signs were then used by the son in communicating with the research personnel (United Press Int. 1979). Francine Patterson, on the other hand, maintains that Koko has been trying to assist in the sign language instruction of Michael, a younger male gorilla, but so far the ape's coaching has achieved little success.

It should be noted that Columbia University psychologist Herbert S. Terrance has challenged the claims of those who believe that apes can use language. After spending four years teaching sign language to a chimpanzee named Nim Chimpsky, Terrance now claims that the success of his own and similar efforts to teach language to apes can be explained as merely prompting on the part of experimenters, plus mistakes in reporting their data. In spite of the claims that have been made for Washoe, Terrance suggests that apes do not use signs with other apes unless a teacher coaxes them to do so (Terrance 1979).

There seems to be evidence that chimpanzees and gorillas have some capacity for language but it must be remembered that these animals had to be taught language by human beings; they did not initiate the complex communication system they are reported to be able to use. Moreover, some people doubt that they are capable of using symbols outside the training context, which, of course, involves human experimenters. It would appear that the question of whether or not apes have a capacity for language is far from settled, but there is no question that such communication is far more important to humans than apes. While Washoe, Koko, and other experimental animals apparently have the mental capacity to communicate with some degree of abstractness, no primates other than humans have proven themselves capable of vocal communication utilizing sound symbols (as opposed to signals). The vocal tract of human beings has a number of special features useful in speech—an efficient voice box (larynx), a network of muscles controlling fine movements of the lips and tongue, and above all, a specialized brain capable of handling complex and abstract symbol usage.

HOW SPEECH BEGAN

We do not know exactly when language began, but we can assume that during late Pliocene or early Pleistocene times hominids with larger and more convoluted brains than others of their generation began the experimentation which would lead to the creation of language, culture, and modern humans. The origin of language may have resulted from a situation such as that hypothesized by Hockett and Ascher (1964). They see the origin of language as resulting from the blending of calls or signals which had been serving as the system of communication of primates. These calls, which were probably much like those of modern apes and monkeys, represented reactions to immediate situations or to emotional states and were relatively few in number.

Now let us suppose, say Hockett and Ascher, that an early human ancestor wanted to communicate the fact that he had found food but that there would also be danger involved in getting it. If evolution had supplied him with a sufficiently efficient brain he might have emitted a single call which combined part of the food call with part of the danger call. If the members of his group had comprehended the new call he might have gone on to produce more composite calls in the future. In essence this would have opened up a closed call system and paved the way to language.

If this assumption concerning the origin of language is correct we would also conceive that the new pattern of communication would have been taught to offspring who would in turn continue to invent new signal combinations with more and more subtle and abstract meanings.

LANGUAGE AND CULTURE—SOME PARALLELS

Since it has been established that language is vital to culture it might be helpful in our analysis of culture to look at some of the characteristics of language. To begin with, language is a product of culture, and many of the same things that can be said about culture can be said about language. For example, language, like culture, is shared, learned behavior. One can hardly have a language by oneself, and even a communication system known only to two individuals is more of a code than a language. Language is a kind of tool which facilitates cooperation and allows members of a society to work toward common goals. If people are going to get things done, they have to exchange ideas and decide upon proper methods. The Biblical story of the Tower of Babel points up this important function of language. The story relates that when the builders of the tower no longer shared a common language all work stopped.

Malinowski (1930) made the point that language not only helps people coordinate their actions in getting tasks completed but it provides a feeling of security and social solidarity for society members. He feels that the mere exchange of words—what he calls *phatic communion*—is a reassuring factor and that silence may be viewed as a reflection of hostility, suspicion, or tension.

Human beings are born with the type of brain and vocal ogans that enable them to speak, but they are not born with language. Language is learned within society, and particularly within the family much like culture is learned. While researchers have found that children do not consciously imitate linguistic forms and that very little actual language instruction is given in the home, a study by Cazden (1967) suggests that the richness of the child's verbal environment greatly influences its grammatical development.

Both language and culture are found in all human groups, but the forms of each are widely varied. Languages differ both in their structure and in the way that they direct attention to the world of reality.

LANGUAGE STRUCTURE

Language is structured just as culture is structured. There are linguistic elements, combinations of elements, and patterns. The patterns, or established ways of making sounds and putting words and sentences together, are learned as a part of culture and like other aspects of cultural behavior these learned patterns in time become habits. Children in our culture, for example, speak effectively for years before they learn the structure of their language in English-grammar classes in school.

The study of hundreds of languages of literate and nonliterate societies has shown that no two languages have been put together in exactly the same way, and the sounds used to convey meaning in some tongues sound extremely strange to our ears. For example, the

Bantu and Bushman people of South Africa utilize lip and tongue noises, called "clicks," as Americans use consonants. Polynesians assign special meaning to no sound at all when it is used to interrupt a word. In the Samoan language *sao* means "to escape," while *sa'o* means "straight." The latter word contains a glottal stop (indicated by ') which is executed by choking off sound through the closure of the glottis. Some languages use tone to alter the meanings of words as in the case of the Sudanese who make a single word mean many things by raising or lowering the voice in different ways in the pronunciation of a word. The word *"aro,"* for example, can mean "symbol" (*aro* mid tone), "lamentation" *(arò),* "store house" *(àró),* "hearth" *(âro),* and "cooperative work" *(ǎró).*

Phonemes and Morphemes. The basic, or significant, sounds that make up a language represent only a portion of the total number of sounds that the human organism is capable of producing. Some languages use as few as 3 vowel sounds (Arabic and Mesoamerican Totonac) while others have as many as 12 (Danish and Haitian Creole). English and Persian utilize 24 consonants while Hawaiian manages to get along with 8. The Zulu, on the other hand, put 48 consonants to use. The maximum number of basic sounds used by any single language is about 75 and the minimum number is about 15. The number of basic, or significant sounds, called *phonemes*, which a language employs has nothing whatsoever to do with the effectiveness of communication or the general level of cultural development of its speakers.

The significant sound units (phonemes) are the component parts of more complex and often larger linguistic units, called *morphemes*. A morpheme is a language feature made up of one or more units of sound plus a unit meaning. There are "free" morphemes, such as "boat," "box," or "suppose" which can stand alone, and there are "bound" morphemes such as "ing," "es," or "pre" which do not make sense unless used in larger constructions as in the case of "boating," "boxes," or "presuppose." Languages vary in the extent to which they feature bound and free morphemes. Eskimo, Algonkian, and French make great use of bound morphemes while English and Chinese tend to emphasize the use of free morphemes. Bound morphemes are used at the beginning of a word (as a prefix), at the end of a word (as a suffix), or in the middle of a word (as an infix) and they do a variety of jobs. They may alter the tense of a verb, indicate singular or plural, serve as an adjective or an adverb, change a verb to a noun, or indicate who carried out the action.

Morphemes represent the basic vocabulary of a language. Although some peoples have larger vocabularies than others, every group has developed a language adequate for its communication needs. Although Western speakers have a huge stock of words for gadgets, tools, machines, and mechanical processes, they have only one word for coconut (Tokelau Islanders have nine, indicating various degrees of ripeness) and one word for potato (Peruvian and Bolivian Indians have over 200 words for potatoes, indicating differences in size and quality). Lapps do not have just a single word which means "snow"; rather, they have 41 terms which relate to various types, properties, and conditions of snow. To the city dweller the word *horse* is quite adequate but a cowboy must have a more extensive vocabulary relating to that noble beast. He needs such terms as *mare, stallion, gelding, grey, sorrel, piebald, strawberry roan, whiteface, pinto, palomino, Appaloosa, quarter horse,* etc.

While we have generic terms for our material objects, the Maori of New Zealand give specific names to each thing they own. We name our children and our dogs but rarely our shoes, houses, or lawn mowers.

Languages also differ in the number of verbs utilized. The Tamo of New Guinea have no verb which means only "to go," but since the direction of movement is regarded as of vital importance there are separate verbs meaning "going north," "going south," "going east," and "going west."

To merely count the words employed in a given language and then make inferences concerning its superiority or inferiority is also invalid on the grounds that in some languages a very few words can do the same work as a whole paragraph in others. For example, in the Eskimo language the six words *"Anilerunik kammiut tingussaat anaataralongo qimmit torsooneetaommata"* do the same work as the following 29 words in English: *When they were about to go out/the boot stretcher/they would take it/using it to thrash with/the dogs/because they usually stay in the entrance passage* (Goldschmidt 1954:28).

Syntax. The way in which morphemes are strung together in an utterance or a sentence constitutes the syntax, or the grammatical structure. All languages have definite underlying principles about where the verbs (or their equivalent) should appear, where the nouns (or equivalent) should be located, and whether linguistic units like adjectives and adverbs should come before or after the words they modify. While some languages, such as Latin, depend to a great extent on morphology (word formation or structure) thus requiring word order to carry a light load in determining meaning, some languages such as Mandarin Chinese and English depend heavily on syntax. Consider, for example, how rearranging the word order in the following sentence alters its message.

Only I threw the ball.

I threw the ball only.

I threw the only ball.

The basic differences in syntax between languages can readily be appreciated when we read a Pennsylvania Dutch phrase like "Throw mother from the train a kiss." When words of one language are used with the syntax of another the result is confusing and occasionally amusing. While every language allows some variation in the order of its linguistic units, there are fixed limits to their juxtaposition if proper meaning is to be achieved.

PERCEPTION OF REALITY

The structure of a language does more than determine how sounds and words go together; it also influences the way in which its speakers view the world and understand their places within it. As Edward Sapir says, "The worlds in which different societies live are distinct worlds, not merely the same world with different labels attached" (1929:209). The reason for this is that different languages direct their speakers' attention to different kinds of phenomena. Men and women do not perceive as mechanical recording devices perceive. A spectrometer, for example, defines color in terms of wavelengths, but the human's perception of color tends to be influenced by the terms available in the language. In some societies people do not tend to think in terms of shade differences between pinks, oranges, and reds because all of these hues are lumped together under a common term, but they may make minute differentiations concerning shades of green because their language supplies them with many words for this end of the spectrum. Some societies speak and think only in terms of light colors as opposed to dark colors.

Not only do different peoples categorize colors differently but they respond in different ways to those colors. The black actor Ossie Davis has pointed out that in *Roget's Thesaurus* there are 120 synonyms for "blackness" and most of them have unpleasant connotations, while the 134 synonyms for "white" carry pleasant connotations. It is his contention that racism is, in part, imposed on our society by the nature of our language. Of course the practice of dividing skin color into black and white categories is a distortion of reality in the first place, for a truly black man or a truly white man does not exist even though we talk and think in these terms.

Another example of how thoughts and actions follow channels that have already been dredged by language concerns the way Chinese and English speakers conceptualize social and ideological phenomena. While Western languages tend to be two-valued and deal in such polarities as "good" as opposed to "bad," "innocent" as opposed to "guilty," "conservative" as opposed to "liberal," the Chinese language is multivalued and permits its speakers to talk and think in terms of intermediate values. Charles F. Hockett relates, for example, that "Chinese adjectives most normally handle qualities overtly as matters of degree of difference, rather than as matters of kind (pigeonhole)." (1954:121). Chinese religions have traditionally been tolerant and it has been hard to maintain doctrinal conflicts in China. Because the Chinese speaks in terms of "shades of gray" it has been more difficult for him to think that one political or ideological position is completely right and another is completely wrong. Chinese ideology today represents something of an enigma to the two factions of the West—the United States and the Soviet Union —who think primarily in terms of a capitalistic—communistic dichotomy.

Careful analyses of the many linguistic worlds which shape the thoughts, perceptions, and actions of people reveal vast differences in the manner in which different cultures view such abstract concepts as time and space. English speakers view time as an unending, flowing stream which can be divided in terms of past, present, and future, while Hopi Indians make no distinction between past, present, and future. The Hopi language has no tenses, and anything that exists in the senses—the memory of an event, the present observation of an event, the realization that an event is taking place even though an individual cannot see it, and the mental expectations of an event in the future—is undifferentiated as far as time or tenses are concerned.

Equally confusing to the English speaker is the Navaho tongue's emphasis on action and the attention focused on verbs as opposed to nouns or adjectives. the Navaho's interest in the nature of action can be seen in the precision permitted him by his language in describing events. For example, while we would make the statement that "We rode into town on a horse" and would ignore the particulars of the act, the Navaho has four verbs that he can use depending upon whether the horse walked, trotted, galloped, or ran. When a Navaho goes somewhere he also makes certain that he identifies his mode of transportation. His verbs indicate whether he goes by foot, wagon, airplane, boat, or horse, and he even splits up the generic idea of "going" by using words that make clear the difference between "starting to go," "going along," "arriving at," "returning from a point," and so forth. Of course every language has ways of relating these particulars but it is easier in Navaho. Our language does not make it as easy to say such things because we are not oriented to think in terms of such action details.

Folklorist Alan Dundes (1969) believes that our language as well as our culture has future orientation and consequently a preoccupation with ends to the exclusion of origins. With an eye to the future Americans constantly insist someday their "ship will come in," "someday their prince will come," or that they are "saving for a rainy day," or that "there is a Ford in their future." And even Tin Pan Alley has picked up the future theme in such lyrics as "She'll be comin' round the mountain," "There's going to be a great day," "Someday sweetheart," and "I'll be seeing you."

Americans don't always say "goodbye" when they leave one another but instead emphasize their future reunion with "Be seein' ya," "See you later," "See you around," or "Come back." They are so interested in the shape of the future that past mistakes are of little concern. What is important is the forthcoming action. They say, "Don't worry about it," "Let bygones be bygones," "Forget it," and often admonish with "Don't let it happen again." When we go to the ball park we are so *end* oriented that we emphasize that "The game isn't over until the last man is out," and so *future* oriented that if the home team doesn't win the pennant, all we have to do is "Wait 'til next year."

If language is a window to a society's values, then this future orientation in American language indicates that her citizens have hopes for success in an achievement-status system, a system that honors deferment of gratifications.

SOCIOLINGUISTICS

Sociolinguistics is a relatively new branch of linguistic science that attempts to investigate the manner in which people use language in various social and cultural contexts. Concerned with language usage in "speech communities" (language patterns shared by particular class, ethnic, occupational, or geographic groups), sociolinguists are interested in understanding the interaction of the several sub-cultures with the greater society. Just as European language students long ago called our attention to "high German" (literary) and "low German" (common speech), so American linguists mark the differences between middle-class and lower-class grammatical usage and vocabulary and differences between the speech patterns of minority or ethnic groups and those who identify with the cultural mainstream.

University of Pennsylvania sociologist E. Digby Baltzell has compiled a list of middle-class and upper class word usage in which the former appears strangely pretentious. Examples are:

Middle Class	Upper Class
I feel ill	I feel sick
davenport	sofa
formal gown	long dress
perspiration	sweat
tuxedo	dinner jacket
wealthy	rich
positions	jobs
launder	wash (1958:50–55)

In order to get some insight into how language reflects status considerations in social interaction, let us follow a physician and a college student as they make their normal social contacts during the course of a day. When the physician stops for gas on his way to work the station attendant addresses him as "Doctor" while the medical man calls the attendant by his first name. The next stop is the hospital and here the doctor is greeted by his colleagues on a first name basis but the nurses will be very careful to use his title, *Doctor*. In making his rounds, some of his wealthier and more successful patients (perhaps fellow country club members) will call him by his given name but most will respond in terms of their status perception of him and use the title.

It would be equally informative to follow a college student about as he goes first to his professor to ask for a letter of recommendation to enter graduate school, then to the campus chaplain to discuss a personal problem, then to his room to borrow money from his roommate, and then to the bike shop to talk to a mechanic about a problem with his Honda. Undoubtedly he would use different forms of address in each conversation, different vocabulary, and perhaps even different sentence structure and grammar, as each of his conversations would represent different social and cultural contexts.

Also reflecting status differences in America are the subtle linguistic overtones which are generated by sexist and racist attitudes. At marriage, for example, it has been traditional for a woman to take her husband's name, all of it. Society pages list only "Mesdames" followed by men's first and last names for the women whose pictures appear on the page. Another linguistic peculiarity relating to sex is the fact that it is possible to know immediately by the terms *Mrs.* or *Miss* whether a woman is married or not, while the same invasion of privacy is not perpetrated on men who use the title *Mr.* whether they are married or single.

The slang terms commonly used to refer to women also reveal, in their negative quality, the position of women in America. There are three times as many slang terms for women (most of them references to animals) as there are slang terms for men. While a few terms for men draw upon animal names, the following are typical for women: dog, bunny, fox, cow, bitch, bird, chick, hen, shrew, lamb, bat, snake, filly. As one observer has put it, "Men think about women a lot; the quality of most of the terms, however, suggests they don't think a lot of them." (Hammond 1977:8)

Further reflections of a dominant male world are such references as "man-hours," "man o' war," "manpower," "man to man," "man of God," and "man the lifeboats" which are not generic but mean to exclude women. Had not the English language been a vehicle mirroring differences in the status of the sexes the famous message from the moon might very well have come through "One small step for a human being and one giant step for all humanity." In the language of America the phrase "ladies first" seems strangely out of place in a communication system that normally puts them last, for example, "men and women," "Mr. and Mrs.," "husband and wife," "boys and girls," or "male and female."

The ways in which our words and combinations of words disparage black people also reveals how language is central to the process whereby we define ourselves and our attitudes toward the people around us. Terms like *culturally disadvantaged* or *culturally deprived*, so frequently used when describing black schoolchildren in America, imply that black people do not have a culture that is of worth. Universities often publicize that they are seeking "qualified black students" and companies often advertise for "qualified black employees" whereas the term *qualified* is not used when talking about whites. Furthermore, people of African descent are frequently referred to as "nonwhite" whereas Caucasians are never referred to as "nonblack." This is significant since the population of the world consists of three times more people of color than people who are white.

Gestures. The study of communication involves more than just human speech and its meanings. Shrugs of the shoulders, movements of the head, facial expressions, and motions of the hands and arms also convey meaning and are a vital part of any communication system. Sometimes such appendages to speech speak for themselves and may even subvert linguistic communication. These aspects of "body language" are, of course, forms of learned, shared behavior just like the units of language, and their precise overtones are known only to those people who share or are familiar with a given cultural system.

Enculturation and Socialization

Those things that set humans apart from the lower animals and make them unique creatures—their ability to use language and develop culture—seem to be acquired through the process of learning. In anthropology, the learning of one's language and tradition is known as *enculturation*. It is a learning process unique to people because only they have culture. Through enculturation the random behavior of children is directed into acceptable channels. Enculturation is, you might say, a conditioning process wherein values, conventions, and symbolic meanings of a culture are transmitted to the young or, in some cases, to new adults who have recently joined the society. As this learning process goes on, the values, ideals, and ethics of a society are internalized so that the individual will automatically operate in terms of the norms of the society even if others are not present. The values of society become the individual's and make up a sort of social conscience that will then serve as the basis for what in turn will be taught to offspring when the time comes.

In addition to enculturation there is another type of learning that is important in the development of a human being. This is *socialization*. It is a different kind of learning experience, but it goes hand in hand with enculturation. Unlike enculturation, socialization is not unique to humans but is characteristic of social animals in general. While enculturation has to do with learning a cultural tradition, socialization refers to learning to get along with the unique personalities making up the social groups into which the individual is born or which he has joined. No two families are exactly alike; father may be strict and mother lenient, or vice versa. Both may be strict or both lenient. There are different adjustment situations for the eldest child, the youngest, or the only child. Over a period of time the child must learn to discriminate between individuals and adjust its behavior accordingly.

DIFFERENCES BETWEEN ENCULTURATION AND SOCIALIZATION

While differentiating between the processes of socialization and enculturation, we must keep in mind that the two are intimately tied together. To a great extent one learns how to get along with the individuals that make up one's group by drawing upon the values or patterns of accepted behavior that prevail within the culture. Sociologists often lump these two types of learning experience together as socialization, but this leaves something to be desired.

A good example of the difference between the processes of enculturation and socialization is to be found in the college pledge situation. Each semester the fraternities on our college campuses add new members to their groups. These new members are called pledges. For a certain period these pledges are on probation while they learn to become good fraternity members. To begin with they must be enculturated—that is, they must learn the nationwide heritage, or traditions, of the fraternity. Second, the pledge must learn how to get along with the "brothers" who live with him in the fraternity house. He must learn, for example, that Joe is very sensitive about his excess weight. Pete is very easy to get along with; nothing bothers him. Jim, on the other hand, likes to sleep late in the morning and is pretty mean if disturbed. Still another "brother," Bill, is very serious about his grades and doesn't want people wandering into his room when he is studying. If the pledge is ever to become an "active," he must learn to get along with these people and their idiosyncrasies. In other words, he must be *socialized.* If he does not choose to learn the fraternity's traditions, or if he does not learn to adjust to the patterns of behavior that prevail within the group, he will not be allowed to become a member in full standing. Even in this situation it may be seen that enculturation and socialization are closely associated. The pledge is aided in his socialization process if he has learned the fraternity traditions well, as they tend to define how fraternity brothers should act toward one another and toward outsiders.

The experiences of the fraternity pledge and the growing child are alike in this respect. The child growing up in a culture finds that it gets along much better with its parents if it observes certain norms concerning respect and obedience that are dominant in its culture. Beyond this point it is a matter of individual differences. Some parents demand more respect or obedience than others, and the child must learn, as the pledge did, to adjust to its particular group.

Material and Nonmaterial Culture

The cultural world in which the child grows up is composed of two types of reality—nonmaterial and material. Thus far our discussion of culture has dealt primarily with the individual's nonmaterial environment—patterns of thought and behavior, the moral code that regulates behavior, and the values and goals that motivate a person. Nonmaterial culture concerns the ideas people live by and the principles that they will die for. The nonmaterial aspects of culture are often the most difficult for the anthropologists to describe, because they often exist at the covert level—that is, below the level of observation. People are often quite unaware of the values that motivate their behavior, and therefore, the anthropologist must try to discover them through prolonged observation and analysis of behavior.

The material aspects of culture, on the other hand, are much more easily observed and documented. Every society tends to produce and use a special set of material objects—houses, clothes, tools, weapons—which also must be considered as part of the traditional way of life.

Although we have recognized material and nonmaterial culture as separate and different types of phenomena, in reality, it is almost impossible to study them as separate entities. Material and nonmaterial culture are functionally related in every society and it is extremely unwise to consider the one without making reference to the other.

A society's religion includes not only a set of spirits or deities and a set of beliefs but also a set of religious objects—altars, carved images, fetishes, shrines—which are part and parcel of the total religious configuration and can hardly be separated from the nonmaterial aspects of worship. The interrelationship of material and nonmaterial culture can also be seen when we look at the way material objects and technological processes affect the total worldview of a people. Europeans who have the technical abilities and inventions to change the course of rivers, turn deserts into productive farm land, and transform swamps into cities look upon nature in a very different way from fatalistic pre-industrial people who must take nature as it comes and adjust to its whims. The person on the assembly line who merely turns a single nut on a truck or solders a single connection in a television set cannot help but have a different attitude toward the work and the product being produced from the craftsperson who begins with a set of raw materials and alone fashions them into a finished product. A society that regulates its behavior by the clock has a very different pattern of living and a very different set of values from one where time is less accurately kept. Punctuality and tardiness, "saving time" or "wasting time," are significant concepts only to people who live by the clock.

The artifacts making up the material culture of a group have proved to be valuable objects of study for anthropologists concerned with the reconstruction of the history of prehistoric cultures. The various diffusionist schools of anthropological thought dealt almost entirely with the material products of primitive people. House and canoe types, weapons, and tools served them as evidence in their efforts to trace the spread of peoples and ideas about the world. One of the main objections to diffusionists' schemes, however, is that even identical artifacts do not always have the same function in different societies. This is a very important principle to keep in mind in studying the relationship between material and nonmaterial culture. A paddle that propels a canoe in one society may serve as a dance baton in another. To know a people's way of life one must know not only about their artifacts but also how they put them to use. Every aspect of life—economics, religion, family, government—has its material equipment as well as its principles and modes of behavior. All are tied together in a meaningful and consistent whole.

Culture and Biology

If a group of anthropologists were asked for a simple statement of why people have culture, they would probably say that it provides them with certain time-tested methods or procedures for satisfying basic biological, psychological, and sociological needs. It provides a pattern for behavior that will ensure or greatly enhance chances for survival. Culture provides people with readymade solutions for keeping themselves fed and sheltered, satisfying their sex drives, understanding the mysteries of the universe, and regulating society. Life without culture would be very much like putting a TV or stereo kit together without instructions. Each step would have to be worked out through trial and error rather than by depending on a prescribed procedure.

Once a person has been thoroughly enculturated, behavior becomes highly automatic. The person develops habits of eating, driving a car, putting on clothes, lighting a cigarette. If people stopped and thought about each action, life would indeed be complicated and filled with no end of confusion. The situation would be like that of the centipede who, upon being asked what foot it put out first became so confused it couldn't manage its many legs at all.

Although culture ordinarily provides solutions for life's problems and is, in general, a response to a set of biological as well as other derived needs, the various aspects of culture are not determined by the biological necessities of human beings. Culture often modifies or even inhibits biological needs. Rather than always seeing to people's comfort, culture often complicates life and disciplines efforts to satisfy needs. For example, every culture provides for some method whereby the need for nourishment is satisfied, but almost every culture stipulates what foods should be eaten, how they will be prepared, and when they can be eaten. There are probably few if any societies in the world that do not have a concept of "meal time." Polynesians eat twice a day, at 10 A.M. and 7 P.M., while Americans eat three times a day, at 8 A.M., 12 noon, and 6 P.M. In each case these meal times represent a regulation of eating. In no society are people able to satisfy hunger in the simplest and most direct manner. Depending on the culture, one must manage knives and forks, chopsticks, or, if no utensils are used, one must eat with one's hands in a special "polite manner." Although humans have a more diverse diet than any other animal, every society considers certain foods unpalatable or actually taboo.

Similar regulations are imposed on people's attempts to satisfy other biological needs. The drive for sexual satisfaction is controlled by a myriad of special restrictions. There is always a time and place for sex activity. Some societies restrict sex to marriage while others do not. Strict rules regulate whom the partners may be. There are often special taboos in regard to sex relations with relatives, members of different castes, or persons below a certain legal age.

While culture provides a person with a means of protecting oneself from the elements, it frequently clothes the individual in styles and materials that are not in tune with the geographical environment or with normal activities. Certain men in European societies, regardless of the heat, are expected to wear coats and ties in public, while women, for the sake of fashion, are often grossly underclothed in the most frigid temperatures. Many an American saleswomen has remarked at the end of the day that her feet are killing her or that she has a headache. Her problem usually stems from the fact that she has spent long hours wearing shoes that, because of extremely high and slender heels, are not suited to her activities. Her grandmother also suffered discomforts in the name of beauty. She cinched in her waist so tightly that her swooning was probably more the result of lack of air than it was an affectation to be called forth in times of shock or emotional crises.

Some cultural ideas do more than just cause discomfort; they actually reduce one's chances for survival. In time of war or other crisis, cultural values such as courage or patriotism often cause people to sacrifice their lives. If one's main purpose is to survive, one would certainly not respond to such values as courage and patriotism but would rather take the easiest and safest way out of each crisis situation.

Thus, we can see that a human being's behavior is more than just a response to certain physical or animal needs. The biological dimension represents only one influence. All human beings are of one species, but there are almost as many kinds of culture as there are societies. Therefore, it is plain that biological needs may be satisfied in a variety of ways. At this point it is quite pertinent to ask, "If biology alone is not responsible for culture, what are the other factors involved?"

Culture and Geography

Geography is always a factor to be considered in any attempt to understand the nature of a given culture. While geography does not determine what form a culture will take, it definitely has a limiting influence. Eskimos, for example, can never become farmers unless they build greenhouses (an unlikely possibility), for the arctic earth never thaws out for long enough periods to make agriculture possible. The conditions of their environment pretty much point them in the direction of hunting, although there are peoples of Siberia who herd under almost the same climatic conditions. While the form of economy, and family and political organizations of a people are often influenced by the nature of the region, people often persist in following customs that seem quite out of tune with their environment. This persistence might derive from a stubbornness against being controlled by a climatic environment that no longer exists when a people have shifted their habitat. An example of this is to be found in the division of labor ideas of the reindeer-herding people of Siberia, the Chuckchi, Koryak, and Yukighir. When their animals have exhausted the sparse tundra vegetation in one area, they must move. The men drive the herd to a new area, leaving the women to move the skin tents that make up the camp. Once the men have driven their animals to a suitable location they merely sit down and wait in the cold until the women arrive to build fires and set up the tents. Rather than engage in what they consider woman's work—building some type of crude windbreak or building a fire to warm themselves—the men sit and suffer in the cold. This division of labor may appear strange from our cultural perspective, but the customs of many peoples seem curious to those outside the culture.

Culture grows not only from the ideas that people originate themselves but also from the ideas they acquire from others. Using American culture as an example, we find that only a small proportion of the culture content has actually been developed by Americans. Ralph Linton estimated that at least 90 percent of our ideas and objects have come to us from foreign sources. Since prehistoric times, societies have come into contact and have given or borrowed ideas about how people should organize their lives.

Culture and Historical Accident

Nearly every culture in the world has probably at one time or another been influenced by historical accidents—events that have taken place that could not have been predicted by the people themselves and for which they were not prepared. The coming of Europeans to North America greatly altered the nature of Indian cultures. They brought the Indian the horse, the gun, and the fur industry, but they also brought them the Indian reservation and the status of underprivileged minority group. The arrival of whites in the South Pacific was accompanied by the spread of both Christianity and influenza. Whole populations were wiped out and others, like the people of the Marquesas, were so demoralized that they almost completely lost their will to live. Earthquakes, floods, epidemics, drastic climatic changes, and a variety of other crises have drastically altered the cultural configurations of a variety of cultures around the world.

In summary it can be said that the unique history of each group determines the manner in which biological, psychological, and social needs will be satisfied. Individuals and societies must survive, but the manner in which they accomplish this is infinitely varied.

An Individual with Culture Is Like a Group

Culture, in providing ready solutions for human problems, allows each of us to confront the environment as though we were a group. Even though we may be completely alone we carry in our head the solutions to problems that have been discovered by people in many places at many times. We do not have to work out each solution for ourselves and we can recall what we have read or have been told that someone else did in a similar situation. Many an air force veteran is alive today because he read one of the government's survival booklets which give emergency instructions for downed flyers. These booklets represent a composite of knowledge known to nonliterate and industrial societies about how to deal with specific problems in specific environments. Much of the knowledge that is so important to us today—how to use fire, how to farm and raise livestock—were ideas first developed within prehistoric societies and perpetuated through culture from one generation to the next for centuries.

The Superorganic

Culture is often referred to by sociologists and anthropologists as the *superorganic.* The term was first coined by the social philosopher Herbert Spencer but more recently has been elaborated by A. L. Kroeber. The term is useful to the beginning student of anthropology, because its sheer composition tells something of the nature of culture. First we can think of *super* as meaning "other than" or "apart from." Considered in this way the word tells us that culture is not part of the organism; it is not passed on through the genes but rather through the processes of learning. Second, it is possible to think of *super* as meaning "greater than" or "more permanent than." *Superorganic* considered in this way reminds the student that culture outlives the organism—that is, the life of culture is greater than a single generation. Culture may be considered to be "greater than" the individual organism in still another way. When we look at culture in a certain light, it almost appears to be a Frankenstein's monster. Although human beings create culture, in the end, culture molds and controls them. A newborn baby has little to say about what language it will learn, what religion it will observe, or how it will be disciplined. Its parents have equally restricted lives. If they do not raise the child according to cultural prescription there will be pressure from relatives and neighbors to do so. Culture seems to dictate when the child shall give up its bottle, when it shall be toilet trained, and when it will begin to date. There may be things about culture that people do not like, but whether they like it or not they must conform. If they deviate too far society will take a stand and force them back in line.

Melville J. Herskovits likens the cultural situation to an escalator and society to those who ride on it. The escalator, of course, remains quite permanent while the people who ride it tend to change. People get on, ride for a time, and then get off, but the escalator goes on and on. Some people may try to walk up the steps but their efforts are insignificant compared with the movement of the escalator itself. Stepping onto the moving stairs is much like being born into a culture. For a time the riders are like the members of a society; they are part of the culture. Although, figuratively speaking, at death a person gets off the escalator, this does not mean its end, for there are others just getting on and others in the process of riding it. Those who have just stepped off the moving stairs were a part of it for a time, but once the ride is over the escalator goes on, little changed by who was once a part of it.

Although we have made the statement that individuals, in general, do little to change the fundamental form of culture, it is important to realize that culture does change. Culture is relatively stable in its main outlines, but it is constantly changing. There is an old saying that there are two things that one can always be sure of—death and taxes. It would be valid to add still a third thing—change. The only unchanging cultures are those being studied by archeologists—that is, dead ones. Change occurs in certain areas and within certain limits. For example, many of the basic values of American culture derive from the Judeo-Christian tradition, but there have been superficial changes. There are some areas in which changes are welcomed and other areas where new ideas and interpretations find stiff resistance. Each autumn Americans rush to showrooms to observe new automobiles with new designs and new gadgets. The inventor in American culture has high prestige. The area of technology is one in which change is desired. However, other aspects of our culture such as family organization or basic political and religious ideology are relatively conservative and slow to change. Innovators in these areas are often branded as immoral, subversive, or heretic.

Change comes to a culture either from within the society itself or from the outside. Although various aspects of a culture may have been added at various times, culture cannot be described as being a hodgepodge of behavior patterns and nonmaterial objects. Nonfunctional aspects in the culture may persist through the force of tradition but the bulk of culture tends to be meaningful and useful to members of the society, and all parts are related in some degree to all other parts. Even though an item, such as fire, discovered nearly a million years ago, coexists with the most modern of innovations, the many elements making up culture are woven into a remarkably consistent, intricately patterned fabric.

Norms of Society—Folkways, Mores, and Sanctions

In every society there are attitudes about the importance of following the dictates of culture, and there are attitudes about what things are right and what things are wrong. Sometimes these attitudes, which are also a part of culture, are very inconsistent. A thing may be right in one situation and wrong in another. In American culture, for example, a person may wear very scanty clothing on the beach, but is required to be fully clothed on a downtown street. The *mores* and *folkways* require citizens to walk a fine line of discretion and to understand there is a time and place for everything. The concepts of folkways and mores were developed by William Graham Sumner in 1906 but remain meaningful concepts today in spite of great advances in sociological and anthropological theory. In Sumner's theory, folkways are expected but not compulsory customs (e.g., Scots wearing kilts or Americans tipping their hats) and mores are customs considered vital to the welfare of the society (e.g., Americans having but one wife at a time). Further insight into the operation of these principles may be seen by returning for a moment to the matter of decent or indecent dress.

Let us say that it is a very warm day and a man decides to remove his coat. No real harm is done as far as society is concerned, but we *are* entering the realm of folkways. In most places society would take no notice of this man's notion, but if he were ushering in church, a few eyebrows might be raised. This is because culture says that it is customary to wear one's coat if ushering in church. Now let us suppose that the man feels compelled to take off his tie. Again no real harm is done, but in his coatless and tieless condition he would probably be refused entrance to certain restaurants. Now let us imagine that our friend takes off his shirt. This action has restricted his movements still further. He may go without his shirt in the privacy of his home, or backyard, or on the beach, but if he were to walk down the street this way in most urban centers there might indeed be talk about his propriety. So far, we have been in the area of folkways, but we are about to enter the realm of mores. The man now takes off his pants! He is standing there only in his shorts. If these shorts were tailored in a certain way and if the design were an Hawaiian print, he could get by at the beach, but as he is now, he is pretty much restricted to his bedroom or the locker room at the YMCA. If he should go out on the street like this, he could expect to be hustled off to jail or perhaps to a mental institution, for he has broken a cardinal principle of society.

Culture carefully defines what is proper to do where, and it sets limits within which people have some latitude for deviation. These principles, which involve folkways, mores, and sanctions, perhaps are best labeled *norms.* They are the shared attitudes of what is legitimate or what is normal behavior for a given individual in a given situation. Certain individuals are expected to follow some norms more rigidly than others. The limits that culture sets for the minister or priest are much narrower than for the artist. If a clergyman were to do some of the things an artist might do, he would be considered mentally ill, for he has a well-defined role that is associated with him, restricting the types of residences he may occupy, the kinds of friends he can have, the hours he must keep, and the type of family life he can enjoy.

Both men have a good deal of choice that they can exercise, but these choices are within the limits defined by culture. The choices open to the artist, while broader than those of the clergyman, do not include cutting off one's ear as Vincent Van Gogh did. There is a point where society steps in and says "You have gone far enough." Even people who are notorious for their nonconformity are operating within the safe limits that have been defined by their culture. The bearded young poet who lives in a garret is actually differing only superficially from the solid citizen who takes pride in his conformity. Both might speak the same language, sit on chairs, sleep in beds, use knives and forks when they eat, and operate in terms of many of the same American cultural principles. Both want recognition—one in the area of business and the other in the area of the arts. Both will work hard and sacrifice to achieve their ends. Actually, the bearded poet is conforming as much as the businessman. He is wearing a beard, living in a garret, eating bread and cheese, and drinking wine because this is a recognized pattern for struggling young poets to follow. He may not be much of a poet, but he is determined to look and act like one.

REAL AND IDEAL CULTURE

The norms of society are often ideal standards of behavior that are really followed by a small number of people, although everyone gives lip service to them. If, for example, a team of foreign anthropologists should come to the United States to study the cultural patterns of its citizens people might very well volunteer that in this country people are assumed to marry for life, that it is proper for unmarried people to remain celibate, and that our system guarantees that there is complete equality among all regardless of race, religion, or national origin. In the course of their investigation the anthropologists might also look into the laws of the land. Informants, for example, might explain that there are traffic laws that say a red light means stop and a green light means go and that there are eight-sided red signs that do not have a light but demand a full stop from the motorist. The anthropologists would write all these responses from Americans in their notebooks and then, according to anthropological methods of study, go and observe the people actually living their lives. They would also go to the libraries to see what the literature could tell them about American culture.

Chances are, they would be somewhat surprised by what they would see and read. To begin with, they would find out that in reality there is, in a single year, about one divorce for every two marriages. If they were to look through the published works of the Institute of Sex Research they would find that unmarried people are far from celibate. If they really dug deeply into the situation of equality and equal rights, they would find that American Indians and American blacks do not have equal opportunities with whites in getting jobs or justice, in finding adequate housing, or in getting an education. They would also find, if they stood on a corner for any amount of time that the eight-sided red sign reading "Stop" is but haphazardly obeyed. Their observations would no doubt be much like those of the psychologist Floyd Allport (1934). Approximately 75 percent of motorists literally obey a stop sign and come to a complete stop. Twenty-two percent reduce their speed and proceed very slowly. Another 2 percent will slow down slightly, while about 1 percent will proceed as though the sign did not exist.

Thus, it is important to realize that what people say they do is not necessarily what they actually do. There is often a great gap between the ideal and the real patterns of culture. It is because of this discrepancy that anthropology utilizes both interview and observation techniques. Using both of these approaches in collecting data, the anthropologist has a chance to verify information recorded in interviews and to assess the degree of conformity or nonconformity that is sanctioned by the society.

Summary

Culture is the most important single concept in anthropology. Defined generally as the learned, shared behavior that people acquire as members of a society, it is considered by anthropologists to be the achievement which more than anything else sets the human animal apart from others in the animal kingdom. As anthropologists have focused more and more on urban society the concepts of *subcultures*, *ethnic groups*, and *cultural scenes* have become important, and this emphasis on cultural pluralism has led to a more cognitive approach wherein culture is defined as a set of rules, skills, and attitudes which people use to generate and interpret social interaction.

Since culture is learned rather than genetically inherited, language is essential to its development and transmission. Although some levels of culture may be acquired through observation and limitation, the use of symbols and abstract concepts which characterizes human culture requires high-level communication. Since about 1966, primatologists have elaborately experimented with the capacity of apes to use human language. While they are not capable of human speech there have been numerous reports that chimpanzees and gorillas have been able to learn and use sign language. Many of these claims have been challenged but there is evidence of apes having some capacity for language even though they, of course, did not initiate the system and their use of it tends to be largely confined to their interaction with the experimenters.

Language is considered so vital to understanding culture and human interaction that there is a specialization within anthropology known as linguistics. Linguists are interested in such things as language structure and they make analyses of phonemes, morphemes, and syntax of the world's languages; or they direct their attention to language and culture and investigate the extent to which language shapes thought and thought shapes language. A relatively new research area is *sociolinguistics*, which studies the way in which people use language in various social and cultural contexts.

Culture is learned, and this process is called *enculturation*. It is differentiated from *socialization* in that the latter pertains to learning how to relate to individuals within one's group rather than learning the cultural norms of the whole group. Generally, learning a culture contributes to an individual's survival because culture provides human beings with time-tested procedures for satisfying basic biological, psychological, and sociological needs. It must be realized, however, that culture often modifies or even inhibits the satisfaction of needs. Just as culture is not dictated to by human biological considerations neither is it a direct response to the physical environment. Geography influences and limits culture but does not determine its nature.

Culture is sometimes referred to as the *superorganic*, and this reference attempts to emphasize that culture dominates, exists longer than, and is little affected by the people who are its carriers. In every society there are moral judgments about the importance of following the dictates of culture and there are attitudes about what is right and what is wrong. These are *mores* and *folkways*, but these norms of the society are often *ideal* standards of behavior which are not actually followed by everyone although most people give lip service to them. This disparity is referred to as the *real* as opposed to the *ideal* conformity to culture.

The Units of Culture 7

The structure of culture

    Traits and elements

    Cultural complexes

    Cultural patterns

    Cultural adhesions

    Configurations

The culture area concept

    Culture areas of Oceania, Africa, and Asia

    North American culture areas

    Culture areas of modern industrial America

The ethnographic present

Institutions

    Aspects of culture

    Definitions of ''institution''

    Origins of institutions

In the previous chapter we have discussed the importance of the concept of culture in studying the behavior of human beings, but culture is a very abstract and elusive idea, and anthropologists setting out to make an orderly and scientific study of any cultural system must have a basic set of theoretical tools to aid in that research. It is all well and good to say to students that anthropologists study culture, but when the students ask, "How?" they are inquiring as to the methods and procedures that are the earmarks of a scientific discipline. Over the rather short but vigorous period of its development, anthropology has devised systematic ways of breaking down total cultural configurations so that their structures may be studied more carefully.

To begin with, we must keep in mind that anthropology is a cross-cultural or comparative science. But it is difficult to handle simultaneously all the facts that have been learned about each and every culture because there are literally thousands of separate cultural systems in the world. From the very beginning of the discipline this diversity has posed a serious problem, and anthropology, like every other science, has had to develop methods for ordering vast quantities of data.

Traits and Elements

One of the first concepts developed to make anthropological materials more comparable was that of the cultural *trait*, or cultural *element*. These have been defined as the minimal significant components of culture; that is, the smallest identifiable units of culture.

Ordinarily, thinking in terms of traits is difficult, for nearly all reality as we perceive it is composed of bundles of interrelated elements, the individual items of which seem meaningless and insignificant when removed from their natural context. The average college student is very much aware of the colorful autumn Saturday afternoon extravaganzas that are known as "football games." The football game is actually a bundle or cluster of integrated traits, but ordinarily we do not think of it as such. We do not arrive at the stadium and set about analyzing the elements which make up the spectacle. As long as all of the right things are found in the stadium, we take the whole show pretty much for granted. The only time a fan would take notice of an individual trait would be if it were foreign to the normal state of affairs. A few years ago a professional football team appeared in a game wearing tennis shoes instead of cleated football shoes because they felt it would be easier to keep their feet on the frozen ground. This fact was written up on every sports page in the country. People were in this case made very much aware of one trait (a certain kind of footwear) in the football-game complex.

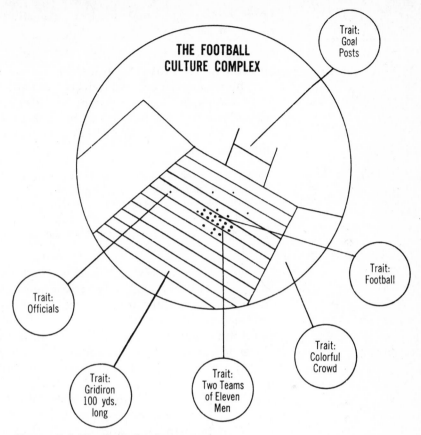

Figure 7-1 The football culture complex.

Whereas we do not ordinarily look for traits at a football game, a visiting anthropologist from another country might do so. In analyzing this great American custom he might record in his notebook such things as

1. 11 men on a team
2. helmets
3. jerseys
4. cleated shoes
5. yard markers
6. 100-yard field
7. officials with striped shirts
8. cheers
9. cheerleaders
10. megaphones
11. dozens of rules (each an individual trait of the game)

12. marching bands making clever formations during half time
13. drum majors and majorettes, etc

A careful inventory of all the traits in the football complex would probably number into the thousands.

The concept of cultural traits or elements was one of the first theoretical tools developed in scientific anthropology. Ruth Benedict has pointed out that the reason for this is to be found in the procedures used by the early students of culture. She reminds us that the early anthropologists

> were armchair students who had at their disposal the anecdotes of travellers and missionaries. . . . It was possible to trace from these details the distribution of the custom of knocking out teeth, or of divination by entrails, but it was not possible to see how these traits were embedded in different tribes in characteristic configurations that gave form and meaning to the procedures. (1959:54–55)

Such works as Frazer's *Golden Bough* or Sumner's *Folkways* are classic examples of analytic discussions of traits that tend to ignore their integration in the total culture. While pioneers in the science of custom had little choice but to deal with traits, subsequent scholars found the concept useful, and it continues to be a tool of anthropological research today. The cultural evolutionists Morgan and Tylor singled out certain traits found among various primitive and civilized groups as being representative of stages of either savagery, barbarism, or civilization. German, British, and American anthropologists alike were concerned during the 1920s and 1930s with the spread (diffusion) of both material and nonmaterial elements of culture units over great areas of the world. Herskovits recalls how American anthropologists

> traced the details of the Sun Dance among different Plains Indian tribes to ascertain with precision what elements of this complex rite were found in what cultures; studies which enabled them to draw conclusions not only as to what had been diffused, but how the elements that moved from tribe to tribe had been adapted and readapted in each new setting. (1953:59)

In the course of research of this type elaborate distribution maps were made in terms of single traits, and Figure 7–2, originally drawn up by Clark Wissler (1923:54), is an example of this approach.

In the process of drawing up a trait inventory of any group, the student of culture cannot help but be impressed with the great complexity of any cultural system. It is soon apparent that in studying humans there are no simple answers, and, above all, there are really no "simple" cultures. Even a culture as unsophisticated technologically as the Australian aborigines seems infinitely complex when one attempts to list the hundreds upon thousands of traits that make up

Figure 7-2 Variations in dress patterns among Indians of western United States (after Wissler).

the social, economic, and religious institutions of their society. William Bascom (1948) did much to change ideas about the "simpleness" of West African culture by describing the many traits that make up such complexes as divination, folklore, medicine, cult activity, and certain aspects of art among the Yoruba of Nigeria.

In the area of divination (soothsaying) Bascom claims that no diviner can practice professionally until he has committed to memory at least 1000 verses and their accompanying sacrifices and charms. The better diviners know up to 4000 verses. Over 3000 Yoruba proverbs have been published, and it is not unusual for a Yoruba to be able to recite 250 or more at a single sitting. Better than 3000 remedies for diseases have been recorded, and about an equal number of charms and medicines having to do with wealth, good luck, safe journeys, marriage, and hunting have found their way into anthropologists' notebooks. The Yoruba worship some 132 deities, each of

"The college classroom complex." (Courtesy Wichita State University.)

which has a separate cult group presided over by approximately 16 priests. In the area of arts and crafts, 13 patterns of men's weaving and 14 forms of women's hairdress are known.

The Cultural Complex

Although traits are useful tools for research, we must remember that they are not meaningful units by themselves, and, what is more, no culture is made up of just so many traits gathered up haphazardly by a society over a period of time. There is always a compatible integration of traits into complexes, patterns, and total configurations of culture.

We have mentioned the football game as a composite of associated traits—that is, a complex. It is but one of several thousand that are part of our daily lives. The college student is quite familiar with the classroom complex, which is composed of such traits as desks, books, blackboards, lectures, a professor, a philosophy of education, students, notebooks, and so on. As we read on we will become acquainted with many of the cultural complexes known to people in other parts of the world—the Kula trading complex of the Trobrianders, the Sun Dance complex of the Sioux, and the Snake Dance complex of the Hopi Indians.

Culture Patterns

The culture pattern has been a significant concept ever since it was brought to the attention of the anthropological profession by Ruth Benedict in her now famous book *Patterns of Culture.* In this work she analyzed the Zuni, Dobuan, and Kwakiutl cultures and showed how specific traits and complexes fit together in a particular way to give a certain set or direction to each of these cultures. Culture patterns, defined as structural regularities in culture, can perhaps best be illustrated by analyzing the phenomenon of language. Of course, linguistic behavior is like any other type of cultural behavior—it is learned and shared by the members of a particular society. Spoken language is made up of sounds (traits) and combinations of sounds (complexes), but no two languages are put together in exactly the same way. The unique, but consistent, manner in which the linguistic elements are linked together represents the pattern of the language. For example, in the English language adjectives always precede the noun, plural subjects always require plural verbs, and if a *q* appears in a written word, it must be followed by the letter *u.* Similar types of regularities occur in all languages.

Every society has a certain set of distinctive culture trait and culture complex linkages that set it apart from other societies. Most of these unique combinations of cultural elements represent reality meaningfully to the members of that society and tend, therefore, to persist over many generations. In every society there are, for example, shared patterns of motor behavior, family organization, dress, and ceremonial life. In our own society families are typically composed of one husband, one wife, and their offspring. Very little importance is placed on kin relationships outside this small, intimate group. The wife theoretically has equal status with the husband and their main purpose aside from the reproductive function is the pursuit of happiness. The West African family, on the other hand, is patterned along very different lines. "Blood" or kinship ties are considered more important than marriage ties. The preferred form of family among the more traditional West Africans is a husband, several wives, and their children. Wives have a much lower status than do their American counterparts, and the economic function of the family is more highly emphasized than the affectional. Romantic love is not a meaningful concept. Men are more concerned with finding compatible, industrious childbearers than they are with finding personal companions.

CULTURAL
ADHESIONS

In discussing the linkage of traits and complexes which form the patterns of culture, something should be said about those traits and complexes that naturally seem to hang together in a variety of cultures. As early as 1888 the British anthropologist Edward Tylor became aware that certain features of culture frequently are found in association with others. In a survey of 359 cultures (1889) he found that where there is matrilocal residence—that is, where a married couple resides with the wife's parents—there also tends to be a custom forbidding the son-in-law to look at, speak to, or enjoy any social relationship with his wife's mother. Subsequent investigations have demonstrated that pottery-making is frequently associated with maize cultivation; wife-purchase with pastoral economy; infanticide and wife-lending with hunting economy; and human sacrifice with agricultural economy. Tylor referred to these complexes that tend to go hand-in-hand as *adhesions*. His investigations not only provided anthropologists with greater insight into the way cultures are structured, but they represent the first use of correlation statistics by an anthropologist.

CULTURAL
CONFIGURATIONS

Actually we may talk about patterns within patterns. A pattern may have to do with aspects of culture, such as family structure and behavior, or it may be used to refer to the total configuration of the culture. It was Benedict's point in *Patterns of Culture* that if the overall emphasis of the culture was either cooperative, materialistic, or hostile, each and every pattern within it bore the stamp of the total culture. She claimed that "the whole determines its parts, not only their relation but their very nature" (1959:57). She also pointed out that "a culture, like an individual, is a more or less consistent pattern of thought and action" (1959:53).

Figure 7–3 portrays this idea graphically. Note that the form of the individual units making up the culture is consistent with the overall configuration. In illustrating how a culture is oriented in particular directions, Benedict reveals how, in the culture of the Zuni Indians of New Mexico, there is a general consistency of patterns, which in their totality constitute a cultural configuration that places stress or importance on cooperation, group (rather than individual) action, sobriety, and serenity. The nature of all of the various aspects of this culture is consistent with the overall emphasis of the culture.

For example, the family, according to Benedict's description, is a

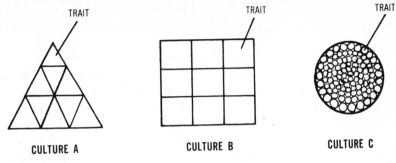

Figure 7-3

highly regulated institution with little regard for individual action.[1] Marriages are arranged; the couple's place of residence is determined by custom; and there is no place in the system for such emotions as jealousy, revenge, or deep and lasting attachment. Status is derived from clan membership rather than wealth, and even the important position of priest is determined by kin relationship rather than individual qualifications.

Typical Zunis avoid positions of leadership. They accept responsibility but don't enjoy being placed in the limelight. Zuni culture, however, is consistent in that it does not expect its leaders to exercise individual authority over their fellows. Since everyone cooperates, leaders are not required to exert authority.

In this Pueblo society everything is done in concert with the group's interests always paramount. Even dancing is ritualistic, orderly, and performed in unison. Worship takes the form of group ritual, and prayers to the deities are mild, prescribed, and ceremonious in form. They are appeals for "orderly life, pleasant days, (and) shelter from violence" (1959:66). The ideal Zuni is inconspicuous in the community, where drunkenness, crime, and other forms of violent behavior are virtually unknown.

The Culture Area

Another tool that has greatly aided the study of cultural anthropology is the concept of *culture area*, commonly defined as regions of common culture. This concept allows for a systematic approach to the study of cultural similarities and differences. There are literally thou-

---

[1] Benedict's characterizations of Zuni life in *Patterns of Culture* have been the subject of much controversy. Other investigators who have worked among these people feel that many of her statements are oversimplifications that ignore a great deal of individual variability.

sands of societies in the world, each practicing a way of life unique in certain respects even from their nearest neighbors. If cultural anthropology—the cross-cultural study of Man—were to try to deal with each and every one of these cultures separately and try to compare their ways of life with all the others in the world the task would be impossible. Therefore, some method of grouping or classifying cultures together is necessary. The concept of culture area satisfies this need. The technique of classifying cultures is like that developed by the Swedish naturalist Carolus Linnaeus in 1758 for classifying the animal kingdom. In an effort to create some order in the scientific study of animals, Linnaeus developed a taxonomic system—that is, a method of grouping animals according to the degree to which they resembled one another in their morphological makeup. Of course, he divided the animal kingdom into various categories such as phyla, classes, orders, families, genera, and species, but for our purposes let us look at what he did in the case of a special group of animals that he labeled mammals.

Mammals are a class of animals having certain characteristics in common. Some of these characteristics are that the female suckles the young, they have two sets of teeth (a milk and a permanent set), they have warm blood and a hair- or fur-covered body, etc. In spite of these similarities there are thousands of varieties of mammals. Believing that systematization and order is a necessary part of scientific investigation, Linnaeus divided them into suborders (again based on common morphological characteristics) such as ungulates (hooved animals), rodents (gnawing animals), primates (apes, monkeys, and humans), carnivores (flesh-eaters), and so on.

In similar vein, the grouping of cultures according to culture areas is a taxonomy of cultures. Although culture area classification has not been developed to the degree that animal classification has, it nevertheless has proved a useful tool for acquainting students with the varieties of cultures throughout the world without resorting to a description of each and every culture. We can talk about types of cultures rather than individual cultures. Just as a variety of animals showing the feature of hoofs—giraffes, cattle, horses, camels—are grouped as the suborder *ungulata*, cultures which share but a few cultural similarities are often identified as belonging to a common culture area. Cultures grouped together geographically are more alike than are those groups who live farther apart. When we say, for example, that the Indians of the Northeast Woodlands of North America lived in bark longhouses, we do not mean to imply that every single tribe used this identical type of house; we merely mean that it is characteristic of the people of that area.

It has sometimes been claimed that the concept of culture area grew out of the rather concrete problem of how to display artifacts in anthropological museums. There may, indeed, be something to this claim, as the man who is generally credited with the development of this system of classifying culture was Clark Wissler, head curator of anthropology at the American Museum of Natural History in New York. Although the first application of this technique was used in connection with American Indian societies, anthropologists have subsequently classified the cultures of nonliterates all over the world. (See Figs. 7–4, 7–5, 7–6, and 7–7.)

In his book *Man and Culture* (1923), Wissler gives us some indication of the methods used in deriving his set of culture areas of North America. First, he made a survey or analysis of the food resources and methods of subsistence. After this information had been plotted, Wissler turned to such factors as methods of transportation, varieties of textiles, and ceramic types. The distribution of house type and other forms of native architecture was then considered along with the characteristics of stone and metal work. Although Wissler did attempt to categorize the distribution of social institutions, ritual behavior, and mythology, note that the first culture areas were drawn up mainly according to distributions of material cultures. The fact that food resources and subsistence methods were of primary importance made geographical and climatic conditions figure heavily in the results. Boas was quick to recognize the weaknesses in this method and pointed out that "The student interested in religion, social organization, or some other aspect of culture would soon discover that the culture areas based on material culture do not coincide with those that would naturally result from his studies" (1938:671). Another feature of Wissler's methodology was the identification of culture center—that is, the point within the culture area that best characterized the area as a whole. As one moved away from the culture center, one would find less and less of the characteristic elements of the area and "the tribal cultures lying at the boundary between two distinct culture areas are mixtures" (1923:57).

To better understand the concept of culture area and learn something of the variety of culture among North American Indians, let us look at the nine areas that have been differentiated. In the following presentation a traditional set of areas will be described, not only in terms of material aspects of culture, but in terms of nonmaterial factors as well.

CULTURE AREA 1—ESKIMO AND ARCTIC

The Eskimo peoples represent the latest of the Asiatic migrants into North America. The harsh environment of the arctic region imposes certain restrictions on the cultures of the area and results in a general uniformity of culture. In certain respects, however, it is possible to differentiate Eastern from Western Eskimo culture.

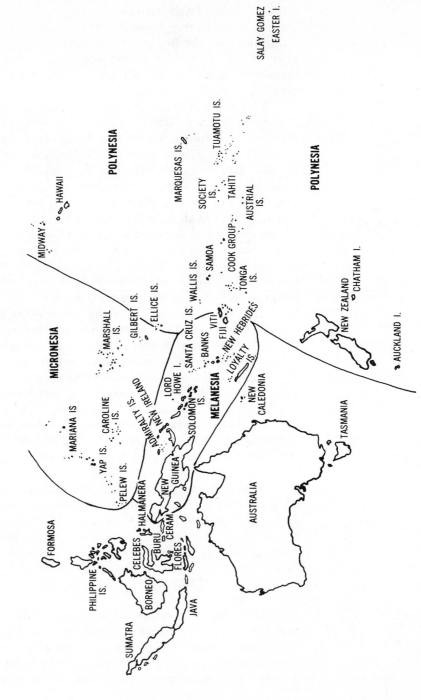

Figure 7-4 Culture areas of the Pacific (after Linton).

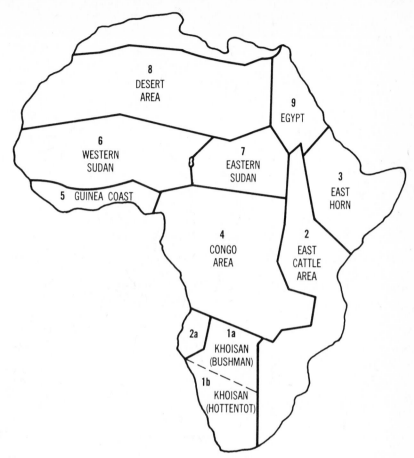

Figure 7-5 Culture areas of Africa (after Herskovits).

The major subsistence activities in most areas are sea mammal hunting in the winter, when the people camp near the sea, and caribou hunting in the summer, when they go inland. Common weapons include the harpoon and bow and arrow. The diet, made up mostly of fat and meat (frequently uncooked), is supplemented from time to time with fish. While men are dominant in subsistence activities, women are essential in the household since they dress hides, make clothes, and prepare the food. The realization that a man cannot survive on a hunting trip without a woman greatly encourages the Eskimo custom of wife-lending.

During the summer months skin tents are universal with all Eskimos, but in the winter Alaskan Eskimos live in rectangular earth-covered homes while the Eastern groups live in domed snow igloos. Certain objects of material culture—kayaks, woman's knives, bow-

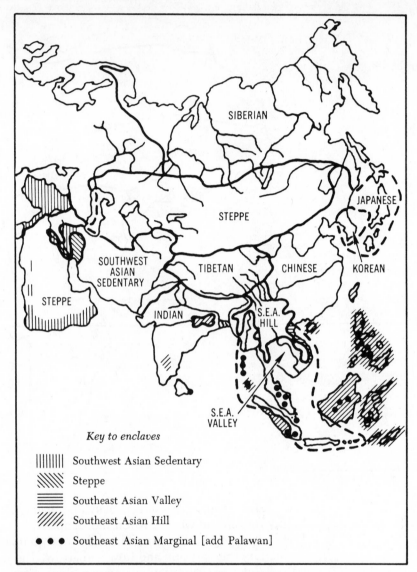

Figure 7-6 Culture areas of Asia (after Naroll 1950).

drills, snow goggles, dog sleds (fan hitch in the East, tandem in Alaska)—are found throughout the entire area.

The Eskimo family is typically monogamous, but wife hospitality and wife-lending are common features. The immediate family is the significant social unit, and kinship, emphasizing kinship ties with both the male and female lines, is not unlike that found in the modern American family. Formal political organization is nonexistent and

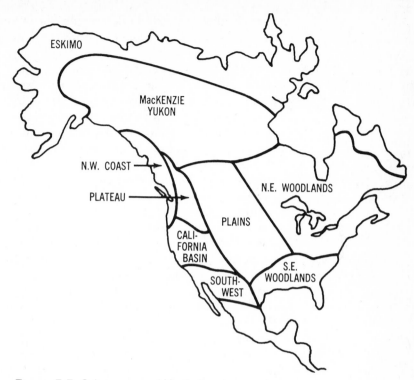

Figure 7-7 Culture areas of North America.

group activities involving leadership are confined to activities such as communal seal hunts.

Eskimos believe that all animate and inanimate objects have souls, and there is a concept of an impersonal supernatural force known as *sila* that resembles the *manitou* concept of Indian groups or the *mana* concept of Pacific islanders. Mythology is simple and centers about tales of Sedna, the goddess of whales, seals, walrus, and everything that lives in the sea. Shamanism (medicine men, see chapter 15) is prominent, but the only ritualistic ceremonies involving groups of people consist of yearly gatherings in which masked men impersonate the gods.

CULTURE AREA 2—NORTHWEST COAST

Although there is some variation from north to south within this region, the cultures are definitely maritime-oriented. The dominant subsistence activity is fishing, and during the time of the year when salmon swim upstream to spawn, great numbers of them are taken with weirs, nets, or spears. Thus these tribes are provided with what is literally a harvest of fish. Fish are preserved by smoking and sun-drying and constitute the year-round staple foodstuff. Additional items in the diet include the meat of sea mammals, deer, and rabbits, as well as wild plants, berries, and camass bulbs, which are collected by the women.

The Northwest Coast tribes have great wealth by American Indian standards. There is an emphasis on private property, and rival chiefs often compete for status and prestige by trying to outdo one another in the destruction of valued objects.

Since the climate in most of this area is mild but rainy, clothing for men consists merely of breech clouts, soft soled moccasins, fiber rain ponchos, and curious basket hats, not unlike those worn in certain parts of China. Women are attired in bark or skin skirts and sleeveless jackets in the north and skin aprons in the south of the region.

Planked rectangular houses, quartering several families, feature gabled roofs in the north, conical in the south. Typical household property includes wooden containers and baskets, but pottery is unknown. For purposes of travel and whaling, cedar dugout canoes are produced, some over 100 feet in length.

The Northwest Coast family traces kinship through both sides of the family (bilateral descent),[2] and it is common for the newly married to take up residence in the village of the husband's kin. Clan organization is strong, and the head of the ranking clan serves as community chief. Villages are autonomous and warfare between these sovereign political units is common.

Secret societies dramatize myths concerning a host of deities including supernatural animals that can take human form. There is a belief in life after death and in spirits who serve as guardians.

Perhaps the most outstanding feature of the Northwest Coast culture pattern is its unusual art tradition. Highly stylized and symbolic animal motifs emphasizing bilateral symmetry are common decorative elements of totem poles, Chilkat blankets, and dance masks. Without doubt the artisans of the Northwest Coast are as fine woodworkers as may be found anywhere in the world.

CULTURE AREA 3—CALIFORNIA BASIN

The California Basin has been referred to by one author as the "tower of Babel" because at least 104 separate languages are known to exist in this area. A. L. Kroeber divided the area into four subdivisions, each representing a subculture, but for our purposes we will take the people of the central portion of the region as representative of the area. Although the tribesmen of this region hunt for certain varieties of small game, the most important source of food is the acorn, which is collected by the women and ground into meal for making bread.

---

[2] See Chapter 13 for more precise definition of kinship terms.

Living a nomadic existence, these people possess little in the way of material goods. Houses are brush structures, easily and quickly constructed, and clothing is scanty. Both sexes go barefoot, and small aprons of shredded bark satisfy their modesty requirements. On certain occasions men wear headbands or crowns of brilliant feathers. While these people do not practice the potter's art, they are world renowned for their basketry. In spite of their material poverty, there is a definite concept of private and group property.

Families consist of a man, one wife, and their children, with kinship being reckoned through both sides of the family. Married couples tend to settle down with the wife's family. Clan organization is nonexistent and there is little in the way of class distinction. Tribes in this area are small and political organization informal.

A variety of shamans, each associated with the spirits of different animals or natural objects, are revered. Girls' puberty ceremonies and secret initiation ceremonies for men are common practices. The most important ritualistic activity, however, is the annual Kuksu ceremony wherein dancers, instead of wearing masks, drape and crown themselves with feathers. Among the northern tribes of the region there is a body of mythology that includes stories of a single creator deity.

CULTURE AREA 4—THE PLATEAU AREA

Although the Plateau culture area has a number of distinct characteristics, it must be thought of as a zone of transition between the culture areas of the Northwest Coast and the Plains.

The inhabitants of the Plateau subsist primarily by hunting and fishing; the former being of greater importance in the east, the latter in the west. The hunting people, who are somewhat more nomadic than the fishermen, use bows and arrows, spears, and a variety of snares and deadfalls to take deer, elk, beaver, and mountain sheep. The fishermen of the west, however, subsist mainly on salmon and follow the lead of their Northwest Coast neighbors in the use of seines, dip nets, spears, and hooks. Gathering, an activity of the women, centers around the search for berries, bitterroot, and particularly camass bulbs.

In prehistoric times the people of this region wore rabbit-skin robes or nothing at all. In historic times, however, they have adopted a pattern of dress where males wear shirts, thigh length leggings, and soft moccasins and women wear belted and fringed tunics, leggings, and stockings made of cedar and sage fiber. Rabbit-skin robes and caps continue to be worn by both sexes in winter.

The typical Plateau house consists of a circular pit, four to five feet deep, over which is built a conical or pyramidal thatched roof covered with a layer of earth. A smokehole at the top serves as exit and entrance for the several families occupying the house. Basketry is, in some places, a fine art, but there is little in the way of pottery.

The Plateau people have no clans, and descent is counted on both sides of the family. Some polygyny is found, particularly in the north. Village organization is loose and chiefs are chosen on the basis of their ability. In the west, there is a tendency toward hereditary offices and in the east, where Plains influence is felt, chieftainship often depends upon war exploits.

The most important religious ceremony is the Spirit Dance wherein frenzied dancers are possessed by their guardian spirits. However, most Plateau ceremonies are simple, featuring songs, prayers, and short dances in honor of the spirits of wild plants or the first salmon of the season. Purification rites for hunters and puberty ceremonies for both sexes are common. Mythology consists of little but a few simple explanatory and trickster tales. Shamans, often women, cure illness and even recover guardian spirits that have been lost or stolen.

CULTURE AREA 5—MACKENZIE— YUKON OR WESTERN SUB-ARCTIC

In this vast wilderness area of Northwest Canada are to be found a group of nomadic caribou-hunting tribes that, except for certain minor features of their social organization and material culture, exhibit great cultural uniformity throughout the area. Men hunt and women gather, but agriculture is absent. It has been stated that the lives of these people are as dependent on caribou as the lives of Plains Indians are on buffalo.

Clothing, tailored from caribou hide and decorated with quills, features shirts and leggings with moccasins attached. Clothing for men and women is much the same, but women wear knee length shirts. Conical skin tents and double lean-to huts suit their nomadic way of life, and household objects include baskets but not pottery. Encampments are commonly made along rivers or lakes, and travel is facilitated by bark and skin canoes in summer and toboggans and snow shoes during the winter months.

Monogamous marriage is the pattern, but wife hospitality is common. Individuals consider themselves as closely related to their father's family as they are to their mother's. The location of marital residence, however, varies from region to region. It is with the wife's family in the south, with the husband's family in the north, and optional in the east. Clan organization is weak and the normal social grouping is the hunting band, chieftainship being a hereditary office.

Religion is not highly developed. Medicine men perform magic rites and healing rituals, but there is an absence of group ceremonies. These Indians have a concept of supernatural spirit guardians, which appear to them in dreams and to whom they make sacrifices.

CULTURE AREA 6—THE PLAINS

No Indian culture is better known to the average American than that of the Plains. Actually, most Americans erroneously believe that all American Indians lived like the people of this area. Prior to about 1700 the Plains inhabitants cultivated maize and hunted buffalo and other large game on foot, but by this date most tribes were in possession of horses and as a result became highly nomadic people living almost exclusively off the vast buffalo herds that roamed the western plains.

Since these people are constantly on the move, material goods have to be light and easily portable. Dwellings are buffalo skin tepees, which can be folded up and transported by travois (lodgepoles with platforms, drawn by horses). Prior to the advent of the horse, dogpacking and dog travois were used. In place of pottery, these people utilize a hide envelope for various kinds of storage. Clothing, made exlusively of buffalo and deerskin, features shirts, hip-length leggings, breech clouts, and soft moccasins for men, and ankle-length T-shaped dresses with soft moccasins and short leggings for women. Famous articles of men's attire are the eagle feather war bonnet (the symbol of membership in a military society) and buffalo robes. Bows and arrows and lances are used in both hunting and warfare, but the most prized possessions of the men are their horses.

The hunting band is the significant social and political unit, although tribes function as units on certain occasions. The majority of families are monogamous, although it is reported that about 20 percent of the men have more than one wife. Since women play a rather insignificant part in the economy, they are married for their beauty rather than their industry. Kin relationship is traced through the mother's side of the family (*matrilineal*) among the Crow, Hidatsa, Pawnee, and Mandan, but through the father's side (*patrilineal*) among the Omaha, Ponca, Iowa, Kansa, and Osage. In most places (except the western edge of the Plains) marital residence is *patrilocal* (with the husband's family). Clans are *exogamous* (forbidding marriage to a fellow clan member) and most tribes place great emphasis on voluntary association groups, such as secret societies, age grades, or military or soldier societies. There are definite status differences; however, positions of prestige are not inherited but, rather, earned through war exploits or through amassing wealth (in the form of horses) by raiding other tribes. Great stress is placed on the individual in this society and competition for war honors is keen. Even the religion is highly individualistic. Every man has his own private guardian spirit which appears to him in visions. Visions are induced through the ingestion of drugs or through self-torture. The Sun Dance is by far the most important of the religious ceremonies of these people. While the ceremony varies somewhat from tribe to tribe, generally it is a rite in which great numbers of men torture themselves so that they might establish communication with the spirits. War dances of various kinds, including the scalp dance, follow each encounter with the enemy.

CULTURE AREA 7—THE NORTHEAST WOODLANDS

The Northeast Woodlands area is the largest of the culture areas and one that presents a number of problems of classification. The Iroquois tribes, located at the very heart of the region, have a number of features—principally in the areas of social and political organization—that are not shared by other groups in the area. There has also been a tendency to set apart the Great Lakes, or Calumet, tribes because of unique cultural features.

Throughout most of the region, maize cultivation, a woman's occupation, is the dominant form of subsistence. Hunting is an important activity in the Great Lakes area but shows decreasing importance as one moves east. Whereas tribes like the Iroquois live a sedentary village life, the Great Lakes people live in villages during the summer but break up into nomadic hunting bands during the winter.

In the warmer months, Northeast Woodlands men commonly wear soft moccasins and a breech clout, but Iroquois frequently add a kilt and tunic, and tribes in the north wear thigh-length leggings with moccasins attached. Winter, of course, necessitates the addition of shirts and robes. Women throughout the area are outfitted with skirts and moccasins, but Iroquois women also wear a sleeveless shirt. Shirts and even leggings are worn by Great Lakes women during cold weather.

Birch bark is a valuable resource throughout the whole area, and containers, canoes, and even houses are made of it. The Iroquois longhouse, constructed of bark over a pole framework, measures as much as three hundred feet in length, and houses a number of related families in separate apartments. The Great Lakes house is known as a wigwam. It is dome-shaped with a covering of bark, mats, or hides. In the northern parts of the culture area conical tepees are found.

Family organization varies in form. The Iroquois place great importance on the mother's line, while Great Lakes people trace kinship through the father's family. Northern tribes stress relationship with both sides of the family. Clans and groups of clans (moieties) are found among all tribes and in some, clan membership is a determining factor in the selection of leaders. The Iroquois elect their chiefs, but they are always members of a special clan. An outstanding phenomenon in this culture area is the League of the Iroquois, a confederation of six tribes created for the purpose of maintaining peaceful coexistence among its members.

Shamanism and guardian spirits are common features of North-eastern Woodlands religion as are planting and harvest festivals. The Iroquois believe in a variety of deities, among them being gods of thunder and rain, grains, fruits, and the Earth Mother, and the Three Sister spirits of maize, beans, and squash. Many of these deities are worshipped by members of secret societies, the most famous of which are the False Face and Bear Societies.

CULTURE AREA 8—THE SOUTHEAST WOODLANDS

The Southeast Woodlands is the home of the "Five Civilized Tribes"—the Creek, Chickasaw, Choctaw, Cherokee, and Seminole. If any group of North American Indians deserves the designation "civilized," it is certainly the people of this region. Greatly influenced by Mayan civilization, these Indians built earthen pyramids, developed complex religious, social, and political systems, and lived in what might be described as urban communities.

The Southeast Woodlands region is one where intensive agriculture is practiced. Corn, beans, and sunflowers, the principal crops, are cultivated on family plots by the women. A town plot is also worked in order to support the ruling chief (*mico*), who presides over the town council of chiefs and gives all of his time to civic responsibilities.

Some hunting for deer and small game is carried on by the men, but these activities are definitely secondary to the work of the women. The major activity of the men is making war. Like the Aztec of Mexico these Southeast Woodland people built their culture around warfare. In these highly stratified tribes the highest honors and ranks are given to those most successful in battle. Great warriors are permitted to wear special costumes and tattoos and to be addressed with honorific titles.

Houses have thatched roofs and clay-daubed walls and, in the case of chiefs, are built on mounds. An exception is the Creek people, who live in semisubterranean dwellings. Household items include cane baskets and mats, coiled pottery, and wooden bowls, mortars, and stools. The bow and arrow is the sole weapon of the hunt, but warfare is carried on with bows and arrows, wooden clubs, shields, cane armor, and lances.

Summer clothing for men includes breech clouts and ankle-high moccasins. Winter temperatures, however, necessitate the addition of leggings and poncho-like shirts of buckskin. Women wear cloth or fiber wraparound skirts and winter shawls of skin or fiber. Chiefs have the privilege of wearing feather robes and turbans of swan or eagle feathers. Dugout canoes are the principal mode of transportation, and frequently they are used in making extended trading trips.

In spite of the relative wealth of the area, polygyny is rarely prac-

Temple mound complex among the Natchez of the Southeast Woodlands culture area. Diorama by Frederick Blaschke. (Courtesy Field Museum of Natural History.)

ticed. Families are mainly matrilineal and matrilocal—no doubt reflecting the importance of women in the economy.

The great emphasis on warfare is definitely reflected in the religious life of the people. No one can lead others in warfare unless he has first experienced a vision promising supernatural aid. Every village has its war bundle—a collection of bear claws, bird skins, and deer hooves—which through its magical properties makes warriors strong and brave. This bundle is so sacred that it is not allowed to touch the ground.

In thatched temples, built atop huge earthen mounds resembling pyramids, a special class of priests tend sacred fires and direct rituals to the sun, corn, and war gods that often include sacrifices of human lives. Like many other agricultural Indians, a first-fruit celebration, known in this case as the Green Corn Ceremony, is an annual occasion of great importance.

CULTURE AREA 9—THE SOUTHWEST

Two major culture patterns may be distinguished in the American Southwest. One pattern, the Pueblo (Zuni, Hopi, and Rio Grande peoples), features maize agriculture and permanent village life, while the other, the Nomadic (Apache and Navaho), emphasizes hunting and herding.

The principal agricultural products of the Pueblos are maize, beans, squash, and cotton, and, contrary to the usual North American Indian pattern, these activities are in the hands of men. Other subsistence activities include some small game hunting with bows and arrows and a throwing stick, much like a boomerang, and gathering— primarily of piñon nuts. Maize, the staple food, is ground into meal and made into bread by the women.

Gathering and hunting play a much greater part in Apache economy than in Hopi, but even these people do some cultivating of corn, beans, and squash. The Navahos also farm, but since 1680 they have been primarily concerned with sheepherding.

Pueblo villages are highly organized with elected governors and war chiefs, but, in spite of the existence of the latter, these people are far from being warlike. The Navahos and Apaches, however, represent a constant threat to the peaceful Pueblos. The Apaches, because of their plundering habits, well deserve the name that was given them—"enemies of the cultivated fields." The Navaho were also a tribe of marauders until about 1868, when they were forced by the United States government to settle down to their herding and weaving and a more peaceful existence on the reservation.

A variety of housetypes can be found in the Southwest, but three major forms may be noted. Most Pueblos, as their name would indicate, reside in apartment-house-style dwellings of adobe while the

Navahos prefer the hogan. These homes are actually only a tripod frame of logs covered with sticks, bark, brush, and a six-inch layer of earth. The Apaches live in still another kind of house, a dome-shaped structure thatched with bear grass, known as a wikiup.

Quite characteristic of Pueblo dress modes are kilts of cotton, ankle high moccasins, and blankets of cotton or wool for men, and cotton or wool dresses with one shoulder bare and boot-type moccasins for women. Male Navahos typically dress in buckskin leggings and shirts, hard sole moccasins, and blankets, while their women wear dresses made from two small blankets sewn together at the shoulders and sides and belted. Buckskin, fashioned into shirts, leggings, and moccasins for the men and into skirts and poncho-type blouses for the women, represent the usual Apache apparel.

Although the Pueblos and Navahos utilize woven cloth, the art of weaving has never been an Apache accomplishment. In Pueblo societies, cotton and wool are made into cloth by men on an upright loom, but among the Navahos the women are the weavers. Using looms very similar to those of the Pueblos, they produce remarkably fine blankets in a variety of colors. Pottery and baskets are made by both nomads and village dwellers in this area, but no Indians in North America produce more superbly formed and decorated pottery than the Pueblo peoples.

In Pueblo society men go to live at the home of their bride where they serve as a friend to their children rather than a stern family head. The mother's brother is the disciplinarian. Maternal clans and matrilineal descent are universal. Monogamy is the rule among all Southwest peoples.

Western Apache and Navaho family systems are much alike. Both have mother clans, residence with the wife's family, and mother-in-law avoidance. Eastern Apaches (Jicarilla, Chiricahua, Mescalero), however, have no clans at all and descent is figured through both sides of the family rather than just through the women. Marriage residence is at the home of the wife.

For the Pueblos, religion is the most important thing in life. They have an advanced theology that includes ideas about a Mother Earth and a Father Sky and a special creation myth that tells of men emerging from the Womb of Earth with the assistance of two supernatural brothers, the War Gods. A special class of priests, as well as numerous secret societies, participate in a year-round calendar of ceremonies. One of the most famous Southwest dances, the Snake Dance, is performed by Hopis in the hope that the gods will send rain. Offerings of maize are made at special sand-painted altars located in underground ceremonial chambers called kivas. All Pueblo ceremonies are orderly and involve great ritual detail.

The religion of the Navaho differs greatly from that of the Pueblo peoples in that all ceremonies are carried on for the benefit of individuals rather than for the sake of the group. Most Navaho rituals are for the purposes of curing illness or of purification of those who have come in contact with outsiders. The Enemy Way ceremony is such a rite. No Southwest people have more magnificent ritual poetry (performed as chants) than the Navaho, and their sand-painting far excels that of the Pueblos.

Apache and Navaho religious systems have many things in common. Among these are sand-painting, curing rites and similar myths, but, in general, Apache religion is less elaborate in form, and the ceremonies are somewhat shorter.

The Ethnographic Present

In looking over the culture areas of the world and their unique forms of culture, the newcomer to anthropology will soon notice that many of the characteristics mentioned as typical for a region can no longer be observed. Representations of the Central Andean region of South America, for example, describe the culture as it existed during the florescence of the Inca Empire. Although some remnants of this way of life may still be found in the area, the present picture is hardly characteristic of the civilization as it existed prior to Pizarro's conquest in 1532. The answer to why this is done in working out culture areas is that the characteristics of these regions of common culture are those that existed at the time of European contact, or at least at the time when the first adequate descriptions were made. Thus all cultures are placed on a common time plane that can be referred to as the ethnographic present. This type of procedure is necessary if cross-cultural comparisons are to be made, because it would be impossible to compare the Hawaiians who live in Honolulu and are almost completely Westernized with the natives of the Amazon Basin, who have had almost no contact with Europeans. All cultures must be rendered comparable and this means that we must analyze the culture as it was before coming under the influence of the industrial societies of the West. Thus, when anthropologists use the present tense in describing the culture of the Aztecs, they are fully aware that this culture no longer exists. They are merely using the *ethnographic present.*

Culture Areas of Modern Industrial America

In 1973 Dr. Stanley D. Brunn, a geographer from Michigan State University, demonstrated that the concept of cultural area was far from obsolete. He proposed that rather than having 50 states we should move to a culture area type system where we would have 16 regions

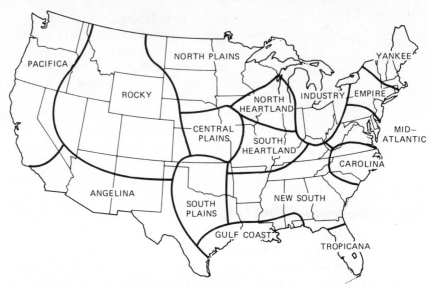

Figure 7-8 Stanley Brunn's modern cultural areas (after *National Observer*, 1973).

of common culture based on similarities in economic outlook, social and cultural heritage, and political ideology (see Fig. 7–8). Maintaining that states are really barriers to effective legislation and political progress, he stated a number of advantages in regional, or culture area organization. Such an arrangement could more effectively deal with problems of air and water pollution that now cross state lines (like the pollution of major river arteries or the Great Lakes) as well as port authority, law enforcement, school district, or energy utilization issues. Just as each culture area, in Wissler's methodology, had a culture center (a point that best characterized the region as a whole), Brunn identifies a metropolitan area as the nerve center of each of these zones of regional culture specialization. The region Tropicana, for example, has Miami as its capital city. This modern cultural area includes all of the state of Florida except the panhandle and includes both Puerto Rico and the Virgin Islands. It has an economy and culture which Brunn describes as "geared to sun and water," and there is a considerable investment in tourism and recreational activities, especially catering to senior citizens. Space research and related defense industries make the region district from north Florida and the rest of the South.

Institutions

For many years it has been traditional in the social sciences to divide culture into units that are even more inclusive than the *complex*.

These major divisions of culture are referred to either as *institutions* or *aspects* of culture. In any general textbook in anthropology or sociology a reader can find separate chapters entitled Family, Government, or Political Organization, Economics, Education, and Religion. Thus, certain types of behavior are arbitrarily defined and set apart for purposes of study. The social scientist is very much aware, however, that institutions have no reality in themselves. They are, in other words, abstract categories of norms, actions, and values extrapolated from the total configuration of culture. It is probably very unlikely that the representatives of any two cultural systems would ever make the same arbitrary divisions of culture. This is because culture is an interwoven fabric of elements and actions, in which family life has its economic and religious aspects; government cannot help but influence, and be influenced by, economics, education, religion, and so on. This problem of dividing up cultures into appropriate categories for study is somewhat less difficult for the sociologist than it is for the anthropologist. This is because the former is engaged to a greater extent in the study of Western industrialized society, and in such society behavior tends to be much more compartmentalized than it does among primitives. By this we mean that the average American male is involved primarily in economic behavior between nine and five o'clock each day. He is involved in religious behavior from eleven to twelve o'clock on Sunday morning and on the first Tuesday after the first Monday in November he performs his political function. This, of course, is an extreme oversimplification of what happens in our lives, but for a moment let us compare our compartmentalized lives with those living in pre-industrial societies.

Suppose we were to approach an American Indian working in his fields. He is planting corn, but he is doing something rather unusual; he is placing a fish in each hillock. If we were to comment to him that he is engaged in an economic activity he might correct us by saying that he is really engaged in a religious activity. For the placing of fish in the hillock of corn might appear to us to be an act of fertilizing the plant but would be a religious act—an offering to the spirit of the maize—in his terms. The feast-giving phenomenon of the South Seas is another example of behavior that is hard to classify. A feast is a social event, but it is also a means of obtaining power and prestige for a chief and is therefore political. The fact that the event has involved the economic activities of an entire family or clan makes it still more difficult to decide whether a feast should be defined as a family, recreational, political, or economic activity. The same thing might be said of many of our own activities. Going to college may be at the same time (1) a way of getting a husband or wife, (2) a way of increasing one's earning potential, (3) a way of gaining social prestige, (4) a way of becoming educated, (5) a way of training one's self to become a religious specialist, (6) a way of having a good time, or (7) a way of meeting the right people (a political function in its broadest sense). If we were to study the phenomenon of higher learning, we would no doubt say that we were studying the institution or aspect of culture known as education, but we would also have to admit that attending college has many ramifications and extensions into other categorical areas of behavior.

While every social scientist approaches culture as a fabric of interwoven ideas and actions, it is nevertheless necessary to concentrate on separate categories of behavior, since everything can't be studied at once. While the British functionalist Malinowski made a special point of stressing the interrelationship of institutions, his studies stressed one institution at a time and showed how various aspects of that institution related to other institutions. In his book, *Coral Gardens and Their Magic*, he concentrated primarily on the economic activities of gardening, but he also showed how gardening was related to family behavior, religion and magic, and political authority and prestige.

ASPECTS OF CULTURE

Some anthropologists would prefer not to use the term *institutions* but instead apply the word *aspects* to the several categories of culture. This is because they think of *institutions* as being primarily a sociological term that stresses patterns of interrelationship of individuals—that is, hierarchies or structures of individuals such as church or political groups. Anthropologists, with their orientation toward the concept of culture rather than society, look upon culture as a set of values and customs that necessitates in some cases interaction of individuals and organization of groups. Much of culture, they would point out, does not involve organizations of individuals at all. While one can hardly have a language by oneself, the use of language does not necessitate a specific social organization. Although artists must have public acceptance of their products, they do not necessarily have to interact with others in the creation of esthetic products. In many societies religion is an entirely private matter. There is no elaborate theology, no class of priests, no religious equipment, but merely a tradition that, through a vision sought by the individual, a unique guardian deity is encountered.

THE AMBIGUITY OF THE TERM "INSTITUTIONS"

For most people *institutions* is a confusing term. Sociologists Leslie, Larson, and Gorman point out:

> Laypersons are likely to use the term "institution" very loosely, regarding churches, hospitals, jails, and many other things as institutions. They are likely, also, to consider buildings to be institutions—as, for example, a penitentiary or a certain "mental institution." Sociologists reserve

the term "institution" to describe certain complex normative systems.
(1973:109)

And then they go on to describe normative systems that operate
in five basic areas of life. The systems (1) determine kinship, (2) provide for the legitimate use of power, (3) regulate the distribution of
goods and services, (4) transmit knowledge from one generation to
another, and (5) regulate a people's relation to the supernatural.
However, some sociologists also describe institutions as social systems or associations of organized people. Therefore, even social scientists get confused as to whether we are dealing with configurations
of customs or with arrangements of people. Perhaps our problem
might be solved for the present if we think of *cultural institutions* as sets
of values, customs, and principles handed down within societies from
one generation to the next; and *social institutions* as those special areas
of cultural and social behavior where group interaction and social organization are significant.

At this point the student has a right to ask: Why is the term used
at all, if it is so confusing? The answer seems to lie in historical reasons.

INSTITUTIONAL ORIGINS

Interest in the "institutions" of groups goes back to the beginnings of
anthropology. The primary concern of early pioneers in anthropology, and even some of the social philosophers who came before
them, was speculation on the origins of the family, religion, government, and so on. These categories of behavior were defined as "institutions" and designated as the proper and natural units for study.
They believed that the European forms of these cultural entities
represented the zenith in cultural development and they searched for
institutional forms among primitives that they thought were furthest
removed from European norms. A simple belief in souls and spirits
(*animism*), found among a number of technologically simple tribes,
was believed to be probably closest to the belief system of "primeval
man." In time animism evolved into a belief in a variety of deities
(polytheism). The final development, characteristic of civilized societies only, was a belief system that honored a single all-powerful god
(monotheism). While some scholars were manipulating the ethnographic data to prove their theory of the evolution of religion,
others were concerned with theories for reconstructing the history of
marriage and the family. Lewis Henry Morgan, John F. McLennan, and
Sir John Lubbock maintained that the promiscuous horde was the first
or earliest social unit, while Alexander Westermarck, a Finnish anthropologist, observing the male-dominated permanent families
among even monkeys and apes, postulated a similar union or situation of mates and offspring among the earliest of humans. Still other

scholars proposed a matriarchal family preceded by a patriarchal form, and nearly all sociologists and anthropologists assumed that, since European families were monogamous, this must be a more advanced form than a polygamous family.

Modern anthropologists, although still interested in institutional behavior, have very different interests from their nineteenth-century forerunners. The greater accumulation of ethnographic data, and the more objective approach to those facts that mark modern anthropology, has resulted in the position that there has been no universal uniform sequence of institutional forms. Furthermore, the futility of looking for institutional origins has long been recognized.

Every modern anthropologist could probably venture an opinion of what the first form of family or religion might have been like, but such speculation is hardly conceived to be vital to the development of the science of anthropology. The number one concern in modern anthropology is: What is the function of family, government, property, or religion in human society? Research today centers around studies of institutional behavior and how it satisfies social, biological, and psychological needs. Through an understanding of what family does in Masai society or Fiji Island society, it is believed that ultimately we will know more about the role of family among the human species in general. This is the goal of anthropological science and the reason for its cross-cultural and comparative approach.

Summary

In the study of culture, there are several levels of analysis that can be utilized, each representing different abstractions. The smallest unit of culture is the *trait* or *element*. There are traits of nonmaterial as well as material culture but they do not exist in isolation. Traits are combined into *cultural complexes*. This linking of traits into complexes is what people naturally perceive on a day-to-day basis. The football game with its dozens of interrelated traits is such a complex. The way that traits are linked gives the anthropologist insights into the ethos and thought processes of a society. Certain complexes may be consistently linked together in more than one culture, and this phenomenon is what the British anthropologist Edward Tylor referred to as "adhesions." Ruth Benedict, on the other hand, called attention to the interrelated patterns which characterize the total culture. Her approach was to discover configurations of culture and how traits reflected the nature of the whole.

One of the more important concepts in American anthropology

has been that of *culture area.* This is defined as a geographic region within which societies share a common culture. While these cultures may actually differ in detail, the overall patterns will be similar because they represent similar responses to the environment. Culture areas have been defined for the Pacific area, for Africa, Asia, and North and South America.

In order to standardize the comparative study of culture in terms of time lines, anthropologists use the concept of the *ethnographic present.* This is a device where comparisons are made of societies in their aboriginal state, before contact with more complex societies (the industrialized West in particular) has altered the nature of the indigenous way of life. In comparing cultures in terms of this common reference point (pre-contact) it is not unusual to find numerous time dates being equated, since some societies remained unaffected by Western influence longer than others.

Perhaps the most inclusive unit for analysis in the study of culture is the *institution* or the *aspect.* Examples are government, family, religion, economics, enculturation or education, and esthetics. These include the traits, complexes, and patterns of culture and operate to meet basic human societal needs in groups with various degrees of cultural complexity. Like many other conceptual tools used by cultural anthropologists, institutions are abstractions wherein normal day-to-day activities are categorized for purposes of study.

The American Cultural Configuration 8

Architecture
Football
Resolving the paradoxes

Anthropologists today commonly show as much interest in the cultural patterns and processes of their own society as they do in foreign, exotic ones. To nonscientists this might seem strange, and they might ask why, if you live in a society day after day, would you have to research its culture? The answer is, of course, that often the most significant things about the way a people behave are so taken for granted by them that they have difficulty talking about them. Individuals who grow up and live in a particular society are commonly the least aware of its culture.

While there is a significant number of anthropologists who believe that foreign cultures should be studied by one of their own rather than by an intruding foreigner, for many years most anthropologists assumed that it is difficult to be objective about or even fully aware of the details and patterns of one's own culture. It is the old problem of not being able to see the forest for the trees. Much of life for the average individual (of any culture) consists of following certain customary routines and procedures, almost without thinking. Robot-like our Mr. or Ms. Average American rises at a prescribed hour, dresses in the appropriate way, eats the usual breakfast, and then drives an automobile along the regular route to the office or factory. If there is a detour on one of the streets usually taken, our subject will probably become upset and frustrated at having to work out an alternate route.

Once at work our Average American participates in the usual job routine, which might have been difficult to learn at first but after a time can be performed with a minimum of thought or imagination. Our friend is quite conscious, however, of the impression he or she makes on the boss because, after all, the important thing is to "get ahead." On weekends it is likely that the family is loaded into the car and they drive to the church of their choice—probably the denomination one or both of the parents were raised in. The sermon reaffirms many of the beliefs that he or she has always ascribed to, and the phrases of the minister are familiar and orthodox. Once every four years our Average American exercises a cherished rite that is guaranteed by the Constitution, but in most cases takes little notice of the real political issues at stake. If, for example, our Average American happened to be raised in a Republican family, this is probably the way he or she will vote, and there will be a tendency to find the looks and personality of the party candidate attractive and those of the opposite candidate offensive.

The point that we are trying to make is not that Mr. or Ms. Average American is stupid or abnormal in any way. The point is that he or she is a product of culture and social environment, and culture provides ready-made solutions to almost all one's problems. A person doesn't always have to think about how and why one does things. It is easier and often more efficient to follow the regularly accepted procedure. That is what culture does for people.

Because it is natural for people to be like this, they find it fascinating when an anthropologist describes how and why they behave in a certain way. After reading about themselves in a monograph on American culture by Margaret Mead, or any number of other anthropologists, they might make the comment "She seems to have us pegged pretty well. I just never thought about it in that way." The real point is that our Average American seldom stops to analyze his or her own values and motivations.

A Culture of Paradoxes

The cultural pattern of the United States is one involving numerous paradoxes and ambiguities. This is probably the case in any complex civilization characterized by rapid change. Although we claim to be a peace-loving people we have fought four major wars and twenty-three limited military actions during the twentieth century, and we spend more than a quarter of our tax dollar for military purposes. While some would characterize our society as a welfare state others would label it a warfare state. Americans believe in rugged individualism, and yet we have been described as a "nation of sheep." There is a basic belief in human equality and a lauding of the "common man," and yet there is great preoccupation with class, racial, and ethnic differences. On the one hand we express faith in the need for mass education, and on the other we exhibit a general undercurrent of anti-intellectualism and an unwillingness to meet the essential cost of mass education. Americans are great humanitarians full of missionary spirit, but they are frequently hostile to welfare, national health insurance, guaranteed income, or foreign aid programs designed to relieve human suffering.

The interesting thing about these cultural contradictions is that the opposing attitudes and behavioral patterns cited above do not necessarily represent the views of different subgroups but are found simultaneously in the value system and behavior of the "average" American.

The Average American

At this point we feel it proper to ask who the Average American is and how one can possibly single out a set of cultural ideas and behavior patterns and maintain that it represents the "American Way."

America has long been called a melting-pot nation although it has literally hundreds of subcultures. There are class differences, ethnic differences, racial differences, regional differences, and even occupational differences, but social scientists have come to consider the relatively homogeneous values and customs of middle-class America as being most representative of the American pattern of culture. In spite of the social and economic complexity of our society four out of five Americans like to think of themselves as middle-class and to a large extent ascribe to a certain set of values and effect a particular lifestyle. Even those who identify with the lower classes either aspire to middle class status or use it as a measuring stick for behavior. Bellah maintains that "not only are middle-class values understood and respected but lower-class people explain their inferior position in terms of circumstances that have prevented them from behaving in a middle-class fashion." (1985:151). Sociologist Martin Loeb once described the middle class as having the "real American way of life." They are the families in the suburban row houses, with the brood of well-scrubbed children, the picture window with its ribbon-trimmed lamp, the 23-inch color television console set, the recreational vehicle parked in the driveway, and on the dinner table, hamburgers or other "bland foods." Such families Loeb believes are particularly puritanical about what they consider "proper," and this culture, with its stress on cleanliness, respectability, hard work, and conformity, is much the same all over the United States. Geographical or regional traditions affect this middle-class pattern very little, and in the South, for example, only the lower and upper classes eat typical Southern food. While visiting in the South the middle-class Northerner will have no trouble finding a meal exactly to his tastes at the local McDonald's, Pizza Hut, Bonanza Steak House, Kentucky Fried Chicken, Sirloin Stockade, Taco Tico, or Long John Silver restaurant.

The middle class is the set of people who determine our life style, pay the majority of federal taxes, vote in and out the politicians, and dominate the local and national power structures. It is their support that is courted by the politicians. These are the people who have been referred to as the "silent majority" or the "Establishment" and who therefore are seen as representing what is "normal" and "proper" in American life. Theirs is a pattern of life which is expected to endure in spite of opposition from the radical pressures of the "far left" and the "far right" or from such special crusades as the National Organization of Women, Gay Rights Movement or SANE.

The middle-class pattern of respectability is primarily that of white, Anglo-Saxon, Protestant America but has also been adopted by other racial and ethnic groups who have been fortunate enough to "make it." Although some black and brown faces are now evident in suburban areas, few Afro or corn-row hairdos, or dashikis are found on commuter trains. Suburban America has still not completely accepted people of color but it finds them somewhat more palatable if they keep their lawns well manicured, drive late-model cars, barbecue in the back yard, and keep their children well-dressed and immaculate.

The middle-class life style represents the image that is most frequently exported by way of U.S. Information Service brochures, World Trade pavilions, movies, and television series. This is also the pattern that social scientists from foreign countries seem to perceive as most typical when they come to America to study our way of life. Although a considerable number of middle-class America's offspring took excursions into the counterculture during the 1960s and early 1970s by "dropping out" or "sitting in," most of these temporary radicals have now returned to the fold, to the Junior Chamber of Commerce, and to the mainstream of American values. The generation gaps have narrowed and the heated dinner-table debates over morality, ethics, and civil rights have greatly moderated. Young middle-class America has returned to professional educational interests — pre-med, pre-law, nurse's training, computer science, engineering, accounting — leaving the philosophy, world religions, and literary criticism courses to the more well-to-do or the more impractical of their peers.

Conformity

Numerous American and European observers of American culture have noted the American compulsion to conform. This conformity is of a particular type, however. Margaret Mead describes our culture as *co-figurative*—meaning that the prevailing model for members of the society is the behavior of their contemporaries (1978). David Reisman, on the other hand, describes our behavior as *other-directed* (1950).

We are concerned primarily with what other people of our social position or age-set have, think, or do, and in order not to appear strange or peculiar, we tend to try to "keep up with the Joneses," or in the case of some counterculture or intellectual groups, to ridicule the value system that motivates us to "keep up with the Joneses." We are careful to adhere to popular trends, to join book clubs so we will read the best sellers, to listen to top-20 radio stations so we are familiar with the most popular record releases, and we try to make sure our houses, clothing, and cars are acceptable to our particular social reference group. In the 1960s and early 1970s there was a pronounced pattern of dual conformity—one model for the Establishment and one model for the anti-Establishment or counterculture. Both were concerned with identification with a particular group and style of life, and both had rigid standards in regard to appropriate dress, values, and loyalties to particular ethical and behavioral codes.

People of all cultures tend to conform, but not always in the ways found in America. Francis Hsu describes Chinese conformity as *situation-centered* and maintains that Chinese people are psychologically and socially dependent on, and conform to, the family, and not on unrelated peers as is the case in America. Europeans conform also, but more to standards and conventions of the past. While Paris and Rome may represent centers of innovation and vogue in dress design, art, and industrial design, most citizens of these countries seem more concerned with traditional ways than are most Americans. In America advertisers have learned that the way to sell a product is to convince the buyer that it is "new" and "everyone is buying it." Few items of tradition have an equivalent appeal. In England, however, one need only recall the British coronation ceremony with the ancient horse-drawn carriages and their footmen and military escorts in sixteenth-century costume to see how these people respect and dote on the past. Ancient castles, noble families, coats of arms, and ceremonies conferring knighthood are cherished elements of most European cultures. Peasants cling to ancient folk dances, time-tested recipes, and honored customs, and occasionally derive pleasure from donning the costumes of their ancestors. There is a great deal less of this type of thing in America. American centennial celebrations often feature beard-growing contests, but in most cases men neglect their razors on these occasions not so much because their ancestors did, but because everyone else is doing it.

Perhaps the American pattern of conformity is different from that of Europe because of our long-term love affair with the machine. Max Lerner has suggested that the machine and mass-production methods have certainly made conformism as a way of life easier. To buy and use what everyone else does and to behave and think like everyone else certainly reduces the strain of thinking for oneself. He writes,

> Most American babies are born in standardized hospitals with a standardized tag put around them to keep them from getting confused with other standardized products of the hospital. Many of them grow up either in uniform rows of tenements or of small-town or suburban houses. . . . They are sent to monotonously similar schoolhouses, where almost uniformly standardized teachers ladle out to them standardized information out of standardized textbooks. . . . As they grow older they dance to canned music from canned juke boxes, millions of them putting standard coins into standard slots to get standardized tunes swung by voices with standardized inflection of emotion. They date with standardized girls in standardized cars. . . . They spend the days of their years with monotonous regularity in factory, office, and shop, performing routinized operations at regular intervals. . . . They die of highly uniform diseases, and to

the accompaniment of routine platitudes they are buried in standardized graves and celebrated by standardized obituary notices." (1957:260—61)

David Potter, on the other hand, believes that America's style of conformity is associated with the belief that everyone is of equal worth and that no one has a right to impose their will on anyone else. But if the majority have adopted an opinion on a particular matter anyone who questions the wisdom of that opinion is, in effect, setting themselves up as being better than the majority. It is an accepted fact that the majority must not force a person to conform but it is also that person's responsibility to voluntarily accept the will of the majority.

The American cultural configuration fosters, in Ashley Montagu's opinion, a "rigid set of requirements to which children are forced to subscribe by their parents, teachers, church, peer groups, and other socializing agencies. Under the pressures of such socializing agencies it is difficult for most individuals to escape becoming anything other than the echo of other people's voices." (1967:35)

Not only is individual variation in behavior frowned upon in educational systems but also in recreational activities. Such group-oriented organizations as Boy and Girl Scouts, Campfire Girls, Little League, and 4H Clubs offer regulated programs of recreational and educational activities designed to meet the needs of the "American boy and girl." The assumption is that all young people should enjoy camping, group games, summer camps, team athletics, and handicrafts. The child who does not enjoy this kind of program is considered somewhat abnormal, if not even delinquent. And even older girls are subject to these kinds of pressures. In reporting the Miss America Pageant Judith Martin made the following observations in her *Washington Post* (1969) article,

> Miss America girls do not smoke, drink, date, discuss controversial topics or go around unchaperoned during the pageant—the winner agrees to behave that way for a year—and they are very polite to their elders. They support their government, condemn dissent, and set their goals on spending a year or two in traditional female occupations—modeling or elementary school teaching—until the right man comes along. . . . They (the judges) called them "true representatives of American youth." For a few magic days the drug scene, the sexual revolution and the civil rights, antiwar, female liberation, and student protest movements seemed to them to have been just bad dreams populated by "a tiny minority of kooks". . . .
> The past and present Miss Americas looked very much alike—both with blond hairdos, green eyes, pale skin and wide smiles. They are both, said Bert Parks, "composites of positive wonders. All Miss Americas are."

If Americans cannot make people conform to certain types of standards in any other way they will pass a law. "There ought to be a law" is a well-known American cry of anguish. A host of ordinances and laws regulate areas of life that most European societies view as personal matters. City and state laws regulating advertisement and sale of liquor and tobacco, litter laws, Sunday closing laws, curfews, and movie and book censorship are but a few of the methods used to produce uniformity in thought and behavior. While on the one hand, Americans savagely demand "liberty" and "freedom," on the other hand, they are constantly restricting liberty through their own law-making devices.

The Common Man

The tendency to conform is associated to a certain extent with the American "cult of the common man and woman." In America some people can admit they are more fortunate than others but not that they are better than others. While the majority of our citizens are motivated to "get ahead" socially and economically, it isn't nice to make too big a point of it. "We are great ones for playing up regional differences," writes Robert Heilbroner, "but equally avid on playing down economic ones. The banker goes out of his way to talk baseball to the gas station attendant. The richer we are, the more we insist that we are just like everybody else (except that we pay more taxes)" (1976:37). No one engenders greater enmity than the person who makes it known that he/she is better than other people. Some of our most popular public figures — people like Woody Allen, Johnny Carson, Willie Nelson, Willard Scott, Bill Cosby, John Denver — have been extremely successful but are admired because they identify with the common people and in some cases give the appearance that "they haven't got a dime." While equal opportunity seldom is realized by racial minorities, the average American theoretically holds to the precept that all men are created equal. Americans have almost deified log-cabin-born Abraham Lincoln while the wealthy aristocrat George Washington runs far behind in national popularity even though he was the "father of our country."

Many a presidential candidate has learned that if he wishes to succeed in politics he must show the voters that he has something of the common man in him. This has often been achieved by developing a public image that will be well received by farm populations, blue collar workers, and "just plain folks." It would appear that the image of farmer is highly representative of the common man, and President Franklin D. Roosevelt often gave his occupation as "farmer" although his estate on the Hudson was hardly what the common man would consider a farm. President Herbert Hoover had been an engineer and it wasn't difficult for the common man to take to a man who had spent several years wearing engineer's boots, khaki pants, and a flannel work shirt. His rural Iowa background and his humble birthplace were also valuable assets. Franklin Roosevelt was very much aware that clothes (particularly old ones) can make a president. A common FDR symbol was his battered campaign hat. Wendell Willkie did not wear a hat but showed his lack of concern for fastidious grooming by letting his hair fly. John F. Kennedy as well as his brother Bobby appeared to be advocates of this particular campaign technique as well. President Roosevelt, however, had one urbane habit and this was a vulnerable point of attack. He used a cigarette holder. No cartoon of criticism ever left out the cigarette holder. Presidential candidate Adlai Stevenson, definitely an urban intellectual, found great difficulty relating to the common man. In spite of numerous pictures of Adlai perched atop a tractor on his Illinois farm, he never quite convinced the people that he really belonged there.

President Lyndon B. Johnson made a Texas ranch his "second White House" and further related to the common man with his "down-to-earth rhetoric," his love of coon dogs, and his preference for "down home" barbecues. President Richard Nixon did little more than emphasize a humble beginning in Whittier, California, but his running mate Spiro T. Agnew developed a calculated campaign approach which has frequently been labeled anti-intellectual. Although Hubert Humphrey had himself photographed visiting farms and factories and kissing babies, and although Mr. Humphrey stressed his beginnings in the Farmer-Labor Party in Minnesota, problems within his own party did much to negate his appeal.

Jimmy Carter, in turn, presented himself to the voters as the peanut farmer made good with numerous "down home" attributes such as a less than intellectual brother who pumped gas for a living, an evangelist sister, and a personal commitment to a fundamentalist "old time religion" faith. His advisors were all "good old boys" from small towns in Georgia and their "poor but honest" approach to national problems was too much for the Gerald Ford people. Ronald Reagan's 1980 campaign posters presented him in a worn and slightly soiled wide-brimmed felt hat appropriate for doing chores on a small ranch. Reagan's "Aw shucks" rhetorical style plus his stock of popular cliches such as "Win one for the Gipper," "Make my day," and "Tell it to the Marines" created the illusion that a multi-millionaire President was really just one of the common folk. And illusion is very important in politics. Weatherford writes in *Tribes on the Hill*, "When politicians become actors, actors also become politicians. At least the actor is a professional capable of making the performance *look* genuine." (1981:268).

While everyone makes a great point of being the common man, (a Yankelovich survey revealed that 82 percent of the people in the United States claimed middle-class affiliation), we also seem motivated to move up the social ladder and show that we are better than average, even if we do have the common touch. Our nation abounds with "just plain Joes" trying to get into country clubs with exclusive memberships.

It is a fine line that must be walked. As David Potter observes, "It is permissible for an American to have servants (which is a matter of function), but he must not put them in livery (which is a matter of rank); permissible to attend expensive schools, but not to speak with a cultivated accent; permissible to rise in the world, but never to repudiate the origins from which he rose" (1964:241).

Authority

One drawback of the "common man" idea is that it makes the exercise of authority difficult when one's role demands it. Pulling rank has always been considered a cardinal sin against American democracy, and probably no army in the world has had greater difficulty in its officer-enlisted man relations than the American army. A common remark of GIs in response to orders from superiors has been "Why should that guy tell me what to do? All he ever was in civilian life was a shoe salesman." In the Vietnam War authority problems ranged all the way from movements among enlisted men to establish a practice of electing their officers to actual refusals to accept officers' orders under fire.

Arthur Asa Berger, an anthropologist who believes that comic strips are an excellent avenue to cultural value analysis, has examined how military authority is treated in American and Italian comics. Concerning Mort Walker's *Beetle Bailey*, Berger writes:

> In this strip, currently one of the most popular in America, the common soldier consistently engages in the battle of wits with his superiors and generally emerges victorious... It is the enlisted men who have the "upper hand" most of the time because they have the brains and because *authority is not* seen as *valid*. The sergeant is a good-natured, boisterous glutton, and the lieutenant is foolish and childish. (1973:47).

But in a "contemporary Italian military strip dealing with the adventures of Gibernetta and Gedeone," writes Berger, there is humor but "a reverential and respectful attitude toward authority." (*Ibid.*)

Some scholars have conjured up some very mystical explanations for this resentment of authority in Americans. They maintain that in rejecting authority the American is symbolically rejecting the authoritarian European father. It would seem perfectly logical, however, to explain this phenomenon by the idea developed on the frontier and in the colonies that every man was his own master and no person had any right to exert his will over any other. In the New World, man had to earn his place in society; he couldn't inherit it. Alexis De Tocqueville (1805–1859) was but one of many historians and social scientists who have pointed out that emphasis on personal autonomy and a distrust of authority are basic requirements in a working democracy. Americans, of course, think of themselves as devotedly democratic.

Not only do enlisted men find it hard to respect the authority of their officers, but officers feel somewhat uneasy giving orders. Frequently, they are rendered completely inadequate for their job because they worry too much about being "democratic" or being viewed as a "good guy."

The problem of authority is also encountered in the world of business and industry. It is not unusual in our culture for the boss to take the office staff out for an evening and act like "one of the boys." Similarly, the factory picnic is a sort of day of atonement, when department heads, foremen, and even the boss take part in the interdepartmental baseball game in order to show that "bossing" is all part of getting the work done, but otherwise bosses are really people after all.

Of all the success stories in America those of the movie star, the pop music performer, and the sports hero are the most cherished by the public. Their appeal lies in the fact that the achievement connotes no authority but still dramatizes the possibility of a rapid rise to fame and fortune through hard work and the kind of opportunity available only in America.

Youth and Progress

America is a country where youth and change are valued on the one hand and distrusted on the other. "What's new?" is almost as frequently asked as "How are you?" and responses to the first question may bring discussions of new dances, new child-raising techniques, new hairdos, new kitchen gadgets, or new public personalities. To keep up with new trends and new ideas is to be young in spirit, and no one in America ever really looks forward to growing old. "Middle age" extends right up to senility or death. In a civilization where each generation is exposed to a whole new set of technological facts and social conditions, elderly people are not respected for their greater experience but rather are considered "old fogies" and out of date.

Something of America's youth fetish can be inferred from the fact that Betty Crocker had her sixth face lift in 1986. The imaginary homemaker whose portrait has served as the General Mills trademark since 1936 has been getting younger and younger over the last fifty years. While the 1936 version was middle-aged, the most recent appears barely 30.

The American accent is on youth because the future belongs to the youth of a nation and America is future-oriented. There is no other nation in the world that dotes more over baby pictures, concentrates as much on developing new and different (and often educational) toys for children, or stresses as highly that parents should devote great amounts of their time and energy to seeing that their children are amused and provided with music and dancing lessons or programmed recreational activities. In America, parents usually play the role of spectators while their children take the spotlight. In England and in European countries in general children are seen and heard as little as possible. When parents have guests, the small fry are relegated to the kitchen, where they are expected to stay unless called by the parents, and they are seldom called.

Although America has been the land of the young for a long time, there are indications that this is beginning to change. Because we have greatly reduced the birth rate, and because people are living longer today, the median age of our population promises to rise gradually. In 1983, it was 30.9 years, but by the year 2023 it will be 38 years.

An aging population will result in a number of changes, besides the obvious ones involving Social Security financing. James Mann and Alexander Astin (1977) suggest, for example that a graying population will eventuate fewer fads in dress and pop music, a decline in junk food popularity, less childish programming on television, fewer traffic accidents and crimes, and a revival of more sedate athletic pursuits. He sees the return of ship cruising and ballroom dancing, and a movement of more and more people to the Sun Belt. For those who chose not to move out of town, he predicts a shift from apartment living to residence in single family dwellings.

In most pre-industrial societies population profiles and culture remain remarkably stable over many generations. Change takes place slowly, and "youth" is synonymous with "inexperience." Government is frequently in the hands of village elders, and the older citizens of a primitive society serve as storehouses of tradition and as authorities on proper behavior. In such cultures individuals are secure in their knowledge of culture. There is no question about how children should be reared and disciplined. Proper methods are those their mothers and grandmothers employed.

Such confidence is seldom found in American culture. Each generation lacks confidence in the methods of the former but has no dependable solutions of its own. Since there is no faith in the old solutions, Americans turn to the "experts," but even they cannot agree on such things as how to rear, discipline, and educate children, or what the proper husband-wife relationship should be. There is no lack of advice, however. Every magazine for women has at least one article on one or all of these subjects. Self-styled experts on family problems write syndicated columns, and even a number of government agencies will furnish anxious wives and mothers with authoritative literature on these matters at nominal cost.

The anxieties of parents in the area of child-rearing and education are heightened by their desire to provide their children with better opportunities for success than they had. This desire to see that one's children have opportunities and advantages that were not available to oneself is part of the American faith in progress. It has often been pointed out by students of American culture that the constant pursuit of material wealth is not so much a desire to have things for their own value but rather an attempt to provide evidence for one's friends and neighbors that one is succeeding and getting ahead. Therefore, the $200,000 home or the Mercedes is not valued because it represents, in the first case, additional living space or increased comfort, or in the case of the car, better engineering or better transportation. These material possessions are valued as symbols of hard work, ability, and achievement.

It is inconceivable for a person who identifies with the American middle class ever to refuse to accept a better position with his/her firm whether it means taking on added responsibility, working longer hours, or even selling the house and moving to another community. The prospect of hard work is no obstacle to this average American if there is any opportunity at all to succeed. Hard work is, for Americans, not only a means to an end but to a great extent an end in itself. A survival of puritan philosophy is the association of idleness with sin and industry with virtue. In commenting on this principle, Margaret Mead stated, "Within traditional American culture, leisure is something that has to be earned and rearned, except for the very old. . . . Unearned leisure is something which will have to be paid for later" (1957:11).

The hard work ethic appears as operative for the younger generation today as it was for their parents, despite a temporary lapse during the late 1960s and early 1970s when young people raised in comfortable middle-class homes rejected the ideas of striving for material wealth in favor of promoting such noble causes as the eradication of war, poverty, and bigotry. While these high ideals have not been completely abandoned, a survey of college freshmen in 1976 found 61 percent of men and 45 percent of women maintained that they were seeking the goal of "being very well-off financially" while five years earlier only 50 percent of freshman men and 28 percent of women claimed pursuit of such an ambition (Mann and Astin 1977).

Americans traditionally are content with simple answers to complex questions, and an example is the belief that there is a positive correlation between hard work and success. Although a commonly heard statement is "It isn't what you know, it's who you know," the behavior of most Americans would indicate that the real axiom that motivates their behavior is "It isn't who you know, it's how hard you work." The failure in business is viewed by the mainstream American as an object of contempt rather than of sympathy. America has always liked winners and has believed that everyone is a potential winner if he puts forward sufficient effort.

Still another facet of this work-success belief is the idea of the "self-made man or woman" and the idea of "pulling oneself up by the bootstraps." A large portion of Americans thoroughly believe that anyone can pull off the bootstrap stunt if he really wants to and they refuse to admit that racial type, lack of educational opportunities, socio-economic background, or sex are obstacles for the really motivated individual. Fortunately, there aren't many self-made people around these days. The concept is, of course, ridiculous. The self-made man is really the egocentric one with the short memory in regard to all the people who have helped him along the way. Surveys show that most owners of big companies today are the sons of founders rather than the founders themselves. The boot-strap concept of self-help is still with us, however. The great popularity of charm schools, positive thinking and assertiveness training, manuals on how to succeed in business, and executive leadership courses testify to the strength of the belief in some circles that people can become more popular and more successful with a minimum of direction and instruction. With a little knowhow, they are prepared to take it from there.

It was pointed out earlier that while America values youth and welcomes change, both are looked upon with a certain amount of suspicion. While the generation gap has been around for a long time there was probably no time in history when the average parent and his adolescent or young adult offspring have been farther apart in their basic ideological frames of reference than in the late 1960s and early 1970s. Representative of this communication chasm is the exchange quoted by Margaret Mead in *Culture and Commitment, The New Relationships Between the Generations in the 1970s.* She records a typical elder's remark: "You know, I have been young and you never have been old." But then she quotes an equally typical young person who counters, "You never have been young in the world I am young in, and you never can be" (1978:33). The world that the youth is referring to is, of course, very different from the one in which his father and mother gained their experience for living. It is a world of hydrogen bombs, space exploration, world-wide satellite communication, air and water pollution, and energy crises.

During the 1960s this existential awareness prompted the emergence of a set of values and a configuration of behavior which social scientists labelled the "counterculture." Theodore Roszak described it as a "cultural constellation that radically diverges from the values and assumptions that have been in the mainstream of our society at least since the scientific revolution of the seventeenth century" (1969:xii).

Symptomatic of this new cultural perspective were the civil rights movements (involving demonstrations, boycotts, and civil disobedience) of the early 1960s, the student revolts which began in the mid sixties, and the anti-war sentiments and demonstrations which continued up until the American withdrawal from Vietnam in 1975, although the Nixon White House had announced in 1970 that nothing the young could do or say would influence public policy in any way.

The avant-garde of this movement for cultural revision had been a small minority of college and high school young people who were the sons and daughters of those middle-class parents whose traditional value system and behavioral patterns are the subject of this chapter on the American cultural configuration. Margaret Mead referred to this group as the "children of electricity and electronics who believed they could make the world new overnight." They were accustomed to pushing buttons "so there would be light" (1978:95).

A major reason why this configuration of values and behavior developed is explained by Mead as being associated with the creation of a massive generation gap between those born and raised before the advent of the atomic bomb and those who grew up under the shadow of its holocaustic potential. Wars had now become for the first time in the history of mankind a proposition where everyone stood to lose everything. Mead explains,

> As the world became one inter-communicating whole, the experience of all those, everywhere on earth, reared in the post World War II world, became a shared experience and differentiated them from all their elders. The colleges and universities had exploded under the pressure of their fresh vision. Empowered by this freshness and by the new ethics of shared responsibility, sufficiently alienated from the Establishment—from all establishments—the post war generation demanded a changed world. (1978:100)

But what has happened to the counterculture today? The end of the Vietnam War in the spring of 1975 brought an end to the draft and to anti-war demonstrations, but now there were financial problems associated with a deepening economic recession. Jobs became scarce and so did the quotas for law and medical schools. Now the children of the upper middle class were faced for the first time with a very personal problem—how to make a living. Students on college campuses gave up the luxury of philosophy, English literature, and art appreciation and began to take accounting, industrial education, and business administration. No longer was there outspoken opposition to outmoded methods and undemocratic university procedures. Mead describes that university environment, an environment drastically different from that surrounding the dissenting counterculturers:

> Activists are almost as rare as they have traditionally been on American campuses. Undergraduate life is again seen as a perpetuation of adolescence, a postponement of choice, or where a professional choice has been made, for a determined pursuit of its academic requirements. Saving the world, like earning a living, can be postponed until later—when once out of law school, one can take up advocacy or out of medical school, one can work for free clinics. . . . The new graduates will not retire to the suburbs any more than their predecessors did. The campuses look more like the 1950s but the questioning generated on the campuses of the 1960s is still with us. (1978:107)

To what extent this questioning remains today is indicated by a recent survey of college students. Although undergraduates have a greater tendency to think of themselves as "middle-of-the-road" rather than liberal, 75–80 percent supported "liberal" positions on energy, pollution, consumer protection, women's rights, student autonomy, and legalization of marijuana. (Mann and Astin 1977). A number of observers of the American cultural scene believe that the ferment of the 60s is lying dormant and could be revived again given the right set of circumstances—perhaps over an issue such as nuclear power, intervention in foreign military conflicts, administration policy on Apartheid, or government infringement of civil rights.

The Paradox of Education

One of the simple answers that Americans have singled out to solve complex problems is that almost any social problem can be solved through education; and most Americans value the type of education that most directly deals with practical problems. Parents often object to their children majoring in philosophy, history, or anthropology because, after all, "What can you do with that kind of an education?" Training in medicine, law, engineering, or business administration can clearly be seen as avenues leading to good jobs and the material wealth that symbolizes success. There is less emphasis on what one learns in college than on what one can do professionally with a college diploma. There have even been those who were "smart" enough to short-cut the whole process by purchasing a sheepskin from a "diploma mill" and therefore have not had to waste all that time being educated. Much is made also of the fact that the average college graduate will make about $300,000 more during his lifetime than the average high school graduate.

Although there is great faith in the necessity for education in America, it can hardly be said that we have a nation of scholars. People in this country read book reviews and digests of articles rather than spending the time on the original. While every English and French hamlet has at least one book store, it is almost impossible to find such an establishment in most of the small towns of America. A recent poll of international reading habits sought to discover how many people were currently reading a book. In England the figure was 55 percent; in West Germany, 34 percent; in Australia, 33 percent; in Canada, 31 percent and in the United States the figure was a pathetic 17 percent.

Intellectuals have been much-publicized in this country as "eggheads," impractical dreamers, or just plain eccentrics, and they are frequently suspected of being subversives. Many states insist that educators at all levels take loyalty oaths to state or national constitutions while the same demands are not made on ministers, lawyers, trade or business people. College professors are generally pictured in films and on television series as absentminded, cloistered, and terribly impractical. Few awards in America have met with such public approval as Senator Proxmire's Golden Fleece Award which is conferred on researchers whose projects are considered of dubious value by the Wisconsin legislator. A number of churches look upon colleges and college professors as corruptors of young people's faith and morality, and working with the mind is often considered to be somewhat less honorable and fatiguing than working with the hands. Jules Henry believes "there is no more vulnerable white collar group than educators. For the most part without unions—subject to the whims of principals, superintendents, boards of education, and local parent organizations—elementary- and high-school teachers stand unprotected at the bottom of one of the most extended pyramids of power in the country" (1971:160).

Although there is faith in what education can do to increase the prospects for success for one's children, there is also a reluctance to pay for education. Teachers as a group are the lowest paid professional people in America, and the defeat of school bond issues at the polls has become more the rule than the exception. While many citizens find no difficulty in purchasing a new car every year, they think that the cost of a college education for their son or daughter is nothing less than bankrupting.

Technology—Our Sacred Cow

America is a machine-and-computer culture. It is a culture where machines think, talk, teach our children, put people out of work, inform on us when we are lying, predict the outcome of elections from 2 percent of the returns, and carry us through space on missions to the moon at 18,000 miles an hour. This is a country where improving education means buying more overhead projectors, tape recorders, computers, and phonographs. Americans own three times as many motor vehicles, radios, and television sets and twice as many telephones as any single country of Europe, including England.

Technology influences our national policy, our motor behavior, our ideas of cleanliness and punctuality, and it influences our whole philosophy of life and our world view. Howard Stein contends that technology is our "impersonal animism and personal diety. Our love (and love-hate) affair with our machines and computers resembles the so-called 'primitive's' love affair with Nature, Fate, and the Cosmos." (1985:8).

Of all the cherished technological artifacts in the United States, none is more loved than the automobile. Arthur Asa Berger suggests that "the automobile dominates us economically as well as physically, and has affected the pattern of our housing (the suburb), consumption (the shopping center), and even our sense of who we are in the world — and where we are going." (1937:166). He further submits:

> There may be an inverse correlation between a person's sense of "self" and the size of the engine in his car. People who feel petty and insignificant, for whatever reason, may need gigantic V-8s, and people who feel weak may need "muscle" cars. Choosing options for cars may be one of the few ways left in which individuals can make decisions that count, and for many it is the only means at their disposal for displaying creativity, as well as status. (1973:168).

Ours is a nation that places high value on energy, efficiency, orderliness, and precise measurement, and much of this can be directly attributed to the machines that we control and the machines that control us. Marshall McLuhan once suggested that our answer to a machine world was to become one, (1951:102), and Howard Stein maintains,

> Believing ourselves to be machine-like, we create machines to be replicas of ourselves, only to conclude that the human mind is a computer and the body is a sublimely engineered specimen of machinery." (1958:8).

It is interesting to note how when seven astronauts reached out for technological progess and failed in our worst space disaster, the values of the "common man" and the "work ethic" were called upon in the creation of a moving eulogy. *Time* reporter Paul Gray wrote about the Challenger tragedy:

> They would not have seemed out of place at a supermarket check-out or standing in line to see a movie. They could have come together by chance just about anywhere in the United States. Nothing odd here, in this assemblage of sexes and ethnic strains and religions, except maybe the extraordinary American experiment in equality inching forward, for the nation and the world to see, and being taken largely for granted.
>
> They were, all of them, human like us. Their courage and ambition took root in the familiar, sustained by circumstances and routines that everyone can recognize. On that last morning they were in pre-flight isolation but still a part of us. They got up and dressed, had breakfast and went to work. (1986:32).

When the author was doing anthropological research in the Samoan Islands, he became aware of two kinds of time—"*fa'asamoa* time" and "white man's time." *Fa'asamoa*, or "the Samoan way" time, was far from being precise because it tended to be calculated by the position of the sun or the length of the shadows. Whether a Samoan's calculations were a half hour or so in error didn't make too much difference because the nature of the culture was such that there was little need for keeping appointments at a precise time. On Sunday morning, church services were supposed to start at eight o'clock, but no one really minded if the church bell rang at seven o'clock or at nine. There was not a single thing in the culture that had to be done exactly at an appointed hour.

The same lack of precision was also found in lineal measurement. The length of a man's forearm or the length of a man's outstretched arms(the fathom) were sufficient standards of measurement. Houses varied a bit in size because of the various sizes of carpenters' forearms, but no one got very upset over this. Measurement in the production of a finely balanced machine must be accurate to the thousandth of an inch, however. One would hate to ride in a commercial airliner, for example, that had been built on the basis of forearm measurements. Mass production of complex products with interchangeable parts must feature precision and accuracy.

It is interesting to see how this necessity for precision has been transferred to American culture in general. The batting ability of baseball players is measured quantitatively down to the third place past the decimal point. Weather forecasters tell us that there is a 65 percent chance of rain within the next 24 hours. Each of us has been assigned a social security number, a car registration number, a driver's license number, a zip code number, an area code number, and a dozen or more credit-card numbers.

Many American mothers believe that the feeding of infants must be by strict schedule even if it means waking the baby at a definite time during the night. People do not sleep until they are rested; they attempt to get eight hours of sleep as though that were a magic number. One soft drink even specifies on its bottle that it should be consumed precisely at 10, 2, and 4.

Our educational system also bows to technology. To begin with we have gotten into the habit of referring to college graduates as "products" of their *alma mater* and to a large extent the university is a large assembly line wherein individual professors perform their specialized function on the student and send him down the line to the next specialist. In most schools letter grades have a corresponding numerical equivalent. A's are worth four points, B's three points, etc. Upon graduation a grade-point average such as 3.548 is recorded on the student's record. Far too often a student may lose a valuable scholarship to graduate school because some other student surpasses him in his grade point average by two or three thousandths of a point. The giving of grades is a most subjective task, to say the least, but once the grades are recorded and averaged, the result becomes an infallible, precise "measurement" of the student's academic and intellectual ability.

The wealth of American technical knowledge has without doubt created a more comfortable existence for its citizens—that is, up to now. But it has made America into a "throw-away" culture, notorious for its capacity for waste. Marya Mannes asks what future archeologists some hundreds of years hence may find as the monuments of our civilization. She writes,

> And what will we leave behind us when we are long dead? Temples? Amphora? Sunken treasure? Or mountains of twisted, rusted steel, canyons of plastic containers, and a million miles of shores garlanded, not with the lovely wrack of the sea, but with the cans and bottles and light-bulbs and boxes of a people who conserved their convenience at the expense of their heritage, and whose ephemeral prosperity was built on waste. (1962:167)

The Individual Versus the Family

Fifty years ago the American had a much greater sense of family than he does today. In the 1920s more than half of our households had an additional adult relative in residence. Today only 5 percent of homes have a grandmother, uncle, unmarried sister or some such kinsman living in. Many Americans have never even met all of their cousins and aren't particularly upset about it. The family reunions of yesterday are now rare, and when they occur they are generally not a success. In the old days, families tended to be localized, and reunions were occasions when relatives could get together and compare crop successes and failures. With the geographical mobility of people today when such get-togethers occur the various family members are so different in their interests and occupations that there is little to talk about.

In 1963 Dr. Francis Hsu pointed out in *Clan, Caste and Club* that the American family is definitely individual centered and that personal happiness is stressed over family welfare or family solidarity. Recent evidence documents an even greater emphasis on individuality at the expense of family structure. According to Bronfenbrenner, "Although family is a core institution the world over, for most Americans it takes a backseat to the 'individual.' We talk about disadvantaged *individuals*, *individual* achievement, discovering ourselves as *individuals*, and "the individual vs. the state" (1977:39). In America marriages are contracted to make two individuals happy; not for economic, political, social, or procreative reasons as in other societies. Based largely on the principle of romantic love, marriage is in effect a continuation of courtship. There is a constant need for the marriage partners to keep reassuring their spouses that they still care. One of the worst crimes in domestic life is to take one's husband or wife for granted. Wives become upset when their husbands forget anniversaries or birthdays, and husbands believe that their wives should "fix themselves up" in preparation for the husband's arrival home from work. Going out now and then to eat in a restaurant and perhaps also to take in a show is very much like the couple's courtship and is considered vital to the happiness of the wife.

The "happiness marriage," based as it is on a fragile foundation of romantic love and personal independence, could become an endangered species. Not only are divorces three times as frequent today as 30 years ago, with 40 percent of modern marriages destined to dissolve; but interest and attention devoted to care of children has been greatly curtailed. Less and less affection is forthcoming from parents. Bronfenbrenner reports that a recent study of middle-class fathers of one year old infants revealed that they spent an average of only 20 minutes a day with their babies. A U.S. Department of Commerce survey in 1984 discovered that 57.2 percent of mothers with school-age children now work outside the home as compared with 28 percent in 1950. And better than one-third of mothers of tiny infants had outside employment. Not only are parents spending more time outside the home, but a fair share are leaving for good. One youngster out of five under the age of 18 lives with only one parent, usually the mother.

Our lack of interest in children is also reflected in national policy, in spite of Reagan administration pronouncements that it is pro-family. The United States is the only industrialized nation in the world that does not ensure health care or a minimum income for every family with young children and the only one that has not established a program of child-care services for working mothers.

Indeed, the members of the American family see that social unit as a source for obtaining personal happiness. The partners marry for happiness, refrain from having children for happiness, and have little concern for family tradition or continuity. The family is something to be exploited rather than sacrificed for. Why are we like this? Alexis de Tocqueville once said that our zeal for democracy and personal freedom made us so. In *Democracy in America* he wrote:

> Among democratic nations new families are constantly springing up, others are constantly falling away, and all that remain change their condition; the woof of time is every instant broken and the track of generations effaced. . . . As social conditions become more equal, the number of persons increases who, although they are neither rich nor powerful enough to exercise any great influence over their fellows, have nevertheless acquired or retained sufficient education and fortune to satisfy their own wants. They owe nothing to any man, they expect nothing from any man; they acquire the habit of always considering themselves as standing alone, and they are apt to imagine that their whole destiny is in their own hands.
>
> Thus not only does democracy make every man forget his ancestors, but it hides his descendants and separates his contemporaries from him; it throws him back forever upon himself alone and threatens in the end to confine him entirely within the solitude of his own heart. (1899, Vol. 2:105–6)

Religion in America

America is primarily a Protestant Christian nation with roots well planted in a Puritan tradition. A 1985 survey recorded American religious affiliations as being 55 percent Protestant, 37 percent Roman Catholic and 4 percent Jewish. It took 184 years for the people of this country to bring themselves to elect a Roman Catholic president, John F. Kennedy, and then there were grave misgivings, particularly among Protestant clergy. Eighty-eight percent of the directorships of business and industry, 83 percent of the directorships of America's largest banks, and 80 percent of the directorships of large insurance companies are held by Protestants, and on college campuses, 80 percent of the members of their governing bodies are of this religious persuasion. America has a long history of Protestant domination because the value system of its people finds Protestantism more acceptable than Roman Catholicism. Americans have never been much for ceremony or ritual, they tend to reject authority and rigid, absolute doctrine, and they could not tolerate an institution that is controlled in part by foreigners. There are in America more than 250 distinct denominations. Free to interpret the Bible as they see fit, each of these groups has placed special attention on certain interpretations. Many represent splinter groups from the major denominations or, in some cases, entirely new denominations. The demand for doctrinal freedom appears to be basic in America. Bellah notes its presence even in the eighteenth century. "Thomas Jefferson said, 'I am a sect myself,' and Thomas Paine, 'My mind is my church.' Many of the most influential figures in the nineteenth century American culture could find a home in none of the existing religious bodies, though they were attracted to the religious teaching of several traditions. One thinks of Ralph Waldo Emerson, Henry David Thoreau, and Walt Whitman." (1985:233).

A *Glamour Magazine* (May 1986) survey of 25,000 readers 18 to 35 years of age reported that while 77 percent pray and 87 percent believe that God has and continues to help them through difficult periods of their lives, there was considerable evidence that respondents seem to choose aspects of their religion they can live with and ignore those they can't. Nearly half disagree with their church's position on premarital sex, and a third (42 percent of single women) disagree with their church's stand on abortions.

The independent spirit of Americans is seen in many other aspects of religion. There is a relatively complete separation of church and state, and a lack of an established church such as the Church of England in the British Isles, the Lutheran church in Sweden, or the Roman Catholic church in Spain. Furthermore, even among the major denominations, seldom is there any central authority or control. In nearly all American churches (including the Catholic) there is a great deal of district and church autonomy. Most churches are quite democratic and often give lay officials as much or more power than the ministers. Still another aspect of the opposition to authority is the tendency in many churches not to require theological training for religious leaders. People without any formal religious training establish churches of their own or declare themselves evangelists.

Being great advocates of tolerance and fair play, Americans generally believe in religious freedom. People tend to respect the rights of others to worship as they wish, although they may disagree violently with their beliefs. Whether or not they want an individual of a certain denomination in a position of authority in business or government is another matter.

In spite of frequent references to America being a Christian nation and in spite of the high proportion (60 percent) of adults claiming church membership, students of American culture agree that America is not a particularly religious nation. With the exception of certain rural areas, where the church continues to influence the social and moral aspects of life, religion tends to be a Sunday-morning phenomenon. Generally, religious precepts have little influence on business ethics or social issues. The organized church all too frequently stays aloof from political struggle and tends to support public opinion. Some of the basic principles of Christianity—the brotherhood of man, the renunciation of struggles for riches and wordly goods—are not popular causes in America, and therefore very little is said about these things from the average pulpit.

A national survey conducted by the Knight-Ridder newspaper syndicate found that those who identified themselves as having "strong religious convictions:"

1. Do not consider themselves "liberals."
2. Feel civil rights progress is proceding too fast.
3. Favor laws against abortion.
4. Believe that jobs are available for those that want them.
5. Are for restricting free speech when its content is obscene.
6. Believe that the solution to crime is more severe penalties.
7. Are against reducing marijuana penalties.

Many churches go out of their way to cultivate a wealthy membership. Those white pastors who have taken strong stands against segregation or other forms of social injustice are in the minority, and they find little support in their congregations.

Generally churches provide a comfortable atmosphere with emphasis on maintaining the status quo. Local religious leaders don't take stands on certain moral issues for fear it will offend members of the congregation who will then sever their membership connections. One major denomination recently reported a loss of more than 250 ministers in a two-year period. When asked why they left the ministry, a large share of them listed dissatisfaction or disillusionment with the organized institutional church. Individual ministers commented on their congregation's "greater interest in buildings, real estate, and statistics than in people" or on the "smallness, insincerity, and untruthfulness of church people."

Demands for change in religious attitudes and practices have become vital issues among a new breed of theological students and young clergymen who have become critical of the failure of the organized church to address itself to the urban and racial crises and to the moral question of American military involvement.

Critics of the organized church in America claim that too much time is spent on social activities and group fellowship. Men's clubs, ladies' aid societies, scout troops, bowling teams, young people's recreation groups, athletic programs, and fellowship dinners have come to be recognized as essential parts of any church program although they may be quite unrelated to the spiritual activities of the church. In regard to the fellowship aspect of American religion, Harry Golden wrote, "The first part of a church they build nowadays is the kitchen.

Five hundred years from now people will dig up these churches, find the steam tables and wonder what kind of sacrifices we performed" (1955:295).

An editorial in *The Economist* following the tragedy at Jonestown, Guyana, speculated on the meteoric rise of religious cults over the last decade. It explained,

> The last third of the twentieth century is a period in which the familiar forms of organized religion have lost their hold on most . . . members of the educated middle class. . . . This is probably the first time in history in which . . . to be intelligent and educated is also to be without religious belief.
>
> The disintegration of the old religious institutions has not produced a world in which everybody is contented to live in the confines of an existence without gods. . . . The market place of religious innovation is one of the last and best examples of free enterprise in the world today. (1979:11)

Demands for new forms of spiritual experience have spawned a startling number and variety of cults, some of which recruit and hold their membership through disturbing techniques of social conditioning and mind control. When orthodox religion decays, those who most hunger for the certainty of faith often find it in the Unification Church, in The Way, in Sun Myung Moon, or at worst, in people like Rev. James Jones. *The Economist* reported that when seeking God in a secular world "it is all too easy to blunder into the arms of Satan instead." (1979:11)

Americans generally do not think deeply about religion. With the exception of a few professors and students of theology, there is little searching or questioning of religious beliefs. Most Americans are content to accept the interpretation and traditions of their denomination. Like swallowing a capsule; no chewing is required. A great number of Americans are quite ignorant, however, of the doctrine of their own denomination, although they are quite sure that it is better than the others. Michael Argyle found that although 95 percent of Americans claim some church affiliation, only 35 percent are able to name the four gospels.

While most social scientists agree that Americans are not particularly religious, they also feel that they are not antireligious. Our country has never experienced any anticlerical movements. Our pastors and priests, although poorly paid, are usually treated with respect. Those who do not participate in the activities of a church tend to do so out of indifference rather than opposition to religion.

Reflectors of American Value

THE COMICS   There is an increasingly large group of anthropologists and folklorists who believe that popular culture, or mass culture as it is sometimes called, can reveal much about the value system and behavioral proclivities of those who are drawn to and partake of it.

Operating on the theory that for a thing to be popular it must be meaningful, a number of social scientists are now turning to the comics as a means of reading the value priorities of our culture. The colorful and amusing "funny paper" strips, particularly the ones which have survived for long periods of time, are looked to as a kind of folk mythology which communicates life information, cultural assumptions, and the charter for social interaction. And as White and Abel have pointed out they appeal to "all classes and areas of our society" (1963:13).

One anthropological student of American culture, Arthur Asa Berger, has produced a book, *The Comic Stripped American*, in which he calls attention to the "All-American" messages conveyed by such perennial favorites as *Blondie*, *Dick Tracy*, *Bat Man*, and *Peanuts*, and Ellen Rhoads, also an anthropologist, has, in another publication, made a Levi-Strauss type analysis of *Little Orphan Annie*, an American favorite since 1924.

Blondie.   According to analyst Arthur Berger, *Blondie* deals with the tragedy of the American family, specifically the irrelevance of the American Husband. Pictured as infantile, weak, greedy, and inadequate to the responsibilities of family life, Dagwood Bumstead (whose very name brands him as a fool), has completely abdicated any role of authority or leadership. Concerning the antics of this short-tempered, hedonistic, immature "family head" Berger writes, "The relationship between Dagwood and Blondie is a parody of that existing in many families, in which there is a domineering figure who tends to do the decision making (and 'holds the marriage together') and a passive figure who is acted upon, subservient and submissive" (1973:108).

With the coming of the industrial revolution in America the ability to make money became the symbol of masculinity. Money meant power and potency, but to make money a man had to spend long hours on the job and this required him to turn over many of the family functions to his wife—household finance, disciplining children, and community service. In spite of frequent claims that "it's a man's world," (particularly by the New Feminists) most social scientists would agree that much of what is learned in the home is learned at mother's knee (until recently, that is, when many of the mothers marched off to work). In other words, the vital enculturation and socialization processes are largely controlled in America by females. This means that to a great extent the young learn their culture and social adjustment from the woman's viewpoint. The hospital nurse, the Sunday-school teacher, the grade-, and junior high-, and high-school teachers are predominantly women, and at home, the greater amount of the child's development—in eating habits, toilet-training, walking, and talking—is under the close scrutiny and supervision of the mother. Primarily the mother decides what things the child must be disciplined for, and she often does the disciplining. If she is not the dispenser of corporal punishment, the father does it at her order. This domestic matriarchy is hard to compete with. The biological role, plus the role as protector, comforter, and provider, make the mother the dominant parent for most Americans. The value of the father's breadwinning role is more easily overlooked since most of his activities are carried on outside the home. "Dagwood," writes Berger, "is in the tragic situation of being an irrelevant male, and feeling it, but not knowing it. To the extent that he is an archetype for American men, who find that many of the situations in the strip somehow 'strike a chord,' it is a tragedy of the most profound dimensions" (1973:108).

Dick Tracy and Batman.   *Dick Tracy* touches on various aspects of our evangelical Protestant tradition, a tradition which conceives of the world as a sinful, corrupt, and degrading place wherein eternal vigilance must be maintained to hold evil—in thought and deed—in check. In this strip our square-jawed detective represents a moral champion, an instrument of society's justice, for all decent God-fearing people. Tracy is a culture hero who undergoes excruciating ordeals with a series of criminal stereotypes, and although he invariably suffers pain and temptation, his eventual victory proves again and again that God is in His heaven and that ultimately goodness will triumph. It is, in effect, a modern-day morality play, and Dick Tracy is the avenging angel of a stern and righteous society.

Batman, on the other hand, represents another facet of basic American moral and ethical thought. After wealthy young Bruce Wayne witnessed the brutal murder of his parents, he swore to avenge their deaths by spending the rest of his life warring on *all* criminals. Described by Berger as a "pietistic perfectionist," *Batman* reflects a typical American belief that everyone is responsible for deciding the morality or immorality of every issue in terms of a higher moral law. This is the mentality of the crusader. It is the type of thought which dispatches missionaries to "heathen tribes" and the Peace Corps to underdeveloped countries. It is the commitment which motivated Carrie Nation to smash saloons, Right to Life people to picket and even harass abortion clinics, and Jimmy Carter to speak out about violations of human rights in the Soviet Union and in a score of other nations around the world. This American belief that it is one's duty to right all wrongs helps explain Vietnam, our intervention in the Middle East, and the activism of the 1960s by young people who perhaps had learned their absolutism from strips like *Batman.* For millions of Americans Batman represents hope in a seemingly hopeless world—hope associated with the return of the hero and the heroic.

Peanuts. In *Peanuts* we find still more food for thought for a puritan nation, this time in the weakness of human flesh and the doctrine of Original Sin. But *Peanuts* is not so much a comment on American culture alone as it is on the human condition in general. Berger comments that Schultz's "characters tend to be monomaniacs who pursue their destinies with all the zany abandon of divinely inspired zealots. . . . The characters in *Peanuts* exist after the fall of man from the Garden of Eden. They are corrupted by original sin and therefore can be selfish egoists without any strain on our credulity" (1973:183).

Through the antics of its petty but lovable tyrants the strip openly acknowledges human frailty and false pride and accepts the human animal for what it is and not what it claims to be. *Peanuts* boldly reveals the absurdity of such sacred shibboleths as "big man on campus," "winning is everything," or the folly of the temperamental artist or the domineering female. It is court-jester humor which through its clever wit makes social criticisms acceptable. Could it be, asks Berger, "that perhaps we have reached the stage in which we live vicariously through Snoopy and all the other characters in the strip. . . . *Peanuts* helps to assuage our hunger for *personality* in a world that is full of dehumanizing forces and in which identity is so much under attack" (1973:193).

Little Orphan Annie. Of all the comic strips, *Little Orphan Annie* is perhaps the most "All American" in its preoccupation with American values. Personifying what some observers of American culture see as America's core value, self-reliance, the child Annie, accompanied only by her dog, Sandy, successfully struggles her way through harrowing episode after harrowing episode, revealing the rewards and satisfactions of hard work, patriotism, social acceptability, honesty, responsibility, and independence. Her foster father, Daddy Warbucks, who apparently acquired his millions through wartime profiteering, is pictured as a hardworking captain of industry struggling to protect capitalism, earn large profits, and act charitably toward the needy.

THE MOVIES

In 1977 millions of Americans stampeded the box office to see *Star Wars*, the first of several outerspace fantasies that would emerge as the biggest entertainment attractions since *Gone With the Wind*. Although there seemed nothing remarkable about the acting or the plot of *Star Wars,* and it dealt with a subject that had been treated many times before with only moderate success, this space melodrama, according to Conrad Kottak, brought "together cultural themes, motifs, symbols, and meanings that are familiar and significant to the natives." (1978:12). A sequel titled *The Empire Strikes Back* appeared in 1980, followed by *Return of the Jedi* in 1983.

In an age when Americans have almost given up trying to deal with the explosion of technology, when human events seem unmanageable, and when the forces of nature seem to threaten to overpower us (e.g. Mt. St. Helens eruption, earthquakes and Carribbean hurricanes) *Star Wars* and its sequels showed human creatures re-establishing control. The films mark the return of the hero (after two decades of anti-heroes) who can still triumph over seemingly impossible odds. After having been defeated in *2001:Space Odyssey* by a computer gone bad, in *Poseidon Adventure* by a tidal wave, in *Jaws I, II* and *III* by a seemingly uncontrollable sea monster, and in the *Exorcist* and *The Omen* by spiritual forces out of control, the *Star Wars* films put human beings back in the driver's seat. *Star Wars* was a fairy tale full of hope and innocence that pitted sharply distinguished good and evil characters against one another with the forces of good being ultimately triumphant. The moral of the tale was that advanced technology is not enough to ensure success; we must also rely on our inner strengths. Technology can be benevolent as well and malevolent (in that it can create amiable droids like R2D2 and C3PO). Conrad Kottak sees the space fantasy as a modern day *Wizard of Oz* maintaining that "The major themes of hope and eventual triumph are common to the two films. With Vietnam and the Nixon era behind us, we are ready again for heroes who are clearly good, and villains who are unambiguously evil. We are ready to cheer rebels in just wars against powerful technology and perverted governments." (1978:106).

The third in the *Star Wars* series, *Return of the Jedi*, is also seen as a specially meaningful statement of American values and attitudes. Arthur Asa Berger (who usually searches the comics for dominant themes) writes:

> The *Return of the Jedi* may be popular all over the world, but its value system is quintessentially American. First, we find youth triumphing and, what is more, teaching adults about love and goodness. This notion that young people are wiser and perhaps even nobler than adults, is one that is particularly American. It is connected, indirectly, to our egalitarian ethos. Young people are not only equal to adults, but morally superior since they have not been corrupted by the "real world."
>
> The second important theme involves faith in oneself. That is what Luke needs — actually all he needs — to become a full-fledged Jedi knight. In America we used to call it willpower. In a society in which we believe we all have equal opportunity (since we have, we believe, no rigid class system and no aristocracy), achieving success is essentially a function of individual effort and faith in oneself. This is behind what is sometimes called the middle-class "effort-optimism" syndrome. (1984:73-74).

FOOD

Octavio Paz is a Mexican poet, writer, and perceptive observer of the culture of the United States. He contends that the nature and culture of a people is revealed by their food preferences. The Yankee meal, claims Paz, is a product of a puritan tradition which in its preoccupation with purity and origins reveals an underlying racism. We insist on simple, spiceless, nutrients which we fanatically maintain should be kept identifiable and not all mixed together. This seems to parallel our insistence on maintaining a separation of our people according to age, class, sex, and color. Institutions that use metal trays with separate compartments instead of dishes ensure that none of the foods can contaminate the others. North Americans want straight-forward, honest, and sensible food just as they are drawn to straight-forward speech patterns. They don't want shadings introduced as the French do with sauces or as intellectuals do with fancy words. And unlike the French, Yankees do not eat for pleasure, but for health. Paz believes that American meals are designed to preserve health and repair the body after it becomes fatigued through hard work. Puritans honor hard work but not pleasure. Few things in rural North America were more honored than the sanctity of the full-to-overflowing harvest table for the thrashing crews or the sanctity of the Thanksgiving feast which marked the end of the season of hard agricultural work. The food-for-health concept also explains post-football-game meals where huge steaks are the only appropriate antedote for four grueling quarters of physical exertion. Yankees also lead the world in their interest in, and purchase of, expensive health foods and in their insistence on balanced diets for growing children.

But Paz sees signs that the Yankee culinary picture is changing. He explains, "The acceptance of rare sauces, strange condiments, marinades, dressings, and seasonings reveals a change not only in taste but also in values. Pleasure, in its more instantaneous form, taste and smell, displaces traditional values. Pleasure is the opposite of work and saving. This change modifies the very idea of time. The *now* is the time of pleasure; work sacrifices the now for the sake of the future" (1972:80).

FAST FOOD
CHAINS

Not only does the kind of foods eaten tell us something about the citizens of the United States but the way in which it is dispensed is equally revealing. Few Americans manage to ignore the golden arches of McDonald's, a fast food restaurant chain rapidly taking its place beside Mom, apple pie, July 4th, and Chevrolet as an American institution. Stressing personalism, fast service, and uniformity in setting and food-fare, McDonald's is the perfect place for Americans who do not care for the exotic or even for variety in their meals, and who do not see eating as pleasurable enough to be worthy of the investment of much time. The efficiency of the entire operation is undoubtedly also appealing to the natives of the land of assembly lines and computer analyses. Furthermore, McDonald's advertising stresses good American values like the importance of nuclear family companionship, clean-cut sincere employees, and healthful recreation complete with Big Macs; and there is frequent reference to McDonald's contributions to charitable organizations. Kottak suggests, "In a land of tremendous ethic, social, economic, and religious diversity we proclaim that we share something with millions of other Americans. . . . By eating at McDonald's we say something about ourselves as Americans, about our acceptance of values and designs for living that belong to a social collectivity" (1982:72). We affirm our identification with the common man.

ARCHITECTURE

Architect Stephen Kliment has referred to architecture as "frozen music"—the physical and permanent expression of a society's values. He maintains that "there is no better place to look for a society's values than in what it chooses as its monuments. The ancient Egyptians, in their obsession with death, built the pyramids as huge burial mounds. The Greeks erected their temples to worship their many gods. Medieval Europe had its cathedrals and its castles to represent the apex of power of the Church and the feudal barons" (1976:27). And if today's monuments follow the pattern, then we might assume that our structures acclaim the value of size, power, money, speed, self-conscious culture, mass spectator sports, belief in the corporation as the source of good and evil, education, growing dependence on government, withdrawal from the threatening impersonal world, and an official concern for the poor and underprivileged. What monuments of modern American culture in particular would lead us to identify these as the major aspects of national concern and interest? Kliment suggests the Las Vegas Strip with its lights and luxury; the Sears Roebuck and John Hancock stratoscrapers in Chicago; New York's Lincoln Center for the Performing Arts; numerous superdome athletic complexes; Dallas-Ft. Worth Intercontinental Airport; the massive marble and granite government buildings in Washington (especially the Pentagon) and Albany, New York; university campus buildings for business and engineering schools (almost always bigger than quarters for the liberal arts); Levitt House and hundreds of high-rise apartment blocks that offer subsidized housing to the poor.

Perhaps nowhere in America does architecture carry a more obvious symbolic message than in Washington, D.C. Architecture critic for *The Washington Post*, Wolf Von Eckardt, writing about such buildings as the James Madison Memorial Building, the Sam Rayburn House Office Building, the FBI Building and the Kennedy Center, charges that the "architecture seeks not to please and serve people, but to impress them. It seeks simplistic solutions to complex problems. It seeks a massive monumentality symbolizing powers. Manifestations of power, in architecture as in politics, can make no allowance for complexity or humane concerns." (1981:61).

Even the Kennedy Center, he writes, "is perceived, not as an art center, but merely as a nondescript monumental monolith. It does not symbolize the joys of music, drama, opera, but wealth, authority — in short, anything but the spiritual values it ought to represent." *(Ibid.).*

Football, a mirror for American values. (Courtesy Wichita State University.)

FOOTBALL

It would be difficult to think of any cultural trait more characteristic of the American scene than football. While this sport has a European origin in the game of rugby no other nation in the world (including Canada) plays the game with the will, or in precisely the manner, that we do. As William Arens has phrased it, "We share our language, kinship system, religion, political and economic institutions, and a variety of other traits with many nations, but our premier spectator sport remains ours alone" (1976:77). As something uniquely our own, its features tend to be compatible with major aspects of our thought and behavior. Arens maintains that more than any other sport, football incorporates the qualities of group coordination through a complex division of labor with highly developed specialization. Furthermore, success in the game demands extensive reliance on sophisticated electronic technology (from telephones to computers). Football is especially appealing also for people who place a high value on time, who pride themselves on using time to the best possible advantage. "Time is of the essence in football," writes Arthur Asa Berger, "but, unlike in baseball and other sports, in football time can be manipulated. And it is this manipulation of time in tightly fought games that leads to the incredible tension generated by the sport... Many football games are decided in the last minutes and often even the last seconds of the game." (1982:124).

Finally, the sport involves a level of aggressiveness and violence that Americans seem to enjoy. It is an appetite well served by television crime and detective series as well as Hollywood cowboy and Indian and war films. America is a place where movies involving murder, physical assault, and even rape get PG censor ratings but where movies involving scenes of physical lovemaking get X ratings and are often liable to confiscation by the police.

Since group coordination through specialization, reliance on electronic technology, and an emphasis on violence all cluster in this sport there is a tendency for it to strike a responsive chord in the average American. Violence alone would not make a sport our national pastime, however. Boxing is violent but it draws a much smaller audience than the gridiron spectacle. Corroborating Octavio Paz's point that America tends to segregate its population according to age, sex, and color, Arens stresses that football emphasizes the "division between the sexes. The game is a male preserve that manifests and symbolizes both the physical and cultural values of masculinity" (1976:77).

From the uniforms that accent the male physique (stressing an enlarged head, narrow waist, broad shoulders, and bulging genital region) to the taboos on sexual activity or even fraternization with women before a game, the result is an exaggeration of maleness and separatist values. When folklorist Alan Dundes speculated whether football might be a "homosexual ceremony" because of the "unequivocal sexual symbolism of the game," one college-football player responded "I was so angry, I just wanted to get my hands on the guy—I mean on his neck."

Is football a mirror for American values? Susan Montague and Robert Morais think it is. They write, "There is good reason to conclude that Americans watching football are watching a model of their own work world. . . . The values that are held up to this widely diversified audience (the whole of America) are strikingly similar to the values of the traditional success model. The greatest football coaches are not seen to work with talent significantly superior to that on other teams. Rather, fine coaches inspire their men on to greater heights of dedication, hard work, and self-sacrifice." (1976:39-40).

Fermin Diez maintains that players are told "if you do not do your job well, the other team will take advantage of it, and the trick is to do your job better than the opposing team. You must nullify their offense and overpower their defense; otherwise they will do it to you. If this not what competition among industries and corporations is all about? Football games reassure spectators that business/industry really works." (1982:262).

Resolving the Paradoxes

At the beginning of this chapter a number of cultural contradictions was cited. Although social scientists have long recognized and discussed these apparent paradoxes, few have provided any explanation of how or why they exist. This very perplexing matter is, however, discussed in articles (1961, 1966) and in a book (1953) by Francis Hsu, an anthropologist of Chinese extraction, who in his many articles and books on American character has proved to be a very competent observer and theorist.

Hsu maintains that many of our cultural contradictions can be understood in terms of a single important core value, *self-reliance*, which is primarily manifested in a fear of dependency. Self-reliance is considered the key to all individual freedom, and it is the ruler by which Americans measure all mankind. Self-reliant people consider themselves their own masters, controlling their own destinies through their own hard work and planning. Since the American seems to adhere to the "boot strap" theory, people who are forced to collect welfare money or the dependent aged are viewed with hostility and are considered misfits. Absolute self-reliance denies the importance of others and explains the rather unique phenomenon of the "self-made man." This denial of the value of others has a tendency to produce instability in ascribed relationships within the family and in achieved relationships as between business partners or between husbands and wives.

American self-reliance prompts people to compete and to value individualism on the one hand but demands conformity on the other. In order to be deemed a success, a man must belong to the right status-conferring organizations, but to do so he must conform to their standards and involve himself in their time- and energy-consuming organizational activities.

Self-reliance is also indirectly responsible for the coupling of such laudable values as Christian love, equality, and democracy with the less desirable values of religious bigotry and racism. This is because religious affiliation in the United States and in the West generally has become mostly a matter of associational affiliation. The successful man is drawn to the successful church that others of his social position attend. Hsu believes that the church is most frequently valued because of its social importance and this consideration greatly overshadows its doctrinal position or spiritual qualities.

The history of Western religion is believed to have always been marked by a search for original purity in both ritual and belief and this has led to the Reformation, the rise of multiple denominations, and even the Holy Inquisition. Dr. Hsu asserts that:

> This fervent search for and jealous guard over purity expresses itself in the racial scene as the fear of genetic mixing of races which feeds the segregationist power in the North as well as in the South. . . . When religious affiliations have become largely social affiliations, this fear of impurity makes religious and racial prejudices undistinguishable. (1961:222–23)

In an open society like America there are no fixed or permanent places in the social structure. People have an opportunity to climb, but so do others who are below them socially or economically. Thus self-reliant persons are afraid of being contaminated by those considered inferiors. They can be accepted as long as their upward mobility is prevented, but when they have the opportunity to share desks in their child's school, live in their neighborhood, or share the pews in their church as equals, insecurity mounts. Since discrimination against particular racial or socioeconomic groups runs contrary to both democracy and Christian theology, the self-reliant American must disguise their objections. In the South they have evaded the real issue by stressing states' rights and in the North by stressing property values.

The only security in a society stressing self-reliance is in personal success, superiority, and personal triumph, but unfortunately these achievements must of necessity be based upon failure or defeat of others, for there can be only one winner in every race. People are not valued for their mere participation.

In spite of its several shortcomings self-reliance is the key to progress. Because of this emphasis, the United States and the West generally have prospered and developed a great technological and industrial civilization. Leaders of developing nations are beginning to realize that if they wish to compete for recognition with Western nations they will have to develop the value of self-reliance in their people. Thus we have the final paradox—that the core value of American culture, self-reliance, is parent to both the best and the worst in us.

Summary

The United States is a society made up of many subcultures, but it is possible to describe "the American way of life" with some accuracy.

The Average American is the middle-class individual—hard working and respectable—who elects our presidents, establishes public opinion trends, and participates in the life style sometimes referred to as that of the "Establishment" or the "silent majority," a way of life that values peer conformity and standardization. The American hero is the "common man," and even the wealthiest of people feel they must appear to assume his role. Presidents succeed or fail according to how successful they are at convincing voters that they are "common men." This egalitarian value, however, makes exercise of authority difficult, particularly in business and in the military.

America is a culture which eulogizes youth and progress, and progress is believed to be tied to hard work and self-discipline. The concept of the "self-made man" is associated with this work-success ethic. Education is both valued (as a teacher of practical skills) and disparaged (as pretentious and impractical). Great confidence is placed in the machine and the computer, and technology influences every aspect of American life. Emphasis is placed on precision and efficiency. But America's technological genius has produced a "throw away" culture notorious for its capacity for waste.

America's core value is self-reliance and this has resulted in an emphasis on the rights and privileges of individuals over families or groups. It is a tendency which de Tocqueville noted as early as the 1830s and perhaps explains the American's passion for independence.

Religion in America is founded on the Puritan tradition. It is basically Protestant because Americans find the less structured, less authoritarian nature of Protestantism more to their liking.

Analyzing a complex civilization like that of the United States is a difficult proposition, but analysis of popular culture—in film, comics, literature, sports, food habits—has been seen as a fruitful avenue of investigation.

How Anthropologists Study Human Culture

9

The holistic, relativistic, scientific approach

    Acceptance by the group

    The language

    The key informant

    Nondirective and directive interviewing

    The hypothetical situation

Anthropology's uniqueness

Researching our own tribe

Survey research and questionnaires

Postulate analysis

Ethnosemantics

Quantification

The genealogical method

Technical aids to research

The goal of anthropological research

The life of an anthropologist, in the eyes of many, is one filled with adventure among strange and exotic people. Most people realize that it is the job of anthropologists to live in far-off places, participate in the lives of the peoples, and return with accounts of their customs and manners that will ultimately find their way into books gracing the shelves of public or college libraries. What many people do not quite understand is just why such foreign excursions are considered so essential to the perpetuation of the science of anthropology.

There are two reasons for field trips to foreign cultures: first, in anthropology a field trip is considered a kind of internship experience for budding anthropology students. It provides them with a certain insight or "feel" for the nature of culture. When people live their whole life in one culture, they tend to take their customs for granted and they are rarely aware of the force of these customs in shaping behavior. If, however, students go to work and live in another culture, they are immediately struck by the fact that things can be done in a very different way from what they have been used to. Patterns of culture stand out and have reality for them as they compare the foreign customs with their own cultural legacy. In addition to what the fieldwork does to the students' own scientific orientation, there is the matter of the fieldworker's contribution to the discipline of anthropology. As has been pointed out earlier, anthropology cannot gather facts from accounts by people who have not been scientifically trained to observe and record the details of people's living habits and value orientations. Something of the value of ethnographic descriptions as produced by untrained writers may be seen in the list of character traits assigned to Samoans by early voyagers, traders, administrators, and missionaries: "happy, proud, self-opinionated, suspicious, impudent, daring, social, decorous, polished, turbulent, threatening, treacherous, ferocious, respectful of old age, fond of children and travelling, sedate and dignified when chiefs, cunning, ungrateful, full of intrigue, expedient in truth and falsehood, cruel to animals, lacking in physical sensitivity, jealous, deceitful, generous, untrustful, arrogant, egotistical, loquacious, unstable, unenterprising, lazy, vain, cowardly when alone, superstitious, boastful, assertive, generous, hospitable, communalistic, lacking in ideas, capable of being led, unable to be bullied, subtle, diplomatic, patient, badly-treated, maladjusted . . ." (Stanner 1953:305–6). This very contradictory list compiled from early literature by Stanner gives some indication of the objectivity and the value of these reports.

The missionary Hiram Bingham upon seeing the Hawaiians for the first time records his doubt as to whether these strange people were even human, and if they were, would it be possible ever to civilize them. (1848:125)

Anthropologists know that they have to study human cultures in a scientific way. Their observations must be reliable, valid, and free from bias. The facts of foreign cultures must be brought in from all corners of the world so that they may be analyzed, combined, and compared. The flow of such facts cannot stop, because cultures are continuously changing, and the changes are also of vital significance. Because a culture has been studied once does not mean that the job is done.

The Holistic, Relativistic, Scientific Approach

Anthropologists do not go to another culture just to see what they can find out. They go with a definite theoretical frame of reference, one that has been acquired through years of college training in the discipline. The anthropological perspective not only helps interpret behavior but it shapes the approach to investigation. The anthropologist goes into the field with a unique set of research tools, part of which is a way of looking at other cultures. Their approach will undoubtedly be holistic, relativistic, and scientific. By holistic we mean that they will look for the *Gestalt* or the whole view of the society. They will look at the culture as an entity with functionally related components. Although they may be studying something quite specialized, like folklore, they know that this aspect of culture cannot be completely understood unless they have some grasp of the total way of life. They know, for example, that legends often constitute history for a primitive people and often regulate their political organization. Folktales and proverbs are frequently used as educational devices for training the young in the values of a society. Songs or riddles are often considered private property and lead one, therefore, into studies of economics. It is only when one approaches a culture as a consistent whole that true insights may be acquired. When any custom is viewed in terms of the total cultural configuration, its meaning and utility become more apparent and its bizarre and baffling qualities diminish. To the anthropologist, seeing the whole of a culture—that is, the general configuration—is often more important than knowing all of its intricate details.

Relativism, one of the most difficult attitudes for anthropologists to assume, is essential to truly good fieldwork. Anthropologists must try to divorce themselves from those value judgments that grow out of their being raised in a society that may have a very different set of moral, ethical, and for that matter, sanitary standards. Even the experienced anthropologist must get over an initial "culture shock" that comes when forced to alter living patterns and tastes to those of the native hosts. Few non-Western people have value systems approximating those of Europe and America, and their behavior cannot be judged in terms of ideas and values entirely foreign to them. The anthropologist must maintain a liberal open-minded position at least until the local norms of behavior are discovered. This approach to foreign cultures has become so much a part of anthropological fieldwork that anthropologists are often jokingly referred to as people "who have respect for every culture in the world except their own."

Although there has been some debate as to whether or not anthropology is a true science, anthropologists insist fiercely that their methods are as scientific and objective as those used in any social or behavioral science. With an eye to objectivity and careful control of data, anthropologists have, over a long period of time, developed through experimentation and experience a number of specialized methodological techniques that allow them a penetrating and accurate study of foreign cultures. While fieldworkers are constantly developing new avenues of investigation the following techniques have stood the test of time and might be said to represent the fieldworker's standard set of research tools.

PARTICIPANT OBSERVATION

The most widely used technique in anthropological field research is *participant observation*. Essentially this amounts to living with the people, participating in their lives as much as is permitted, and keeping one's eyes and ears open. A more formal definition would be that of Florence Kluckhohn, which reads:

> Participant observation is conscious and systematic sharing, in so far as circumstances permit, in the life activities and on occasion, in the interests and affects of a group of persons. Its purpose is to obtain data about behavior through direct contact and in terms of specific situations in which the distortion that results from the investigator's being an outside agent is reduced to a minimum. (1940:331)

For best results, the anthropologist prefers to secure native housing right in the middle of the village as this gives a more natural situation for observation. Without any great effort they can experience the daily routine—the quarrels, disciplining of children, and entertainments of the people-going on all around. Since anthropologists in the field depend for a great share of their information upon what they see, they must be more observant than the average human being and they must also be able to organize and categorize observations.

Much can be learned about a people's way of life from observation alone, but when carefully tied in with interviewing, observation becomes even more valuable. Observations suggest questions or topics for interview as well as serving to verify interview data. Ceremonies can, for example, be described in great detail from observation alone, but what they mean or what is happening may not be completely understood. By questioning knowledgeable members of the culture, the meanings, symbolism, and function of the ceremony may be added to the description. On the other hand, misinformation about a ceremony may be corrected when the anthropologist is permitted to see the event.

Participation in the society's way of life, if properly done, is an excellent way of establishing rapport, but more than that, by actually helping to build a house or canoe, by helping out with work in the fields, the anthropologist begins to understand the people's problems and his descriptions of the culture are in some degree more from their point of view. It should be remembered, however, that participation in a culture does not add up to "going native." Regardless of what anthropologists might believe, they can never truly become a part of the culture they are studying, and they will be more respected if they live as tolerant but respectable representatives of their own culture, governing their behavior by their own cultural norms but with a sensitivity to those of the hosts.

They should be sensitive to just how far they can go in their participation. The amount of participation permitted often varies according to the sophistication of the people in regard to strangers. Even very acculturated people have confidential areas of culture. Good fieldworkers will realize this and not insist on going where they are not wanted. In comparing his opportunity to participate in Nuer and Azande culture, E. E. Evans-Pritchard writes:

> Azande would not allow me to live as one of themselves; Nuer would not allow me to live otherwise. Among Azande I was compelled to live outside the community; among Nuer I was compelled to be a member of it. Azande treated me as a superior; Nuer as an equal. (1940:15)

ACCEPTANCE BY THE GROUP

Before any field researcher can begin to participate in the culture he/she must, of course, be accepted by the people. A number of avenues of approach have been used successfully. In Samoa, the role of the anthropologist is well-known, and they welcome him/her as the *a'o a'o aganu'u* (one who studies the customs of the country), but in many areas the fieldworker must communicate satisfactorily the reason to move in with notebooks, cameras, and tape recorder. In some cultures the role of teacher has proved the best to assume—there to study their way of life because one's students are particularly interested in knowing about them. Equally effective has been the assumption of a role of historian who wants to write a history of the culture so their own grandchildren may know how people lived in the "old days." This approach is becoming an increasingly effective explanation, for more and more people, under the contact of the West, are realizing that their traditional customs are slowly being lost.

THE LANGUAGE

Of equal importance with participation and observation is the acquiring of information through interviews with native informants. This aspect of fieldwork, of course, immediately involves us in the rather serious problem of how this communication is to take place. The problem is greatly increased by the fact that in 90 percent of the cases the people will speak languages that cannot be learned in college courses or through the aid of language records. Some ethnographers maintain that learning the native language is desirable but not essential, since in most areas where fieldwork is likely to be carried on there are school teachers, or other educated persons who can serve as interpreters. The majority of anthropologists, however, feel that it is absolutely essential that the ethnographer have an adequate grasp of the native language so that checks might be made on interpreters, or even that work might proceed in the native tongue without the use of interpreters. One Australian anthropologist, R. G. Crocombe, has stated this quite emphatically:

> It is my firm belief that top class fieldwork cannot be done anywhere without a good knowledge of the language. I have seen many fieldworkers try to do without it, and construct formidable rationals for not learning the language, and from an examination of their work as well as from my own experience I am of the opinion that a fieldworker who is not prepared to learn the language should not be allowed into the field (at least not sponsored by any reputable institution). (Holmes 1962:5–6)

The struggle of anthropologists with native languages is usually one of their greatest tribulations. Clyde Kluckhohn, who was one of America's most outstanding anthropologists, claimed that he spoke Navaho only imperfectly, although he had been actively involved in learning and using the language for 25 years. While it is difficult for any anthropologist to attain proficiency in a native language in a one-year field trip, there are some definite advantages in making an effort. Margaret Mead (1939) points out that a few words of greeting, a sign of recognition at the mention of a technical cliché uttered in the native tongue make all the difference as to whether the anthropologist is accepted as a sympathetic visitor or an unwanted intruder.

THE KEY INFORMANT

Regardless of whether the anthropologist has decided to use an interpreter or to learn to speak the language there is the knotty problem of from whom to get information. An anthropological fieldworker seldom must proceed in the manner of the sociologist—ascertaining the composition of the population and making up a representative sample. In a small primitive community composed of, say, 300 people almost any intelligent knowledgeable person will know much of the way of life of the community and can serve as a representative sample of the people. Great care must be exercised in choosing such

Interviewing a key informant in American Samoa.

people since it is always possible to select a deviant who will not share the values of other societal members.

There is no rule of thumb as to how many informants must be used to ensure a good study. This depends to a great extent on the knowledge of the informants and the nature of the research. If the anthropologist is primarily interested in magico-medical lore and there is only one practitioner in the society, then that person will of necessity be the sole informant. In most studies, however, several persons should be used for cross-checks and verification of data. Since the anthropologist is essentially concerned with documenting regularities and shared behavior patterns, a few well-chosen key informants might be sufficient to communicate the general cultural patterns that prevail within the society. The success of the research does not depend so much on how many informants are used but rather on their proper selection.

As the research with a few well-chosen informants proceeds, it will often be necessary to consult specialists. In many societies there are religious specialists, professional fishermen, commercial traders, or specially qualified craftsmen. While one's key informant will probably know how to build a house, he doesn't know the fine details that are known only to professional carpenters. A good key informant will often tell the anthropologist who is best able to provide accurate and detailed information in these specialized areas. In time, the research will usually become a collaboration between anthropologists and their key informants. While working with the ethnographer, many informants develop a very keen interest in their own culture and do everything in their power to help the field worker describe it accurately and completely.

NONDIRECTIVE AND DIRECTIVE INTERVIEWING

In working with informants the ethnographer utilizes two types of interview, (1) the nondirective or open-ended interview and (2) the directive. The first type involves asking the informant to discuss a general area of culture. Typical questions might be "Tell me about your life as a child" or "Explain to me how your family is organized" or "Describe the religious beliefs of your people."

The nondirective interview is frequently used in the early phases of research as it allows informants to discuss freely the things that seem important to them. It brings to light many things that the anthropologists might overlook because of a lack of an equivalent situation in their own culture. One type of nondirective procedure is the collection of autobiographical material. When invited to tell the anthropologist his or her life story, the informant has the opportunity to reveal his or her own personality. For the anthropologist it is a personal document of one individual's values, goals, and motivations. When a variety of such personal documents have been collected, the norms of the society and the extent to which persons are permitted to deviate can be described. Invaluable in culture and personality research, autobiographies also have had great value in discovering dominant patterns of culture.

The directive, or structured, interview involves asking a series of prepared questions that systematically attempt to cover a specific area of the culture. After the anthropologist acquires a general "feel" of the culture by letting informants talk about broad aspects of culture, detailed questions about customs or traditions that might have been mentioned only briefly in the nondirective interviews must be asked. The ethnographer's daily observations will also prompt these specific questions.

Over a period of many years several publications such as *Notes and Queries on Anthropology* (1874), *Outline of Cultural Materials* (1950), *Field Guide to the Ethnological Study of Child Life* (1960), *Ethnocentrism Field Manual* (1973), and others have been developed to aid the anthropologist in framing questions and in making sure that questions are exhaustive in scope. These outlines of cultural content serve as handy *aide-memoire* for the trained anthropologist; questions are seldom taken directly from the books as each culture must have its own custom-tailored schedule of questions. A paragraph from *Notes and Queries* will, however, give the reader a vague idea of the kind of questions asked in the directive interview. On the subject of cooking, the structured interview might run something like this:

> What articles of food are eaten raw? Is food preferred fresh or "high"? Is meat preferred slightly or well cooked? Are there any spots where it is definitely forbidden to cook? Is cooking performed exclusively by one sex, and are there any rites or beliefs connected with it? Is the food for men and women cooked together or separately? (1951:242–3)

In spite of the many aids to interviewing that have been published, structured interrogation in a foreign culture involves many pitfalls for the inexperienced ethnographer. An example of the kind of thing that can occur has been related by S. J. Campbell, who worked in the Tonga Islands of the South Pacific. He warns that in response to a question like "Weren't these slabs used for burials?" the native would probably answer "Yes" but actually mean that they were not. Campbell points out (Holmes 1962:12) that in a case like this "The 'Yes' agrees with your statement equivalent which was 'These slabs were not used for burials.' " Another problem involved in getting accurate information is, strangely enough, the amiability of the natives. Most informants are very friendly and anxious to please. If they think the interrogator would like a certain answer, they are quite willing to give it in order to please, even if it is incorrect. To avoid this kind of thing, the ethnographer must always avoid the leading question.

HYPOTHETICAL SITUATION

As part of the interview situation the ethnographer can often use the "hypothetical situation" to good advantage. This technique, which has been discussed at some length by veteran ethnographer M. J. Herskovits, represents a method of getting information about practices or traditions without making reference to specific persons, places, or events. It is, for example, more judicial to ask "What would happen if a boy were caught stealing bananas from someone's land?" than to ask "I understand your cousin got caught stealing last year. What happened to him?"

Herskovits points out that the hypothetical situation

> brings forth responses that are in the nature of projections of the informant's experience against the background of his culture, it affords the investigator a heightened sensitivity to those relations of person to person in the group being studied. . . .

By this method the informant is

> released to tell of happenings to himself or to others that, in any other terms, he would be loath to reveal were he naming "actual" persons. Thus both in the personal and the cultural sense, he can go further, and will go

further in expressing reactions than conventions of approved conduct
would otherwise permit. (1950:40)

Success in interviewing is not so much a matter of using specific
techniques, however, as it is developing good rapport between the
interrogator and his informants. As Pacific ethnographer R. G. Crocombe put it, "The only information of value is that which people
give freely. People do not speak freely unless they feel at home with
the interviewer" (1962:8).

Anthropology's Uniqueness

Anthropologists and other social scientists sometimes study the same
kinds of phenomena with much the same methods. For example, W.
Lloyd Warner, an anthropologist, moved from his initial study of Australian aborigines to a lifetime study of social stratification in the
United States. William Foote Whyte, the author of *Street Corner Society*, identifies himself as a sociologist but admits that most of his
research methods might best be labeled "anthropological." Although
anthropologists and other social scientists occasionally invade one
another's territory, anthropology as a discipline advocates a somewhat less statistical, more personal approach. It seeks to document
patterns of behavior while sociology is more concerned with particulars of behavior. Anthropology tends to sacrifice precision for significance.

A comparison of the methodology of anthropology and that of
the other social sciences is brought into clear focus by the following
parable by John W. M. Whiting:

An anthropologist has just returned from studying the Mbongo-
Mbongo and is having a drink with some of his friends, one of whom is an
experimental psychologist, another a sociologist and the third a psychoanalyst. After the first drink and the amenities have been exchanged, the anthropologist says, "Say, let me tell you what I found out on my field trip!"
and gives an impassioned and enthusiastic account of some of his findings.
When he has finished, all his friends show polite interest, and then comment as follows:

THE EXPERIMENTAL PSYCHOLOGIST: "Your ideas are very interesting, but
let me ask you some details. Just what was your independent variable, and what control groups did you run?"
THE SOCIOLOGIST: "Yes, and I would like to ask you something too. I've
often been worried about anthropological field work. Tell me, what
was your sample size, and was it random or stratified?"

And you can guess what the psychoanalyst said.

> The anthropologist, of course, has to admit that he has met none of their criteria but replies with some anger, "Have any of you ever lived with your subjects for two years?" (1960:150–51)

Researching Our Own Tribe

Today anthropologists, often in league with sociologists, psychologists, and political scientists have broadened their perspective to include the study of their own (American) cities, neighborhoods, occupational subgroups, ethnic enclaves, and class identities. It is not a bit unusual these days to see anthropological monographs entitled *Fun City: An Ethnographic Study of a Retirement Community; The Cocktail Waitress: Woman's Work in a Man's World; The Vice Lords: Warriors of the Streets; The Portland Longshoremen: A Dispersed Urban Community; You Owe Yourself a Drunk: An Ethnography of Urban Nomads.*

SURVEY
RESEARCH AND
QUESTIONNAIRES

As anthropologists move into more literate and urban communities for their investigations they have sometimes felt the need for methods which are more quantitive and can obtain information from a larger number of informants than is possible through traditional participant observation/informal interview techniques. This is frequently achieved through the use of survey techniques and questionnaires. The *survey* is an investigation wherein a representative sample is queried on a series of precise questions, the answers to which may be utilized to assess "public opinion" on particular issues, or behavioral responses to certain social situations. Questions are carefully standardized, and everyone is asked the same questions. This makes it possible to do computer analyses of the data to derive elaborate statistical measurements of the groups' responses.

Questionnaires are frequently used in survey research but their usefulness depends upon the respondents' ability to read and write. In Western communities questionnaires are usually mailed to respondents who in turn return them by mail, but distribution and collection often pose a serious problem in non-Western societies. Also, people attempting to answer the questions may not understand them but, of course, have no one to clarify the meaning. While anthropologists sometimes use this method of data collection to elicit information on particular issues from particular segments of the population, they almost always combined it with other investigative techniques.

SOCIAL
NETWORKS

If an anthropologist is studying a remote village or an island society the concept of community is not difficult since the boundaries can be clearly defined. The community consists of the people who live together within a certain area and who interact on a day-to-day, face-to-face basis. But once anthropologists begin to move into plural societies and urban settings the situation becomes complicated, particularly if it is a highly integrated society. The viable community is represented by only a network of social and economic linkages or cliques. Since every individual plays many roles—for example, worker, worshipper, father, son, bowling team member, lodge member, friend—each of these identities connects the individual with others. Thus the community of interaction may be highly covert and may be discovered only through social network or interaction analysis.

The problems of network analysis are described by J. A. Barnes as follows, "The study of networks calls for information about a plurality of persons who are in contact with one another, and consequently the traditional methods of selecting respondents individually are inadequate" (1972:23). Social networks are interconnecting links among chains of individuals who do not sort out into bounded groups. They are personal networks that members of a society utilize in trying to realize personal goals.

POSTULATE ANALYSIS

One method which Adamson Hoebel suggests for understanding the basic principles on which a modern society is built is to use *postulates.* He defines *postulates* as "ethnographically derived distinctions made in each culture," and maintains that "every society must of necessity choose a limited number of behavior possibilities for incorporation in its culture, and it must peremptorily and arbitrarily reject the admissibility for its own members of those lines of behavior which are incompatible with its selected lines as well as those which are merely different" (1954:12).

The postulates are *norms* and *preferences* of a society. They are indications of what is and also what ought to be. Since the study of large impersonal societies cannot always use simple one-to-one observation of behavior coupled with informal or formal interview, Hsu suggests the following sources for deriving postulates:

1. Writing on social, religious and educational philosophies and ethics;
2. Laws and legal trends;
3. Literary works (such as novels) and their most frequent problems and solutions;[1]
4. Advice books and columns;
5. Sociological and anthropological researches;

---

[1] And we might add analysis of comics, food preferences, sports interests, and perhaps architecture. See chapter 8.

6. Studies on abnormality, crime and other forms of breakdown;

7. Personal experience.

Hsu goes on to explain the postulate research technique as follows: "In making use of such data it is essential to check one source against another for correspondence or disagreement. Postulates flow from the points of convergence among the various sources" (1969:63). And what, we might ask, are some of the American postulates that might be gleaned from this procedure? The following are a few listed by Hsu.

> **Postulate 1:** An individual's most important concern is self-interest: self-expression, self-development, self-gratification, and independence. This takes precedence over all group interests.
>
> **Postulate 2:** The privacy of the individual is the individual's inalienable right. Intrusion into it by others is permitted only by his invitation.
>
> **Postulate 3:** Because the government exists for the benefit of the individual and not vice versa, all forms of authority, including government, are suspect. But the government and its symbols should be respected. Patriotism is good.
>
> **Postulate 4:** An individual's success in life depends upon his acceptance among his peers.
>
> **Postulate 5:** An individual should believe or acknowledge God and should belong to an organized church or other religious institution. Religion is good. Any religion is better than no religion.
>
> **Postulate 6:** Men and women are equal.
>
> **Postulate 7:** All human beings are equal.
>
> **Postulate 8:** Progress is good and inevitable.

Ethnosemantics

Another recent approach to data collection has developed out of linguistics and the *emic/etic* differentiation and has become known as the New Ethnography, or *ethnosemantics*. Believing that culture is "the knowledge people use to generate and interpret social behavior" (Spradley and McCurdy 1972:8), New Ethnographers attempt to determine a group's knowledge base and the way they utilize that knowledge to organize their behavior. Spradley and McCurdy recommend that "instead of asking, 'What do I see these people doing?' we must ask, 'What do these people see themselves doing?' " (1972:9)

Seeking to discover how informants understand and classify their experiences, the investigator begins by recording categories as indicated in the people's language. Spradley and McCurdy explain, "Every category of person, place, time or object simplifies our world. Once a person is placed in a category, be it 'student,' 'professor,' 'shaman,' or 'mother's brother' it is easier to anticipate his behavior" (1972:60).

After establishing major categories, that is, objects, acts, or people who are treated as equivalents, the next step is investigation of *inclusion*. Let us say that the category we have established in our investigation is *tramps*. Spradley, who has done extensive research on these homeless nomads, has discovered that there are eight varieties of tramp and that one of the varieties, *working stiff*, has five inclusions—mainly "harvest tramp," "tramp miner," "fruit tramp," "construction tramp," and "sea tramp."

If, on the other hand, we were to establish a category of food, "the goal of the anthropologist is to discover how his informant classifies and sorts . . . terms into a taxonomy of food. He wants to know what characteristics an apple and a banana share that make Americans consider them to be members of the more general category fruit. . . . For this information the anthropologist can build both a system of classification and the rules for the classification" (Edgerton and Langness 1974:38). The people who utilize this kind of methodology assume that the categories detectable through analysis of language reflect what is important to a people and the way they encode reality.

Quantification

Traditionally, cultural anthropology has fallen far short of her sister discipline sociology in the quantification of data. There has never been a strong tradition in cultural anthropology of framing problems in quantitative terms, and many anthropologists, interested in humanistic or historical problems, have expressed contempt for quantitative field measurements. In general, however, anthropology is becoming more scientific and more quantitative. More and more anthropologists are maintaining that if anthropology is ever to make a major contribution to the knowledge of human behavior, data must be more comparable and measurable.

Although there have been early examples of statistical analysis of cultural materials (Tylor's adhesions in 1889 and Boas's use of chi square in folklore analysis in 1895), it has not been until quite recently that there has been a major breakthrough in the use of truly scientific methods of control and analysis of field data. In Clyde Kluckhohn's study of Navaho ceremonial participation he states why a quantitative field approach is necessary. He writes:

> In anthropological literature one continually reads such statements as the following: "The Navaho are a very religious people," or more specifically, "The Navaho spend a great deal of their time in ceremonials." It would seem to me interesting and perhaps useful to examine such statements as these on the basis of fairly full information about this particular group of Navaho during a particular period of time. (1938:359)

In his research on this subject, Kluckhohn found:

1. One summer 41 individuals spent a total of 93 days attending 4 different Enemy Way ceremonials.
2. From March 15 to September 15, 9 singers spent 62 days in conducting 20 ceremonials.
3. Twenty out of 69 adult men of the community conduct ceremonials and 9 women and 7 men serve as diagnosticians in the healing ceremonies.
4. The most popular ceremonial singer participated in 29 ceremonials, totaling 81 days, during the 6-month period.
5. In this period there were 148 ceremonials with a time involvement of 389 nights (more than one might be going on in a single night).

As a result of his detailed observations and interviews, Kluckhohn could do more than just comment in a general way on Navaho religiosity or ceremonial involvement. Instead he could state, ". . . During this six month period, the average adult man in the community spent 0.32 of his waking hours in ceremonial activity, the average adult woman, 0.18" (1938:364).

Quantitative measurement of a different type but no less important was that utilized by Oscar Lewis of the daily round of activities of a Mexican family in Tepoztlan or by Thomas Weisner of Kenyan children's social behavior (See Field Observation Protocol, Table 2). Lewis carefully recorded the activities of each and every member of the family throughout the day, giving precise amounts of time devoted to each of their activities. The presentation of these data in the form of a chart allows anyone to see at a glance (1) the family division of labor, (2) tasks performed individually or shared by the family, (3) exact time allotted to work, rest, and recreation, etc. The Wiesner chart utilizes a similar technique although the observation is more limited in scope. Their methods are much more effective than the usual type of generalization that appears in most anthropological monographs. While the generalizations may be correct, they often lack the precise quality that will make them valuable in comparative analysis.

TABLE 1   A synchronic record of the activities of each member of a Tepoztlan family (Lewis 1951:63)

	Father	Mother	Eldest daughter	Second daughter	Youngest daughter
A.M.					
6:00–6:30	In bed	Rises, makes fire and coffee	In bed	In bed	In bed
6:30–7:00	Rises, feeds cattle, takes them to pasture	Goes to buy bread, sweeps patio	Rises, sweeps kitchen, prepares utensils	Rises, goes for milk	In bed
7:00–7:30	Drinks coffee	Serves husband and self coffee	Grinds corn, makes tortillas	Drinks coffee, cuts and stores fish	Rises, washes, combs hair
7:30–8:00	Hauls water, shells corn for mules	Resumes sweeping patio	Grinds corn, makes tortillas	Smooths and folds laundered clothes	Breakfasts
8:00–8:30	Breakfasts	Combs hair, breakfasts, serves others	Grinds corn, makes tortillas	Breakfasts	Goes to school
8:30–9:00	Talks with investigator	Cuts squash for animals, cooks squash, shells corn	Grinds corn, makes tortillas	Makes beds	At school
9:00–9:30	Goes to bed	Arranges squash in market basket	Breakfasts	Sweeps porch	At school
9:30–10:00	In bed	Arranges squash in market basket	Washes dishes	Washes arms and feet, combs hair	At school
10:00–10:30	In bed	Goes to market to sell corn and squash	Prepares corn for grinding	Accompanies mother to market to make purchases	At school
10:30–11:00	In bed	At market	Prepares and cooks stew	At market	At school
11:00–11:30	In bed	At market	Prepares and cooks stew	At market	At school
11:30–12:00	In bed	At market	Prepares and cooks stew	Returns home, polishes nails	At school

P.M.					
12:00–12:30	Feeds mules	At market	Grinds corn	Talks with recorder	Returns home
12:30–1:00	Rests	At market	Makes tortillas	Feeds chickens	Does nothing
1:00–1:30	Rests	Returns home, prepares lunch	Makes tortillas	Helps making tortillas	Does nothing
1:30–2:00	Eats and talks with recorder	Serves and eats	Makes tortillas	Eats	Eats
2:00–2:30	Eats and talks with recorder	Serves and eats	Eats	Eats	Goes to school
2:30–3:00	Reads prayers	Serves and eats	Eats	Sews	At school
3:00–3:30	Goes to bed	Hauls water for animals	Washes dishes	Sews	At school
3:30–4:00	In bed	In bed	Washes dishes	Sews	At school
4:00–4:30	In bed	Cleans dried gourds	Shells corn, prepares dough	Sews	At school
4:30–5:00	Reads prayers	Cleans dried gourds	Shells corn, prepares dough	Sews	At school
5:00–5:30	In bed	Cleans dried gourds	Mends her clothes	Sews	Returns home
5:30–6:00	In bed	Feeds turkeys	Mends her clothes	Sews	Reads
6:00–6:30	In bed	Cuts squash for animals	Knits	Sews	Talks to friends
6:30–7:00	In bed	Mends blouse	Knits	Sews	Talks to friends
7:00–7:30	In bed	Goes to visit mother	Grinds corn	Goes for bread	Knits
7:30–8:00	In bed	Sits in kitchen, talks with girls	Makes tortillas	Prepares coffee	Knits
8:00–8:30	Gets up for coffee	Serves coffee to family and self	Eats	Eats	Eats
8:30–9:00	Goes to bed, takes medicine and foot bath	Prepares medicinal drink and foot bath for husband	Washes dishes	Knits	Knits
9:00–9:30	In bed	Goes to bed	Goes to bed	Knits	Knits
9:30–10:00	In bed	In bed	In bed	Goes to bed	Goes to bed

TABLE 2 Field observation protocol used by Thomas Weisner in Kenyan children study

FIELD OBSERVATION PROTOCOL

Name _____ Charles _____ Sex __1__ Age _8_ Date _21-8-72_

17208   Name   30

Homestead & ID _____ Observer _____ Time elapsed _____

Time	Personnel		Activity	Location/Act Act	Behavior Code	
		Sequence				
12:30	S-17208		P. talks with John and Geof		Yard	
12:31	O-17207		about playing football			
	17209			01	SO	02
	17202					
	S-17208		P. and John start pulling	02	PL	00
	O-17207		each other and laughing			
		S1				
12:32	S-17202		Ma tells them to be careful		ST	01
	O-17208		not to hurt Pat		PS	03
	17207			03	C	01
		S9				
	S-17208		P. and John continue talk-	04	SM	08
	O-17207	S1	ing. P. asks John to come		C	01
			with him. John complies			
12:33	S-17206		P. and John pick up some	05	SI	01
	17207		leaves and talk to Ma about		EG	03
	O-17202	S9	them. Ma C.		C	01
12:34	S-17208		P. asks Geof for sugar cane	06	EG	052
	O-17209		to eat. Geof C.		C	1
	S-17208		P. tells John to take soap	07	ST	01
	O-17207				NC	14
		S1			PS	01
					CH	01
	S-17202		Ma says no	08	ST	02
	O-17208				EG	11
		S9				
	S-17202		Ma tells P. to get the basket.	09	PS	01
	O-17208		P. does not hear		C	07
12:35	S-17208		P. stands near Oba fiddling	10	IN	00
			with stick and stands			
			around			
12:36	S-17208		P. asks Peter to play foot-	11	ST	01
	O-17206		ball. Peter says nothing		SM	08
					NC	06

TABLE 2   (*cont.*)

Time	Personnel		Activity	Location/Act		
				Act	Behavior	Code
		Sequence				
	S-17208		P. runs after a sheep and	12	EG	07
	O-00082		hits her		ST	09
					NC	19
	O-99991		John and the kids tell P.	13	SO	01
	S-17208	S1	they are going			
12:37	S-17208		P. looks after them as they	14	IN	11
		S2	move down the path			
	S-17208		P. tells John to wait for	15	SM	08
	O-17207		him. John keeps walking		ST	01
		S9			NC	6

Notes: S = subject of act; P. = child being observed; O = object of act; Ma = Mother of P.; C. = complies (to a mand); NC = non-compliance; ST = style or way in which an act is done by subject; S1 . . . S9 = sequencing of behaviors.

One of the major incentives for collecting measurable and more comparable data has been the availability of electronic computers. Anthropologists Edgerton and Langness see the use of these devices as a revolutionary contribution to the science of anthropology. They state:

> Aided by the growth of computer technology, they (i.e. anthropologists) were able to develop new methods for use in making cross-cultural comparisons of a large number of societies. Comparison enabled them to test their explanations of the influence of such factors as environmental conditions, child-rearing practices, or technological knowledge on various other aspects of culture, in order to produce better theories about man and culture. (1974:94)

The Genealogical Method

Another traditional method that allows a concrete and analytical approach to abstract phenomena is the genealogical method developed by W. H. R. Rivers, a British anthropologist, in 1910. The method consists of diagramming (see Fig. 13—1) the kinship relationships of every individual in the group as many generations back as they can remember, noting those living and dead, as well as those residing outside the community. The value of this method is, in Rivers's own words, as follows:

> The genealogical method makes it possible to investigate abstract problems on a purely concrete basis. It is even possible by its means to formulate laws regulating the lives of people which they have probably never formulated for themselves. (1910: *passim*)

With the genealogical method it is possible to study marriage regulations, laws of descent and property inheritance, succession to chieftainship, ceremonial functions of particular relatives, and even such biological data as ratio of sexes, fecundity, and mortality. Aside from the concrete information it provides, the genealogical method gives the anthropologist a wealth of general background data and also aids in establishing rapport with subjects. As *Notes and Queries* states,

> The data in the genealogies will not only give the investigator the names and relationship to one another of all those whom he will meet in daily work, but will further give him information about individuals not present in the community. Such knowledge is a great asset. There are few people who are not flattered by the personal attention that is shown to them when greeted by their correct names; the skilled fieldworker will use the data he has gained from a few informants to make many more personal contacts (1951:50).

Village Mapping

A valuable companion to the genealogical diagram is the village or regional map that the anthropologist constructs to record the plan of village housing, agricultural land, and fishing or hunting territories of the group. If there is individually or family-owned land ownership or use, the boundaries or divisions are carefully plotted and related to genealogical or census data. Where aerial photographs are available, maps of this type may be constructed for quite large areas. Maps can be valuable contributions to field data for a number of reasons. They force the anthropologist to analyze closely the spatial dimensions of his village, the precise arrangements of habitations of kinsmen, the number, size, and variety of buildings, and the natural features of the area.

The maps included in this chapter, one by the author of a Samoan village, and two by Raymond Firth of a village in Tikopia record quite different details and show how maps can supplement ethnographic field reports. In the sketch of Ta'u village the reader will note the different symbols for houses of traditional native construction and those utilizing European materials and design. Since the latter type of construction represents a departure from indigenous culture methods, the map is useful in measuring one aspect of cultural change. A series of such maps drawn for the same village over a period of years could show the rate of change as well as its direction. The author, for example, returned to Ta'u village 22 years after the map (Fig. 9–1) was made and found that less than two dozen traditional style houses remained of the 133 indicated on the map. Approximately 68 "hurricane houses" stood in their places. Numbers appearing on the map represent separate households. Thus an analysis of the number and type of structures in each household gives some indication of its relative prosperity.

The Tikopia maps are valuable in the study of land tenure, ecology, and the physical-environmental aspects of the culture and the change that can take place in land usage over a period of 23 years.

Technical Aids to Research

Western technology has provided the field anthropologist with a number of devices to increase his/her efficiency in recording ethnographic data. In recent years cameras and tape recorders have become considered almost essential equipment, for, in a manner of speaking, they allow anthropologists to bring a little bit of the culture home. Both still and motion pictures capture events that can be studied again and again. Many times they will provide them with information neglected in the field. If, for example they failed to see how a certain type of lashing was made in house construction, they can have their pictures of housing enlarged and study this technique in detail. Many times a complete set of photographs can be useful to others doing cross-cultural comparisons of certain cultural features. An example of this might be the study of comparative motor behavior from motion pictures with a number of sequences showing native peoples dancing or working. Although the anthropologist who originally recorded the sequences may not have been interested in this aspect of the culture at all, the visual record allows others to analyze this facet of culture without actually going to the area themselves.

No matter how carefully an anthropologist tries to record the details of an intricate ceremony, the motion-picture camera has far greater documentary capabilities. The photographic record is, in effect, a set of notes that will allow the ultimate in precision in writing descriptions of the proceedings. One anthropologist confessed that he "couldn't make head nor tail" out of a particular weaving process he observed and therefore took a movie of the whole procedure so he could figure it out when he got home.

Margaret Mead has also shown that photographs can be ex-

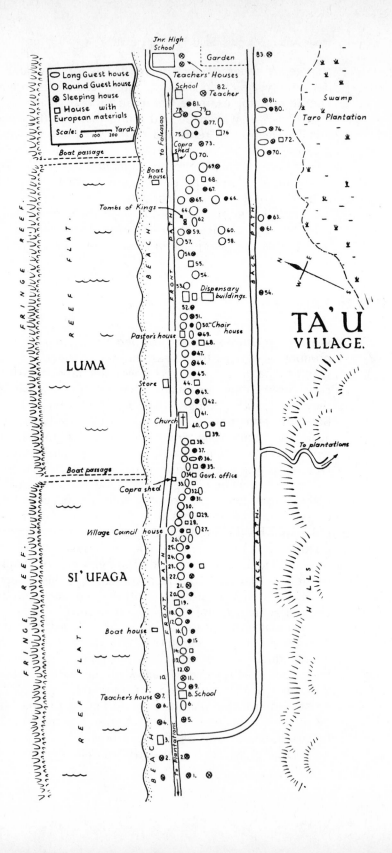

TA'U
VILLAGE.

tremely useful in the study of native personality. In her study of Balinese personality she took hundreds of photographs of body attitudes and facial expressions of people as they expressed love, sympathy, fear, anxiety, or hatred.

A set of still pictures or a reel of movies can become, in effect, museum specimens recording aspects of a culture that have disappeared upon increased contact with the Western world. Many of the details of American Indian house types and costumes are known to modern anthropologists only because of ancient yellowing photographs that have been preserved in museum archives. An interesting set of photographs in this respect is that to be found in Margaret Mead's book *New Lives for Old.* Between her visits in 1928 and in 1953, revolutionary changes took place in the Manus island community described in this volume. The then-and-now photographs clearly show

VILLAGE LAND OWNERSHIP

The following numbers correspond to numbers on the village map and indicate the various families who own the village plots.

1. Lauofo	29. Nua	57. Niumata
2. Seu	30. Mailo	58. Tuumalo
3. Salausa	31. Salevao	59. Aiasau
4. Mua	32. Tuia'ana	60. Seumae
5. Talavale	33. Solia	61. Atiu
6. Su'afo'a	34. Faaea	62. Tafa
7. Mailo	35. Tufele	63. Pese
8. Aufotu	36. Upega	64. Fuatuua
9. Ulugalu	37. Saveena	65. Tulifua
10. Atuelua	38. Lauofo	66. Tago'a'i
11. Salevao	39. Liliu	67. Vivao
12. Leaai	40. Pomele	68. Mua
13. Fualau	41. Liliu	69. Ale
14. Salausa	42. Tuialu'ulu'u	70. Togotogo
15. Tuito'elau	43. Leui	71. Moliga
16. Pomelo	44. Mau'u	72. Tuimanufili
17. Li	45. Faumina	73. Tunupopo
18. Fiame	46. Gaoā	74. Ui
19. Aufotu	47. Siva	75. Taula
20. Savini	48. Manulauti	76. Ale
21. Pomele	49. Ioelu	77. Tauala
22. Seu	50. Tiāligo	78. Gogo
23. Aufotu	51. Lepolo	79. Maui
24. Mua	52. Taule'ale'a	80. Moliga
25. Atuelua	53. Milo	81. Ve'a
26. Sei	54. Lemau	82. Vivao
27. Lefiti	55. Faumina	83. Ve'a
28. Se'a	56. Taua	

Figure 9-1 (From Holmes, 1957).

Figure 9-2 Cultivation in Rakisu. (From *Social Change in Tikopia* by Raymond Firth. Copyright 1959 by Allen & Unwin Publishers, Ltd. and reproduced with their permission.)

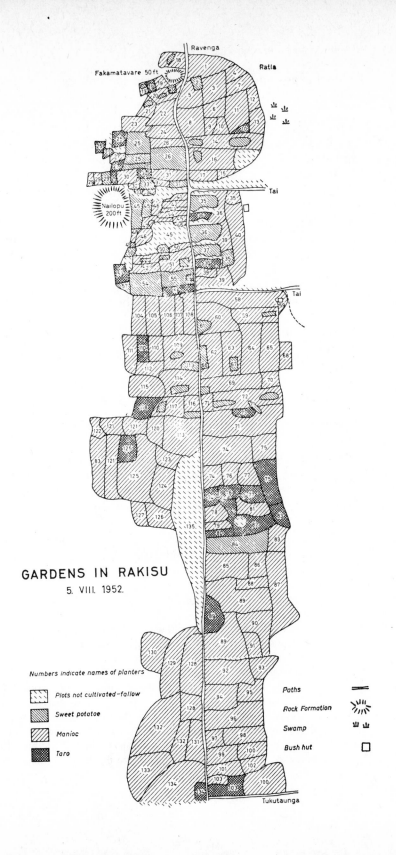

GARDENS IN RAKISU

5. VIII. 1952.

Numbers indicate names of planters

Plots not cultivated - fallow

Sweet potatoe

Manioc

Taro

Paths

Rock Formation

Swamp

Bush hut

the changes and record for all time the culture of 1928, which is no more.

The tape recorder is a new addition to the fieldworker's set of scientific gadgets, but it has great research possibilities. Kenneth Emory of Bishop Museum in Honolulu states that "the tape recorder is the greatest boon to the field worker" (Holmes 1962:6). He points out that a recorder enables the anthropologist to get native text (useful in linguistic analysis) and samples of music for ethnomusicological research. Emory also suggests that the tape recorder might prove extremely valuable in the interview situation, especially if the fieldworker is having difficulty using the native language. He recommends, "Let them talk freely. You can miss much at the start before you have the language in hand, but later you can go back on this record" (1962:6). While the fieldworker is frequently in an area where electrical power is not available, this is no great obstacle to using a recorder, since a number of small battery-operated instruments have been developed which are adequate for research purposes.

The Goal of Anthropological Research

We have mentioned only a few of the more traditional anthropological field methods; there are many others, and as anthropology matures as a discipline many more methods will be developed to ensure more penetrating and productive research. Although the ways and means of studying cultures may be refined, the anthropologist will continue to pursue the goal that was described as early as 1922 by the British anthropologist Malinowski. It is

> to grasp the native's point of view, his relation to life, to realise *his* vision of *his* world. We have to study man, and we must study what concerns him most intimately, that is, the hold which life has on him. In each culture, the values are slightly different; people aspire after different aims, follow different impulses, yearn after a different form of happiness. In each culture, we find different institutions in which man pursues his life-interest, different customs by which he satisfies his aspirations, different codes of law and morality which reward his virtues or punish his defections. To study the institutions, customs, and codes or to study the behaviour and mentality without the subjective desire of feeling by what these people live, of realising the substance of their happiness—is, in my opinion, to miss the greatest reward which we can hope to obtain from the study of man. (1961:25)

Summary

Although more and more anthropologists are studying their own society today, they have traditionally studied other cultures to acquire data concerning the total range of cultural activities characteristic of human beings. Anthropology continues to be comparative, relativistic, and holistic in its approach and therefore it requires a particular set of investigative techniques. The most important of these are participant observation and interview.

To live among a people and participate as fully as possible in their lifestyle gives the anthropologist insights into what it is like to be a member of that society. This is often referred to as the *emic* perspective. Interview is also important, for investigators sometimes do not completely understand what they are seeing or how it should be interpreted. There is also a great deal of important information about a culture which cannot be observed at all—ways of categorizing reality, attitudes and feelings, and worldview. With interview come the problems of learning the local language, choosing appropriate informants, and phrasing questions to ensure useful and reliable information. Technological equipment like tape recorders and cameras aid in the collection of valuable ethnographic data, but the most important factor in successful fieldwork is the establishment and maintenance of good rapport with the people by a sensitive, well-trained, and perceptive anthropologist.

Culture and Personality 10

Cultural change and psychological response
Revitalization movements
Acculturation and modernization
Samoan Personality—a diachronic analysis

The study of personality is commonly thought to be the prerogative of the psychologists, but for some 30 or 40 years anthropologists have been interested in the development of personality, particularly from the point of view of how it is influenced by the forces of culture. More than any other scientist, the anthropologist has been struck by the many directions that personality development can take throughout the world. Observing that behavior and temperament can be radically different from one place to another, the anthropologist has become very wary of such popular statements as "It's just human nature to want to get ahead," or "Human nature being what it is, what can you expect." While the layperson glibly makes such pronouncements, students of anthropology, who have been able to view many cultures, would doubt that as far as temperament and behavior are concerned, there is any such thing as a common "human nature" shared by all. People who assume that "human nature" is the same everywhere are so involved in their own ways of life that they begin to feel that everything they do is natural for the species. Perhaps a much more valid term to refer to the way people typically think and act and feel in a given culture would be "cultural nature." A culture may shape a person to be selfish, generous, mild, pugnacious, cooperative, modest, or boastful. Margaret Mead found that culture can even influence the behavior and personality which are considered masculine or feminine in a society.

Because the term "human nature" has been erroneously used does not mean that it is a bad concept; on the contrary, it is a useful concept if used correctly. In order to understand the relationship between human nature and cultural nature let us look at the following statement by Kluckhohn and Murray:

> Every man is in certain respects
>   a. like all other men,
>   b. like some other men,
>   c. like no other man. (1949:35)

Like All Other Men

People are in certain respects like all other people in that they *do* have a human nature. This is the nature of the human animal arising out of the fact that Man is one species and shares the same kind of basic physiology. It is the nature of human beings to experience live birth, feel pain, meet with hunger, respond to feelings of sexual excitement, weaken with age, and finally die. The human animal walks upright on the earth; it does not burrow in the ground, live in the trees or under the sea, or fly through the air under its own power like the birds. People have a certain set of needs that must be met, certain physical and mental limitations, and certain abilities. At the moment of birth, every child of every race and culture inherits these needs, abilities and limitations; they are its heritage as a human, its human nature. From that moment on, however, this bundle of raw material will be shaped by its group and its culture. The processes of developing a human being might be compared to the process of a sculptor carving a statue out of wood. The sculptor knows the limitations and strengths of his material, and must work in terms of its nature. By observing certain precautions, the sculptor can develop a finished product. Two sculptors, however, both working in terms of the nature of the same raw material, might fashion quite different products, one producing a heavy and strong figure, the other a delicate, fragile, and beautiful one. The two figures will be alike in some respects—in their material, with its color and grain, but they will also differ greatly in their appearance due to the different approaches of the two artists. For human beings, this development of a finished product from a raw material amounts to growing up in a culture with its own unique material artifacts, ideologies, system of family, and configuration of values.

Like Some Other Men

Since all people in a given society share much the same culture, they will have had similar experiences and therefore can be expected to demonstrate similarities in personality. Even in very heterogeneous cultures fellow members share a common language with its inherent values and a similar ideological orientation. In less heterogeneous cultures they will have experienced a similar childhood training experience. Keeping in mind that culture is but one of many forces helping to mold personality, let us look at the experiences of the Alorese child learning the culture and see how it helps shape adult behavior.

ALORESE CULTURE AND PERSONALITY

Alor is an island in Indonesia, but its inhabitants are Oceanic Negroes. The village of Atimelang, lying high on a volcanic ridge, was the site of one of the first detailed studies of culture and personality carried out by a cultural anthropologist. The investigator, Cora DuBois, reports that these people are agriculturalists, deriving their daily food requirements primarily from corn, peas, rice, and squash and occasionally from chickens, pigs, and dogs. The women are the principal cultivators, and the men concern themselves mainly with raising pigs. The village is largely self-sufficient, but food is a source of much anxiety. The people might be described as highly materialistic, and every trading transaction within the society involves the expectation of profit. There is very little hospitality. Wealth determines status, and marriage is accompanied by financial exchanges of dowry and bride price.

The child growing up in this society experiences many frustrations, the most severe being connected with food. Since the women are the tillers of the soil, and thus are frequently away from the village, small children are placed in the care of older siblings, who are often careless about providing them with nourishment. Weaning is described as being done "gradually and simply by pushing the child gently away from the breast" (1961:40). The overly insistent child, however, is likely to get slapped. Should these measures not prove sufficient, the child is taken to live in the household of a relative for a few nights.

Toilet-training is also described as a gradual and easy process. An occasional child may get a rap on the head with the mother's knuckles for his lack of control, but generally this aspect of training is rather smooth and without incident. Alorese parents appear to be little concerned about whether or not their offspring get sufficient rest. Lack of proper bedtimes and numerous sleep-disturbing activities in the average household result in children learning to sleep whenever and wherever they can.

Discipline often involves shaming, ridiculing, and even frightening children by brandishing knives and threatening to cut off ears or hands. While children are not, in general, treated harshly, the kind of discipline is so inconsistent that they are never able to "establish a clear image of punishment for 'being bad' or reward for 'being good.' They are just as likely as not to be rewarded for the 'badness' of excessive crying" (1961:51). There is little in the way of rewards for being good, and on such occasions when children are promised a reward for good behavior, the promise is rarely kept.

Rages and tantrums are commonplace among the children of this society, a common cause being desertion by the mother when she leaves to work in the fields. Like discipline in general, her reaction to the wailing child is one of inconsistency. Concerning the mother's responses DuBois writes, "On successive days I have noted her ignore him, return to comfort him, return to slap him, and return pretending to stay for the day, only to slip away when he had been diverted" (1961:51).

Later childhood is a period when some of the child's earlier anxieties are reinforced. Food still remains a problem. Children are fed at

7 A.M. and 7 P.M. but between these hours they have to learn to forage for themselves. In time, they learn any number of ingenious ways, including theft, of getting midday nourishment. Parents are not above appropriating the property of their children, who must stand helplessly by without any source of redress. Another cause of frustration among prepuberty children is the continuation of teasing, ridicule, and deception as a form of both discipline and amusement. DuBois records, "I have seen youths in their late teens and early twenties send boys on fool's errands and deceive them with false promises of rewards for services, and then guffaw with laughter when the crestfallen child returned" (1961:65).

The consequence of such behavior is that lying is taken as a matter of course and to call a person a liar is not an insult or a reproach but merely a statement of fact. While children in late childhood no longer are deceived by bogeymen stories or threats of amputating ears or hands, they respond to suggestions that they will be sold into slavery. There is little in this period of their development that would allow them to develop feelings of trust or loyalty toward others, and "the lack of training and praise, as well as the presence of teasing, ridicule, and fear, combined with lack of privileges and esteem, must create in the child an essential distrust of itself" (1961:79).

As the child approaches adulthood, it is possible to see the effect of childhood cultural experiences on its attitudes and behavior toward marriage partners. As young men begin their search for a wife, they unconsciously, or consciously in some cases, seek a mother image. As her chief interpreter related to Cora DuBois, "Wives are like our mothers. When we were small our mothers fed us. When we are grown our wives cook for us" (1961:96). Since women do most of the farming, they tend also to be the backbone of the economy.

One of the many problems in Alor relationships, however, is that the male tends to be somewhat ambivalent toward his "mother image," for childhood recollections of the mother are not altogether pleasant ones. Mother was a somewhat unreliable and uncertain provider. Women, on the other hand, are somewhat reticent to accept the role of provider with its greater economic responsibilities, especially where this added burden brings little increase in status. In order to obtain a wife, a young man must produce a rather substantial bride price, which is paid to her kinsmen, and frequently a new bride will refuse her husband sexual privileges if his financial arrangements with her family have not been satisfactorily settled. Wealth is of great importance both in obtaining a good provider and in establishing self-esteem, through freedom from dependency on the woman. Thus, DuBois concludes that "the culture fosters a linkage of food, sex, and wealth. All three of these are associated with many avenues of possible frustrations and prepare the ground for instability and distrust in the marital relationship" (1961:115).

Keeping the cultural experiences of the Alorese childhood, adolescence, and young adulthood in mind it is interesting to note some of the more commonly found personality characteristics of adults. Abram Kardiner, a psychiatrist who analyzed much of DuBois's data, finds the following traits to be typical: (1) anxiety, (2) suspicion, (3) mistrustfulness, (4) lack of self-confidence, (5) lack of strong parental fixations, (6) over-valuation of sex and food, (7) lack of enterprise, and (8) repressed hatred.

The DuBois study did not take into consideration only the very early years of the child's life—the period of toilet-training and weaning—but also considered how personality was built through an interaction of an individual with the culture and with other individuals over a period of some twenty years.

Childhood Experiences

There has been a tendency in studies of culture and personality in past years to rely heavily on the theories of Sigmund Freud that personality formation is almost entirely determined by the child's early experience in weaning, toilet-training, and discipline. Geoffrey Gorer, for example, maintains that behavioral patterns established early in life influence subsequent learning. Thus Gorer feels that experiences of early childhood must be carefully documented. Attitudes of a child toward father and mother and siblings will greatly influence attitudes toward others met later in life. In one study of the personality characteristics of the peasants of Great Russia, Gorer postulated that many adult personality traits could be related to the fact that as infants the average peasant was swaddled with long strips of cloth that restricted movement of the limbs.

The rationale behind this approach is that in these early years a human organism experiences its first contacts with its environment. It is believed that during this period the child's sensitive and highly impressionable nervous system is most vulnerable to trauma. Furthermore, it is a time when both pleasant and unpleasant experiences become associated with people, objects, and situations.

In recent years there has been much less emphasis placed upon the deterministic character of the early years of a child's life. Infant experiences are thought of as providing certain potentialities, but whether such potentialities are realized depends to a great extent on the individual's subsequent life experiences. Although experiences of early childhood are undoubtedly of great importance in shaping personality, there are any number of influences, such as ideological environment and material culture, that the individual is not likely to be exposed to or at least be greatly influenced by until later in life.

One study which supports this idea is that of James W. Prescott who investigated the relationship of deprivation of physical sensory pleasure during infant and adolescent years with the presence or absence of physically violent behavior during adult years. From a sample of 49 societies he found that 22 societies clearly featured high infant physical affection (fondling, caressing, playing with infants) and also had low adult physical violence (in terms of theft, killing, and torturing or mutilating enemies). Fourteen societies had low infant affection and high adult physical violence. Thus adult physical violence was accurately predicted in 36 out of 49 societies. This 73 percent rate of accuracy could occur by chance only 4 times out of 1000.

But, according to Prescott,

> Thirteen of the 49 societies studied seemed to be exceptions to the theory that a lack of somatosensory pleasure makes people physically violent. It was expected that cultures which placed a high value upon physical pleasure during infancy and childhood would maintain such values into adulthood. This is not the case. (1975:66)

Prescott explains the exceptions by another variable, not associated with early childhood experience but with experiences in adolescence—premarital sexual behavior. It was discovered that the societies characterized by both high infant affection and high violence exhibited premarital sexual repression and high valuation of virginity; and in the societies characterized by both low physical affection and low adult violence there was a permissive code relating to premarital sex.

Thus the investigator concluded that on the one hand, "the beneficial effects of infant physical affection can be negated by the repression of physical pleasure (premarital sex) later in life," and on the other hand, "the detrimental effects of infant physical affectional deprivation seem to be compensated for by sexual body pleasure experiences during adolescence" (1975:67).

IDEOLOGICAL ENVIRONMENT

The influence of varying ideologies upon the personality structure is well illustrated in the comparative value systems of Athens and Sparta. Every society has an idea of what an ideal man is and all the training and teaching in these societies were dedicated to what each held up as the proper way to behave.

While the people of Sparta and Athens were rival city-states over a period of years, they developed quite different philosophies of life, although each society attempted to instill in its individuals a sense of patriotism and a high valuation of bravery. Sparta placed maximum emphasis on military virtues; Athens stressed the acquisition of knowledge, appreciation of beauty, and development of the body through physical exercise and sports. Since the Spartans glorified the courageous and ingenious warrior, the training of youth centered about military tactics, resourcefulness, and endurance of hardships. It is reported that after eating at the public mess in Sparta one visitor remarked, "Now I understand why Spartans do not fear death." Spartan boys were often required to steal their food in order to develop their ingenuity, and one of the favorite Spartan folktales, told and re-told to boys, was about the boy who stole a fox and hid it under his coat. While making off with his prize, he was stopped by a man who engaged him in conversation. Giving no indication of his theft, the boy stood and talked with the man until he fell dead as the result of being repeatedly bitten by the pilfered animal. The Spartan boy received no intellectual education but was impressed with the desirability of modesty, obedience, and courage.

Sparta, with a constitution but very little democracy, stood in strong ideological contrast to her neighbor Athens. Pericles in a famous funeral oration pointed up many of the differences that shaped the minds and manners of Athenians and Spartans:

> We admit anyone to our city, and do not expel foreigners from fear that they should see too much, because in war we trust to our own bravery and daring rather than to stratagems and preparations. Our enemies prepare for war by a laborious training from boyhood; we live at our ease, but are no less confident in facing danger. . . . We love the arts, but without lavish display, and things of the mind, but without becoming soft.

MATERIAL ENVIRONMENT

In American culture children grow up in a world of rapid transportation, congested urban centers, overstuffed furniture, porcelain plumbing, and clocks with accuracy ensured by Western Union. Since a majority of Americans are reared, or at least feel at home, in such an environment, it probably contributes to our personality configuration. Although this factor is often overlooked in studies of dominant personality, Malinowski has recognized it as a vital influence. He states:

> The secondary environment, the outfit of material culture, is a laboratory in which the reflexes, the impulses, the emotional tendencies of the organism are formed. The hands, arms, legs and eyes are adjusted by the use of implements to the proper technical skill necessary in a culture. The nervous processes are modified so as to yield the whole range of intellectual concepts, emotional types and sentiments which form the body of science, religion and morals prevalent in a community. (1931:622)

In a similar vein, but concerning the impact on American personality of mass production and assembly line technology, Geoffrey Gorer writes:

> From the point of view of the engineer, the man is part of the machine, performing movements which no machine—so far—has been devised to do. This view is perforce accepted by the worker; he has no choice but to admit that his body can be used as an adjunct to a machine, that his muscular strength and coordination are raw materials to be exploited in the most efficient and economical way, that his work should consist in learning a few routines and repeating them endlessly. It would appear that this is not consciously felt to be humiliating or degrading by the majority of workers, but is rather accepted as a necessary condition of life. (1964:142)

VARIATION WITHIN CULTURE

Although common cultural experiences tend to standardize personality and make "every man in certain respects like some other men," we cannot carry the influence of uniform cultural experience too far. Culture is not a mold that turns out its participants as exact facsimiles. There is always a great variety and range of personalities even in the simplest of cultures. This fact has been well documented by C. W. M. Hart in a character analysis of five brothers of the Tiwi tribe of Bathurst Island, Australia. Although the younger two of the five brothers had a different father, all had the same mother, a common family conditioning, and an almost identical cultural environment. According to Hart's very detailed accounts of their personalities, each was extremely different from his siblings. Antonio, the eldest, was "insecure" and "uneasy." As heir to his father's social position, he was "a man pushed into a position rather too big for him to fill. He was not by nature particularly aggressive or domineering."

Mariano, the second brother, was a great contrast to the firstborn. He was a "forceful, domineering, self-important, introverted man" whose gloomy and hostile behavior resulted in his having no intimates or close friends. Equally lonely was Louis, who wanted no friends and sought only to be left alone. He was "completely devoid of humor" but a man of great intelligence and dedication. Louis was dedicated to but one cause—the seduction of other men's wives.

Brothers Tipperary and Bob were slightly younger (late twenties) than the other three and vastly different in personality. Tipperary was "gay, completely relaxed, and unselfconscious," always looking on the brighter side of things and always surrounded with friends; while Bob, the youngest, was completely lacking in color—a "born follower" and a complete conformist.

Hart concludes that "we should expect to find, in any culture in the world, a pretty similar range of variation in what must roughly be called 'types of people.' The anthropologist on the other hand who is looking for 'stereotyped personalities' in even the simplest culture must expect to be disappointed'' (1954:261).

Unfortunately, statements of the variety of personality types have all too often been neglected in the writings of culture and personality researchers, and often the factor of variation has been disguised by the very method of presentation. For example, in Ruth Benedict's national character study of Thai men she portrays them as cheerful, easy-going, jolly, gay, indolent. She claims they accept subordination to higher rank or power without either resentment or servility; they do not cringe. They respect and obey authority without demanding return or assistance from it. They are self reliant in a quiet, careless way—without much sense of responsibility for others (1943). In reading such a description the student is tempted to think that *all* Thais behave in exactly the same way, as there is no statement of variation or range of personality. Certainly there must be personality subtypes that could logically develop from various roles or statuses to be found within the society.

Modal Personality. The term *modal personality* has been useful in the proper understanding of personality variation. Modal personality may best be understood by calling attention to the concept of the *mode* in statistical measurement. The mode is a type of average that is derived by ascertaining the value appearing most frequently in a series of numbers. Let us say that we are interested in the average size of family in a suburban area and as we go from house to house making inquiry we receive the following responses: 5, 6, 5, 4, 3, 2, 5, 2, 4, 9, 5, 7, 5, 3, 4. One way of figuring the average size of family would be to find the number that appears most frequently—in this case, 5. Transferring the concept of mode to the area of personality we would say that modal personality is that personality that is found most commonly among a variety of personality types. There may be a whole range of personalities just as there were many other numbers in our series. Those enjoying the modal personality might very well represent a small percentage of the total number of personalities represented.

A study of modal personality of Tuscarora Indians by Wallace (1952), utilizing Rorschach ink-blot tests, illuminates the concept of modal personality and gives greater understanding of the extent to which personality is shared within a society. In Wallace's study, the personality traits of 70 adults were ascertained from their performances on 21 scoring categories normally used in Rorschach interpretation. Although some traits, such as ability to make use of the entire blot (index W), were shared to the extent of 86 percent, when all 21 trait indices were considered cumulatively, only 26 people were calculated as making up the modal class.

National Character.   Modal personality when applied to the people of complex industrialized societies is often referred to as *national character*. Studies of this phenomenon, as explained by Margaret Mead, are "like all culture and personality studies, . . . focused on the way human beings embody the culture they have been reared in or to which they have immigrated" (1953:642). Just as all members of a given nation tend to share certain cultural traits (e.g., the American heritage), this approach assumes that, being exposed to somewhat similar cultural experiences, they will also tend to share certain personality traits, even though they come from numerous subcultures. Some investigators tend to think of these national character descriptions as "scientifically drawn stereotypes" of personality. We must remember, however, that although culture is a powerful determinant of personality, it is but one of many influencing factors—among them body structure and constitution, family situation, class, caste, and employment status.

Like No Other Man

In stating that every man is in certain respects like no other man, Kluckhohn and Murray are commenting on the uniqueness of every individual personality. This uniqueness might be accounted for partially by constitutional determinants—that is, the state of the human organism at a particular time in terms of general body build, sex, age, and the health and well-being of the body. The possibilities for variation in each of these several factors are enormous when a total population is considered, and thus the possibilities for personality variation as influenced by these factors are great.

Roger Williams, who has sometimes been referred to as a "chemical anthropologist," has pointed out the great variation in physiological factors that definitely affect personality in a given population. Glands, for example, do not control but certainly influence our behavior. In normal individuals the size of thyroid glands may vary from 8 to 50 grams and the amount of thyroid hormone in the blood may vary in perfectly healthy individuals over a five-fold range. Pituitary gland secretions vary in normal individuals over a forty-fold range. Taking such factors as sensitivity to pain, nutritional requirements, size, performance of the heart, and gland secretion into consideration, Williams tells us that there is one chance in 6,500 of being "average."

While Sheldon's findings (see constitutional anthropology chapter 1) on the effect of somatotype on personality are far from conclusive, we can certainly assume that body type, at least in extreme cases, has some influence on personality. We may be sure that a seven-foot Watusi has a very different world view from a four-foot six-inch Pygmy. One's height, strength, and how close one's body approaches what is considered beautiful by a society greatly influences how the world and one's fellowmen are viewed. The constitutional factor includes considerations of age and health, and all of us know that our personalities are quite different depending on whether we are ill or healthy. It is also possible to observe changes in personality in a given person as he advances in age.

FAMILY ENVIRONMENT

There are probably no two people in our society who have been exposed to exactly the same combinations of personalities in the family. The overprotective mother, the domineering father, the happy-go-lucky, the neurotic, or even the psychotic parent can all be found in family groups in our culture. There is also the factor of sibling order; the eldest child in a family is quite likely to have had different training and treatment from the youngest, and both have probably had different life experiences than an only child. The social status of the home also provides a special environment for personality development.

Twins Reared Apart.   In a study of identical twins reared apart, carried out by Newman, Freeman, and Holzinger, there is a case of sisters separated at the age of three months and raised for fifteen years in two vastly different socioeconomic environments. Mildred grew up in the home of a bank president and former mayor of a town of five thousand population, while her twin, Ruth, was reared in a large city where her foster father was a foreman of day laborers. While Mildred was encouraged to make friends and play with groups of older children, Ruth was overly sheltered by her foster mother, who discouraged any contacts with other children. Mildred's home environment was intellectually stimulating, and she had an opportunity to read widely, take music lessons, and come into contact with highly educated people. Although Ruth had as much formal education as her sister, her home was depressing, with nothing in the way of good books, good music, or stimulating companions. When examined at the age of fifteen, the girls differed little in their health records, and there were "no marked contrasts in physical characters." In regard to personality traits, however, they were quite dissimilar. The investigators describe the two as follows:

> Observation of the sisters revealed a marked difference in their overt behavior. Mildred was sociable and relatively easy in her manner and conversed freely. While not at all bold, she seemed to show no signs of timidity or embarrassment. Her diction was good and her enunciation clear. Ruth, on the contrary, was excessively timid, would not converse, never spoke except when questioned, and then spoke with a pronounced lisp. (1937:225)

The reader should remember, of course, that identical twins have exactly the same genetic heritage and if there are differences in the personalities of twins who have been reared apart it is the result of variation of nurture rather than nature.

Still other factors may produce variation in personality and explain why in some respects "every man is like no other man." Even in pre-industrial societies we cannot expect every individual to have had exactly the same set of life experiences in terms of successes and failures, inquiries, and harrowing experiences. In modern nations the situation aspect is magnified in terms of class, region, and occupational differences in experience. Taking all these into account it is understandable why the anthropologist feels that personality may be dealt with in terms of general national or cultural tendencies, but not without recognizing a wide range of variation.

Normal and Abnormal Personalities

The fact that early studies of culture and personality were highly influenced by Freudian and other psychiatric theories has led many to believe that anthropologists are more interested in abnormal than normal personality. This is not true. By far the greatest number of psychological studies done by anthropologists have been concerned with documentation of representative or modal personality types in the cultures of the world. In a normally functioning society one could hardly expect the representative personality to be abnormal. Since anthropologists felt that their studies tended to be "vague, impressionistic, subjective, and not amenable to check or transubjective verification" (Spiro and Henry 1953:418), they turned to the instruments utilized by psychologists and psychiatrists for measuring personality in an attempt to be more scientific and objective. In most cases these instruments had been used more in diagnostic tests of mental illness than as ways of studying normal personality.

Anthropologists believed, however, that certain tests used in clinical psychology could be used as originally developed or altered slightly so that they could be used cross-culturally to challenge the individual to reveal his inner thoughts, feelings, emotions, and fears. Those tests that have been selected and used most extensively for this purpose have been (1) the Rorschach test, (2) the Thematic Apperception test (usually modified), (3) free drawings, and (4) doll play.

THE
RORSCHACH
TEST

The Rorschach test consists of a series of 10 cards on which ink blots of varying form and color have been reproduced. Developed by Swiss psychiatrist Hermann Rorschach, it is essentially a test wherein the subject reveals his personality by his verbal responses to the amor-

Modified TAT developed by William Lessa for use on Ulithi.

phous blots. This form of projective test has been used widely by anthropologists in foreign cultures because the equipment is simple, does not require literacy, can be used on either adults or children, and does not have rigid administrative standards. Spiro and Henry maintain that the test:

> elicits material covering a wide range of personality characteristics. Among these are: sensitivity to inner promptings as contrasted with responsiveness to outer stimuli; degree of control over emotions; capacity to relate effectively to other people; capacity to see total situations as contrasted with absorption in petty details; tendencies to submit as contrasted with tendencies to react vigorously to the environment; various aspects of sexuality; degree of hostility; degree of imagination, conformity, originality; tendencies to psychopathy. (1950:419)

THE THEMATIC APPERCEPTION TEST

The TAT, as it is commonly called, consists of 30 thought-provoking pictures and a blank card, to which the subject is to respond by telling a story of what each picture represents. The theory behind the test is that every author reveals him or herself in his work, and the pictures are used merely as a stimulus to the less imaginative person. Since the set of TAT pictures used in clinical diagnostic situations shows people in European dress and Western settings, many anthropologists have modified the pictures to match the circumstances of their native subjects. For example, see William Lessa's drawing for use on the Micronesian island of Ulithi.

One of the most extensive uses of the modified TAT was a study of 1000 children in 6 different American Indian cultures conducted by the U.S. Office of Indian Affairs and the University of Chicago in 1947. Using a series of 12 pictures representing varying social situations within the everyday experience of Indian children, the test studied such things as emotional orientation to the physical world; characteristics of interpersonal relations, particularly those of family members; the extent to which individual spontaneity was encouraged or restricted by the group; the influence of white contact on personality; and the influence of cultural training at various periods of a child's life.

FREE DRAWINGS

This test of personality simply involves giving children an opportunity to draw anything they desire. By analyzing content as well as the characteristics of rendition, it is believed that much can be learned about self-image, sibling and parental relations, the fantasy life of the child, as well as his conceptions of the physical universe and of his society.

DOLL PLAY

In this test situation a child or group of children are given dolls, usually representing members of a family. The children are free to do anything they want with the dolls, but the manipulations of the dolls and the children's comments are closely observed and recorded. It is believed that the manner in which the children play with the dolls will reveal their attitudes toward their own parents and siblings, their conceptions of sexual behavior, and their tendencies toward aggressive behavior.

CROSS-CULTURAL VALIDITY

In European culture, norms have been developed so that the above devices for studying personality may be used to identify psychotic and neurotic individuals, but these criteria are seldom, if ever, valid when testing in foreign cultures. Although Cora DuBois feels that the Rorschach can be used cross-culturally if properly handled and interpreted (1961:xx), many anthropologists insist that responses considered abnormal in one society may be considered perfectly normal and desirable in another. A good example of how a different set of values can greatly affect a subject's test responses is the case of a Quaker girl in our own culture, who made an error on a test where she was to tell what was wrong with a picture in which a frontiersman was shooting distant Indians while those close to him were about to take his scalp. Instead of writing that one should always shoot the closest Indians first, the girl answered "One shouldn't shoot Indians." This was not the expected answer, but in terms of the girl's pacifistic ideological background it was her natural and normal response.

An example of the kind of problems which can appear when

European-developed tests are applied cross-culturally may be seen in P. H. Cook's use of Rorschach in Samoa. In the analysis of some 50 protocols of young Samoan men it was soon apparent that there were problems relating to the interpretation of S (white space), C (color), and F (form) categories. If Europeans had given responses similar to those of the Samoan subjects they would have been regarded as abnormal, but the Samoan responses were considered normal because of the Samoan's different color preferences and associations and because Samoa is a very formal society, stressing elaborate etiquette and careful attention to ceremonial detail.

Abnormality

One of the most difficult problems in psychology today is how to define what is abnormal in our own culture let alone in foreign or non-Western cultures. Something of the dilemma may be seen in Yehudi Cohen's discussion:

> We generally tend to think of psychotics as people who are confined to a psychiatric ward or hospital. This is a misconception, since psychiatrists generally hospitalize a psychotic only when he is in danger of hurting himself or others or when he is incapable of functioning by himself. There are many people labeled by psychiatrists as psychotic who are perfectly capable of performing everyday functions, including earning a living, and for whom hospitalization is not required. Because there is no definition of psychosis which is universally applicable, we must have an operational criterion of psychosis which is meaningful in the context of the data which social scientists are capable of gathering. Hence, we shall say that a person is psychotic when, because of personality or psychological factors, he is unable to perform his roles as a member of the society or group of which he is a member. (1961:469)

A slightly different but equally sound solution to defining normal and abnormal is the suggestion of Alexander Leighton that abnormal mental behavior consists of "patterns of behavior and feeling that are out of keeping with cultural expectations and that bother the person who acts and feels them, or bother others around him, or both" (1969:180).

With these definitions in mind we must recognize that in many societies certain mental states that are by our definitions abnormal may allow or even specially qualify a person to perform his role as a member of society. Among certain California Indian groups, as well as among Siberian Eskimos, the individual who has hallucinations and cataleptic seizures is not pitied but rather regarded as a very important religious practitioner. Since it is believed that the spirits possess and speak through him during seizures, he enjoys a great amount of authority over his fellow society members.

Another example of behavior that would be termed psychotic or at least abnormal by European standards, but in no way hinders a person in the performance of social roles, is cited by Herskovits, who relates that:

> In West Africa and Brazil the gods come only to those who have been designated in advance by the priest of their group, who lays his hands on their heads. . . . The terminology of psychopathology has been readily applied to these states of possession. Such designations as hysteria, auto-hypnosis, compulsion, have come to rest easily on the tongue . . . (but) . . . in these Negro societies the interpretation given behavior under possession—the meaning this experience holds for the people—falls entirely in the realm of understandable, predictable, normal behavior. (1949:67)

Opposing this view is that of Derek Freeman, who feels that Herskovits's relativistic approach is an erroneous doctrine that seriously hinders the proper understanding of human culture. Freeman's position is that

> to assert . . . that behavior is normal because it is set in a cultural mold, is to say no more than it is shared and accepted by the members of the culture concerned, but dereistic thinking and irrational behavior are not one whit the less dereistic because they happen to be shared and accepted. (1962:273)

A middle ground position in this controversy is that of Yehudi Cohen, who writes,

> There can be little doubt that the hallucinary experiences of a Plains Indian young man in quest of personal supernatural power is as much as "clinical" manifestation or entity as are the hallucinations of a hospitalized psychotic. Somehow or other, however, the Indian's membership within a bounded societal group keeps this hallucination encapsulated so that it remains within its proper cultural place and does not intrude upon or flood the rest of the personality. (1961:469)

Much of this trance and hallucinary behavior, which appears abnormal in European terms, is quite normal in the eyes of the members of a particular society if it remains in the proper context. If we define normal behavior as that which is expected and predicted, then possession in African cult ceremonies and hallucinations in the Plains Indians' vision quest are normal. If Africans have seizures or trances in areas of behavior where they are not expected or if Plains Indians have hallucinations about things other than guardian spirits, then even their fellow society members would consider them psychotic. Every society does recognize certain kinds of behavior as being abnormal and considers those who exhibit these traits as being psychotic. While mental illness might generally be thought of as a matter of losing touch either temporarily or permanently with reality and behaving in unpredictable ways, this concept is not entirely valid; for it would appear that the mentally ill have enough of a grasp upon reality that they follow culturally prescribed patterns of psychosis.

In Latin America "magical fright" is the common mental malady, and its symptoms are "depression, withdrawal from normal social activity and responsibility, and signs of temporary collapse of the ego organization" (Gillin 1948a:387). In Ulithi one who is mentally ill swims about in the lagoon for hours with an old rotten log under his arm. An Ojibwa Indian suffering with *Windigo* shows signs of "melancholia, violence and obsessive cannibalism" (Landes 1960:24). The mental disturbance known as *Pibloktoq* among Greenland Eskimos produces such symptoms as singing until one becomes unconscious, imitating the calls of birds, throwing things about, tearing off one's clothing, and sometimes running out of the house into the snow (Foulks 1973). In Samoa anyone can easily recognize one afflicted with *ma'i aitu* (spirit sickness) for they talk in their sleep, run aimlessly about, yawn repeatedly, compulsively count their fingers, and frequently pick flowers and sing.

CAUSES OF PSYCHOSIS

An even more difficult problem to tackle than defining "normal" and "abnormal" behavior is the task of isolating cultural or environmental factors that seem to precipitate mental illness. Studying the problem cross-culturally, anthropologists have come up with a series of factors that they believe may contribute to psychological disorganization. They are (1) the presence of conflicting values, (2) heterogeneity of culture, (3) discontinuity of life experiences, and (4) too rapid cultural change accompanied by a loss of norms.

Conflicting Values.   Modern America, which psychiatrists claim has an alarming rate of one out of ten persons with some degree of mental illness, is a perfect example of a society with conflicting values and ideologies combined with rapid cultural change. The United States is a country that advocates brotherly love, yet fights at least one war every generation, sanctions ruthless business competition, and tacitly sanctions racial segregation. It holds up monogamy and chastity as ideals and yet has one of the highest divorce rates in the world and is obsessed with sex in literature, motion pictures, and advertising.

In comparison with Samoa, Margaret Mead finds America an exceedingly difficult place in which to come of age. She describes our society as one

> which is clamouring for choice, which is filled with many articulate groups, each urging its own brand of salvation, its own variety of economic philoso-

phy, will give each new generation no peace until all have chosen or gone under, unable to bear the conditions of choice. The stress is in our civilization, not in the physical changes through which our children pass, but it is none the less real or less inevitable in twentieth-century America. (1928:235)

Cultural Discontinuity.   Closely associated with the phenomenon of conflicting values is the discontinuity of cultural conditioning, which is found in our society and others and represents a source of great emotional stress. Ruth Benedict has dealt with this problem at some length (1938) and points out that in our society a child advancing from childhood to adulthood experiences very different demands—many of which he/she has not been prepared for by the culture. In our society childhood is considered a time for play, and the child is asked to assume very little responsibility. High-school students are often discouraged by their parents from seeking part-time work on the grounds that they should go to all the high-school dances, sporting events, and other social events they can because they have the rest of their lives to work. On the other hand, the moment a young person completes his schooling he/she is expected to know how to work hard, efficiently, and responsibly. Concomitant with this change in roles is also a change in submission-dominance behavior. Many societies, including our own, require or at least expect perfect obedience and submission from children. If this is not forthcoming, the child is punished. In our society this pattern continues as long as the children live under the parents' roof. When they manage to leave the nest, however, they are supposed to be able to "stand on their own two feet," stick up for their rights, and show signs of dominance and leadership. Becoming an adult also involves developing a sexual role. In our society especially, children are shielded from knowledge of sexual functions, and yet young people are expected to establish normal and satisfactory marital sex relationships.

Each of these changes in role represents an almost complete reversal of attitude and behavior from earlier conditioning, and, although it is true that the majority of individuals take these major hurdles without great difficulty, many others for one reason or another never adjust. Sometimes this inability results in our branding individuals as immature, but in other cases these maladjustments can be a real source of psychic disturbance.

Homogeneity and Heterogeneity.   Ordinarily we assume that the more homogeneous a culture and the fewer its discrepancies and discontinuities, the lower its incidence of mental illness. In such a society people tend to be in pretty much "the same boat." There is little class distinction, little difference in economic position, little disparity of values, little mobility or change; and childhood experiences tend to be supported and reinforced as the individual grows older.

Although we are not sure whether heterogeneous societies attract or produce abnormal individuals, the fact remains that in cities like New York, Chicago, and Detroit approximately 10 percent of all hospital admissions involve severe or moderate personality disturbances, and approximately one person out of five in the United States visits a doctor every year for some nervous disturbance.

No attempt to assess the many causes for this phenomenon will be made here, but they surely lie in societal anonymity, in the diversity of values in its many subcultures, in whirlwind change, in the demand for efficiency and production, and in the breakdown of family ties that prevails in our urban and industrial areas.

Although a number of studies have shown that the lot of the pre-industrial or rural community member is somewhat better as far as maintaining mental balance, homogeneous societies are not always free from the shadow of psychosis just because life is simpler and more uniform. For example, the nature of the values held is also an important factor.

The Hutterites. The Hutterites, an Anabaptist religious group who inhabit sections of the Dakotas, Montana, and the prairie provinces of Canada, live a simple communal life in 98 small agricultural communities. As a group they believe in pacificism, adult baptism, and communal ownership of property. They reject jewelry, art, comfortable household furnishings, radios, and movies. Although they see no need for education beyond the primary grades, they read newspapers, utilize outside medical and legal services, and engage in highly mechanized agriculture. In regard to their cultural homogeneity, Eaton and Weil write:

> In the Hutterite social order people are exposed to a large number of common experiences. Their indoctrination begins in infancy and is continued by daily religious instruction and later by daily church-going. Hutterites spend their entire life within a small and stable group. Their homes consist only of bedrooms, all furnished in an almost identical manner. The women take turns cooking and baking for everybody. Everyone wears the same kind of clothes; the women, for example, all let their hair grow without cutting, part it in the middle and cover it with a black kerchief with white polka dots. The Hutterite religion provides definite answers for many of the problems that come up. (1953:37)

In spite of this great cultural homogeneity and stability, the Hutterites do have mental illness. Eaton and Weil discovered in 1950 that about one in forty-three individuals either had active symptoms of or had recovered from mental illness. Although this incidence is not particularly high, it is somewhat greater than many other less homogeneous groups with which they were compared by the investigators. It is of interest that very few of these cases ever manifested delusions, hallucinations, or other schizophrenic symptoms. There was, however, a high incidence of manic-depressive reactions. To a certain extent it is possible to find an explanation for this in the ideological system of these people. Eaton and Weil explain:

> There was much evidence of irrational guilt feelings, self blame, withdrawal from normal social relations and marked slowing of mental and motor activities . . . Religion is the focus of the Hutterite way of life. Their whole educational system, beginning with nursery school, orients the people to look for blame and guilt within themselves rather than in others. (1953:34)

Personality and Cultural Change

For some time there has been a controversy in regard to the effects of cultural change on personality structure. Some scholars like Hallowell, Spindler, Bruner and others feel that personality structure is relatively tenacious and that considerable change can take place in the cultural institutions without a corresponding alteration of the representative, or modal personality. Barnouw, Mead, and others believe that one of the characteristics of modal personality is that it is adaptable to change. Barnouw writes, for example,

> When the culture of a society changes and it develops new institutions, the members of the society must adapt themselves to the new conditions. Such adaptation may involve changes in personality which may, in turn, lead to further changes in culture. (1979:361)

PSYCHOLOGICAL CONTINUITY DESPITE CULTURAL CHANGE

In a study of 217 Ojibwa subjects using Rorschach protocols A. Irving Hallowell reported "that in the case of the Ojibwa a considerable amount of acculturation actually has taken place without any major change in their modal personality structure" (1955:351). And Spindler, in commenting on the matter of psychocultural adaptation, maintains that the Blood Indians of Alberta have undergone a great deal of acculturation without a great change in their personality characteristics because they already had a psychological orientation compatible with the direction and demands of cultural change (1968:332).

Reviewing data gathered among the Mandan-Hidatsa Indians of North Dakota in regard to the impact of acculturation on traditional cultural patterns and personality, Edward Bruner advanced his "early learning hypothesis" which holds that "that which was traditionally learned and internalized in infancy and early childhood tends to be most resistant to change in contact situations" (1956:194). If the advocates of "Basic Personality" (who hold that most indoctrination in culturally appropriate modes of thinking, feeling, and behaving occurs early in life) are correct then this hypothesis would suggest that there would be great tenacity in traditional personality configurations.

CULTURAL
CHANGE AND
PSYCHOLOGICAL
RESPONSE

More characteristic of anthropologists' views is the idea stated by Margaret Mead in *New Lives for Old* that "it has been a thesis of modern anthropology that there is a systematic correspondence between the institutions of a society and the character structure of the individuals who embody those institutions" (1956:362). Let us look now at various situations involving various kinds of change in order to better understand cultural modification and concomitant personality alteration.

REVITALIZATION
MOVEMENTS

In recent years a good deal of attention has been paid to the psychological ramifications of a special kind of change phenomenon commonly identified as "nativistic," "messianic," or "revitalization" movements. Included in this category are such happenings as the cargo cults of Melanesia, the Ghost Dance and Handsome Lake movements of the North American Indians and even perhaps the Russian Communist Revolution of 1917 or the Cultural Revolution of the Red Chinese in 1966. The characteristics of such movements were brought to our attention in 1943 by Ralph Linton in an article dealing with "nativistic movement" typology, and in subsequent publications (1956, 1970) Anthony F. C. Wallace explored the concept further and introduced the term *revitalization.* In his analysis Wallace compared society to a living organism and maintained that if it is threatened by some traumatic experience—war or rapidly imposed change—a revitalization movement might develop to restore societal order or balance.

Revitalization movements are of interest to psychological anthropologists because they usually involve a leader with charisma (but often a deviant personality) who rises to power and establishes a new order—and usually a new national character in his followers. It is not uncommon for such leaders to claim to have had visionary experiences with a deity, and to have received a special commission to serve as a prophet, to seek followers, and to launch a special movement to right perceived wrongs. Not only might we find personality changes occurring in the leader in this process but ultimately in his converts as well. Revitalization movements are usually responses to periods of stress and disappointment, and frequently they facilitate cultural change through their reactions to the deliberate attempts of a leader to create a more satisfying culture. A good example of this kind of a movement is the New Way phenomenon in the Manus Islands described by Margaret Mead in her book *New Lives for Old.*

In the village of Peri in the Manus Islands, a nontraditional leader named Paliau came from Rabaul in 1946 and led the people in a deliberate and successful attempt to revitalize their society which was marked by post-war discontent. The citizens of Peri are described by Mead (who studied them originally in 1928) as being on an economic treadmill in which adults functioned within an elaborate and annoying system of sanctions and taboos. But with the onset of World War II an influx of Americans passed through the islands bringing with them models for a new way of life. What the leader, Paliau, introduced was a bold new plan to "Americanize" the society and do away with the onerous restrictions and the materialistic values that had plagued its members for generations. The revitalization movement, we are told, "changed the entire pattern all at once—houses, costumes, ceremonies, social organization, law—making up the new pattern out of the accumulated bits of European civilization which they had learned through the previous twenty-five years" (1956:287).

With these changes in institutions and material culture went a deliberate attempt to turn around specific kinds of attitudes and emotions. They inaugurated prohibitions against anger, lustful thought, and slander. Laughter was encouraged and quarreling became a civil offence under the code of New Peri. In the old culture children never participated in adult activities because adults wanted to spare their offspring the burdensome obligations and restrictions of adulthood as long as possible. In New Peri, children and adults interacted freely and with enjoyment. There is no doubt that this revitalization made an impact on the personality structure of the Manus Islanders, for Mead writes:

> Today they are friendly where formerly they would have been harshly competitive; they are actively concerned with the prevention of types of behavior which they would formerly have regarded as natural and desirable; they are relaxed and unworried where they would formerly have been tense; they are rearing their children with a kind of indulgence which would have been unheard of twenty-five years ago. (1956:362)

ACCULTURATION AND MODERNIZATION

Esther Goldfrank (1943) has given us an excellent example of personality change under changing external conditions in Teton Indian society in the nineteenth century. In analyzing patterns of cooperation and hostility among these people, Goldfrank found that prior to 1850, when the white man was not yet a threat, there was a great deal of ingroup violence growing out of rivalries between individuals for war and hunting honors.

Between 1850 and 1877 caravan travel west brought immigrants into the area who killed the buffalo and thus threatened the Indians' basic economy. Faced with this common threat from outside, the Teton neither fought nor quarreled among themselves and instead developed a sense of tribal solidarity where individuals took greater pride in giving than getting.

The period of 1877 to 1885 was one in which the spirit of the tribe was broken. The buffalo had disappeared and thus the traditional economy was gone. The people were poverty stricken. With the complete collapse of the tribal structure, the sense of cooperation and tribal solidarity also disappeared and internal strife, even to the point of a series of murders, once more developed.

From 1885 on, the Teton again managed to develop a sense of solidarity. The people were now one in their economic deprivation. Either they would help each other or none would survive. Hospitality became a cardinal virtue, and the Protestant church became an important institution in that it provided both solace for the bulk of the Teton and opportunity for prestige for those young men who entered the ministry.

Ashley Montagu believes that personality is a pattern of behavior that can change not only from one generation to another but within the same person in a single generation. He points out that history supports his position. Montagu writes:

> Consider . . . the seafaring Scandinavians of the Bronze Age, undoubtedly the ancestors of the modern Scandinavians: how different is the cultural behavior of the modern relatively sedentary Scandinavians [who have not fought a war in more than 165 years] from that of their raiding forbears!
>
> The boisterous joy in life of the English of Elizabeth I's period is very different from the attitudes of the English in the reign of Elizabeth II. The lusty libertinism of the Restoration contrasts sharply with the prudery of the Victorian Age. The Englishman's "nature" was different in the sixteenth as compared with that which he exhibited in the seventeenth century. In the centuries preceding the middle half of the nineteenth the English were among the most aggressive and violent peoples on the face of the earth, today they are among the most law-abiding. (1956:77—78)

Many anthropologists would agree that the people of Fiji are among the happiest, friendliest, and most cooperative and peaceful in the world. And yet, as late as 1878 Fijians were still practicing cannibalism, raiding their neighbors, schooling their children in revenge, and making a specialty of massacring shipwrecked mariners. How such a drastic change in attitude and action came about in less than a century is a mystery. Norman Cousins (1964) suggests that perhaps the Fijians might be persuaded to send missionaries to the rest of the world and inform all of us how we might also develop their pacifistic personality traits.

It is still possible to use the old cliché that "You can't change human nature," for that can be done through evolution alone. But cultural nature, the product of given cultures at given times, is as dynamic as culture itself.

A number of broad impressionistic studies have probed the impact of great historical events on personality structure. Examples are Burckhardt's study of the influence of the Italian Renaissance (1958), Fromm's analysis of Lutheranism and Calvinism (1941), Riesman's examination of American population cycles and national character (1950), McClelland's study of the psychological manifestations of economic growth in "achieving" societies (1961) and Mead's investigation of the psycho-social effects of an American Generation Gap resulting from differential awareness of the realities of nuclear technology (1978).

What is desperately needed in order to improve our knowledge of the psychological effects of change are systematic, quantitative studies of culture and personality in given societies over extended periods of time. Very little in the way of longitudinal studies such as this have been produced by psychological anthropologists, but one study of this type by Holmes, Blazer, and Tallman documented Samoan personality modification over a 12-year period in which there was rapid cultural change.

SAMOAN PERSONALITY—A DIACHRONIC ANALYSIS

A generation ago the average Samoan boy grew up in a large extended family, was educated to be a good fisherman and agriculturalist, and participated in a world where rank and ceremony were focal points. Service and obedience were required of young untitled men, and dignity, responsibility, and wisdom were synonymous with chiefly rank. Samoan children today come of age in a very different world. European technology and economics have created new values. Instead of looking forward to the time when he may become the chief of his extended family, administer family lands and properties, and participate in the sacred ceremonies of old Samoa, many a Samoan young man is looking forward to learning a trade or even receiving a college education and a job in government or industry. He finds the old system of communal ownership of land stifling and life in his remote village dull. His travels to the port towns of his archipelago show him what luxuries money can buy, and these are often more attractive to him than the security and prestige he can attain by remaining within the traditional system. Since the young man is literally a part of a different cultural world from his father, it is little wonder that he thinks and behaves in a different manner. There are a number of

Order—a major characteristic in Samoan personality.

behavior patterns learned in childhood that tend to dominate the young man's actions even now, but many of his childhood values do not bring rewards in the European world and thus they are modified or replaced.

In order to investigate the psychological dimensions of Samoan life style Lowell D. Holmes tested 68 senior students at the high school in American Samoa using the California Test of Personality, the Edwards Personal Preference Schedule, and the Rogers Test of Personality Adjustment. This was in 1962. The tests were given in the Samoan language by a Samoan teacher, and they were altered slightly to render them valid cross-culturally. Test results produced a personality profile that was very nearly identical with impressions gained by Holmes during 26 months of participant observation of the culture. The profile revealed that Samoans have strong tendencies toward Deference (accepting the leadership of others), Order (enjoying organization), Abasement (being timid in the presence of superiors), Endurance (keeping at a job until finished); but weak tendencies toward Autonomy (independence in decision-making), Dominance (directing the actions of others), Exhibition (being the center of attention), Aggression (getting angry or disagreeing with others), and Achievement (doing one's best to be successful).

Holmes returned to Samoa again in 1974 and with the aid of another Samoan high-school teacher gave the Edwards test to 31 subjects and the California test to 47 subjects. In the period from 1962 to

Edwards Personal Preference Schedule

Subsection	Samoan '62	Samoan '74	American norms
Achievement	13.368	14.000	15.66
Deference	13.157	15.967	11.21
Order	14.763	15.000	10.23
Exhibition	11.368	13.419	14.40
Autonomy	10.026	11.483	14.34
Affiliation	12.000	14.096	15.00
Intraception	14.315	15.741	16.12
Succorance	8.500	12.161	10.74
Dominance	12.815	13.290	17.44
Abasement	18.657	16.645	12.24
Nurturance	14.657	15.548	14.04
Change	12.236	13.419	15.51
Endurance	15.868	16.387	12.66
Heterosexuality	7.552	11.096	17.65
Aggression	8.184	11.451	12.79

1974 there was great cultural change in American Samoa. Twenty-six consolidated elementary schools, three high schools and a junior college were built, and educational and entertainment television was introduced. A tourist hotel was built on the shores of Pago Pago Bay and airport and harbor facilities were improved. A tuna-fish cannery had been established in the early 1950s but a second one, established after 1962, brought the Samoan labor force canning tuna up to 1100 workers. Other enterprises—watch, underwear, and food processing factories—were luring more and more Samoans away from subsistence agriculture and into wage labor. The 1970 census figures showed that the wage labor force totaled 4939, with the largest share (3515) being government employees in the schools, the hospital, the government offices, and in public works.

In comparison with 1962 Samoan personality-test scores, the 1974 results revealed Samoan modal personality to be changing in the direction that stressed modern traits more and traditional traits less. Movement toward American norms was noted on 10 out of 15 test variables on the Edwards test and on 14 out of 15 test variables on the California test. The general tendency was for the strongest Samoan traits—Deference, Order, Endurance—to persist whereas the weakest tendencies, without exception, moved in the direction of American norms. Change was seen to be due to an adaptation to Western influences, since the majority of variables had moved in that direction.

California Test of Personality

Subsection	Samoan '62	Samoan '74	American norms
Personal adjustment	47.602	53.936	76.64
Self-reliance	8.764	8.829	11.92
Sense of personal worth	9.455	12.617	13.75
Sense of personal freedom	7.602	8.404	13.13
Feeling of belonging	9.382	10.936	13.74
Withdrawing tendencies	5.911	8.659	12.41
Nervous symptoms	7.852	8.297	11.69
Social adjustment	51.250	56.170	79.20
Social standards	10.529	10.936	14.41
Social skills	10.470	10.042	12.41
Antisocial tendencies	8.088	8.106	13.78
Family relations	5.779	8.808	13.34
School relations	7.529	8.212	12.77
Community relations	9.514	9.617	12.89
Total adjustment	94.779	110.212	155.84

The persistence was also believed to be a type of adaptation to Western influence but here it is believed that traditional traits have found an increased usefulness in the new situation.

Summary

Culture and personality explores how the development of temperament, or personality, is influenced by growing up in a particular cultural system. This anthropological area of specialization differs from psychology in that it is less concerned with the individual, and more concerned with normal rather than with abnormal personality.

Culture and personality scholars Kluckhohn and Murray have proposed that everyone is, in certain respects, (1) like all other people (in that they share a common human nature and a common set of biological needs); (2) like some other people (in that they share a culture or other life circumstances); and (3), like no other people (in that everyone has in some respects a unique social and cultural environment and that there is great variation in human populations in personality-influencing anatomical characteristics).

Studying the psychological aspects of human behavior cross-culturally can present numerous problems, not the least of which is defining personality deviance and mental illness. There is also the problem of the cross-cultural validity of personality-assessment tools. There has been some use of projective tests (sometimes modified) by cultural and personality fieldworkers but most of the past research in this area has utilized the traditional anthropological methods of observation and interview. Early research in psychological anthropology centered on analysis of childhood experiences (toilet training, weaning, discipline) in explaining "basic" or modal personality. There was also considerable interest in national character profiles, often drawn from a distance by analyzing the dominant culture themes in films, literature, or other varieties of popular culture.

In recent years there has been considerable interest in assessing the impact of cultural change on personality structure, and this has prompted studies of revitalization movements, revolutions, acculturation, and modernization situations, as well as cases of forcefully imposed change. While some scholars believe that personality is tenacious and therefore little-affected by such change, others see human personality as flexible, and their interest is in understanding the direction and dynamics of personality alteration.

Science, Technology, and the Environment 11

Although human beings are basically animals in their biological makeup, they have the distinction of being cultural animals. Therefore, they are able to interact with their environment in a way not open to those animals standing below them on the taxonomic pyramid. By this we mean that humans did not have to grow a heavy pelt to survive in a cold climate; they merely devised a garment of fiber or skins and built themselves shelters. Human animals did not have to grow sharp teeth or long claws to hunt or to protect themselves from their enemies; they merely invented a weapon of the hunt or of defense. Nor do people have to have a special body structure to do certain kinds of work. Tasks beyond their physical abilities are accomplished through their genius for making tools or for utilizing leverage, gravity, or other natural principles. Because of culture, the solutions to technical problems become the heritage of subsequent generations who are then free to perfect and refine the techniques of their ancestors.

This chapter will not discuss all of the material inventions and discoveries of the world's peoples, but rather will attempt to describe how human beings as a species respond to their needs for tools, shelter, and clothing, and to show the extent to which people, even in nonliterate societies, are scientists in solving their basic survival problems.

Tools

One of the outstanding characteristics of human beings is that they are toolmakers. Although animals have proved themselves capable of utilizing natural objects to accomplish things that require something beyond their biological endowments, only the human animal managed to develop methods of developing and using tools of any complexity. In recent years the subject of tools has filled the anthropological spotlight. Some anthropologists have argued, and very convincingly, that the use of tools has made a great difference in determining the direction of human evolution. *Homo sapiens*, the toolmaking and tool-using animal, has protected itself and domesticated its environment through its tools so that it does not face many of the environmental pressures of the lower animals. Of course, humans have in their hands, in their stereoscopic vision and in their complex brains a set of built-in tools that help them survive. Their hands, for example, are very efficient tools. Prehensile fingers and opposable thumbs give a viselike grip that is sure and powerful. At the same time humans have an acute sense of touch and little treads or ridges (which produce fingerprints) to aid them in delicate manipulations.

Their flat nails allow them to pick up the smallest and flattest of objects. With these multipurpose tools attached to arms that rotate in an arc of 360° human animals can grip, strike, oppose motion, and accomplish a variety of complex manipulations that require coordinated movements. In spite of the great utility of human hands as tools, they also have their limitations.

The skin that covers the palms and fingers is tender and the nails are frail. If one is to chop wood, skin animals, or cut flesh, it is obvious that something more than merely the hand is required. Originally, prehistoric folk probably picked up objects of nature that suited their tool requirements.

As the human species developed in its capacity for culture, there came a time when it realized that something more than natural objects would be required if it were to sustain life by converting natural resources. The problem that was probably faced, however, was what kind of tools should be developed to satisfy daily needs? Some of the earliest tools were simple, indeed, in that they were pebbles with a few flakes struck off to produce a sharp cutting or striking edge. For example, these earliest of tools, which date back nearly 2 million years, have, because of their crudeness of manufacture, produced many an argument. Many claim that these eoliths, or pebble tools, were not made by human beings at all. One man went so far as to throw a quantity of pebbles into a cement mixer in order to show that the tumbling action could produce stones of identical form as pebble tools. Another fact which added fuel to the argument was that there was no record of any kind of prehistoric human living at the time these tools were supposed to have been produced. However, in 1960, L.S.B. Leakey found numerous bone fragments and several tools of *Homo habilis*. These materials from Olduvai Gorge in East Africa were dated as being 1,850,000 years old. The tools were sharpened pebbles much like the eoliths that had been found earlier in England. It was therefore, quite apparent that humans have long been toolmakers and that there was a tradition of tool manufacture, implying the existence of culture at a very early date.

About 1 million years ago human beings developed a very efficient all-purpose tool, the hand or fist ax. With this tool they could saw, chop, scrape, drill, and slice. The implement must have proved to be very effective because varieties of this hand ax have been found in all parts of the world. It probably appealed to hunters and gatherers, who were always on the move and needed a single tool to do a number of tasks.

As culture developed and hunting techniques became more refined, people realized there was a need for a greater variety of spe-

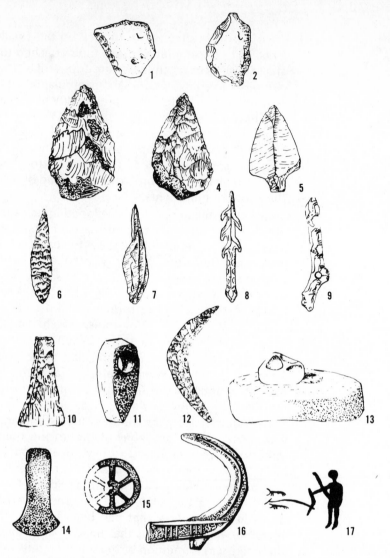

Figure 11-1 Tools of early prehistoric peoples.

cialized tools. Thus we find a great florescence of tools, particularly in the Upper Paleolithic—that is, the latter portion of the Old Stone Age. The basic hand ax shape was reproduced in smaller size and often hafted to a shaft, thus making a spear that could be thrown. Truly efficient axes were developed by the Neanderthal, and it was probably these people who first attached a blade to a handle and thus had increased striking power. The old hand ax was not as efficient as it might have been in slicing or sawing operations, so the Aurignacian peoples, living in France, developed long flint knives and end scrapers to handle the removal of hides and the dressing of game. Among the Solutrean peoples, another European group, flakes actually were produced with serrations or teeth to facilitate sawing operations.

Eoliths and Pebble Tools
1. Knife (England)
2. Sidescraper (E. Africa)
   Lower Paleolithic Core Tool
3. Chellean hand ax (France)
   Tools of Neanderthal Man
4. Mousterian hand ax (France)
5. Mousterian point (N. Africa)
   Upper Paleolithic Tools of Cromagnon Man
6. Solutrean point of knife (France)
7. Aurignacian Burin—engraving tool (France)
8. Magdalenian harpoon point of antler (France)
9. Magdalenian arrow shaft straightener (France)
10. Flint ax (Denmark)
11. Stone ax-hammer (Denmark)
12. Flint sickle blade—notched for hafting (Denmark)
13. Mealing stones (France)
    Bronze Age Implements
14. Ax blade (Denmark)
15. Wheel for votice chariot (Switzerland)
16. Sickle blade (Hungary)
17. Petroglyph of man plowing with oxen (Sweden)

Upper Paleolithic developments in toolmaking not only included refined methods of secondary chipping but new materials were introduced. Bone and antler were used for needles, harpoon points, and shaft straighteners. The introduction of these new materials, in turn, required the development of specialized tools. Engraving tools called burins were developed, and flint drill points, often set in shafts and twirled between the hands or rotated as part of a bow drill, were invented to work bone and antler.

The Neolithic, or New Stone Age, brought new subsistence methods (agriculture and herding) and also new kinds of tools and new tool-making procedures. Flaking and chipping methods held on in many areas, but there was the addition of grinding and pecking techniques that produced smooth, even surfaces on the tools. The more reliable subsistence provided by agriculture and herding allowed for greater craft specialization, and, as people began to work exclusively at special trades, they developed new specialized tools. An example of this would be the many varieties of wedges, axes, and adzes used in woodworking. Agriculture required special kinds of tools, and a whole variety of sickles and grinding stones have been found dating from the Neolithic period. The Bronze Age, which followed, introduced a new material for tools, and many of the Neolithic tool types were merely reproduced in metal. This period also brought the plough, the potter's wheel, the wheeled vehicle, the lathe and, most important of all, the concept of draft animal power. The new metal tools were stronger and more enduring; tasks could be performed more quickly and more efficiently.

The next great upheaval in toolmaking did not occur until approximately 150 years ago when the industrial revolution introduced mechanical and electrical energy. When one looks at the modern power lathe, drill press, planer, or band saw, one realizes that we have come a long way from the days of the multipurpose hand ax. Our ingenuity has brought us from a condition when every day was a struggle to keep alive, to a point where we are so rich in technological knowledge that we have become arrogant in our relationship with nature.

FIRE

The story of tools would not be complete without mentioning mankind's servant and comforter—fire. We do not know when the use of fire was first discovered, but the first concrete evidence of its existence is a fire-hardened hearth in a cave occupied by *Homo erectus* some 700,000 years ago. This prehistoric man probably did not know how to produce fire but very likely borrowed and used it when a forest or field of dry grass was ignited by lightning or some other natural cause. The first method of actually making fire was perhaps a heat-through-friction method. Such methods are most widespread in the primitive world today. The Australian aborigines produce fire by making a sawing motion on a log of soft wood with a boomerang of hardwood. North and South American Indians use the bow or pump drill, and the people of the Pacific kindle a spark with fire graters or fire plows. This Pacific technique consists of rapidly rubbing a pointed hardwood stick back and forth in a grooved piece of soft wood until the resulting sawdust begins to smolder. Upper Paleolithic peoples used pyrites and flint to strike a spark, and the people of Borneo developed a fire pump or fire cylinder that compressed a column of air and thereby raised the temperature to a point sufficient to ignite tinder.

Fire has been such a valuable tool throughout human history that it has often been considered a sacred object. Many peoples have myths that associate fire with the gods. Greek myths relate that Prometheus stole the precious substance from Zeus; the Polynesian peoples have a tradition that fire was given to us by the demigod Maui. Fire has been worshipped, anthropomorphized, and even considered private property. The Buryat, of the steppes of Asia, feel that fire has a spirit that must not be offended by having refuse thrown upon it.

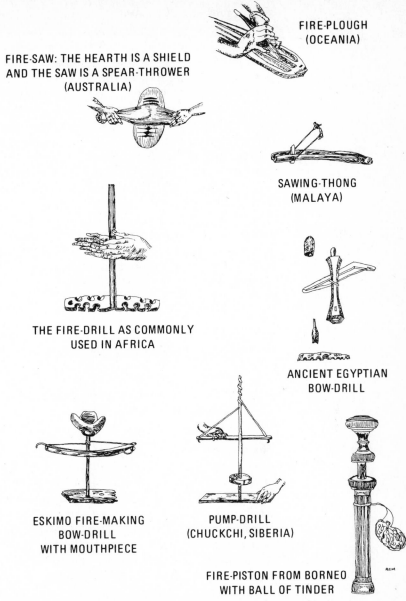

Figure 11-2 Fire-making methods around the world (after Harrison).

These people also consider fire to be the property of the clan, and no stranger may take so much as a spark away from the family hearth.

It is not difficult to understand people's reverence for fire, as it is perhaps their most valuable tool. It has provided warmth, cheer, and light for untold numbers of men and women in habitations ranging from caves to castles. With fire brands, Polynesian peoples attract fish to the surface where they may be speared in night fishing. On the Northwest Coast of North America smoke was used to cure the annual harvest of fish so that the Indians could depend on a year-round supply. Every people in the world cook at least part of their food through boiling, baking, broiling, or steaming. Without fire, simple tropical forest peoples would find the clearing of land difficult or even impossible. In Ice Age times, fire was used to drive herds of animals into corrals or over cliffs, and many people today still rely on fire to flush game. The ancient Maori used fire to attract sea birds to catch in nets. Fire is used by primitive peoples to hollow out canoes, harden pottery, smelt ore, and consume the dead.

HUNTING TOOLS

No group of technological inventions better reveals the technological aptitude of pre-industrial hunters than their traps, snares, and dead-falls. Concerning these various devices, Julius Lips comments:

> Long before Archimedes, [primitive man] invented, based upon the application of the laws of leverage, the important relay and release mechanisms whose analogous application in modern machinery can easily be observed by any layman, even if their construction has undergone considerable improvements (1956:54)

Lips sees these hunting "machines," so widely used by hunting peoples even today, as falling onto four basic categories. These he labels (1) the gravity trap, (2) the snare trap, (3) the spring-pole trap, and (4) the torsion trap.

The Gravity Trap.   The gravity trap makes use either of the weight of the animal itself or the force of an object that when released will fall and hit the animal. This category of traps would therefore include camouflaged pits into which an animal might fall and be impaled upon pointed sticks in the bottom, as well as a whole variety of log traps where the animal springs a release mechanism resulting in its being crushed by one or more falling timbers. A slightly different variety is the East African Lango elephant trap where a weighted spear falls on the elephant when he trips the release rope.

The Snare Trap.   This device depends on the forward motion of the animal to tighten a noose about its neck or one of its legs. Set either horizontally or vertically on frequently traveled game trails and partially hidden by grass or brush, the trap capitalizes on the animal's fear and effort to get away for its effectiveness. The greater the struggle, the tighter the noose is drawn, and if the neck is involved, the result is often death from strangulation.

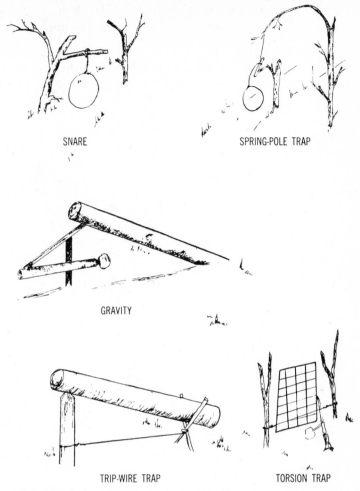

Figure 11-3 Snares and traps (after Gatty).

The Spring-Pole Trap. The spring-pole trap combines the features of the snare with the power of a bent tree or a branch that when released serves as a spring that will jerk the animal up into the air, killing it instantly and keeping the carcass out of the reach of other animals. This spring-pole principle also finds application in fishing, but, of course, in this case the snare is replaced with a hook or a basket.

The Torsion Trap. The torsion trap utilizes the power generated when a twisted sinew, root, or fiber is permitted to regain its original form. One variety of this trap uses a board twisted in a leather thong, which, when released, is forced down upon an animal. Another variation of this trap utilizes a net in place of the board and, instead of the animal being killed, the descending net merely captures it.

WEAPONS OF
THE CHASE

Man-Operated Hunting Weapons.   The more conventional tools of the hunt—the spear, harpoon, bow and arrow, and so on—although often less ingenious than the traps and snares in their conception and construction, do nevertheless in their manufacture and use involve an acute awareness of physical principles as well as a thorough knowledge of the habits of the game on which they will be used. The hand and missile tools of the hunt have served as the backbone of hunting economies since the beginning of culture and, although snares and traps have an important place in the activities of hunting, their utility has been secondary to the man-operated types of hunting weapons. The tools of the chase can, like snares and traps, be separated into several categories. One such system of classification is that of Daryll Forde (1954), who divides these weapons into (1) crushers—clubs, throwing-sticks, sling stones, (2) piercers—knives, spears, javelins, harpoons, arrows, blow-gun darts, and (3) entanglers—lassos, bolas, and nets.

Crushers.   Of the several crusher-type weapons the club has perhaps the least effectiveness in the chase. It has great usefulness, however, in dispatching animals wounded or entangled by other weapons. The throwing stick, which increases its crushing effectiveness by virtue of its being a missile, has wide distribution throughout the world. The Hopi Indians and South African Bushmen use such devices for hunting birds and other small game, but the most outstanding example of native ingenuity is the Australian boomerang, which returns to the thrower if it has missed its mark.

Sling and missile stones have been more of a weapon of war than of the hunt, but their effectiveness is well known to anyone who has

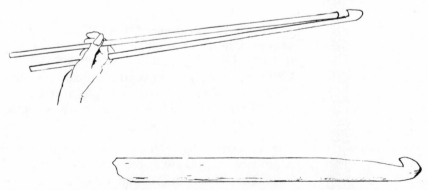

Figure 11-4 Spear throwers (*atlatl*) (after Braidwood).

read the David and Goliath story. Such people as the Navaho and the Ona of Tierra del Fuego find that the sling-delivered missile makes an effective hunting weapon and is an improvement in terms of speed, power, and range over the hand-thrown stone.

Piercers.   The first piercing weapon was undoubtedly the knife or blade, since such implements made of flint date back to the Lower Paleolithic. Like the club, the knife is limited to close-at-hand encounters with game. These are rarely possible in hunting unless the animal is either wounded or caught in a trap. Of the several piercer missiles the spear or lance has the greatest antiquity. The first spears were, very likely, stripped saplings with a sharpened point that might have been fire-hardened. There is evidence that Neanderthals used stone spear heads lashed to wooden shafts for purposes of throwing and thrusting. Although this type of weapon was highly effective, the Magdalenian people of the Upper Paleolithic improved its utility by inventing a special launching device commonly known as the spear-thrower or atlatl. Usually made of wood or ivory, the spear-thrower has a grip, or handle, at one end and a peg, or notch, at the other to take the butt of the spear. These spear-throwers, which measure from 1 to 3 feet in length, act in the manner of a sling, thus increasing the force and effective range of the missile. The same leverage principle was used by the New Caledonians and Roman soldiers in their spear-throwing lanyards. The knotted end of the cord fit into a notch at the butt of the spear while a loop in the other end was attached to a finger. The lanyard had the effect of increasing the length of the arm and therefore allowed the weapon to be thrown with greater force.

Another significant invention of the Upper Paleolithic period was the harpoon. In many cases, an animal wounded by a spear could use the leverage provided by the weight of the shaft to dislodge the head of the spear. The distinguishing feature of the harpoon is its detachable head. In many cases, the head is not only detachable but is supplied with a line that, like a fishing line, may be paid out or can be attached to a float as in the case of the Eskimo seal harpoon.

European cave painting, dating from approximately 13,000 B.C., includes scenes of hunters using bows and arrows. Although such weapons were probably widely used during the Upper Paleolithic, they became especially important in the Mesolithic when the retreating glaciers resulted in Europe changing from a tundra to a forest area. This change in climate and vegetation also brought a change in the animal life in central and western Europe. The great herds of reindeer had disappeared and in their place were elk, deer, and aurochs, the hunting of which required a good deal of skill. The bow and arrow, with its accuracy, powerful impact, and low trajectory at a range of several hundred feet, was the ideal hunting weapon. Many

Figure 11-5 Cave art from Spain depicting hunters with bows.

anthropologists believe that the concept of the bow was inspired by the spring-pole trap, since both utilize the power principle of the potential energy stored in a temporary bent stick. The arrow also derives from earlier weapon forms. It is a miniature of the javelin. The bow may be made of either a single piece of elastic wood, or, as in the case of the Siberian and New World Eskimo composite bow, it may be constructed of several pieces of wood or horn held together with glue and sinew.

The final type of piercing weapon with which we shall be concerned is the blow-gun dart. The blow gun is found mainly in Southeast Asia and South America, and, in spite of the wide separation of these two areas, the form and function of the weapons are remarkably similar. Whether this is the result of independent invention or diffusion has not as yet been settled. Wherever the weapon is found, its operation depends upon the propulsive force of the human thorax. Tylor points out that the blow-gun principle is basically what was employed in the development of the musket or the cannon. He writes, "When . . . gunpowder was invented in China, its use was soon adapted to make the blow-tube an instrument of tremendous power, when instead of a puff of breath in a reed, the explosion of powder in an iron barrel drove out the missile" (1894:197). Although the blow gun is quite accurate up to 150 feet, the darts are too small to be a very effective weapon against large game. To correct this fault, most people dip the darts in poison.

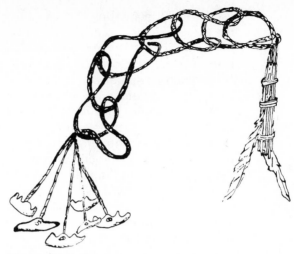

Figure 11-6 Eskimo entangler (after Beals and Hoijer).

Entanglers.   The most interesting of the entangling weapons is the bola. L. S. B. Leakey has discovered that weapons of this type were used in Kenya as early as Acheulian times (450,000–250,000 B.C.). The bola stones that he discovered were three in number, about the size and shape of baseballs, and grooved. This type of device is still used by gauchos in Argentina. The South American variety consists of three stone or clay weights joined by thongs of leather. To operate the contraption, the Pampas cowboy holds one weight in his hand, whirls the other two about his head, and at the appropriate moment lets the whole thing fly at the animal he is pursuing. The whirling device entangles the animal's legs, trips it, and holds it securely. The bola as a hunting weapon is used today by the Tehuelche people of Patagonia and the Eskimos of North America. The Patagonians use a three-weight bola for hunting guanaco and rhea, while the Eskimo weapon is used for birds and has five ivory weights, shaped like birds, seals, or bears. The latter weapon has a handle with feathers that serve to guide its flight.

The line with a running noose at one end is used as a hunting weapon in every part of the world in one form or another. Polynesians catch sharks and moray eels by luring them into a noose; Tierra del Fuegians use a long stick with a noose on the end for capturing birds. The lasso, truly a missile weapon, was employed by early Egyptians, Minoans, and New World pre-Columbian peoples in the hunting of large game.

While normally thought of as fishing devices, nets have been used widely in hunting. The fishing net probably originated during the Mesolithic period in Europe (7000 B.C.), but when it was first used for land animals is unknown. A relief decoration of a Grecian cup from 1600 B.C. depicts a bull caught in a net secured to two trees, and an Assyrian bas-relief dating from 700 B.C. shows deer being hunted with nets. Contemporary Witotos, of the Amazon jungle, reportedly stretch great nets 1000 feet or more in length among the trees and then drive large animals into them. In Uganda the people use the same methods in hunting antelope. Vancouver, and other early explorers in the Puget Sound area of North America, recorded the existence of "flagpoles" in many of the Indian villages. Actually the forty-foot poles they discovered were used for stringing bird nets. Teal, mallard, and canvasback ducks have a habit of flying 20 to 30 feet above the ground, and early in the morning or at twilight when the light was poor they would unwittingly fly directly into the nets. Waiting men would then seize them and wring their necks.

LIFTING MACHINES

Especially noteworthy was the ability of ancient peoples to handle blocks of stone weighing many tons with only human labor as a source of power. Monuments which particularly command our admiration are the pyramids of Egypt, the Stonehenge, and menhirs, dolmens, and other megaliths of western Europe, the huge Olmec heads, the great stone figures of Easter Island, and the wall of Cuzco. Very likely the engineering feats of creators of these marvels were the result of trial and error, rather than of theories of mechanics, but in each case there was an amazing perception of many basic mechanical principles, among these being the lever, the ramp and wedge which served in major ways as lifting machines.

It is believed that the Stone Age Polynesians of Easter Island erected their large stone figures with an earthen ramp. The statues were produced from stone quarried on a mountainside and were carved in a prone position. Then with the use of rollers they were transported by human labor to platform sites upon which they were to be raised. A ramp was built, and the figures were rolled to the edge of a shallow ditch, base foremost. They were gradually brought to an upright position by a system of lever and cribbing and slid into the ditch. The ramp was then made taller so that a large stone cap or crown could be rolled into place atop the figure.

Some of the major stones of the temple at Stonehenge on Salisbury Plain in southeastern England were probably erected in similar fashion, although these stones were much larger and heavier than those on Easter Island. Even more impressive was the technology required to place large lintel stones athwart pairs of vertical monoliths. These stones were quarried far away and transported to the

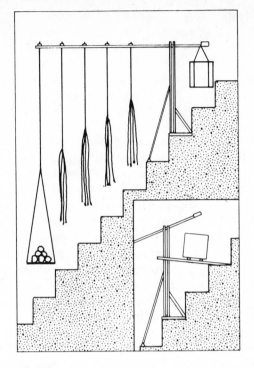

Egypt

Pallet is piled with rocks until weight is almost equal that of block. Then men add their weight by hanging on ropes. This raises the block to the level where a ramp may be put in place and the block is rolled away.

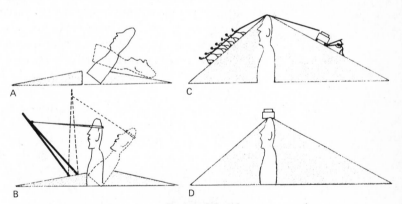

Easter Island

A. Stone statues are brought on rollers and tilted from ramp into ditch.
B. Ropes are used to bring it to erect position.
C. Ramp is raised for positioning of red stone hat.
D. Hat in place. Now earthen ramp is removed.

Figure 11-7 Lifting machines. Egypt and Easter Island (after Strand 1979).

erection site partly on water.

It has long been assumed that the great pyramids of the Old Kingdom of Egypt were built using enormous ramps to raise the stones to the proper levels. The building of the ramp's, however, would have been an engineering feat rivaling the building of the pyramids. Recently a Scandinavian engineer, Olaf Tellefsen, has suggested an alternative method, one within the capabilities of a limited technology and one which Tellefsen claims can be observed being used by modern Egyptians. The machine he believes they used is a form of lever known as the *weight arm*.

The weight arm consisted of a heavy timber which pivoted on a fulcrum about 6 feet high. The placement of the arm on the fulcrum was such that a short portion was about 3 feet long and a longer part was about 15 feet long, thus giving a large mechanical advantage. A pallet was placed at the end of the long arm upon which rocks were piled to form a counterweight. A sling attached to the short arm encircled the blocks of stone to be lifted. Rocks were piled on the pallet until the arm almost balanced. Then the men added their weight to lift the block to a position high enough to place a ramp and rollers under it. Once lowered onto the rollers by removing counter weights it was pushed to its proper place in the structure. (See Fig. 11-7) If indeed this was the method used in building the pyramids, it would have required many fewer laborers than previously assumed and would have been within the technical capabilities of the Bronze Age Egyptians. Theories that these monuments were massive public-works enterprises used to stabilize the economy by providing work for large numbers of farmers during the off seasons may have to be revised.

THE MAGNIFICENT CHINESE COOKING MACHINE

Few utensils developed by the world's societies are more compatible with the circumstances and needs of their users than the Chinese *wok.* Developed hundreds of years ago to cope with shortages in both food and fuel, the *wok* may have made the difference between starvation and survival in ancient China. China has always had more population than the land (only 10 percent is arable) could support and therefore food was always in short supply. They also have always had a desperate lack of fuel. Fortunately they were long on ingenuity and imagination, for they conceived of a wonderful cooking method which would utilize every morsel of food and very little fuel in the preparation of a palatable and healthful meal. This was accomplished through the invention of the *wok,* which merely means "cooking vessel." This utensil was unique however in that it was made of very thin metal and was shaped like a modern-day round bottomed salad bowl with handles. The vessel was made to rest on top of the traditional Chinese brazier and even a tiny bit of fuel (wood, charcoal, straw, or dung) would produce a flame that would diffuse heat up through the thin metal of the *wok* and cook the food in a matter of a few minutes. A very small amount of oil in the vessel prevented the food from burning and gave it flavor. The food was cooked just long enough to sear the cut surfaces of the vegetables and bits of meat, thus sealing in the natural juices and ensuring both flavor and the preservation of nutrients.

Housing

Although an aborigine standing in front of a thatched hut with a stone-tipped spear in his hand hardly looks like a scientist, we have seen that he can do some remarkable things in adjusting to his environment. Scientific behavior involves observing certain regularities of the physical universe and utilizing this knowledge to solve life's problems. If we look at the problems primitives must overcome and the resources they have at their disposal, we find that they can accomplish some remarkable things. A good example of this is in the area of native architecture. Fitch and Branch (1960) and Rapoport (1969) have made a thorough analysis of the architectural characteristics of the housing of contemporary primitives and find that these people, on the whole, show a greater awareness of climatic problems than the so-called "civilized" peoples who make such a point of their technical proficiency. They point out, for example, that far too often we have produced buildings that are beautiful to look at but are functionally very poor. Glass-walled skyscrapers are as modern as tomorrow, but unfortunately they often leak badly during rainstorms and in nearly every case they require special types of air conditioners and blinds to compensate for the excessive heat and glare produced by the glass.

Fitch and Branch, and Rapoport describe the characteristics of native housing in all parts of the world, but for our discussion we shall focus attention on shelters in (1) arctic climates, (2) deserts, (3) equatorial zones, and (4) grasslands.

THE ARCTIC

Eskimos live in a variety of houses, but the snow igloo is architecturally the most fascinating. The hemispherical shape of the dwelling offers the maximum amount of resistance and the minimum obstruction to winter winds. At the same time it offers the largest volume with the smallest structure. An oil lamp, centrally placed, can, in a structure of this shape, effectively heat every cubic foot of the inte-

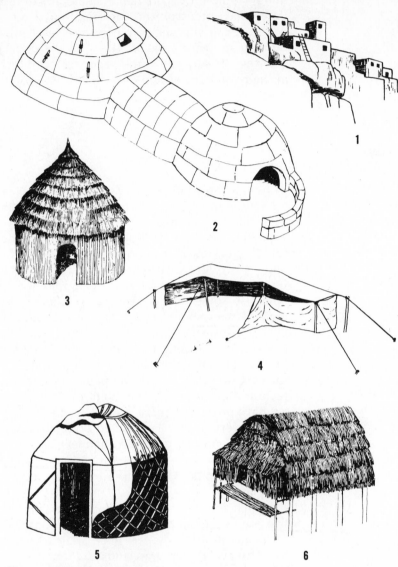

Figure 11-8 Houses of preindustrial peoples.

1. Southwest Indian Pueblo
2. Eskimo igloo (after Fitch and Branch)
3. African thatched hut
4. Bedouin tent
5. Central Asian Kazuk yurt
6. Melanesian stilt house (after Fitch and Branch)

rior. When the house is first occupied, the combination of lamp and body heat causes the interior face of the snow blocks to melt slightly. In time a glaze of ice develops on this interior surface, thus insulating the house and serving as a radiant heat reflector. When the walls are covered with skins, the tiny house represents the maximum in comfort possible under these difficult climatic conditions. By digging the entrance tunnel at a level below that of the house floor the Eskimo shows that he understands that cold air is heavier than warm and thus keeps the unheated entrance tunnel from chilling the main house interior.

THE DESERT

Desert conditions such as those encountered in the African Sudan, in Iran and Iraq, or in the southwestern part of the United States also present serious house-construction problems, but apparently none are too great for the ingenuity of the native builders. While there is no problem of protection from the rain, there are the problems of excessively hot and sunny days, rather cool nights, and a shortage of certain kinds of building materials. Fortunately there is a great abundance of clay and stone in such areas, and there is no material any better for desert housing than these. The adobe houses found in all of these areas are constructed so that the roof and walls absorb the sun's heat during the day but lose it slowly during the night. Thus the range of temperature for the occupants of the house is reduced. The mud construction does not stand up well under heavy rains, but since rain is at a minimum in desert areas this is not a problem. In parts of West Africa where there are heavy seasonal downpours the mud walls of the houses must be protected by overhanging thatched roofs. Nomadic peoples in desert areas must of necessity utilize easily portable materials. The Bedouin tent, for example, is made of woven goat hair supported in the form of a canopy by half a dozen poles. The shelter serves primarily as a sunshade, but side walls may be attached to provide a shield against blowing sand.

EQUATORIAL ZONES

In equatorial zones houses must primarily keep out the rain and provide shade. The beehive-shaped roofs of Pacific island dwellings are very efficient in this respect. Frequently these houses are entirely open on the sides, thus allowing maximum ventilation. In Melanesia, floors are often raised on stilts, partly for better exposure to the trade winds and partly for protection from rats, snakes, and crawling insects. The Nigerian dwelling is an interesting example of adaptation to the environment. Here the natives have developed a double-roofed dwelling. An inner roof of clay has projecting pegs to receive an outer layer of thatch. The thatch sheds water and protects the clay. The clay dome conserves heat for cold nights, and the air space be-

Housing in the tropics stresses ventilation and shade. (Courtesy Bill Short.)

tween the two serves as insulation from the heat of the afternoon sun.

GRASSLANDS OR PRAIRIES

In many of the grassland or prairie regions of the world we find nomadic herders like the Kazaks of the Asian steppes or nomadic hunters like the Plains Indians of North America. While the prairie environment poses certain architectural problems, nomadic activities further complicate the housing situation. Most of the prairie or grassland regions have great seasonal differences in temperature, strong winds, and shortage of trees for use as a building material. Furthermore, the nomadic economies of the inhabitants demand a type of house that is easily portable and simply and quickly erected. Both the Kazak yurt and the Plains Indian tepee appear to be quite adequate solutions to these problems.

The Kazak tent somewhat resembles a domed pillbox. The framework of the house has walls made up of crossed saplings tied together in such a way that they may be folded up like a child's safety gate. This feature allows the tent to be set up or dismantled in half an hour's time. Over the sapling framework is stretched a covering of felt that sheds water and insulates the interior. Ropes running in various directions over the outer surface of the house hold the felt in place. In summer the felt wall panels may be rolled up, thus allowing the occupants a maximum of ventilation.

The overhanging thatched roof of the West African dwelling protects the mud walls from the torrential rain. (Courtesy Field Museum of Natural History.)

Plains Indians tepee—made of buffalo hide and easily portable. (Courtesy Field Museum of Natural History.)

Similarly, the Great Plains tepee utilizes saplings that can be taken from place to place thus solving the wood shortage problem. Instead of felt they used the hides of buffalo as a weather-resistant covering. The heavy winds of the plains bothered the structure little, as it was well anchored to the ground with pegs, and furthermore, the conical shape provided a maximum of stability with a minimum of exposed surface. The hide covering could, with various adjustments, be closed up tight or opened to provide increased ventilation. When the house was dismantled, the lodge poles became part of a kind of trailer (travois), which was drawn by a horse, thus providing a means of transporting all of the material goods of the people.

Clothing

Why do people wear clothes? The most obvious answer, that clothing keeps them warm or protects them from the sun, wind, or rain, is but part of the explanation. We cannot go very far in explaining the variety of men's and women's costumes throughout the world in terms of an instinctive feeling of modesty. Modesty is not innate—it is learned cultural behavior—and Lowie has even suggested that it was the wearing of clothes that prompted the idea of modesty in the first place. To some people, it is indecent to show any part of the body other than the hands and face. Women in Moslem countries are very particular about covering their faces, but they sometimes leave their breasts exposed. Samoan women are likewise not embarrassed about being nude above the waist but consider it quite improper to expose the knee. Among the Tuareg of the African Sudan, it is the men who believe they must cover their faces. In this society, it is considered very immodest for any male to expose his mouth, particularly while eating, and thus they have adopted a style of dress that has resulted in their being called "The People of the Veil." The story is told that an anthropologist traveling in the Amazon jungles encountered a group of people where the women wore nothing save lip ornaments. The anthropologist persuaded one of these women to sell him her labret. Upon removing this ornament, she ran away and hid because she was ashamed of her nude appearance.

With all these variations in the concept of modesty and with the fact that some people give no thought to wearing nothing at all, it is doubtful that man's widespread use of clothes is prompted to any great extent by moral considerations.

Clothing usually reflects the environmental conditions of the wearer, and it is the development of protective clothing and housing as well that has allowed people to inhabit all parts of the globe. The presence of the two basic types of clothing, tailored and loose-hanging, seem to show a definite relationship to the kind of climate to be coped with. Where retention of body heat is important, the former seem to be found, but where there is a need to facilitate heat loss or where special protection from the sun is important, we more frequently encounter loose-fitting garments.

CLOTHING AND CLIMATE

During World War II Paul Siple[1] conducted research for the United States Government on ideal clothing for the many climatic zones in which American troops were fighting. Realizing that the ability of servicemen to function effectively is greatly reduced if they are inadequately clothed it was hoped that research into climate and clothing requirements could provide a satisfactory solution. Siple designated seven types of climatic zones running from "humid tropical or jungle" through "temperate" and into "arctic." The clothing recommendations designed to meet the demands of the various climatic conditions were based on a "layer principle" (a layer of clothing being one-fourth-inch thick).

Researchers recommended that one layer was appropriate for the "subtropical" zone with additional layers being added until four layers were recommended for inhabitants of the "subarctic winter" zone.

In 1971 Ellen Rhoads compared clothing styles of 18 pre-industrial groups in a variety of climates with the "ideal" as determined by Paul Siple and his researchers. It was discovered that about half of the cultures whose clothing styles were analyzed in regard to protective effectiveness had clothing that could be considered "ideal" or "nearly ideal" for the environment. And correspondence between climate and clothing increased with the severity of the climate. Reasons for less than "ideal" clothing for the particular climatic zones were found to be explainable in terms of cultural phenomena—retention of earlier practices established in a different climate, status considerations, and acculturative influences. There were several documented examples of undesirable results of changes in clothing resulting from contact with traders, government administrators, missionaries, or other agents of change. Generally Rhoads's study concluded that "primitive man is exceedingly efficient in dealing with his environment, although he almost always operates within a context of relatively limited material resources and often within a restricted scope of technological alternatives (1971:144)".

---

[1] Paul Siple was the Eagle scout who accompanied Admiral Byrd on his expedition to Antarctica.

There are, however, numerous examples of curious and even uncomfortable fashions that seem to relate little to the climatic problems or cultural activities of their wearers. The Ona people of Tierra del Fuego live in a region where the average temperature is 45 degrees, and yet their normal dress includes a small otter or seal skin cape and a thin layer of grease and clay smeared over the body. The Tungus people of Siberia, who also live in a very cold climate, fashion their clothing out of fur, but seem to let style or tradition stand in the way of complete comfort. The Tungus fur coat greatly resembles a European morning coat. It could be a very warm garment, but it is always worn open, thus giving no protection to the chest, abdomen, or upper legs. One need not think that primitive peoples are the only ones who develop strange impractical fashions. The hobble skirt, the wasp waist, the high heel, the necktie, the dinner jacket, the celluloid collar, and the powdered wig are European inventions that, in spite of their obvious impracticability, attracted millions of wearers for the sake of fashion.

Obviously clothes do more than satisfy modesty requirements and afford protection from the elements. They can represent objects of allure or they can serve as indicators of sex, age, occupation, wealth, caste, or class. Clothes can be used to indicate religious or political affilations.

CLOTHING AND STATUS

Perhaps the most important factor for determining particular kinds of clothing to be worn is the matter of prestige and position. Few societies do not have some method of indicating who are the important people, either by special garments or by body decoration. The amount and the type of design of tattooing set apart the Polynesian nobleman from the commoner. The feather war bonnet told everyone that its wearer was a member of an honored Plains Indian soldier or military society. Nootka chiefs on the Northwest Coast of America showed their high status by wearing gaudier and more elaborate costumes than anyone else. They were the only ones who could wear dentails or abalone shells, and only their robes could be trimmed with sea otter fur.

Turning to our own culture we can see that clothing provides valuable status clues for us as well. We talk about "white-collar" workers and "blue-collar" workers as representing various levels in our class system. The college graduate can, by style of dress, be easily distinguished from shop or office workers of comparable age, and the college professor frequently sets him or herself apart by a certain "tweediness," distingushable from the banker, the salesperson. The minister of course, is easily identified by one article of clothing—the clerical collar.

In one area of women's apparel we find the greatest status indicator, the coat. As a rule, it is a matter of how much fur and what kind of fur. There is the cloth coat, the fur-collared cloth coat, the fur coat, and then, most prestigious of all, the mink coat. Mink coats are desired primarily because they indicate that the wearer is of the upper classes, or more important, the wife of a very successful member of the middle class. They are not necessarily more beautiful than other kinds of furs, nor are they any warmer, but merely more expensive because mink fur is rarer than other kinds. If the mink coat were worn for warmth, it would come equipped with buttons (which it usually is not) and it would have the fur on the inside. Viewing the situation very objectively, it would appear that mink will have to be assigned to the category of "conspicuous consumption." This was a term first used by the American sociologist and economist Thorstein Veblen (1899), who pointed out that tight-fitting knee breeches, powdered wigs, and lace cuffs served to identify certain colonial men as aristocrats or men of wealth who did not have to work for a living. Their impractical apparel was obviously not suited to any kind of physical exertion.

Clothing styles also seem to be influenced by factors of which people are not even aware. Anthropologists A. L. Kroeber and Jane Richardson once painstakingly analyzed 300 years of European dress styles noting such features as length and width of skirts and position of neckline and waistline. They found that in spite of all the dress designer's and manufacturer's efforts, fashions follow a pattern of cyclic change. In times of peace and prosperity dresses featured a fitted bodice, a full skirt, and the waistline at the natural waist. In troubled times such as the Revolution, the Napoleonic era, and World War I and during the depression of the 1930s dress styles were extreme, featuring either ultra-high or ultra-low waistlines and skirts that were narrow or short or both. They concluded from their study that, "since the periods of dress-pattern instability were also periods of marked socio-political instability and churning, there is presumably a connection" (Kroeber 1948:334). The events of the late 1960s lend support to Kroeber and Richardson's hypothesis. Not only was it a period of marked social and political unrest but it was also a period characterized by the shortest (mini) and the longest (maxi) skirts, the most plunging necklines, and generally the most unorthodox dress fashions to appear in the twentieth century.

Pre-industrial Scientists

We have learned from a brief cross-cultural inventory of tools and technical methods that everyone, whether "primitive" or "civilized," has the ability to work out solutions to quite complex problems by using a type of scientific behavior involving observation, experimentation, and generalization. Where irrational types of behavior occur, such as in the quirks of clothing styles, "civilized" folk seem to be as guilty of these follies as are pre-industrial peoples. It is fair to ask, however, why the latter who have shown such great ingenuity and ability in many areas of culture have been so overshadowed by the technical accomplishments of the West. This is a fair question because it was not always the case. When Northern Europeans were still chipping stone for their weapons, the West Africans were smelting iron. In the twelfth century, a Negro university in Timbuktu was equal to or better than, any in Europe at that date. When the conquistadors conquered the Mayan territory of Yucatan, Guatemala, and Southern Mexico in 1562, they found that these Indians had developed a scientific body of knowledge, at least in the area of astronomy, that surpassed that of Europeans at that time. Approximately 100 years before the peak of the Italian Renaissance, Inca craftsmen in Peru were weaving priceless tapestries of gold and silver cloth and producing unbelievable objects of sculpture. One Spanish account describes a great golden garden on the grounds of the Inca emperor's palace where llamas and their herders, flowers, and birds were wrought life size out of gold. The garden was complete even to tiny golden butterflies with filigree wings, which fluttered like tiny kites over the flowers.

One of the great adventures in human history and aboriginal science was the peopling of Oceania. About 1500 B.C. the ancestors of today's Polynesians and Micronesians left the mainland of southeast Asia and began to move eastward in search of new islands. Their frail catamarans and outrigger canoes, measured 100 feet or more in length. Great lateen sails, woven of pandanus fiber, drove these ships at remarkable speeds toward new homes among the Pacific islands. Voyages from one major island group to another often were thousands of miles long, and many were through reef-infested waters; and remarkably, navigators achieved their landfalls without the aid of compasses, sextants, nautical almanacs, chronometers, or any of the aids so vital to modern navigation. Another 2000 years would pass before comparable feats would be accomplished by Europeans (Vikings) and Arabs.

The most common Polynesian method of navigation consisted of laying a course that kept the bow of the vessel pointed toward a star near the horizon which lay in the direction of the desired destination. Instead of using a single star as a navigational beacon, Polynesian captains thought in terms of moving bands of light. Those bands were actually a series of stars which rose one after the other at a given point on the horizon. When one star climbed too high to be useful, the helmsman would shift to one lower on the horizon. A given series of stars was associated with particular islands and the stars were named accordingly. It is difficult to visualize exactly how these associations between stars and islands were made in the first place, but we may assume that on voyages of exploration, close attention was paid to stars rising ahead of the vessel and setting astern, for this information was vital to a safe return.

All of the native navigators in Oceania also had to be able to know the prevailing wind and wave directions in the various seasons of the year to orient themselves when an overcast sky made it impossible to steer by the stars. Wind pennants of feathers or palmetto bark were used, but normally the run of the sea was a more dependable indicator, as winds can shift direction more quickly than can waves or swells.

Why have these outstanding primitive technicians not gone beyond a certain point in their development? The answer is to be found in a single factor—isolation. Through some quirk of fate, Europe has been a great mixing bowl of peoples and ideas. Armies of every nationality have surged across the continent like waves on the sea. They have often brought destruction, but they have also brought new ways of doing things and making things. Trade routes crisscrossed the area bringing goods from afar. Europeans have not had the opportunity to isolate themselves from new ideas, even if they had wanted to.

Compare this situation with that of the Astralian aborigines who entered the continent of Australia about 25,000 years ago and remained almost completely cut off from contact with other people until the first European contacts in about 1788.

The remoteness of the islands of Polynesia and Micronesia made contact difficult with other Pacific peoples, let alone contact with peoples with foreign cultures. Although there was always some intertribal contact and trade in Africa, this continent remained a rather remote and isolated area until its coasts were explored by the Portuguese in 1415. Even today, movement from one part of Africa to another is difficult without air transportation.

Complex technological inventions do not grow out of thin air; every new idea rests on a base of accumulated knowledge. The invention of television, for example, could not have taken place until the way was paved by the discoveries of electricity, metallurgy, glass manufacture, sound and light wave theory, and hundreds of other innovations, which we forget about because they are so much a part of our daily lives. Inventions breed inventions, and the larger the technological base of knowledge the more likely it is that still newer and more ingenious inventions will appear; history books estimate that the really significant technological inventions and discoveries between the years A.D. 1000 and 1400 were about 10 in number, these same references set the figure at 2100 for the years 1800 to 1899.

Cultures that have been forced to develop in a world continually exposed to new ideas will be more responsive to change than those who have not had this experience. In most European cultures, the fact that father and grandfather did it that way is no reason at all for continuing, if a better method is available. Pre-industrial people, however, who have worked out their technology painfully, through the process of trial and error, tend to find an acceptable method and stick to it for generations. Change takes place slowly and deliberately. The new and the different hold no fascination for pre-industrial people. Cultural stability is so fundamental that Harding has postulated that "a culture at rest tends to remain at rest" (1960:54).

Summary

Human beings are toolmaking and tool-using creatures, and their tools are responsible, in part, for the development of their humanity. Beginning with the simple pebble-tool tradition known as Oldowan, and developing to the refined and specialized implements of the Industrial Revolution, mankind has displayed an ability to alter the environment, and at times even create an artificial one, thereby improving comfort and chances of survival.

Not ordinarily thought of as a tool, but something that has literally made the difference between life and death for humans, is fire. Dating back to at least *Homo erectus*, fire has been used to process food, warm habitations, provide light, and aid in hunting. It is so valuable that it is worshipped in many societies.

Human beings have long been extraordinary in their ability to discover scientific principles in solving practical problems. Examples are the ingenious use of natural materials and architecture compatible with climate in the construction of housing, the development of hunting and lifting "machines," and the fashioning of protective clothing. But clothing does more than protect; it also identifies—indicating sex, status, and occupation.

Scientific procedures are not the exclusive property of Western industrial peoples and can be found in the experimentation and careful, controlled observation which have allowed pre-industrial peoples to navigate by the stars, build magnificent edifices, smelt iron, and develop a metalurgical art tradition in gold and silver.

The Economic Aspect of Culture 12

The role of economics in society

    Urban versus rural economics

    Shifting economic roles

Types of economic systems

    Hunters, fishers, and gatherers

    Specialized hunters and fishers

    Pastoralists

    Simple cultivation

    Advanced cultivation

    Sedentary highland cultivators in the New World

    Oriental agrarian societies

    Occidental economics

Economic organization

    Organized system of productions

    Economic value system

    Methods of product distribution

    Monetary symbols

    Property

New approach to economic life

    Energy usage

    Ecological approach

Many changes occurred in the economic life of America as the trend to urbanization intensified in mid-twentieth century. When one of the authors (WP) married an Iowa farm girl in the early forties, the rural community in which she lived was a closely knit social unit, revolving around a rural church, already almost a hundred years old. This community was relatively stable, with farms remaining within families for several generations, and considerable intermarriage occurring between families. In the period before combines became numerous (after World War II), much of the harvesting of cereal grains was done by binders and threshing machines, requiring a large number of laborers to shock the grain and to bring it to the machine after it had dried.

A "threshing machine," which was both the engine (at first steam then gasoline powered) and the separator, was usually owned by a couple of men, who received cash for the grain that was threshed, at so much per bushel. The rest of the crew was made up of men and boys of the families whose grain was being harvested, and who received no cash wages though each farm also provided horses and wagons for the operation. The wives and daughters provided the noon dinner on the days their crops were being threshed, and usually they helped other women on the days the other farms were being served. Much rivalry existed between women as to who could serve the best dinner. No matter which woman excelled, the men always won.

The sharing of work carried on in activities during the entire year. Whenever a farmer needed a hand he called one of the neighbors in this co-op ring and if the neighbor couldn't come himself, he would send a son or hired man to help. No one kept books on the time given—it was all a part of being a "neighbor", and one suspects the accounts would probably have balanced quite well. If a man consistently avoided his responsibilities, he would probably have found no one who would help him.

During World War II with so many men in military service and only older men and young boys remaining on the farm, it became necessary to recruit labor from town or at least from outside the neighborhood. Payment in hourly wages became the rule, and the farm wives had little interest in feeding strangers, so the laborers either had to bring their own dinner or they went to a restaurant in town for dinner. The ring of sharing of farm work has now almost totally disappeared, except for enclave groups like the Amish or Hutterites, who live eighteenth century-like peasant lives in the midst of the twentieth century.

The basic economy of a people is an integral part of their way of life and cannot easily be separated from their patterns of family, government, and, to a certain extent, religion. Patterns of subsistence correlate with certain kinds of movement and settlement, and the relative amount of wealth made possible by the use of certain subsistence methods supports varying degrees of specialization and facilitates trade.

The problem of studying economics cross-culturally is not an easy job as there are literally hundreds of separate combinations of methods of getting a living. For purposes of study it will be convenient to utilize a scheme of classification of economic types or models. Such a scheme has been developed by J. H. G. Lebon, a British human geographer. Although the following eight categories do not embrace every single society in the world, they do represent significant types of economies and they help us to see the influence of economic activities on the nature of culture.

Economic Types

Lebon (1969) divides the economies of the world into the following categories:

1. hunters, fishers, and gatherers,
2. specialized hunters and fishers,
3. pastoralists,
4. simple cultivators,
5. advanced cultivators,
6. sedentary highland cultivators of the New World,
7. Oriental agrarian civilizations, and
8. Occidental economies.

HUNTERS,
FISHERS, AND
GATHERERS

Hunting and gathering were ways in which humans got a living throughout the Paleolithic period, but as food producing skills and herding developed, hunters and gatherers began to disappear, and today they exist only in marginal areas of the world. The nonliterates who are identified with this type of simple economy include such peoples as the Andaman Islanders, the Semang and Sakai of the Malay Peninsula, the African Bushmen of the Kalahari desert, and the Australian aborigines. Although these peoples live in a variety of climates and their cultural histories vary greatly, there is a general similarity in their lives that derives from the nature of their economic activities.

Generally, these people make intensive use of the environment. Everything that is edible, except traditionally taboo foods, makes up the diet. This may include such things as a wide range of fruits, nuts, eggs, rodents, reptiles, and even insects. The weapons of the hunt are manufactured mainly of wood and stone, and fishing is done with spears, hooks, or traps. Pottery, weaving, and metalworking are unknown arts, and there is little specialization of labor other than sex or age differentiations. Every man is a hunter and every woman and child a gatherer of wild plants. The only systems of trade known to these peoples are irregular barter or silent trade activities carried on with neighboring sedentary peoples.

Since hunting and gathering activities can seldom provide more than a meager and unreliable living, hunters and gatherers must limit their numbers. Often a single extended family makes up the hunting band. With autonomous bands of only a dozen or two dozen people, government is informal. In a manner of speaking, family structure and political structure are one.

Hunting and gathering peoples are commonly nomadic. They must constantly move from one place to another in search of new supplies of game. These movements seem to be patterned. No hunting people ever wanders aimlessly from place to place. Hunting is a difficult activity at best, but it would take on added difficulty if carried on in unfamiliar terrain.

Because of this mobility, these bands seldom live in more than temporary shelters constructed of brush, bushwood, and leaves. All hunting and gathering people seem to have well-established ideas of territoriality. Boundaries of hunting and gathering areas are recognized by the groups that occupy them and are jealously guarded against trespass from outsiders, although often in times of duress, permission to hunt and collect will be granted upon request to outsiders, and of course exchange of marriage partners, food, and services takes place between bands.

SPECIALIZED HUNTERS AND FISHERMEN

As examples of this kind of economic life we might point to the Indians of the Pacific Northwest, Alaska, and northern Canada; a number of hill and forest peoples of India and Southeast Asia; and the fishermen of Malaya and the East Indies. A specialized hunting and fishing economy differs from the former category in that subsistence comes from a few abundant species. Pacific Northwest Indians depend upon salmon and sea mammals, Northern Canadian Indians utilize caribou as the main food source, and the "Sea Gypsies" of Indonesia completely eschew agriculture and subsist entirely on fish.

With a dependable source of subsistence and with efficient methods of exploiting it, these cultures have a relatively high standard of living as hunting and fishing cultures go. Weapons, clothing, houses, and their furnishings are quite elaborate, since a certain degree of specialization in arts, crafts, and industries can usually be supported by the dependable and stable economy. In modern times many of these cultures have become involved in commercial hunting or fishing enterprises for European entrepreneurs, and therefore acculturation and acquisition of European goods have been accelerated.

Settlements often include assemblages of as many as 50 families, and tribal groupings are even found among some of these peoples. The Northwest Coast Indian societies occupied permanent villages, and Canadian Eskimos and Indians utilized sizable winter camps. Where mobility is found, movements tend to be seasonal and traditionally patterned. Hunting and fishing areas are considered group or community property and are jealously guarded against trespass by other groups.

PASTORAL ECONOMIES

Although pastoral economies are found in a great variety of environments, and the animals domesticated differ greatly from place to place, the very nature of this kind of economy imposes a certain pattern of culture that is roughly similar in all of these areas. In Africa, the Masai and Fulani keep cattle, the Siberian Tungus tend reindeer, the Bedouins of Syria and Arabia herd camels, and the Siberian Kazaks live mainly off their herds of horses, sheep, and goats. In most of these societies the cultural patterns may generally be described as follows:

Movements of societies, dictated by the needs of animals for fresh pasture or water, are basically seasonal ones. All these cultures have concepts of either summer and winter pasture or wet and dry season areas of grazing. Aside from the seasonal migrations there are constant movements from place to place, and material goods are consequently limited. Housing takes the form of tents in many of these cultures—materials ranging from felt to skins, or cloth of wool or cotton. Frequently, herding peoples are able to establish trade relationships with sedentary agricultural peoples, thereby enriching their diet and material wealth. Herding peoples do little themselves, however, in the way of developing craft specialization.

The significant social unit among pastoralists is typically the clan or group of related families with patriarchal rule. Permanent settlements are seldom found, and it is difficult for them to maintain social or political units larger than the clan. Loosely organized tribal units have been known, however, and in the case of nomads of the Asiatic steppe lands, "hordes" and even nations were formed under the Khans.

SIMPLE CULTIVATORS

This rather rudimentary type of economy, sometimes called "swidden farming" which greatly resembles that found during the Neolithic, is represented by the cultures of peoples living in the hill regions of India, Indonesia, and Central America as well as any number of Ama-

African advanced cultivation supports craft specialists like this Bura potter.

zon river societies. The societies practicing this way of life occupy warm forest regions where they cut away and burn the underbrush in order to clear small plots of land for the cultivation of root crops and grains. The hoe and the digging stick (dibble) are the principal tools of subsistence, but weapons of the hunt are also present, as both gathering and small game-hunting activities appear in combination with farming.

Life is simple, and textiles, pottery, and housing are rudimentary. Settlements, which include from five to twenty families, tend to be impermanent, as soils are often infertile and erosion, caused by the simple cultivation methods, forces these people to move periodically to new locations with virgin soil. In some areas a pattern of weak tribal organization exists, but the usual pattern is village autonomy. Trade relationships between villages are seldom of a regular nature and most economic exchanges take the form of simple barter.

ADVANCED CULTIVATORS

Somewhat more advanced agricultural methods characterize the cultures of the people of the Southwest Pacific and the agricultural regions of Negro Africa. While most of these people utilize hand cutlivation methods, there is a greater dependence upon crops than is found among the cultures in the simple cultivator category. Forests are permanently cleared and there is a regular pattern of resting land after a few seasons' cultivation. Agriculture is often combined with stock-raising, but there is little hunting or gathering. Tribal government is often well developed, and some villages are very large, with populations numbering in some cases into the hundreds and even thousands. Land tends to be clan or village property, but individuals or families are given land-use rights. In some areas, particularly West or Central Africa, an elaborate system of markets and trade relationships may be found. These agricultural methods support a good deal of specialization in the areas of government, religion, and the arts and crafts.

SEDENTARY HIGHLAND CULTIVATORS OF THE NEW WORLD

The Aztecs, Incas, Chibchas, and Quechuas prior to Spanish conquest lived by a type of economy that, although limited to one area of the world, is significant enough to warrant a special category. These cultures, specializing in maize, potatoes, beans, and other subsidiary crops, irrigated dry lands and terraced fields located on hilly slopes. Land was permanently cleared, and intensive agrarian methods supported substantial permanent towns as well as organized political states. Hand cultivation was a universal characteristic with domesticated animals being found to any great extent only in the Peruvian area, where llamas were raised for their wool and as pack animals.

A well-established system of trade, made possible in part by a network of permanent roads, enhanced the standard of living. Specialization in the areas of arts and crafts, religion, science, and government reached a zenith with the substantial support made possible by maize agriculture.

ORIENTAL AGRARIAN CIVILIZATION

For examples of this type of economy the reader's attention might be directed to the civilizations of India, Burma, Java, Thailand, Cambodia, China, and Japan. In most of the Oriental cultures, the greater bulk of the population is supported by irrigated rice cultivation, but in a few cooler and drier regions millet or other Western cereals take on major importance. In addition to the cereal staples, fruits, vegetables, spices, oil-producing seeds, and fibrous plants bolster the economy. Plough cultivation is characteristic in all of these cultures, but there is not a great deal of emphasis placed upon domestication of animals although the water buffalo is a very important part of this system. It provides draft power, and fertilizer, and it lives off the produce of the land—that is, it requires no exotic fuel, spare parts, or other maintenance resources not found in the society.

Arts and crafts are elaborate, and local and regional trade is highly developed. In most of these areas there is evidence of an early

Indonesian farms with water buffalo. (Courtesy Willis Tilton and Wichita State University.)

development of this rather advanced economic complex, with the result that well-organized political states have existed for hundreds of years.

Rice-growing areas have, under this form of subsistence, been able to support as many as 1500 people per square mile. In most of these cultures the permanent village is the significant settlement unit and land is usually privately owned, either by peasant farmers or by a land-owning class that controls large estates. In all of these Oriental countries, towns or cities developed as centers of craft specialization, trade, and government.

OCCIDENTAL ECONOMIES

Although anthropology to a great extent concentrates on cultures outside the Western tradition, it has been our purpose throughout this book to study the human animal cross-culturally, and therefore some note must be taken of the industrial economies of Europe, Brazil, Argentina, the United States, South Africa, Australia, New Zealand, and other areas of the world that have been influenced in their economy by the presence of European emigrants.

Even though there are obvious differences between the European peasant farmer and a farmer in Iowa or Illinois, whose investment in land, machinery, and livestock may well exceed 500,000 dollars, both are more like each other than either is like the Oriental farmer. Basic in the Western economy is nonirrigated plough cultivation of Western cereal crops with mechanized equipment and the large-scale raising of domesticated animals. The most characteristic feature, however, is the widespread use of mechanical power in mass production industry. Still another support of the Occidental economy is the exploitation of oil, natural gas, mineral, water, and timber resources. Efficient production and management techniques in all facets of agriculture and industry make for abundance, a high standard of living, and adequate support of well-organized states with world economic interests. Because of mechanization and advanced scientific knowledge in the areas of plant and animal production, it has been possible in most Occidental cultures for a small percentage of agriculturalists to support large urban populations who engage in highly specialized occupations in industry, commerce, the arts, and sciences. Such economies as these must for purposes of product distribution feature networks of roads and railways, and transoceanic commerce is a vital aspect of the economy.

Economic Organization

Morton Fried has remarked that "from the point of view of anthropology, economic studies have three primary facets: the description of the tools and techniques of production, the designation of the particular means and level of subsistence, and the analysis of the social relationships which involve the movement of goods and services" (1959:114). Having already dealt with the first two facets in this chapter and Chapter 9, we shall now consider how individuals interact to facilitate the economic production and distribution of goods in a society. Our discussion of the eight model types of economy has shown us that economies in various parts of the world can vary greatly in detail, but a second look will reveal that all economic systems have a great number of things in common. These things are called *universals* and they arise out of human needs and the nature of society. The term *universal* does not imply identical features in all societies but rather similarities in classification of economic behavior. Requesting the reader to keep this fact in mind we may move on to a statement of what these worldwide economic features are. No economic system in the world is without (1) an organized system of production, (2) an economic value system, (3) methods of product distribution, (4) common monetary symbols, and (5) a concept of property.

Economic Universals

AN ORGANIZED
SYSTEM OF
PRODUCTION

No society can long exist without a traditional formula for what kind of work will be engaged in for its support and who is going to do that work. In a society where there is great surplus, people may pretty much choose what they want to do, but where precise organization

The work of women—cooking, weaving, gathering firewood, working in the cultivations, washing, and pounding flax fibres.

Men at work, snaring rats, digging with the ko, fishing, fighting with taiaha, canoe building, and thatching the roof of a whare.

Figure 12-1 Division of labor among the Maori of New Zealand. (Courtesy Reed Methuen Publishers, Ltd.)

TABLE 3   Sex division of labor in 224 societies (from Murdock 1937:551)

Activity	Number of societies in which activity is performed by:				
	Males only	Males mostly	Males or Females	Females mostly	Females only
Pursuit of sea mammals	34	1	0	0	0
Hunting	166	13	0	0	0
Trapping	128	13	4	1	2
Fishing	98	34	19	3	4
Gathering shellfish	9	4	8	7	25
Gathering fruits and nuts	12	3	15	13	63
Preserving meat and fish	8	2	10	14	74
Gathering herbs, roots, and seeds	8	1	11	7	74
Cooking	5	1	9	28	158

and utilization of talent may mean the difference between life and death by starvation the culture carefully prescribes who shall work at what.

The most basic organization of productive labor, found even among hunting and gathering people, is a sex division. This represents an attempt at least to produce specialists in jobs they are capable of doing, and at the same time it has the effect of reducing duplication of activities and needless competition between the sexes.

Sex Division of Labor.   An inventory of sex divisions of labor among the world's peoples would reveal that there is no great uniformity in what should be the jobs of men or the jobs of women but that there is a tendency for women to be given those jobs that keep them relatively close to the home (a necessity while nursing and caring for small children) and require less physical strength. Men, on the other hand, not being biologically tied to small children, often engage in activities that might require an absence from home of several days or even weeks and require great endurance and physical strength and often the ability to cope with a measure of danger as well. It will be noted in the analysis of 224 cultures made by Murdock (Table 3) that while men may cook and women may trap, it is more common for men to hunt, fish, and trap and for women to gather, preserve food, and cook. Wherever the patterns runs contrary to this, it is usually possible to find special cultural reasons. In Samoa, for example, men do the major part of the cooking, but food is often involved in matters of high ceremony. Many of the foods are considered too sacred to be handled by anyone other than titled or especially authorized untitled men. Not only are men the cooks in this society, but often the serving people as well.

Division of labor between men and women among the Bura of Nigeria is quite rigid. In general those duties involving food and drink are women's; house building and duties pertaining to clothing are men's. Both sexes cooperate in planting and harvesting of the staple crop, guinea corn. Drawing and carrying water is women's work and no self-respecting male would be caught in this kind of work. The importance of work allocation by sex was noted when during a drought, the women who usually carried water to fill the barrels of a group of missionaries were unable to keep up with the demand. One of the young men was being trained as a mechanic and driver, and was utilized in hauling water from the river in 55-gallon barrels in an old truck. However, he was not hauling water (a female role) but driving a truck (emphatically a male role)!

Age Division of Labor.   In addition to dividing the jobs between men and women, most societies also do so according to age. To a certain extent this organization reflects the relative strength, experience, and temperament of people at various ages. In most societies children are given light tasks like baby-sitting, running errands, and collecting firewood, while postadolescents and adults handle the heavy work—the hunting, cultivating, or house-building. As a man advances toward middle age, his experience is of great value to his society, but his strength is beginning to wane. In many societies it is at this time that a man enters the village council of elders and helps deliberate vital issues concerning the welfare of his community. The aged are often recognized as storehouses of tradition and knowledge and as people who have experienced much of life. Thus, they are often the educators of the young and the advisors of the village political leaders. The elderly are often given light tasks so that they might keep themselves busy, but in most societies (excepting those to be found in difficult environments where everyone must do his share or be abandoned) the aged are felt to have earned their rest.

Other Divisions.   Still another way of dividing labor duties is according to family, caste, or class. In parts of Africa, working in iron or manufacturing salt is the special prerogative of certain families or clans, a concept also held in Europe until comparatively recently. Craft specialization was handed down from father to son in particular families. A survival of this period is to be seen in such family names as Carpenter, Mason, Hostler, Miller, etc.

Among the East African Bikitara people, class completely determines occupation. Nobles are pastoralists and peasants are agriculturalists. In India one of the most striking aspects of the *jati*, or caste, is its labor specialization. Alan R. Beals lists the various *jati* in the southern Indian village of Gopalpur, as priest, farmer, carpenter, blacksmith, saltmaker, shepherd, barber, butcher, weaver, stoneworker, basket weaver, and leatherworker (1962:36).

As we move from primitive societies to peasant and industrial ones, we find that labor specialization becomes more diverse. Redfield says:

> With the development of tools and techniques, with increase in population, and with the advancement of communications and transportation, the division of labor has become far more complete and complex. In the Guatemalan village of San Pedro de la Laguna, fifty-nine different kinds of specialists are to be recognized in a population of less than two thousand. A classified telephone directory suggests but by no means completely lists the thousands and thousands of kinds of specialists that make up a modern city. (1956:346)

Cooperative Work.   The organization of labor extends beyond a mere designation of who should do what job. In some societies labor is organized around an individualistic and competitive pattern whereas the members of some others could not imagine working under anything but a cooperative group situation. In Dobu, farmers work alone and in competition with everyone else, even the members of their own lineage. Harvesting is done in strictest secrecy so that no one can see how prosperous a man might be, for a "good crop is a confession of theft" (Benedict 1959:135). If a man has harvested many yams, it is because he has used powerful charms to attract his neighbors' yams into his own garden.

Eskimos are quite individualistic in their work patterns. Most men hunt separately in their own kayaks while their wives stay at home working alone at cooking, tailoring, and processing hides. The family, however, tends to work in a joint cooperative effort, and several families on occasion can work together successfully in communal caribou drives or in spring seal hunts. Plains Indians often went out alone to hunt deer or antelope, but the society insisted that buffalo hunting be done communally. Police societies enforced this regulation and imposed penalties upon private hunting.

The West Africans are almost completely cooperative in their labor patterns. Agricultural work is done by groups who help each other in turn, and even in the village, women often like to pound grain, cook, and wash clothes in groups. Although there may be no special advantage to working in groups, the people say that the social aspect makes the work seem lighter. There is, however, some reason to believe that more work is accomplished with group cooperation. While this proposition has never been tested, it is logical that in

The members of a cooperative work group among the Kofyar of northern Nigeria share the task of planting ground nuts. (Courtesy Robert M. Netting.)

group work there is great pressure to work up to the standard of one's co-workers. A much quoted statement by Hogbin gives us the impression that cooperative work has its advantages in increased productivity. He writes:

> A man who toils by himself pauses every time he feels like having a smoke. . . . But when two men work together each tries to do the most. One man thinks to himself, "My back aches and I feel like resting, but my friend there is going on: I must go on too, or I shall feel ashamed." The other man thinks to himself, "My arms are tired and my back is breaking, but I must not be the first to pause." Each man strives to do the most, and the garden is finished quickly. (1938:296)

While America prides itself on its competitive spirit, there is and has been a good deal of cooperative work found in this society as well. The rural barn-raisings, quilting bees, and threshing parties were not unlike the communal activities of many West African peoples, and our modern contractors really control what, in effect, is a kind of cooperative work group. While each man operates in terms of his specialty—carpentry, plumbing, plastering—the work is coordinated and complementary and results in the final product, a house.

AN ECONOMIC
VALUE SYSTEM

Every society, in addition to having an established system of organizing the productive efforts of its members, has a traditional set of economic values. Every people must decide how best to direct their efforts and where to invest their scarce means in order to derive the maximum satisfaction. All people are somewhat like the schoolboy standing in front of the candy counter trying to decide how to get the most for his money. Maximizing one's satisfactions thus involves making choices, and choices are made in terms of one's set of values. In attempting to understand any people's economic system the place to begin is at the level of learning what things they deem most valuable.

The Irrational Primitive.   From the European point of view the actions of primitive people often seem quite irrational and often this assumption leads to the conclusion that primitives do not have standards of economic value. Actually, primitive people have quite adequate reasons for what they do, but their actions are based on their own value system. Samoan islanders have often been criticized for what has been called their "church-building mania" while their water supplies and sanitation systems go neglected. But apparently having a beautiful place to worship is more important to them than having good water and sanitary villages. The Indians who sold Manhattan Island for 24 dollars, a few trinkets, and a barrel of rum did so, not out of ignorance, but rather because of their different concept of land tenure, their valuation of the few acres involved (they still had hundreds of square miles for their own use), and the attraction of the novel, foreign goods that could be purchased with the money.

It is the common practice for Eskimo hunters to refrain from killing animals considered sacred by their family, even if it means that they must go hungry for days. Faced with the choice of filling the belly or respecting the spirit of their totemic animal, they will choose the latter every time.

Jerry Martin, a former graduate student of the authors', spent a summer doing field work in the interior highlands of Fiji, studying a credit union in an extremely traditional, conservative village. Credit unions have not been successful in many areas of the non-Western world, especially in peasant villages where suspicions usually set sharp limits on trusting one's money to someone else, especially a nonkinsman. Even more of a problem is allowing one's kinsmen to learn one's economic status. Traditional values of sharing with one's kinsmen impose great financial burdens, since there is a decidely low rate of loan repayment when it is owed to a relative. Several attempts to establish a credit union in the village had been unsuccessful in spite of sponsorship by a Roman Catholic mission.

Martin found that this credit union was succeeding at the time of his investigation in spite of previous failure and that the account manager was operating the system very efficiently, refusing loans to poor risks regardless of kinship, and working in the interest of the members. Further, he was making money for the investors. To an outsider from the West, it looked as if good management according to basic credit-union rules was the reason for success. However, interviews revealed that the manager was also a chief of very high status in this stratified society, and that the people believed it was the *mana* ascribing to his status that was responsible for the success of his operation. Thus assured, the people willingly brought their money for investment, and the proof of his great *mana* lay in the fact that he was making them money. According to the villagers, management had nothing to do with it.

Among the Sukuma of the Lake Victoria region of Tanzania it is believed that there is a very finite amount of wealth, expressed in terms of cattle and agricultural products, and it is desirable to have an equitable distribution of this wealth. Any person who has considerable more than the average is strongly suspected of having utilized sorcery or sinister powers to gain more than what is "rightfully" his.

Why People Work.   Still another phase of the system of economic values concerns why people work and also the amount of effort they will expend. The fact that Americans work so hard that they get coronaries and ulcers is, from an objective point of view, rather irrational. Few people, regardless of culture, really enjoy the physical exertion involved in work, but all normal individuals do it. Why? Aside from the rather obvious reason that most people work to eat, the following reasons have been given:

> AMERICAN—"To be counted a success you have to have money. That means work . . . It's habit, I suppose. We don't like to be seen on the streets or around home doing nothing because we think people will talk about us." (Keesing 1958:229)
>
> "For many people, work is simply the best way of filling up a lot of time. . . . It takes a highly intellectual individual to enjoy leisure. Most of us had better count on working." (Gerstner 1974:24)
>
> HOPI INDIAN-"Work provides pleasure through group activity marked by joking and laughter, gossip, singing and perhaps recital by the old people of folk tales." (Keesing 1958:228)
>
> MAORI-"Successful completion of a certain piece of work will raise a man in the esteem of his fellows and give him a feeling that he has done his duty in the community." (Firth 1929:156—59)
>
> OMAHA INDIAN-"If a man is not industrious he will not be able to entertain other people. A lazy man will be envious when he sees men of

> meaner birth invited to feasts because of their thrift and their ability
> to entertain other people." (Fletcher and LaFleche 1911:331—33)
>
> SAMOAN ISLANDER-"I get satisfaction out of seeing things grow which I
> have planted with my own hands. People work because it is some-
> thing that people admire and respect. It brings them prestige."
>
> ALMOST ANYBODY-"One works because one must; because everyone
> else works; because it is one's tradition to work." (Herskovits
> 1952:122)

In every society goals are different and the means of attaining
goals are different. We cannot expect someone of another culture to
exert himself equally to achieve the goals important to us. Franz Boas
(1938) has pointed out that while the primitive often appears unreliable and disinterested in his work habits, the only fair way to compare
primitive and civilized man's work incentive is to observe them both
in undertakings that are equally important to each. In such cases, it
has been seen that the native can proceed with just as much purpose
as the white man.

Some people work because it gives them enjoyment, self-
respect, and prestige, or they work because it is the thing to do. We
have noted in the several statements from men of various cultures
that the prestige motivation greatly overshadows the profit one. In
the Northwest Coast of North America, Kwakiutl chiefs used to work
and save all year so they could compete successfully with other chiefs
in the destruction and distribution of property at the annual potlatch
ceremony. The chief who could destroy and give away the most property and thereby embarrass the other competing chiefs had very little
material to show for his year's work, but he had a giant measure of
prestige to glory in. Prestige is often of greater importance than profit
in our society also. While white-collar jobs are considered prestigeful
and are sought after by the majority of high school and college graduates, salaries are notoriously poor when compared with blue-collar
jobs. The old joke about the boss not being able to give his clerk a
raise but only a bigger title expresses a basic value principle in ours as
well as many other societies.

Not only is incentive to work tied in with status but so is the distribution of economic products in many primitive societies. As a matter of fact, Robert Redfield categorizes economies as being based either on a status system or on a market system. He states,

> In primitive societies most of the production . . . is brought about not
> because somebody sees a chance to make a profit in some market, but
> because it is part of the traditional status of that man or woman to hunt or
> farm or make baskets. And what is made is shared with others according to
> status. (1956:353)

1. THE SHARE OF THE VILLAGE ORGANIZATION OF UNTITLED MEN (AUMAGA)
2. THE SHARE OF THE VILLAGE PRINCE (MANAIA)
3. THE SHARE OF THE VILLAGE ORGANIZATION OF UNTITLED MEN
4. THE SHARE OF THE HIGH TALKING CHIEFS
5. THE SHARE OF CHIEFS OF LOWER RANK
6. THE SHARE OF CHIEFS OF LOWER RANK
7. THE SHARE OF THE PARAMOUNT CHIEF
8. THE SHARE OF THE FAMILY OF THE PARAMOUNT CHIEF
9. THE SHARE OF THE VILLAGE CEREMONIAL HOSTESS (TAUPOU)
10. THE SHARE OF THE CHIEFS OF LOWER RANK
11. THE SHARE OF THE CHIEFS OF LOWER RANK

Figure 12-2 Ceremonial food distribution in the Manu'a Islands of American Samoa.

METHODS OF PRODUCT DISTRIBUTION

Every economic system must of necessity include methods or means of product distribution. This distribution, as Redfield points out, may be based on status considerations or it may involve markets and money. A man may, because of his status as mother's brother in a matrilineal society, be required to provide food for his sister's children while his own are fed by his wife's brother.

In Samoan society individual chiefs gain great prestige by giving food to the village council of elders. Each council member is the head of a village family, and the food he is given will be taken home and distributed among the members of the family. Gifts to the council serve to feed the whole village, but the food presentation itself in the council-meeting is formal, ceremonial, and status-rewarding. Tradition has established a voluminous set of distribution regulations, and pigs and fish are carefully divided by the village talking chief according to an age-old system. (See Fig. 12–2)

Gift Exchange. Distributions of products within a society or between different societies often take the form of reciprocal gift exchanges. At marriages, funerals, or title installations of a new chief, Samoans are required to give gifts to the families involved. After much ado about thanking the guests for the gifts, each guest is given a gift to take away with him which is roughly equal in value to but different from what he brought. In the case of weddings, the family of the bride and the family of the groom are required to exchange goods. The bride's family must bring finely woven hibiscus fiber mats and tapa cloth and present them to the groom's family. In return they will be given pigs and other kinds of food. The exchange is reciprocal, but the important thing is that goods are circulated throughout a certain segment of the society and a number of people have had an opportunity to gain prestige through their generous giving.

The gift exchange phenomenon of Samoa has the effect of rescuing the society from economic stagnation. Since each family is actually economically independent of every other, there is normally no need for trade and no need for producing beyond the family's daily requirements. The exchange system stimulates economic interaction within the society and provides a strong motivation for individual family initiative.

Gift exchange can operate on an intersociety basis also. Not only does this type of transaction serve as a means of trade, but it is often an effective means of maintaining peaceful relations between a number of villages.

Christmas Giving. If, as Marcel Mauss has contended, gift-giving is a "cement" holding the elements of a society together, does the practice of gift exchange in American society at Christmas, and to a lesser degree, at other ceremonies marking the rites of passage (birthdays, graduations, marriages, etc.), help to hold our society together? Or are these practices nonfunctional remnants of long-forgotten cultural elements, carried on by inertia, because "we've always done it," or perpetuated out of fear that we will be in some manner ill thought of if we don't send the "proper" (translate that in economic value) gift to fit the occasion? Although Christmas giving has some function in serving as a stimulus to our economy and in symbolizing one aspect of the Christian religious heritage, the practice is also somewhat irrational and psychologically confusing in regard to its reciprocal aspects. Concerning this, Marvin Harris writes:

> Gift giving at this time of the year is a terrible threat to one's sanity. Everybody has to pretend that he wants to give away valuable items without expectation of equivalent items or anything at all in return. . . .
>
> So the first rule of Christmas gift giving is that all price tags and sales slips must be removed from the gifts. This proves that the giver doesn't want the receiver even to think about the possibility of a return gift of equal value. But everybody knows that Christmas shoppers are experts at judging prices. . . .
>
> As in true reciprocity, failure to match the value of a Christmas gift for

a short time need cause no embarrassment. But a persistent imbalance, either above or below the actual price, will eventually lead to corrective action. Either the party on the high side lowers his desire to give, or the party on the low side raises his. Some of my informants have told me that close relatives and friends attempt to avoid this sort of unpleasantness by calling each other and agreeing beforehand on what kind of present each will give the other. Apparently, they may even indicate brand preferences. These items, however, can scarcely be called gifts, since the mode of exchange is closer to barter than to reciprocity. (1972:24—25)

Perhaps we should envy the Nuer tribesman who knows exactly which cattle will go to whom in the traditional bridewealth exchange and who will get these particular animals back if the marriage fails.

The Kula Ring.   Often gift exchange is only one ceremonial aspect of a greater complex involving barter. Such is the case with the Trobriand Island kula ring. Malinowski describes this now-famous trade complex as follows:

> The Kula is a form of exchange, of extensive, inter-tribal character; it is carried on by communities inhabiting a wide ring of islands, which form a closed circuit. . . . On every island and in every village, a more or less limited number of men take part in the Kula-that is to say, receive the goods, hold them for a short time, and then pass them on. Therefore every man who is in the Kula, periodically though not regularly, receives one or several *mwali* (arm-shells), or a *soulava* (necklace of red shell discs), and then has to hand it on to one of his partners, from whom he receives the opposite commodity in exchange. . . . The ceremonial exchange of the two articles is the main, the fundamental aspect of the Kula. . . . Side by side with the ritual exchange of arm-shells and necklaces, the natives carry on ordinary trade, bartering from one island to another a great number of utilities, often unprocurable in the district to which they are imported, and indispensable there. (1961:81—83)

There are several intermediate stages between reciprocal gift exchange and true market distribution of products where money and prices are present. We do not imply, however, that a given society will evolve through these various stages. The trade continuum presented here is merely a means of classifying data and is not meant to represent an evolutionary sequence.

Barter.   We have already made passing reference to barter, the exchange of goods for goods. In this kind of transaction members of different families or villages or even different societies come together and through much haggling and bargaining effect an exchange of, say, pottery for spearpoints or yams for fish. Such exchange often takes place between coastal and inland people where each has a special kind of commodity which the other wants but does not produce. Barter may also include trading services for services.

Barter has been known to take place even where the trading parties are feuding or at war. If a symbiotic relationship exists between two societies but warfare prevents their meeting face to face, a procedure known as *dumb* or *silent* barter may be brought into play. In this kind of transaction one society places their trade objects in an agreed upon spot and then departs so that their trading partners can take the products they want and leave objects of equivalent value in their place. Such transactions are reported as occurring between the Veddas and the Sinhalese of Ceylon where exchanges of meat for arrow points take place during the night, among the Bantu and the pygmies of Africa, and among the Christian tribes of Northern Luzon and their Negrito neighbors.

Still a further step in the direction of a market distribution economy is the phenomenon of *money barter*, where a useful consumption commodity serves as a standard value for all goods exchanged. In Nicobar the commodity is coconuts; in Kenya, cattle and goats; in China, bricks of rice; and most unusual of all, in Easter Island, rats (eaten raw).

While barter may prove quite sufficient for a small isolated society, it is quite likely that an expanding society can arrive at a place where it has outgrown a simple exchange of goods through barter. As craft specialization becomes more diverse, something more efficient must be developed. In his book *Principles of Political Economy*, J. S. Mill wrote, "A tailor who has nothing but coats might starve before he could find any person having bread to sell who wanted a coat; besides he would not want as much bread at a time as would be worth a coat, and the coat could not be divided" (1898:287).

The statement is, of course, a gross exaggeration of the problem. Even the simplest of minds could work out some arrangement where bread would be provided over an extended period in payment for the coat. The statement does, however, emphasize the fact that something more than simple barter is required when an economy expands and a high degree of labor specialization exists.

The Market. True market exchange seems to be found mainly among agricultural and industrial people. In describing its characteristics, Redfield writes:

> In larger communities, where people do not know each other personally, and more and more kinds of goods appear, the market may be more fully a matter of an effort to sell at the highest price and buy at the lowest; then buyer and seller alike "shop around," and who the man is who buys or sells does not matter as compared with the opportunity to get the best price. (1956:354)

Thus we may see that compared with gift and ceremonial exchange, market transactions tend to be impersonal and often hostile. The sense in which such transactions can be considered hostile may be seen in the following quote from a series of articles about salesmen which appeared in *Fortune Magazine.* A veteran salesman is reported as advising an unsuccessful novice—"Fella," he finally said in exasperation, "you're not going to sell a damn thing until you realize one simple fact: The man on the other side of the counter is THE ENEMY" (*Consumer Reports* 1958:546).

"A market," writes Redfield, "can to some degree operate by the exchange of one sort of goods for another, but money, as a universal measure of value, is an enormous help in facilitation of market exchanges" (1956:354).

COMMON MONETARY SYMBOLS

We may be quite certain that Redfield would have maintained that the use of money, however, is not restricted to market economies. Actually, many forms of currency that we shall discuss facilitate economic transactions where there is no concept whatsoever of an organized market.

Although some economists insist that true money must have the qualities of portability, durability, homogeneity, divisibility, and stability of value, we find that any number of monetary symbols used in the market and informal trade transactions of primitive peoples fall far short of the criteria listed. These incomplete monies have been labeled "primitive money" as opposed to "modern money" by Paul Einzig, and in regard to their utility, Einzig states that an object may function as a primitive money, in spite of its defects, if a large portion of the community accepts it as "sufficiently valuable to be acceptable in payment for goods and services" (1966:322). A study of the function of some of these monies in particular societies reveals many parallels in our own economic system.

Melanesian Diwara—Banks and 10 Percent Interest.   One of the most efficient forms of currency used among primitive peoples is Diwara shell money of New Britain. The standard unit is the fathom-long string of half-inch-long shells, but prices are also quoted in fractions of units. A fathom is sufficient to purchase 60 to 80 taro roots, but chickens cost only one fourth of a unit. Even individual shells may be taken off the string to make small purchases such as a handful of betel nuts. While the people of New Britain carry on a great deal of barter with neighboring villages and islands, transactions involving Diwara are definitely considered purchases.

Diwara is stored in special money houses in coils of 50 to 200 fathoms. This capital is rarely drawn upon but instead provides its owner with prestige when it is frequently exhibited. Not only are there large shell fortunes but there are also bankers in each of the villages with whom wealthy men place money to be loaned at a 10 percent interest. Money is loaned without security, but the man who fails to repay his debt pays a heavy price in loss of prestige. He is considered an embezzler and never will be able to secure another loan. As in the case of American installment buying, the wealthy men of these Melanesian villages make it easy for villagers to have the things they want. Rich men often distribute food, weapons, and ornaments among the members of the community. Then, on a given day, a festival is held and those who have accepted the goods have to make payment by laying strings of Diwara at the feet of the village banker.

Wampum—Multipurpose Money. When the New England colonists arrived in America, they found that the Indians were using beads as Europeans "use gold and silver" (Einzig 1966:170). The clam shell beads known as wampum were an effective medium of exchange and were used even by the colonists in their transactions, but they also had many other uses: wampum served as a measure of wealth, as ornaments, as a method of conveying important messages and recording historical events, as tokens of friendship, and as a pledge of honor in treaties.

The value of a wampum string was determined partly by the number of beads it contained and partly by the color of the beads— purple and white having different values. Since the production of wampum involved great amounts of time, skill, and patience, it tended to maintain a high value and did not experience inflation until faked porcelain beads were introduced by fur traders in the nineteenth century.

The utility of wampum lay in the fact that its value was highly standardized throughout eastern North America, it was to a great extent imperishable, and it was small in bulk, light in weight, and easily divisible. The standard unit of monetary value was the fathom-length string, but for small transactions wampum beads were measured in smaller units, notably in wooden spoons.

Kwakiutl Coppers—Big Bank Notes of the Northwest Coast Indians. In the United States no one carries around a $10,000 bill, but it is a necessary unit in our complex monetary system. The same was true of copper shields among the Kwakiutl Indians of British Columbia. The actual unit of exchange in this area was a cheap white woolen blanket with a value of about fifty cents. Everything was valued in blankets, and loans made at 100 percent interest were repaid in blankets. Most important, blankets served as one form of wealth to be given away or destroyed when chiefs vied for prestige in the potlatch ceremonies. The really big operators at these ceremonies bothered less with blankets than they did with copper shields. These "coppers" were worth thousands of blankets, and the higher the rank of the purchaser the greater their price in blankets. The sole function of these copper shields was ceremonial exchange. Each had its own name and separate history. After a wealthy chief had succeeded in crushing his rivals by giving away several of these "big bank notes," he basked in the glory of his conspicuous consumption and planned for his next "battle of wealth."

Sudanese Cowries—Discount on a Car Load.   Shell money was also important in Africa, and white cowries served as standard monetary symbols in much of West Africa and the Congo. In the Sudan there never have been enough cowrie shells in circulation to meet trade requirements. But even though other currencies are used, the value of everything is quoted in cowries. One of the most peculiar characteristics of Sudanese cowrie transactions was the method of counting out shells for large purchases. Einzig describes the procedure as follows:

> Nominally the decimal system was in operation: Nevertheless 8×10 was reckoned as 100; 10×80 (nominally 100) was reckoned as 1,000; 10×800 (nominally 1,000) was reckoned as 10,000 and $8 \times 8,000$ (nominally 10,000) was reckoned as 100,000, so that what they called 100,000 was really only 64,000. (1966:133)

While this system may seem a little strange to us, it was merely a means of selling wholesale. If a trader made a big purchase of, say, five large bars of salt for 100,000 cowries, he actually only had to lay out 64,000. However, in his retail sales small quantities of salt were sold for five or ten cowries. When all the salt was sold, the trader had 100,000 cowries, which meant a profit of at least 36,000 shells.

One of the great difficulties in using cowries was that in big transactions counting was a major chore, and then transporting the currency was even more of a problem. C. H. Robinson describes in his book *Hausaland* the problem he ran into in Nigeria when one of the horses used in his expedition became ill and could not go on. He writes, "The trouble is that we cannot sell it, as its value in cowries would require fifteen extra porters to carry, to whom we should have to pay all the money they carried and a great deal more besides" (1896:46).

Yap Money Wheels—Micronesian Bank Accounts Subject to Inflation.   One of the most peculiar monetary standards ever devised is the "stone money" of Yap. Although this "money" is neither portable nor divisible, it certainly is durable and its function on this Micronesian island is not unlike that of a European bank account. This currency was produced in various sizes (silver-dollar size to 12 feet in diameter) from aragonite, a calcite rock quarried on the islands of Guam and Palau. A hole in the center for the insertion of a carrying pole facilitates their transport. The value of the money depends upon three factors: (1) scarcity, (2) cost of production, and (3) risk.

One could hardly expect these money wheels to be very abundant since the material had to be quarried at least 300 miles away (550 miles in the case of Guam stone) and then transported by frail outrigger canoes. Not only did production crews have to be paid in food but gifts had to be given to the island sovereigns for permission to quarry. Once the stones were in the boats the chances of getting them home were not the best. Often whole crews were lost along with their hard cash cargoes. Naturally, the larger the wheel the more it was worth, and Guam money was worth more than Palau money.

When the newly quarried money arrived on Yap, it was rolled or carried to a special place where it could be admired by the island populace. While silver-dollar- and plate-sized stones circulate, the larger stones are not moved. They serve mainly as stores of wealth and sources of prestige for their owners. The owners of the stones change but the stones remain in place. A 12 to 14 inch diameter stone of good quality will purchase 50 baskets of taro, yams, and bananas or a pig weighing approximately 80 to 100 pounds. Owning a large money wheel is very much like having a large bank account. When an American businessman makes a large purchase he merely writes a check on his account and the money is credited to the account of the seller, but neither man actually handles the money. The same thing happens with Yap money. In the event that a man wants to buy another's plantation, the purchase is made with the large money wheel. The stone money is not moved from its usual location beside the village path; only its title is transferred from one man to another.

In the 1880s an Irish trading schooner captain by the name of O'Keefe called at Yap and got the idea that with enough stone money he could become its king. He immediately set sail for Palau and Guam and returned with a whole boat load of large money wheels. While the natives of Yap were quite impressed with his cargo, his money was immediately labeled "O'Keefe money" and he found that it would buy very little. The problem was that his methods of obtaining the money had inflated it. The cost of production and the risk of transport were, through his methods, greatly reduced and so was the money's value. Just as United States currency was once backed by gold, Yap money has to be backed up by considerable expense, labor, and risk.

PROPERTY

One cannot talk about the economic organization of any people without taking into consideration their concepts of property. In our analysis of the "common understandings . . . which attach to things that may be used, enjoyed, or disposed of" (Redfield 1956:356) we immediately are involved in a consideration of the rights and obligations of individuals in regard to one another and to their society. It is easy to be guilty of oversimplification, however, in the analysis of particular societies' attitudes toward property ownership. As *Notes and Queries* states:

> Ideas concerning property may vary, not only in different societies, but even within a single society according to the nature of the property and the type of ownership right involved. A full understanding of these ideas calls for careful analysis; simply to label a system as "individualistic" or "communistic" is never adequate and often miseading. (1951):49

There is probably no society in the world that makes more of individual ownership of property than that of the United States, but even here there is much communal property. Visitors to every National Park, for instance, are reminded "This is your park. Keep it clean." People also talk about "our town," "our postal system," and "our church."

On the other hand, no naturally evolved society is totally communistic, not even the Soviet Union. There is always the recognition of some private ownership of tools, weapons, clothing, or ornaments. Linton has pointed out that "the only exceptions are a few completely communistic societies established by sophisticated individuals as a part of religious movements and no society of this sort has ever had a long duration" (1952:657).

Primitive people generally are more communal in their property concepts than industrialized people. Many pre-industrial people faced with rigorous environments where hunger and danger are always present have found that they cannot afford the luxury of private property. One cannot be selfish when the very existence of the group is at stake. Sahlins suggests, "It is a demand of group survival that the successful hunter be prepared to share his spoils with the unsuccessful. 'The hunter kills, other people have,' say the Yukaghir of Siberia" (1960:86). Even in the less rigorous climate of Southeast Asia, the same kind of awareness of group needs prevails. Of the Semang, Lisitzky writes:

> The common principle seems to be that the catch is the private property of the successful hunter, but the food is expected to be shared among those who have less than himself. The reason is, of course, everywhere the same: No man is always fortunate, and he who lets his neighbor starve while he has plenty will have no one to help him survive in future times of need. But the generosity of the Semang does not come from a cool calculation of this principle. He shares as naturally and spontaneously among his kinsmen as do the members of our own smaller families among themselves. (1960:49)

What actually operates in many primitive societies is what Sahlins calls "kinship-friendship" economics or what Redfield labels "status" economics. In this kind of system there is a set of obligations arising from one's position in society or one's kinship relationship. After these obligations have been met, then and only then can one consider oneself. In Western culture the conditions concomitant with industrialization have broken the kinship structure and have produced an atmosphere of anonymity that has reduced one's sense of obligation to his fellows.

Although we have pointed out that some private property exists in all societies, the exact interpretation of what private property means varies greatly. The man of Western culture emphatically states that "what is his is his!" and he has a title, a deed, or a no trespassing sign to prove it. In many primitive societies, however, a man may refer to an article as "his" because he made it and has the sole right of disposal, but if a kinsman should ask to use the object he is obligated to loan it. In the Samoan Islands there is communal family land and also private land that a man has carved out of the virgin bush for the support of his immediate family; but since such private lands are left to all of one's heirs, in time they also become communal.

Many non-literate people must consider Western concepts of ownership a personification of the "dog in the manger" parable, for to them ownership is validated primarily through use. A man owns a piece of land if he clears it and plants a crop, but if, after the harvest, he allows the bush to take over again, he has lost his claim to that land.

In many parts of the world property consists of things that we ordinarily do not think of as property at all. Weaving or pottery designs are often owned by individuals or their families. In Samoa every chief has a special name for the location of his guest house, and that name is the exclusive property of his family. Bush doctors in a variety of societies "own" their power to heal. In many areas of Polynesia family heads own their family legends and genealogies and have the exclusive right to their recitation.

Property and Prestige. It would seem that a common human desire is for recognition—to be singled out by members of society as someone worthwhile, someone important. A number of people throughout the world see property as an avenue through which this recognition may be obtained. But how property is used for this purpose is an interesting story when considered cross-culturally.

Having a $75,000 home, two cars, and a multifigure bank account is a major goal for many an American, but, as we have seen earlier, for the Kwakiutl Indian prestige and recognition come from giving property away rather than hoarding it.

Many times people are far less concerned with the products of their labors than with the applause they receive for a job well done.

Eskimos consider the kill the private property of the successful hunter, but the animal must be divided equally among the whole party. The fact that the slayer of the animal gets to choose his portion first is of little consequence compared to the prestige he derives from being the skillful hunter. Merely being designated as the owner of the kill is more important than the meat.

In still other societies prestige comes through holding no property at all. Asceticism places great value on turning one's back on wealth. This was an important principle in early and medieval Christianity and is found today to some extent among Roman Catholic clergy and monks. Scorn of worldly wealth is also an important principle followed by Buddhist and Brahman priests whose practices of self-denial gain for them the maximum of respect and prestige among the laity. Having, giving, or doing without property can bring to peoples of various cultures the acclaim of their fellowmen and represent a portion of the panorama of values that motivate people and determine solutions to problems that demand their decisions.

Human Ecology—Societies and Resources

The ecological approach is one of the more promising theoretical approaches in anthropological research, applicable to archeology and ethnology alike. Ecology, defined in biology as the interrelationship between organisms and the environment, applies to humans as well as other organisms but with a special dimension—the biocultural. For much of human history the impact of people on the environment differed little from that of lower animals. Human hunters and collectors made light demands on environmental resources. However, since the Neolithic, when people first became food producers, human society has undergone a logarithmic expansion in regard to population and technological development.

A particularly important event occurred during the eighteenth century with the advent of the industrial revolution. This technological milestone, which fostered the development of a culture of consumption, not only affected the course of human cultural development in the Western world but resulted in industrial nations outgrowing their boundaries and devouring their natural resources so they began a long history of seizing the underdeveloped lands and resources of tribal peoples. For example, pre-industrial England lived within its own resources for thousands of years but in only approximately a century industrial England developed shortages of grain, wood, fibers, and hides. With incredible ethnocentrism and spurious benevolence England and other "civilized" Western nations linked programs for "progress" with extraction of tribal resources. Missionaries were often pacifying agents.

The resource crisis of the 1970s in the Western world involved fossil fuels. Their availability has been conditioned by political concerns and the attitudes of vested interest groups. Predictions for the future range from sceptical optimism to warnings of a catastrophic fall of civilization. With the enormously greater expenditures of fossil fuels for automotive vehicles and for the generation of electricity in the Western world, little attention has been paid to the non-Western (emerging or third world) countries. Energy usage in these societies with nearly two-thirds of the world's population equals that of the Western world. They utilize more immediate organic sources of energy however. Plants, which depend on solar energy for photosynthesis, are an important food and energy source for humans and animals. Heating and cooking fuel sources are also very basic substances such as wood, dung, and plant residues.

Summary

All societies have some form of economic organization, and the range of organization from relatively simple hunting and gathering societies to economic systems of industrialized, urban societies is enormous, both in technology and in social organization. Some factors seem to be almost universal, though differing in details from one people to another. Included are: division of labor by sex, age, kinship, caste, etc. Cooperation in work exists with competition. Westerners who have been taught academic concepts of economic allocation of resources are often confused by the values of non-Western people, whose economic systems include elements which are influenced by kinship and religion.

Methods of distribution of goods include forms of barter, both open and "silent," and the giving of gifts may solidify social relationships in all societies. Market places serve many social and other noneconomic functions, and monetary symbols may take many forms besides currency. Profits may be individually or cooperatively owned or may be a matter of prestige as much as utility, while economics may be measured in terms of energy usage as well as response to the requirements of the environment.

Kinship and the Human Family 13

Evaluation of forms of the family
The conjugal family of marriage
The consanguine family of birth

There is no "right" or "wrong" way for societies to be organized. In fact most society members are probably not aware that they are organized at all, and the particular framework of organization is more a concern of the anthropologist studying the system than of the people living within it. Throughout the world both individuals and groups think of themselves in terms of kin relationships and they organize themselves accordingly. In the same sense a "society" can be viewed as a network of interrelated kinsmen, both near and distant, related consanguineally (by blood), or affinally (by marriage). This organization is both longitudinal in that it involves many generations and lateral in that it links nuclear families and collateral relatives at a particular period in time.

Anthropologists know of no society in the world that does not have some form of family, and this grouping is so vital to the survival of both individuals and groups that it may be assumed that the family in some form has always existed. Since we may observe various types of male-female bondings among other primates and among other animals, we may assume that this type of bonding is rooted in the pre-hominid stages of human evolution. To think of people without the family is to consider them as something other than human.

Even though in America the "right" or natural family is thought of as being (1) *monogamous,* uniting one husband and one wife, (2) *conjugal,* placing emphasis on the marital bond over blood relationships, and (3) *nuclear,* consisting only of biological parents and their offspring, the American family is only one of many forms in the world, each of which is also considered "right" within the context of its society. While the monogamous family may be "right" for Americans it is not the only feasible form although it is by far the most common type of marriage. *Polygamy* (plural marriage) is found as a permitted alternative (for those who can afford it) in many more societies than the number insisting on monogamy. Murdock (1949:24) found only 43 societies out of a sample of 195 demanding strict monogamy. Of these 195 the majority permitted *polygyny* (one husband, plural wives) and less than 2 percent condoned *polyandry* (one wife, plural husbands).

Among certain Tibetan societies a child may grow up in a family that consists of its mother and her husbands, who are usually brothers. This is called *fraternal polyandry.* The child will look to the eldest of the brothers as its "father," although any of the men may be its actual biological parent. While it may not be possible to determine precisely the reasons for the existence of polyandry, the arrangement seems to be associated with a shortage of women arising from the practice of infanticide. This in turn is usually associated with economic or technological deprivation which enhances the value of male children over females. Such conditions often characterize marginal agricultural or hunting and gathering societies.

On the other hand, a child born into the Bura society of Nigeria or into any number of West African societies might have to distinguish between members of its family with terms which mean "son of my mother" (brother) and "son of my father" (half brother). The child's father may have two or more wives in a polygynous household, and the child will share a house with its mother and siblings, while its half brothers and half sisters live with their respective mothers in other houses, and the father resides in his own, although all those dwellings are usually enclosed within a large walled compound. The child will share its mother with other children of the family although its feeding and care will come primarily from its biological mother. The other wives of the father are also "mothers" to the child, disciplining, nurturing, and even nursing it if need be.

The pre-revolutionary, traditional Chinese family represents yet another type of organization. Here the child has but one father and one mother, but it lives in an *extended family* in which the child and its parents share the house with grandparents, other relatives of the parent's generation—aunts and uncles—and their children (cousins). These additional kin, which represent extensions of the nuclear family laterally and longitudinally, are referred to as *collateral relatives.* The Chinese family is *consanguineous*, which means that the most important ties are those of blood rather than those by marriage. A father-son or a mother-son relationship, for example, is much more important than a husband-wife relationship. A wife must defer to her mother-in-law during the older woman's lifetime, and she will acquire a measure of authority only when her son brings home a wife to be her daughter-in-law. Chinese marriages are usually arranged by the parents of the bride and groom, and much more importance is attached to the girl's thrift, industry, and potential compatibility than to her beauty, charm, or romantic attraction to the groom.

Descent Patterns

Families vary greatly throughout the world in the manner in which they determine kin relationships. Americans are so accustomed to reckoning kinship through both the mother's and the father's families that other kinship systems seem very strange indeed. The American system, where both family lines are important in determining kinship is known as a *bilineal* or *bilateral* one. In many cultures, however, the people may recognize dual biological descent but may stress a single line of social inheritance. This kind of system is known as a *unilineal* or *unilateral* one. If the emphasis is placed on the father's side of the

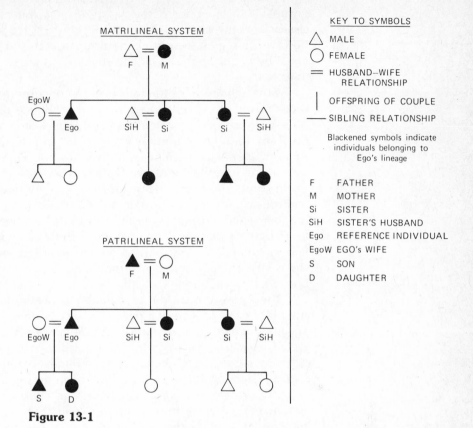

Figure 13-1

family, the system is referred to as *patrilineal*, but if the mother's side is stressed, the system is *matrilineal*. In the latter situation, a man would inherit his name, property, and occasionally family secrets from his mother or his mother's brother. In such a system a person does not ignore the biological relationship to the father or the father's relatives, but the person would recognize that their major social obligations are to relatives on the mother's side.

There is no satisfactory explanation of why one form of descent is preferred over others. Nor is there any substantiating proof of the priority of any particular form, since archeological evidence rarely indicates these types of data. Contemporary societies rarely have knowledge of why they do things in a specific way or particular interest in trying to explain the reason for their perpetuating a system, which in their terms is the only "correct" way to do things. No adequate geographical explanations are valid, since a variety of kinship systems are found all over the world and often in close proximity. For example, *matrilineal* descent is found among such American Indian groups as the Pueblos, Crow, and Iroquois, but the Cheyenne were *bilineal* and the Osage, Omaha, and Ponca were *patrilineal.* There is, however, a region in south-central Africa that is known as the "matrilineal belt" although not all societies in this area trace descent matrilineally.

Although there is little information concerning possible origins of these forms of descent, there is some evidence that where societies have been in contact with either Christianity or Islam (both related to Judaism) there is a tendency to favor patrilineal descent. Even in America there is a patrilineal emphasis in our bilineal system, particularly in the inheritance of family names.

It should be noted that matrilineal descent does not imply female control. In most societies men are dominant over women in matters of inheritance of property or titles or in the arrangement of marriages for daughters or sons. In patrilineal societies a woman is subordinate first to her father and then to her husband; in matrilineal societies she is subordinate to her maternal uncle prior to marriage and to her brother after the uncle's death.

There is a rather close association between descent patterns and the place of residence of a newly married couple. In general, in those societies which are patrilineal, residense is *virilocal,* or as formerly called, *patrilocal.* This is where they will take up residence with the husband's people. In like fashion matrilineality tends to be associated with residence with the wife's family—an arrangement known as *uxorilocal* (formerly *matrilocal*) residence. An alternative to the strict adherence to either of these systems is found in *bilocal* residence, where the couple reside with both kin groups, usually in some pattern of alternation, that is, a year with the husband's family and then a year with the wife's. In some societies like our own, which recognizes bilateral descent, the problem of which family to live with is often solved by residing with neither and setting up one's own household instead. This is *neolocal* residence. This situation tends to stress the importance of the nuclear family over the extended family and is typical of the West and a few developing societies well on the road to modernization.

A *lineage* is a descent group which traces relationship patrilineally or matrilineally from a known ancestor. This may require people to remember back many generations, but since kinship is so important in pre-industrial societies, great attention is given to keeping trace of relatives past and present. In literate societies, however, written records make it possible to keep accurate accounts of genealogies over many generations. The current interest in genealogies is to a large extent encouraged by the excellent records available in genealogical libraries maintained by the Mormon church and by Congress and by the birth and death documents available in government archives. Often the roles and statuses or the achievements or ancestors in pre-literate societies are remembered more than the personal characteristics of an ancestor, however.

A *clan* is a more inclusive kinship grouping than the lineage in that it represents a composite of two or more lineages of people who consider themselves at least distantly related to a common mythical ancestor. It is a bit like everyone with the name of Adams claiming that they belong to the Adams clan. It may be highly legendary who the original Mr. Adams was or when he lived, but all Adams believe they are kinsmen by virtue of the common surname. On the other hand, some Adams, interested in genealogical research, may be able to trace their family line back to an American president named Adams. This isn't exactly the same as what we find in most non-Western clans, however, since the Adams trace descent bilineally.

The mythological founder of a clan may not have even been human. The sacred mythology of the group may relate that the founder of the clan was a remarkable godlike animal or bird, and the clan may therefore revere contemporary representations of that creature as the clan *totem* (See totemism, Chapter 15). Clan members are often not allowed to eat of this animal or bird which is so sacred to their heritage. Clan members also may refer to themselves as "eagles," "grizzly bears," "deer," "beavers," etc. Sometimes the mythological ancestor is a culture hero or even a god, and there may be an elaborate oral history associated with this extraordinary human or divine forebearer.

In addition to clans being held together by real or imagined kinship ties, clans also tend to share common residence; an entire village may be made up of a single clan. An exception to this was the Iroquois who had parallel segments of eight clans in most of the six tribes comprising the Iroquois Confederation (Morgan 1877:70). In some cases villages may have the feature known as dual organization and consist of two clans which compete or cooperate with each other, depending on the enterprise. Clans are often *exogamous* (forbidding marriage within the group) since all members are theoretically relatives.

Kinship Classification Systems

Patterns of descent have long been important bases for family classification. Lewis Henry Morgan (1877) established a principle of classification based on the kinship terms used in describing one's relatives. If the terms defined precise relationships of individuals, they were called *descriptive*; if the terms tended to put kinsmen in groups or classes, they were called *classificatory*. Later writers such as Rivers (1910), Kroeber (1909), Lowie (1948), and Murdock have developed systems of kinship terminology based on the relationships of kinsmen as defined by *ego* (reference individual), that is, they are asking, What do I call each of my kinsmen; do I have a separate term for each or do I use a common term in referring to several of them; or do I do a bit of each?

Both Kroeber and Murdock have considerably influenced the defining of kinship terminology. For example, in 1909 Alfred Kroeber set down eight principles on which all kinship systems draw. The kinship system of modern Americans, for example, utilizes four of the following principles (1,3,4, and 7):

1. Differences in generation level (e.g., father, son, grandfather)
2. Differences in age levels (e.g., younger brother, older brother)
3. Differences between lineal and collateral relatives (e.g., father, uncle, brother, cousin)
4. Differences in sex of relatives (e.g., brother, sister)
5. Differences in sex of speaker (often different kin terms are used by males and females)
6. Differences in sex of person through whom relationship is established (e.g., father's brother, mother's brother)
7. Differences in genetic relatives and those related by marriage (e.g., sister, sister-in-law, mother, husband's mother)
8. Differences in life status of person through whom relationship is established (e.g., identifications of living or dead, married or single)

George Peter Murdock (1949) has recognized six basic systems for classifying kin. Each uses its own combination of the above principles and each represents a scheme for merging kinsmen under common terms or separating (bifurcating) them by utilizing different terms. They are:

1. Hawaiian System (Figure 13-2): This scheme involves five categories of kinship. They are: (1) grandparents, (2) parents (3) siblings, (4) offspring, and (5) grandchildren. Sex distinctions are made, but closeness of relationship is ignored. For example, dis-

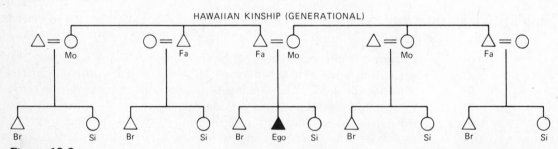

HAWAIIAN KINSHIP (GENERATIONAL)

Figure 13-2

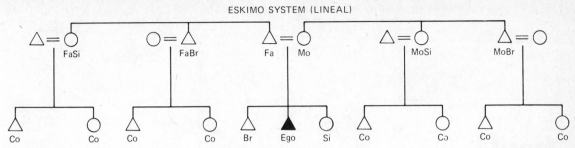

Figure 13-3

tant cousins are referred to as "brothers" and "sisters," just as if they were true siblings. This system is highly classificatory.

2. Eskimo System (Figure 13-3): This system does not distinguish between cross-cousins and parallel-cousins (see Figure 13-8), but does have different terms for cousins and siblings. American society basically follows this system of kin classification.

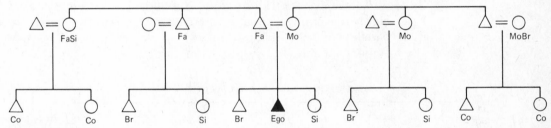

Figure 13-4

3. Iroquois System (Figure 13-4): This system equates siblings and parallel-cousins by using a single term, but cross-cousins are identified by another term.

4. Crow System (Figure 13-5): The Crow, who are matrilineal, ignore generational differences, but do differentiate between lineal and collateral relatives. For example, the word for "father" is used for

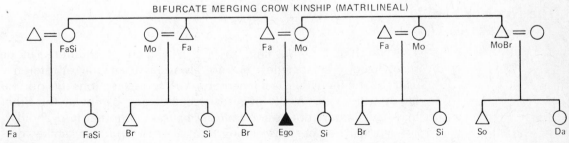

Figure 13-5

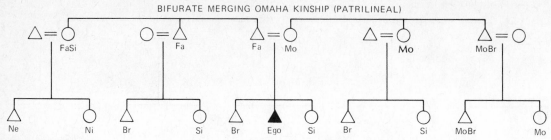

Figure 13-6

ego's father, his father's brother, and for his father's sister's son. More correctly, the term means "male of my matrilineal lineage," rather than our term "father."

5. Omaha System (Figure 13-6): The Omaha, who are patrilineal, follow a system which is basically a mirror image of the Crow system. In this scheme the term for "mother" is applied to mother's sister, and mother's brother's daughter and actually means "female of my mother's patrilineage," rather than "mother."

6. Sudanese System (Figure 13-7): The Sudanese system is the most highly descriptive of all, with separate terms for cross- and parallel-cousins, siblings, uncles, aunts, nieces, and nephews. Understandably, this system is quite rare.

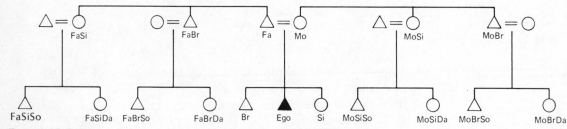

Figure 13-7

The Nuclear Family

The social unit of husband, wife and unmarried children can be recognized in all societies, but not always as the family of reference as far as the individual is concerned. With few exceptions this nuclear family will be the family of residence, but one parent or the other may have important ties and obligations to kin in other households.

Normally all persons belong to at least two nuclear families dur-

Eskimo nuclear family. (Courtesy Willis Tilton and Wichita State University.)

ing their lifetime, the exception being those who remain unmarried (a relatively rare situation in non-Western society). First, everyone is born into an already existing nuclear family (the *natal* family), and second, one becomes part of another nuclear family (the *conjugal* family) at marriage. Obviously there is a linkage between these two in that ego's natal family is the conjugal family of the parents.

The nuclear family is essentially also the nurturing family even where a man has responsibilities to his sister's children as in the case of the arrangement known as the *avunculate*. But even here the man maintains vastly more continuing and affective relationships with his own children, especially when they are young, than he does with his sister's children.

The *family of reference*, that is, "the" family to which a person "belongs," is far more apt to be his natal, nuclear family (the one based on consanguineal ties) than the one based on marriage ties. This seems bizarre to those raised in Western society because they are accustomed to think of "the" family as the nuclear family formed at marriage. This is because Westerners reckon descent through both parents equally. This is rare among human societies as a whole, for *unilineal* descent (primarily through one parent) tends to be the rule. The Western system works well because bilateral kinsmen are largely ignored and the small nuclear unit is considered to be the proper family of residence and economic responsibility.

Minimal Functions of Family

We can see that many forms of family can and do satisfy human needs. The important thing to note is that all of these families perform a number of functions that are essential to the survival and perpetuation of the human species. The minimum functions that family must perform in this respect are seen by anthropologists to be the following:

1. The family must make provision for legitimate sexual outlets for adults.
2. The family must perpetuate the species through controlled reproduction.
3. The family must educate and socialize the children.
4. The family must serve as a unit of economic cooperation and as an agency for the transfer of titles and property.

THE SEXUAL FUNCTION OF FAMILY

One of the most basic and necessary functions of the family is providing sexual outlets for the adults of a society. While the need for such outlets is not as demanding as the need for food, water, or shelter, it is nevertheless a strong motivating force in behavior, and, if we are to explore the reasons for the universal existence of family, we must not forget the nature of human sexuality.

Among humans and primates in general, sex activity is continuous. It is not limited to mating seasons, rutting periods, or heat cycles as it is in nearly all animals. This ever-present attraction between sexes makes for continual association and in part explains the existence of a permanent union of males and females in all human societies. Among many animals there is only seasonal association of the sexes for the purpose of breeding, but after the female has conceived, the male departs since there is no promise of continued sexual activity. Among such animals as lions, the association will continue until the young are suckled. During the nursing period the males will hunt for the females, but in the case of deer or buffalo and domesticated dogs and cats, the female can get her own food and the union is immediately ended when the mating is over.

We must not, however, be lured into explaining too much in terms of sexual behavior, particularly in the case of humans. They are far from being dominated by their sexual feelings. In human society the sex act cannot be engaged in irresponsibly, because there is always the possibility of conception. In such an event the resulting child must be carefully nurtured for a prolonged period until it is capable of caring for itself. Thus, sex behavior is considered serious business, and there is no society in the world that does not impose some kind of controls on such activity. These controls stipulate whether or not the couple must be married and they define what constitutes an incestuous relationship but there are always clear statements concerning what is sanctioned and what is taboo. There is a time and a place and a certain kind of partner for sex behavior in all societies. While it is often felt to be a natural human function, sexual behavior tends to be learned behavior, and its forms vary greatly from culture to culture.

There are also other reasons for the existence of a permanent family among humans. In nearly all cultures there is a high valuation placed upon offspring, and particularly sons by their fathers. Whether this is a matter of passing on a name, property, or family traditions, or whether it is a matter of the father's considering the child his property, or perhaps even an image of himself, a feeling of special attachment is usually present. The situation varies from society to society, of course, but human males generally take pride in their offspring, cherish them, and want to watch them grow and develop. There are few societies where a father would not lay down his life to protect his children. These ideals and emotional feelings that tie the father to the children no doubt account in great measure for the maintenance of a compact family unit.

The attachment between mother and her children is the result of somewhat different factors. There is no evidence to support claims of a special motherly instinct in women, but there is some evidence that there is a biological basis for a mother's love and concern for her child. Niles Newton, for example, points out that "research . . . indicates that motherly behavior is related to menstrual flow, breast feeding, hormonal changes, and some other physical and social factors" (1955:70–71).

Of course, cultural ideas can always overrule biological pressures of this kind. There are societies, the Marquesas, for example, where children are nursed but are shown little affection. Mothers merely provide the nutritional necessities but then leave the children to others to care for their other needs. On the other hand, many modern European mothers do not nurse their babies and the mutual satisfaction of both mother and child is not experienced, but their behavior is highly influenced by cultural attitudes that make it mandatory that they consider their babies to be "cute," "lovable," and "dear." The family relationship can be considered as a triangle of affection and dependency. The mother is drawn to the child through physical satisfactions and cultural ideals, the father through pride and identity of blood. The parents are drawn together through sexual satisfaction, economic necessity, and a shared sense of responsibility for the welfare of the child. There are always those who do not feel their responsibilities, those who deviate from the societal norms or those who never develop an emotional feeling for their spouses or their children, but these are exceptions; and while such behavior should be considered, it hardly alters our explanations of the nature of universal family cohesion.

NURTURE OF THE YOUNG

It is more important for humans than for any other type of animal to have a permanent and intimate family organization. This is because of the nature of the offspring that we produce. The human infant is born completely helpless, without many instincts and without the ability to effectively use its body. For many years the child must be protected and cared for while learning to obtain a living and while learning the culture's system of customs, ideals, values, and attitudes. This takes time and it takes intimate association with the members of a permanent group who have a special concern for the child. Aristotle once stated that "What is everybody's business is nobody's business." This was, of course, a criticism of Plato's idea of a communal group that would have resulted in a de-emphasis of parent-child ties. We find, however, that the adults who care for and educate the children need not be the biological parents. In many societies "sociological" or surrogate parents actually have more to do with the rearing of children than do the actual parents. As long as someone shoulders the responsibilities, the true relationship doesn't really matter.

SOCIOLOGICAL "PARENTS"

In societies that trace kinship through the mother's family only, the *avunculate* phenomenon is often present. In this situation the most important adult male in the lives of the children is not the biological father but the mother's brother, or maternal uncle. Such an arrangement can be found among the Trobriand Islanders of the Southwest Pacific. Concerning this system Malinowski writes as follows:

> As he (the child) grows up . . . the mother's brother assumes a gradually increasing authority over him, requiring his services, helping him in some things, granting or withholding his permission to carry out certain actions; while the father's authority and counsel becomes less and less important. (1929:7)

Still a different surrogate situation is that labeled the *amitate*. Here we find a counterpart to the mother's brother's position. The amitate refers to a special relationship which prevails between the father's sister and his children. Lowie describes this family feature among the Haida as follows: "The paternal aunt of a Haida appears in every critical phase of life, fulfilling some obligation, but also receiving compensation therefore. Thus, when a girl comes of age, this aunt cares for her, and at a youth's wedding she conducts the bride to him" (1948:74).

Among the Canella of Brazil "a little girl spends much time at her aunt's and the sentimental tie between the two is likely to grow stronger than that between the nephew and uncle" (1948:74).

In the Samoan Islands a variety of "parents" provide for the needs of the children. Margaret Mead describes this arrangement as one where children are "reared in households where there are a half dozen adult women to care for them and dry their tears, and a half dozen adult males, all of whom represent constituted authority" (1928:209). The Samoan household is actually an extended family unit wherein all adult relatives feel a certain responsibility for and exert a certain amount of control over all the children. It doesn't matter how many "mothers" and "fathers" there are, so long as they definitely feel and attend to their responsibilities toward the children.

PARENTS AND SOCIALIZATION

Aside from the love and care that the parents give to the child, the mere association of these adults with the children is important in their personality development and in their learning to get along with others. The desirability of having a father and mother in close association with the child is well pointed up in the family situation in American culture. The American nuclear family represents the maximum extent to which the size of family can be reduced without adversely affecting the personality development and socialization of the child. When this bare nucleus of family becomes smaller, it may be defined as a "broken home." The family may be broken in a number of ways—by death, divorce, separation, or desertion. How the family is broken is not as important as the fact that it is an incomplete family unit.

Statistics show that most American "broken" homes are homes without a father. Although the father exerts less influence over his children today than in generations past, the family in which the mother must be both mother and father to her children is less than satisfactory. Sociologists generally agree that young people from "broken" homes in America are more likely to engage in deviant behavior than those who come from complete families. Koller (1971) found a rather high correlation of between broken homes and delinquency. Other studies have shown that deviant behavior is also more frequent in complete families where there is hostility on the part of a parent toward the children or where one or both of the parents refuse to accept their responsibilities in rearing and educating the children. In either of these cases, the situation is roughly the same: The family either is incomplete or is functioning as an incomplete unit and therefore the enculturation and socialization of the children is impaired.

Why is it that problems sometimes arise where one of the parents is missing? Since "broken" home situations more frequently involve a missing father than an absent mother, let us consider for a moment the importance of the male parent in the family. Not only is the father important as a provider but his mere presence and interest in the children are valuable for their development. The father represents for them a model of adult male behavior. Sons learn what is expected of them as men, husbands, and fathers by observing the behavior of their fathers.

Sociologists have found that sons raised in families where there was a happy relationship between the father and mother will themselves be quite likely to develop a satisfactory marriage relationship. Many a modern father in America takes an interest in the activities of his sons because his own father took an interest in him. The father also establishes for the son a pattern of masculine behavior and aids the child in understanding his own sexuality. Green and Money, in a study of effeminacy, have observed that "many men do not realize how important it is for a boy to identify with his father and impersonate him, which is made easier when the two participate in activities and recreation together. In the absence of a father, a grandfather, uncle, stepfather, brother or other male may serve as a father substitute" (1961:289).

A number of psychological studies have shown that homosexuality in males is often associated with mother dominance or with situations where the father-son relationship is a hostile one and therefore only a minimum of association and identification is possible. Barclay and Cusumano (1967) found that boys from fatherless homes may often try to cover up their sex-role confusion by a compulsive denial of anything they defined as feminine. They often prized a football jersey or a motorcycle jacket and wore it as a badge of masculinity, but in spite of these acts the evidence of a research study "pointed firmly to one conclusion-that these boys tend to relate to their surroundings in the passive way that our society has, at least until now, considered typically feminine" (1967:35).

The presence of a father in the family is almost as important for the daughter as for the son. The daughter needs this association so that she may have some insight into male behavior, particularly that associated with the role of husband and father. In this way she gets some idea of what to expect from her husband in her own future marriage. Furthermore, a father represents an example of men in general. He has a man's point of view and although a girl may consider her father terribly old fashioned, his opinions about a new hairdo or dress are often more valuable to her than her mother's. She doesn't expect dad's point of view to correspond exactly with that of her young man, but at least it is a male opinion.

The Nayars—A Family Without a Father.   Although we have made the generalization that in order to rear children adequately the family unit should be a complete one involving both male and female parents (either biological or sociological), there are one or two notable exceptions. The most interesting example of a well-functioning but incomplete family is that of the Nayar of India. The Nayar are a warrior caste that prior to 1792 served the local feudal rulers. Since the men were engaged in this extremely dangerous occupation, and since they were often away from home for extended periods of time, a form of family developed wherein men played a very insignificant role in family life. The significant social unit in Nayar society is the matrilineal lineage, or as it is sometimes expressed, the uterine family. This is a group of related women, their children, and occasionally a few men—the brothers of the women. No relatives by marriage are included in the Nayar households—not even husbands. The eldest woman in the lineage is its head and administrator of its house, lands, and other property. Every 12 to 15 years there is a ritual marriage ceremony for all the adolescent girls. On this occasion ritual husbands give the girls gold ornaments, called *tali*, and this legitimizes the marriage. Following this ritual marriage ceremony the couples separate, but from this time on the girls are considered mature and therefore ready to engage in a series of casual unions, called *sambandham* "marriages," with men of her own subcaste or with those of higher castes. *Sambandham* relationships are hardly marriages, because they only involve *sambandham* "husbands" giving their "wives" gifts of cloth and then being entitled to share the girl's room for the night. The men leave their weapons outside so that other "husbands" will know enough to stay away. The men do not support the women in any way, nor are they obligated to aid in the rearing of any children that might result from their meetings. Nayar children often do not know their fathers and even if they do, there is no sense of a relationship between them.

While this family apparently represents an exception to all we have said about the importance of a family with both a father and mother, it represents a unique situation. This form of family was developed to cope with the rather serious problem of the absence or even loss of adult males as a result of their activities as soldiers. The system solves the usual economic problems by placing all property and wealth in the hands of the mother's lineage, and the fact that the lands are cultivated by an inferior caste, subservient to the Nayar, ensures that the needs of all will be satisfied. Since the female lineage does include the brothers of the women, something of the role of surrogate father is undoubtedly assumed by these men for the many children residing within a given household.

The Family as An Economic Unit

It has been pointed out that one of the more important functions of the family is its activities as an economic unit. The family is a unit of both production and consumption. In some societies every family member has a share in the production, but in others only certain members shoulder the responsibilities of production for the entire group. Production may mean actually growing the food that the family will eat, or it may mean earning a wage so that the goods that the family consumes can be purchased. Whatever the economic problems, the family seems to find a way of organizing itself so that satisfactory adjustments may be made. An example of the influence of economic matters on family form and function may be seen by contrasting the urban American family with that of the rural areas. Traditionally the farm family has been one where all its members contributed to the family welfare. Mother kept chickens and sold eggs; the children had their chores and often had a calf, the raising of which was their responsibility alone; and father was the main laborer and director of economic activities. The more children there were, the easier it was to run the farm; thus, farm families were traditionally large.

In the city, however, we find that the structure, organization, and even size of the family are very different. In the city, people are involved in an industrial or commercial way of life, and more often than not, there is but one wage earner per family. The mother has an important role to play as homemaker but she and the children are actually economic liabilities in that they consume but do not participate in the production, or wage-earning activities. In the city therefore the size of the family is limited by the earning power of the single wage earner and the fact that the cost of living is higher in the city. The cramped living conditions which usually prevail in urban areas also tend to restrict the number of children wanted.

MATE SELECTION   The influence of economics on family life may also be seen in the matter of mate selection. In contrasting European with primitive society, Marshall Sahlins writes, "Marriage and family are institutions too important in primitive life to be built on the fragile, shifting foundations of 'love.' The family is the decisive economic institution of soci-

The family as an economic unit. Among the Kung Bushmen of the Kalahari Desert region of Southwest Africa, men hunt and make weapons and their wives gather wild plants and care for the home and the children. (Courtesy L. K. Marshall Expedition, Peabody Museum of Harvard University —Smithsonian Institution.)

ety. It is to the hunter and gatherer what the manor was to feudal Europe, or the corporate factory system is to capitalism: it is the productive organization" (1960:82). "The economic aspect of primitive marriage," he continues, "is responsible for many of its specific characteristics. For one thing, it is the normal adult state; one cannot economically afford to remain single. . . . The number of spouses is, however, limited by economic considerations among primitives" (1960:83). While premarital sex is permitted (or more commonly ignored) in many societies, the rules of mate selection usually dictate that those for whom some barrier to marriage might exist, should avoid sexual relationships.

BRIDE PRICE

Throughout much of the world some form of payment is given by a man to the family of the woman he wishes to marry. The term *bride price* has long been associated with this practice, but *progeny price* and *bridal wealth* have also come into usage. No simple explanation for this activity exists since it is so deeply ingrained in the cultural values of people practicing it that they rarely have any explanation beyond it's being "the proper thing to do." Certainly no girl is demeaned by her father's bargaining for her hand. To the contrary, she would be humiliated if he did not. In fact, the validation of her marriage may well depend upon it.

In trying to find an explanation for this practice, some of the difficulty lies in the term *bride price* itself, particularly *price*, a word in

English usage denoting a purchase of a commodity or service, that is, an economic term. Obviously one does not "buy" a wife in the sense that something is bought in the market. One of the authors, while in Nigeria, noted that his informants used the same verb to discuss buying in the market and in the bridal arrangements and asked if this meant the girl was purchased. He was told with some surprise by his informants that it most certainly was not the same, but gave no further explanation. What to them was obvious (though not to the anthropologist at first) was that the context of the transaction established the meaning, though in the economy of language, one verb could be used in several contexts without confusion.

The term *progeny price* has been suggested in lieu of *bride price*, the implication being that the payment is recompense for the children the woman will bear to the family of her husband. This might serve to explain the payment in patrilineal societies, where descent is from the father to the children, who are in his lineage alone. But progeny price seems to make little sense in matrilineal societies, where the children are a part of the mother's lineage, not the father's. However, this economic exchange takes place in matrilineal societies as much as in patrilineal, and in the same fashion, with the male paying the bill.

Some anthropologists are using the term *bride wealth* as an alternative. This is useful, especially where cattle or some other monetary wealth is used, though this does not do much to solve the problem of what is meant by the transaction. Perhaps as good as any is the view that the economic services of a woman are what are being purchased, a view not restricted by either unilineal concept mentioned above. At any rate, this transaction is vastly more than simply an economic one. There is a wide variety of social obligations and relationships involved, not only validating the marriage, but also establishing a reciprocal network of obligations which strengthen and unify the kin group.

POLYGYNY

While polygyny is allowed in almost all societies except Western, only in economies of surplus can men mass enough wealth to afford more than one wife. In many agricultural societies women do much of the cultivating and actually can increase the wealth of a man, but in most societies where polygyny is practiced the main problem is having enough money to obtain extra wives in the first place. There is often the matter of bride price. Since a man must save enough money to "purchase" a wife and since the price is usually high, most men in polygamous societies practice monogamy as a matter of economic necessity. Plural marriage is seldom prompted by sexual desire; in most cases a man wants extra wives because of the increased status

Polygynous Ifugao Family.

and prestige they will bring. In West African society, for example, no man who really wants to be somebody would ever be content with having but a single wife. In many families it is the wife who urges her husband to acquire extra wives because her own work will then be lighter and she will be known around the village as one of the wives of a very important man. The situation may be compared with the American wife who wants to keep up with the Joneses by having her husband buy a second car.

While polygyny is found much more frequently in surplus rather than subsistence economies, it would not be correct to say that wealth is the only factor involved. Of all the societies of the world the one with the highest standard of living and the greatest amount of wealth is undoubtedly the United States, and yet we have laws to prevent polygamy. Bengt Danielsson, the anthropologist who accompanied the Kon Tiki expedition, in his book *Love in the South Seas* suggests, in a tongue-in-cheek manner, that we are making a mistake in limiting our number of spouses to one. He explains his position as follows:

> In the first place, there are great individual variations in the strength of the sexual impulse, so that for many people one partner is simply not enough. In the second place, certain people, for example, captains of industry, politicians, large landowners, etc., have very heavy social and economic duties which are often too overwhelming for one unfortunate wife. (1956:275)

Such an idea would be quite shocking to most Americans, because their Judeo-Christian tradition labels any form of polygamy immoral. Danielsson considers such a reaction as rather inconsistent, however, and reminds us that "from the moral standpoint . . . there can be no difference between being married to several wives in rapid succession and being married to them at the same time" (1957:275). Regardless of the inconsistencies involved, cultural norms, often based on religious ideals, can overshadow the influence of the basic economy on the form and function of family.

RESIDENCE

There is also some evidence that economic factors play a part in influencing the location of marital residence and the way kinship is reckoned. William I. Thomas found in one study that temporary matrilocal residence tends to be found in hunting and gathering societies. In other words, hunters and gatherers commonly live with and serve their parents-in-law for a time before taking their brides to their own family group. This practice is believed to occur where bride wealth is paid in installments. Once having paid for his bride, the husband moves to the community of his own people.

In primitive societies permanent matrilocal residence, and matrilineal descent as well, is to a great extent associated with large sedentary groups that subsist primarily from the agricultural activities of women. A typical example is found in Iroquois society. Underhill describes the role of women as follows:

> Women were important people in an Iroquois village. They owned the fields, an arrangement which is often found in agricultural tribes where women do the field work. Since property went down in the female line, descent also was counted in that way. . . . Iroquois women also owned the houses. A matron with her daughters, her younger sisters, and the husbands of all of them often occupied a longhouse, while the brothers and sons moved away to live with their wives. (1953:90)

In herding societies and in those where plough agriculture is present, married couples tend to reside with the husband's people, and kinship is generally traced through the male line. Where cattle are kept or where the plough has been introduced, the men's subsistence contribution tends to be greater than that of women, and there is a desire to keep the control of the property in the hands of the father and his sons. Furthermore, since the main source of family support is with the father's family, a bride would naturally go to live with the family of her husband. The Nilotic people of East Africa illustrate this relationship between herding and male inheritance very well. As Ralph Linton points out, "Cattle were the emotional and cultural center of native life. All work with them was pre-empted by the men, and all cultures having this economy were strongly patriarchal and patrilineal" (1955:432).

LEVIRATE AND SORORATE

In studying the economic ordering of family some mention should be made of two widely found customs known as the *levirate* and the *sororate.* The levirate is an arrangement where at the death of a husband the wife is expected to marry a brother of her deceased husband. In the case of the sororate, on the other hand, a man who has lost his wife will be expected to marry one of her sisters. There are undoubtedly many plausible reasons for such customs, but one of the better explanations can be made in terms of economics. Let us imagine a matrilineal, matrilocal situation where throughout a man's entire married life he has been living with his wife's family and through his labor has been contributing to that family's welfare. The family has effectively worked him into its labor force and he has become a valuable asset to the family. He works well with his wife's brothers and they have come to accept him as one of them. At the death of the man's wife, however, the whole situation might be changed. With his wife gone there is little to hold him in the family. If he leaves to go home to his own family group where he has some property, he might insist on taking his children, and perhaps they too have developed into real economic assets for the family. In order to remove the possibility of such a disorganizing occurrence, the society has developed a way of retaining the individual and his children within the group, thus ensuring the economic and social continuity of the family. While we shall not make an analysis of the reasons for the levirate, it conceivably works in much the same way, only in this case there is pressure to retain the wife of the deceased and her children within the group.

The Family as a Unit of Society

The role of the family in the total society might be likened to that of a brick in a great masonry structure. The whole is dependent upon the strength and durability of its component parts, which fit together in a particular way to produce the desired total configuration. Just as the characteristics of the individual bricks influence the color and style of the total structure so the individual families influence and reflect the tone and quality of the total society.

In general we can say that the values learned within the family represent the values of the society as a whole. The child who learns to interact successfully with the members of his family and learns to regulate his behavior in terms of family concepts of what is right and wrong, what is important and unimportant, will have little trouble making a successful adjustment to society as a whole. In our culture, only-children are listed as poor marriage risks by sociologists who specialize in family studies. There is no doubt that such children find it difficult to adjust to a marriage partner because they have never experienced the give-and-take situations that characterize larger families. They have never had to share with others or work out compromises with their siblings.

A good example of how the nature of family is reflected by the society and vice versa may be seen in an analysis of traditional Chinese social organization. Lin Yutang tells us that in pre-Communist China

> the family system is the root of Chinese society, from which all Chinese social characteristics derive. The family system and the village system, which is the family raised to a higher exponent, account for all there is to explain in the Chinese social life. Face, favor, privilege, gratitude, courtesy, official corruption, public institutions, the school, the guild, philanthropy, hospitality, justice and finally the whole government of China-all spring from the family and village system, all borrow from it their peculiar tenor and complexion, and all find in it enlightening explanations for their peculiar characteristics. (1935:175–76)

As strong a statement as Lin Yutang's could probably not be made about the relationship between the American family and American society, but certainly there are resemblances between family values and the cultural values of our nation. For example, the democratic nature of our total culture is reflected to a very great extent in our patterns of family behavior. While the father is nominally the head of the American family, he can seldom exert autocratic rule. He controls the family through persuasion and gives reasons for the demands he makes on family members. Geoffrey Gorer carries this concept of the democratic family even further. He says:

> To a certain extent the pattern of authority in the state is reproduced in the family: it is as if the father represented the Executive, the mother the Legislative, and the neighbors, headed by the school teacher, the Judiciary authority. The child is in the position of the public, playing off one authority against another, invoking the system of checks and balances to maintain his independence. Although this is a somewhat far fetched comparison, it more nearly represents the structure of the ordinary American family than does the patriarchal picture derived from Europe, or the mirror image of that picture, with the father's authority transferred wholesale and unaltered to the mother. (1964:44–5)

Carrying our family-building block analogy further, we must point out that building blocks or bricks are not just piled one on top of the other with nothing holding them together. They require mortar if the structure is to last. The mortar holding the individual family units of society together is kinship and marriage. We have already discussed how kin relationship traced matrilineally, patrilineally, or bilineally can tie families and generations together and promote mutual aid and cooperation. The part that kinship plays can further be seen in a commonly found phenomenon known as the *classificatory system*. A common form of this is the generation system where the majority of relatives of one's own age and lineage are referred to as "brother" or "sister," while relatives of one's parents' generation are collectively known as either "mother" or "father." Relatives of the generation of one's offspring are referred to as "son" or "daughter." Since specific kinship terms require appropriate corresponding behavior, this system tends to pull the group together and promote cooperation and respect. Under such a rule one's uncle and aunt have equivalent status with one's parents and expect to be treated accordingly.

Occidental societies, on the other hand, tend more toward *descriptive* kinship terminology. This kind of system uses separate terms for designating particular degrees of relationship. Instead of referring to all relatives of one's own generation as "brother" or "sister," relatives are singled out as "brother," "cousin," and "second cousin." By thus designating inner circle relatives from those further removed, civilized societies display their lack of concern for family and the reduced function of kinship as a force for social solidarity. Where specialists perform the functions of social control and where formal agencies control economic cooperation, kinship assumes a less important role in the organization of society. In many primitive societies, however, kinship is everything. It determines all social, economic, and religious interaction within the group. It has been said that many primitive groups consider a stranger an enemy unless they can establish some kinship relationship between him and the group. The practice of adopting individuals into a group as "blood" brothers derives from this concept.

THE INCEST TABOO

Stressing the importance of marriage bonds in the organization of society, John Layard states, "The whole structure of human society, in whatever form it may be found or wherever it may be . . . is based on something extremely concrete; namely, the incest taboo" (1961:51).

The incest taboo is the prohibition of marrying or mating with someone within one's own circle of kin. It is a universally prevalent taboo that has interested anthropologists for years. Westermarck, one of the first to investigate the phenomenon, maintained that inbreeding is biologically bad and a man or woman is therefore instinctively repulsed by the idea of marrying a relative. The main problem with this theory is that inbreeding does not necessarily produce harmful effects. A great deal of inbreeding has occurred in isolated Swiss villages and on Pitcairn Island, without any noticeable ill effects. Hawaiian, Egyptian, and Incan monarchs even married their sisters, and yet these royal lines were remarkably sound biologically. We might also ask Westermarck why a taboo must be installed to restrain people from doing what they instinctively abhor; also, among many primitives, individuals are often permitted and even encouraged to marry partners no farther removed genetically than those they are forbidden to marry. To understand how this can occur in primitive society it will be profitable to analyze the concepts of "cross" and "parallel" cousins.

Cross- and Parallel-Cousins. *Cross-cousins* are defined in anthropology as offspring of siblings of the opposite sex—that is, the children of the families of a brother and a sister. Parallel-cousins, on the other hand, are offspring of siblings of the same sex—that is, the children of the families of two sisters. In many societies where kinship is traced either matrilineally or patrilineally, parallel-cousins are considered siblings, and therefore, cannot marry; but cross-cousins in such societies are allowed to marry because they belong to different lineages or clans and are therefore considered less closely related than parallel cousins. It is not unusual to find cross-cousins considered ideal marriage partners because when such a marriage takes place every generation it permanently links two kin groups. The diagram in Figure 13-8 will help to explain the different kinship status of the two varieties of cousins and will also provide evidence of their biological affinity.

Another theory of incest holds that familiarity breeds contempt or at least a lack of sexual interest. Bentham insisted that siblings raised in the same home would find it impossible to want a brother or a sister as a marriage partner. Perhaps the most extraordinary theory of incest is that of Sigmund Freud. He postulated a mythical human horde existing in a primeval era that was led by a jealous and powerful father (the "old man"). In keeping all the females for himself he incurred the hatred of his sons and they in turn banded together and slew and ate him. Each of the sons would have liked to have taken over the role of the "old man," but none was strong enough to seize control and expel the others. In order to survive as a group they removed the source of their temptation by establishing an incest prohibition on all the women of the group. This prohibition has in some mysterious way been handed down through hundreds of generations

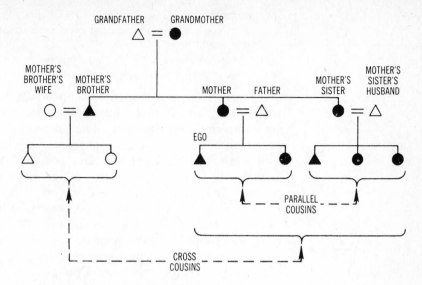

GRANDFATHER GRANDMOTHER

MOTHER'S BROTHER'S WIFE MOTHER'S BROTHER MOTHER FATHER MOTHER'S SISTER MOTHER'S SISTER'S HUSBAND

EGO

PARALLEL COUSINS

CROSS COUSINS

Note: Blackened symbols indicate all individuals who consider themselves related through the grandmother's lineage.

Figure 13-8

so that today people instinctively have a horror of incest.

Moving to more logical explanations of the universality of the incest taboo we read that Edward Tylor believed that by forcing men to seek brides outside their own group they established ties with other groups. This, of course, has the effect of reducing intergroup hostilities and at the same time creates larger social and economic groupings. Supporting evidence for Tylor's theory comes from the account of the anthropologist who asked a primitive why the men of his tribe didn't marry their sisters. After an initial shock reaction the native replied, "If we married our sisters, what would we do for brothers-in-law?" For this man, and for primitives all over the world, brothers-in-law mean additional strength in cooperative labor enterprises and aid in time of trouble or warfare.

The cultural consequences of marrying one's sister can be much more serious than just being without brothers-in-law. Nadel describes the extent to which certain groups might be disorganized by such a move.

> If any man married in disregard of the [incest] rule, the others would fail to work also. The bride-price would have to be paid within the same descent group, while in the people's conception it is a payment suitable only between such groups, being meant (among other things) to indemnify the bride's group for the loss of her prospective progeny. The offspring of such an irregular union would forfeit the double assistance from two kin

groups since the father's and mother's kin now coincide, and would be less advantageously placed than the offspring of customary marriages. And there would be various other, minor but no less confusing, complications; for example, rules of avoidance (obligatory towards in-laws) and intimacy (towards blood relations) would now apply to the same people. (1953:269)

Thus we can see that Layard's idea that the concept of incest has the concrete result of building a structure of society is a profound insight into the understanding of social organization. Leslie White concurs with Layard's position that forcing people to marry outside the group tends to "increase the size, and therefore the strength of the group." He feels, however, that exogamy (marrying out) is more important "in preliterate societies than in literate cultures, whereas the reverse is the case with endogamy (marrying in)."

The latter arrangement has the effect of "fostering solidarity and integrity." Endogamy tends to be found in more advanced types of society "based upon property relations, ones having occupational groups, the political state, and a police force, than in a society based upon kinship" (1959:116). Hindu society, with its emphasis on caste endogamy, or our own with emphasis on marriage within religious, racial, or class divisions, is an example of the situation in question.

Is One Form of Family Better Than Another?

We have seen that all known family types perform the minimal functions required for the survival of man and society, but it is only fair to ask, "Is one form of family better than others?" The answer to this is that the various forms each have their own distinctive strengths and their own weaknesses. Let us compare, for example, two major categories of family organization—the *conjugal* and the *consanguine*—in order to illuminate this problem.

THE CONJUGAL FAMILY

The *conjugal* form of family, found so frequently in Western society, provides its members with the greatest amount of personal freedom. There is usually freedom of choice of mates, and the power to control the family activities and destiny lies in the hands of those directly involved: a married couple and their offspring. There is little concern for the larger extended family or with family lines of descent and kinship, and it is rare that any great emphasis is placed on family lands or property.

While this form of family organization offers its members maximum freedom and minimum concern for distant relatives or extended family affairs, those who participate in this kind of social organization must pay for that freedom by having reduced family stability and a lack of family continuity. The conjugal family is formed when a married couple has produced their first child and it exists as a complete unit for a period of only sixteen to twenty-five years. Since there is little stress placed on the parent-child relationship, children are expected to develop an independence from their parents, and upon marrying to set up their own homes and maintain only minimum contacts with parents. When all the children have married and moved out of the home, the parents are left alone and the life cycle of the conjugal family is completed. The conjugal family not only lacks continuity but also efficiency. Each generation must start anew to obtain its own property and experience and to expect little or nothing from their relatives.

The American form of conjugal family places great emphasis on severing the parental ties, and it is seldom that a man and his bride will want to move in with either set of parents. They will instead be eager to start their own home and make their own way. The major problem, however, is that these young people have no experience in running a home. In addition to this, the earning power of the young father is at a minimum as he and his wife raise their children. He is too proud to ask his parents for help at this time when expenses are great and income is small. Independence from parental authority also carries the responsibility of self-support.

By the time the children start to move out of the home, the father, by virtue of his experience, has in many cases reached his maximum earning capacity, but now he does not need the money. His children, in turn, want their chance at making their own way. Thus the cycle begins anew.

THE CONSANGUINE FAMILY

The *consanguine* family, characteristic of many Oriental cultures, presents a very different picture. A typical consanguine situation involves a family consisting of several generations living together in a common household on family land that has supported the family for dozens of generations. This family unit shares both the work and resources. The eldest male may very likely direct the family activities and serve generally as the family patriarch. As the sons marry they will tend to remain at home. As long as the family head lives, the sons must obey him and work the land according to his wishes. When the patriarch dies, however, the eldest son will take over the authority of his father as well as the control of the family property. Since the son is often middle-aged by this time, he has long observed the manner in which the household must be run and he merely takes over the management of its material and human resources. Neither the efficiency nor the continuity of the family has been disturbed. In such families, however, individual action is discouraged. Personal considerations must be subordinated to family considerations, and men must often take directions from their older relatives when they themselves are mature adults.

Who is to say which of these families is *better*. One offers maximum freedom and the other offers maximum stability. Those who grow up in each prefer their own system and are anxious to have it perpetuated. Both kinds of families satisfy needs, but each places emphasis on different areas of satisfaction.

Summary

Although some form of family is found in all human societies, there is considerable variation in form and function. What is considered "right" and normal in one society, in terms of the proper number of spouses, the manner of figuring descent (*bilineal* or *unilineal*), or the appropriate place of residence after marriage, may be considered quite improper and abnormal in another. The primary functions of the family include the production, nurture, and enculturation of offspring. In many non-Western cultures mate selection is not based on romantic attraction of two individuals. Rather, it is a total family concern, and in some cases even a societal concern, that the conventional roles and responsibilities be fulfilled, thereby ensuring the survival and perpetuation of this basic social unit, the human family. The family is also an economic unit, both in production and consumption, and there is a division of labor between the sexes and between the members of various age levels. In a select number of societies some economic consideration (bride price or dowry) validates the marriage of two individuals, but this is in no sense a sale of a chattel.

In many parts of the world kinship is still the major organizing principle about which societies are structured. Every person is a member of two families, the *consanguine* family of birth and the *conjugal* family of marriage. In addition, they are connected to collateral relatives in various ways and this to a large extent determines the nature and quality of reciprocal relationships. Identities, responsibilities, and privileges are assigned and defined through the web of kinship.

Government and Law 14

International relations

    Necessity for international relations

    Economic and social ties

    Religious ties

    Conquest

Democracy

    Definition of democracy

    Distribution of democracy

The maintenance of order is a necessary concern in all societies, from small nomadic hunting and gathering bands to the most complex urbanized industrial societies. Within the face-to-face relationships of the small band of hunters and gatherers (which are united by ties of consanguineal and affinal kinship) the rules governing relationships between kinsmen function to maintain order most of the time, and any person violating these rules would be subject to sanctions applied directly and immediately. Ordinarily these measures bring the offender back into conformity, and only the most reprobate individual would fail to recognize the advantages of conformity or the problems arising from disobedience.

When the size of the society reaches the point where it is no longer possible to maintain the close scrutiny found in the kin group or the band, more formal measures of control become necessary. When the informal authority associated with age and sex roles (essentially male) no longer suffices to maintain order then some delegation of power becomes associated with social positions or *offices*. The persons filling these positions are *officials* and hold the power only as long as they are functioning in that role. This delegation of power from *persons* to *offices* marks the emergence of a formal political system.

One of the problems of control in kin-oriented societies is often the reluctance to discipline a kinsman, especially if the crime calls for a severe punishment. Theoretically, an official does not have to consider this problem, for his responsibilities are to discharge the duties of his office regardless of who the offender is. Actually, a conflict of interests can easily arise, but the tradition of governance and the authority of the office relieves the official of personal accountability.

The Origin of Government

Observing that every society in the world has some formal or informal governmental system, social scientists and social philosophers alike have long pondered the source of the concept of government. Although modern anthropology is less concerned with origins than it is with the role of government in human society, it is interesting to look at some of the more popular theories of genesis which have been put forward. Aristotle claimed that people are by nature political animals, implying that it is instinctive for them to live under some system of societal control. The origin of humans and the origin of government could not be separated in time. Other scholars have maintained that government was merely a human-conceived idea through which the selfish and cunning were able to impose their will upon their fellows.

The "contract theory" advanced by Hobbs and Locke postulated a deliberate agreement, in some primeval period, between the dominant and subordinate members of society which established mutual respect for one another's rights. Each had responsibilities as well as privileges.

The idea that government was given to humans by the gods is a concept that has appeared time and time again in human history. It explains the "divine right of kings" and serves as a sanction to theocratic systems in Mesopotamia, Egypt, Japan, and numerous primitive societies where rulers are looked upon as the descendants of deities.

Most social scientists today would explain government as being a natural outgrowth of group living. They would maintain that the larger and more complex the group the greater the need for satisfactory controls over behavior. In all societies, primitive or civilized, some means must be provided to enforce rules, punish wrongdoers, settle disputes, and protect private and group property. Political organization facilitates the growth of society by mobilizing its resources, providing a sense of unity, and serving as a source of decisions designed to promote the general welfare of the group. As Redfield puts it, "Formal political institutions not only keep societies going in the good old ways; they also provoke a challenge of those ways" (1956:361).

Authority and Social Control

Whether government decisions are in the hands of a paramount chief, a council of elders, or an elected legislature, there cannot be government without authority. Authority may be seized, inherited, or accorded, but if it is to be effective it must be backed up by force or the threat of force. Goldschmidt (1960) refers to authority as the *power* to govern and Mair maintains that "there is no society where rules are automatically obeyed, and . . . every society has some means of securing obedience as well as of dealing with offenders" (1962:18). In every society there are various levels of rules and regulations and various degrees of punishment for their infraction. Not all rules that control behavior, however, are enforced by political authorities. Many of the controls are built into the culture. Many societies have neither formal law nor a police force, but in their absence public opinion serves as a powerful deterrent to unruly citizens.

The least obvious forces of social control are folkways, or manners. Only the force of tradition backs up these customs, but it is a very thick-skinned person who can ignore them. If a person is expected to attend a party or dance in a dinner jacket and black bow tie, an uninformed guest can suffer untold agonies in a business suit and four-in-hand tie.

Even more powerful instruments of social control than manners are *mores,* or morals. As in the case of manners, they are a product of a cultural tradition although associated with only a certain aspect of that culture. An example would be the strong stand taken against divorce and interfaith marriage by some churches in the United States. Infractions of these taboos are not considered a crime against the society but only against the church.

Laws are the most formal and obvious instruments of social control. They are rules enforced by the authority of the state and they are often supracommunity and suprainstitution. This may best be seen in the case of United States Supreme Court and federal law pronouncements concerning integration. Although these legal orders run contrary to the sentiments of the people of many communities and contradict *mores,* they nevertheless have precedence. Law often overrules the systems of folkways or *mores* developed within certain institutions. When a number of religious sects advised their young men to ignore the draft, the offenders were prosecuted under federal law. In Utah, state law overruled Mormon church canons by forbidding the practice of polygamy. However, cases of polygamy periodically come before the courts, indicating "conservative" Mormons have not abandoned the practice.

Checks and Balances

Societies must have leaders, and leaders must be granted authority. A society that withholds the power to govern from its leaders robs itself of effective government. On the other hand, the leader who is given too much authority can in some cases further his own selfish interests and ignore the rights of those under his authority. The answer to this, of course, is the creation of a set of checks and balances whereby authority can be given but where it can also be controlled. Leaders must not only have rights but responsibilities as well.

The reader is no doubt well aware of the system of checks and balances that operates in the government of the United States. The executive branch may curb the legislative through the power of the veto, but the executive authority is in turn held in check by the legislature's power to override a veto and in extreme cases, to remove the executive officer through impeachment. The judicial branch has the power to declare legislation unconstitutional, but the legislature has the right to pass on judicial appointments. Still another factor, the voting franchise of the people, directly or indirectly serves as a control over all three branches of government. Most modern governments have a system that employs devices of a similar nature to ensure human rights and maximum participation of citizens in their government. However, a system of checks and balances is not a characteristic of civilized societies alone. A large number of primitive societies have very effective systems of controlling authority; indeed, it seems to be a natural requirement of stable and just government.

The Samoan Islanders of the southwest Pacific have lived under a very ingenious system of governmental checks and balances for centuries. Instead of the Samoans having three separate branches of government, the executive, judicial, and legislative functions are carried out by a single body, the village council. Each of the members of the council is the head of a separate extended family group and is known as a *matai*. Mataiship carries with it the rank of either Chief or Talking Chief depending upon the traditional status of the family. Actually, these chiefs are arranged in a hierarchy, and their power and authority in the village vary with their status—a matter to a great extent determined by tradition. The paramount chief of the village is a High Chief, and it is he who presides over the village council meetings (*fono*) and to a great extent influences its decisions.

The checks and balances in this system work as follows. Each Chief or Talking Chief is elected to his position of family head (*matai*) and council representative by the members of his extended family. Unlike many societies of Polynesia, primogeniture plays little or no part in his selection. More important is his leadership ability, general intelligence, knowledge of Samoan lore, and his past service to the family. Just as a *matai* may be elected to his position of family leadership, he can be removed from it by his family if he proves to be an autocratic or an ineffective leader. The chief's role in the village council is not unlike that of the elected congressman who goes to Washington to represent his district or state.

Even if a man holds the paramount chief title in the village, he will not have free rein to do as he pleases. While he has much authority and will receive great respect, his actions are regulated by the rest of the council. To begin with, in most villages his authority is balanced by the only slightly lesser power of the village High Talking Chief. These orator chiefs are known for their power to persuade and are frequently referred to as the "hard" or "difficult" people. It is not a bit unusual for a political question to be completely deadlocked when a paramount High Chief and a High Talking Chief are on opposite sides of the issue. Since all village council decisions must be unanimous the High Chief is careful to nurture the Talking Chief's support.

If a paramount chief should prove to be an autocrat, the village council merely votes to remove him and informs the surrounding

Samoan Talking Chief with orator's staff.

villages that they no longer look to him as their village leader. Once such drastic action has been carried out, the family of the former paramount chief will begin to exert pressure on their deposed representative. Since they do not want to be robbed of their powerful voice in the council and since their prestige has been impaired by his high-handed actions, they will in many cases threaten him with title removal unless he manages to re-establish himself in the good graces of the council. This is usually enough to make the chief go to the village council, ask their forgiveness, and mend his ways in future interaction with his fellow council members. The system that has evolved in Samoa is ingenious in that it represents the ultimate in representative government and provides for effective leadership although holding in the background the threat of removal of authority if misused.

In some societies it appears that a leader has tremendous unchecked authority because all of his decrees are immediately and unquestioningly obeyed. This is often deceiving and the leader may have less power than it appears; a universal principle of successful leadership is that one should never give an order that one knows will not be obeyed. The shrewd leader knows just how far he can go in making demands on his followers; and, even in the most autocratic of governments, there are always methods to bring the most despotic of leaders to terms. An example of this is cited by Vernon Dorjahn in his writings on the Temne of Sierra Leone. In precolonial days, when a paramount chief used his tremendous power to oppress the people, or as the Temne put it to "eat his chiefdom," a common defense was recourse to supernatural means. Dorjahn records that

> The use of swearing medicines was usually secret, for if word of it reached the chief he would take steps to protect himself, by supernatural means, and employ a counter-medicine. . . . Nevertheless, the belief was strong that swearing medicines employed by a man who had been wronged were especially powerful, and fear of such was said to have been a powerful deterrent on a chief's behavior. (1960:136)

Another method of bringing pressure on an errant chief was to appeal to the officials of the powerful Poro or Ragbenle secret societies or to subchiefs who were the paramount chief's confidants and advisors. If all this failed, there was always the threat of withdrawal of military support by the war chiefs, or even threats of assassination.

Primitive Law

There was a time when the basic requirement in the definition of law was that a society have writing. The unwritten norms known as folkways and *mores* were felt to be the limit to which nonliterate societies had evolved in achieving social control. Only a literate society would possess the capability of establishing and maintaining a code of rules and sanctions appropriate to infractions with consistency. But as anthropologists studied the normative structures of nonliterate societies, it was frequently found that a remarkable degree of consistency was maintained despite the lack of written codes.

Many years ago Radcliffe-Brown stated his belief that law was a matter of "legal sanction," and a sanction was legal when enforced by a "political society." Those societies lacking a political organization imposed and maintained their obligations on persons by "custom" and "convention," rather than by law. However Radcliffe-Brown did consider that in all societies if the recognition of an offense brought an organized and regular response in fixing responsibility and punishment then this should be called a "penal sanction," its purpose being to restore the social equilibrium upset by the infraction (1933).

E. A. Hoebel, also a pioneer in the anthropological study of law, defined law according to three basic principles that distinguished law from generalized social norms. Law, in his terms, must involve (1) the legitimate use of coercive force or economic deprivation; (2) allocation of official authority; and (3) regularity or consistency. Hoebel adds that the real core of law lies in the legitimate use of force, although the *threat* of force is usually adequate to maintain order. Law exists primarily to channel behavior into socially accepted means and ends, not to punish. But as a last resort, the application of force in appropriate forms may be invoked (1954).

Hoebel's concept is challenged in part, by Leo Pospisil, who considers the method of enforcement of less importance than the act of enforcement. Even more significant is a controlling authority to see to enforcement. Pospisil believes that there are many effective sanctions other than physical force, that is, those with psychological aspects— gossip, ridicule, ostracism, avoidance, or denial of favors. Some of these are obvious and overt, some are subtle and covert, but all are very effective (1958).

In writing on government and politics in Bantu societies Isaac Schapera (1967) considers that the establishment of courts, including those of African societies where the local chief (who is also the magistrate) sits to adjudicate civil and criminal, is the major criterion in determining the presence of law.

One of the authors observed such a court in a Bura village in Nigeria. Here the *joro* (chief) had total judicial power and sat in judgment whenever necessary. On one occasion a hearing involved alleged adultery, and there appeared to be little question of guilt. The woman involved sat with a very distressed expression, sobbing quietly while her husband and lover argued violently. Her husband had obviously beaten her severely, and he also wanted to punish the lover. It was difficult to determine if the lover was confessing or boasting, but finally the chief called an abrupt halt. He asked the woman if she were guilty and her answer was another sob, interpreted as a "yes." He asked the lover if he were guilty and received an affirmative answer. The chief levied a fine of five pounds (about $13.50) which, of course, he claimed, and then he adjourned the court. The husband had his revenge in that he had beaten his wife and caused her lover to be fined. One would assume that the woman and her lover had already had their pleasure, albeit with painful results. The chief had the money, and the case was closed. Adultery would seldom if ever result in a divorce among the Bura, however, for premarital and extramarital sex is very common.

Max Gluckman, writing on law among the Lozi in Barotseland, feels that the rules and procedures established by judges constitute law. This is similar to what is found in Western law, where precedents are so important, and where law is a matter of interpreting previous judicial decisions. In theory, there is a known body of law, previously unwritten, and judges are supposed to know it; but obviously no one person is able to do this, because so much latitude is employed in individual cases, and because the "law" is frequently amended to fit the situation. This flexibility allows for equity and reason in that it considers the evidence carefully and the personalities of those involved (1955).

PUNISHMENT

In traditional societies there are rarely any facilities available for long term incarceration, and if there were, they would not necessarily have the same effect on criminals as loss of freedom might have on our own. One of the authors knew an African hunter who was thrown into jail annually during the dry season for the crime (established by the British forestry office) of setting fire to the bush. The hunter did this so he could see the game more easily. Spending three or four months lying around with little to do but visit with other prisoners and passers by, and having his food prepared and brought to him with no effort on his part, were hardly punitive measures when compared to the rigors of earning one's living outside of prison.

Where pre-industrial societies are operating under their own indigenous systems punishment is usually corporal for lesser offenses and capital for major, especially if the crimes have been against the supernatural or against the king (often considered blasphemy against a divine being). There is no need for a holding facility since in either case retribution comes swiftly. An example of this kind of justice was seen in the punishment of the defilers of the Grand mosque in Mecca in 1979. All were quickly and efficiently beheaded.

OATH TAKING

One of the most important of all principles of law is that ensuring the truth of testimony. Proof of this importance is seen in the severity of punishment meted out to those who give false testimony. In some cases this perjury warrants the same punishment as that for the offense for which the accused person is standing trial, including the death penalty. Normally the assistance of the supernatural realm is evoked so that the gods or spirits might bring retribution. In effect, the swearing of an oath is a prayer inviting death if the testimony is not the truth. Just how seriously this concept is taken is hard to determine absolutely, but among traditional societies like the Bura of Nigeria, their particular form of oath (licking the *hoptu*—a stick with a leather ball on one end and feathers and beads attached to the other) is taken very seriously. This *hoptu* is presented to the person about to testify. He touches his tongue to it and asks the spirit of the *hoptu* to kill him if he is untruthful. He believes implicity in the power of the *hoptu* to do this, so there is little chance that the witness will intentionally tell a lie.

Whether to extend this concept to the case of the Bible for oath swearing in American courts might be questioned, but there is little doubt that the sanctity of the religious book is supposed to ensure the truth of the testimony. That the oath administered by the clerk of the court is usually garbled and unintelligible matters little, since it is the hand being placed on the Bible that seems to establish the necessary connection with the supernatural. Quakers and other dissidents who object to an oath and make a statement of affirmation instead, are still subject to the penalties for perjured testimony, and presumably divine retribution as well.

Levels of Government

To obtain an understanding of the universal features of government as well as those that become necessary as societies grow in population and in complexity of culture, we will survey its forms in various geographical and cultural regions of the world. Of the various levels of political complexity known, the kinship-based government is perhaps the simplest. In such a system it is difficult to see where family leaves off and government begins. This type of political organization is found in many parts of the world—primarily among hunters and gatherers—but we shall look to the Bushmen of the Kalahari desert of South Africa as being somewhat typical of this form.

BUSHMAN GOVERNMENT— A KIN-BASED SYSTEM

The Bushmen follow a hunting and gathering way of life in the Kalahari desert in southwest Africa (Namibia). They are organized into bands of 25 to 50 individuals who in many cases are the members of a single extended family. Their leader is usually the head man of the dominant extended family, a position that he inherits in the male line. His actual authority over the group is slight, and anthropologists who have worked among these people describe his role as that of a leader rather than a ruler. While this man is in a sense the "executive officer" of the group, his main functions are those of directing the band's movements, officiating at certain ceremonies, and providing leadership in time of warfare. There is some variation in the authority of these headmen from band to band, but this is largely dependent upon the man's personality and leadership ability. He is expected to hunt like everyone else, as this kind of society cannot afford specialists of any variety. He has no judicial functions, and even his "executive" proclamations are subject to veto by the other adult males of the band. The Bushmen may be described as having a completely classless and democratic society. There is great freedom of action within the group, and individuals are free to do much as they please as long as it does not work a hardship on the group or infringe upon some traditionally honored law or custom. The enculturation and

Among the Kung Bushmen of Southwest Africa, kinship and political structures are nearly one and the same. Here the father and headman of the band (hand to face) discusses plans with his three sons-in-law. (Courtesy L. K. Marshall Expedition, Peabody Museum of Harvard University—Smithsonian Institution.)

socialization processes place major stress on conformity to the norms and regulations of the group, and there is little need for law enforcement among adults. The head of each nuclear family is responsible for the behavior of his wife and children. Since there is no recognized judiciary authority, disputes between families tend to be settled through feud.

A major distinction is often made between primitive and civilized governmental systems in the emphasis placed on territoriality. Although territorial boundaries of modern nations are extremely important in determining citizenship and in defining jurisdiction of authority and sovereignty, ideas of territoriality are far from lacking among the Bushmen. Each band has a clearly defined territory of approximately 200 square miles which they fiercely defend against encroachment by neighboring bands. While bands may be allowed to cross the territorial boundaries of one another, settlement or hunting without permission brings conflict.

THE HOTTENTOTS —MULTIPLE-KIN GOVERNMENT

To the south of the Bushmen lives a group known as the Hottentots. While these people are racially related to the Bushmen, their economy and political organization are different. The Hottentots are a pastoral people who primarily herd cattle and sheep but carry on some hunting and gathering activities. The government of these people is somewhat more complex that that of their Bushmen neighbors and might be described as being of the *multiple-kin* variety.

The Hottentots are organized into tribes of roughly 500 to 2500 people. Each tribe is autonomous and composed of a number of clans. All the members of a particular clan claim a common ancestor and think of themselves as being related through the male line. One of these clans in considered senior and paramount and the chief of the entire tribe is drawn from this clan. The office of tribal chief is a hereditary one, handed down from father to son. Although the status of chief commands great respect, his executive authority is subject to the advice and rulings of a tribal council. Council members are "elected" at a mass meeting of all the married males, but they actually are the normal heads of the several clans making up the tribe. Senior officials, such as subchief, magistrate, and war chief, are appointed from this body of clan heads. While this council has been described as the tribal executive, its votes on specific issues are frequently influenced by the chief's desires, particularly if he is an individual of strong character. The main functions of the council are those of making wars and treaties, and formulating rules and regulations for intra- as well as intertribal relations. Judiciary matters are handled primarily by the magistrate or the subchief, but the total council often serves as a court of appeal.

At this level of government the council is a formal body of officials with tribally sanctioned powers and responsibilities. While the adult males in Bushman society no doubt serve as a type of council, they are not recognized as an official governmental body to which one might be elected.

Even at this somewhat more advanced level of government we still do not find full-time political specialists. Apart from the fact that the Hottentot chief is generally the wealthiest man in the tribe, he is not distinguished in dress or size of house and household from his subjects. He and the other tribal officials have to tend their own animals the same as anyone else.

Tribal boundaries are not as clearly defined for these people as they are for the Bushmen, but there is a concept of use rights of water holes. If one tribe were to enter the area of another, application for rights to use grasslands and water holes has to be made to the resident chief. If friendly relations exist between the two groups, permission will be freely given; otherwise a tribute might be demanded for using the land and the water. Thus we can see that something in the way of intergroup diplomacy takes the place of feud where there is a conflict of interests.

THE TRIBE

Multiple-kin units are often referred to as "tribes," but tribes need not have a kinship principle of organization. It is also true that the word "tribe" does not necessarily imply a centralized form of government. Often it is hard to lay one's finger on why a group of relatively self-governing bands is collectively referred to by this term. Some would maintain that a tribe is merely a group of individuals who share a common language, culture, or territory. Mandelbaum feels that

> The important basis for the existence of a tribe is not any one of these factors, but the combination of them that gives every person in the tribe a feeling of belonging with the other men and women of the tribe. The real bonds which hold any group together, whether it be tribe, clan, or state, are the attitudes which the individuals in that group have toward each other, and the behavior patterns of reciprocal help, of cooperation, which are the tangible demonstrations of those attitudes. (1956:296)

The word *tribe* does not imply any specific form of government but instead singles out a group of people who work together for the common good. Tribes may be headed by a hereditary chief of a senior clan, or leadership may be entirely independent of kinship.

ASSOCIATIONAL TRIBES

Many Plains Indian tribes, for example, elected the chiefs for their council from the bravest and most reputable men of their communities. In addition to this decision-making body, there were political units that actually held greater authority in controlling the society than did the council chiefs. These were the soldier or military societies. Of the Cheyenne, Llewellyn and Hoebel write:

> There were six military societies . . . the Fox Soldiers, Elk Soldiers, Shield Soldiers, Bowstring Soldiers, Dog Men and Northern Crazy Dogs. These were free associations in which membership was voluntary and at the discretion of the individuals. Open to all men of all ages, they were of the ungraded type.[1] (1941:99)

The leaders of these military societies were generally appointed by the chief's council and given almost supreme authority to maintain law and order. Any order issued by them had to be obeyed—frequently on pain of death. While the main function of these societies was to police tribal buffalo hunts and make sure that no one would spoil the hunt, their duties often extended to matters of everyday village control as well. Typical of the functions of military societies was the adjusting of quarrels between village members, forbidding gathering parties from going out when enemies were near, preserving order when villages moved to another campsite, and restraining war parties from going out on inopportune raids. Often they served as judge, jury, and penal authority over thieves and murderers.

---

[1] From *The Cheyenne Way* by Karl N. Llewellyn and E. Adamson Hoebel. Copyright 1941 by the University of Oklahoma Press, p. 99.

AGE-GRADE
TRIBES

Still another type of tribal organization involves a system of government based upon various age categories. Among the Nandi, Masai, and Kikuyu tribes of East Africa, political roles are not allocated according to lineage or clan units but according to age grades. An age grade is a group composed of all those men who passed through manhood initiation ceremonies together. The members of these groups share a common status and this status changes as they grow older. After their initiation they share a common lot as warriors, and then, after they marry and raise their families, they pass on to elder status. In the tribes where this kind of organization is found, the many segments of the tribes are widely scattered and nothing in the way of centralized authority was ever developed. The territorial groupings that cross-cut family and clan organization look to their elders to settle disputes, direct the group in ritual matters, mobilize the warrior grades in time of war, and generally serve as decision-making authorities in local and territorial matters.

TRIBAL
CONFEDERATIONS

Sometimes independent tribes with similar cultures are drawn together for purposes of their mutual welfare. Although the groups might have strong pride in their own sovereignty, commonly when people are threatened by external forces they tend to forget their minor differences for the sake of their common defense. This was the case with the League of Five Fires, a multitribal grouping of Plains Indians organized for the purpose of driving off the ever-encroaching white man. Although this defense organization was shortlived and not very effective, the League of the Iroquois represents a classic example of a primitive confederation of sovereign nations.

League of the Iroquois. The League of the Iroquois represented a federation of northeast woodland tribes—the Onondaga, Mohawk, Oneida, Seneca, Cayuga—in the area that is now upstate New York. A sixth tribe, the Tuscarora, was added after the initial charter was formed. While the League is sometimes referred to as the first United Nations, its actual operation was more like that of the North Atlantic Treaty Organization (NATO). These six Iroquois-speaking tribes were interested in maintaining peace only among themselves, and they often took to the war path as a group against their neighboring tribes.

The political structure of the League greatly resembled our own Federation of States, and it has been suggested that the authors of the United States Constitution might very well have borrowed certain features from the League, since they had knowledge of its organization. Each of the tribes was autonomous in local affairs, but matters that concerned the League as a whole, such as declarations of war, were under the jurisdiction of a council of fifty representatives, or *sachems.* Some tribes sent as many as fourteen *sachems*, while others sent as few as eight; but since all council decisions had to be unanimous the unequal representation was not a drawback. In each of the tribes there were eight matrilineal clans—the Wolf, Bear, Beaver, Turtle, Deer, Snipe, Heron, and Hawk—of which the *sachems* were representatives. Although the legislators were always men, they owed their appointments to the clan matriarchs; the kinship bond between a man and the representatives of his clan in other tribes helped stabilize the confederation. The traditional capital of the League was in Onondaga territory, where representatives assembled to settle disputes and thus maintain peace within the group, make treaties, send and receive ambassadors, regulate the affairs of subjugated tribes, and decide on matters pertaining to the general welfare.

CHIEFDOMS

Scholars who take an evolutionary approach to culture argue that a form of transitional political organization exists, intermediate between egalitarian tribal societies and states. Chiefdoms, they claim, possess a somewhat theocratic orientation, with the leader being both priest and chief, and the position is hereditary and aristocratic; however, the chiefdom lacks a formal legalized structure to administer force, a central criterion of the state. There is a distinct hierarchy of statuses for other roles in the society (Service 1975:15–16).

MONARCHY

As in the case of the tribe, the nature of monarchy can't be generalized, for it may exist in very primitive societies with fairly small populations or in complex industrial states. In most cases, however, it represents a form of kin-based government in that the ruling monarch usually derives from a royal family or clan. A king may receive his position by virtue of primogeniture or, as in the case of Samoan kings, be chosen from a special group of candidates by a traditional body of "kingmakers." In a number of Bantu societies where ruling monarchs have numerous sons because they have many wives, succession is decided by fighting.

In a monarchy, government is centralized, with decisions originating with the king, whose authority usually has both sacred and secular sanctions. We are all familiar with the concept of "divine right" of kings, which was so emphasized by the Stuart kings of England. In Egypt the king was himself a god, and in a number of primitive societies myths can be called upon to prove that the royal line extends back to a time when its members were supernatural. The Shilluk of the African Sudan believe that their king, the Reth, is a living representative of the partly divine culture hero Nyikang, who is credited with leading them to their present home. It is believed that the spirit of Nyikang enters the body of each new king at the time of

A faithful subject bows before his king in the Cameroons. (Courtesy Field Museum of Natural History.)

his installation and from this time on he exhibits some of the supernatural characteristics of the mythical founder. Because he embodies these qualities he is considered incapable of poor judgment. Should bad decisions be made, the blame is always placed on his advisors who gave him bad counsel.

The secular power of a king is acquired through a system of clientage that Mair describes as the process of "building up a body of persons who depend upon their leader in such a way that their first loyalty is to him" (1962:166). This may be done by giving people economic advantages or by rewarding them for special service. Samoan kings rewarded their chiefs for outstanding service with lands, honorific titles, and special privileges. The talking-chief title Lolo, of Sili village, for example, carries the special privilege of wearing a turban in the village—a prerogative withheld from all other chiefs regardless of their rank.

The power of kings varies a great deal. In some cultures they hold life and death power over their subjects while in others they are merely figureheads or ceremonial leaders—for example, modern European sovereigns. Monarchy is almost always associated with pomp, ceremony, and symbolism, all of which serve as a method of drawing upon sentiments of national pride, thus creating a more unified nation.

CHARACTERISTICS
OF THE
POLITICAL
STRUCTURE OF
THE STATE

"The state" is a designation indicating complex government. While it is possible to enumerate several characteristics of "state" political structure, not every complex government incorporates all of them in its organization. Generally, most of these features are essential to the operation of political systems in densely populated areas with urban communities.

Centralized Government with Delegated Authority.   In attempting a definition of a state, Lucy Mair writes: "If we were to try to put in a a single sentence the essence of the state system we might say that it consists in the delegation of power by the ruler who holds final authority, in such a way that he can expect his orders or decisions to be carried out throughout the land which he claims to rule" (1962:138).

Elman Service, in *The Origin of the State and Civilization* writes, "Civil law and formal government, elements that characterize states, are distinguishable from the usual forms of political power in primitive society by the fact that they are institutionalized, enacted, official, and they employ, threaten, or imply the actual use of force" (1975:12).

Complex governments must of necessity delegate authority in order to tend to the many problems that develop at all levels. Since no single man can carry the whole burden of authority, hierarchies of officials are created who are directly responsible for certain portions of the population and for various areas of activity. Often these lesser authorities are appointed by the central ruler, elected by the people, or in some rare cases these positions are hereditary. At this level of government, kinship almost ceases to enter into the political structure.

There is perhaps no more clear-cut picture of the delegation of authority in a state system than that which existed among the Incas, a government that employed literally hundreds of officials with graduated spheres of authority. Chapple and Coon describe the Inca bureaucratic system as follows:

> The administrative hierarchy consisted of nine ranks of officials beginning with the Inca. The empire was divided into four quarters, and each of these had a ruler who was directly responsible to the Inca. In each quarter were officials who ruled an area containing 40,000 households, and under them were officials who ruled 10,000, 1000, 500, 100, 50, and 10. Each rank of official was appointed by those immediately above him in the scale. (1942:352)

Political Specialization.   As has been noted in other areas of culture, advanced societies tend to be characterized by specialization of occupation. It is true in religion, in the arts and crafts, and also in government. In simpler societies the political leader earns his own living by hunting, herding, agriculture, or whatever the prevailing economy might be. His political activities take little of his time, and he is well paid for them in prestige and in the respect accorded him by his followers. In more complex societies the political leader is called upon more frequently to settle disputes, coordinate group activities, and maintain order, and he finds less time for tending to the support of his own family. As the demands on the paramount ruler become more oppressive, there is a delegation of power to specialists such as war leaders, judges, advisors, diplomats, and ambassadors whose full-time activities must be supported by the citizens they serve.

Taxation.   One of the consequences of complex government is that someone must pay the bill. Taxation, which provides a nation's fiscal power, is the natural outgrowth of bureaucracy and political specialization. If leaders are expected to devote themselves full-time to the affairs of government, they expect to be rewarded. Support for state projects and state officials is not always in money but may very likely be in the form of goods or services. In many societies the first fruits of the harvest go to political and religious leaders, and among the East African Ganda it is common practice for the more important families to give tribute in the form of young women who become the wives of the king. In Egypt every able-bodied man was expected to donate a few months' labor each year to the building of royal monuments. In the Inca empire, taxes in the form of food were required of the people, but the value of labor performed for the state was deducted. A similar phenomenon is still found in the laws of the state of New Hampshire where it is possible to work on public roads in lieu of paying taxes.

In a number of Copper Age civilizations of the Middle East, such discoveries as writing and mathematics are believed to have developed out of the necessity of keeping records of royal tribute. In Mesopotamia tax records were incised in wet clay and then baked into permanent documents.

The Athenians had a unique tax system that had the effect of making the burden somewhat less objectionable. While the rich were heavily taxed, the system was not as impersonal as modern income tax procedures. It was not uncommon for a man of wealth to be charged with the operation of a particular naval vessel for a year. If he chose, he could even serve as its captain. Greeks with theatrical interests were given the opportunity to serve as patrons of the state-supported plays. In this fashion, government enterprises took on the nature of private hobbies for affluent citizens.

Territoriality.   At one time it was believed that this factor set apart simple and complex political systems. We find, however, that even a simple hunting band like the Bushmen are territorial in the sense that they claim a certain territory as their own and drive all trespassers from it. Gearing points out that "almost all groups which act politically . . . possess or control territory; but gypsies and Shoshonis do not" (1962:71).

The aspect of territoriality that we can invariably associate with complex government is something quite different. Meyer Fortes and E. E. Evans-Pritchard explain that in more complex societies "the administrative unit is a territorial unit; political rights and obligations are territorially delimited" (1940:10). The political machinery, whatever its form, has total administrative and judicial authority within a certain set of geographical boundaries; everyone living in the defined area is subject or citizen and owes loyalty and economic and military support to the territorial government. The Greek city-state, or *polis*, had this concept of a centralized government with jurisdiction over a fixed territory. The Athenian people occupied a territory technically known as Attica, consisting of many villages. A citizen of any of these villages was known as a citizen of the state of Athens and subject to its laws. This concept of citizenship is much the same as that which prevails in the United States or any modern complex nation.

Professional Military.   A characteristic feature of the state is its ability to engage in total war. One aspect of this capacity is the necessity of maintaining a professional body of full-time soldiers. Among American Indians the only society of sufficient complexity to support such a force was the Inca, who had a standing army of about 10,000, which essentially served as bodyguards to the emperor. A few African societies, such as Dahomey, had a standing army, and it is to be found in several of the more complex societies of Asia. Japan, for instance, had a special class of professional soldiers, the samurai. In many European countries where a standing army was a common phenomenon, military leaders were drawn from the prominent families in which it was traditional for one son in each family to enter the army as a career.

While the Spartans maintained a society that was almost a military camp, the Athenians represent an exception to our generalization. Warfare for Athenians was a civilian enterprise, and mobilization meant that everyone went home and got his shield, spear, and rations. The citizen assembly formulated war plans and directed the military. While the Athenian fighting man was both brave and intelligent, campaigns were anything but efficiently planned and executed. An example is the decision of the Athenian assembly to invade Sicily during the Peloponnesian War, when most of the legislators knew neither the size of the Sicilian army nor the location of the island. Warfare was so much of a civilian enterprise that campaigns were planned to be short in duration so that the soldiers (mostly farmers) could return to attend to their harvesting activities.

A Court System. Whereas in simple kin-based political systems headmen or chiefs settle disputes and punish offenders, complex governments extend their services to include specially established courts with professional judges. In Inca society, officials who governed the various-sized political units included as part of their regular duties the function of magistrate, but in Aztec society an extremely elaborate system of courts existed. The least important of these was the merchants' court, which regulated the business of the market. It consisted of a body of 12 men who sat each day in the market and settled disputes between the various vendors of merchandise. The courts hearing civil suits of all types, located in the four quarters of the city, were more formal. Each district had its court presided over by a body of judges, who derived their support from the products grown on special sections of government land. If there were need to appeal a decision, this could be done in a special appellate court located in the emperor's palace. Appeals of noblemen were channeled to a still higher court, the supreme court of the land. Its presiding officers were the Aztec war leader and a body of 13 elders.

In England under the Norman conquerors special courts had to be established to relieve the king of this increasingly time-consuming task. When originated, these courts remained under the king's supervision, but in time they became separate specialized organs of government with their own administration.

International Relations

In addition to providing methods of controlling the behavior of the members of a society, the political authority must also work out ways of dealing with the sovereign nations with which it comes in contact. In some cases satisfactory peaceful relations cannot be established and a continual state of war or feud exists. The Willigiman-Wallalua people of the highlands of New Guinea wage war almost weekly with their neighboring tribe, the Wittaia. Although the two tribes practice the same culture and speak the same language, each thinks of the other as subhuman. Their weekly battles last only a day but they go on month after month, year after year, as there is always a death on one side or the other that must be avenged.

In many other societies the people have managed to escape the constant threat of aggression from their neighbors by establishing with them diplomatic relations of some variety. These methods of maintaining the peace may in some cases be strictly political arrangements (e.g., the League of the Iroquois) worked out by the authorities of the groups, but in other cases amiable relations may grow out of trade interaction, intermarriage, or common membership in ritual associations.

ECONOMIC AND
SOCIAL TIES

People who have developed an economic dependency with adjacent tribes will often go to great lengths to work out treaties so that war will not leave each without sorely needed commodities. In the case of the Trobriand Islanders, although two communities might be engaged in hostilities, kula partners do not take up arms against one another.

Although any sovereign groups find difficulty in yielding to a greater authority, it is often done when some material advantage is envisioned. So it was at the annual buffalo hunts of Plains Indians. At this time ordinarily independent hunting bands came together and submitted to the paramount authority of soldier societies who regulated and policed the hunt. Since it had often been proved that a carefully co-ordinated operation would result in more game than when each band hunted on its own, even these fiercely independent people worked out a system of intergroup cooperation.

European dynasties, as well as the royalty of the Maori and others, have long utilized international marriages as a method of establishing goodwill and cooperation. There are any number of cases in the anthropological literature of adjacent villages with separate political authorities becoming a single entity through the intermarriage not only of chiefly families but of commoners as well.

RELIGIOUS TIES

Just as an American college student can find sanctuary on a rival campus in the house of the fraternity to which he belongs, so members of ritual associations or secret societies in primitive groups can expect friendship from members of a common cult when they are traveling through foreign territory. In Sierra Leone a Temne tribesman who is a member of the secret association known as the Poro Society has something in common with Poro members in distant parts of his own tribal territory and even with members in the adjacent Mende country. In Western culture an example of the power of religion to produce political allies is to be seen in the Crusades, when the nations of western Europe combined to free the Holy Land from Moslem control. Chapple and Coon add that "in Morocco at the time of the Riffian War, the Spanish deserters would be spared if they approached their captors shouting, 'There is no god but Allah, and Mohammed is the messenger of Allah!' " (1942:343).

CONQUEST

One system of establishing workable relations with a hostile group is by conquering it. Conquest is almost always undertaken for economic reasons—to obtain either natural resources or additional tribute—and usually conquerors interfere in the internal affairs of a subjugated nation only to the extent necessary to keep the peace and to collect the desired tribute. Often the conquerors impose an oligarchical rule and establish themselves as a sort of landed gentry, living off the fruits of the vanquished population. This situation was common in medieval Europe and can be found today in East Africa in the relations between the aristocratic Tusi and the Hutu commoners.

Conquest empires are rarely able to establish serene administrations. In a United Nations building in Geneva, Switzerland, there is a mural bearing the title *The Burden of Conquest* that depicts an inevitable result—that the vanquished will plot revenge. One of the most successful conquest empires was that of the Incas, who ruled an area about the size of most of western Europe (380,000 square miles) and attempted to allay any possible resistance by systematically breaking down conquered cultures through a juxtaposition of population. Even in this extremely efficient totalitarian state, internal dissension was not eliminated and the empire had already begun to disintegrate when Pizarro dealt it a deathblow in 1532.

Democracy

One method of delegating authority in government is by means of a representative democratic system. Democratic government may be differentiated from other forms by the fact that those in positions of political power acquire them through election rather than inheritance or appointment. Although representative government is common to a large number of complex governmental systems, it is found at other levels as well. It is present among the Samoans, the Yakut of Siberia, and the Cheyenne of North America.

The democratic system, of which the United States is justifiably proud, has been heralded as the most stable and effective of governmental forms. The democratic process might at times appear agonizingly slow and inefficient, but its strength lies in that there is a maximum of interaction between the governors and the governed. This interaction and the concomitant communication allow for constant adjustment in the system to meet current needs. Chapple and Coon see democracy as having greater staying power than either autocratic or totalitarian forms. They state: "The democratic governments . . . are so constituted that they can weather adversities of warfare or technological changes which would destroy the equilibrium of others" (1942:363).

As scholarly as any evaluation of the democratic system are the remarks delivered by Adlai Stevenson in January, 1963, before the

Center for the Study of Democratic Institutions in New York City. A portion of his speech reads:

> There is precious little dignity or equality in our natural state. Most human beings have to spend their lives in utter vulnerability. All are born unequal in terms of capacity or strength . . . and survive only through the restraint shown by more powerful neighbors. For nearly three thousand years "Western man" has struggled to create a social order in which weak, fallible, obstinate, silly, magnificent man can exercise his free and responsible choice.
>
> Whether democracy can prevail in the great upheaval of our time is a valid question. We have good reason to know how clumsy, slow, inefficient and costly it is compared to the celerity, certainty and secrecy of absolutism. But the important thing is that even the absolutists masquerade as democrats; even the military and quasi-military dictatorships strive in the name of democracy to manage the public business. And all of them say that authoritarianism is only a necessary transition to democracy. . . . The enemies of freedom, whatever the magnificent ends they propose—the brotherhood of man, the kingdom of saints, "from each according to his ability, to each according to his needs"—miss just the essential point: that man is greater than the social purposes to which he can be put. He must not be kicked about even with the most high-minded objectives. He is not a means or an instrument. He is an end in himself.
>
> This is the essence of what we mean by democracy—not so much voting systems or parliamentary systems or economic or legal systems (though they all enter in), as an irrevocable and final dedication to the dignity of man. In this sense, democracy is perhaps mankind's most audacious experiment.

Summary

Since the maintenance of order is necessary in all societies, some form of structure designed for that purpose is found everywhere. In small societies interpersonal relationships are frequent and there are strong traditions about how people should treat one another for the good of the society. Order in such a society can be maintained by direct and informal means, with the family and village applying pressure to ensure proper behavior. In larger societies up to the complexity of industrial ones, more formal means are necessary to maintain control, and there is a delegation of authority to officials who replace kin and neighbors in ensuring conformity to local *mores*. Anthropologists define "law" in terms of (1) legitimizing the use of force, and (2) allocation of authority, involving the application of sanctions, punishment, and oath-taking.

The simplest form of political organization is based on kinship. Beyond this, levels of government include tribal societies, chiefdoms, and states. States have centralized political networks, delegation of authority, political specialization, taxations, territoriality, a professional military, and a court system. International relationships are derived from the necessity of maintaining social and economic ties for mutual welfare, and this includes the reduction of tension and likelihood of warfare.

Religion 15

Religion and economics

> Magic in hunting and collecting societies
> Magic in agricultural societies

> Economic rewards for being religious

Religion and morality

> Separable concepts in many human societies
> Strongest in Judeo-Christian-Islamic religion

Magic and religion

> Magic as power to compel
> Contagious principle in magic
> Homeopathic principle in magic
> Magic as pseudoscience

Religion is many things to many people. Its forms are so varied that it is even difficult to describe what the institution of religion is except in very general terms. Anthropologists recognize religion as a universal aspect of human behavior and one that is very difficult to study, because religion is highly personal, and the emotional content is at least as important as the intellectual. Religion is the means through which human beings can acquire some of their most profound and meaningful experiences and by which they handle some of their most fundamental personal problems. One's own cultural background will tend to affect how religion is perceived and defined. For some, religion is only Christianity, Judaism, Islam, Buddhism—that is, the major historic traditions—and all else is idolatry and false belief. But there is no such thing as a "true" or a "correct" belief, as there is no way to evaluate qualitatively the validity of a particular religion. The strength of religion is to be found in the fact that it is accepted and perpetuated although its tenets cannot be tested empirically; they must be accepted on faith. One's cultural background also influences responses to the introduction of new religions. Belief systems which feature polytheism (belief in many gods—like the 365 million honored by one Hindu sect) are more tolerant in accepting new deities than monotheistic ones which tend to operate on a "Thou shalt have no other gods before me" premise. Polytheists believe that if the foreign god is as good as missionaries say it is, it will make an excellent addition to their already-established pantheon.

While religion must be thought of as being in the realm of the nonempirical, it often functions in areas in which people also apply scientifical principles. In the area of illness, for example, prayer and the consolations of religion may be seen by some people as having as much value as scientific medicines or surgical procedures. Occasionally religion is even more effective than science in its ability to explain human events and why they occur.

Religion represents a system which, in may ways, runs parallel to and also in opposition to the logical and empirical tenets of science. There is a tendency, however, for those who live in technologically advanced societies to believe that their forms of religion are somehow more valid than the belief systems of nonliterate, pre-industrial people. The latter's sacred convictions are often dismissed by "civilized" folk as mere "superstition."

While the anthropologist sometimes uses the term superstition, he does not apply it to meaningful sacred beliefs. Superstitions are survivals of an earlier age that people no longer believe in but observe anyway (like our fear of the number 13). When applied to religion, superstition is a derogatory and unscientific term. Many Americans have no qualms about calling a West African's beliefs superstition but are greatly upset when they hear Soviet Marxists refer to Christianity as such. People who insist on dwelling upon the "primitive" and "irrational" religious behavior of primitives should think seriously about the following items found in a newspaper "chuckle" column. "Natives who beat drums to drive away evil spirits are considered stupid (and heathen) by Europeans who honk horns to break up traffic jams."

Religion has been defined as "a set of earnest policies," "a philosophy," "a special mode of behavior," "a pragmatic attitude," but in all cases it has to do with the realm of the supernatural. It has been argued, however, that Confucianism regarded the supermatural aspects of religion as unimportant and felt that religion was a device for unifying society and supporting its values. Generally, however, we shall follow the view of Finegan, who has written, "Religion . . . has to do with something more than the obvious surface of things. . . . In religion . . . there is an attempt to relate life to a dimension of existence other than that with which common sense and science are concerned" (1952:6). What this "something more" is may be defined differently in different cultures, and the attitudes and acts judged appropriate in relation to it may likewise vary widely. One thing is certain: This "something more" is of vital importance. Lessa defines religion as a "system of beliefs and practices directed toward the ultimate concern" of a society (1958:1) and Redfield concurs by relating that religion is "about what most matters" (1956:362).

Thus, we find that almost all people in the world have a supernatural belief system and a category of behavior which we might call religious but each and every religious system is unique, satisfying that particular culture's needs. When any religion moves from one cultural setting to another, it becomes something quite different from what it was in the parent culture.

Since religion reflects culture it is not easily transferable and thus can only be completely understood in context. An example is the understanding of the Twenty-Third Psalm by the Khmus tribe of Laos. Literally translated it would read something like this:

> The Great Boss is the one who takes care of my sheep
> I don't want to own anything.
> The Great Boss wants me to lie down in the field.
> He wants me to go to the lake.
> He makes my good spirit come back.
> Even though I walk through something the missionary
>   calls the valley of the shadow of death, I do
>   not care.
> You are with me.
> You use a stick and a club to make me comfortable.
> You manufacture a piece of furniture right in
>   front of my eyes while my enemies watch.

You pour car grease on my head.
My cup has too much water in it and therefore
overflows.
Goodness and kindness will walk single file behind me all my life.
And I will live in the hut of the Great Boss
until I die and am forgotten by the tribe.[1]

Why People Have Religion

As we look about the world and see that all peoples are drawn to a belief in something greater than everyday reality, we find justification for asking why religion of some variety is found everywhere. Religion, after all, is not a response to any biological need and, as far as simply living out one's three score and ten, man *can* live by bread alone. And yet, religion must satisfy some basic psychological need. It appears that all religious behavior represents a response to the wonder and the fear of the uncontrollable forces of nature; awed by the overwhelming power of the wind, waves, lightning, and thunder, people perhaps develop an idea of a supernatural deity on which they can call in order to deal with these forces.

Religion supplies answers to things that people do not understand—such things as creation, ill fortune, illness, and especially death. When the Australian aborigine asks "How did men come into being?" the sacred myths of his society tell him that the Numbakulla spirits created them out of animals and plants. When the Samoan child asks "Where did the islands come from?" his mother draws upon mythological traditions and answers that they were created as resting places by the god Tagaloa. When the Hopi Indian wonders what will become of him after death, he recalls the teachings of his tribe, which maintain that his "breath body" will journey to the underworld where it will live as a Hopi but never have to worry about a lack of water. In time it may return to the village as a kachina to reward or punish Hopi children or bring needed rain to their parents.

Religion provides solace when one faces important crises of life. The well-known statement that there are no atheists in foxholes backs up this point as does the fact that in many primitive societies dangerous activities, such as going to war, were always surrounded by numerous ceremonies and supernatural taboos (religion-derived restraints) applied to the warriors.

Other scholars have explained the universality of religion by the fact that people turn to the supernatural to get those things that they

---

[1] From an interview with Dr. William Smalley. *Wichita Eagle*, January 7, 1960.

cannot get themselves. Still another explanation is that religion develops in order to satisfy a need for moral and ethical order. Customs and value systems that have supernatural support are always more powerful than those with social sanction alone. These important values are maintained through the ceremonies and rituals of the society, which bring them ever closer to the individual.

The French sociologist Durkheim believed that religion is an outgrowth of crowd excitement and the thrill that people feel when large tribal gatherings take place. Religion, according to this definition, is actually nothing more than man symbolically worshiping his own group unity and *esprit de corps.*

Culture and personality specialist Francis Hsu explains the universality of religion in terms of the parent-child relationship. The infant, helpless to do things for itself, calls upon a greater power, the parents, who tower above it and who care for all its needs. As the child grows older, it exchanges its parents for a supernatural deity or force when strength greater than that of mortals is required.

Speculations about the *raison d'etre* of the many world religions are interesting but offer no concrete answers in our study of religion. The more important question—one which can be observed and documented—is, what part does religion play in people's lives and in the functioning of human society? What forms does it take in satisfying human needs?

Human and Cultural Factors

Wherever religion is found, it is always related to human experience. This is certainly not a new conclusion, for around 500 B.C. Xenophanes wrote:

> Yes, and if oxen and horses or lions had hands, and could paint with their hands, and could produce works of art as men do, horses would paint the forms of their gods like horses, and oxen like oxen, and make their bodies in the image of their several kinds. . . . The Ethiopians make their gods black and snub-nosed; the Thracians say theirs have blue eyes and red hair.

Concerning the total variety of religious practices today, we can say, with all due respect to its Biblical counterpart, that *man creates his gods in his own image.* This, of course, is not surprising as our finite mind which can only think in terms of our own cultural experience, paved the streets of heaven with gold and saw heavenly rewards in terms of jewels in a crown. Many a Sunday school lesson pictures God as a man with a long white beard very much like great-grandfather, only more stern, more knowing, and more enduring.

Man creates his gods in his own image. Buddhas in a Thai Wat.

Gods often have human emotions and human behavior patterns. Norbeck has called attention to this tendency to humanize the supernatural in Judaism, Christianity, and Islam and he points out that the important deity in each

> is often conceived as having human form, and is consistently regarded as being sentient, as having a will, wishing, watching, judging, feeling anger and joy, and meting out punishments and beneficences in accordance with individual and group morality—in short, acting as men act. (1961:45)

While the deity in these religions embodies those characteristics which are considered good and proper, a number of religions present their gods as having human weaknesses and failings. Greek and Roman gods caroused, seduced, lied, and often stole, and generally were no more virtuous (perhaps a little less) than the mortals they dominated. The Yoruba explain that the god Obatala missed the honor of being the creator of the world because he got drunk and fell asleep. His brother, Odudua, finding him, took the creation articles—a chicken and a chain—and created the world himself by lowering the fowl to the surface of the sea where it scratched up earth and formed the major continents.

In Chinese society, as well as others with polytheistic religions, hierarchies of gods reflect family and political structures. In China there are gods of varying degrees of authority and jurisdiction not unlike the bureaucratic hierarchy of the ancient dynasties. Gods are conceived of as having kinship ties, and they observe patterns of respect which have parallel in the mortal Chinese family.

All people, however, do not conceive of the supernatural in entirely anthropomorphic terms. Some look to supernatural power totally divorced from human characteristics and believe it to be in an impersonal force or spirit such as *mana* or *manitou*. Still other cultures seize upon natural phenomena—rain, thunder, the sun, or winds—and give them human attributes although not human forms.

Mana

The concept of *mana* was first brought to the attention of the scholarly world in a book entitled *The Melanesians* (1891) by a missionary, R. H. Codrington. Codrington found that in certain Melanesian religions there was a belief in an impersonal supernatural force that could reside in human beings, animals, or places. Viewed as an invisible mysterious force like electricity, it can flow from place to place, be stored up, and even be inherited, and through the use of magical acts gained and controlled.

Although this concept was first observed in Melanesia, it is perhaps more typical of Polynesia. Here, kings and high chiefs (frequently believed to be descendants of the gods) were often regarded as having so much mana that it was dangerous for commoners to approach, much less touch, such an individual. In the Manu'a Islands of Samoa, the king could only be served his meals by his wife, as it would have been dangerous for those of low rank to touch his food. In Tahiti, chiefs were not allowed to walk where commoners might tread on their footprints, and thus such nobility had to be carried on litters when they went out in public to protect the lives of their subjects.

The association of the power of mana with status also figured heavily in the ascribing of divinity to rulers in the early civilizations of Egypt, Peru, and sub-Saharan Africa. In some parts of West Africa this concept continues even today. As in the case of Pacific island kingdoms, these rulers are secluded and specially attended, because it is believed that the power of mana can be attained or lost. The ruler must protected against loss of mana and the populace must be protected from their leader's power. A basic concept of divine-rulership (monarchs were often women) was that the welfare of the land is embodied in the sovereign. If he or she remains healthy and sexually virile the land will prosper; if he or she sickens, the fertility of the land will diminish. Aging and ailing monarchs must be replaced, but how does one eliminate a divine being? The sacred blood must not be spilled, and poison, strangulation, or some other technique of execution that would not involve the loss of blood must be used. Ideally, the monarch should commit suicide by swallowing poison or by selfhanging, but if he or she does not accommodate the people, then an executioner must perform the duty. Executioners are often condemned criminals, since the executioner must also die, having killed a divine being. In the arid climate of certain regions of West Africa the divine sovereign is also responsible for rain-making, and success as a ruler may depend greatly on ability to bring rain. A prolonged drought is interpreted as a loss of potency and a signal that the monarch must be done away with.

Much of the cannibalism reported in Polynesia and Melanesia was directly tied in with mana. A warrior ceremonially ate certain parts of a valiant enemy so that he might add his victim's mana to his own. Actually, success in almost any venture—war, fishing, house- or boat-building—was believed to be an evidence of mana. All societies believing in mana have personal deities or spirits as well but often these supernatural beings also are believed to have varying amounts of mana depending upon their position in the pantheon; and one can be given mana by a personal deity. There is no society where impersonal force constitutes the total religious belief of a people.

Animatism

Intermediate between the concept of a personal god and a completely impersonal supernatural force like mana is the concept of animatism. This term, developed by Marrett, describes those situations where primitives endow inanimate objects with life. The South African shouts at the hurricane, the Crow Indians attribute power to reproduce to a stone, and the Australians revere a piece of wood (*churinga*) and perhaps even, in many cases, endow it with a spirit.

Animism

The essence of religion is supernaturalism, and a universal aspect of this is belief in spirits, souls, and life after death. The cultural evolutionist E. B. Tylor felt that belief in a spirit in people, animals, and even inanimate objects represented the earliest form of religion. It developed, he believed, from dream and trance experiences. When early people slept, they often dreamt that they went places and did things. Upon discovering that their bodies had not left the house during their slumber, they hit upon the idea that the soul or spirit had had the experiences recalled from dreams.

Totemism

One of the curious and little-understood manifestations of religion is the concept of totemism. This is the recognition of some special spiritual relationship between a clan or other social group and some animate or inanimate object of nature. We are all familiar with the totem poles of the Northwest Coast Indians. These are, in effect, coats of arms of the various clans, symbolizing (or commemorating) supernatural experiences that remote ancestors had with animals or objects of nature.

There is often the tendency to explain totemism in terms of economics, that is, it reflects the concern with animals, which would be natural in a hunting society. The only problem is that totemism is found more frequently in agricultural societies than in hunting or gathering ones. There is even evidence that something of the nature of this category of religious behavior is present in industrialized societies. What seems to be involved is a tendency to associate the group with some natural object or phenomenon that typifies the *elan* or the goals of the social group. Thus, we find athletic teams proudly bearing such names as Wildcats, Wolverines, or Lions, but never Kittens, Mice, or Lambs.

One of the most interesting developments of totemistic-like behavior emerged during World War I in connection with the 42nd, or Rainbow, division, in which, under stress, American soldiers adopted the rainbow as almost a protective deity or guardian spirit. Linton describes the developing totemistic attitude as follows:

> A feeling of connection between the organization and its namesake was first noted in February, 1918, five to six months after the assignment of the name. At this time it was first suggested and then believed that the appearance of a rainbow was a good omen for the division. Three months later it had become an article of faith in the organization that there was always a rainbow in the sky when the division went into action. A rainbow over the enemy's lines was considered especially auspicious, and after a victory men would often insist that they had seen one in this position even when the weather conditions or direction of advance made it impossible. (1924:296)

Linton feels that this rainbow totem and the manifestations of totemic beliefs among many primitive peoples represent a common social and supernatural phenomenon. In all cases, the prevailing characteristics are: (1) a distinct grouping conscious of their identity; (2) an exclusively possessed object of veneration derived from nature; (3) a reverent attitude toward, and a faith in, the object to function as a guardian spirit capable of giving omens.

It would be unfair to say that religion is a response only to human insecurities and fears. If religion amounted only to solace, we would be hard pressed to explain the elaborate ceremony that usually accompanies appeals to the supernatural. Even societies without a basic defined theology have a set of shared beliefs about the nature of the universe and their relation to it. More than the mental activity required in holding such beliefs, all religions seem to require action—participation in the manner of prayer, praise, adoration, or sacrificing.

Both existence of belief systems and the ubiquitous ceremonials have been explained by many as giving support to the existing social structure of a society and to its configuration of culture—its moral and ethical system as well as its social institutions. Most religions stress group participation perhaps because group ritual gives "psychological assurance and promotes societal unity through joint action and common aims" (Norbeck 1961:132).

Myth

In our obsession with empirical facts, rooted in centuries of experience developing science and the scientific method, we have tended to equate "myth" with falsehood or fantasy. But factual explantations for natural and cultural phenomona are not always easy to come by, and in much of the non-Western world eminently satisfactory explanations take the form of myth or legend. Strictly speaking a myth deals with the supernatural, and legend deals with "real" events and human beings. Obviously, these two categories, can overlap since the accounts of events and persons often directly or indirectly involve the supernatural.

Myths provide explantations for all types of questions but there are some themes which seem to be almost universal. These are the narratives which explain the creation of the world and humans, the origin and migrations of particular societies, why suffering and death came into existence, the rationale for separation of gods and humans, and how foods of various kinds were given to human beings.

Role in Economics

In addition to reflecting the structure and values of society the nature of its deities, to a great extent, also reflects the economic level of a society. Radin has remarked that

Cave art from Niaux, southern France. (Courtesy Field Museum of Natural History.)

no correlation is more definite or more consistent than that between a given economic level of society and the nature of supernatural beings postulated by the tribe at large or by the religious individual in particular. (1957:192)

On the walls of the caves frequented by Paleolithic hunters we find paintings of bison, deer, and mammoth. These animals often appear with spears protruding from their sides and some of the paintings have holes in them made by actual spears. While these sketches might only record the events that took place in memorable hunts, the more common interpretation is that they represent examples of contagious magic—that is, it was believed that a symbolic wound on the drawing would become a real one on the next hunt.

One cave painting from southern France, often called the "sorcerer," depicts a man in reindeer costume. Very likely this is the kind of religious practitioner who officiated in ceremonies designed to ensure a successful hunt. Some of the earliest forms of religion plainly centered around the worship of animal spirits. One of the oldest altars of sacrifice thus far discovered dates to Neanderthal times. Upon it the skulls of cave bears are neatly arranged on slabs of rock.

Possibly this altar formed a part of a religious complex something like that of the Eskimo. These arctic hunters believe that the soul of the polar bear is sacred and that they must apologize to this spirit when the animal is killed. After the animal is skinned, the skull is painted red or black, offerings are made to it, and the bones of the animal have to be put into the fire in a specific order.

The hunters of the Gravettian period called upon the supernatural power of magical charms to ensure an abundant supply of game. These charms are described by Childe as being:

> small figurines of women, carved out of stone or ivory. Normally the bodies are excessively fat and the sexual features exaggerated, but the face is almost blank. It is assumed that such were fertility charms. The generative powers of women would inhere in them, and through them be canalized to provide food for the tribe by ensuring the fertility of game and vegetation. (1951:56)

Hunting and gathering societies almost universally are served by part-time religious practitioners known as shamans which Benedict describes as follows:

> The shaman is the religious practitioner who, by whatever kind of personal experience is recognized as supernatural in his tribe, gets his power directly from the gods. He is often, like Cassandra and others of those who spoke with tongues, a person whose instability has marked him out for his profession. In North America shamans are characteristically those who have the experience of the vision. The priest, on the other hand, is the depository of ritual and the administrator of cult activities. The Pueblos have no shamans; they have only priests. (1959:93)

Radin (1957) feels that the existence of true deities and theology as opposed to indistinct spirits and ghosts is associated with societies that have enough economic surplus to support a priest class, which finds it both necessary and profitable to develop elaborate theology and ritual. Such specialists are, of course, seldom found in societies that do not have an agricultural base for their economy. Since religion is seldom separated from the daily lives of primitive people, the form of economy is often directly or indirectly connected with kinds of deities and ceremonies that comprise the religious complex. Let us look, for example, at what is sacred to the predominantly agricultural Hopi Indians.

The Hopi ceremonial calendar reads something like this: The first important ceremony of the year is at the winter solstice—a ceremony to ensure the return of the sun. Then, in February comes the Powamu ceremony of germination and early growth. This is climaxed by the return of the spirits of the rain, the *kachinas* (bearing bean sprouts and ears of corn) from their winter retreat in the San Francisco Mountains. In July the Home Dance marks the departure of the *kachinas* to their winter homes, carrying the Hopi prayers for rain and good health to their cloud parents. At this time the dancers impersonating the spirits

A Dyak priest makes supplicatory food offerings to the spirits to ensure a successful harvest. From the roof hangs an offering to the omen birds to induce them not to give evil omens. (Courtesy W. R. Geddes.)

distribute the first green ears of corn and melons fresh from the fields.

In August the most spectacular of the Hopi ceremonials is held. This Snake Dance is designed to bring the rain that is so essential to the growth of the last crop of corn. The final major ceremony of the year is the Wuwuchim, which serves as an occasion for the initiation of young men into adult status and also ensures, through the kindling of New Fires, the advent of the winter solstice and the rebirth of the sun.

Even in Christianity, a religion that grew up in an agrarian and pastoral economy, the important ceremonies in the church calendar tend to be synchronized with the annual agricultural cycle of the Middle East. Many of the New Testament parables depend for their proper impact upon an understanding of agricultural terms: *shepherds, lost sheep, mustard seed, sowing, reaping, vineyard, flock, rocky ground, wineskins, etc.*

Although economic level is invariably reflected in the religious activities of a people, we do not conclude that industrial societies literally worship the machine or the dollar. However, German sociologist Max Weber, in describing what he refers to as the Protestant Ethic, maintains that there is a connection between the fundamental

IF YA GOT SOMETHIN'
IT'S CAUSE YOU'RE GOOD

IF YA GOT NOTHIN'
IT'S CAUSE YOU'RE
BAD...
ASK SANTA
CLAUS

The Protestant Ethic. (Reproduced by permission.)

religious ideas of Protestantism and the ideal of behavior compatible with industrial capitalism. He asserts that stress has come to be placed on such conduct as frugality, honesty, industry, respectability. Far too often these are seen not so much as virtues in themselves as for their utility in attaining economic goals. Typical of the Protestant Ethic emphasis is the verse "Seeth thou a man diligent in his business: He shall stand before kings" (Proverbs 22:29).

As insecurities of life disappear, so their reference tends to disappear from the religion; however, our economic insecurities have been replaced by other kinds that are equally reflected in religion. Many a day of prayer for peace has been proclaimed, and religion becomes more and more the only solace against the possibility of annihilation by hydrogen blast. A noticeable rise in the interest in religion and its activities has been seen in the 1970s with various cult movements becoming very active, including the pathological Jonestown cult, which caused the mass suicide and murder of more than 900 persons.

We must not go overboard in our correlations of specific forms of religion with specific economies. As Lowie writes:

> Nothing is more proper than to stress primitive man's insecurity, but that is only in part the result of a specifically economic situation. The very fact that shamans are almost everywhere primarily curers shows that man's

physiological risks are at least as significant in this context as his dread of an inadequate food supply or an insufficient accumulation of pelf in any form. (1952:334)

Morality

For those raised in the Christian tradition religion is apt to be thought of as a keeper of the morals of society; and one of the basic tenets of Christianity and its parent, Judaism, is the struggle between good and evil "in the hearts of men." This feature is not found, however, in all religions; many leave moral and ethical matters to society and individuals to work out. This was certainly true of the old Samoan religion: it explained such mysteries as how the world was created, who controls the universe, and what happens to a man after he dies, but it left definitions and judgments of proper behavior to the village council and to individual families. Adulterers were not punished by the gods but by the injured family or by the village council of chiefs. There are some religions, on the other hand, like Buddhism and Confucianism that deal so much with conduct and spiritual qualities that they do not center about a god at all.

We can say that in nearly every society religion embodies an expression and reaffirmation of its central values. It "contributes to the operation of society through the power and authority and sacred meaning which it provides to the support of man's conduct and to his understanding of his place in the universe" (Redfield 1956:363).

Although religion may not deal with matters of morality as we define it, every society has its set of sanctions (actions it approves) and taboos (actions it forbids), which are made more powerful by the threat of supernatural punishment. These acts are considered so important that some supernatural power must enforce them. Francis Hsu points out that

Although taboos have a tremendous variety, they pertain to a few basic matters: food, sex, life's crises (such as birth, initiation, marriage and death), sacred persons and potent things. What is common to these categories?—Danger. These are objects or occasions of danger to the individual and danger to the society of which the individual is a member (1958:13)

He explains that food can give life, but the wrong food can bring death. Although sex is the origin of life, sexual jealousy is a source of tragedy the world over. Life's crises involve a rearrangement and realignment of individuals and events that can disorganize individuals or groups if not properly managed. Sacred persons have a great power over the destinies of their fellow men, whereas potent objects may affect one's life or fortune.

"All of these matters," writes Hsu, "are of greatest concern to every individual and his society. Each society, in order to safeguard the individual and the group, has a particular set of symbols with which to express its corporate concern in the problems of existence. This concern has two facets: the solidarity of the group at any moment; the survival of the group through time" (1958: 14).

W. W. Howells, in his book *The Heathens*, included as part of his definition of religion that "religion is a set of earnest policies which a group of peoples adopts . . . in order to tidy up their distraught relationships with one another and with the universe. . . ." (1948:22).

Certainly the taboos and sanctions that Hsu writes about are part of these "earnest policies." Many religions seem to have these policies, which comment day to day on social relationships as well as relationships to the deity or whatever form the supernatural assumes. The Ten Commandments are, to a certain extent, a statement of taboos and sanctions that comment on a person's proper behavior toward God and fellow humans. Not only do they instruct a person in the proper relationship to the deity, but they represent as good a formula as can be found for maintaining a well-organized social system.

The Power Struggle

Religion is not only closely tied to the social and economic dimensions of a society, but it also has a part in its struggles for power. Seldom does a coup, revolution, or war not carry with it claims that its actions, motives, and goals are god-directed or -inspired. Thomas Jefferson, in penning the Declaration of Independence, justified dissolution of political bonds with Great Britain on the grounds that all men are "endowed by their Creator with certain inalienable rights, that among these are life, liberty, and the pursuit of happiness."

Also claiming supernatural support for their position, Confederacy Vice-President Alexander Stephens stated in a discussion of the South's constitution that "this, our new government, is the first in the history of the world based upon this great physical, philosophical, and moral truth [that the Negro is not the equal of the white]. The great objects of humanity are best attained when there is conformity to the Creator's laws and decrees."

Deities often play a rather significant role in warfare either by portending omens or by sanctioning the action. In old Samoa, for example, *Le Sa*, the Forbidden One, was a war god incarnate in the lizard. Before an impending battle the actions of a lizard were carefully watched. If it ran around the outside of a bundle of spears, it was a favorable sign; but if it worked its ways into the center, a victory could not be expected.

Not only did the chief god of the Aztecs sanction their warlike behavior, but hostilities were actually made necessary by its demands for human blood. Believing this god had to be nourished with human hearts, as many as 20,000 war captives were put to death at a single ceremony. "A martial success," writes Vaillant, "could be achieved only through the exercise of divine favor. Thus, sacrifice led to war, and war back to sacrifice, in an unending series of expanding cycles" (1962:169).

Even in modern times nations involve their deity in power struggles. During World War II the popular song *Praise the Lord and Pass the Ammunition* indirectly implicated God in a gun-crew action. The Germans, also claiming supernatural support, provided uniforms with belt buckles inscribed with the words *Gott mit Uns* (God is with us).

In April, 1970, a high ranking admiral on the Joint Chiefs of Staff gave testimony at a U. S. District Court supporting the policy of compulsory chapel attendance at West Point, Annapolis, and the Air Force Academy. His testimony included the statement that "an atheist could not be as great a military leader as one who is not an atheist," and he declared that he didn't think "you will find an atheist who has reached the peak in the Armed Forces (*Washington Post*, April 29, 1970).

Magic and Religion

One of the oldest controversies in anthropology has been the relationship of magic to religion. Magic has been defined by Redfield as

> That activity directed toward accomplishing some special limited end and one in a form which is determined not by the real effectiveness of the act to bring about the result but by the desires and fears and general thinking and feeling of the man who performs them. (1956:365)

Magic is the manipulation of symbolic material objects or words in order to achieve desired practical results. The assumption in magic is that, if a rite is performed correctly, the expected results will be automatic.

"Magic is characteristically colorful, even dramatic. Magical rites are little pictures of what one wants" (1956:365). A well-known form of this magic is imitative magic, found in West Africa and the Caribbean, where the image of one's enemy is formed out of wax, and pins are stuck into it in the belief that supernaturally caused illness and even death will overtake the intended victim. The idea behind this is that the magician can produce any effect he desires merely by imitating it. Imitative magic is not always carried out with malevolent goals. Among the Bering Strait Eskimos, barren women often consult a practitioner of magic (a shaman) to obtain a doll-like image imbued with magical properties, which is placed beneath the woman's pillow so that in time she may produce a baby of her own. Imitative magic not only pays attention to form but also to color. In Germany, folk remedies prescribe yellow turnips, gold coins, gold rings, saffron, and a variety of other yellow things as remedies for jaundice.

Still another category of magic, contagious magic, operates on the principle that things that were once associated will remain so even when they are separated. One of the most widespread fears among primitive peoples is that an enemy will be able to obtain nail clippings, excrement, or hair cuttings to use against them in witchcraft magic. Even in comparatively recent times, varieties of contagious magic could be found in England. Frazer tells us that "if a horse wounds its foot by treading on a nail, a Suffolk groom will invariably preserve the nail, clean it, and grease it every day, to prevent the foot from festering" (1958:48).

In comparing the many forms of magic with the characteristics of religion, many scholars have considered magic as psychologically simpler, more specific, and more impersonal than religion. Since magic lacks a church and a communion of the faithful, some propose that it represents an early form of religion. Other students of religious behavior recognize magic as a part of religion and feel that too much has been made of minor differences. Goode (1951), for example, points out that both magic and religion (1) are symbolic, (2) have a ritual system, (3) are concerned with nonempirical phenomena and thus stand in the same relationship to Western science, and (4) call forth similar psychological responses in those who participate.

Almost all religions, including Christianity, have magical aspects woven into their institutional fabric in that they combine both praise and propitiation of their deity or conception of the supernatural with a means of harnessing supernatural power for the solution of human practical problems. If we look at Christianity very objectively we must admit that it includes many practices that would qualify under our definition of magic. In all Christian denominations some rote prayers are said with the belief that the repetition of such set formula will result in God providing for daily needs. Christian prayers are more frequently requests than they are statements of adoration, faith, or praise. Often, as Finegan puts it:

> A prayer may be uttered with a belief in the automatic efficacy of the pronouncement of certain syllables or in the compulsive effect of a sufficient number of repetitions, and thus the line of demarcation often remains indistinct between magic and religion (1952:7)

Frontier families used the Bible for divining (another form of magic): the Bible was opened at random and the finger placed on the first verse that caught the eye. The contents of the verse supposedly provided direction for making decisions on difficult problems.

Not too many years ago the Christopher medal was worn in the belief that it afforded absolute protection from danger while traveling, and many a driver still places a plastic icon on the dashboard in hopes that it will keep him safe from mishap.

In the folklore of Eastern Europe we find that the cross was an effective device for warding off evil spirits and the "evil eye," providing protection against witches, vampires, and werewolves and as a means of neutralizing the activities of sorcerers.

Although every religion has these magical aspects, there is great variation in the importance placed upon a set formula and symbolically potent objects in the world's religions. The historical or major religions have tended to throw off much of their magical content. While we can dwell upon the manifest differences in behavior called forth by the two aspects of supernatural belief, it is almost impossible to separate them in the thoughts and actions of the believers. Finegan stresses this point when he observes that "magic and religion are coexistent and even more inextricably interwoven in too many instances to make it possible to believe that the one was the predecessor and the root of the other" (1952:6).

Magic and Science

Whereas religion has often been considered in conflict with science, magic has sometimes been called pseudoscience. Some would contend that at a certain level magic takes the place of science. The Hopi Indians, for example, explain the coming of rain as the result of their dancing with snakes rather than as the result of certain winds and barometric pressure systems. The Arunta say, "Our magic rites are just as necessary and efficacious in keeping up the supply of emus and grubs, as the digging and weeding done by wretched cultivators."

Childe points out that magic involves

> an act of faith, and that is what distinguishes a magical operation from a scientific experiment. In judging its results, negative instances, i.e., failures, are simply ignored. Or rather objective judgment gives place to hope and fear.

. . . Feeling very helpless, he just dare not let that hope go. And just in so far as Nature seems alien and unknown is man afraid to omit anything that might help him in that menacing environment. (1951:50−51)

In the Hopi snake dance, the performers believe beyond question that if the ceremony is performed correctly it will surely rain. Hopis have certainly seen much evidence of the power of the ceremony to produce rain. Some years it has rained so hard that visitors were stranded for days by muddy impassable roads. From the scientist's point of view, however, the Hopis do not subject religious beliefs to the same rigorous tests required in science. They do not count how many times they have danced and how many times it has rained. They do not question the causal connection between the two events. They do not ask if there could possibly be some other factor (such as proper weather conditions) that brought the rain. They merely have faith in the power of the ceremony, and if it doesn't bring the desired result they will explain that the fault was theirs because there was something improper about their performance. One failure, or even many, is not sufficient for them to reject their religious beliefs. The important fact is that for the Hopi, and for anyone else, science and religion represent quite different categories of behavior. It is impossible to disprove religious phenomena to the same extent as it is possible to test and reject scientific data.

Pre-industrial people, in their approach to the supernatural forces that control their universe, behave very much like average Americans in their approach to the scientific explanations of their surroundings. Both lack understanding of the nature of the phenomenon, but both have taken on good faith the teachings of their sacred tradition and thus both believe. Let us say, for example, that a man returns to his apartment and upon opening the door throws the light switch. Although he has performed the correct action, the light does not come on. In most cases, this man does not understand the nature of electricity or how his electric circuit works, but he believes that there is a causal relationship between switch-throwing and illumination. When the light does not come on, he does not reject the presence of this causal relationship or his belief in it; he merely says that there is something wrong in the circuit—a short, a blown fuse, a faulty switch, or a burned-out bulb.

This is the same kind of faith that pre-industrial folk have in their magic and religion and is the reason that it is not easy for them to drop their magical concepts in favor of more scientific ones. In our own culture, there have been many religious explanations replaced by scientific ones, but the transition has always been a difficult one. When we look at the religious and magical behavior of primitives, untenable from a scientific point of view, we must identify with the primitive and realize that scientific and religious behavior are sometimes quite indistinguishable. An example of this may be seen in the following exchange between a medical doctor and an African rain-doctor as described in Livingstone's *Missionary Travels*:

MEDICAL DOCTOR: So you really believe you can command the clouds? I think that can be done by God alone.

RAIN-DOCTOR: We both believe the very same thing. It is God that makes the rain, but I pray to him by means of these medicines, and, the rain coming, of course it is then mine. . . . If we had no rain, the cattle would have no pastures, the cows give no milk, our children become lean and die, our wives run away to other tribes who do make rain . . . and the whole tribe become dispersed and lost; our fire would go out.

MEDICAL DOCTOR: . . . you cannot charm the clouds by medicines. You wait till you see the clouds come, then use your medicines, and take the credit which belongs to God only.

RAIN-DOCTOR: I use my medicines, and you employ yours; we are both doctors, and doctors are not deceivers. You give the patient medicine. Sometimes God is pleased to heal him by means of your medicine; sometimes not—he dies. When he is cured, you take the credit of what God does. I do the same. Sometimes God grants us rain, sometimes not. When he does, we take the credit of the charm. When a patient dies you don't give up trust in your medicine, neither do I when rain fails. If you wish me to leave off my medicines, why continue your own? (Livingstone 1858:25–27)

Summary

Religion, defined as belief in the supernatural, has been a part of human culture at least as far back as the time of Neanderthals. Its importance lies in its ability to answer questions that cannot be answered by empirical observation. These are questions regarding the origin of the universe, the origin of mankind, explanations of illness and death, and a rationale concerning the functioning of the natural world. Although the forces of nature appear beyond comprehension, some sense of understanding of these forces has been forthcoming through religion. And magic, which is the ability to compel the supernatural, provides humans with an avenue of control over nature, human crisis, and the perils of getting a living.

The impersonal, supernatural power called *mana* among the Melanesians has its counterparts in many societies around the world.

Acquisition and control of this force enables spirits, deities, and humans to work magic and miracles. Divine monarchs, high chiefs, successful warriors, and successful healers are believed to possess great *mana*.

Myths provide explanations of religious and other cultural matters, and rituals re-enact the myths. Though these explanations rarely are factual or verifiable, they are a powerful force in motivating human behavior. Morality, which is considered a vital aspect of the Judeo-Christian-Islamic religious context, is not necessarily an important part of other religious traditions. In many cultures the gods' punishment comes from violating supernatural edicts and not from violations of society's laws or injuries to kinsmen or neighbors. Often matters of morality are the sole concern of the village council or the local courts but are seen as outside the realm of the gods or spirits.

For many years anthropologists have debated the difference between magic and religion. Magic has been defined as the manipulation of symbolic objects to achieve practical ends. It is seen as psychologically simpler and more impersonal than religion and it lacks a church and a communion of the faithful. Religion has important integrating powers, in that through religious participation, humans are joined together with the supernatural world. However, religion and magic are both symbolic, they both involve ritual, and they both call forth similar psychological responses among believers.

The Arts—Forms and Functions 16

The anthropological approach to art

The principal arts

    The graphic and plastic arts

    The verbal arts

    The performing arts

Style

    Representative art

    Stylized art

    Abstract art

    Style in music and dance

    Ceremonial symbolism

Art for art's sake

Art and economics

    Specialization

    Airport art

    Folklure

Art and social organization

Art and religion

Art and communication

Art and education

Art as an aid in science

The artist in society and culture

    The Maori carver

    The Balinese artist

    The American composer

Through artistic works human beings create monuments to their own uniqueness, ingenuity, and spirit. Whatever motivates the desire to create and beautify, it is distinctly human. While lower animals have shown themselves capable of altering their environments to suit their needs, only human beings do so to suit their tastes. This need for expression seems to extend beyond the activities of practical day-to-day existence, and no matter how hard people struggle merely to survive, they still have a desire for expression in prose, poetry, song, the dance, or the graphic and plastic arts.

For a working definition of art we may say that it is the production or expression of what is considered beautiful or what appeals to the canons of taste. While art is universal, concepts of beauty and taste vary from culture to culture and within cultures. They are the products of those cultures. Culture even defines what is and what is not art. There are any number of primitive art forms that would motivate a comment like "Do you call that art?" from the average American.

Art, being a cultural product, cannot be influenced by race. The art of African Negroes, South Sea islanders, or Western Europeans is different not because it was created by representatives of different races but because the historical art traditions are different in each of these areas. People tend to reproduce objects familiar to them and people of different areas are sometimes limited or influenced by the materials they have available, but ideas of how best to handle line, form, and color are a matter of learning and experience within a given art tradition. Living in different parts of the world, peoples have had different life experiences and therefore their ideas of what is beautiful, what is esthetically satisfying, and what is in good taste are varied.

Art is more than mere expression: it is expression with skill and with some measure of originality. Our culture, as well as others, recognizes the difference between a mere paint dauber and a real artist. In one of America's major literary arts, the production of novels, the distinction has facetiously been made between "typing" and writing.

Although the idea of beauty is usually included in any definition of art, art doesn't express but one feeling or search for but one result. An artist may find as great a pleasure in creating something that he considers grotesque and horrifying as in creating something which his culture defines as beautiful. The paintings of Francis Bacon, Ivan Albright, or Jean Dubuffet fascinate audiences because of their nightmarish quality and their superbly created moods of despair.

Art is the result of conscious intent (to please an audience, to entertain, to inspire, to make money); it is not something that just happens by accident. It has pattern, order, and unity, and it evokes emotion (sadness, joy, disgust). The emotional effect of the work may be within it or it may be related to the meanings associated with the object. This is often the case with religious art. Art is a form of communication wherein artist and audience share culturally meaningful symbols, perspectives, and experience.

Anthropological Approach to Art

Many people are surprised to find that the study of art is an integral part of anthropology. Art is not commonly an area of study for a scientific discipline, but since anthropology is the science of culture it cannot ignore any cultural activity. The anthropological approach to art is somewhat different from that of the artist or the art critic. Whereas the major concern of the art critic is the art product itself and how it was produced, the anthropologist considers the function of art in the total cultural configuration more important. Since function often affects form, the anthropologist realizes that a complete understanding of an art object may only be obtained by probing into the reason for its production. No less important is the study of the role and status of the artist in society.

The art critic is also interested in the psychological process of creativity and in the artist's expression and communication of emotion and experience as well as in an evaluation of the quality of a work according to certain traditional or current standards of esthetics. It is very difficult to extend these interests cross-culturally, and some of the most sophisticated art specialists in anthropology have confessed their inadequacy in this respect. E. R. Leach states:

> When you or I first encounter a carving from New Guinea or West Africa or British Columbia we automatically see it as if it were a work of European art. One may like it or dislike it, but in either case judgment is based on an assumption that the primitive artist is trying to "say" the same sort of thing as European artists try to say. (1961:26)

Although the problem is admittedly difficult, anthropologists feel that by concentrating on the role of art and the function of the artist and by seeking standards by which to evaluate art works from the people themselves, they can attempt to translate for the viewer of primitive art just what the primitive artist is trying to "say" and how well it has been said.

The Principal Arts

Any creative activity performed with some measure of excellence which serves as an emotional outlet for its author and as a source of pleasure or satisfaction for the observer is art. The activities that may be covered by this definition are so many and varied that it will be convenient to arrange them in some categorical system. For purposes of analysis the following divisions might be considered: (1) the graphic and plastic arts, (2) the verbal arts, and (3) the performing arts.

THE GRAPHIC AND PLASTIC ARTS

This broad category is used to designate those activities connected with the production or decoration of cultural artifacts that are considered esthetically pleasing. Varying from Gravettian Venuses to totem poles to Henry Moore productions, sculpture is probably the most universally practiced art in this category. Painting follows a close second in world importance. Some of the most famous varieties are Bushman rock paintings from the Kalihari, Polynesian tapa cloth decoration, exterior wall designs among the Mangbetu of the Congo, or the frescoes of ancient Mayan ceremonial centers.

Weaving, a plastic art, dates back at least to the Neolithic and includes, in various parts of the contemporary world, basketry, matting, and production of textiles from various vegetable and animal fibers through the use of the loom. In the Andes, gold and silver threads were utilized for tapestry production.

Although architecture, when applied to the construction of ceremonial structures or monuments, has been considered a fine art the world over, only in the West has the artistry been carried over into the design of dwellings. In most pre-industrial societies house structures are more the work of the artisan than the artist. Houses may be beautifully and intricately constructed, but originality is not an important factor. House types are usually traditional and are more in tune with temperature than with taste.

Of the many wonders of megalithic architecture throughout the world none are more astounding than those produced by the isolated nonliterate people on the island of Nias in Indonesia. Nias villages often contain stone-paved plazas with bathing pools and altars, great walls, majestic staircases, and superbly sculptured statuary of enormous size which are truly marvels of architectural and stone-cutting art.

Although pottery is often thought of as confined to strictly useful objects, the treatment of the surfaces and even the form of the pots have afforded much opportunity for artistic expression. Each tribal group in the American Southwest has its distinct tradition of form and surface decoration, and in South America ceramics approached sculpture in the form of effigy vessels. In Mexico it is possible to date a number of pre-Aztec cultures by small modeled ceramic figures which still may be found around ceremonial sites. Ceramics were also used in making toys in this area, and the only example of the use of the wheel in pre-Columbian America is found in a little toy horse that might have served as a pull toy.

Artistic work in metals appeared somewhat later in the history of culture than most of the arts previously described, but it is nevertheless widespread today among the peoples of the world. Most frequently the production of art objects in brass, bronze, or precious metals has utilized the "lost wax" process similar to that employed by modern dentists in casting inlays or bridges. Not all art metal work employs casting, however. The Pueblo and Navaho silversmiths have long produced belts, bracelets, and necklaces from silver pellets by using a hammer and cold chisel, and in many parts of Mexico and Asia today, primitive people produce delicate filigree ornaments from precious metals in wire form.

Also classed as a form of graphic and plastic art is body decoration. Serving as a source of beauty, as a symbol of rank, or as an indicator of family or tribal membership, tattooing and scarification are widespread. The decoration of the body is nearly always the job of a specialist. His duties do not always call for originality or creativity, but they always demand skill. Hairdressing also attains the status of a fine art in some areas—notably in the Congo, in the Southwest, and, of course, in Japan and in much of the Western world.

THE VERBAL ARTS

The verbal arts, which might also be referred to as folklore, are often less apparent to the average American than the graphic and plastic arts. Aside from a group of Old English and Early American folksongs that have enjoyed recent popularity, literature in America has largely been restricted to the printed page. Primitive cultures, with their lack of writing, have quite naturally been the main exponents of oral or verbal literature, which maintains its immortality by being passed down by word of mouth from generation to generation.

From the standpoint of the people, *myths* are often the most important variety of verbal art. Essentially, these are narratives that deal with the remote past before the world was in its present condition. The principal characters are usually gods or culture heroes, and their activities and personality characteristics represent—sometimes symbolically—an exposition of the basic value system of the society.

Legends are sagas of individual humans or societies and are considered to be true historical accounts. *Folktales*, on the other hand, are stories of anthropomorphic animals or exceptional humans which are told for entertainment and frequently for educational purposes since they often contain a moral. Sometimes coupled with a narrative but more frequently used independently, *proverbs* are brief epigrammatic statements suggesting a course of action consistent with a society's system of values. Since statements like "A stitch in time saves nine" or "Honesty is the best policy" represent consensuses of opinion about what is culturally acceptable behavior in a society, they are sometimes used in court litigation as precedents for judgment of conduct. Mankind reveals its capacity for humor in the universal existence of the *riddle*. Riddles are, of course, cryptically phrased questions or statements that demand an answer based on association, comparison, and perception of likeness and difference in natural or cultural phenomena.

Closely approximating music in its rhythm and choice of word tones is poetry. Many societies consider the poem the most dramatic form of narrative and assign their most sacred lore to the realm of the rhyme and the meter.

THE PERFORMING ARTS

The division between folklore and the performing arts is an arbitrary one, for certainly many a story teller is essentially a performing artist. The performing arts, however, in our classification are represented by such artistic genre as oratory, music, the dance, and drama. In each of these activities the performer draws heavily on the forms of the other categories. The dance, for example, may utilize masks or brilliantly designed costumes, and drama usually draws upon the significant mythology of a society. In the Samoan Islands oratory tends to be mainly political in nature, but every orator liberally utilizes proverbs, poetry, and allusions to myths and legends to sway his audience. To a certain extent every artist must please the audience, but the performing artists are more directly subject to their demands. Although there are many cases, particularly in the area of the dance, in which total participation by the group is present, most often performing artists are involved in a performer-spectator situation in the practice of their art. The performer and the audience are frequently psychologically very close, since the dance often expresses the emotional state of the group; the songs may represent songs of anguish or joy and dramatic performances play out the desires, anxieties, and satisfactions of a whole society.

Style

Artists in every culture tend to maintain a continuity in the form and quality of their art. There also seems to be a tendency, at least in non-Western culture, for artists to work within a traditional framework of form, quality, and mode of expression. This consistency, called *style*, allows us to identify the work of a certain artist and also to place his work in a specific cultural context. In analyzing style traditions of the

Magdalenian cave drawings were masterpieces of line and perspective. (Courtesy Field Museum of Natural History.)

world we shall begin by establishing three categories of art: (1) representative, (2) stylized, and (3) abstract art.

REPRESENTATIVE ART

Representative art is often described as "photographic" or "naturalistic," that is, closely approximating nature. Good examples of this kind of art are to be found in magazine illustrations and to a large extent in portrait-painting. This is the kind of absolute reproduction that many artists disdain, maintaining that it can better be done with a camera.

Actually, the term *representative art* is not a very objective one because not even a photograph is a true copy of nature. Anthropologists have reported that nonliterate people, upon being photographed and given the print of the picture, turn it one way and another without being able to recognize themselves; they cannot reduce their three-dimensional world to the two-dimensional one of the camera.

Many examples of art forms are naturalistic or realistic to the artist but might appear very abstract to a viewer from another culture. A good example of this is the X-ray-like bark paintings of the Australian aborigines. These paintings, usually of fish or kangaroos, show not only the outer form of the animal but the skeleton as well. To the eyes of a European the painting looks abstract but to the Australian it represents an accurate representation of nature.

A similar concept of representative form is found in the art work of the Indians of northern British Columbia. Their subjects, usually animals, are portrayed as though one were viewing their hides stretched out to dry. This kind of treatment was considered very realistic by the artists, and their reasoning is described by Boas:

> It is easily intelligible that a profile view of an animal in which only one eye is seen and in which one whole side disappears may not satisfy as a realistic representation. The animal *has two* eyes and *two* sides. When it turns I see the other side; it exists and should be part of a satisfying picture. (1955:72)

STYLIZED ART

By stylized art we merely refer to those art traditions following a general pattern of deviation from what is commonly recognized as naturalistic within the culture. This deviation may in some areas consist of such techniques as simplification of forms such as the bird and deer forms found on Zuni pottery or the abbreviated drawings characteristic of modern American advertising and cartoon art. Still another variety of stylization is distortion—that is, emphasizing certain significant aspects of an object by purposely altering form or perspective. An example of this kind of stylization is found in a special kind of little wooden figurines carved by Yoruba artists in West Africa. Each of these depicts a different occupational status and features size distortion of the characteristic tools of each trade; the missionary carries a huge Bible, the magistrate wears a gigantic wig, and the anthropologist comes complete with an oversize pencil and notebook.

Northwest Coast Indian art utilizes the stylistic principle of distorting the normal arrangement or location of anatomical parts of an animal in order to achieve a desired design. While the eyes, mouth, ears, paws, and other parts of the body are realistically drawn, they are set into the design without regard for their normal arrangement in life.

ABSTRACT ART

Among nonliterate peoples abstract art almost always carries one into the realm of symbolism. Although there are undoubtedly numerous examples of primitive artists merely getting satisfaction from experimenting with line, form, and color, in most cases art products that are not recognizable as representations of objects from nature are produced for their symbolic quality. On occasion, as in Arapaho bead-

Yoruba figurines representing a magistrate and a missionary. Stylization is found in the exaggeration of the size of the symbols of their occupational roles. (Courtesy Milwaukee Public Museum.)

work symbols, we are not sure whether the abstract designs such as a diamond for "man" or a cross for "star" were created to symbolize objects or whether the designs were created first and meaning read into them secondarily. The Arapaho Indians utilized color symbolism as well. Red stood for "blood," "man," "earth," and "sunset"; blue represented "sky," "smoke," "distant mountains," or "night"; and white carried the meaning of "snow," "sand," or "water."

Symbolism is one of the most important aspects of Navaho sand-painting. Concerning this form of Southwest ritual art Bunzel records,

> The figures of masked gods are greatly elongated; male gods are symbolized by round masks, females by square masks. . . . There is a fixed color symbolism associated with the four cardinal points: white for east, blue for south, yellow for west, black for north. The clothing of the Gods and the corn plants which are conventionally represented are of the colors appropriate to the directions with which they are associated. . . . The same system of symbolism which appears in the sand paintings is even more fully developed in myth and song. (1938:580—81)

In Samoa, young men obtain tattoos that extend from the knee to the small of the back. The designs consist of a series of straight and

Traditional Samoan tattooing patterns
for the legs (after Kramer).

curved lines interspersed with sections of solid color. There is little variation in the traditional pattern from individual to individual and nearly every design element is symbolic. A solid section extending across the small of the back is called the "boat" or "canoe," while other aspects of the design symbolize "the head of a bird," a "centipede," and important beams and ribs of the traditional Samoan house framework.

Art symbolism also carries over into the area of Samoan architecture, for various components of the Samoan house with its beehive-shaped roof have symbolic references. The ridge beam is referred to as "a sleeping barracuda," the curved, parallel beams of the eaves as "the rainbow," and the numerous house posts that support the roof are referred to as a "school of fish in shallow water." Symbolic representation, however, has found its way into few other Samoan arts. Contrary to the situation encountered in the Hawaiian *hula*, the Samoan *siva* does not attempt to tell a story. Tapa cloth designs likewise have neither symbolic color nor design.

STYLE IN MUSIC AND DANCE

Music is difficult to categorize in the same manner as we have the graphic and plastic arts, as the category "representative" can not be meaningfully applied to it. The closest approach to this, however, is to be found in the structure of the Chinese and Hindu musical scales, which mythology relates were first developed by imitating the sounds of nature—mostly bird and animal calls. The important consideration in this area is conventional style, which involves differences in scales, rhythm, tone quality, relative importance of harmony and melody, and so on.

In the area of singing alone, the styles of the world's cultures are so diverse that it would be impossible to decide which was most naturalistic. A few characterizations of vocal styles by Lomax will give us some idea of the variety to be found.

> AMERICAN INDIAN: The solo singer uses a chesty voice, wide rather than narrow, yet with strong characterizers of nasal resonance and throaty burr and with forceful accent.
>
> ORIENTAL: He (the solo voice) performs highly complex strophes composed of many long phrases, with maximum ornamentation . . . in a voice that is usually high and falsetto, narrow and squeezed—with maximum nasality, raspy, and often characterized by forcefully precise articulation.
>
> POLYNESIAN: One of the most notable traits of old Polynesian music is the choral performance (rather than solo performances) in perfect tonal and rhythmic unison of long and complex texts, where every syllable is clearly enunciated. In some areas, a rudimentary form of polyphony occurs: one of the voice parts rises in pitch and maintains this level while the chorus continues to sing at the original pitch, thus creating a simple drone harmony. (1962:*passim*)

CEREMONIAL SYMBOLISM

Among the performing arts none is more replete with symbolism than dramatic ritual and the dance. Whereas the Western world has long been accustomed to idea plays with symbolic plots and characters and there is a well-established pattern of interpretive dancing, we are often surprised to learn the extent to which nonliterate people rely on dramatic ceremonies and dances to perpetuate the basic values of their culture.

The Sun Dance.   Of the many colorful ceremonies performed by native American peoples none is more symbolic and dramatic than the Sun Dance of the Sioux Indians. The Sun Dance is essentially a ceremony of self-torture in which dancers offer their bodies and souls to the Sun (Wakan Tanka) in order that the people of the Sioux nation might be revitalized. The ritual also ensures an abundance of buffalo as well as success in hunting them.

Every action, every word, every bit of paraphernalia associated with the dance carries religious and social symbolism. The lodge in which the Sun Dance is performed is constructed of 28 poles (the number of days in each moon). At the very center (symbolic of the center of the earth) is planted the most sacred object of all—a cottonwood tree to which a buckskin bag filled with fat is attached. The cottonwood, selected because its leaves resemble the outline of a tepee, is said to unite the earth and the sky, and the fat-filled bag serves as a petition to the sun deity to make the earth fat and plentiful. The tree, referred to in the chants as the "standing person," is "captured" and cut down by a Sioux war party. Just as in actual battle, the four warriors and the war chief who fell the tree receive war honors (coup). As the tree is carried into camp, the warriors howl like coyotes—the Sioux symbol of victory. After reverently planting the tree in the dance lodge, the men proceed with detailed preparations for the dance itself.

Rawhide is cut into circles, one colored red symbolizing the sun; another blue, representing the moon; and still others are produced and decorated to stand for Mother and Grandmother Earth, and for the buffalo—the source of Plains Indian subsistence. A five-pointed star-shaped piece is produced symbolizing the desire that the people might receive knowledge as they received light, from the Morning Star. These and other sacred objects such as buffalo skulls, a calumet, leather thongs, and skewers are taken to a sweat lodge where they are purified by tobacco smoke and prayed over. It is at this time that the dancers volunteer to endure suffering and give their flesh so that their people might flourish.

The actual ceremony begins at dawn with a procession of dancers led by a woman, the White Buffalo Cow Maiden, who carries the sacred calumet. The dancers repeat a simple chant requesting Wakan Tanka to reward their suffering with longevity for their people. Soon the spectators take up the chant. As the drums begin to add their rhythm to the chant, special attendants seize the dancers, pierce the skin of their chests, and insert pegs that are fastened by long things to the top of the cottonwood tree. With faces raised to the sun the dancers circle the sacred tree tugging at the thongs until the pegs tear out the flesh of the chest leaving bloody wounds. When all the dancers have pulled free of the thongs, they return to the sweat lodge where they are commended for their courage and promised that their sacrifices will not readily be forgotten.

Art for Art's Sake

In non-Western society there is very little "art for art's sake"; most art is utilitarian and is produced for religious, economic, social, or other purposes. Art in a sense always has utility even when it is produced with no purpose in mind but enjoyment. Anyone who has worked with the mentally ill will attest to the therapeutic value of creative activities. The psychological factor in art has been summed up by John Lewis as follows: "Art releases tensions by enabling the artist to externalize some of his emotions and ideas in an objective way; and this makes him the emotional leader and representative of his tribe" (1961:115).

The artist's sheer pleasure in creating beautiful forms is witnessed in the decoration of a particular kind of rawhide box or wallet produced by the Sauk and Fox Indians. The artists of this tribe took great pains in laying out a beautifully balanced and symmetrical design on a rectangular piece of rawhide. The colors were chosen to give a harmonious, pleasing effect. However, the design was laid down with no thought to the folding of the box. When the proper folds were made, the original effect of the design was destroyed. To the artist the *parfleche* (as the box was called) was a work of beauty, but to its owner and user it was merely a useful object made more valuable because effort had been spent in its decoration.

A similar situation is encountered in the legging decorations made by the Thompson Indians of British Columbia. In that culture, beads of various kinds are strung on legging fringe in such a way that they give a rhythmic design. While the artist may gain a good deal of pleasure from her creation, the beauty of the leggings is not actually enhanced, for when they are worn, the fringe hangs down in such a way that the elaborate design is not visible.

There are many cases of apparent art for art's sake in which the tendency to create a thing of beauty actually detracts from the usefulness of the decorated object. This mystic psychological phenomenon can be seen in the manner of producing stone hand axes in the Lower Paleolithic. In an attempt to achieve symmetry, these tools were flaked on both faces all around. While this produced an esthetically appealing form, it also reduced the implement's utility, for its user undoubtedly had to use a piece of hide or some other form of protection to keep his hand from being cut by the sharp butt edge.

While doing research among the Bush Negroes of Surinam in Dutch New Guinea, Melville Herskovits discovered that the people had in their possession "rice-winnowing trays" that their artists had rendered useless by carving designs completely through the wood. Since they obviously would not even hold grain, they represented only a Surinam decorative object.

In the Cook Islands of Polynesia "art for art's sake" is represented in the ceremonial adzes, which feature wooden handles so delicately carved that they have an appearance of filigree work. While the stone head of the adze is exactly like those used in house or boat construction, the artist's treatment of the handle has relegated the implement to the ceremonial sphere.

One may argue, however, that the artistic embellishment of this tool has merely removed its utility in one aspect of culture and has created a useful object in another—in this case, in the area of religion. This is one of the problems involved in making flat statements about the existence or non-existence of an "art for art's sake" concept. Even in our own culture it is possible for a given work of fine art to be (1) a thing of beauty to be enjoyed in a museum, (2) a symbol of affluence to a private collector, or (3) an aid to retailing when used in a magazine advertisement.

Although artists in all cultures produce works of art to gratify a creative impulse, in most non-Western societies art is usually produced for a particular purpose. Art objects must often be more useful than ornamental. Ruth Bunzel tells of a Pueblo potter who rejected a piece of pottery with the statement "It is beautiful but not strong" (1938:538). A wooden figurine carved by a West African may be esthetically satisfying, but its major function is an abode for a spirit. A Navaho sand-painting is an appealing creation even to the Western eye, but its main purpose is healing. A dance may thrill dancers and spectators alike with its grace and beauty, but the first thought of the choreographer is its function in the worship of the gods. In primitive society it is difficult to view art as an isolated activity. It is always an integral part of the total cultural configuration. Art may be an adjunct to economics, social organization, religion, communication, education, and any number of cultural aspects.

Economics

The quantity and quality of art as well as the role of its authors is often related to the form of subsistence of a society and the amount of its surplus. Boas explains the dearth of art in some societies by the fact that a hunter's life is so taken up with obtaining life's bare necessities that there is little time or energy left for the luxury of artistic expression. Even if the required leisure could somehow be found, hunting peoples must constantly be on the move and they cannot be burdened with unnecessary or unfinished art products. Thus, art activities often take the form, in these societies, of decoration of clothing or weapons or occasionally small carved objects such as Eskimo needlecases which can easily be transported (1938:589).

An apparent contradiction to this generalization is to be found in the hunting and fishing peoples of the Northwest Coast of North America, who were prolific and proficient carvers and weavers. Their dependable supply of salmon and sea mammals provided the surplus leisure necessary for a full concentration on their art activities. Their heavy wood sculpture—totem poles, mortuary posts, and house posts—was made possible by their sedentary village life.

SPECIALIZATION

The great art traditions of Mesopotamian, Egyptian, Mayan, and Incan civilizations were made possible only by economic systems where there was sufficient surplus to support specialized craftspeople and artists in the full-time pursuit of their activities. Each of these societies not only supported great numbers of artists but actually trained them through art apprenticeships or in government-supported schools of fine art.

In some cases economic security leads not to art specialization but to a general raising of art interest and production in a population as a whole. This has been the case in Bali. According to Covarrubias:

> Everybody in Bali seems to be an artist. . . . The effervescence of artistic activity and the highly developed esthetic sense of the population can perhaps be explained by a natural urge to express themselves, combined with the important factor of leisure resulting from well-organized agricultural co-operatism. However, the most important element for the development of a popular culture, with primitive as well as refined characteristics, was the fact that the Balinese did not permit the centralization of the artistic knowledge in a special intellectual class. (1937:160−62)

Economics and art are related in still other ways. For example, it is not unusual for art products to serve as repositories of wealth or even as units of exchange. The delicately woven hibiscus-fibre fine mats of Samoa, North American Indian beadwork in the form of wampum belts, and Banks Islands crimson-dyed feather ornaments are examples of esthetic currency. Undoubtedly, trade relationships have been closely tied in with the development of the arts in many areas. In ancient Crete the development of fine pottery vessels as well as their decoration with floral and marine designs is directly traceable to trade relationships with Greece and Egypt. The pottery served to package Crete's principal export—olive oil.

Oral art has its economic tie-in also. In parts of Melanesia it is believed that there is a direct relationship between the nightly telling of folktales during certain seasons and the success of the garden harvest. Further to the West, in Indonesia, one Celebes tribe believes that riddles may be asked only during the period when the rice crop is developing. At this time the farmers sit in the fields and ask each other riddles. When a correct answer is given, the assembled group chants, "Let the rice grow." It is believed that a man's success in riddling has a very definite effect on his success as a rice farmer.

AIRPORT ART

The art of pre-industrial peoples used to be referred to as *primitive art*. It was never a good term for it was also the term used for the naive and childlike creations of Seraphine, Henri Rousseau, and Grandma Moses. When applied to foreign and exotic cultures the word *primitive* implied that either the artists or their products were inferior in comparison with the serious art of the Western world. Now Graburn maintains that there is an even better reason for dropping such terminology. Labels such as *primitive* or *folk* are inadequate for contemporary art analyses. What is called for is a more realistic and flexible approach, taking into account (1) the intended audience to whom the art is directed, (2) the particular functions (if any) that the art may serve beyond its function as art; and (3) the sources of both the formal and esthetic characteristics portrayed in the art, that is, whether "traditional" or "transitional." (1976:30)

What we must consider now is that there is another form of art emerging which cross-cuts the categories of "primitive" or "Western." It is art produced by artists in pre-industrial societies, not for their own consumption, but to be sold to visitors from industrial societies. This is *tourist* or *airport* art. With the rise of tourism and the demand for souvenirs of trips to far-off places (even if the airport was as far as the traveler penetrated the culture) the world has seen, since World War II, the rise of a class of art objects especially produced for the tourist market. While the souvenir art objects are similar to indigenous creations used within the culture, they are modified by the nature of the marketing operation.

To begin with, Graburn says, all the objects are extremely uniform. One East Africa carved salad fork is almost identical to every other one. Because of this standardization it is now impossible to recognize the work of individual craftsmen or families of craftsmen. In the indigenous arts it has always been possible to recognize the work of individuals, although most of the motifs, stylistic features, and subject matter are determined by tradition. While airport art must retain enough of the traditional to symbolize to the outsider a few central characteristics of the culture and make it salable, the art pieces must also be (1) cheap, (2) portable, (3) understandable and (4) dustable. (1976:30) It also helps in some cases if they are useful and will have meaning in the home environment of the traveler.

The impact of these newly emerging economic opportunities on the pre-industrial artist and his works is difficult to comprehend. It is, according to Graburn, a "most powerful source of formal and aesthetic innovation, often leading to changes in size, simplification, standardization, naturalism, grotesquery, novelty and archaism." (1976:15)

One of the marketing problems is that airport art must compete with imported souvenirs (like plastic totem poles, post cards, and slide sets) therefore necessitating a low unit price. This has led to smaller sized pieces which can easily be sold, stored, and transported. The miniaturization, a universal characteristic in airport art, has a number of ramifications—economy of materials, expansion of their use as decorative objects, but also omission of important symbolic details which the buyer may not be aware of but will alter the meaning and genuineness of the art object as a representative of an art tradition.

The need to mass-produce also leads to greater use of power tools, and even greater standardization of products. These could conceivably lead to tourists ceasing to admire the objects as handicrafts. Pre-industrial peoples are often thought of as "natural artists" but if their art begins to take on assembly line characteristics the mystique may be lost.

FOLKLURE

American artists have for some time been more patronized by Madison Avenue than by fine-art collectors or marble-hall museums. Stained glass windows do not sell nearly as well as billboard layouts and textile designs. There is more money and status to be achieved from writing a musical jingle for radio or television commercials than from writing a cantata.

And now, still another form of art, mythology, is being called upon to do service in the pursuit of capital gain. Priscilla Denby has designated, this phenomenon where characters and motifs from mythology are used to market foods, washday products, and automobiles as "folklure." Probably the most effective of these merchandizing myths involves the Jolly Green Giant, who promotes the vegetables grown in the Le Sueur Valley of Minnesota. Drawing on traditions of spring fertility symbols such as Jack in the Green in England and such Continental characters as Green George, Leaf King,

Grass King, and Whitsuntide Lout, Jolly Green Giant seems to revive an age-old human response to the land and its bountiful promise.

Almost as effective as the Giant are the Keebler elves who bake "uncommonly good" cookies in their little factory in the forest. A perusal of the literature reveals that elves live only in subterranean areas, and so the Keebler elves must really be fairies (Sullenberger 1974). But then fairies do not bake cookies, but only bread (which must be consumed the same day or it turns to toadstools).

Whatever the identity of the elves, they, like the Jolly Green Giant, produce a "curious aura of credibility that allows us to accept their presence without consciously questioning the implausibility of the incidents they depict." (Sullenberger 1974:56) Perhaps the willing suspension of disbelief which fairies and folklore characters promote makes us more susceptible to the fictions and fairy tales of Madison Avenue.

The list of folklore characters selling soap gets longer every day. There is the White Knight of Ajax (the foaming cleanser) drawn from the Trojan War accounts of Homer; Mr. Clean, obviously an oriental genie from Arabian mythology; and the muscular arm of Action rising out of the automatic washer—not a far cry from the image of the sword Excalibar rising from King Arthur's lake or a magical genie rising from a well to do a master's bidding.

Detroit has also been quick to pick up on the mythological sales pitch with the Plymouth Fury (Furies Tisiphone, Megaera, and Alecto are found in Greek creation myths), the Thunderbird (from North American Indian mythology), the Firebird, and Phoenix cars of Pontiac (borrowing from tales of the magically immortal bird that is resurrected from its own ashes), and finally the Gremlin of American Motors (the supernatural airborne imps first discovered by military pilots). Although folklore has been a good investment for the market place, has the market place been good for the art? Undoubtedly some increased interest in folklore will result from bringing it into the mass media but the sad thing is that the "folklure" presented to the public is such a poor substitute for the real thing.

Social Organization.

Art in its various forms contributes materially to the maintenance of the social organization of any society. One reason for this is that art can represent a strong unifying force. Consider for a moment emblems of family, clan, and national solidarity that have come from the hand of the artistic craftsperson.

For the European, family unity is often symbolized by a coat of arms, while Northwest Coast Indians expressed pride in their clan and family traditions and heritage by raising a totem pole. Nations have also utilized graphic symbols (the French fleur-de-lis and cockade or the German swastika or Maltese cross), national anthems, and traditional folk or fatherland songs to arouse patriotic feelings in their citizens. No country is without its flag, pregnant with symbolism, or its emotion-stirring paintings and sculpture—for example, *Washington Crossing the Delaware*, the statue of the Flag Raising on Iwo Jima, the seated Lincoln in the Lincoln Memorial.

Lomax believes that music, and particularly folk music, is a great source of personal and cultural security:

> The primary effect of music is to give the listener a feeling of security, for it symbolizes the place where he was born, his earliest childhood satisfactions, his religious experience, his pleasure in community doings, his courtship and his work. . . . (1959:929)

Art has been used not only to symbolize *esprit de corps*, but it has also fortified prevailing social structures by serving as a designator of role and status. In the New Hebrides, each social grade carried the privilege of wearing a special mask made of cane and clay and decorated with the colors appropriate to his rank; men purchased their way up the social ladder with payments to the village elders of a special breed of pigs.

In the Samoan Islands, tapa cloth is considered the ceremonial clothing of the chiefs only, and the exalted village *taupou* (ceremonial hostess) is easily distinguished by her garments of the most finely woven hibiscus bast. On her head she wears an artfully constructed head ornament of human hair, sticks, and small pieces of mirror. Of the Aztecs Vaillant writes:

> The warriors frankly gloried in their costumes. Rich mantles and ornate feather head-dresses were not enough for some, who carried on their shoulders a harness of wicker supporting an elaborate structure in feather mosaic. Others wore costumes modelled on the appearance of an ocelot or an eagle. (1956:140)

Religion

Art has long been the handmaiden of religion. Without artists there can be no idolatry. Whether it be the earliest cave art of Lascaux or Altamira, the chants of Gregory, the murals of Michaelangelo, or the Sallman *Head of Christ*, art has served a common function in religion—to express awe and adoration of the supernatural. Believers have exhibited a pronounced tendency to require something material upon

Navaho sandpainter. (Courtesy Arizona State Museum, The University of Arizona; Fred Stevens, Photographer.)

which to focus their worship. Whether we look at a stained-glass window, a nine-branched candlestick, or a Polynesian *tiki*, art provides us with symbols of faith and unity in a given religious system.

Frequently art shades into religion to such an extent that the two are inseparable. Such is the case with the Navaho. Lee describes this fusion as follows:

> The sand-paintings are no more art than they are ritual, myth, medical practice or religious belief. They are created as an integral aspect of a ceremony which brings into harmony with the universal order one who finds himself in discord with it; or which intensifies and ensures the continuation of a harmony which is already present. Every line and shape and color, every interrelationship of form, is the visible manifestation of myth, ritual and religious belief. (1959:167)

Communication

Before humans recorded their thoughts and experiences in words, they did it in pictures. Many peoples, known only through the findings of archeologists, would remain inarticulate except through their art.

In North America, Ojibwa Indians drew quite recognizable pictures of gods, birds, and animals on bits of birchbark in order to remember the sequence of songs in ceremonies. One of the most interesting bits of early American art is the wampum belt given to William Penn by the Leni-Lenape Indian chiefs at the Treaty of 1682. This belt, made predominantly of white shells (the color of peace), depicts Penn and an Indian with joined hands and represents a record of the agreement between whites and Indians to live in peace. In the West, Plains Indians covered the outsides of their tepees with story pictures of memorable hunts or victorious battles using symbolic colors and figures to spell out the accurate details. The Sioux Indians even developed a way of keeping historical records of the tribe over a period of years. By looking at their chronological picture record, it was possible for them to recall years in which specific births, deaths, wars, and epidemics took place.

In a great number of civilizations it is possible to trace an evolution of writing from a pictograph stage to one in which abstract characters were used. Of Aztec civilization Vaillant states:

> The priesthood . . . instructed youth in the mysteries of writing and keeping records. . . . There was no alphabet, but a picture of an animal or thing could be combined with the picture of another animal or thing to give a third meaning in terms of its sound value. . . . The Aztecs wrote the name of their capital by drawing stone *tena* from which sprouted a napal cactus, *nochtli,* or the town Pantepec, by drawing a flag, *pantli,* on a conventionalized hill, *tepec.* Color, position, puns and abbreviations all contributed to recording sounds by this means. Conventionalized signs, like footprints to show travel or movement, a shield and club for war, a bundled corpse for death, gave simple connotations of action. (1956:201)

The Aztec numerical system also depended upon art work. The number 1 was indicated by a dot or a finger; 20 by a flag; 400 (20 × 20) by a fir tree, 8,000 (20 × 20 × 20) by a bag commonly used for carrying cacao beans.

Education

Some form of communication is essential in socializing and enculturating the young people of any society; so it is difficult to separate the communication and educational functions of art. Audiovisual aids are hardly new to humankind, and the concept of a "picture being worth a thousand words" probably emerged during the Stone Age.

The Micronesians used as their principal aid in teaching navigation delicately fashioned frameworks of bamboo and shells. These were supposed to instruct novices concerning prevailing winds and

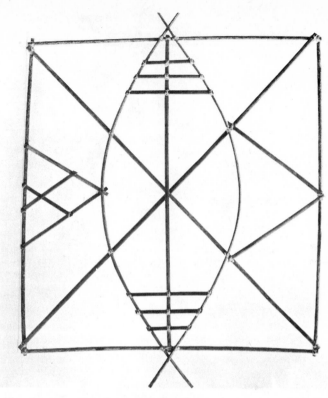

Elements of artistic design may be observed in the Micronesian sailing chart. (Courtesy Field Museum of Natural History.)

currents. While some do not consider these bamboo charts works of art, they do feature in many cases bilateral symmetry and artistic arrangements of sticks and shells often at the expense of accurate scale.

In Pueblo cultures one of the more significant forms of art is the Kachina dolls, which are carved by the men with great concern for accurate detail and are often given to children as gifts. When the men teach their children to carve these faithful models of Kachina dancers, dress, color, and posture have to be correct or the spirits will be offended. Thus, the children learn through the creation of these playthings the important elements of their religious heritage.

Turning to other forms of art, we find that among the Lamba of Africa there is one class of proverbs that is used especially for the training of children. And Reichard records:

> Almost every tribe has stories which they consider children's tales, or moralizing stories for the main purpose of inculcating virtue. . . . The fact that the very rehearsal of the tales by adults with the children present, as

Hopi Kachina dolls. These figures are representations of supernatural beings living in the surrounding mountains. (Courtesy Field Museum of Natural History.)

well as frequent reference to the tales in various situations of daily life, exerts a potent influence in the teaching and learning process. Children learn the right and wrong of a matter by implication and inference and by repetition, and it would be difficult, if not impossible for them to tell how they know many things (1938:478)

Myths serve as repositories of values in every society including our own. Just prior to the turn of the century fifty million young people were reading about the life and times of a number of American culture heroes created by the novelist Horatio Alger. Sociologist R. Richard Wohl, who has made a study of the impact of Alger's works, points out that the myth usually went something like this: A respectable country boy goes to the city to make good in order to assist in the support of his recently widowed mother, who is being threatened by mortgage foreclosure. Through clean living, thrift, honesty, and hard work he is victorious over bullies, thieves, and economic difficulties.

In trying to understand Alger's great popularity Wohl suggests that (1) Alger's novels appeared at a time of great mobility from farm to city; (2) Alger helped define the aspirations of a nation of farm boys—to make money, to get ahead, to make good; (3) the principles of proper conduct found in the novels were reinforced from the pulpit, in the press, and in the advice of the average American to his children; and (4) the stories have universal appeal for every generation that would like to believe "push" and not "pull" is the secret to success. The Horatio Alger stories represented a primer for success for millions of Americans and incorporated the basic principles of the "great American dream."

Art as an Aid in Science

Scholars will probably never develop a very satisfactory science of art. The value of art lies in unpredictable nature. However, art objects and art processes have provided data important in developing a science of anthropology. In the study of New World archeology, for example, ceramic analysis has been one of the major methods of recognizing and dating prehistoric cultures and civilizations. In Mexico and Central America, frescoes and books of polychrome pictures (known as codices) have given us a glimpse into Mayan and Aztec life as it existed prior to the destruction or abandonment of many of the ceremonial centers.

Analysis of folklore motifs appearing in a variety of cultures has been utilized to study cultural diffusion, and ethnomusicological studies have provided evidence of cultural contact where historical records are missing. When cultural evolutionists were claiming that art progresses from the representational to the abstract, Franz Boas demonstrated that at least in Eskimo needle-cases this had not been the case. He found that originally the cases carried only geometric incised designs but "the various parts of the needle-case excite the imagination of the artist" (1908:337) and in time certain portions were decorated with realistic animal forms. Ackerknecht (1953) and Kerley and Bass (1967) have pointed out that art works have served the physical anthropologist well in his studies of paleopathology. Egyptian paintings and statues provide evidence (corroborated by mummies) of the presence of congenital clubfoot and both achondroplastic and cretinistic dwarfism. Art objects from both hemispheres indicate the presence in prehistoric populations of poliomyelitis and Pott's disease (tuberculosis of the spine). Aztec codex pictures accurately depict both dwarfs and hunchbacks, and pottery and clay sculpture from the Peruvian Andes throws light upon the antiquity of certain skin diseases in that area.

In the study of contemporary peoples analysis of works of art has been utilized in studying personality structure in primitive as well as industrialized cultures. Honigmann describes the theory behind such analysis as follows:

> Professional works of imagination do not only reveal the character structure of their creators, as might be thought. Successful stories, plays, films, and similar creative products contain themes that appeal to existing

needs and aspirations of the community. Popularity indicates that the expressive product satisfies audience needs and suggests a relationship between that product and character structure. (1954:129)

Still other studies have revealed how basic value systems may be investigated by analyzing the peculiarities of a culture's art works. For example, in China, where rank and station were of paramount importance, the costumes and other emblems of rank of emperors were painted in detail by portrait artists, but little attention was paid to the distinct facial characteristics of individuals (Hsu 1953). In colonial America, however, where the "rugged individual" was extolled, itinerant portrait painters used to paint clothing in advance leaving only the accurate representation of the face of the customer to be painted in at the time of the sitting.

Frankfort (1948) has called attention to the fact that in Egyptian paintings of battle scenes the pharaoh was always the dominant figure, being represented in much larger size than fellow warriors. In Mesopotamian art, however, the king is not easily distinguishable from his subjects. This difference is significant because Egyptian kings were regarded as gods while those of Mesopotamia were merely highly honored mortals.

The Artist in Society and Culture

The role of artists in non-Western society has often been neglected in favor of interest in their products. To gain some insight into the creative experience and how it grows out of, and relates to, the cultural context let us look at the role of the artist in three societies—Maori, Balinese, and American.

THE MAORI CARVER

In approximately 1350A.D. a mass migration from central Polynesian arrived in New Zealand. Having an agricultural economy, they brought a great variety of plants on their double-hulled catamaran vessels; but much to their surprise, the tropical plants could not survive in the temperate climate of New Zealand. Therefore, these migrants (which anthropologists call the Classic Maori) experienced a difficult period of adjustment. Not only was the source of subsistence different, but the colder climate forced them to change their clothing styles and methods of house construction. It was during this period, strangely enough, that the magnificent art of the Maori was born. They created the art of weaving, and produced cloaks, dresses, and kilts from yarn made from flax fibers. Since more substantial houses were needed to keep out the cold a special new class of artisans fash-

The Maori carver today.

ioned stout houseposts, rafters, and gables; plaited lattice panels to cover the interior walls; and painted vivid designs on the rafters in red, black, and white.

As Classic Maori society developed in size and complexity differences in wealth and status began to appear, and the art of tattooing body decorations became an important method of identifying people of wealth and authority. The most important Maori art however was woodcarving, and carvers were believed to work under a special supernatural charter from the god Rua. The carvers, their tools, the wood they used, and their finished products were believed to have magical power and personalities, and consequently they were given personal names.

The classic Maori carvers were also blessed with excellent materials with which to work. Totari and Kauri woods were soft and durable; they were easily worked and free of knots. Chisels, gauges, and adzes were made of nephrite, a variety of jade found in New Zealand. After an initial adjustment to the temperate climate, life became more secure and in time the population expanded to such a point that both food and land were in short supply. Disputes between communities over land boundaries and over fishing and fowling rights led to intertribal wars. Gradually the activities of carvers were directed toward the needs of a society at war. Handsomely carved spears and war clubs were produced; great war canoes were built and ornamented with decorative magical carvings. Stockades were built around villages and many of the vertical timbers were capped with figures of famous warriors with out-thrust tongues mocking the enemy. Memorials to legendary heroes in the form of free standing sculpture in the round stood about the village square. Chieftainship in this society was handed down from father to son but if the heir did not have both the qualities of a great warrior and of a skilled carver he was often passed over for the next in line.

Ancestors were the most important subject of Maori art. Although the subjects were mostly secular, the products (imbued with mana) were sacred. More concerned with politics than religion, the Maori carvers' major efforts went into decorating the village council house (*whare whakairo*) with carvings of past heroes and founding fathers.

The *whare-whairo* was the Maori artists' gallery. The structure itself symbolized the body of an early ancestor. The rafters were ribs, the frontal boards his outstretched arms, the mask at the peak his face, and the ridge beam his spine. The central beam of the structure was supported by carved pillars representing the captains of the canoe in which the community originally arrived. Carvings on panels along the walls were of important ancestors. The house was truly an archive of tribal history.

The training of a carver began early. When only a boy he would be apprenticed to a priest-carver and his instruction was acquired through watching and assisting his mentor. He had to learn the traditional motifs, how to select the proper woods, how to obtain permission from the forest god Tane to remove the timber, and above all, how to make and use his kit of adzes, chisels, and gauges.

There is an old Maori proverb which says, "The art of the wood carver is the art of Rua." But now the Maori gods (including Rua) are dead and the Maori woodcarver's art is dying. Revivals have been attempted from time to time—like the establishment of the Rotorua School of Maori Arts and Crafts in 1927. The craftsmen trained in this school have built many magnificent council houses and churches in Maori communities but today the handful of traditional carvers who remain find it difficult to obtain contracts for new council houses, and it is difficult to attract serious apprentices. Commissions for this sort of work are almost always less lucrative than the wages offered in the regular building trades. The role of the Maori carver will soon be only a historical fact to be read about in connection with the products of his artistry hopefully protected and treasured in New Zealand museums.

Balinese dancer.

THE BALINESE ARTIST

In Bali everyone is an artist. It seems to matter little whether one is a peasant or a prince, a man or a woman, a youngster or an elder; the world of art is shared by all. Some of the finest orchestras (*gamelans*) are found in very remote villages, and tiny hamlets are famous for their families of painters, sculptors, actors, story tellers, and dancers. There is almost no differentiation between the most and least gifted or between the professional and the amateur artist.

Painting, sculpture, and music-making are the arts reserved for men; women weave, dye (batiks), and make beautiful offerings for the gods—palm-leaf cutouts, flower and fruit arrangements, cakes and other special foods. Women of all ages take part in ritual offering dances but only little girls are trained to do the important *Lelong* dance pantomines that tell one of the many famous Balinese "Thousand and One Nights" epic narratives. These dance dramas which the audience know by heart but still enjoy, are an elaboration of another art form, the archaic shadow-plays, called *Wayang Kulit*.

The artist in Bali strives for excellence and hopes to enhance the reputation of his or her village but does not expect to be singled out and acclaimed: art is produced for the community and not for personal gain or notoriety. The actors and musicians who perform at village festivals do so without pay, and even when they appear at private feasts they are wined and dined but not paid. Artists belong to musical or theatrical clubs, and whatever money might be received for performances is given to the club to buy new costumes or musical instruments, or to fund a party for its members.

The art of Bali is in a constant state of flux and few art objects or art traditions are thought of as permanent. The soft soapstone sculpture is expected to crumble in a matter of a few years; temples and their relief carvings must constantly be renewed; ants destroy wooden sculpture; and the humidity does away with paper and cloth treasures. While Balinese are proud of their traditions they are also progressive. Foreign influence on Balinese art includes Indian, Chinese, and Javanese concepts but all these influences are reinterpreted to suit Balinese esthetics. New styles in music, theater, or graphic and plastic arts come and go but there are also traditional ideas that persist. Local styles are maintained, although a certain amount of individuality is permitted and innovations are soon copied by others as nothing remains private property in this communal society.

Balinese art is realistic without being photographic. There is no attempt to give the optical illusion of the real thing. There is no perspective in painting, and sculpture is highly stylized. Balinese admire technique and craftsmanship above all else. Their art is not pretentious—it is for the masses, to be produced and enjoyed by all. Although Balinese arts serves religion it is not a religious art. The Balinese artist carves or paints or dances the only stories they know—the ones created by the learned religious teachers of long ago.

THE AMERICAN COMPOSER

In turning to contemporary America let us look at the role and status of a musical artist—the serious composer. From a cross-cultural perspective this is a somewhat unique role, for the composer as a specialist does not exist in many non-Western societies. Often the person in these societies who composes is also a performer, a priest, or another variety of religious practitioner. American composers are often reputed to be great innovators, but they must be innovative within a framework of a fairly well-established tradition. Anything that breaks with tradition too radically will probably not find acceptance.

In America composers tend to be men. This, according to Dennison Nash, "may be due to the fact that specialization tends to weed out women who, because of the value placed on their reproductive and child-rearing functions, cannot devote themselves sufficiently to

Some American composers combine compositions with performance.

training for, and practicing in, the role to achieve eminence."
(1961:83) Although there is a folk belief that one need not bother with
music unless a kinsman has established the fact that talent is present
in the line, an analysis of life histories of 23 eminent American composers shows that none of them had parents who were composers
and only 8 of them had parents who were performing musicians.

Composers in our society come from families of above average
status and income with the exception of a number of black jazz composers who have come from families of lower class identification.
Some people claim that proficiency in composition correlates with
maladjustment to the culture but no particular type of personality is
characteristic of the composer and it cannot be said that they are abnormal or even borderline.

Composers tend to live permanently or semipermanently in
urban centers, such as New York, because of the "affluence of these
centers and their evaluation of music which have brought about the
congregation of various musical specialists and a sophisticated air—
the essentials of a highly developed and complex art." (Nash 1961:87)

In America almost no composers earn their living by producing
original music. Most survive by doing jobs other than their "calling."
Virgil Thompson's tongue-in-cheek discussion of perils of composing
is probably more truth than humor. He writes of serious composers:

> They have arrangements or they don't. If they don't, they take pupils. If they can't get pupils they starve. If they get tired of starving they go on relief. Unemployed musicians of high ability and experience are shockingly numerous in America. A surprisingly large number of composers are men of private fortune. Some of these have it from papa, but the number of those who have married their money is not small. Many composers are able to live for years on gifts and doles. Include among these all prizes and private commissions. The number of composers who live on the receipts from their compositions is very small. Royalties and performing-rites fees are . . . comparatively rare . . . since composers are nothing like as powerfully organized for collecting them as electrical and banking interests are for preventing their being collected. (1962:76 *passim*)

Most composers enjoy very little commercial success during their lifetimes. The role of a serious composer in America is a precarious one indeed because most of the audiences for serious music would be quite content not hearing *any* modern original music whatsoever. They like familiar forms and recognizable melodies.

In America the principal patrons for both jazz and serious music are the wealthy. Although patrons seldom exercise control over the activities of the composer, other people connected with the music industry do—specifically conductors and instrumentalists who often cater to popular tastes, musical businessmen (with no taste), and critics. American music is marked by pronounced specialization and an ever-expanding gap in musical taste between the composer and his audience.

In Western music, composition is considered to result from a combination of inspiration and conscious craft. It is a solitary act carried out in private and not actualized until the creation is performed much later. Even then it is the performer who tends to take the bows, not the composer. In American musical art there is a differentiation made between "serious" music (for the few) and "popular" music (for the many). Most serious composers hold popular music to be inferior and it is unlikely that a serious composer can write a serious work that will also be popular and commercially lucrative.

Summary

Art is a uniquely human activity which for most cultures represents the production or expression of what is considered beautiful or what appeals to the canons of taste. The anthropological approach to art is somewhat different from that of the art critic or historian in that the science is primarily concerned with the function of art in the total cultural configuration and with the role of the artist.

In analyzing art, anthropology groups creative works into the following categories: (1) the graphic and plastic arts, (2) the verbal arts and (3), the performing arts. Regardless of the variety of expression, all artists maintain a continuity of form and quality. This is called style, and it is possible to talk about representative, stylized, and abstract style traditions. All three varieties can be found in most societies throughout the world.

There is a much greater tendency for non-Western art to have utility, although "art for art's sake" does exist outside of Western culture. More often art has economic utility (as money or as trade items), social value (as emblems of family or societal unity), religious significance (as symbols of faith), or communication functions (as pictographs or educational aids). While art forms vary greatly from society to society, art is an activity wherein the artist and the audience share culturally meaningful symbols, perspectives, and experiences.

Cultural Change 17

An American mission group established a station at Garkida, in northern Nigeria, in 1922 and inaugurated work in education, medicine, industrial and agricultural training, as well as in religious activities. The people of the area were the Bura, a tribal society of 175,000 to 200,000 people living in a territory about 100 miles from east to west and 50 miles from north to south. Their subsistence base was hoe agriculture, with guinea corn as the principal crop. The Bura were "traditional" in the anthropological sense, having successfully resisted long-term attempts to convert them to Islam by the neighboring Kanuri. They had also managed to retain their village-oriented social organization, but they had no concept of political identity above that level. Lacking a centralized political organization, they had long been prey to raids by the Kanuri, the Pabirs, and other neighboring tribes, who did have more centralized governments. In 1914, the British, who had established the protectorate over Nigeria, ended this predation.

The influences of the American mission group were both direct and indirect. Direct influences included those of Western medicine, education, and religion. The basic economic structure of village agriculture was modified by employment opportunities at the mission. Major roles were filled by Bura as soon as they were trained. Indirectly, Western goods—cars and household goods—and technology brought by the missionaries had an enormous cultural impact on the Bura.

Twenty-five years after the establishment of the mission one of its founders, looking across the Hawal River valley, with its schools, hospital, and other evidences of civilization standing in sharp contrast to the village housing, stated that in 1922 he had watched a herd of roan antelope cross that same valley to drink from the river. Although the mission station had changed Bura life in that valley, villages a few miles away were still very traditional. Elaborate courtesies were used in greeting one's neighbors, the age-old cycle of planting and harvesting was the people's most important concern, and they had little or no interest in the white man's world.

In a period of 25 years the village of Garkida had left the Neolithic and had entered the twentieth century in a number of ways. Young men who had been in the British armed forces in the Southeast Asian campaigns and elsewhere returned to the village with service pay amounting to several hundred pounds sterling—more wealth than their fathers would see in a lifetime of farming. A few of the veterans gave their money to their elders in the traditional ways of family support—to be used for the benefit of all—but for others the money meant that they were free to bypass the need to ask the total family for assistance in getting bridewealth. Ordinarily this assistance would have obligated the groom to return the favor and to give the family the choice of who the bride would be. The veterans, however, made their own choices, paying cash for the women. All this wealth also allowed them to buy liquor which led to fights and to abuse of wives and children. When the money was gone (all too soon), rather than return to the family farm they migrated to the city or resorted to stealing. The Bura saw theft as a most heinous crime, and prior to the coming of Western influences it had been possible to leave anything of value unattended indefinitely without fear of having it stolen.

The post-war period also brought motor transport to the village on a weekly schedule. Goods arrived from the outside world and village people now had the opportunity to go to the cities or to other villages. Even though the roads were primitive by Western standards (impassable at times during the rainy season and dusty beyond description during the dry season) people and goods came and went. The trip to Jos, the railhead, was 400 miles (at 25 m.p.h.) and all food, gasoline, and other necessities had to be carried along since service was nonexistent along the road. But as bad as conditions were everyone commented on how much things had improved since the mission began 25 years earlier. A close friend and a former student of one of the authors is today a family head and teacher in Garkida. He writes that the dirt roads are now blacktop and buses run regular schedules. Everyone has a transistor radio, and the news of the world reaches them as quickly as it does anyone else.

An anthropological description depicting the way of life of a particular society freezes the action, so to speak, at a given point in time. Thus, no anthropological work is a completely accurate account of a contemporary culture, for that culture today is not quite the same as it was when it was visited and studied by the enthnographer. Although tribal societies are undoubtedly more conservative than Western ones, there is no culture in the world that remains completely static, year in and year out. We might also add that some pre-industrial societies are more conservative than others, and in every culture some aspects or institutions tend to change more rapidly than others. In discussing this phenomenon of human society, Raymond Firth (1958:149) maintains that the "bony structure," that is, the basic underlying principles that give a culture form and meaning, is not easily altered, but the "flesh and blood," the traits and complexes that fill out the cultural configuration, can and do change quite rapidly.

The validity of this principle can readily be seen by looking at our own American cultural system. There are certain moral, religious, social and political principles that are nearly as strong today as they were when our country was founded. The puritan morality of early New England survives in various parts of the country in the form of

Blue Laws, Prohibition, and anti-evolution movements and parties, Sunday closing laws, movie and book censorship, and dozens of other restrictions.

Although these underlying principles remain recognizable, there have been alterations and realignments of the associated cultural elements. The church remains a dominant force in our culture as far as morality is concerned, but there have been changes in its role. While the church continues to minister to the spiritual needs of its members, it also provides recreation, education, and even social and psychological counseling. It is often the sponsor of Scout troops, drama clubs, and athletic teams.

Our ideal of what the American family should be socially and morally has prevailed for some time, but the family itself has certainly changed from colonial and frontier days—in size, in function, and in structure.

Lower animals are born to behave in a given way and the behavior of a species is subject to change only if subsequent generations experience a genetic change. Humans, however, are cultural animals and one of the most characteristic things about their manners and mores is that unique circumstances within the culture or exposure to the ideas of another culture can cause them to drop old ideals and adopt new ones.

Internal Change

Changes that spring from within a society may be either of a technological or a social nature. In other words, they may involve new kinds of gadgets like helicopters or microwave ovens or they may involve new and different values, ideologies, or social procedures. Detente is a social invention just as were the ideas of laissez faire, universal suffrage, and social security. These things may be termed inventions because, like artifacts, they represent new cultural ideas that did not previously exist in the society. Sometimes inventions, social and technological, represent an entirely new principle, or they may merely involve a special or novel application of a known principle to a new situation. An example of the latter is the military prep school, where the principles of military training and discipline have been borrowed from the armed forces and applied to the area of elementary and secondary education.

CAUSES OF INTERNAL CHANGE

What are the reasons for a society altering an institution that has perhaps remained quite stable for many generations? Here are a few of them.

Population Pressure.   Population pressure may force a change in social structure or in residence or subsistence patterns. One of the most striking examples of the effect of population growth on culture occurred in Europe during the nineteenth century. For hundreds of years Europe had remained stable in its population and mode of life, but during the last century:

> a combination of factors, no one of which can be completely isolated from the whole and weighed independently, began to disturb the balance. One factor of outstanding significance was clearly the growing pressure of the population itself. It was that as much as anything which was responsible for the breakdown of the old established order. For a succession of crises was thereby created, necessitating new forms of economic, political, and community organization, new institutional and technical developments, new ideologies and programs of reform. Much of Europe was in fact remade as a result. The old bounds of community and cultural life were literally burst asunder. European society could not reorder and readjust itself rapidly enough to meet conditions and at the same time contain itself; it therefore overflowed. Tens of millions of people began to migrate to the new world. In this movement appeared the evidence that profound change was sweeping through the whole social structure. (Sims 1939:247–48)

Change in Climate.   A change in climate may cause a society to adopt new subsistence methods, clothing styles, and diet. For an example of this we may take what happened at the end of the great Ice Age period. V. Gordon Childe describes the situation:

> Ice Age Europe . . . produced a dazzling culture . . . made possible by the food supply bounteously provided by glacial conditions. . . . With the end of the ice age these conditions passed away. As the glaciers melted, forest invaded tundras and steppes, and the herds of mammoths, reindeer, bison and horse migrated or died out. With their disappearance the culture of societies which preyed upon them also withered away. . . .
>
> By contrast to what had passed away, the mesolithic societies leave an impression of extreme poverty. (1948:43)

The most important aspect of the Mesolithic changes in climate was the growth of forests. In place of the great herds of game that had been characteristic of the Upper Paleolithic, Mesolithic species consisted of the stag deer, aurochs (wild cattle), wild boars, and hares. The majority of these animals had to be hunted individually rather than in herds. No doubt this circumstance brought about the domestication of the dog as an aid in hunting. The people of Mesolithic Europe, many of them no doubt the descendants of the Paleolithic hunters, also came to depend upon shellfish, fish, and waterfowl. During this time habitation sites were first located along beaches, at river mouths, and on the shores of lakes. We must not suppose that these changes in culture took place overnight or even within one's lifetime. Those people who remained in Europe gradu-

Maori migration required the development of a house suitable for a temperate climate.

ally altered their culture to meet the problems of their environment over a period of a thousand years or more.

An example of a slightly different type involves the Maori of New Zealand. This is a case of changes required of people who migrated from a tropical climate in central Polynesia to a temperate climate. Changes had to be made more rapidly than in the case of the people of the Mesolithic, and greater adjustment was required on the part of the individual South Sea islander. Perhaps the most drastic change concerned their basic diet. Breadfruit, bananas, and coconuts would not grow in New Zealand. Taro and yams could be raised, but only with great difficulty and only in certain regions. The people adjusted by developing the fern root as a vegetable staple and preyed upon sea birds and the giant ostrich-like moa for their protein.

While the temperate climate of New Zealand forced drastic changes in Maori living habits, certain areas of the culture continued in the traditional central Polynesian form and the institutions of family and government. Religion and mythology remained stable elements; language changed so little that even today it can easily be recognized as a central Polynesian dialect.

Innovators and Reformers. Especially gifted individuals may be born into a society, and their inquiring minds, searching for new and better ways of doing things, may conceive programs of reform or technological experimentation. It must be pointed out that such individuals are rare in primitive society, for the pressure is to conform, not to innovate. Progress and reform are to a great extent Western inventions. Robert Redfield has remarked that in "primitive societies uninfluenced by civilization the future is seen as a reproduction of the immediate past" (1953:120)

However, innovators and reformers have lived in every century and in every society. Legend tells us that Hiawatha one day conceived of an idea whereby all the warlike Iroquois tribes could live at peace with one another. He foresaw a time when they would come together in a great league or confederacy whereby they might work together rather than fight among themselves. Fired by this idea, he is supposed to have spent years traveling from tribe to tribe until he finally succeeded in persuading the tribal chiefs to try his unique idea. The League of the Iroquois, once established, lasted for more than 400 years.

Whereas there is little chance of verifying the above legend, an incident concerning another reformer is a matter of recorded history. In the journals of the James and Bell expedition to Nebraska in 1818 there appears the story of a rather unusual young man, Petalesharoo, the son of Knife Chief of the Loup band of the Pawnee. The issue on which this young man broke with tradition and truly established himself as a reformer is described as follows by Redfield:

> By ancient custom, this group of Pawnee each year sacrificed a captive to Venus, Morning Star, to ensure abundant crops. The victim, fattened and kept uninformed of the fate ahead, was on the proper day bound to a cross or scaffold, tomahawked, and shot with arrows. For several years Knife Chief "had regarded this sacrifice as an unnecessary and cruel exhibition of power, exercised upon unfortunate and defenseless individuals whom they were bound to protect; and he vainly endeavored to abolish it by philanthropic admonitions."
>
> A young girl from another tribe was brought captive to the Pawnee village. . . . She was bound to the cross when Knife Chief's son stepped forward "and in a hurried but firm manner, declared that it was his father's wish to abolish this sacrifice; that for himself, he had presented himself before them, for the purpose of laying down his life upon the spot, or of releasing his victim." He then cut the victim's cords, put her on a horse, mounted another and carried her to safety. (1953:130–31)[1]

Culture Fatigue. Still another reason for internal change is suggested by A. L. Kroeber, who maintains that people may merely tire of a certain institution. A prime example of this kind of "cultural fatigue" concerns the sudden decision of the Hawaiians in 1819 (pre-missionary days) to abolish their ancient taboo system and repudiate their Polynesian gods. Of this incident Kroeber writes:

---

[1] Copyright, 1953, by Cornell University. Used by permission of Cornell University Press. Reprinted 1969.

Strangely enough, the high priest of the islands was also active in the coterie, and in fact subsequently took the lead in extending the movement from mere abolition of the taboo (system) to the overthrow of the gods whose representative he was. This man seemingly had everything to lose by the change, and it is difficult to imagine what he could have had to gain. . . . He evidently represented, therefore, an element in the population that was psychologically ready for a breach with established religion, from internal reasons. (1948:403)

Kroeber further suggests that this kind of "cultural fatigue" or disillusionment finds parallels in the defeatist attitude in France in 1940, the attitude toward the 1929 depression in America which brought on the New Deal, the Japanese Emperor's renunciation of divinity at the end of World War II, or the emergence of a counterculture in America in the late 1960s.

While we have pointed out a number of ways in which the members of a culture may be prompted to find new solutions for old problems, it must be remarked that most societies, if left entirely to themselves, will remain quite stable. Once pre-industrial people have found workable solutions to the challenges of everyday living, they show little interest in inventiveness or experimentation. However, Nadel reminds us that such people show "little hesitation in copying (or borrowing) novel methods, that is, in adopting them when they can be seen *in use*. The pull of tradition, then, means in fact reluctance to abandon a safe routine for risks that go with untried methods" (1953:267).

External Change

ACCULTURATION
AND DIFFUSION

The borrowing of ideas from a neighboring society has been referred to in anthropology as *diffusion* or *acculturation*. Although people disagree on the proper definition of these terms, we will make the following distinction: acculturation represents a situation where borrowing and lending of cultural traits takes place between two societies living in continuous first-hand contact. Notable examples are white-Indian relations as they existed for some 400 years of American history, the Maori and English contacts in New Zealand, or those of Arabs and Jews in the Middle East. *Diffusion*, on the other hand, is also a borrowing phenomenon, but, as Winick defines it in his *Dictionary of Anthropology*, it may involve only "a part of a culture (spreading) to other areas" (1958:167). What might be spread may be only a single institution, invention, trait, or complex. A major distinguishing factor is that "although it is found in every example of acculturation, it can take place without the contact necessary in that process" (1958:168).

Herskovits, however, makes still another distinction between diffusion and acculturation. "Diffusion," he maintains "is the study of achieved cultural transmission" (1949:525). He reminds us that frequently such questions as "how," "when," "where," and "by whom the change was brought about" are only matters of conjecture in diffusion studies. Having relegated diffusion to the past tense, Herskovits defines acculturation as "cultural transmission in process" (1949:525). In other words, acculturation is, in most cases, a contemporary phenomenon and the historical facts of contact are either known or obtainable.

Studies of acculturation and diffusion have become a major pursuit of anthropologists today. While an interest in culture change and culture transmission is as old as anthropology itself, never before have so many people come under the influence of Western culture and never before have people had such easy access to the ideas of others. The days are over when an enthnographer can settle down among an isolated untouched people and study their age-old traditions. In the course of field study, every anthropologist today will find that if one wants to record truly indigenous customs and beliefs, they are to be found—if at all—only in the minds and memories of the old men and women. All too often the young people care little for the "old ways" and are more interested in dressing, behaving, and making money like the "white man." Thus, an accurate study of almost any nonliterate people today must of necessity take into consideration the influence of foreign (usually Western) cultures on the way of life.

Most anthropologists feel they can make their greatest contribution in studying the processes of culture change. Change is certain, but the results of change cannot always be foreseen. Anthropology may never formulate *laws* of cultural change but, as Gillin puts it,

> If we know the conditions under which culture operates and the lines of its internal integration and coordination, we are able to predict within certain limits what form and direction cultural change will take. . . . As prediction becomes possible, so control and manipulation of changes are possible. (1948:568—69)

PRINCIPLES OF CULTURAL DYNAMICS

Although anthropology has just scratched the surface in its understanding of cultural dynamics, the following are well-agreed-upon principles.

Selective Borrowing. Borrowing is always selective. If a trait or a trait complex is to find acceptance in another culture, it must have utility, compatibility, and meaning in the adopting culture. What is more, it must lie within the area of culture where change is acceptable. We in America are exposed to all sorts of foreign ideas, but we incorporate only some of them into our cultural system. We accept Schiaparelli gowns from the French but not national socialism from the Swedes or hari-kari from the Japanese. The fashion world, like the world of mechanical gadgets in America, is one where the new and the novel have high prestige. But even here there is the matter of compatibility and meaning to be considered. The Schiaparelli dress has features that are definitely Western and in harmony with many American accessories. It is doubtful if a Siamese or Japanese fashion house utilizing traditional style features of those countries in their dresses could ever become as sought after as this famous French house. The Oriental dress with the slit skirt·or the Indian sari may have brief fad acceptance in America, but it is unlikely that their influence would be lasting.

National socialism, on the other hand, appears, to the majority of Americans who value rugged individualism and a Jeffersonian variety of democracy to be a direct threat to personal freedom and individual initiative. Not only is hari-kari or any form of sanctioned suicide in direct opposition to the very foundation of American religious principles, but its practice is completely inconceivable to Americans. It involves a concept of "face" that has never become institutionalized in Western culture.

A new element coming into a culture has a tough gauntlet to run. It faces the vested interests, the difficulty of finding a congruous slot in an integrated cultural configuration, and also the temporal factor—it may be introduced before its time is ripe.

Rates of Transmission. Cultural transmission takes place at different rates. This point is closely tied to our earlier one concerning the selectivity of borrowing. Also, a thing that is immediately seen to be more useful than an existing trait stands a good chance of gaining quick adoption, provided it can easily be integrated into the system and provided that it does not encounter the force of vested interests. The anthropological literature would tend to support the fact that simplicity in a cultural element facilitates transfer. Also, a trait of a nonsymbolic nature can be digested more rapidly by a culture than a symbolic one, and form transfers with greater speed than function, a fact known all too well to missionaries in various parts of the world who have been very encouraged by the speed with which church attendance, hymn singing, and Bible reading have been accepted by a native people, but have then found that the outward forms of Christianity are much more quickly acquired than the regenerating influence it is meant to have in their lives. Furnas recalls a number of incidents in Oceania where this phenomenon was present:

> The newly-converted natives of Anaa (Tuamotu) seized and plundered a ship suspected of pearling without a license, and then trooped in a body to church to give thanks for their loot. (1948:277)

> On Tubuai (Australs) natives converted by L. M. S. teachers from
> Raiatea fought bloodily with natives converted by L. M. S. teachers from
> Tahiti over whether hymns should be sung standing or sitting, a matter
> which the L. M. S. had neglected to standardize. (1948:279)

Melville J. Herskovits has called attention to the concept of *cultural focus* as being a major consideration in the rate of cultural transmission. Herskovits believes that

> the greatest variation in form is to be found in the aspect of a culture that is
> focal to the interests of a people. This variation, by implication suggests that
> the focal aspect has undergone greater changes than other elements. . . .
> We find that where cultures are in free contact, the focal aspect will be
> likely to be the one where new elements are most hospitably received.
> (1949:549–50)

In a work entitled *Cultural Dynamics and Administration* (1953a) the late Felix Keesing analyzed a number of acculturation situations and generalized that the areas of culture that tend to resist change are those pertaining to basic survival, security, integrity, value, and problem-solving. Specifically, he found the more conservative aspects to be those having to do with:

1. Psychosomatic conditioning—traditional bodily training patterns relating to digestion, elimination, rest, energy expenditure, or mental sets such as friendliness, enjoyment, curiosity, worry, or fear.
2. Communication—vocal and written language habits by which people share and transmit experience.
3. Primary group relations—ascribed statuses of age and sex, crisis points in the life cycle, and intimate rights and responsibilities of household and immediate kin groups.
4. Prestige status maintenance—conserving established superior statuses, entrenched authority, and monopolistic skills.
5. Territorial security—historically entrenched solidarity and loyalty of a people sharing common living space and common leadership.
6. Ideological security—basic intellectual and religious beliefs and their ritual and emotional associations.

On the other hand, Keesing found that the areas which prove most malleable in the face of change are those concerned with (1) technological techniques for solving problems, provided the new approaches are demonstrably superior; (2) cultural elements of taste and self-expression which can be chosen voluntarily—dress styles, art styles, recreational activities, and other luxury goods and services; and (3) mass social structures over and above the primary group level—neighborhood and tribal relationships.

From the writings in personality and culture comes still further light on the problem of conservatism and the lack of it. There is a good deal of evidence to support the theory that those aspects of a culture learned through conditioning as a child will tend to be more resistant to change than those things acquired as an adult. Examples of stable elements are language, facial expression, moral and ethical standards, and basic food preferences.

An interesting example of how things learned as an adult can be more easily changed than those things learned as a child, is to be found in Margaret Mead's writings about cultural change in the Manus Islands. In 1938 Mead found the Manus people plagued with a variety of taboos and avoidances, a great inequality between the sexes, and a puritanical sex code that equated the sex act with excretion. She also found that most of these unpleasant and restricting aspects were part of the adult world only. One might say that the young were exposed to the better side of the value system. From mere babies they were trained to be independent, alert, and resourceful. Children did not play at adult activities, and therefore the adult world of ritual, taboo, and fear was little known to them. Thus, when change came crashing down on these Melanesian people through the medium of World War II, the personality traits gained in childhood aided them in accepting new ideas and techniques. The later-acquired values of the adult world were replaced by a European value system, which proved to be more satisfying.

Involuntary Change

The relative difference in rate of adoption of culture items also depends to a great extent on whether change is voluntary or involuntary. As Keesing states: "The fieldworker . . . is likely . . . to encounter numerous case examples of artibrary manipulation in terms of governmental, missionary, or other outsiders or by internal elites or other authorities: the process is doubtless as old as human history" (1953:81).

Examples of such change are easily found. If it had not been for the insistence of Hiram Bingham and his Yankee missionaries, the Hawaiian women would probably have taken considerable time in exchanging tapa cloth wrap-arounds for Mother Hubbards. And many a South American Indian has given up headhunting prematurely at the request of government officials. However, Herskovits maintains that there are certain areas of culture which are resistant to any amount of manipulation. While it has been pointed out that the *focus* aspects of a culture are often areas where there is great interest in new ideas. Herskovits also observes that "in situations where one people is dominated by another, and pressure is brought against customs lying in the focal aspect, retention will be achieved by devious ways. . . ." (1949:550). What is meant by "devious ways" is that the customs will either go underground or they will be reinterpreted so that they will appear less objectionable to the dominant culture.

Reinterpretation

Because no two cultural configurations are exactly the same, and because a cultural configuration is an integrated and compatible bundle of meaningful traits, complexes, and patterns, a borrowed item will often have to be reinterpreted to have meaning and utility in the borrower's culture. Reinterpretation may be defined as the process whereby either the form or the function of a trait is altered to enhance its meaning or compatibility in the borrowing culture. An example of this principle at the level of material culture is the case of the New Guinea canoe paddle that moved inland. A common pattern in parts of this island is for new ideas (perhaps obtained through voyages to other islands) to originate in the coastal villages. As members of the inland tribes come to the coast to trade, they also observe the new artifacts, ceremonies, and ideas of their more sophisticated seagoing neighbors and often carry home a few new ideas to try out themselves. On one of these visits an inland native became enamoured with a canoe paddle he observed in one of the coast villages. The laurel-leaf shape of the blade pleased him greatly so he purchased it and eagerly bore it home with him. The main problem was that in his area there were no navigable rivers or lakes, thus no canoes to propel. If the paddle were to catch on in this new setting, its function would have to be changed. In this particular case our story has a happy ending, for a few weeks later when a large ceremony was held several of the men appeared twirling dance batons shaped very much like laurel-leaf-bladed canoe paddles.

A number of cultural traits have undergone reinterpretation before they could be adopted into American culture. A fascinating example is the form of Italian pizza in the Middle West. Pizza probably diffused to the United States in the twenties or thirties but remained a localized delicacy in certain eastern seaboard states until the end of World War II. At this time it rapidly spread to every part of the country. Originally, this Italian pie was made with mozarella or scamorza cheese, tomatoes, highly spiced sausage, oregano spice, and a crust made of flour, water, olive oil, and yeast. Although this type of pizza is still found in most eastern cities, and in midwestern ones as well, in many cases the dish has been reinterpreted to meet midwestern taste preferences for bland food. Authentic Italian pizza in such states as Kansas, Missouri, Iowa, Nebraska, or the Dakotas is often considered

Reinterpretation—a Samoan *fale* of traditional design is "thatched" with galvanized iron rather than sugar cane leaves.

too spicy; therefore, restaurants or supermarkets sell pizzas that are topped with American process cheese, have no oregano at all, and, in place of spiced sausage, hamburger or even tuna fish rounds out the Americanized version. In many home recipes, the crust is made of biscuit mix. Although the Italians would hardly recognize it, it still carries the name pizza and has become extremely popular.

A final example of reinterpretation in American culture concerns the Maori greenstone fertility pendants, which are known as *hei tiki*. This borrowing situation is described by the Maori anthropologist Sir Peter Buck as follows:

> The Red Cross in Auckland brought joy to the hearts of numbers of convalescent American soldiers during World War II by giving each one a small nephite *tiki* as a good luck talisman. As a result a new myth was born, for in the United States the *tiki* is regarded not as a fructifying symbol for women but as a protective war amulet for men. (1950:301)

Borrowing Is Reciprocal

Whenever two societies live in continuous first-hand contact, borrowing is a two-way process. For a long time it was believed that prolonged contact between a "civilized" and a "primitive" culture resulted in the latter's soaking up all of the ideas and traits of the former but having none of its own borrowed. This, of course, was built on the idea that a "superior" culture had nothing to learn or take from an "inferior" one. No anthropologists today would venture such a statement, for they know that advanced technology does not necessarily make a culture superior. We know that when members of different cultures meet day after day, both give and take cultural traits. We may be certain that the New England colonists considered themselves vastly superior to the American aborigines with whom they lived side by side; yet we know that 300 or more years of contact have resulted in a great deal of cultural borrowing in both directions. The white man brought the horse but borrowed the canoe; many American Indians today live in European style houses, but many Americans spend at least their two weeks' vacation living in a tent. American Indian Jim Thorpe was a nationally known All-American college and pro-football player, while many an Ivy League college student plays on a varsity lacrosse team. In the area of foodstuffs, the white man got somewhat the better of the deal. He borrowed corn, beans, squash, hominy, popcorn, wild rice, melons, cocoa, tomatoes, pumpkins, potatoes, and turkeys. Probably no other American product has experienced such mass consumption or created such wealth for its producers as tobacco—also a gift from the American Indian. One often wonders what the names of scores of towns, rivers, counties, and states might have been if it had not been for their Indian namesakes, and one even wonders if our constitution might not have been somewhat different if it had not been for its prototype in the League of the Iroquois. Shifting our focus from North American to South American acculturation, and considering Negro-white as well as Indian-white contacts, we find in the writing of Melville J. Herskovits that the same type of mutual borrowing existed there. He writes:

> Negroes who were brought to Brazil influenced the culture of the dominant Portuguese, themselves migrants, and subject to Indian influence as well. These varied influences are to be seen merged in such widely differing aspects of modern Brazilian life as the cuisine, the social structure, beliefs of various sorts, current musical forms and linguistic usages, to say nothing of the extensive retentions of African belief and behavior that were maintained by the Africans themselves. (1949:533)

Borrowing and Fusion of Cultures

Where there is continuous first-hand contact between groups with different cultures we might expect, although it is not inevitable, that the two will eventually fuse their cultural systems. Just because two people live side by side does not mean that they will accept each other's ideas. History records that the Hakka and Punti people lived side by side in a valley of Southern China for nearly a thousand years without exchanging any cultural traits whatsoever.

More typically, however, two peoples living in such circumstances would be involved in much mutual borrowing that would lead ultimately to a fusion of culture known as *assimilation*. Assimilation represents a situation not where one society abandons its culture in favor of its neighbors but rather where the two will fuse to form a new society and culture. When this happens, the final product will be a culture having elements of the two contact societies represented in varying proportions. There will also be some new traits that were found in neither of the parent cultures. An example of assimilation in America is cited by Linton:

> Thus the Italians in America usually lose their identity as a distinct society by the third or fourth generation and accept the culture in which they then find themselves. At the same time this culture is not the same which their ancestors encountered on arrival. It has been enriched by the American acceptance of such originally Italian elements as a popular interest in grand opera, spaghetti dinners. . . . (1936:355)

and we might add art movies and Ferrari sports cars.

And of Europe, Kroeber writes:

> The Norman and Saxon fusion after 1066 is a familiar instance. Within three centuries these two strains were assimilated in culture, speech, and mainly in blood. English civilization was greatly enriched by the infusion of the large Norman-French element into the Anglo-Saxon, so that by say 1400 it had come to approximate more nearly French culture in its level; but of course it remained definitely distinct from French. (1948:429)

PITCAIRN ISLAND ASSIMILATION

One of the most controlled scientific studies of cultures in contact was that carried out by Harry Shapiro on Pitcairn Island. The reader will perhaps recall that in the year 1789 a mutiny occurred on H. M. S. *Bounty* while it was under the command of Lt. William Bligh. Immediately after casting Bligh and several loyal crew members adrift in the *Bounty's* cutter, the 25 mutineers led by Fletcher Christian sailed to nearby Tahiti where they took aboard 12 Tahitian women and 6 Tahitian men. Selecting Pitcairn Island as their retreat from justice, the fugitives founded a society that would exist in complete isolation for nearly 70 years. The Pitcairn culture that emerged had, as might be expected, traits that were partly Tahitian, partly English, and partly original. Shapiro, who studied the society and culture in 1934, describes the strange blend of traits in the construction of their houses. He writes,

> We find them . . . building houses ingeniously put together, the frame mortised, the walls ingeniously constructed of roughly hewn planks fitted into slotted uprights, the interiors provided with bunks as in a ship's cabin. The roof, however, was thatched in the Tahitian manner. (1953:41)

Table 4 describes the kaleidoscopic nature of assimilation.

TABLE 4 Origin of elements of culture in Pitcairn (Shapiro 1953:42)

	Tahitian	English	Original
The household arts:			
Underground oven	+		
Food preparation	+		
Tapa-making	+		
Use of calabash	+		
Dress style	+		
Hats	+		
Houses:			
Building materials		+	
Structure		+	+
Roof thatch	+		
Arrangement			+
Household equipment:			
Furniture		+	
"Linens"	+		
Lighting	+		
Fishing:			
Gear		+	
Methods	+	+	
Boats	+		+
Agriculture:			
Tools		+	
Methods	+	+	
Family life			+
Social life:			
Social organization		+	
Separation of sexes at meals	+		
Position of women			+
Dance	+		
Music	+	+	
Surf-riding	+		
Kite-flying	+	+	
Private ownership of land		+	
Common fund			+
Education		+	
Religion		+	+

Diffusion and Culture Complexity

A previous chapter pointed out that the more complex societies of the world have been those most exposed to the cultures of others, for the cross-fertilization of ideas enriches any culture by providing it with innovations it may not develop itself; but too frequently differences in the level of cultural accomplishments have been explained in terms of superior or inferior intelligence. Ralph Linton points out the embarrassing fact that even the most sophisticated of societies have invented only a small percentage of the cultural traits they utilize. To get some idea of the amount of borrowing that has been necessary in order to produce our complex American culture let us look at the day of an average American as humorously described by Linton:

> Our solid American citizen awakens in a bed built on a pattern which originated in the Near East but which was modified in Northern Europe before it was transmitted to America. He throws back covers made from cotton, domesticated in India, or linen, domesticated in the Near East, or wool from sheep, also domesticated in the Near East, or silk, the use of which was discovered in China. All of these materials have been spun and woven by processes invented in the Near East. He slips into his moccasins, invented by the Indians of the Eastern woodlands, and goes to the bathroom, whose fixtures are a mixture of European and American inventions, both of recent date. He takes off his pajamas, a garment invented in India, and washes with soap invented by the ancient Gauls. He then shaves, a masochistic rite which seems to have been derived from either Sumer or ancient Egypt.
>
> Returning to the bedroom, he removes his clothes from a chair of southern European type and proceeds to dress. He puts on garments whose form originally derived from the skin clothing of the nomads of the Asiatic steppes, puts on shoes made from skins tanned by a process invented in ancient Egypt and cut to a pattern derived from the classical civilizations of the Mediterranean, and ties around his neck a strip of bright-colored cloth which is a vestigial survival of the shoulder shawls worn by the seventeenth-century Croatians. Before going out for breakfast he glances through the window, made of glass invented in Egypt, and if it is raining puts on overshoes made of rubber discovered by the Central American Indians and takes an umbrella, invented in Southeastern Asia. Upon his head he puts a hat made of felt, a material invented in the Asiatic steppes.
>
> On his way to breakfast he stops to buy a paper, paying for it with coins, an ancient Lydian invention. At the restaurant a whole new series of borrowed elements confronts him. His plate is made of a form of pottery invented in China. His knife is of steel, an alloy first made in southern India, his fork a medieval Italian invention, and his spoon a derivation of a Roman original. He begins breakfast with an orange, from the eastern

Mediterranean, a canteloupe from Persia, or perhaps a piece of African watermelon. With this he has coffee, an Abyssinian plant, with cream and sugar. Both the domestication of cows and the idea of milking them originated in the Near East, while sugar was first made in India. After his fruit and first coffee he goes on to waffles, cakes made by a Scandinavian technique from wheat domesticated in Asia Minor. Over these he pours maple syrup, invented by the Indians of the Eastern woodlands. As a side dish he may have the egg of a species of bird domesticated in Indo-China, or thin strips of the flesh of an animal domesticated in Eastern Asia which have been salted and smoked by a process developed in northern Europe.

When our friend has finished eating he settles back to smoke, an American Indian habit, consuming a plant domesticated in Brazil in either a pipe, derived from the Indians of Virginia, or a cigarette, derived from Mexico. If he is hardy enough he may even attempt a cigar, transmitted to us from the Antilles by way of Spain. While smoking he reads the news of the day, imprinted in characters invented by the ancient Semites upon a material invented in China by a process invented in Germany. As he absorbs the accounts of foreign troubles he will, if he is a good conservative citizen, thank a Hebrew deity in an Indo-European language that he is 100 per cent American. (1936:326−27)

Modernization

In the last two or three decades there has been an overwhelming impact on the lifestyle of pre-industrial peoples emanating from a special kind of cultural change called *modernization*. As early as 1966 S. N. Eisenstadt wrote, "Modernization and aspirations to modernity are probably the most overwhelming and the most permeating features of the contemporary scene. Most nations are nowadays caught in its web" (1966:1).

Just what modernization represents for people and societies that come under its influence is best summed up by Donald O. Cowgill who sees it as a change from a relatively *rural way of life* based on (1) use of animate power, (2) limited technology, (3) relatively undifferentiated institutions, and (4) a parochial and traditional outlook and set of values, toward a predominately *urban way of life* based on (1) use of inanimate sources of power, (2) highly developed scientific technology, (3) highly differentiated institutions matched by segmented individual roles, and (4) a cosmopolitan outlook which emphasizes efficiency and "progress."

Modernization might be described more concisely as a movement in the direction of urbanization, industrialization, and secularization although not necessarily "Westernization." While modernization involves total societies, it also affects the individual. Individuals accept modernity in varying degrees and in various aspects of their lifestyle. In other words, the process is not unidimensional and involves many variables—standard of living, religious belief, personal aspirations, literacy and education, political behavior, economic participation, and world wisdom.

Modernization is not a simple phenomenon, and anthropologists and scholars in a number of disciplines are just beginning to understand its dynamics and effects. Everett Rogers, for example, in his book *Modernization Among Peasants, The Impact of Communication* (1969) points out that

> Modernization has often been equated with Europeanization and/or Westernization. . . . This implies that the source or impetus for change necessarily comes from Europe or from the Western nations. . . . Such a view is much too limiting and in many ways inaccurate. . . . Modernization is a *synthesis* of old and new ways and, as such, varies in different environments.
>
> It has often been implied that all modernization is "good." No such value judgment is intended in our definition. Modernization brings change, which may very well produce not only benefit but also conflict, pain, and relative disadvantage. (1969:14–15)

Ramifications of Change

Before closing our discussion of cultural change, it will be worthwhile to comment on the ramifications of change in terms of social integration, emotional stability of the individual, and group morale. In situations of change, people and cultures must adjust and the problem is to achieve the least amount of personal and group disorganization with the amount of change that is inevitable in our modern industrial world. There are anthropologists who might favor a "keep primitives primitive" policy believing that they will be better off in the long run. While this is probably true, it is a most artificial and unworkable solution that most primitives would themselves oppose. The answer is not to stop change but to channel it, or at least attain some measure of success in predicting what will happen under certain conditions of change, as for example if the wrong kind of change is forced upon a people or if it comes too rapidly. Societies can become so disorganized through revolutionary change that they can completely lose their cultural identity. The Inca made it a policy to destroy the cultures they conquered. By moving out great numbers of the population and replacing them with people from foreign cultures they were successful in dividing peoples and imposing both their rule and their culture on them.

A similar but perhaps less studied result occurred in much of Melanesia. Here, colonial administration coupled with blackbirding, economic exploitation, and mission ardor succeeded in breaking down the culture to such an extent that many of the people lost their will to live. Rivers reported in 1922 that some peoples were unwilling to bear or care for children and they took no interest in educating or socializing them. Thus, they existed as a people without hope and without faith in their old culture or an understanding of the new.

STEEL AXES IN AUSTRALIA

The effects of what might be considered a very minor change are often unpredictable and may be demoralizing to a highly integrated cultural and social system. Such was the case among the Yir Yoront group of northeastern Australia. One would hardly think that a change in ax blades could precipitate a chain of events that would undermine the foundations of the whole society, but that is exactly what happened.

Lauriston Sharp, who studied these Australian aborigines from 1933 to 1935, tells us that prior to the introduction of steel ax blades, the blades were made of stone. They were produced and owned only by the men but used to a great extent by the women and children, and there was a pattern of borrowing axes from specific male relatives. This helped maintain a system of superordination-subordination. During the dry season fiesta-like tribal gatherings were held which featured exchanges between traditional trading partners. These occasions were anxiously awaited as it was sometimes possible to acquire a whole year's supply of stone ax heads from one's trading partner.

When steel axes began to appear in the area, the local mission purchased a supply of them and began to dispense them to worthy parishioners. "By winning the favor of the mission staff," Sharp writes, "a woman might be given a steel axe. This was clearly intended to be hers. The situation was quite different from that involved in borrowing an axe from a male relative, with the result that a woman called such an axe 'my' steel axe, a possessive form she never used for a stone axe" (1952:83–84). Not only were the steel axes introducing new linguistic forms but also a more serious social situation "in which a wife or young son . . . need no longer bow to the husband or father, who was left confused and insecure as he asked to borrow a steel axe from them" (1952:86).

The whole concept of ownership became confused, and stealing and trespassing began to occur. The annual festival, so anticipated by trading partners, declined because a single steel ax might last several years. As this festival waned, so did interest in the religious and social events that were associated with it. Thus, we see that a steel ax blade introduced by people who conscientiously wanted to help the Yir Yoront produced a situation that is summed up by Sharp as follows:

> The most disturbing effects of the steel axe, operating in conjunction with other elements also being introduced from the white man's several subcultures, developed in the realm of traditional ideas, sentiments and values. These were undermined at a rapidly mounting rate, without new conceptions being defined to replace them. The result was a mental and moral void which foreshadowed the collapse and destruction of all Yir Yoront culture, if not, indeed, the extinction of the biologic group itself. (1952:85)

Profiting from the experience of what happened to the Yir Yoront and other broken cultures, students of change such as Felix Keesing have drafted generalizations about cultural change and disorganization such as the following, which prove very valuable rules of thumb:

> So far as groups and individuals in a dynamic situation have their self-esteem little impaired, retain confidence that they are keeping in touch with the best sources of security, power and prestige, and so maintain a high level of morale, they will tend to remain "well integrated"; cultural fundamentals are likely to be highly persistent, and voluntary cultural change may occur with a minimum of tension and disorganization. So far as they feel superior, in relation to groups and individuals with whom they are in contact, their culture may be held to the more firmly, or change may go further with little tension. By contrast, to the extent that groups and individuals come to feel themselves inferior, lose confidence in their basic sources of security, power and prestige, and so lapse in morale, the way is opened for extensive and even drastic change. Unless reasonably satisfying cultural substitutes can be found, extreme disorganization and emotional stress will occur. (1953:89)

In ancient Samoa there was a sport for high chiefs known as *seuga lupe* (pigeon-netting). The platforms on which the chiefs stood while trying to snare the birds were often set up out on the reef. On rough days there was always the possibility of being washed off the platform. This explains the meaning of the Samoan proverbial saying *Seu le manu ae taga'i le galu* (Catch the pigeon but look out for the waves) or in modern terms as the motto of American Samoa "Progress with Caution." Many a trusteeship or colonial or newly independent government would do well to bear this proverb in mind, for every culture that fades away and dies, no matter how unimportant it is in world affairs, is a loss to humankind as a whole.

Survival and Identity Societies

In 1975 a California psychologist, William Glasser, wrote *The Identity Society* in which he presented a four-stage scheme of human development based on survival and identity considerations. The first stage,

Religion, ceremonials, dancing, and singing developed in the Primitive Identity stage. (Courtesy Willis Tilton and Wichita State University.)

which Glasser called the "primitive survival society," began about 4 million years ago and lasted until about a half million years ago. During this period the primary goal of early hominids was survival in a rigorous, hostile environment. The theme of survival was cooperation, and natural selection favored those individuals and societies with sufficient intelligence to recognize the advantages of cooperation and who had the willingness to implement it.

As early hominid forms evolved into higher levels of intelligence a half million years ago, awareness of the advantages of cooperation was supplemented by insights into the need for humans to be involved as individuals in one another's affairs, and this laid the groundwork for the second stage, the "primitive identity society." At this stage humans found time to have fun, to love and be loved, to recognize loneliness and how not to be lonely. Ties of kinship, elaborate rituals and ceremonies, dancing, singing, and religious belief systems developed. The pleasures of sex led to large numbers of offspring, but there was room in the system for all. When an area became overcrowded some people would move to new areas, retaining ties with the old group in clan and extended family relationships. Wars and conflicts arose, not to acquire territory, but for personal status and glory. Glasser believes that remnants of this stage are to be found among the Kalahari Bushmen and the Cheyenne and other American Indian groups as they existed during the nineteenth century.

Physical needs of the primitive identity societies placed little strain upon the environment, but as societies developed an agricultural base 10,000 years ago, the concomitant expansion of population demanded ever greater production. Land used for farming became valuable and possession of land or the lack of it motivated wars of conquest. This, according to Glasser's scheme, ushered in the third stage, the "civilized survival society." Rather than reverting to cooperation as in the savage survival stage, societies and individuals now saw each other rather than the physical environment as the hostile adversary. Aggressors plundered, enslaved, and destroyed all who opposed them. Any guilt could be overcome by believing that these measures were essential to one's own survival. Primitive identity societies were eliminated by the power and hostility of the conquerors. The disappearance of the American Indian exemplifies this: the invading whites armed with a concept of Manifest Destiny were survival-oriented and ruthless.

Paradoxically, only after a society had made itself relatively secure from aggression from others could it again concern itself with identity, that is, with human rights and privileges. In a few nations like Switzerland, Sweden, Canada, and the United States this concern has been implemented at least to some degree. All civilized survival societies are and have been power hierarchies with the top strata being composed of the strong few, the bottom represented by the powerless masses bearly at the subsistence level, and the middle classes, obedient and committed to the system, in between. For 10,000 years this has been the order of things and many believe it will always be so because it is the natural order of things, a divine decree.

Although a great deal of energy has been expended on perpetuating this myth, within the last quarter century a new stage has begun to emerge which is labeled by Glasser, the "civilized identity society." This is a society motivated by respect for human welfare and dignity. Led by the youth of the world, this new society is recognizing that many problems are global in scope and that no single nation should be the sole recipient of the world's benefits, privileges, or problems. Pollution, famine, disease, warfare are everyone's problems and it is impossible to isolate their effects. The civilized identity society recognizes that everyone has a right and a responsibility to participate in both problems and solutions, that our resources are finite, and that limitations must be placed on the expenditure of resources that are nonrenewable. It also believes that limits must be placed upon population growth.

Glasser's scheme of changing conditions and changing values may not be altogether accurate historically and may be more important philosophically than scientifically but it does explain a great deal about the happenings of history and it provides us with a unique frame of reference for interpreting human annals.

Summary

Both in newly emerging nations and in well-established industrial ones, the forces of cultural change are operative. This has always been the case, but the rates of change have accelerated enormously since the middle of the twentieth century. Social and cultural changes result from both internal forces and from forces outside the society. Such things as climate changes, population pressures, the introduction of new elements by innovators and reformers, or the little-understood phenomenon known as culture fatigue may contribute to change within the society. Outside influences include military invasion, missionaries, traders, or simply the borrowing from neighboring societies. However, traits are selectively accepted: some will be readily incorporated into the system, others will be accepted slowly and deliberately, ignored, or openly opposed. Each of the cultures in contact will be both borrower and donor regardless of their differences in the level of technological development. Cultural fusion, reinterpretation, and conflict may attend the meetings of cultures. But cultures will inevitably change, and anthropologists believe that this is the area in which their most productive research can take place, for we live in a shrinking world experiencing the impact of modernization and ever-greater global awareness and interaction.

Understanding Other Cultures 18

When a hunting band of Australian aborigines encounters strangers they are immediately considered to be enemies unless someone can discover some kinsman among the party and thus establish some common basis for understanding. If this is not possible, the strangers will be driven off or killed. While this rather narrow and unfriendly point of view has been unanimously condemned by the Western world on the grounds that it is quite uncivilized, the West has given little indication that its learned enlightenment has led it to develop adequate means for understanding the strange and different cultures of the world. It would seem that the tendency to look down on other people with different ways of life as inferiors or even as potential enemies in order to bolster one's own personal or national ego is as old as time itself. Cicero once wrote Attilus, advising him thus: "Whatever you do, do not buy English slaves, for the English people are so dull and stupid that they are not fit to be slaves. . . ." This, of course, was during a period of Roman domination, but at an earlier period, when the Greeks were in a position of power, they referred to the Romans as "barbarians, good enough to kill and fight, but devoid of culture and having base souls." Going back even farther in history we find that the Egyptians felt that the Greeks "are but children . . . who . . . have no history, no past, no adequate civilization."

Usually the claims of superiority have been based on evidence of cultural differences, and always there is the underlying feeling that if another people were of equal quality they would not behave so differently. When Europeans first observed the behavior of nonindustrial peoples living in the remote and isolated corners of the world, they saw very little to admire in their way of life and categorically labeled them "savages," "barbarians," and "primitives." Although the last term is used by anthropologists even today, it *does* carry overtones of crudeness and childlikeness, and many anthropologists prefer more objective labels such as "preliterate" or "nonliterate." When we turn to the early accounts of primitive people written by explorers, government administrators, and even scientists, we find no end of derogatory assessments of native minds as judged by native manners.

In the late eighteenth century the French naturalist Comte de Buffon described the North American Indian as having "no vivacity, no activity of mind; the activity of his body is less an exercise, a voluntary motion, than a necessary action caused by want; relieve him of hunger and thirst, and you deprive him of the active principle of all his movements; he will rest stupidly upon his legs or lying down entire days" (1866:464). In 1839 the American scientist Samuel G. Morton wrote that "the mental faculties of the Eskimo from infancy to old age, present a continued childhood; they reach a certain limit and expand no further." Of the Australian aborigine he said, "It is not probable that this people as a body are capable of any other than their slight degree of civilization" (1839 *passim*).

There is a good deal of evidence that having first-hand experience in dealing with a foreign culture did little to improve cross-cultural attitudes. Take for example the editorial appearing in a Topeka, Kansas newspaper in 1867 which described American Indians as "a set of miserable, dirty, lousy, blanketed, thieving, lying, sneaking, murdering, graceless, faithless, gut-eating skunks . . . whose immediate and final extermination all men, except Indian agents and traders, should pray for." And American Indians, by and large, were no more impressed by white men. We are told that it was a periodic practice of Benjamin Franklin to finance the education of a few Indian boys at Williamsburg College, but one of the tribal chiefs soon put a stop to this, stating that when the "educated" boys returned they were "bad runners, ignorant of every means of living in the woods, unable to bear either cold or hunger, knew neither how to build a cabin, take a deer, or kill an enemy, spoke our languages imperfectly, were therefore neither fit for warriors, hunters, nor counsellors; they were totally good for nothing."

Some scholars have couched their derogatory views of primitive people in elaborate theories. One social philosopher, Lucien Lévy-Bruhl, who was recognized as an authority on the subject of primitive mentality. His position was that primitive people are prelogical. This meant that their minds were entirely governed by waves of emotional force developed in ritual activities. They did not therefore analyze and they did not seek explanations. Primitives, he felt, did not understand cause-and-effect relationships. Westerners, on the other hand, had been able to progress because they had been able to develop a purely rational and scientific pattern of thought, totally divorced from the pressures of emotion. Even today there are many seemingly intelligent people who feel that the majority of aborigines justifiably warrant the name "primitive" because they are more emotional, less reasonable, and less rational than we.

For most people of the Western world their own moral and technological superiority was beyond question and was one of the realities of life to be imparted to one's offspring. We find an example of such Western wisdom even in the nursery literature produced by Robert Louis Stevenson.

> Little Indian, Sioux or Crow,
> Little frosty Eskimo,
> Little Turk or Japanee,
> O! don't you wish that you were me?
>
> You have seen the scarlet trees
> And the lions over seas;
> You have eaten ostrich eggs,
> And turned the turtles off their legs

Such a life is very fine,
But it's not so nice as mine:
You must often, as you trod,
Have wearied not to be abroad.

You have curious things to eat,
I am fed on proper meat;
You must dwell beyond the foam,
But I am safe and live at home.

Little Indian, Sioux or Crow,
Little frosty Eskimo,
Little Turk or Japanee,
O! don't you wish that you were me?

Labels

As is true of many social problems, much of the difficulty in cross-cultural understanding arises out of the use of labels and stereotypes. Although there are quite detailed and objective definitions of such terms as *primitive* and *civilized*, Westerners often think of the latter term as symbolic of total cultural superiority and let it go at that. It is no wonder that anthropologists like Goldenweiser, in trying to tip the balance, suggest that civilization should be synonymous with culture. In keeping with this idea, he makes reference to "Australian civilization," "Hopi civilization," and "Masai civilization" in his writing.

V. Gordon Childe (1950) has drawn up a very adequate set of criteria for recognizing a civilization. They are

1. a great increase in the size of the settlement.
2. the institution of tribute or taxation with resulting central accumulation of capital.
3. monumental public works.
4. the art of writing.
5. the beginnings of such exact and predictive sciences as arithmetic, geometry, and astronomy.
6. developed economic institutions making possible a greatly expanded foreign trade.
7. full-time technical specialists.
8. a privileged ruling class, and
9. the state.

It will be noted that at least six of these criteria depend greatly on technological advance. If we define civilization in terms of advanced technology, there can be little quarrel that the industrial cultures of the West are more civilized than those aboriginal populations of

Africa, Asia, Oceania, or the Americas. If we use civilization as a mere term of classification (similar to industrial), there is no real problem. If, however, we define civilization as an overall superiority in all aspects of culture, then there might be some serious question as to the civilized nature of the West. Man cannot live by gadgets alone, and there is no reason why technology should be a yardstick for evaluating the quality of a culture. It would seem logical that a truly advanced culture should exhibit a high development of philosophy, literature, the arts, and government. Yet we are embarrassed to read that Hindu intellectuals consider Americans incredibly "boorish," "materialistic," "unintellectual," and "uncivilized." While Hindu culture has never been exceptionally noteworthy for its technological developments, it has been renowned for centuries for its high development of music, literature, art, and philosophy.

Western claims of technological superiority are often based on complexity of operations, number of processes, efficiency or effectiveness of tools or procedures, and impact on human lives. When Richard Nixon became involved in the famous "kitchen debate" with Khrushchev he claimed American superiority over the Soviet system because we had produced *more* television sets. If we were to pick some aspect of culture other than technology—family, art, or religion—as a yardstick for establishing relative quality of culture and if we were to use some of the same criteria used in our claims of technological superiority we might find ourselves at somewhat of a disadvantage. Most non-Western families, for example, are larger, are more stable, and play a more supportive, pervasive role in members' lives. Most non-Western societies value art more than we, employ a greater percentage of artists, and respect and utilize works of art to a greater extent than we do. In regard to religion, if our criteria for evaluation were deities acknowledged or number of ceremonies performed (i.e., complexity of content) most religions would surpass Christianity and Judaism; and if we were to evaluate the function of religion in human lives, we would have to recognize that the belief systems of most pre-industrial people influence their every act and their every thought, while religion in America is for many, a once-a-week phenomenon with little effect on day-to-day living.

Cultural Relativism

Closely associated with the proper evaluation of the quality of cultures is the concept of *cultural relativism*. This concept, which has become a dominant theme in anthropology, is defined by Redfield as follows:

> Cultural relativism means that the values expressed in any culture are to be both understood and themselves valued only according to the way the people who carry that culture see things. In looking at a polygamous society and a monogamous society, we have no valid way to assert that the one is better than the other. Both systems provide for human needs; each has values discoverable only when we look at marriage from the point of view of the man who lives under the one system or the other. (1953:144)

Cultural relativism represents a rejection of the bigotry and self-centeredness that quite naturally develops in all cultures. This self- or group-centeredness, commonly known as *ethnocentrism*, is a very natural human reaction, and within limits, a rather essential requirement for group solidarity. If the members of a particular group had no preference for their own group, there would be nothing to hold it together. When this ingroup feeling develops to the extent that the members of a particular society feel that their way of life is so superior to all others that it is their duty to change other people to their way of thinking and doing (if necessary by force), then this attitude becomes a menace.

The concept of cultural relativism as formulated by social scientists first came into fashion some 80 years ago when William Graham Sumner, in his book *Folkways* (1906), shocked his contemporaries by maintaining that even such practices as infanticide, headhunting, slavery, cannibalism, human sacrifice, and religious prostitution were completely understandable in terms of certain cultural settings. Since they represented adaptations to particular circumstances, these customs must be honored as justified and acceptable in an objective, scientific sense.

CULTURAL RELATIVISM AT THE UNITED NATIONS

Believing that the tolerance that comes from an understanding and application of a relativistic point of view is vital to harmonious human relations, the Executive Board of the American Anthropological Association submitted in 1947 the following statement to the Commission on Human Rights of the United Nations:

> 1. The individual realizes his personality through his culture: hence respect for individual differences entails a respect for cultural differences.
> 2. Respect for differences between cultures is validated by the scientific fact that no technique of qualitatively evaluating cultures has been discovered.
> 3. Standards and values are relative to the culture from which they derive, so that any attempt to formulate postulates that grow out of the beliefs or moral codes of one culture must to that extent detract from the applicability of any Declaration of Human Rights to mankind as a whole.

What this statement basically attempts to convey is that it is unfair and undemocratic for any one society to declare that it alone has the right cultural road. It reminds people of all nations that each society should be free to solve certain cultural problems according to their own time-tested methods without condemnation from those who would choose different solutions. It pleads, in essence, not to think too harshly of the Eskimo or Bushman mother who has no other choice but to put a newborn child to death if it is born before its sibling is old enough to fend for itself. The practice of infanticide undoubtedly tears the heart out of the mother, but there is no choice if the group as a whole is to survive. Hunters who live constantly on the edge of starvation cannot be burdened with surplus helpless children. This practice, which we would define as murder, is not too foreign from our own concepts of behavior, however, when we are faced with a matter of individual versus group survival. During time of war there have been numerous occasions when it was necessary to sacrifice an individual to save the lives of an entire company of soldiers or a whole ship's crew.

The relativistic statement submitted to the United Nations further points up the fact that primitives who believe in animistic gods do so because they were raised to believe in them, and it is the cultural deviant who rejects his indigenous religion. Cultural relativism also says that a man raised in Africa has a basic human right to follow the norms of his society and practice plural marriage. It brands as irresponsible such dogmatic proclamations as that of an American industrialist who queried (and not in humor) in a graduation address, "How can we hope to sit down at a conference table and work out a satisfactory agreement for peace with men who have more than one wife?"

DIFFICULTIES OF INTERPRETATION

The United Nations statement on human rights is a good one from the standpoint that it strongly condemns bigotry and ethnocentric attitudes. On the other hand, the statement if taken literally proclaims that all cultures are equally good and all forms of behavior, no matter how destructive or inhumane they might be, should be respected. It implies that the people of New Guinea have a perfect right to take a neighbor's head as part of an ordeal validating manhood, and it would sanction the destruction of all village property standing in the way of the litter on which the corpse of a Samoan king is carried. The statement taken literally gives the nod of approval to *suttee* and other forms of ceremonial human sacrifice. The statement leaves no room for condemnation of racial segregation in America, or apartheid in South Africa, or even of the killing of millions of Jews in Germany during the Nazi regime. The majority of the world's peoples would surely hesitate to sanction much of this behavior, but a strict position of cultural relativism would demand that they respect all customs and cultures as equally good.

In the month of July, 1970 the mass media carried stories of a "tiger cage" prison at Con Son, South Vietnam. The revelation that political prisoners (not prisoners of war) were being subjected to inhumane treatment by a political regime operating largely with the economic, political, and military support of the United States shocked a substantial number of American citizens including some members of Congress. What was perhaps more shocking was a series of statements by high level governmental officials in the United States that we should withhold our condemnation of the local government because they were the outgrowth of its own value system and not ours. In other words, Americans were asked to sanction inhumane treatment of political prisoners because it was acceptable procedure in a society where life is supposedly "cheap" and brutality is more common and therefore more excusable. Life is often reputed to be "cheap" in non-Western cultures. Life is so "cheap" in such countries that a United Press International feature story in October 1979 told that a number of United States corporations were exporting banned drugs and dangerous intrauterine devices to Third World countries after federal watchdog agencies had forced them off the American market.

Few anthropologists reading of the "tiger cages" and attempts to justify them would fail to recognize that here was cultural relativism being employed to soften public reaction to certain kinds of objectionable behavior operating in a society whose value system is very different from our own.

Margaret Mead, in reviewing Melville Herskovits's posthumous book, *Cultural Relativism* (1972), wrote that this philosophical dilemma "becomes sharpest when anthropologists accustomed to espousing, wholeheartedly and without any confusions, the rights and privileges which colonial peoples should be accorded come face to face with those people, now independent nations, who now embrace more virulent forms of ethnocentrism than those under which they themselves suffered" (1974:1328).

Cultural relativism is a difficult concept to deal with and Mead points out that following the classical position rigorously "would mean that if a preliterate people were following a set of health practices that resulted in the death of their children, the anthropologist would stand aside, respecting their beliefs in the efficacy of their own system" (1974:1329). To further complicate this hypothetical situation let us say that the anthropologist *did* believe that the death of the children was necessary to keep the population in balance but let us also say that there were acculturated individuals in the group who wanted modern medicine brought in and asked the anthropologist to support them in their efforts. Now where does the anthropologist turn for guidance? It has been said that it is a lot easier to support a concept of cultural relativism when the culture to be respected is isolated, autonomous, and homogeneous.

Faced with a position of bigoted ethnocentrism at one pole and uncritical cultural relativism at the other, the student of social science often stands bewildered, trying to locate himself on the continuum. Is it possible, he asks, to prefer the benefits of modern medicine to the practices of the bush doctor and still be an objective observer of human culture? Any number of scholars would answer "Yes."

Are Some Cultures More Advanced?

Kroeber for one has stated that there is validity in maintaining that some cultures are indeed more advanced intellectually and have progressed farther than others. In a rather daring attack on the problem he has arrived at "three approaches that seem to yield at least a partial standard of what constitutes 'higher' or more advanced culture, apart from mere quantity of it" (1948:298). His three criteria for assessing cultural level are concerned with (1) magic and superstition, (2) obtrusion of physiological or anatomical considerations in social situations, and (3) cumulative quality of technology, mechanics, and science.

MAGIC AND SUPERSTITION

Kroeber feels, with respect to magic and superstition, that

> in proportion as a culture disengages itself from reliance on these, it may be said to have registered an advance. . . . When the sane and well in one culture believe what only the most ignorant, warped, and insane believe in another, there would seem to be some warrant for rating the first culture lower and the second higher. (1948:298)

Although our own Western society can hardly claim vast superiority over the primitive in the realm of magic and superstition, many primitive societies assign the cause of all physical illness to witchcraft and sorcery. Certain societies believe that charms and rituals can solve all of their problems, but others refuse to give up magical practices and superstitions when their science has proved these invalid. A special stigma should be attached to them. Many of the large medical centers in the United States boast the most advanced therapy and facilities and yet there are few hospitals in our country that have a room or floor 13 for patient use. While nearly every large newspaper in the United States has considered dropping its astrology feature, few have had the courage to do so and face the fury of its sizable public.

The May 3, 1976 issue of *Newsweek* reported that in Morganton, North Carolina, a Mrs. Joann Denton, "middle-aged, miniskirted former go-go-dancer and Sunday school teacher who works at a center for retarded children" was scheduled to go on trial under a 1952 witchcraft law for successfully predicting the date of the death of another Morganton woman at a séance. Los Angeles also has its resident witch, Louise Huebner, who describes herself as the "most successful of her family's long line of witches." She has authored *Power Through Witchcraft, The Witches Cook Book* and a syndicated column on witchcraft. She lectures and casts spells for colleges, senior citizens' groups, and women's clubs. The University of Washington even awarded her an honorary degree.

PHYSIOLOGICAL AND ANATOMICAL OBTRUSIONS

Kroeber feels that a high culture is one that has been able to throw off a preoccupation with blood, death, and decay. Some of the practices that he feels are characteristic of a less advanced culture are blood and animal sacrifice, segregation of menstruating women, anatomical mutilations, puberty rites, mummification, human sacrifice, head-hunting, and cannibalism. Civilized people, he maintains, tend to look upon such practices with "aversion, disgust, revulsion, or the shame of bad taste" (1948:300).

Again, as with the case of magic and superstition, America would have difficulty laying claim to any relative superiority when we consider our preoccupation with blood, death, and anatomical mutilations. Psychologist Karen Paige of the University of California, Berkeley, maintains that the mentrual discomfort suffered by one third of American women is a response, not to biochemical changes in the body but to frustration and anxiety resulting from menstrual taboos—particularly that forbidding sexual intercourse (Scheper-Hughes 1973).

In evaluations of America's place in Kroeber's scheme one must also consider the matter of capital punishment. David Hoekema claims the penalty "involves the planned deliberate killing of someone in custody who is not a present threat to human life or safety. Execution is not necessary to save the lives of future victims, since there are other means to secure that end" (1979:341). Today America is one of the few developed countries in the Western hemisphere with capital statutes still in force. South Africa regularly executes offenders, France uses its guillotine only on rare occasions and England may reinstate the penalty which was abolished in 1965. In America, however, there seems to be substantial support for the death penalty. Sara Terry reports that public opinion polls show that approximately 70 percent of Americans are in favor of capital punishment (1979).

War, of course, has its own set of excesses and forms of madness, but we might note in this discussion of levels of cultural progress that more than 100 badges were awarded to members of a U.S. Army battalion who could prove that they had killed a Viet Cong. One form of evidence of such an accomplishment was an ear of the slain man. A string of such trophies was proudly displayed at battalion headquarters.

TECHNOLOGY
AND SCIENCE

The area in which progress can best be measured is that of technology. Whereas it is difficult to say objectively that monogamy is more progressive than polygamy or that monotheism is more progressive than polytheism, it is possible to say that a steel axe is a better tool than a stone ax and a gun is a better weapon than a spear. The important consideration is the function of the tool. If it is to chop down a tree and a steel ax can do it in one-tenth and the time it takes with one made of stone, then the former is the more advanced tool. While it can definitely be shown that European cultures are far more advanced technologically than African or Oceanic ones, this does not necessarily imply superiority in all aspects of culture. Although the West was able to develop an atomic bomb, the act of dropping it on Japanese cities is considered by some a more savage thing than the sporadic headhunting activities of some primitives. It is somewhat embarrassing to read, in an account by Lowie, of the Eskimo who stated a desire to send missionaries to teach the white man how foolish (and primitive?) it is to go to war with one another.

Kroeber comes to a final conclusion that there *are* advanced (or adult) cultures and infantile ones. He believes that with civilization comes a greater concern for humaneness—for example, opposition to slavery, torture, capital punishment, and slaughter of prisoners of war. When any of these things are done by a supposedly civilized people (the Nazis, for example), there is a tendency to be more horrified than if they were carried out by some South American bush tribe.

Primitive cultures have been so maligned that the anthropologist, somewhat unscientifically, will often take an overly relativistic position and will not admit that Western culture is in any way superior to that of the African, American Indian, or South Sea islander. But J. C. Furnas, a very anthropologically minded journalist, made a point we are forced to consider:

> For generations the western world has bitterly blamed western man for the crime of not understanding the savage. It seems never to occur to anyone that, other things being equal, it would be equally fair to blame the savage for not understanding western man. Since that would obviously be absurd, the two sets of cultures are unmistakably on different levels, a statement that can be made without specifying higher or lower. Western man has something which neither the preliterate nor any of his ancestors possess or ever did possess, something that imposes the privilege and complicating duty of intellectual integrity, self-criticism, and generalized disinterested-

ness. If there is such a thing as the white man's burden, this is it. (1948:488)

Thus, we arrive at what Redfield describes as a "double standard of ethical judgment toward primitive peoples." In such a system, he explains,

> We do not expect the preliterate person to cultivate and protect individual freedom of thought as we expect civilized people to do. We do not blame the Veddah for failing to have a subtle graphic art. We understand how it is that the Siriono husband leaves his wife to die alone in the jungle, and we do not condemn him as we condemn the suburban husband who leaves his wife to die in a snowdrift. We do not expect a people to have a moral norm that their material conditions of life make impossible. (1953:163)

Although we may find a custom or two offensive this is no reason for assuming that the entire culture is backward and incapable of growth and development. Lisitzky suggests that we need not respect a people's cannibalism, but cannibals may have other ideas worth our consideration (1960:23). We must also be careful about condemning pre-industrial people for following customs which to us may seem inhumane or lacking in respect for human life. Their scope of thought has been stunted by isolation and shackled by vested interests, supernatural taboos, and fear of change. They have not had the opportunity to freely select or reject the ideas of thousands of minds like those of Einstein, Goethe, Aristotle, or Jefferson. We cannot completely condemn their head-hunting, infanticide, or cruelty, but we can prefer the enlightened heritage of civilization. If we can respect limitations, understand differences, and emphasize those things held in common, we then have, in essence, a skeleton for developing world understanding.

No set of traits making up any culture can be assumed to be the best possible assemblage. They are only the best combination of traits that the members of the society have conceived of or have had the opportunity to borrow from other societies. Increased contact with other peoples normally results in expanded knowledge and traits formerly considered adequate are dropped in favor of more satisfying ones. Inhumane customs continue, not because they are the best possible solutions to problems, but because within the limited experiences of the members of the society they are the best known solutions. Some customs that have no positive value at all may come into being as a result of peculiar sets of circumstances and continue to be practiced out of habit and lack of awareness of how unproductive they are. However, there can be sick cultures, just as there are sick human beings, and customs which work against the comfort and survival of the society could be products of a kind of cultural psychosis which the society cannot itself heal.

To evaluate customs cross-culturally is, of course, not likely to be simple. While many anthropologists would agree that human sacrifice and human torture must be condemned they would not agree that other customs that people of the West oppose—such as plural marriage or indigenous belief systems—are objectionable. The job of developing standards for moral judgment will be a difficult one but it should be possible to devise some such code from the writings and traditions of hundreds of great thinkers from the East and the West, from "primitive" and "civilized" societies, and from cultural practices most honored and most utilized in meeting human physical, social, and psychological needs. It must be a code based on humaneness, mutual concern, freedom of participation, and the right to live without fear, pain, or hunger. We must develop this universal standard of behavior most appropriate to human survival and happiness and then honor those societies which follow it and condemn those (even our own if necessary) which choose to violate it.

Compromise Positions

Often the cause of failures in cross-cultural understanding is the tendency to dwell too much upon cultural differences rather than attempting to find common denominatiors among cultures. On first acquaintance with any foreign people there is a temptation to be overly impressed with differences in language, dress, food, and customs, but many an anthropologist after studying a group of people for an extended period of time has discovered that in the more important aspects of daily living people are much the same the world over.

There is, in fact, a tenable position between a completely ethnocentric and a completely relativistic point of view, and that is to respect those cultures whose practices tend to correspond to a universal system of ethics and look with disfavor on those who have developed, in one way or another, customs that ignore or violate those common principles that people the world over observe in order to promote the welfare of their group and species. In an essay summarizing these worldwide ethical uniformities Ralph Linton states:

> The resemblances in ethical concepts so far outweigh the differences that a sound basis for mutual understanding between groups of different cultures is already in existence. The present difficulties seem to stem from two main sources: the first is that societies which share the same values often differ considerably in the relative importance which they attach to them. To judge from historic evidence on the changes which have taken place in various cultures, such differences are by no means insurmountable. A greater difficulty lies in the age-old tendency of every society's members to assume that ethical systems apply only within their own

tribe or nation. This attitude is difficult to overcome but the modern world is witnessing a rapid expansion of social horizons. When people learn to think of themselves as members of a single world society, it will be easy for them to agree on a single ethical system. (1952:660)

UNIVERSAL ETHICS

One of the claims frequently laid on primitive people by Europeans is that they are dishonest not only in their dealings with strangers but with each other. Although the first allegation is often true, it should be remembered that all people have a strong sense of in-group as opposed to out-group. This is certainly true in our own society as evidenced by the grocer who will set aside the best produce for his friends, relatives, and good customers but will sell the poorer quality goods to strangers and occasional shoppers. Among many people it is actually considered good fun to cheat the outsider. Linton points out that within the in-group, however,

theft is everywhere regarded as a crime and is severely punished [and] all societies recognize economic obligations of the sort involved in exchange of goods and services and the individual who fails to live up to them is punished simply but effectively by exclusion from future exchanges. Attitudes with respect to sharp practices show more diversity but each society defines the areas in which such practices are permitted and usually has rules as to what techniques are and are not permissible. (1952:657)

Closely associated with dishonesty, at least in the minds of Europeans, is the practice of lying. Although few societies value telling the truth as highly as we do, Linton's research reveals that all societies demand truth in certain areas of personal interaction and some even go so far as to demand that its members take oaths.

The statement is often made that "life is cheap" in primitive societies, but killing or maiming without justification is universally condemned. Again the problem we face is the in-group out-group differentiation. While no headhunter would wantonly take the head of a next-door neighbor, he often feels quite justified in taking one in the next village occupied by a different tribe. He, of course, would strenuously object to a "turn about is fair play" policy. And here the anthropologist feels justified in condemning a people for imposing practices on other people that they do not sanction within their own group. In this respect warfare as carried on by modern nations is as reprehensible as headhunting. When our side kills the enemy it is glorious, but when our soldiers are killed it is an atrocity.

While the attitudes toward sexual behavior vary widely from one society to another, each feels that it must regulate sex behavior. Every society prohibits incest, abhors rape, and punishes adulterers, but beyond this, what constitutes sexual morality is a matter of divergent definition. Sometimes the codes of sexual morality are stricter than those in European society but lay emphasis on entirely different things.

It also appears that every society admires the "good family man" and responsible parent. Linton writes that "Lifelong union of spouses is everywhere the ideal no matter how easy and frequent separations may be in practice. . . . Each parent must make certain contributions toward the economic life of the family [and] loyalty to the spouse is expected in most societies . . ." (1952:652).

Other phases of intrafamily behavior appear universally similar. Ideas on discipline vary widely, but sadistic and irresponsible punishment of children by parents is everywhere condemned, and violence toward a parent is usually a major crime. Every society nourishes its in-group feelings, but the family is the tightest in-group of them all. Feelings that "blood is thicker than water" are standard and ensure family stability and security for its members the world over.

Not only do humans everywhere feel a responsibility to family but we can find similar feelings for fellow group members and for the group as a whole. There are always recognized ways of caring for poor and unfortunate individuals, and as Linton points out,

> Among the values involved in ethical systems, that of ensuring the perpetuation and successful functioning of the society always takes first place. Acts which threaten the group are condemned and punished with greater severity than those which threaten only individuals. . . . All societies also recognize that there is a point beyond which the interests of the individual must be made subordinate to those of the state. (1952:659)

REAL AND IDEAL BEHAVIOR

One of the factors that often brings about intolerance and hostility toward other cultures is the common tendency to compare the worst in another culture with the best in one's own. There is also the tendency, particularly on the part of Europeans, to compare primitive *real* behavior with the *ideal* standards of the West. Americans and Englishmen often allege that Samoans are "not a religious people" in spite of their faithful church attendance, tithing-plus practices, and almost fanatical church-building activities. They maintain that the Samoans only like the ceremonial nature of the church services, and as for their church-building, it is only a method of gaining prestige for themselves and their villages. Some of this may be true, but one can hardly speak disparagingly of Samoan Christianity when one comes from a culture where a large percentage of people go to church only on Easter, and then only to show off their new spring attire.

The same principle would apply to Polynesian morality. Ideally sex activity is confined to marriage in American culture; however, a number of studies have shown that this is far from the truth, and if the actual figures could be obtained they would probably show that in his erotic behavior the average American youth differs little from his South Sea island counterpart. The people of West Africa are often bitterly criticized for their custom of plural marriage, but whether one has several wives at once or several, one after the other, as we sometimes find in America, seems only a technicality.

Wanted—A Standard for Judgment

Anthropologists have often excused their lack of effectiveness in finding solutions to pressing human problems by emphasizing that anthropology is still a young science. They say that they haven't found many answers but "they have asked some darn good questions." Anthropology is a young science (although Tylor set up shop in 1884), and it will continue to exhibit the immaturity of youth until it develops a basis for moral and ethical judgment on a cross-cultural basis. Anthropology continues to respect all cultures merely because they exist. Valuing all cultures equally is as unrealistic as other forms of stereotyping. Unless we have the courage and ingenuity to develop a yardstick for evaluating cultures we cannot judge the adequacy of any given culture to meet the needs and aspirations of its participants. Some cultures work better than others in sustaining human life and in promoting well being. Why are we afraid to say so? The world's peoples are not only objects for study they are human beings and they insist upon being treated as such. They insist upon being accepted or rejected as individuals who differ from one another in personality and behavior. Why can't we approach the multiplicity of world cultures on that basis? Edmund Leach has called for anthropologists to give up "butterfly collecting" and to resort to "inspired guessing" to find true generalizations. To this we might add, it is not enough that anthropologists classify and analyze cultural behavior; they must become critics of it as well.

Universal Stresses and Threats to Societal Survival

One method of evaluating the relative value of cultures is to determine what needs all human beings have or what stresses all human beings feel and then investigate the extent to which the individual cultures meet these needs or alleviate the stresses. In his book *Human Relations in a Changing World*, Alexander Leighton lists a number of basic assumptions derived from psychiatry, psychology, and anthropology concerning general types of stress that are believed to cause anxiety and injury to human beings if not properly dealt with by their cultural system. They are:

1. Threats to life and health.
2. Discomfort from pain, heat, cold, dampness, fatigue, and poor food.
3. Loss of means of subsistence, whether in the form of money, jobs, business, or property.
4. Deprivation of sexual satisfaction.
5. Enforced idleness.
6. Restriction of movement.
7. Isolation.
8. Threats to children, other family members, and friends.
9. Dislike, rejection, and ridicule from other people.
10. Capricious and unpredictable behavior on the part of those in authority upon whom one's welfare depends (1949:76–77).

When the above forms of stress combine to produce frustration of expectations or goals, conflict of choice between mutually incompatible desires and intentions, or circumstances creating confusions as to what is happening or what will happen in the future, then human anguish becomes particularly acute.

Some cultures carry within their value configuration and behavioral norms the seeds to their own destruction, and possibly after a certain time the society will cease to exist. In the meantime the members of that society may be experiencing great hardships and suffering. Some basis for evaluating this possibility has been provided by Aberle and others (1950) in an article in which they enumerated "conditions terminating the existence of a society." These conditions include (1) the biological extinction or dispersion of the members; (2) apathy or cessation of individual motivation (losing one's will to live); (3) war of all against all ("every man for himself"); and (4) the absorption of the society into another with loss of cultural identity but not necessarily the extinction of the members.

One World or Several?

In a book carrying the same title as this chapter, Ina Corinne Brown writes the following solemn warning:

> Our only hope of a peaceful, just and reasonably orderly world lies in the development of sufficient knowledge, insight, understanding, and maturity to live and let live, and work together to solve the common problems that are involved when two and one half billion people attempt to share an evershrinking globe. (1958:v)

Many people have felt that if the whole world were one culturally, our problems of maintaining the peace would be over. The cultural uniformity of America was of little help in maintaining peace in 1860, nor did our common cultural heritage keep us from war with Great Britain in 1775 or 1812. Thus stressing the cultural similarities between all peoples does not really guarantee that we will be able to live together in peace. It has often been said that America and the Soviet Union have trouble getting along not because they have such different cultures but rather because they are so similar. Both are products of revolutions, both have great national pride, both are technologically minded, both are anxious to spread their political doctrine, and both yearn to be world leaders.

UNITY THROUGH DIVERSITY

Although for many years humans have been recognized as part of the animal kingdom, they have a great tendency to consider themselves apart from the world of nature. Diversity is the rule of nature; in our complex world no two leaves, snowflakes, sets of fingerprints, or individuals are exactly alike. To expect all mankind to practice the same set of customs, hold the same values, and be equally motivated by common situations is contrary to this rule of nature.

Margaret Mead pointed out that "we're just beginning to realize that too much homogeneity means death. Whenever possible, life seeks variety, change and diversity" (1978:1). Pluralistic societies have difficulty with diversity, however. Mead suggests that in regard to such things as abortion, liquor use, or water fluoridation there is always someone trying to get a law passed that will make everyone conform to the same set of values or practices.

The anthropologist feels that the only answer to world harmony is unity through diversity, achievable only by an attitude of live and let live. Since all cultures have something to offer, the greatest good can accrue from recognizing the value of each and every culture, and through this proper evaluation of their worth then profiting from cross-cultural fertilization of these different points of view rather than trying to change them to a single pattern of thought and action.

Where to Start

Just "knowing" about people is not the ultimate answer in achieving a peaceful world, but it is surely a start. We have to learn to get along with each other, but the greater share of this is knowing about and being able to predict behavior. No civil engineer builds a bridge and then runs a train over it to test its strength. First they painstakingly investigate the characteristics of every piece of material that will go into the structure. They predict where the greatest stresses and strains will occur and compensate for this in the material. The anthropologist believes that a peaceful world can be achieved only by a thorough knowledge of human beings and how they function within their many cultures.

A number of years ago Mark Twain said that everyone complains about the weather but no one does anything about it. Today through the science of meteorology things are being done about it. Perhaps the actual weather can be changed very little but through accurate predictions, the disastrous effects of its flare-ups can be minimized. In like manner the science of anthropology attempts to understand people, predict their actions, and reduce points of tension. If folks are to live together successfully in an atomic age, they are going to have to learn to do it, and the greater share of this learning centers on knowing the nature of culture and the nature of human beings.

We are often tempted to ask why we must worry about understanding and respecting the way of life of all these foreigners anyway. There are two reasons. One is the moral reason that these people have a right to be respected as human beings of worth, the same as we. If there is to be any freedom or dignity of humankind, it must be shared equally by all human beings and not be considered the heritage of a fortunate few. The other reason for our understanding foreign and primitive people is a practical one. If we do not learn to live with them, we may one day have to defend our lives against them. As one of the wealthiest and most powerful nations in the world, the United States is, whether we like it or not, an example. Whether it is a good or bad one depends on us. We have made a great point of the supposition that our democratic way of life is better than all other forms, as it has at its heart the ideas of the equality and fraternity of all. Only yesterday many of the people of Africa, Asia, and Oceania were dominated by foreign colonial powers but today they are self-governing. As members of newly emerging countries they can follow the way of the free democratic world or choose totalitarianism in its many forms. If democracy advocates that all people regardless of color or culture can live together peacefully respecting each other's rights, we must show them that this is in truth the way it works. Grooming a few dedicated young people in a Peace Corps effort is not enough. We must accept the responsibilities of democracy as a nation and as individuals in our relations and attitudes to people of the whole world. Democracy depends on responsible citizens who are well informed on the issues. The issues of cross-cultural understanding are now of vital importance. Let us hope that through the scientific and humanitarian influence of anthropology and its related sciences we can learn to think clearly and feel deeply about the human species in all its cultural variety.

Summary

All people form judgments about the quality of lifestyles that are different from their own. Every society in the world has a tendency to consider their own customs correct and "natural" and those of foreigners, improper, unnatural, and inefficient. Believing that foreign ways of doing things are inadequate, leads to the judgment that foreign cultures are inferior. This universal tendency is known as *enthnocentrism*.

Although they can't overcome being ethnocentric completely, anthropologists attempt to control their bias and adopt a philosophical position called *cultural relativism*. This is a very important concept to operate under in both the study of another culture and in cross-cultural comparisons. What is right for one group is not necessarily right for another, and cultural relativism pleads for tolerance and understanding of other ways of life and maintains that judgments concerning the worth of a cultural system must be made only in terms of the standards, ethics, and morals of the particular people under investigation. Many anthropologists, however, have carried this idea too far and have held that one has no right to denounce any cultural form of behavior no matter how destructive or inhumane it might be.

Because of the difficulties inherent in evaluating cultures qualitatively, anthropologists have been reticent to condemn certain cultural practices even though they sensed they were less than beneficial. A. W. Kroeber, however, has advanced the idea that cultures can be ranked as more or less advanced and intellectually mature in terms of their involvement with (1) magic and superstition, (2) blood, death preoccupation, and torture, and (3) advanced technology. Technology has long been used as a yardstick for assessing degree of "civilization," and this has tended to foster a belief in the overall superiority of the West. However, many social institutions of pre-industrial people are far more complex and effective than some found in Europe or the United States. An example is the extremely complex and stable kinship system of the Australian aborigines.

A meaningful step toward improving cross-cultural understanding might very well be to search for common denominators among all cultures rather than dwell so heavily on cultural differences. It is possible to identify a kind of universal ethical system which most societies agree makes human interaction more satisfying. There are also specific forms of behavior which some anthropologists believe can be condemned on the basis of being threats to the health and survival of the human species. Some kinds of cultural behavior are seen as threatening to the welfare of societies.

Life can be lived satisfactorily in many ways and human diversity is not necessarily bad. Perhaps one of the best lessons we can learn is that there can be unity in diversity. To expect all people to look the same, act the same, and think the same is contrary to the rule of nature.

Glossary

absolute dating methods which allow assignment of a chronological date to artifacts or features, for example, Carbon 14, dendrochronology, and potassium-argon dating.

acculturation changes occurring as a result of ongoing contact between two cultural systems, with an interchange of cultural elements taking place.

adhesion Edward Tylor's concept that cultural features are found in association with each other, that is, pottery-making with maize cultivation.

affinal kin kinsmen by marriage.

age-grade social categories, usually in hierarchy, which will be occupied by age-sets.

age-set individuals of approximately the same age who will occupy the same age grades. They usually underwent ceremonial of transition to adulthood together.

allele an alternate expression of a gene.

amitate relationship between a child and a father's sister in a patrilineal society.

animatism ascription of life to inanimate things.

animism belief in the existence of souls and indwelling spirits in all things living and inanimate.

anthropology science of humankind; the word derives from the Greek *anthropos* ("man") and *logia* ("science").

applied (action) anthropology application of anthropological knowledge in the solution of social problems.

artifact something created by humans. Formerly called "material culture."

assimilation the ultimate fusion of contacting cultural systems.

avunculate relationship between a child and mother's brother in a matrilineal society.

avunculocal residence of married couple with the maternal uncle of the wife. Found in association with matrilineal descent.

barbarism the state of cultural evolution that is midway between savagery and civilization.

barter to exchange goods for goods.

bilineal (bilateral) line of descent from both parents.

bilocal residence of married couple with either father or mother, sometimes alternately.

carbon 14 radioactive isotope of carbon, whose half-life is used in dating organic materials.

case study approach a method of recording ethnographic data concerning events in the life of an individual or society; an intimate, in-depth analysis of a total cultural situation.

caste a rigid social grouping, usually fixed by birth and usually endogamous.

chinampas artificial islands in Lake Texcoco constructed by the Aztecs.

chopper stone chopping-tools, rather crude in form, found in Southeastern Asia dating from the period of *Homo erectus*, but still used by some tribal groups today.

chromosome DNA — containing units which carry genes; located in the nucleus of the cell.

civilization in cultural evolution, the highest stage of development, implying urban centers, writing, etc.

clan large kin group composed of several lineages tracing relationship back to common mythological ancestor.

classificatory kinship terminology putting kin into classes (e.g. all kinsmen of one's own generation are called "brother" or "sister") instead of differentiation between cousins and siblings.

cognitive anthropology the study of how members of a particular group perceive and categorize their daily experience.

comparative or relative dating dating of an unknown feature by association with one of a known date.

configurationalism the concept that patterns or themes permeate all the levels of a cultural system, molding the personalities of the people into character types.

conjugal family family system stressing marriage ties.

consanguineal family family system stressing descent or "blood" ties.

contagious magic magic based upon the principle that "once in association, always in association" (e.g. nail clippings may be used to work magic against their owner).

core bi-face tools the stone tools formed by removal of flakes from a central core—hand axes, "coup-de-poing."

cross-cousins cousins whose related parents are of opposite sex, that is, the children of a man are cross-cousins to his sister's children.

cultural ecology the study of human adaption to the physical environment.

cultural relativism evaluating a cultural system by its own norms.

culture learned, shared behavior acquired by humans as members of society.

culture area geographic areas reflecting a high level of cultural homogeneity.

culturology a synonym for neo-evolution, especially the views of Leslie White.

cuneiform wedge-shaped writing found in ancient Mesopotamia.

demography quantitative analysis of human populations; statistical analyses of age and sex distribution, birthrates and deathrates, marital status.

dendrochronology dating by analysis of tree rings.

descriptive kinship kinship terminology in indicating precise relationship to ego (e.g. *uncle*, *aunt*, or *cousin*).

deterministic thinking over-simplified statements of causality; explaining cultural phenomena solely in terms of single factor such as race, climate, or economics.

diachronic comparison studying cultural phenomena utilizing several time levels.

diffusion transmission of cultural traits or complexes from one culture to another.

dominant an allele that determines the phenotype of an individual.

double descent descent from both parents, but of different things, for example, inheritance of social or kin identify from one and soul or spirit from the other.

element see *trait.*

emic the society member's (insiders) perspective; derives from word *phonemic.*

enculturation learning of one's language and cultural tradition.

endogamy marriage within culturally defined limits.

enthno-botany the way a society utilizes and classifies the plant life in its environment.

enthnocentrism the preference a society has for its own norms and values.

ethnography the data collecting activities carried out by anthropologists in the field.

ethno-history reconstruction of cultural history of groups through written documents, oral traditions, and linguistic analysis.

ethnology the science of culture; making cultural comparisons in order to formulate and test hypotheses about the nature of human beings.

ethno-musicology cross-cultural analysis of the world's musical traditions.

ethno-science study of emic or folk systems of classification of of phenomena.

etic the scientist's cross-cultural perspective; derives from word "phonetic."

evolution, biological genetic changes which occur in a population over time.

evolution, cultural the belief that culture evolves in a fashion analogous to biological evolution. The mechanism of inheritance learning rather than heredity.

exogamy marriage outside culturally defined limits.

extended family those relatives near to a mated pair and their children, with nearness measured by degrees of interaction.

flake tools stone tools formed by deliberately removing a flake from a core with the intent of using it as a tool.

folktale story of anthropomorphic animals or humans told to entertain or educate.

folkways the customary ways by which societies regulate behavior, enforced by appropriate sanctions.

functionalism concept that the component parts of a cultural system are interdependent at all levels—traits, complexes, and institutions contribute to the operation of the entire system.

gene a unit of inheritance which directs the production of characteristics of an individual.

genetic drift a force of evolution which produces genetic changes in a population due to chance.

gene pool the sum of all genes of a population at a given time.

genotype the sum of all genetic factors that make up the genetic constitution of an individual.

gerontology the science of aging; often with emphasis on latter years.

gestalt or configurational approach analysis of the whole and the relationship of component parts.

hieroglyphic rebus-like picture writing of ancient Egypt.

holistic gestalt approach wherein all possible variables are taken into consideration.

homeopathic magic magic based upon the assumption that objects resembling each other have an influence upon each other, for example, a doll may be burned to give a fever to one's enemy.

incest sexual relations between individuals defined as close relatives.

institution the broadest unit of cultural analysis, includes the various traits, elements, and complexes associated with meeting a basic societal need.

kula ring ceremonial trading of shell bracelets and necklaces practiced by the Trobriand Islanders in Melanesia.

kulturkreis German diffusionist school holding that the cultures of the world had been built by the spread of several core cultures (groups or clusters of traits) diffusing from the Old World.

law social norms whose violation brings a response from a group (or individual) who are socially recognized as having authority to determine guilt and impose punishment.

legend narrative of individuals and societies considered by the people to be true history.

levirate marriage of a woman to her dead husband's brother.

linguistics the study of human language; involves descriptive, historical, language, culture, and sociolinguistic specializations.

lithic refers to stone, for example, lithic tools.

magic the ability to compel or control supernatural powers.

mana a Melanesian term for an impersonal supernatural power.

matrilineal descent through the mother's line.

matrilocal (uxorilocal) residence of married couple with the family of the wife.

midden past people's trash heaps excavated by archeologists.

money barter the use of a consumption commodity as a medium of exchange, for example, coconuts in Nicobar, bricks of rice in China, and edible rats in Easter Island.

monogamy marriage consisting of one husband and one wife.

morals (ethics) sanctioned rules of human behavior.

mores the important or mandatory folkways, enforced by severe sanctions.

morpheme the smallest unit of meaning in linguistic analysis.

morphology the study of body shape and size.

multilinear evolution concept that cultural evolution may occur in several areas, with parallel development in each, independent of the others.

mutation a change in the genetic material (DNA).

myths narratives of the remote past before the present condition of the world which express the value system of the society.

natal family the nuclear family into which ego is born.

natural selection a force of evolution which selects those individuals in a population with features advantageous for relatively higher reproduction.

neo-diffusionism attempts to explain cultural phenomena by improbable migrations (often long distance voyages) or even by contacts from outer space.

neo-evolution a mid-twentieth-century approach to anthropology by Leslie White, V. Gordon Childe, Robert Redfield, and others that general trends in culture change are from the simple homogenous to complex heterogenous.

neolithic a cultural period beginning about 10,000 years ago characterized by food production and pastoralism.

neolocal residence by married couple apart from either father or mother.

nuclear family a social unit of a husband, wife, and their unmarried children.

paleolithic the cultural period from the earliest stone tools to the development of agriculture. A period of hunting, collecting, and gathering.

palynology pollen analysis.

parallel cousins cousins whose related parents are of the same sex, for example, the children of a man are parallel cousins to his brother's children.

participant observation method of field investigation where observer lives among subjects and participates in their lifestyle as much as he or she is permitted.

particulate inheritance Mendel's theory that genetic factors retain their integrity and do not blend or fuse from generation to generation.

patrilineal descent through the father's line.

patrilocal (virilocal) residence of married couple with the family of the husband.

phenotype the total expression of characteristics of an individual resulting from the interaction of the genotype and the environment.

phoneme the smallest unit of sound in linguistic analysis.

pleistocene geological epoch extending from c. 2 million years to 10,000 years ago. Roughly the Ice Age.

polyandry marriage between one woman and plural husbands.

polygamy plural marriage; includes both polygyny and polyandry.

polygyny marriage between one man and plural wives.

polymorphisms different, discontinuous phenotypes or genes present in a single population.

population genetics study of gene frequencies in populations.

potlatch conspicuous consumption or destruction of wealth by the Kwakiutl Indians to enhance personal status.

primatology studies of anatomy and behavior of apes, monkeys, and prosimians.

primitive a vague term, disliked by anthropologists, but still used in the absence of anything better, connoting a simple technology and cultural system. Totally lacking in perjorative implications.

proverb a brief epigrammatic statement suggesting a course of action consistent with the value system of the society.

quipu knotted strings used as aids to memory by the Incas and Polynesians.

recessive an allele which is unexpressed phenotypically when present with a dominant allele in the genotype.

religion belief in the supernatural.

riddle riddles are cryptic statements or questions demanding an answer based on association, comparison and perception of likenesses and differences in natural and cultural phenomena.

savage as used by Tylor, Morgan, and other early anthropologists this implied a simple, low level of cultural development.

silent barter (dumb barter) trading without personal contact that is, goods are left at a place, then the people withdraw, allowing the others to come and examine the goods; this proceeds until a satisfactory arrangement is met.

socialization learning how to get along with the persons of one's social group.

sororate marriage of a man to his dead wife's sister.

state formal and complex government structure featuring centralized authority, bureaucracy, taxation, courts and professional military.

stratigraphy study of the various horizontal layers or strata in archeologic and geologic sites, presuming that those lower are earlier than those in higher levels.

structural anthropology a school of anthropology founded by Claude Levi-Strauss, in which culture, particularly mythology, is analyzed for universal thought regularities.

superorganic synonymous with culture. Concept holds that societal tradition shapes, regulates, and outlives individual participants.

syntax the way in which morphemes are placed together in an utterance or a sentence; the grammatical structure.

taxonomy the theory and practice of classifying organisms.

totem a mythical object or being (sacred animal, plant, or natural phenomenon) associated with a group, often a clan or other kin group.

totemism a religious complex organized around a totem.

trait the smallest significant unit of culture; also called cultural element.

transhumance migration of pastoral peoples in following seasonal availability of grass and water.

tribe a social group identified by a common language and culture.

unilineal line of descent from one parent, either mother or father.

ziggurat a truncated pyramid found in Mesopotamia, with a temple or shrine on the top.

Literature Cited

ABERLE, D. F., COHEN, A. K. , LEVY, M. J., Jr., SUTTON, F. X. 1950. "The Functional Prerequisites of a Society," *Ethics*, **60**:100–110.

ACKERKNECHT, ERWIN H. 1953. "Paleopathology," in KROEBER, A. L. (ed.). *Anthropology Today*. Chicago, University of Chicago Press.

ALLPORT, FLOYD. 1934. "The J-Curve Hypothesis of Conforming Behavior," *Journal of Social Psychology*, **5**:141–83.

ARENS, W. 1976. "Professional Football: an American Symbol," in ARENS, W. and MONTAGUE S. (eds.). *The American Dimension*. Port Washington, N.Y. Alfred.

ARGYLE, MICHAEL. 1959. *Religious Behavior*. Glencoe, Ill., Free Press.

ARGYLE, MICHAEL, and BEIT-HALLAHMI, BENJAMIN. 1975. *The Social Psychology of Religion*. London, Routledge and Kegan Paul.

ALTMANN, J. 1981. *Baboon Mothers and Infants*. Cambridge Ma., Harvard University Press.

ALTMANN, S.A. and ALTMANN, J. 1970. *Baboon Ecology*. Chicago, Ill., University of Chicago Press.

ATTWOOD, WILLIAM. 1953. "The American Male: Why Does He Work so Hard?" *Look*, **22**:70–75 (March 4).

BALTZELL, E. DIGBY. 1958. *Philadelphia Gentlemen*. Glencoe, Ill., Free Press.

BARCLAY, ALLAN G., and CUSUMANO, D. R. 1967. "Testing Masculinity in Boys without Fathers," *Trans-action* (December) 33–35.

BARKER, GORDON H. 1940. "Family Factors in the Ecology of Juvenile Delinquency," *Journal of Criminal Law and Criminology*, **30**:681–91.

BARNES, J. A. 1972. *Social Networks*. Module 92. Reading, Mass., Addison-Wesley Press.

BARNOUW, VICTOR. 1979. *Culture and Personality*. Homewood, Ill., Dorsey Press.

BASCOM, WILLIAM R. 1948. "West Africa and the Complexity of Primitive Cultures," *American Anthropologist*, **50**:18–23.

BASSO, KEITH. 1969. *Western Apache Witchcraft*. Papers of the University of Arizona, Tucson, University of Arizona Press.

BATESON, GREGORY, and MEAD, MARGARET. 1942. *Balinese Character, a Photographic ANalysis.* New York, New York Academy of Sciences.

BEALL, C.M. 1982. "An Historical Perspective on Studies of Human Growth and Development in Extreme Environments," in F. SPENCER (ed.). *A History of American Physical Anthropology.* New York, Academic Press.

BEALS, ALAN. 1962. *Gopalpur: A South Indian Village.* New York, Holt, Rinehart & Winston.

BEALS, RALPH L., and HOIJER, HARRY. 1959. *An Introduction to Anthropology.* New York, Macmillan.

BECK, B. 1980. *Animal Tool Behavior.* New York, Garland Publishing, Inc.

BELLAH, ROBERT N., et al. 1985. *Habits of the Heart.* Berkeley, University of California Press.

BENEDICT, RUTH. 1933 "Continuities and Discontinuities in Cultural Conditioning." *Psychiatry,* **1**:161–67.

———. 1943. *Thai Culture and Behavior.* (Mimeographed. Distributed by the Institute for Intercultural Studies, Inc.)

———. 1959. *Patterns of Culture.* (Preface by Margaret Mead.) New York, New American Library, Copyright 1934, Houghton Miffln.

BENNETT, JOHN W. 1946. "The Interpretation of Pueblo Culture," *Southwestern Journal of Anthropology.* **24**:361–74.

BENNETT, JOHN W., and WOLFF, KURT H. 1956. "Toward Communication between Sociology and Anthropology," in THOMAS, WILLIAM L., Jr. (ed.). *Current Anthropology.* Chicago, University of Chicago Press.

BENNETT, WENDELL C., and BIRD, JUNIUS B. 1964. *Andean Culture History.* Garden City, N.Y., Natural History Press.

BERGER, ARTHUR ASA. 1973. *The Comic Stripped American.* New York, Walker and Company.

———. 1973. *Pop Culture.* Dayton, Pflaum/Standard.

———. 1982. *Media Analysis Techniques.* Beverly Hills, Sage.

———. 1984. "Return of the Jedi: The Rewards of Myth," *Society,* 21(4):71-74 (May/June).

BIERSTEDT, ROBERT. 1966. "Indices of Civilization," *American Journal of Sociology,* **71**:483–90.

BINGHAM, HIRAM. 1848. *A Residence of Twenty-One Years in the Sandwich Islands.* Hartford, Hezekiah Huntington.

BOAS, FRANZ. 1895. *Indianische Sagen von de Nord-Pacifischen Kuste Amerikas.* Berlin, A. Asher and Co.

———. 1908. "Decorative Designs of Alaskan Needle Cases: A Study in the History of Conventional Designs, Based on Materials in the

U.S. National Museum," *Proceedings of the U.S. National Museum,* **34**:321–44.

——— (ed.). 1938. *General Anthropology.* New York, Heath.

———. 1948. *Race, Language, and Culture.* New York, Macmillan.

———. 1955. *Primitive Art.* New York, Dover.

BORDES, FRANÇOIS. 1968. *The Old Stone Age.* New York, McGraw-Hill.

BOTHWELL, D. R. 1961. "The People of Mount Carmel," *Proc. Prehist. Soc.,* **27**:155–59.

BRAIDWOOD, ROBERT J. 1975. *Prehistoric Men.* Glenview, Ill., Scott, Foresman and Company.

BRONFENNER, URIE. 1977. "The American Family in Decline," *Current,* January, pp. 39–47, reprinted from *Search* 2:4–10 (Fall 1976).

BROWN, INA CORINNE. 1958. *Understanding Other Cultures.* Cincinnati. This edition was produced for women's study groups in the Methodist church and is now out of print. A revision has been published under the same title (1963) by Prentice-Hall. Englewood Cliffs, N.J.

BRUNER, EDWARD. 1956. "Cultural Transmission and Cultural Change," *Southwestern Journal of Anthropology,* **12**:191–199.

BRUNN, STANLEY. 1974. *Geography and Politics in America.* New York, Harper & Row.

BUCK, SIR PETER. 1950. *The Coming of the Maori.* Wellington, Maori Purposes Fund Board, Whitcombe and Tombs.

BUFFON, GEORGE LOUIS LECLERC, COMTE DE. 1866. *A Natural History. General and Particular; containing the history and theory of the earth, a general history of man, the brute creation, vegetables, minerals, etc.* Vol. I. (WILLIAM SMELLIE, trans.). London, Thomas Kelley and Co.

BUNZEL, RUTH. 1938. "Art," in BOAS, FRANZ (ed.). *General Anthropology.* New York, Heath.

BURCKHARDT, JAKOB CHRISTOPH. 1958. *The Civilization of the Renaissance in Italy.* New York, Harper & Bros.

BURKHARDT, R.W. JR. 1977. *The Spirit System: Lamarck and Evolutionary Biology.* Cambridge, Cambridge University Press.

BUSHNELL, G. H. S. 1957. *Peru.* New York, Frederick A. Praeger.

———. 1968. *The First Americans.* New York, McGraw-Hill.

CALDWELL, JOSEPH R. 1958. "Trend and Tradition in the Prehistory of the Eastern United States," *American Anthropologist,* Vol. 60, No. 6, Pt. 2.

CAMMAS, R., and BAYLAC, P.   1950. "Découvertes récentes dans les grottes de Montmaurin, Haute-Garonne," *Anthropologie*, **54**:262–71.

CAMPBELL, B.G. 1985. *Humankind Emerging*. Boston, Little, Brown and Company.

CAMPBELL, DONALD, and LEVINE, R.   1973. "Field Manual in Anthropology," in NAROLL, RAOUL, and COHEN, RONALD (eds.), *A Handbook of Method in Cultural Anthropology*. New York, Columbia University Press.

CAZDEN, C. B.   1967. "The Role of Parent Speech in the Acquisition of Grammar," Project Literacy Report. No. 8. Ithaca, New York, Cornell University.

CHAPPLE, ELIOT D., and COON, CARLETON S.   1942. *Principles of Anthropology*. New York, Holt.

CHARD, CHESTER S.   1969. *Man in Prehistory*. New York, McGraw-Hill.

CHILDE, V. GORDON. 1948. *What Happened in History*. Harmondsworth, Middlesex, England, Penguin.

———. 1950. "The Urban Revolution," *Town Planning Review*, **21**:3–17.

———. 1951. *Man Makes Himself*. New York, New American Library. Copyright C. A. Watts and Company, Ltd., London.

CLARK, GRAHAME.   1961. *World Prehistory*. Cambridge, Cambridge University Press.

———. 1967. *The Stone Age Hunters*. New York, McGraw-Hill.

CLARK, W. E. LE GROS.   1959. "The Crucial Evidence for Human Evolution," *American Scientist*, **47**:299–313.

COE, MICHAEL D.   1962. *Mexico*. London, Thames and Hudson.

COHEN, YEHUDI.   1961. *Social Structure and Personality*. New York, Holt, Rinehart & Winston.

CONSUMER REPORTS.   1958. "Confessions of an Appliance Salesman," **23**:546.

COON, CARLETON, GARN, STANLEY M., and BIRDSELL, JOSEPH B.   1950. *Races: A Study of the Problems of Race Formation*. Springfield, Ill., Charles C. Thomas.

COUSINS, NORMAN.   1964. "A Plea to the Fijians," *Saturday Review*, July 25, pp. 14–15.

COVARRUBIAS, MIGUEL.   1937. *The Island of Bali*. New York, Knopf.

COWGILL, DONALD, And HOLMES, LOWELL. 1972. *Aging and Modernization*. New York, Appleton, Century and Crofts.

CRAWFORD, M.H. 1973. "The Use of Genetic Markers of the Blood in the Study of the Evolution of Human Populations," in M. CRAWFORD and P. WORKMAN (eds.). *Methods and Theories of Anthropological genetics*. Albuquerque, New Mexico, University of New Mexico Press.

DANIELSSON, BENGT. 1956. *Love in the South Seas*, New York, Reynal.

DART, R. A. 1957. *The Osteodontokeratic Culture of Australopithecus Africanus*. Transvaal Museum Memoir No. 10.

DART, RAYMOND, and CRAIG, DENNIS. 1959. *Adventures with the Missing Link*. New York, Harper & Bros.

DARWIN, C. 1859. On the Evolution of Species by Means of Natural Selection or the Preservation of Favoured Races in the Struggle for Life. London, Murray.

DAY, M.H. and WICKENS, E. H. 1980. "Laetoli Pliocene Footprints and Bipedalism," *Nature*, 202:321-330.

DE TOCQUEVILLE, ALEXIS. 1899. *Democracy in America*. Vol. II, New York, Knopf. (Vintage ed. 1954.)

DIEZ, FERMIN. 1982. "The Popularity of Sports in America," in CONRAD KOTTAK (ed.), *Researching American Culture*. Ann Arbor, University of Michigan Press.

DIXSON, A.F. and GEORGE, L. 1982. "Prolactin and Parental Behavior in a Male New World Primate," *Nature,* 299:551-552.

DOBZHANSKY, T., AYALA, F., STEBBINS, G.L. and VALENTINE, J.W. 1977. *Evolution*. San Francisco, W.H. Freeman and Co.

DORJAHN, VERNON. 1960. "The Changing Political System of the Temne," *Africa*, **30**:110–39. (Oxofrd University Press.)

DOZIER, EDWARD. 1956. "The Concepts of 'Primitive' and 'Native' in Anthropology," in THOMAS, WILLIAM L. (ed.), *Current Anthropology*, Chicago, University of Chicago Press.

DUBOIS, CORA. 1961. *The People of Alor*. 2 vols. New York, Harper & Bros. Copyright 1944 by the University of Minnesota.

DUNDES, ALAN. 1969. "Thinking Ahead: A Folkloristic Reflection of the Future Orientation in American Worldview," *Anthropological Quarterly*, **42**:53–72.

————. 1978. "Into the Endzone for a Touchdown: a Psychoanalytic Consideration of American Football," *Western Folklore*, **37**:75–88.

DURKHEIM, EMILE. 1915. *The Elementary Forms of the Religious Life* (J. W. Swain trans.). London, Routledge and Kegan Paul.

EATON, JOSEPH W., and WEIL, ROBERT. 1953. "Mental Health of the Hutterites," *Scientific American,* **189**:31–37.

———. 1955. *Culture and Mental Disorders.* Glencoe, Ill., Free Press.

ECONOMIST, THE. 1979. "The Role of Religious Cults," *Current,* January reprinted from *The Economist,* November 25, 1978, pp. 11–13.

EDGERTON, ROBERT, and LANGNESS, L. L. 1974. *Methods and Styles in the Study of Culture.* San Francisco, Chandler and Sharp.

EISENSTADT, S. N. 1966. *Modernization; Protest and Change.* Englewood Cliffs, N.J., Prentice-Hall.

EINZIG, PAUL. 1966 *Primitive Money.* Oxford and New York, Pergamon Press.

ELLIS, WILLIAM. 1831. *Polynesian Researches.* London, Fisher, Son, and Jackson.

ELLISON, JACK. 1963. *The Emergence of Civilization.* Chicago, Anthropology Curriculum Study Project.

EVANS-PRITCHARD, E. E. 1940. *The Nuer.* Oxford, Clarendon Press.

———. 1956. *Social Anthropology.* Glencoe, Ill., Free Press.

EVANS-PRITCHARD, E. E., *et al.* 1961. *Institutions of Primitive Society.* Glencoe, Ill., Free Press.

FAGAN, BRIAN. 1977. *Men of the Earth.* Boston, Little, Brown & Co.

FEDIGAN, L.M. 1983. "Dominance and Reproductive Success in Primates," *Yearbook of Physical Anthropology,* 26:91-129.

FINEGAN, JACK. 1952. *The Archaeology of World Religions.* Princeton, copyright by Princeton University Press.

FIRTH, RAYMOND. 1929. *Primitive Economics of the New Zealand Maori.* New York, Dutton.

———. 1958. *Human Types.* New York (Mentor Books), New American Library. Copyright 1956 by Thomas Nelson & Sons, London.

———. 1959. *Social Change in Tikopia.* London, Allen & Unwin.

FITCH, JAMES MARSTON. 1972. *American Building: The Environmental Forces that Shape it.* Boston, Houghton Mifflin.

FITCH, JAMES M., and BRANCH, DANIEL P. 1960. "Primitive Architecture and Climate," *Scientific American,* **203**:134–44.

FLETCHER, A. C., and LA FLECHE, F. 1911. *The Omaha Tribe.* 27th Annual Report, Bureau of American Ethnology. Washington, D.C.

FORDE, DARYLL. 1954. "Foraging, Hunting and Fishing," in SINGER, CHARLES, HOLMYARD, E. J., and HALL, A. R. (eds.). *A History of Technology.* Vol. I. New York, Oxford University Press.

FORSTER, GEORGE. 1777. *A Voyage round the World . . . Sloop Reso-*

lution, Commanded by Captain James Cook. 2 vols. London, B. White.

FORSTER, JOHN REINHOLD. 1778. *Observations made during a Voyage round the World, on Physical Geography, Natural History, and Ethic Philosophy . . . (Resolution).* London, Printed for G. Robinson.

FORTES, MEYER, and EVANS-PRITCHARD, E. E. (ed.). 1940. *African Political Systems.* London, Oxford University Press.

FOULKS, EDWARD F. 1973. *The Artic Hysteria of the North Alaskan Eskimos.* Anthropological Studies, No. 10. Washington, D.C., American Anthropological Association.

FRANKFORT, H. 1948. *Kingship and the Gods.* Chicago, University of Chicago Press.

FRAZER, SIR JAMES. 1958. *The Golden Bough.* New York, Macmillan.

FREEMAN, DEREK. 1962. Review of *Trance in Bali, Journal of the Polynesian Society.* **71:270**–73.

FRIED, MORTON. 1959. *Readings in Anthropology.* Vol. II. New York, Crowell.

FROMM, ERICH. 1941.*Escape from Freedom.* New York, Holt, Rinehart & Winston.

FURNAS, J. C. 1948. *Anatomy of Paradise,* New York, William Sloane Associates.

GARN, S.M. 1957. "Research in Human Growth," *Human Biology,* 29: 1-11.

GEARING, FRED. 1962. *Priests and Warriors.* Memoir No. 93, American Anthropological Association.

GERSTNER, JOHN. 1974. "The Many Reasons Why We Work," *The National Observer,* June 8, p. 24.

GIDE, ANDRE. 1931. *The Counterfeiters.* New York, Modern Library.

GILLIN, JOHN. 1948. *The Ways of Men.* New York, Appleton-Century. Quoted by permission of author and publisher.

———. 1948a. Magical Fright," *Psychiatry,* **11**:387–400.

GLASSER, WILLIAM. 1975. *The Identity Society.* New York, Harper & Row.

GLUCKMAN, MAX. 1955. *The Judicial Process Among the Barotse.* Glencoe, Ill., Free Press.

GODSELL, GEOFFREY. 1978. "When a Changing World Shatters Traditions," *The Christian Science Monitor,* November 29, pp. 1, 6.

GOLDEN, HARRY. 1955. "Personal Journal." *The Carolina Israelite,* May.

GOLDFRANK, ESTHER. 1943. "Historic Change and Social Character: A Study of the Teton Dakota," *American Anthropologist*, **45**:67–83.

GOLDSCHMIDT, WALTER. 1954. "A Word in Your Ear," in *Ways of Mankind*. Boston, Beacon Press.

———. 1960. *Exploring the Ways of Mankind*, New York, Holt, Rinehart & Winston.

GOODALL, J. 1979. "Life and Death at Gombe," *National Geographic*, 155:597-620.

GOODE, WILLIAM J. 1951. *Religion Among the Primitives*. Glencoe, Ill., Free Press.

GORER, GEOFFREY. 1948. *The American People*. New York, W. W. Norton. Copyright 1948 by Geoffrey Gorer. Revised ed. copyright © 1964. Reprinted by permission.

GORER, GEOFFREY, and RICKMAN, JOHN. 1949. *The People of Great Russia*. London, Cresset Press.

GOUGH, KATHLEEN. 1959. "The Nayars and the Definition of Marriage," *Journal of the Royal Anthropological Institute*, **89**:23–34.

GRABURN, NELSON. 1976. *Ethnic and Tourist Arts, Cultural Expression from the Fourth World.* Berkeley, University of California Press.

GRAEBNER, ROBERT FRITZ. 1911. *Methode der Ethnologie*. Heidelberg, G. WINTER,

GRANT, MADISON. 1916. *Passing of a Great Race*. New York, Charles Scribner's Sons.

GRAY, PAUL. 1986. "Seven Who Flew for All of Us," *Time*, February 10:32.

GRAYBILL, GUY. 1974. "The Archeologist's View . . . Eric von Daniken," *Popular Archeology*, September, pp. 43–49.

GREEN, RICHARD, and MONEY, JOHN. 1961. "Effeminacy in Prepubertal Boys," *Pediatrics*, **27**:286–91.

HAAS, J.A. 1982. "The Development of Research Strategies for Studies of Biological Variation in Living Human Populations," in F. SPENCER (ed.). *A History of American Physical Anthropology*. New York, Academic Press.

HALLOWELL, IRVING. 1955. *Culture and Experience*. Philadelphia, University of Pennsylvania Press.

HAMMOND, GERALDINE. 1977. "Sex and the Word," *Wichita State University Magazine*, **2**:4–9 (Fall).

HARDING, THOMAS G. 1960. "Adaptation and Stability," in SAHLINS, MARSHALL, and SERVICE, E. (eds.). *Evolution and Culture*. Ann Arbor, University of Michigan Press.

HARRIS, MARVIN. 1972. "Bah, Humbug," *Natural History*, December, pp. 21–25.

HART, C. W. M. 1954. "The Sons of Turimpi," *American Anthropologist*, **56**:242–61.

HAYNES, C. VANCE, Jr. 1966. "Elephant Hunting in North America," *Scientific American*, (June).

HEILBRONER, ROBERT. 1976. "Middle-class Myths, Middle-class Realities," *Atlantic Monthly*, October, pp. 37–42.

HENRY, JULES. 1971. "Is Education Possible?" in WAX, MURRAY, DIAMOND, S., and GEARING, F. (eds.). *Anthropological Perspectives in Education*. New York, Basic Books.

HERODOTUS. 1928. "Euterpe," in The History of Herodotus (Rawlinson, trans.). New York, Dial Press.

HERSKOVITS, M. J. 1949. *Man and His Works.* New York, Knopf.

———. 1950. "The Hypothetical Situation," *Southwestern Journal of Anthropology*, **6**:32–40.

———. 1952. *Economic Anthropology.* New York, Knopf.

———. 1953. *Franz Boas: The Science of Man in the Making.* New York, Charles Scribner's Sons.

HIBBEN, FRANK C. 1958. *Prehistoric Man in Europe.* Norman, University of Oklahoma Press.

HILGER, INEZ. 1960. *Field Guide to the Ethnological Study of Child Life.* New Haven, Human Relations Area Files Press.

HOBHOUSE, LEONARD T. 1924. *Social Development.* New York, Holt, Rinehart & Winston.

HOCKETT, CHARLES F., and ASCHER, R. "The Human Revolution," *Current Anthropology*, 5:135-147.

HOCKETT, CHARLES F., and ASCHER, ROBERT. 1964. "The Human Revolution," *Current Anthropology*, 5:135–47.

HOCKETT, CHARLES F. 1954. "Chinese versus English," in HOIJER, HARRY (ed.). *Language in Culture*, Chicago: University of Chicago Press, 1954.

HOEBEL, E. A. 1954 *The Law of Primitive Man; a Study in Legal Dynamics.* Cambridge, Harvard University Press.

———. 1966. *Anthropology: The Study of Man.* New York, McGraw-Hill.

HOEKEMA, DAVID. 1979. "Capital Punishment: the Question of Justification," *The Christian Century*, 96:338–342.

HOGBIN, H. IAN. 1938–39. "Tillage and Collection, a New Guinea Economy," *Oceania*, **9**:127–51, 286–325.

HOLMES, LOWELL D. 1958. *Ta'u: Stability and Change in a Samoan Village.* Reprint No. 7, Polynesian Society. Wellington.

———. 1962. *Methods in Polynesian Ethnography.* (University Studies, No. 50) Wichita, University of Wichita.

HOLMES, LOWELL D., TALLMAN, GARY, and JANTZ, VERNON. 1978. "Samoan Personality," *Journal of Psychological Anthropology,* 1:453–472.

HONIGMANN, JOHN J. 1954. *Culture and Personality.* New York, Harper & Bros.

HOOK, SIDNEY. 1950. *Reason, Social Myths and Democracy.* New York, Humanities Press.

HOOTON, EARNEST. 1945. *A Survey in Seating.* Gardner, Mass., Heywood-Wakefield Co.

HOWELLS, WILLIAM W. 1944. *Mankind So Far,* Garden City, N. Y., Doubleday. Qhoted by permission of the author and publisher.

———. 1948. *The Heathens.* Garden City, N. Y., Doubleday.

———. 1967. *Mankind in the Making.* Garden City, Doubleday.

HSU, FRANCIS L. K. 1953. *Americans and Chinese: Two Ways of Life,* New York, Schuman.

———. 1958, "Taboo," *What's New,* **206**:12–15. Abbott Laboratories Publication. North Chicago.

———. 1961. "American Core Value and National Character," in Hsu, F. L. K. (ed.). *Psychological Anthropology.* Homewood, Ill., Dorsey Press.

———. 1963. *Clan, Caste and Club.* Princeton, Van Nostrand.

———. 1966. "The United States and China: Psychocultural Factors for Mutual Isolation," *Northwestern Review,* **2**:2–10 (Fall).

———. 1969. *The Study of Literate Civilizations.* New York, Holt, Rinehart & Winston.

———. 1972. "American Core Values and National Character," in HSU, FRANCIS (ed.). *Psychological Anthropology.* Cambridge, Mass., Schenkman Publishing Co.

HUNTER, DAVID, and WHITTEN, PHILLIP. 1979. *Anthropology, Contemporary Perspectives.* Boston, Educational Associates.

INSTITUTE OF HUMAN RELATIONS. 1950. *Outline of Cultural Materials.* 3rd ed. New Haven, Yale University Press.

JENNINGS, JESSE D. 1974 *Prehistory of North America.* New York, Mc/Graw Hill.

JOHANSON, D.C. and EDEY, M. 1981. *Lucy: The Beginnings of Humankind.* New York, Simon and Schuster.

JOLLY, A. 1972. *The Evolution of Primate Behavior.* New York, MacMillan and Co.

KARDINER, ABRAM, and PREBLE, EDWARD. 1961. *They Studied Man.* Cleveland, World.

KEESING, FELIX. 1953.*Culture Change.* Stanford, Stanford University Press.

———. 1953a. *Cultural Dynamics and Administration Proceedings,* Seventh Pacific Science Congress. Aukland, New Zealand.

———. 1958.*Cultural Anthropology.* New York, Holt, Rinehart & Winston.

KERLEY, ELLIS, and BASS, WILLIAM. 1967. "Paleopathology: Meeting Ground for Many Disciplines," *Science,* **157**:638–44.

KITTO, H. D. F. 1951. *The Greeks.* Harmondsworth, Middlesex, England, Penguin.

KLEIMAN, D. 1977. "Monogamy in Mammals," *Quarterly Review of Biology,* 52:39-69.

KLIMENT, STEPHEN. 1976. "Architecture: 1776 and 1976—Two Reflections of Values," *Social Education,* January, pp. 26–28.

KLUCKHOHN, CLYDE. 1938. "Participation in Ceremonials in a Navaho Community, *American Anthropologist,* **40**:359–69.

———. 1949. *Mirror for Man.* New York, McGraw-Hill.

KLUCKHOHN, CLYDE, and LEIGHTON, DOROTHY. 1945. *The Navaho.* London, Oxford University Press.

KLUCKHOHN, CLYDE, and MURRAY, HENRY (eds.). 1949. *Personality in Nature, Society, and Culture.* New York, Knopf.

KLUCKHOHN, FLORENCE. 1940. "Participant Observer Technique in Small Communities," *American Journal of Sociology,* 46:331–42.

KOLLER, K. M. 1971. "Parental Deprivation, Family Background and Female Delinquency," *British Journal of Psychiatry,* **118**:319–27.

KOTTAK, CONRAD P. 1978. "Social Science Fiction," *Psychology Today,* February, pp. 12, 17, 18.

———. 1982. *Researching American Culture.* Ann Arbor, University of Michigan Press.

KRAMER, S.M. 1957. "The Sumerians," *Scientific American,* 197:70-86 (October).

KROEBER, A.L. 1909. "Classification Systems of Relationships," *Journal of the Anthropological Institute of Great Britain,* 39:77-84.

———. 1917. "The Superorganic," *American Anthropologist,* 19:41-54.

_____. 1948. Anthropology. New York, Harcourt, Brace.

_____. 1953. *Anthropology Today.* Chicago, University of Chicago Press.

_____. 1959. "The History of the Personality of Anthropology." *American Anthropologist,* 61:398-404.

LAMARCK, J.B. 1809. "Philosophie Zoologique, on Exposition des Considerations Relatives a l'Histoire Naturelle des Animaux," (English translation) H. ELLIOT. *The Zoological Philosophy.* 1914. London, MacMillan and Co.

LANDES, RUTH, 1938. "The Abnormal Among the Ojibwa Indians." *Journal of Abnormal Psychology,* 33: 14-33.

LANGDON, ROBERT. 1975. *The Lost Caravel.* Sydney. Pacific Publications.

LATTER, B.D.H. 1980. "Genetic Differences Within and Between Populations of Major Human Subgroups." *American Naturalist* 116:220-237.

LAYARD, JOHN. 1961. "The Family and Kinship," in Evans-Pritchard, E. E., *et al., The Institutions of Primitive Society.* Glencoe, Ill., Free Press.

LEACH, E. R. 1961. "Aesthetics," in Evans-Pritchard, E. E., *et al. The Institutions of Primitive Society.* Glencoe, Ill., Free Press.

LEBON, J. H. G. 1969. *An Introduction to Human Geography.* London, Hutchinson.

LEE, DOROTHY. 1959. *Freedom and Culture.* Englewood Cliffs, N. J. Prentice-Hall. Quotes from *Freedom and Culture* (pp. 203, 346) by permission of Harper and Row, publisher of *Integrity and Compromise* (MacIver, R. M., ed.) 1957; page 167 by permission of The Ronald Press, publisher of *Religious Perspectives in College Teaching* (Fairchild, H. N., ed.) 1952.

LEIGHTON, ALEXANDER. 1949. *Human Relations in a Changing World.* New York, Dutton.

_____. 1969. "A Comparative Study of Psychiatric Disorders in Nigeria and Rural North America," in PLOG, STANLEY and EDGERTON, ROBERT B. (eds.), *Changing Perspectives in Mental Illness.* New York, Holt, Rinehart & Winston.

LERNER, MAX. 1957. *American as a Civilization.* New York, Simon and Schuster.

LESLIE, GERALD R., LARSON, RICHARD F., and GORMAN, BENJAMIN L. 1973. *Order and Change; Introductory Sociology.* New York, Oxford University Press.

LESSA, WILLIAM A., and VOGT, EVON Z. 1958. *Reader in Comparative Religion.* Evanston, Ill., Row, Peterson.

LEWIN, R. 1984. *Human Evolution. An Illustrated Introduction.* New York, W.H. Freeman and Co.

LEWIS, JOHN. 1961. *Anthropology Made Simple*. Garden City, N.Y. Doubleday.

LEWONTIN, R.C. 1972. "The Apportionment of Human Diversity," *Evolutionary Biology*, 6:281-298.

LEWIS, OSCAR. 1951. *Life in a Mexican Village: Tepoztlan Restudied.* Urbana, University of Illinois Press.

LINTON, RALPH. 1924. "Totemism in the A.E.F.," *American Anthropologist*, **26**:296–300.

———. 1936. *The Study of Man*. New York, Appleton-Century-Crofts. Quoted by permission of publisher.

———. 1943. "Nativistic Movements," *American Anthropologist*, **45**:203–40.

———. 1952. "Universal Ethical Principles," in ANSHEN, R. (ed.), *Moral Principles of Action*. New York, Harper & Row.

———. 1955 *Tree of Culture*. New York, Knopf.

LIN YUTANG. 1935. *My Country and My People*. New York, John Day.

LIPS, JULIUS. 1956. *The Origin of Things*, New York, Fawcett Publications. Copyright by A. A. Wyn. Inc.

LISITSKY, GENE. 1960. *Four Ways of Being Human*. New York, Viking Press.

LIVINGSTONE, DAVID. 1858. *Missionary Travels and Researches in South Africa*. New York, Harper & Bros.

LLEWELLYN, KARL N., and HOEBEL, E. ADAMSON. 1941. *The Cheyenne Way*. Norman, University of Oklahoma Press.

LOMAX, ALAN. 1959. "Folk Song Style," *American Anthropologist*, **61**:927–54.

———. 1962. "Song Structure and Social Structure," *Ethnology*, **1**:425–51.

LOWIE, ROBERT. 1937. *History of Ethnological Theory*. New York, Holt, Rinehart & Winston.

———. 1948. *Social Organization*. New York, Holt, Rinehart & Winston.

———. 1952. *Primitive Religion*. New York, Liveright.

LUCAS, CHRISTOPHER. 1968. "Japan's Remarkable Monkeys," *The Rotarian*, November, 36–37, 56–57.

LUCRETIUS. 1873. *De Rerum Natura*. 5th Book (Munroe, H. A. J., trans.). New York, Deighton, Bell & Co.

LYND, ROBERT S., and LYND, HELEN M. 1929. *Middletown, A Study in Contemporary American Culture*. New York, Harcourt, Brace.

MAIR, LUCY. 1962. *Primitive Government*. Harmondsworth, England, Penguin.

MAITLAND, F. W. 1911. "The Body Politic," in *Collected Papers*, Vol. III. Cambridge, Cambridge University Press.

MALINOWSKI, BRONISLAW. 1929. *Sexual Life of Savages*. London, Routledge and Kegan Paul.

————. 1930. "The Problem of Meaning in Primitive Languages," in OGDEN, C. K., and RICHARDS, I. A. (eds.), *The Meaning of Meaning*. New York, Harcourt Brace Jovanovich.

————. 1931. "Culture," *Encyclopedia of the Social Sciences*. New York, Macmillan.

————. 1935. *Coral Gardens and their Magic*. London, Allen & Unwin.

————. 1961. *Argonauts of the Western Pacific*. Prospect Heights, IL, Waveland Press.

MANDELBAUM, DAVID. 1956. "Social Groupings," in SHAPIRO, HARRY (ed.), *Man, Culture and Society*. New York, Oxford University Press.

MANN, JAMES, and ASTIN, ALEXANDER. 1977. "The End of the Youth Culture," *Current*, November, pp. 3–7.

MANNES, MARYA. 1962. "Wasteland," in ERIC and MARY JOSEPHSON (eds.), *Man Alone: Alienation in Modern Society*. New York, Dell Publishing Co.

MARTIN, JUDITH. 1969. "There She Is . . . Miss America," *Washington Post*, September 14, 1969.

MARTIN, PAUL. 1967. "Pleistocene Overkill," *Natural History*, December, 32–38.

MARX, KARL. 1867. *Das Kapital*. New York, L. W. Schmidt.

MAYO, ELTON. 1933. *The Human Problems of an Industrial Civilization*. New York, MacMillan.

MAYR, E. 1982. *The Growth of Biological Thought*. Cambridge, Ma., Belknap Press.

McCLELLAND, DAVID. 1961. *The Achieving Society*. Princeton, Van Nostrand.

McELROY, A., and TOWNSEND, P.K. 1985. *Medical Anthropology in Ecological Perspective*. Boulder, Co., Westview Press.

McGREGOR, JOHN C. 1965. *Southwestern Archaeology*. Urbana, University of Illinois Press.

McLUHAN, H. MARSHALL. 1951. *The Mechanical Bride*. New York, Vanguard Press.

MEAD, MARGARET. 1928. *Coming of Age in Samoa*. New York, Morrow.

————. 1939. "Native Languages as Field Work Tools," *American Anthropologist*, **41**:189–205.

————. 1953. "National Character," in KROEBER, A. L. (ed.), *Anthropology Today*. Chicago, University of Chicago Press.

————. 1957. "The Pattern of Leisure in Contemporary American Culture," in DOUGLASS, PAUL F.; HUTCHINSON, JOHN L.; and SUTHERLAND, WILLARD C. (eds.), *The Annuals of the American Academy of Political Science; Recreation in the Age of Automation* (September). Philadelphia.

————. 1956. *New Lives For Old; Cultural Transformation-Manus, 1928—1953*. New York. Morrow.

————. 1974. Review essay of M. J. Herskovits *Cultural Relativism: Perspectives in Cultural Pluralism, American Journal of Sociology* **79**:1326–30.

————. 1978. *Culture and Commitment*. New York, Doubleday Anchor.

MEGGERS, BETTY, and EVANS, CLIFFORD. 1966. "A Transpacific Contact in 3000 B.C.," *Scientific American*, **214**:28–35.

MILL, JOHN STUART. 1898. *Principles of Political Economy* (abridged by J. Laurence Laughlin). New York, D. Appleton and Company.

MONTAGU, ASHLEY, 1956. *The Biosocial Nature of Man*. New York, Grove Press.

————. 1967. *The American Way of Life*. New York, Putnam.

MONTAGUE, SUSAN, and MORALS, ROBERT. 1976. "Football Games and Rock Concerts," in ARENS, W. and MONTAGUE, S. (eds) *The American Dimension*. Port Washington, N.Y., Alfred.

MONTESQUIEU, CHARLES LOUIS DE SECONDAT, BARON DE. 1756. *The Spirit of Laws*. Aberdeen, Scotland, F. Douglass and W. Murry.

MORBECK, M.E. 1975. "*Dryopithecus africanus* Forelimb," *Journal of Human Evolution,* 4:39-46.

————. 1983. "Miocene Hominoid Discoveries From Rudabanya. Implications From the Postcranial Skeleton," in R.L. CIOCHON and A.B. CHIARELLI (eds). *Evolutionary Biology of the New World Monkeys and Continental Drift*. New York, Plenum Publishing Co.

MORGAN, LEWIS HENRY. 1877. *Ancient Society*. New York, H. Holt.

MORGAN, STEPHANIE. 1968. "The Sagacious Dolphin," *Natural History*, August–September, 32–39.

MORTON, SAMUEL G. 1839. "Varieties of the Human Species" (preface to), *Crania Americana*. Philadelphia, J. Dobson.

MURDOCK, GEORGE P. 1937. "Comparative Data on Division of Labor by Sex," *Social Forces*, **15**:551–53 (University of North Carolina Press).

———. 1949. *Social Structure.* New York, Free Press.

MURDOCK, GEORGE P., and WHITING, JOHN W. M. 1951. "Cultural Determination of Parental Attitudes," in SENN, M. J. E. (ed.), *Problems of Infancy and Childhood.* New York, Josiah Macy, Jr., Foundation.

NADEL, S. F. 1953. "Social Control and Self Regulation," *Social Forces*, **31**:265–73 (University of North Carolina Press).

NAROLL, RAOUL S. 1950. "A Draft Map of the Culture Areas of Asia," *Southwestern Journal of Anthropology*, **6**:183–87.

NASH, DENNISON. 1961. "The Role of the Composer," *Ethnomusicology*, **5**:187–201.

NEWMAN, HORATIO; FREEMAN, FRANK N.; and HOLZINGER, KARL. 1937. *Twins: A Study of Heredity and Environment.* Chicago, University of Chicago Press.

NEWTON, NILES. 1955. *Maternal Emotions.* New York, Harper & Row.

NISHIDA, T. 1983. "Allopaternal Behavior in Wild Chimpanzees of the Mahale Mts.," *Primates,* 20:1-20.

NORBECK, EDWARD. 1961. *Religion in Primitive Society.* New York, Harper & Row.

OGBURN, WILLIAM, and NIMKOFF, MEYER. 1964. *Sociology.* Boston, Houghton Mifflin.

PACKARD, VANCE. 1959. *The Status Seekers.* New York, David McKay Co.

PAZ, OCTAVIA. 1972. "Eroticism and Gastrosophy," *Daedalus*, **101**:67–85. (Fall).

PERRY, W. J. 1923. *Children of the Sun.* London, Methuen.

PILBEAM, D. 1979. "Recent Finds and Interpretations of Miocene Hominoids." *Annual Review of Anthropology*, 8:333-352.

———. 1984. "The Descent of Hominoids and Hominids," *Scientific American,* 250(3): 84-96.

POIRIER, F.E. 1972. "Introduction," in F.E.POIRIER (ed.). *Primate Socialization.* New York, Random House.

POSPISIL, LEOPOLD. 1958. *The Kapakau Papuans and their Law.* Yale Publications in Anthropology, New Haven, Yale University Press.

POTTER, DAVID. 1964. "Individuality and Conformity," in McGIF-FERT, MICHAEL (ed.), *The Character of Americans.* Homewood, Ill., Dorsey Press.

PRESCOTT, JAMES W. 1975. "Body Pleasure and the Origin of Violence," *The Futurist,* April, pp. 64–74.

RADCLIFFE-BROWN A. R. 1933. "Primitive Law," *Encyclopedia of Social Sciences,* Vol. 9.

———. 1948. *Andaman Islanders.* Glencoe, Ill., Free Press.

RADIN, PAUL. 1957. *Primitive Religion.* New York, Dover Publications.

RAPOPORT, AMOS. 1969. *House Form and Culture.* Englewood Cliffs, N. J., Prentice-Hall.

REDFIELD, ROBERT. 1953. *The Primitive World and Its Transformation.* Ithaca, Cornell University Press. Quoted by permission. (Second Printing 1958).

———. 1956. "How Society Operates," in SHAPIRO, HARRY (ed.), *Man, Culture and Society.* New York, Oxford University Press.

REICHARD, GLADYS. 1938. "Social Life," in BOAS, FRANZ (ed.), *General Anthropology.* New York, Heath.

RHOADS, ELLEN. 1971. *Climates and Clothing; an Ecological Analysis.* MA Thesis, Wichita State University.

———. 1973. "Levi-Strauss and Little Orphan Annie," *Journal of American Folklore,* 86:345-57.

RICHARD, A.F. 1985. *Primates in Nature.* New York, W.H. Freeman and Co.

RIESMAN, DAVID; GLAZER, NATHAN; and DENNEY, REUEL. 1950. *The Lonely Crowd.* New Haven, Yale University Press.

RIVERS, W. H. R. 1910. "The Genealogical Method of Anthropological Inquiry," *The Sociological Review,* 3:1–12.

ROBBINS, MAURICE, and IRVING, MARY. 1965. *The Amateur Archaeologist's Handbook.* New York, Thomas Crowell Company.

ROBINSON, C. H. 1896. *Hausaland.* London, S. Low, Marston and Company.

ROGERS, EVERETT. 1969. *Modernization among Peasants: the Impact of Communication.* New York, Holt, Rinehart & Winston.

ROSZAK, THEODORE. 1969. *The Making of a Counter Culture.* Garden City, N. Y., Doubleday.

ROYAL ANTHROPOLOGICAL INSTITUTE OF GREAT BRITAIN AND IRELAND. 1951. *Notes and Queries on Anthropology.* London, Routledge and Kegan Paul. Copyright 1874.

SARICH, V. 1971. "A Molecular Approach to the Question of Human Origins," in P. DOLHINOW and V. SARICH (eds.). *Background for Man.* Boston, Little, Brown and Co.

SAHLINS, MARSHALL. 1960. "The Origin of Society." *Scientific American,* **203**:76–87.

SAPIR, EDWARD. 1929. "The Status of Linguistics as a Science," *Language,* **5**:207–14.

SCHAPERA, ISAAC. 1930. *The Khoisan Peoples of South Africa.* London, Routledge and Kegan Paul.

———. 1967. *Government and Politics in Tribal Societies,* New York, Schocken Books.

SCHEPER-HUGHES, NANCY. 1973. "Woman as Witch," *Popular Psychology,* January, pp. 57–58, 60–61, 63–64.

SCHMIDT, WILHELM. 1939. *The Culture Historical Method of Ethnology.* New York. Fortuny.

SERVICE, ELMAN. 1975. *Origins of the State and Civilization.* New York, Norton, Inc.

SHAPIRO, HARRY L. 1953. *Race Mixture.* Paris, UNESCO.

———. 1962. *The Heritage of the Bounty.* Garden City, N.Y., Doubleday.

SHARP, LAURISTON. 1952. "Steel Axes for Stone Age Australians," in SPICER, EDWARD H. (ed.), *Human Problems in Technological Change.* New York, Russell Sage Foundation.

SIBLEY, MULFORD Q. 1968. "Anonymity, Dissent, and Individual Integrity," *Annals of the American Academy,* **378**:46–57.

SIEBER, ROY. 1973. "Approaches to Non-Western Art," in D'AZEVEDO, WARREN (ed.), *The Traditional Artist in African Societies.* Bloomington, University of Indiana Press.

SIMS, NEWELL LEROY. 1939. *The Problem of Social Change.* New York, Crowell.

SJOBERG, GIDEON. 1960. *The Preindustrial City.* New York, The Free Press.

SMIL, VACLAV. 1979. "Energy Flows in the Developing World," *American Scientist,* **67**:522–29.

SMITH, GRAFTON ELLIOT. 1915. *The Migrations of Early Culture.* London, New York, Longmans, Green & Co.

————. 1916. *The Influence of Ancient Egyptian Civilization in the East and in America.* New York, Longmans, Green & Co.

SMITH, HARVEY. 1949. *Sociological Study of Hospitals.* Unpublished PH.D. dissertation, Dept. of Sociology, University of Chicago.

SNOW, DEAN. 1976. *The Archeology of North America.* New York, Viking Press.

SPINDLER, GEORGE. 1968. "Psychocultural Adaptation," in NORBECK, E., PRICE-WILLIAMS, D., and McCORD, W. (eds.). *Study of Personality.* New York, Holt, Rinehart & Winston.

SPIRO, MELFORD E., and HENRY, JULES. 1953. "Psychological Techniques: Projective Tests in Field Work, in KOREBER, A. L. (ed.). *Anthropology Today.* Chicago, University of Chicago Press.

SPRADLEY, JAMES. 1979. *The Ethnographic Interview.* New York, Holt, Rinehart & Winston.

SPRADLEY, JAMES, and McCURDY, DAVID. 1972. *The Cultural Experience.* Chicago, Science Research Associates.

STALLINGS, W. S. 1939. *Dating prehistoric ruins by tree-rings.* Santa Fe N. M. School of American Research, Laboratory of Anthropology, Bulletin No. 8.

STANNER, W. E. H. 1953. *The South Seas in Transition.* Sydney, Australiasia Publ. Co. Quoted by permission of Australian Institute of International Afairs.

STANYON, R. and CHIARELLI, A.B. 1982. "Phylogeny of the Hominoidea: The Chromosome Evidence," *Journal of Human Evolution,* 11: 493-504.

STEIN, HOWARD. 1985. *Psychoanthropology of American Culture.* New York, Psychohistory Press.

STEVENSON, ROBERT LOUIS. 1885. "Foreign Children," in *A Child's Garden of Verses.* London.

STEWARD, J. H. 1949. "Cultural Causality and Law: A Trial Formulation of the Development of Early Civilizations," *American Anthropologist,* **51**:1–27.

————. 1956. *Theory of Culture Change.* New York.

STRAND, SIGVARD. 1979. *A History of the Machine.* Nordbok, Sweden.

SULLENBERGER, TOM E. 1974. "Ajax Meets the Jolly Green Giant," *Journal of American Folklore,* **87**:53–65.

SUMNER, WILLIAM GRAHAM. 1906. *Folkways.* Boston, Ginn & Co.

TACITUS. 1942. *The Complete Works of Tacitus.* (A. J. Church, trans.) New York, Random House.

TANNER, J.M. 1951. "Growth and Constitution," in A.L. KROEBER (ed.). *Anthropology Today.* Chicago, University of Chicago Press.

———. 1966, "Growth and Physique in Different Populations of Mankind," in P.T. BAKER and J.S. WEINER, (eds.), *The Biology of Human Adaptability.* London, Oxford University Press (Clarendon).

TELEKI, G. 1973. *The Predatory Behavior of Wild Chimpanzees.* Cranbrook, New Jersey, Bucknell University Press.

TELLEFSON, OLAF. 1970. "A New Theory of Pyramid Building," *Natural History,* November, pp. 10–23.

TERRANCE, HERBERT S. 1979. "How Nim Chimpsky Changed My Mind," *Psychology Today,* November, pp. 65–76.

TERRY, SARA. 1979. "The Death Penalty," *The Christian Science Monitor,* May 4, pp. 14–15.

THOMA, A. 1966. "L'occipital de l'Homme mindelien de Vertesszöllös," *L'Anthropologie,* **70**:495–533.

THOMAS, WILLIAM Jr. (ed.). 1956. *Current Anthropology.* Chicago, University of Chicago Press.

THOMPSON, J. E. 1964. *The Rise and Fall of Maya Civilization.* Norman, Oklahoma University Press.

THOMSON, VIRGIL. 1962. *The State of Music.* New York, Vintage Press.

THOMAS, ADOLPH S. 1943. "Rural Survivals in American Urban Life," *Rural Sociology.* **8**:378–86.

TREFIL, JAMES S. 1978. "A Consumer Guide to Pseudo-science," *Saturday Review,* April 19, pp. 16–21.

TYLOR, SIR EDWARD BURVETT. 1871. *Primitive Culture.* London, J. Murray. 1889. "On the Method of Investigating the Development of Institutions . . ." *Journal of the Royal Anthropological Institute,* **18**:245–69.

———. 1894. *Anthropology.* New York, D. Appleton.

———. 1958. *Religion in Primitive Culture.* New York, Harper Torchbook.

UNDERHILL, RUTH. 1953. *Red Man's America.* Chicago, University of Chicago Press.

UNESCO. 1952. *What is Race?* Paris.

UNITED PRESS INTERNATIONAL. 1979. "Chimps Teaching Sign Language," *Wichita Beacon,* November 19.

VAILLANT, GEORGE C. 1956. *The Aztecs of Mexico.* Harmondsworth, Middlesex, Penguin Books, Ltd.

VALLOIS, H. V. 1955. "La mandibule humaine pré-moustérienne de Montmaurin," *C. R. Acad. Sci.* Paris, **240**:1577–79.

VEBLEN, THORSTEIN. 1912. *The Theory of the Leisure Class.* New York, Macmillan.

VON ECKARDT, WOLF. 1981. "Architecture of Arrogance," *Society,* 18(3):61-62 (March/April).

WALL STREET JOURNAL. 1978. "Reflections after Jonestown," November 30, p. 22.

WALLACE, ANTHONY F. C. 1952. *The Modal Personality Structure of the Tuscarora Indians, as Revealed by the Rorschach Test.* Bulletin 150, Bureau of American Ethnology, Washington, D.C.

WARNER, WILLIAM LLOYD. 1937. *A Black Civilization.* New York, Harper & Bros.

WEINBERG, S. KIRSON. 1952. *Society and Personality Disorders.* New York, Prentice-Hall.

WHITE, LESLIE. 1959. *The Evolution of Culture.* New York, McGraw-Hill.

WHITE, DAVID M., and ABEL, ROBERT H. 1963. *The Funnies: An American Idiom.* Glencoe, Ill., The Free Press.

WHITING, JOHN W. M. 1960. "Totem and Taboo—a Reevaluation," in WASSERMAN, JULES (ed.), *Psychoanalysis and Human Values.* New York, Grune and Stratton.

WHYTE, WILLIAM F. 1955. *Street Corner Society.* Chicago, University of Chicago Press.

WHYTE, WILLIAM H., Jr. 1952. "Help Wanted—Sales," *Fortune* (May).

WILEY, GORDON. 1966. *An Introduction to American Archaeology.* Vol. I. Englewood Cliffs, N.J., Prentice-Hall.

WILLIAMS, ROGER. 1958. "Chemical Anthropology," *American Scientist,* **46**:1–23.

WINICK, CHARLES. 1958. *Dictionary of Anthropology.* New York, Philosophical Library.

WISSLER, CLARK. 1923. *Man and Culture.* New York, Crowell.

WOLF, ERIC. 1962. *Sons of the Shaking Earth.* Chicago, University of Chicago Press.

WOLPOFF, M. 1980. *Paleoanthropology.* New York, Alfred A. Knopf.

WORMINGTON, H.M. 1968. *Prehistoric Indians of the Southwest.* Denver, Denver Museum of Natural History.

YEARBOOK OF AMERICAN AND CANADIAN CHURCHES. 1985. C.H. JACQUET (ed.). Nashville, Abingdon.

Index